Literacy for the 21st Century
A Balanced Approach

Fourth Edition

Gail E. Tompkins
California State University, Fresno

PEARSON

Merrill
Prentice Hall

Upper Saddle River, New Jersey
Columbus, Ohio

Library of Congress Cataloging in Publication Data

Tompkins, Gail E.
   Literacy for the 21st century: a balanced approach/Gail E. Tompkins.— 4th ed.
       p. cm.
   Includes bibliographical references and index.
   ISBN 0–13–119076–8
    1. Language arts (Elementary) 2. Literature—Study and teaching (Elementary)
3. Reading (Elementary) 4. Literacy. I. Title: Literacy for the twenty-first century. II. Title.

LB1576.T657 2006
372.6—dc22
                                                                2004060129

Vice President and Executive Publisher: Jeffery W. Johnston
Senior Editor: Linda Ashe Montgomery
Senior Editorial Assistant: Laura Weaver
Senior Development Editor: Hope Madden
Senior Production Editor: Mary M. Irvin
Design Coordinator: Diane C. Lorenzo
Text and Cover Designer: Kristina D. Holmes
Cover Image: Laura DeSantis
Production Manager: Pamela D. Bennett
Director of Marketing: Ann Castel Davis
Marketing Manager: Darcy Betts Prybella
Marketing Coordinator: Brian Mounts

This book was set in Galliard by Carlisle Communications, Ltd. It was printed and bound by Courier Kendallville, Inc. The cover was printed by Coral Graphic Services, Inc.

Photo Credits: Photo on p. 168 by Anthony Magnacca/Merrill; all other photos by Gail E. Tompkins.

Pearson Education Ltd.
Pearson Education Singapore Pte. Ltd.
Pearson Education Canada, Ltd.
Pearson Education—Japan

Pearson Education Australia Pty. Limited
Pearson Education North Asia Ltd.
Pearson Educación de Mexico, S.A. de C.V.
Pearson Education Malaysia Pte. Ltd.

10 9 8 7 6 5 4 3 2
ISBN: 0–13–119076–8

In loving memory of
Lilly
who filled our hearts with joyful anticipation

About the Author

Gail E. Tompkins is Professor *Emerita* at California State University, Fresno, and she continues to direct the San Joaquin Valley Writing Project. She regularly works with teachers in their kindergarten through eighth-grade classrooms and leads staff-development programs on reading, language arts, and writing. In 1998 Dr. Tompkins was inducted into the California Reading Association's Reading Hall of Fame in recognition of her publications and other accomplishments in the field of reading, and recently she was awarded the prestigious Provost's Award for Excellence in Teaching at California State University, Fresno.

Previously, Dr. Tompkins taught at Miami University in Ohio and at the University of Oklahoma in Norman, where she received the Regents' Award for Superior Teaching. She was also an elementary teacher in Virginia for eight years.

Dr. Tompkins is the author of five other books published by Merrill/Prentice Hall: *Language Arts: Content and Teaching Strategies*, 6th ed. (2005), *Teaching Writing: Balancing Process and Product*, 4th ed. (2004), *50 Literacy Strategies*, 2nd ed. (2004), and two grade-level specific versions of this text: *Literacy for the 21st Century: Teaching Reading and Writing in Pre-Kindergarten Through Grade 4* (2003), and *Literacy for the 21st Century: Teaching Reading and Writing in Grades 4 Through 8* (2004).

She is also coeditor of three books written by the Teacher Consultants in the San Joaquin Valley Writing Project and published by Merrill/Prentice Hall: *Sharing the Pen: Interactive Writing With Young Children* (2004), edited with Stephanie Collom; *Teaching Vocabulary: 50 Creative Strategies, Grades K–12* (2004) and *50 Ways to Develop Strategic Writers* (2005), both edited with Cathy Blanchfield.

Preface

What are my goals to make *Literacy for the 21st Century* the most valuable and relevant literacy text on the market? I have several.

As I revise each edition, working with teachers in the field and with preservice teachers at the university level, I realize more and more that new as well as experienced teachers need the best information about how students learn, ideas to create an environment that engages and addresses the needs of all students, and a deep understanding of the literacy methods that best address those needs. I also recognize that teachers need specific tools to take into the classroom. My goal is to provide all this in a text that speaks directly to new and experienced teachers, modeling effective teaching, and helping you envision yourself using these methods in your classroom.

I have found that the best approach to sharing this information with you is through an authentic vision of today's classroom, a balanced approach to literacy, and the best research-based and classroom-tested practice I can provide.

Authenticity

I regularly visit and work in the classrooms of some very talented teachers, many of whom have been my students, and I am very pleased to profile them in this text. These teachers face the same opportunities and challenges that you will. They, too, have to find ways to be creative and nurturing while being accountable to state and federal mandates.

The classrooms I visit reflect the diversity you'll find everywhere in America. Many of these students are English learners, and they bring background knowledge and cultural understandings that challenge teachers to ensure they prepare learning experiences that meet the literacy needs of all students.

Good teachers, like those who generously share their experiences with me for this text, strive to help struggling readers develop solid literacy strategies and skills. They work with students who are eagerly learning to read and write and others who are unmotivated and resistant. They work to make sure all their students have the foundational literacy knowledge they need to succeed in life, and help them develop a love of reading as well.

- **Chapter-opening vignettes and minilessons** throughout chapters help you envision today's classrooms as I share stories of literacy teachers who work successfully with all their students, including English learners.

- **Student work samples** that appear throughout chapters model assessment and evaluation, helping you recognize the ways students develop as readers and writers.

- *New!* **Instructional Procedures: Scenes from the Compendium** is a new DVD, free with this text, that shares video footage of talented teachers and their compelling classroom scenes. These clips take you right into their classrooms to watch teachers use grand conversations, guided reading, interactive writing, and other procedures discussed in the text.

- Classroom footage showcases masterful teachers using instructional procedures from the Compendium.
- Notes throughout chapters connect DVD clips with chapter content and Compendium procedures.
- Activities on the Companion Website help new teachers deepen and apply their understanding of the instructional procedures illustrated on the DVD.

BALANCE

This new edition strengthens and clarifies the importance of balancing literacy instruction, integrating essential skill development, strategy instruction, literature study, and authentic reading and writing experiences.

You will understand literacy instruction in terms of four foundational instructional approaches: *basal reading programs, literature focus units, literature circles*, and *reading and writing workshop*. Through these approaches, I provide you with strategies and skills within the context of authentic reading and writing experiences. You will find in these pages the principles, skills, strategies, and examples of literature that will empower you to get up to speed quickly.

- **New!** **Components of a Balanced Literacy Program** features in every chapter show how the chapter's topic relates to the 10 components of a balanced literacy program. For example, how does teaching comprehension relate to strategy instruction, fluency, content-area reading, and writing? It's important that you understand how each chapter's topic impacts and supports the entire literacy program, and this feature gives you that information.

Organization

The four parts of the text are organized to build your background knowledge piece by piece, always integrating what you've just learned with new information being covered. I want you to see how a solid literacy program incorporates theory and research into teaching and assessment methods, and how they drive your instructional decisions.

- **Part 1: What Is a Balanced Approach to Literacy Instruction?** sets the stage for the methods and applications to follow. The eight principles of effective reading instruction outlined in Chapter 1 provide a strong, easily understood foundation for the entire book. You'll learn about how children learn and how to create a community of learners, organize instruction, implement assessment, and balance literacy instruction. You will also learn four theories supporting a balanced literacy approach. Chapter 2 builds on this foundation, focusing on the reading and writing processes, and readying you to learn how to work with your students.

- **Part 2: How Do Children Learn to Read and Write?** consists of seven chapters that will help you implement a truly balanced approach to working with young readers and writers, covering phonics instruction, developing fluency and comprehension, and addressing assessment in a developmentally appropriate way.

- **Part 3: How Do Teachers Organize Literacy Instruction?** applies the foundational concepts you learned in Parts 1 and 2, focusing on day-to-day classroom instruction. What does balanced literacy instruction look like in terms of basals, literature focus units, literature circles, reading and writing workshop, and content-area literacy?

- **Part 4: Compendium of Instructional Procedures** completes the text with a bank of classroom-proven instructional procedures that will engage and scaffold your students' learning in reading and writing. The DVD that accompanies this text illustrates many of these procedures.

CLASSROOM PRACTICE

My primary goal in this text is to show you how to teach reading and writing effectively, how to create a classroom climate where literacy flourishes, and how to empower the diverse array of students who will populate your classrooms, helping them function competently as literate adults in the twenty-first century.

Although there are many other useful ideas and strategies that can accomplish the goal of producing literate students, I have deliberately and painstakingly chosen research-based, classroom-tested ideas—the best of the best—as the focus of this textbook. With these in hand, you will be prepared to hit the ground running as you confidently implement effective methods. If you know how to be effective from the first day, you will have the confidence necessary to add to your bag of tricks as your experience guides your practice.

New! • **Nurturing English Learners** features demonstrate how literacy elements, including cueing systems, basals, background knowledge, assessment, and phonemic awareness, must be redirected and aligned to meet the needs of English learners.

New! • **Scaffolding Struggling Readers** features provide pivotal information on topics such as fluency, revising, the difficulty of vowels, vocabulary in content-area texts, and comprehension to help students who struggle make real progress in developing literacy competency.

- **Minilessons** offer clear, concise skill and strategy instruction, ready for you to take right into your classroom!

- **Assessment Resources** model classroom assessment to help you integrate assessment before, during, and after literacy instruction.

- **Part 4's** *Compendium of Instructional Procedures*, composed of dozens of clearly articulated instructional methods, will become an invaluable professional resource and ready classroom reference.

INTEGRATING MEDIA AND THE STANDARDS

Today's school environment is driven by state and federal mandates, and by standards. You will need a handy reference to the national IRA/NCTE Standards for Reading Professionals, as well as access to your own state's standards. You will also need to find ways to integrate these standards into your own teaching. On my Companion Website you will find the quick reference and teaching tools you need:

- An NCTE/IRA Standards matrix will pinpoint chapter-by-chapter standards coverage.

- A complete correlation of NCTE/IRA Standards and chapter content will help you conceptualize a standards-driven literacy classroom.

- Online lessons keyed to the NCTE/IRA Standards will give you classroom tools. Link from these lessons to your own state's standards to adapt the lessons to meet the standards designated for your own state, and save your new lessons to your hard drive or on disk through the Online Portfolio. By the end of the class, you will have compiled a wonderful bank of standards-specific lessons to use with your own students.

SUPPLEMENTS

Companion Website: Available at **www.prenhall.com/tompkins,** this robust on-line support system offers many rich and meaningful ways to deepen and expand the information presented to you in the text.

- **IRA/NCTE Standards Integration,** delivered through chapter correlations as well as adaptable lessons that can be saved to your hard drive or disk through the Online Portfolio, provides classroom-ready lessons that align with national and state standards.

- **Praxis practice questions** help prepare preservice teachers for the Praxis 2 exam. Link to *Literacy for the 21st Century's* Ready for RICA website to cater your prac-tice specifically to California's teacher examination and California's standards.

- **Self-Assessments** help users gauge their understanding of text concepts.

- **Field Activities** help contextualize chapter content in a classroom setting.

- **Web Links** provide useful connections to all standards and many other invaluable online literacy sources.

- **Chapter Objectives** provide a useful advance organizer for each chapter's online companion.

Electronic Instructor's Manual: This useful tool for instructors, available online at **www.prenhall.com** with an instructor's access code, provides rich instructional support:

- **A test bank** including multiple choice and essay questions. Also available as a TestGen, a computerized version (ISBN 0–13–171815–0).

- **PowerPoints** specifically designed for each chapter.

- **A Media Guide** with suggestions for making the most of the text's accompany-ing DVD *Instructional Procedures: Scenes from the Compendium.*

- **Chapter-by-chapter materials,** including chapter objectives, suggested readings, discussion questions, and in-class activities.

Videos: Free to adopters, these videos can add depth to classroom concept cover-age and promote discussion and analysis in class.

- A VHS version of *Instructional Procedures: Scenes from the Compendium* (ISBN 0–13–171816–9) is available upon request to professors whose classroom envi-ronment makes viewing footage from a VHS more convenient than viewing the DVD as a class.

- *Guidelines for Reading Comprehension Instruction* (ISBN 0–13–031405–6) con-tains footage of Gail Tompkins providing guidance for preservice and inservice lit-eracy teachers.

- *Literacy Library: Video A* (ISBN 0–13–042087–5) provides a collection of class-room segments where teachers and students are engaged in developing literacy lessons. Individual lessons include: reciprocal circles, inquiry methods for language and literacy, retelling, higher-order thinking skills, letter-and-sound relationships, and reading for word problems.

- *Literacy Library: Video B* (ISBN 0–13–112395–5) provides clear guidance for practicing guided reading with students.

CD ROMs: Several CDs are available to package with this new edition of *Literacy for the 21st Century*. Users can examine, re-examine, and manipulate genuine classroom footage to develop a deep and lasting understanding of highlighted instructional approaches and the ways they are effectively carried out in classrooms.

- *Writing Workshop* (ISBN 0–13–117590–4). Experience the effective instruction that takes place in classroom communities by analyzing video footage of master teachers who integrate minilessons and strategy and skill development through writing workshops.

- *Literature Circles* (ISBN 0–13–061167–0). Examine footage of a master teacher in an eighth grade literacy classroom. You will have the opportunity to observe the classroom footage, hear from the teachers and students involved, and consider the research behind the teacher's decisions.

- *Primary Grades Literacy* (ISBN 0–13–172133-X). Study a master teacher's approach to a K–3 integrated unit on insects.

ACKNOWLEDGMENTS

Many people helped and encouraged me during the revision of this text. My heartfelt thanks go to each of them. First, I want to thank my students at California State University, Fresno, who taught me while I taught them, and the teacher-consultants in the San Joaquin Valley Writing Project, who shared their expertise with me. Their insightful questions challenged and broadened my thinking. Thanks, too, go to the teachers who welcomed me into their classrooms, showed me how they used literature in innovative ways, and allowed me to learn from them and their students. In particular, I want to express my appreciation to the teachers and students who appear in the vignettes: Eileen Boland, Tenaya Middle School, Fresno, CA; Jessica Bradshaw, Rocky Hill Elementary School, Exeter, CA; Roberta Dillon, Armona Elementary School, Armona, CA; Whitney Donnelly, Williams Ranch School, Penn Valley, CA; Stacy Firpo, Aynesworth Elementary School, Fresno, CA; Laurie Goodman, Pioneer Middle School, Hanford, CA; Judy Hoddy, Hennessey School, Grass Valley, CA; Sally Mast, Thomas Elementary School, Fresno, CA; Susan McCloskey, Greenberg Elementary, Fresno, CA; Nicki Paniccia McNeal, Century Elementary School, Clovis, CA; Jennifer Miller-McColm, Roosevelt Elementary School, Selma, CA; Gay Ockey, Hildago Elementary School, Fresno, CA; Kristi Ohashi, Terry Elementary School, Selma, CA; Jill Peterson, Mickey Cox Elementary School, Clovis, CA; Judy Roberts, Lincoln Elementary School, Madera, CA; Kacey Sanom, John Muir Elementary School, Fresno, CA; Darcy Williams, Aynesworth Elementary School, Fresno, CA; and Susan Zumwalt, Jackson Elementary School, Selma, CA. Thanks, too, to Sonja Wiens, Leavenworth Elementary School, Fresno, CA; Kimberly Clark, Aynesworth Elementary School, Fresno, CA; Laura McCleneghan, Tarpey Elementary School, Clovis, CA; Kim Ransdell, Armona Elementary School, Armona, CA, and their students who also appeared in photos in the book. I also want to acknowledge Jenny Reno and the teachers and students at Western Hills Elementary School, Lawton, OK, and Carol Ochs, Jackson Elementary School, Norman, OK, who have been a part of each of the books I have written. Thanks to R. Carl Harris for creating such an innovative DVD design and successfully showcasing five such exemplary teachers: Susan McCloskey, Kristi McNeal, Jennifer Miller-McColm, Leah Scheitrum, and Susan Zumwalt. I want also to thank the reviewers of my manuscript for their comments and insights: Bonnie B. Armbruster, University of Illinois at Urbana-Champaign; Philip Berryhill, Fairmont State College; Margaret S. Carter, James Madison University; Jean Casey, California State University, Long Beach; Nancy Frey, San Diego State University; Daniel Holm, Indiana University South Bend; Laveria F. Hutchison, University of Houston-Central; Carolyn Jaynes, California State University, Sacramento; Philip S. Kligman, California State University, Northridge; Judy A. Leavell, Southwest Texas State University; Leanna Manna, Villa Maria College; Donna Read, Florida Atlantic University; Laurie Ryan, University of Texas at El Paso; Timothy Shanahan, University of Illinois at Chicago; and Jill E. Steeley, Oral Roberts University.

Finally, I am indebted to Jeff Johnston and his team at Merrill/Prentice Hall in Columbus, Ohio, who produce so many high-quality publications. I am honored to be a Merrill author. Linda Montgomery is the guiding force behind my work, and Hope Madden is my cheerleader, encouraging me every step of the way and spurring me toward impossible deadlines. I want to express my sincere appreciation to Mary Irvin, who has again skillfully supervised the production of this book, and deftly juggled the last-minute details, and to Melissa Gruzs, who has so expertly copy-edited the manuscript and proofread the pages.

Brief Contents

Contents

PART 3
How Do Teachers Organize Literacy Instruction? 329

PART 4
Compendium of Instructional Procedures   467

Note: Every effort has been made to provide accurate and current Internet information in this book. However, the Internet and information posted on it are constantly changing, so it is inevitable that some of the Internet addresses in this textbook will change.

What Is a Balanced Approach to Literacy Instruction?

In a balanced approach to literacy instruction, teachers integrate instruction with authentic reading and writing and experiences so that students learn how to use literacy strategies and skills and have opportunities to apply what they are learning. The 10 components of a balanced approach are:

- Reading
- Phonics and Other Skills
- Strategies
- Vocabulary
- Comprehension

- Literature
- Content-Area Study
- Oral Language
- Writing
- Spelling

In this photo essay, you'll see how Mrs. Peterson uses a balanced approach to literacy instruction in her sixth grade classroom. She is teaching a literature focus unit on *Bunnicula: A Rabbit-Tale of Mystery* (Howe & Howe, 1979), a hilarious novel about modern family life, written from the viewpoint of the family's dog. *Bunnicula*, an invented word made by combining *bunny* and *Dracula*, is the name given to the black-and-white bunny that the family finds at a vampire movie. The pets believe that the rabbit is a vampire and try to warn the family.

Mrs. Peterson shares a box of objects related to the novel—white vegetables, a bunny, and a children's version of *Dracula* as she introduces *Bunnicula: A Rabbit-Tale of Mystery*.

The sixth graders talk about the novel in a grand conversation. They analyze events in the story, make predictions about what will happen next, clarify misconceptions, and make connections.

Mrs. Peterson is sharing information about the author in this minilesson. She has collected photos and information about his life to share with the students.

This boy is writing an entry in his reading log. Sometimes he writes in response to a question Mrs. Peterson has asked; sometimes he writes a summary; and sometimes he reflects on his use of strategies while reading.

Mrs. Peterson teaches a minilesson on invented words such as Bunnicula, and then students practice matching the invented words with the words that were combined to form them at the word work center.

These girls share the "Count Dracula's Vampire Facts" poster with classmates. One girl reads each fact aloud and classmates decide whether the fact is true or false. Then the other girl lifts the red tab to check the answer.

This student practices her presentation skills as she shares vampire jokes and riddles with classmates.

Becoming an Effective Teacher of Reading

- Which theories guide the effective teaching of reading and writing?
- What is a balanced approach to literacy?
- How do effective teachers organize their classrooms?
- Which four instructional approaches do effective teachers use?
- How do effective teachers link instruction and assessment?

Fourth Graders Participate in a Yearlong Author Study

There's a busy hum in Miss Paniccia's fourth-grade classroom. The students are involved in a 40-minute writing workshop; this is the time when students develop and refine pieces of writing on topics they've chosen themselves. They work with classmates to revise and edit their rough drafts and then use AlphaSmart® keyboards for word processing. Next, they transfer their compositions to a classroom computer and print out copies of their drafts for a final editing conference with Miss Paniccia. Afterward, they print out the finished copies.

Today, the fourth graders are putting the finishing touches on the collections of stories they've worked on for 7 months. Each student has written at least seven stories and published them by pasting them into bound books with blank pages. The spring back-to-school night is 2 days away, and these students are eager for the parents to read their newly published books.

The class has been involved in an ambitious yearlong project on Chris Van Allsburg, the popular author and illustrator of award-winning fantasy picture books, including *Jumanji* (1981) and *The Polar Express* (1985). A list of his books is shown in the box on page 5. The students have read some of these stories in their basal readers and some during literature circles, and Miss Paniccia has read others aloud. The stories they've been writing accompany the illustrations and titles in *The Mysteries of Harris Burdick* (Van Allsburg, 1984).

Books by Chris Van Allsburg

The garden of Abdul Gasazi. (1979). Boston: Houghton Mifflin.
A wicked magician turns dogs into ducks, or does he?

Jumanji. (1981). Boston: Houghton Mifflin.
Children play a jungle board game that comes to life.

Ben's dream. (1982). Boston: Houghton Mifflin.
In a dream, Ben and his friend visit the world's major monuments, including the Eiffel Tower and the Great Wall of China.

The wreck of the Zephyr. (1983). Boston: Houghton Mifflin.
A boy's ambition to be the greatest sailor brings him to ruin.

The mysteries of Harris Burdick. (1984). Boston: Houghton Mifflin.
A collection of dazzling illustrations accompanied by titles but no stories.

The polar express. (1985). Boston: Houghton Mifflin.
A boy takes a magical train ride on Christmas Eve to receive a gift from Santa.

The stranger. (1986). Boston: Houghton Mifflin.
Jack Frost visits the Bailey farm one autumn.

The Z was zapped: A play in 26 acts. (1987). Boston: Houghton Mifflin.
An eerie alphabet book showing a transformation of each letter (e.g., the N was nailed).

Two bad ants. (1988). Boston: Houghton Mifflin.
Two greedy, nonconformist ants confront many dangers as they explore a kitchen.

Just a dream. (1990). Boston: Houghton Mifflin.
Ben's dream is a warning about a future ecological nightmare.

The wretched stone. (1991). Boston: Houghton Mifflin.
A mysterious stone transforms a ship's crew into apes, but finally, after a storm, the men return to normal.

The widow's broom. (1992). Boston: Houghton Mifflin.
An old woman outsmarts her neighbors who fear her magical broom.

The sweetest fig. (1993). Boston: Houghton Mifflin.
A mean dentist receives magical figs from a patient and gets just what he deserves when he uses the magic.

Zathura. (2002). Boston: Houghton Mifflin.
This sequel to *Jumanji* picks up where the first story left off: The Budwig brothers take on the fantasy board game, but this time, the game is set in space on the planet of Zathura.

Check the Compendium of Instructional Procedures, which follows Chapter 14, for more information on highlighted terms.

The Chris Van Allsburg unit began in September when Miss Paniccia read aloud *Jumanji* (Van Allsburg, 1981), the story of two children who play a jungle adventure board game that comes to life. She also read aloud the sequel *Zathura* (2002) about a space adventure board game, and students watched the movie version. They also made board games and wrote directions for playing them. She used the story to emphasize the importance of listening to her directions in the classroom, following parents' directions at home, and reading the directions on state achievement tests.

Miss Paniccia regularly teaches minilessons on writing strategies and skills that students then apply in their own writing. She began with a series of lessons on revising and editing that students use in writing workshop. Next, she taught a series of lessons about the elements of story structure: plot, characters, setting, point of view, and theme. Posters about each story element hang in the classroom, testimony to the learning taking place in this classroom. Students apply what they have learned about story structure as they create their own stories because they develop story cards as a prewriting activity. They develop story ideas by sketching out the characters, plot, and setting and share their ideas with a classmate to further expand their thinking before they begin to write. In addition to the lessons about story structure, Miss Paniccia has taught lessons about reports and other writing genres after they are introduced in the basal reading program.

The students use a process approach to writing that involves all five stages of the writing process. The box on page 7 shows the activities that Miss Paniccia's students participate in at each stage of the process. During the second semester of third grade, students at this school take an afterschool touch-typing course, so these fourth graders know the fundamentals of finger placement on the keyboard and are developing typing fluency as they use the AlphaSmart® word processing machines.

Month after month, the students have been drafting, revising, rewriting, proofreading, word processing, and printing out final copies of their stories. Seth's story for the illustration entitled "Mr. Linden's Library" is shown in the box on page 8. The illustration depicts a girl sleeping in bed with an open book beside her; vines are growing out of the book and are spreading across the girl's bed. As you read Seth's story, you will see how his story idea developed from the illustration and how he has applied what he has learned about story structure.

Today during writing workshop, Miss Paniccia is meeting with Alfonso, Martha, and Yimleej to proofread their stories and correct errors. Other students are word processing their last stories or are printing out their final copies and gluing them in their books. Miguel and Lindsey have finished their books, so they're helping their classmates word process, transfer to the computer, and print out their stories. Miss Paniccia is optimistic that everyone will be done by lunchtime tomorrow. She plans to start author's chair during writing workshop tomorrow: Students will take turns reading their favorite stories aloud to their classmates. Author's chair is a popular classroom activity; most students will be eager to share their stories, and their classmates will enjoy listening to them read aloud because the students have learned how to read with expression and hold their classmates' interest.

Last week, the students created this introductory page for their story collections:

Thirty years ago a man named Harris Burdick came by Peter Wenders's publishing office. Mr. Burdick claimed that he had written 15 stories and illustrated them. All he brought with him on that day were the illustrations with titles. The next day Harris Burdick was going to bring the stories to Mr. Wenders, but he never returned. In fact, Harris Burdick was never seen again.

Chris Van Allsburg met with Mr. Wenders and that is where he came across the illustrations. Mr. Wenders handed Mr. Van Allsburg a dust-covered box full of drawings, and Chris Van Allsburg was inspired to reproduce them for children across the nation.

Students' Writing Process Activities

Stage	Activity	Description
Prewriting	Story Cards	Students create story cards to develop their ideas for the story. A story card is a sheet of paper divided into six sections: idea, character, setting, problem, climax, and solution.
	Peer Conference	Students meet with a classmate for a "one-on-one" where they share their story cards, talking out their ideas and answering their classmate's questions.
Drafting	Drafting	Students write their rough drafts in pencil, working from their story cards.
Revising	Peer Conference	Students meet with two classmates to share their rough drafts, getting more feedback about their stories. Then they make revisions based on the feedback they received.
	Conference With Miss P.	They recopy their drafts in pen and have Miss Paniccia read and respond to their stories. Students make more revisions based on their teacher's feedback.
Editing	Proofreading	Students proofread their drafts and correct the errors they notice. Then they have two classmates proofread their drafts to identify and correct remaining spelling, capitalization, punctuation, and grammar errors.
	Word Processing	Students word process their stories using word processing machines. After correcting the errors they notice, they transfer their stories to the classroom computer, put them into their own files, and print out a copy in a legible font.
	Conference With Miss P.	Students meet with Miss Paniccia to proofread and fix the remaining errors.
Publishing	Final Copy	Students print out a final copy and cut the papers to fit into their bound, blank book. They glue the papers into the book and add illustrations.

Right here in room 30, we have worked hard all year creating stories for the illustrations. Even though we have completed our stories, the mystery of Harris Burdick still remains.

It is a class collaboration: Miss Paniccia and the students developed it together, and copies were made for each student. By writing the introduction together, the teacher was able to review writing skills and strategies and ensure that all students had a useful introduction for their books.

Seth's Story About "Mr. Linden's Library"

"I would like to check out this book," Sally Olger said. The book that she wanted to check out was called <u>Adventures in the Wild</u>. She had skipped as she had gone up to the counter. Sally loved to go to this library. It was owned by Mr. Linden, so everybody just called it Mr. Linden's library.

The expression on the man at the counter's face changed when he saw the book that Sally was holding. The man warned Sally that if she left the book out on one page for over an hour, something dangerous would come out of the book.

Sally didn't really hear or care about what the man said. She checked out the book and started reading it in bed that night. The book was really interesting. It had tons of short stories in it. At 12:00 midnight, Sally turned the page to a story called "Lost in the Jungle," yawned, and fell asleep. At 1:00 A.M. vines started to grow out of the book. He had warned her about the book. Now it was too late. Soon Sally's whole room was covered in vines. By 2:00, they were making their way up the stairs.

BBBRRRRIIIIINNNNNNGGGGGG! went Sally's alarm clock.

"AAAAAAAHHHHHHH!" screamed Sally. Now the whole house was covered in vines. Sally slowly made her way to her parents' bedroom through the vines and woke them up. They screamed too. As quickly as possible (which wasn't very fast) the Olgers got out of their house, got in their car, and drove to the library. They told the man at the desk what had happened. He said that the only way to get rid of the vines was to cut their roots (they would be sticking right out of the book) and then haul all of the vines off to the dump. Luckily, the town dump wasn't very far away from the Olgers' house.

By the time Mr. Olger had found and cut the roots away from the book, Sally and Mrs. Olger had rounded up the whole neighborhood to help take the vines to the dump. By 5:00 P.M. in the afternoon they had cleared away all of the vines. Sally had learned her lesson to listen when someone warns you about something.

After beginning the author study in September, Miss Paniccia has continued to read stories each month. In October, she and her students read *The Stranger* (Van Allsburg, 1986), a story included in their basal readers. In the story, the Baileys take in an injured stranger, a man who doesn't speak or seem to know who he is, but he appears to be attuned with the seasons and has an amazing connection with wild animals. The stranger is Jack Frost, although that statement is never made explicitly in the story. They take several days to read the story. On the first day, the teacher introduced the key vocabulary words, including *autumn, etched, mercury, peculiar,* and *hypnotized,* and the class previewed the story, examining the illustrations and making predictions. Miss Paniccia used a shared reading procedure: The students listened to the story read aloud on the professional CD that accompanies the textbook and followed along in their textbooks. Some inferred that the stranger is Jack Frost, but others didn't. That's when she introduced making inferences, which she calls "reading between the lines."

They read the story a second time, searching for clues that led their classmates to guess that the stranger is Jack Frost, and afterward made a cluster, a spider web–like diagram, with the clues. They wrote the words *The Stranger* in the center circle, drew out rays from this circle, and wrote clues at the end of each ray. The clues included that he wears odd clothing, is confused by buttons, and works hard, but doesn't get tired. Afterward, they completed page 156 in the Practice Book that accompanies the textbook as well as other pages that emphasize comprehension.

Then Miss Paniccia asked students to closely examine the illustrations in the story. They noticed how the perspective in the illustrations varies to draw readers into the scenes and create the mood. The students read the story a third time with partners, talking about how Chris Van Allsburg used viewpoint in the illustrations.

In November, students read other books by Chris Van Allsburg in literature circles. Miss Paniccia presented book talks about these four books: *Two Bad Ants* (Van Allsburg, 1988), *Just a Dream* (Van Allsburg, 1990), *The Sweetest Fig* (Van Allsburg, 1993), and *The Wreck of the Zephyr* (Van Allsburg, 1983). Then students formed small groups to read one of the books. They assumed roles and took on responsibilities in the small groups as they read and talked about the book. Then students read another of the four books during a second literature circle in January.

Miss Paniccia read aloud the award-winning holiday story *The Polar Express* (Van Allsburg, 1985) in December. In the story, being able to hear Santa's bells jiggle represents belief in the magic of Christmas, so Miss Paniccia gave each student a small bell to jiggle each time it was mentioned in the story. The students discussed the story in a grand conversation; much of their conversation focused on the theme and how the author states it explicitly at the end of the story. "What an awesome story!" Hunter concluded, and his classmates agreed. They also talked about their own holiday traditions and wrote about them during writing workshop.

They continued to read other books by Chris Van Allsburg: In February, Miss Paniccia read *The Garden of Abdul Gasazi* (Van Allsburg, 1979), and in March, she read *The Wretched Stone* (Van Allsburg, 1991). These books are difficult for students to comprehend because they have to make inferences: In *The Garden of Abdul Gasazi*, readers have to decide whether the magician changes the dog into a duck, and in *The Wretched Stone,* they need to understand that the stone represents television or video games. Miss Paniccia taught a series of minilessons on inferencing, and she modeled how to make inferences as she reread the stories, showing the fourth graders how to use their background knowledge, the clues in the story, and self-questions to read between the lines. Then students reread the stories with partners, talked about clues in the stories, and made inferences as their teacher had.

In March, Miss Paniccia also taught a series of minilessons on the fantasy genre. They developed a chart with these characteristics of fantasies that they posted in the classroom:

Characters have unusual traits.

The setting is not realistic.

Some events could not really happen.

Magic is involved.

Then the students divided into small groups to reread the Chris Van Allsburg books and examine them for these characteristics. They developed a data chart with the titles of the books written across the top of the grid and the characteristics of fantasies written down the left side. Then they completed the chart by indicating how each characteristic is represented in each book.

This month, students are reading Chris Van Allsburg's books independently. Some students are reading those they haven't yet read, and others are rereading their favorite ones. As they read, they search for the white dog that Van Allsburg includes in each book. In some books, such as *The Garden of Abdul Gasazi,* the dog is alive, but in others, he's a puppet, a hood ornament, or a picture. In several books, only a small part of him shows; in *The Wretched Stone,* for example, you see his tail on one page. In addition, they continue to notice the fantasy elements of the stories, they use inferencing when needed, and they notice Van Allsburg's use of perspective in his illustrations.

This author study has been successful because Miss Paniccia's literacy program is balanced with a combination of direct instruction, small-group and whole-class literacy activities, and independent reading and writing opportunities. Her schedule is shown in the box below. By combining several instructional approaches, Miss Paniccia juggles the district's adopted basal reading program with other activities that enrich and extend her students' literacy experiences.

Miss Paniccia's Literacy Program Schedule

8:50–9:30   **Writing Workshop/Literature Circles**
Students alternate writing workshop and literature circles. Currently, they doing writing workshop; during literature circles, they read and discuss chapter books in three ability-based groups while Miss Paniccia circulates, meeting with each group each day. They also write in reading logs, summarizing their reading, making connections, and predicting what will happen next. Students read several Van Allsburg stories in literature circles, and during the last round of literature circles, the groups read *Dogs Don't Tell Jokes* (Sachar, 1991), *Fudge-a-Mania* (Blume, 1990), and *My Side of the Mountain* (George, 1988).

9:30–10:00   **Centers**
Students work in small groups, moving each week through the spelling center, the listening center, the grammar center, and the SRA Reading Laboratory Kit center. In the SRA kit, the students practice comprehension and study skills. Miss Paniccia also administers the spelling pretest on Monday and final test on Friday during this period.

10:00–10:50   **Basal Reading Textbooks**
Students read stories and informational articles in the textbook together as a class, and Miss Paniccia teaches the accompanying vocabulary, decoding and comprehension strategies, and grammar skills. They complete some workbook pages during this period and others at the spelling and grammar centers.

12:50–1:30   **Literature Focus Unit**
Miss Paniccia reads aloud core books, and students participate in literacy activities. Currently, she's reading Laura Ingalls Wilder's *Little House in the Big Woods* (2001). Earlier in the year, she read some Van Allsburg stories as well as *James and the Giant Peach* (Dahl, 1996), *The Trumpet of the Swans* (White, 2000), *The Great Turkey Walk* (Karr, 1998), *Bunnicula: A Rabbit-Tale of Mystery* (Howe & Howe, 1979), and *Esperanza Rising* (Ryan, 2000).

The children of the 21st century will face many challenges that will require them to use reading and writing in different forms. As we begin the new millennium, teachers are learning research-based approaches to teach reading and writing that will prepare their students for the future. Teachers make a significant difference in children's lives, and this book is designed to help you become an effective reading teacher. Researchers have examined many teaching practices and have drawn some important conclusions about the most effective ones: We must teach students the processes of reading and writing, as well as how to use reading and writing as learning tools. Bill Teale (1995) challenges us to teach students to think with and through reading and writing, to use reading and writing to get a wide variety of things done in their lives, and to use reading and writing for pleasure and insight.

Let's start with some definitions. *Literacy* used to mean knowing how to read but the term has broadened to encompass both reading and writing. Now literacy means the competence "to carry out the complex tasks using reading and writing related to the world of work and to life outside the school" (International Reading Association and the National Council of Teachers of English, 1989, p. 36). Educators are also identifying other literacies that they believe will be needed in the 21st century (Harris & Hodges, 1995). Our reliance on radio and television for conveying ideas has awakened us to the importance of "oracy," the ability to express and understand spoken language. Visual literacy, the ability to create meaning from illustrations, is also receiving a great deal of attention.

The term *literacy* is being used in other ways as well. For example, teachers are introducing even very young children to computers and developing their "computer literacy." Similarly, math and science educators speak of mathematical and scientific literacies. Hirsch (1987) called for another type of literacy, "cultural literacy," as a way to introduce children "to the major ideas and ideals from past cultures that have defined and shaped today's society" (p. 10). Literacy, however, is not a prescription of certain books to read or concepts to define. Rather, according to Rafferty (1999), it is a tool, a way to learn about the world and a means to participate more fully in the technological society of the 21st century.

Reading and writing are both processes of constructing meaning. Sometimes children describe reading as "saying all the words right," or writing as "making all your letters neatly," but when they do they are focusing only on the surface features of reading and writing. In actuality, readers create meaning for the words in the book based on their own knowledge and experiences. Similarly, writers organize ideas using their knowledge of spelling and grammar to transcribe their thoughts onto paper or computer screens. Phonics, decoding, and reading aloud are all part of reading, but the essence of reading is the creation of meaning. By the same token, spelling, handwriting, and using capital letters correctly are parts of writing, but without ideas to communicate, neat handwriting isn't very important.

The International Reading Association's position statement *Honoring Children's Rights to Excellent Reading Instruction* (2000) emphasizes that all children deserve excellent literacy instruction and support so that they become competent readers and writers. In that light, this chapter introduces eight principles of an effective reading program; each principle is stated in terms of what an effective teacher does.

Visit Chapter 1 on the Companion Website at *www.prenhall.com/ tompkins* to check into your state's standards for reading and writing.

PRINCIPLE 1: EFFECTIVE TEACHERS UNDERSTAND HOW CHILDREN LEARN

Understanding how children learn, and particularly how they learn to read and write, influences the instructional approaches that effective teachers use. Until the 1960s, behaviorism, a teacher-centered theory, was the dominant view of learning; since then, student-centered theories, including constructivism, have become more influential, and literacy instruction has changed to reflect these theories. In the last few years, however, behaviorism has begun a resurgence as evidenced by the federal No Child Left Behind legislation, the renewed popularity of basal reading programs, the current emphasis on curriculum standards, and the mandated testing programs. The instructional activities that Miss Paniccia used in the vignette at the beginning of the chapter and that other teachers use today represent a balance between teacher-centered and student-centered theories. Figure 1–1 presents an overview of these learning theories.

Behaviorism

Behaviorists focus on the observable and measurable aspects of human behavior. They believe that behavior can be learned or unlearned, and that learning is the result of stimulus-and-response actions (O'Donohue & Kitchener, 1998). This theory is described as teacher centered because it focuses on the teacher's active role as a dispenser of knowledge. Skinner (1974) explained that students learn to read by learning a series of discrete skills. Teachers use direct instruction methods to teach skills in a planned, sequential order. Information is presented in small steps and reinforced through practice activities until students master it because each step is built on the previous one. Traditionally, students practice the skills they are learning by completing fill-in-the-blank worksheets. They usually work individually, not in small groups or with partners. Behavior modification is another key feature: Behaviorists believe that teachers control and motivate students through a combination of rewards and punishments.

Constructivism

Jean Piaget's (1969) theoretical framework differed substantially from behaviorist theories: Piaget described learning as the modification of students' cognitive structures, or schemata, as they interact with and adapt to their environment. Schemata are like mental filing cabinets, and new information is organized with prior knowledge in the filing system. Piaget also posited that children are active and motivated thinkers and learners. This definition of learning and children's role in learning requires a reexamination of the teacher's role: Instead of simply being dispensers of knowledge, teachers engage students with experiences so that they modify their schemata and construct their own knowledge.

Interactive Theory

The interactive theory describes what readers do as they read. It emphasizes that readers focus on comprehension, or making meaning, as they read (Rumelhart, 1977; Stanovich, 1980). Readers construct meaning using a combination of text-based information (information from the text) and reader-based information (information from readers' backgrounds of knowledge, or schemata). The interactive theory echoes the importance of schemata described in the constructivist theories. In the past, educators have argued over whether children's attention during reading moves from noticing the letters on the page and grouping them into words to making meaning in the brain, or the other way around, from activating background knowledge in the brain to examining letters and words on the page. Educators now agree that the two processes take place interactively, at the same time.

The interactive model of reading includes an executive function, or decision maker: Fluent readers identify words automatically and use word-identification skills

Figure 1-1	Learning Theories That Inform Literacy Instruction		
Category	**Theory**	**Characteristics**	**Applications**
Teacher-Centered	Behaviorism	• Teachers provide direct instruction. • Teachers motivate students and control their behavior. • Teachers use tests to measure learning. • Children are passive learners.	Teachers apply behaviorism when they use basal reading programs, post word walls in the classroom, and use tests to measure students' learning. Children apply this theory when they complete workbook pages.
Student-Centered	Constructivism	• Children are active learners. • Children relate new information to prior knowledge. • Children organize and relate information in schemata.	Children apply constructivism when they use K-W-L charts, make personal, world, and literary connections to books they are reading, and choose the books they read and topics for writing.
	Interactive	• Students use both prior knowledge and features in the text as they read. • Students use word-identification skills and comprehension strategies. • Fluent readers focus on comprehension as they read.	Teachers apply interactive theory when they use guided reading and model strategies using think-alouds. Children apply this theory when they use reading and writing strategies and draw graphic organizers to aid their comprehension.
	Sociolinguistics	• Thought and language are related. • Students use social interaction as a learning tool. • Teachers provide scaffolds for students.	Teachers apply sociolinguistics when they read aloud to children, use shared reading, the language experience approach, and interactive writing because the teachers provide a scaffold. When children work collaboratively, they are applying this theory.
	Reader Response	• Readers create meaning as they read and write. • Students vary how they read and write according to aesthetic and efferent purposes. • The goal is for students to become lifelong readers and writers.	Children apply reader response theory when they respond to literature by writing in reading logs and participating in grand conversations and instructional conversations. Other applications include reading and writing workshop.
	Critical Literacy	• Children are empowered through reading and writing. • Readers think critically about books they are reading. • Children become agents for social change.	Children apply critical literacy theory when they read multicultural literature, consider social issues in books they read, write letters to the editor, and pursue community projects. Teachers apply this theory when they create inclusive communities of learners in their classrooms.

when they come across unfamiliar words so that they can focus their attention on comprehension, and the decision maker monitors the reading process and the skills and strategies that readers use. Teachers focus on reading as a comprehension process and teach both word-identification skills and comprehension strategies.

Sociolinguistics

The sociolinguists contribute a cultural dimension to our consideration of how children learn: They view reading and writing as social activities that reflect the culture and community in which students live (Heath, 1983; Vygotsky, 1978, 1986). According to Lev Vygotsky, language helps to organize thought, and children use language to learn as well as to communicate and share experiences with others. Understanding that children use language for social purposes allows teachers to plan instructional activities that incorporate a social component, such as having students talk about books they are reading or share their writing with classmates. And, because children's language and concepts of literacy reflect their cultures and home communities, teachers must respect students' language and appreciate cultural differences in their attitudes toward learning and becoming literate.

Social interaction enhances learning in two other ways: scaffolding and the zone of proximal development (Dixon-Krauss, 1996). Scaffolding is a support mechanism that teachers and parents use to assist students. Vygotsky suggests that children can accomplish more difficult tasks in collaboration with adults than they can on their own. For example, when teachers assist students in reading a book they could not read independently or help students revise a piece of writing, they are scaffolding. Vygotsky also suggests that children learn very little when they perform tasks that they can already do independently; he recommends the zone of proximal development, the range of tasks between students' actual developmental level and their potential development. More challenging tasks done with the teacher's scaffolding are more conducive to learning. As students learn, teachers gradually withdraw their support so that students eventually perform the task independently. Then the cycle begins again.

Reader Response

Louise Rosenblatt (1978, 1983) and other reader response theorists consider how students create meaning as they read. These theories extend the constructivist theories about schemata and making meaning in the brain, not the eyes. According to reader response theorists, students do not try to figure out the author's meaning as they read; instead, they negotiate or create a meaning that makes sense based on the words they are reading and on their own background knowledge. Reader response theorists agree with Piaget that readers are active and responsible for their learning.

Rosenblatt (1991) explains that there are two stances or purposes for reading: When readers read for enjoyment or pleasure, they assume an aesthetic stance, and when they read to locate and remember information, they read efferently. Rosenblatt suggests that these two stances represent the ends of a continuum and that readers often use a combination of the two stances when they read, whether they are reading stories or informational books. For example, when students read *Nature's Green Umbrella* (Gibbons, 1994), an informational book about tropical rain forests, they may read efferently to locate information about the animals that live in rain forests. Or they may read aesthetically, carried off—in their minds, at least—on an expedition to the Amazon River. When students read a novel such as *Sarah, Plain and Tall* (MacLachlan, 1985), a story about a mail-order bride, they usually read aesthetically as they relive life on the prairie a century ago. Students are encouraged to step into the story and become a character and to "live" the story. This conflicts with more traditional approaches in which teachers ask students to recall specific information from the story, thus forcing students to read efferently, to take away information. Reader response theory suggests that when students read efferently rather than aesthetically, they do not learn to love reading and may not become lifelong readers.

Critical Literacy

Critical literacy grew out of Pablo Freire's theory of critical pedagogy (2000), which called for a sweeping transformation in education so that teachers and students ask fundamental questions about knowledge, justice, and equity (McDaniel, 2004; Wink, 2000). Language is a means for social action. Teachers should do more than just teach students to read and write: Both teachers and students can become agents of social change. The increasing social and cultural diversity in our society adds urgency to resolving the inequities and injustices in society. Think about these issues:

Does school perpetuate the dominant culture and exclude others?

Do all students have equal access to learning opportunities?

Is school more like family life in some cultures than in others?

Do teachers interact differently with boys and girls?

Are some students silenced in classrooms?

Do teachers have different expectations for minority students?

Literacy instruction does not take place in a vacuum; the content that teachers teach and the ways they teach it occur in a social, cultural, political, and historical context (Freire & Macedo, 1987; Giroux, 1988). Consider the issue of grammar instruction, for example: Some people argue that grammar shouldn't be taught in the elementary grades because it is too abstract and won't help students become better readers or writers, but others believe that not teaching grammar is one way the majority culture denies access to nonstandard English speakers. Both proponents and detractors of grammar instruction want what is best for children, but their views are diametrically opposed.

Luke and Freebody's (1997) model of reading includes critical literacy as the fourth and highest level. I have adapted their model to incorporate both reading and writing:

1. *Code Breakers.* Students become code breakers as they learn phonics, word-identification strategies, and high-frequency words as they learn to read and write fluently.

2. *Text Participants.* Students become text participants as they learn about text structures and genres in order to comprehend what they read and as they learn to develop coherent ideas in the texts they write.

3. *Text Users.* Students become text users as they read and write multigenre texts and compare the effect of genre and purpose on texts.

4. *Text Critics.* Students become text critics as they examine the issues raised in books and other texts they read and write.

One way that teachers take students to the fourth level, text critics, is to read and discuss books such as *The Breadwinner* (Ellis, 2000), the story of a girl in Taliban-controlled Afghanistan who pretends to be a boy to support her family; *The Watsons Go to Birmingham—1963* (Curtis, 1995), the story of an African American family caught in the Birmingham church bombing; and *Homeless Bird* (Whelan, 2000), the story of an Indian girl who has no future when she is widowed. These stories describe injustices that elementary students can understand and discuss (Foss, 2002; Lewiston,

Flint, & Van Sluys, 2002; McLaughlin & De Voogd, 2004; Vasquez, 2003). In fact, teachers report that their students are often more engaged in reading stories about social issues than other books and that students' interaction patterns change after reading them.

Critical literacy emphasizes children's potential to become thoughtful, active citizens. The reason injustices persist in society, Shannon (1995) hypothesizes, is because people do not "ask why things are the way they are, who benefits from these conditions, and how can we make them more equitable" (p. 123). Through critical literacy, students become empowered to transform their world (Bomer & Bomer, 2001). They learn social justice concepts, read literature that reflects diverse voices, notice injustices in the world, and use writing to take action for social change.

PRINCIPLE 2: EFFECTIVE TEACHERS SUPPORT CHILDREN'S USE OF THE FOUR CUEING SYSTEMS

Language is a complex system for creating meaning through socially shared conventions (Halliday, 1978). English, like other languages, involves four cueing systems:

- the phonological or sound system
- the syntactic or structural system
- the semantic or meaning system
- the pragmatic or social and cultural use system

Together these systems make communication possible; children and adults use all four systems simultaneously as they read, write, listen, and talk. The priority people place on various cueing systems can vary; however, the phonological system is especially important for beginning readers and writers as they apply phonics skills to decode and spell words. Information about the four cueing systems is summarized in Figure 1–2.

The Phonological System

There are approximately 44 speech sounds in English. Students learn to pronounce these sounds as they learn to talk, and they learn to associate the sounds with letters as they learn to read and write. Sounds are called *phonemes*, and they are represented in print with diagonal lines to differentiate them from graphemes (letters or letter combinations). Thus, the first grapheme in *mother* is *m*, and the phoneme is /m/. The phoneme in *soap* that is represented by the grapheme *oa* is called "long o" and is written /ō/.

The phonological system is important for both oral and written language. Regional and cultural differences exist in the way people pronounce phonemes; for example, people from Massachusetts pronounce sounds differently from people from Georgia. Similarly, the English spoken in Australia is different from American English. Children who are learning English as a second language must learn to pronounce English sounds; sounds that are different from those in their native language are particularly difficult to learn. For example, because Spanish does not have /th/, children who have immigrated to the United States from Mexico and other Spanish-speaking countries have difficulty pronouncing this sound; they often substitute /d/ for /th/ because the sounds are articulated in similar ways (Nathenson-Mejia, 1989). Younger children usually learn to pronounce the difficult sounds more easily than older children and adults.

The phonological system plays a crucial role in reading instruction during the primary grades. Children use their knowledge of phonics as they learn to read and write.

Figure 1-2 Relationships Among the Four Cueing Systems

System	Terms	Applications
Phonological System The sound system of English with approximately 44 sounds and more than 500 ways to spell the 44 sounds	• Phoneme (the smallest unit of sound) • Grapheme (the written representation of a phoneme using one or more letters) • Phonological awareness (knowledge about the sound structure of words, at the phoneme, onset-rime, and syllable levels) • Phonemic awareness (the ability to manipulate the sounds in words orally) • Phonics (instruction about phoneme-grapheme correspondences and spelling rules)	• Pronouncing words • Detecting regional and other dialects • Decoding words when reading • Using invented spelling • Reading and writing alliterations and onomatopoeia • Noticing rhyming words • Dividing words into syllables
Syntactic System The structural system of English that governs how words are combined into sentences	• Syntax (the structure or grammar of a sentence) • Morpheme (the smallest meaningful unit of language) • Free morpheme (a morpheme that can stand alone as a word) • Bound morpheme (a morpheme that must be attached to a free morpheme)	• Adding inflectional endings to words • Combining words to form compound words • Adding prefixes and suffixes to root words • Using capitalization and punctuation to indicate beginnings and ends of sentences • Writing simple, compound, and complex sentences • Combining sentences
Semantic System The meaning system of English that focuses on vocabulary	• Semantics (meaning) • Synonyms (words that mean the same or nearly the same thing) • Antonyms (words that are opposites) • Homonyms (words that sound alike but are spelled differently)	• Learning the meanings of words • Discovering that some words have multiple meanings • Using context clues to figure out an unfamiliar word • Studying synonyms, antonyms, and homonyms • Using a dictionary and a thesaurus • Reading and writing comparisons (metaphors and similes)
Pragmatic System The system of English that varies language according to social and cultural uses	• Function (the purpose for which a person uses language) • Standard English (the form of English used in textbooks and by television newscasters) • Nonstandard English (other forms of English)	• Varying language to fit specific purposes • Reading and writing dialogue in dialects • Comparing standard and nonstandard forms of English

In a purely phonetic language, there would be a one-to-one correspondence between letters and sounds, and teaching students to sound out words would be a simple process. But English is not a purely phonetic language because there are 26 letters and 44 sounds and many ways to combine the letters to spell some of the sounds, especially vowels. Consider these ways to spell long *e: sea, green, Pete, me,* and *people.* And sometimes the patterns used to spell long *e* don't work, as in *head* and *great.* Phonics, which describes the phoneme-grapheme correspondences and related spelling rules, is an important part of reading instruction. Students use phonics information to decode words, but phonics instruction is not a complete reading program because many common words cannot be decoded easily and because good readers do much more than just decode words when they read.

Children in the primary grades also use their understanding of the phonological system to create invented spellings. First graders, for example, might spell *home* as *hm* or *hom,* and second graders might spell *school* as *skule,* based on their knowledge of phoneme-grapheme relationships and the English spelling patterns. As children learn more phonics and gain more experience reading and writing, their spellings become more conventional. For students who are learning English as a second language, their spellings often reflect their pronunciations of words (Nathenson-Mejia, 1989).

The Syntactic System

The syntactic system is the structural organization of English. This system is the grammar that regulates how words are combined into sentences; the word *grammar* here means the rules governing how words are combined in sentences, not parts of speech.

Children use the syntactic system as they combine words to form sentences. Word order is important in English, and English speakers must arrange words into a sequence that makes sense. Young Spanish-speaking children who are learning English as a second language, for example, learn to say "This is my red sweater," not "This is my sweater red," which is the literal translation from Spanish.

Children use their knowledge of the syntactic system as they read: They expect that the words they are reading have been strung together into sentences. When they come to an unfamiliar word, they recognize its role in the sentence even if they don't know the terms for parts of speech. In the sentence "The horses galloped through the gate and out into the field," students may not be able to decode the word *through,* but they can easily substitute a reasonable word or phrase, such as *out of* or *past.*

Many of the capitalization and punctuation rules that students learn reflect the syntactic system of language. Similarly, when children learn about simple, compound, and complex sentences, they are learning about the syntactic system.

Nurturing English Learners

Why are the cueing systems important for English learners?

Students who are learning English (often called English learners or ELs) learn to use all four cueing systems as they become proficient in English: They use the phonological system to pronounce English words, the syntactic system to arrange words in sentences, the semantic system to learn vocabulary and idioms, and the pragmatic system to vary how they use English for different social purposes. ELs make errors involving each cueing system; however, their syntactic or grammar errors, especially verb forms, noun-verb agreement, and plurals, can be the most obvious. Through a combination of talking with teachers and English-speaking classmates, learning to read and write in English, and receiving direct instruction on language concepts, most students can become proficient in conversational English during the elementary grades.

Another component of syntax is word forms. Words such as *dog* and *play* are morphemes, the smallest meaningful units in language. Word parts that change the meaning of a word are also morphemes; when the plural marker *-s* is added to *dog* to make *dogs,* for instance, or the past-tense marker *-ed* is added to *play* to make *played,* these words now have two morphemes because the inflectional endings change the meaning of the words. The words *dog* and *play* are free morphemes because they convey meaning while standing alone; the endings *-s* and *-ed* are bound morphemes because they must be attached to free morphemes to convey meaning. Compound words are two or more morphemes combined to create a new word: *Birthday,* for example, is a compound word made up of two free morphemes.

During the elementary grades, children learn to add affixes to words. Affixes that are added at the beginning of a word are prefixes, and affixes added at the end are suffixes. Both kinds of affixes are bound morphemes. The prefix *un-* in *unhappy* is a bound morpheme, and *happy* is a free morpheme because it can stand alone as a word.

The Semantic System

The third cueing system is the semantic or meaning system. Vocabulary is the key component of this system: As children learn to talk, they acquire a continually increasing vocabulary. Researchers estimate that children have a vocabulary of 5,000 words by the time they enter school, and they continue to acquire 3,000 to 4,000 words each year during the elementary grades (Lindfors, 1987; Nagy, 1988). Considering how many words children learn each year, it is unreasonable to assume that they learn words only through formal instruction. They learn many, many words informally through reading and through social studies and science lessons.

Children learn approximately 8 to 10 words a day. A remarkable achievement! As children learn a word, they move from a general understanding of the meaning of the word to a better-developed understanding, and they learn these words through real reading, not by copying definitions from a dictionary. Researchers have estimated that students need to read a word 4 to 14 times

The Cueing Systems

These students are using all four cueing systems as they write and present a puppet show to their classmates based on characters from the Beverly Cleary books they've read: They use the phonological system to spell words while writing the puppet show script, the syntactic system to create sentences for the script and read the sentences during the performance, the semantic system to choose words for the script and to recall these words as they present the puppet show, and the pragmatic system as they create dialogue that is appropriate for the characters. Their classmates are using the four cueing systems, too, as they review the puppet show. You will find that students use the cueing systems in combination for almost every literacy activity.

to make it their own, which is possible only when students read and reread books and write about what they are reading.

The Pragmatic System

The fourth cueing system is pragmatics, which deals with the social aspects of language use. People use language for many purposes; how they talk or write varies according to their purpose and audience. Language use also varies among social classes, ethnic groups, and geographic regions; these varieties are known as dialects. School is one cultural community, and the language of school is Standard English. This dialect is formal—the one used in textbooks, newspapers, and magazines and by television newscasters. Other forms, including those spoken in urban ghettos, in Appalachia, and by Mexican Americans in the Southwest, are generally classified as nonstandard English. These nonstandard forms of English are alternatives in which the phonology, syntax, and semantics differ from those of Standard English. They are neither inferior nor substandard; they reflect the communities of the speakers, and the speakers communicate as effectively as those who use Standard English. The goal is for children to add Standard English to their repertoire of language registers, not to replace their home dialect with Standard English.

As children who speak nonstandard English read texts written in Standard English, they often translate what they read into their dialect. Sometimes this occurs when children are reading aloud. For example, a sentence written "They are going to school" might be read aloud as "They be goin' to school." Emergent or beginning readers are not usually corrected when they translate words into nonstandard dialects as long as they don't change the meaning, but older, more fluent readers should be directed to read the words as they are printed in the book.

Effective teachers understand that children use all four cueing systems as they read and write. For example, when students read the sentence "Jimmy is playing ball with his father" correctly, they are probably using information from all four systems. When a child substitutes *dad* for *father* and reads "Jimmy is playing ball with his dad," he might be focusing on the semantic or pragmatic system rather than on the phonological system. When a child substitutes *basketball* for *ball* reads "Jimmy is playing basketball with his father," he might be relying on an illustration or his own experience playing basketball. Because both *basketball* and *ball* begin with *b*, he might have used the beginning sound as an aid in decoding, but he apparently did not consider how long the word *basketball* is compared with the word *ball*. When the child changes the syntax, as in "Jimmy, he play ball with his father," he may speak a nonstandard dialect. Sometimes a child reads the sentence as "Jump is play boat with his father," so that it doesn't make sense: The child chooses words with the correct beginning sound and uses appropriate parts of speech for at least some of the words, but there is no comprehension. This is a serious problem because the child doesn't seem to understand that what he reads must make sense.

In upcoming chapters, you will learn ways to apply this information on the cueing systems. The information on the phonological system is applied to phonics in Chapter 4, "Cracking the Alphabetic Code," and the information on the syntactic system is applied to words and sentences in Chapter 5, "Developing Fluent Readers and Writers," and Chapter 6, "Expanding Students' Knowledge of Words." The information on the semantic and pragmatic systems is applied to vocabulary and comprehension in Chapter 6 and in Chapter 7, "Facilitating Students' Comprehension: Reader Factors."

PRINCIPLE 3: EFFECTIVE TEACHERS CREATE A COMMUNITY OF LEARNERS

Classrooms are social settings in which students read, discuss, and write about literature. Together, students and their teachers create the classroom community, and the type of community they create strongly influences students' learning. Effective teachers establish a community of learners in which students are motivated to learn and are actively involved in reading and writing activities, just as Miss Paniccia's were in the vignette. Teachers and students work collaboratively and purposefully. Perhaps the most striking quality of classroom communities is the partnership that the teacher and students create. Students are a "family" in which all the members respect one another and support each other's learning. Students value culturally and linquistically diverse classmates and recognize that all students make important contributions to the classroom (Wells & Chang-Wells, 1992).

Students and teachers work together for the common good of the community. Consider the differences between renting and owning a home. In a classroom community, students and the teacher are joint "owners" of the classroom. Students assume responsibility for their own learning and behavior, work collaboratively with classmates, complete assignments, and care for the classroom. In traditional classrooms, in contrast, the classroom is the teacher's, and students are simply "renters" for the school year. This doesn't mean that in a classroom community, teachers abdicate their responsibility to the students; on the contrary, teachers retain all of their roles as guide, instructor, monitor, coach, mentor, and grader. Sometimes these roles are shared with students, but the ultimate responsibility remains with the teacher.

Characteristics of Classroom Communities

Classroom communities have specific characteristics that are conducive to learning and that support students' interactions with literature:

1. *Responsibility.* Students are responsible for their learning, their behavior, and the contributions they make in the classroom. They see themselves as valued and contributing members of the classroom community.

2. *Opportunities.* Children have opportunities to read and write for meaningful purposes. They read real books and write for real audiences—their classmates, their parents, and community members.

3. *Engagement.* Students are motivated to learn and are actively involved in reading and writing activities. Students sometimes choose which books to read, how they will respond to a book, and which reading and writing projects they will pursue.

4. *Demonstration.* Teachers provide demonstrations of literacy skills and strategies, and children observe in order to learn what more capable readers and writers do.

5. *Risk taking.* Students are encouraged to explore topics, make guesses, and take risks.

6. *Instruction.* Teachers are expert readers and writers, and they provide instruction through minilessons on procedures, skills, and strategies related to reading and writing.

7. *Response.* Children share personal connections to stories, make predictions, ask questions, and deepen their comprehension as they write in reading logs and participate in grand conversations. When they write, children share their rough drafts in writing groups to get feedback on how well they are communicating, and they celebrate their published books by sharing them with classmates.

8. *Choice.* Students often make choices about the books they read and the writing they do within the parameters set by the teacher. When given opportunities to make choices, students are often more highly motivated to read and write, and they value their learning experience because it is more meaningful to them.

9. *Time.* Children need large chunks of time to pursue reading and writing activities; it doesn't work well for teachers to break the classroom schedule into many small time blocks. Two to three hours of uninterrupted time each day for reading and writing instruction is recommended. It is important to minimize disruptions during the time set aside for literacy instruction; administrators should schedule computer, music, art, and other pull-out programs so that they do not interfere. This is especially important in the primary grades.

10. *Assessment.* Teachers and children work together to establish guidelines for assessment so that children can monitor their own work and participate in the evaluation. (Cambourne & Turbill, 1987)

Figure 1–3 reviews these 10 characteristics, and explains the teacher's and students' roles.

How to Create a Classroom Community

Teachers are more successful when they take the first 2 weeks of the school year to establish the classroom environment (Sumara & Walker, 1991); they can't assume that students will be familiar with procedures and routines or that they will instinctively be cooperative, responsible, and respectful of classmates. Teachers explictly explain classroom routines, such as how to get supplies out and put them away and how to work with classmates in a cooperative group, and set the expectation that students will adhere to the routines. Next, they demonstrate literacy procedures, including how to choose a book to read from the classroom library, how to provide feedback about a classmate's writing, and how to participate in a grand conversation about a book. Third, teachers model ways of interacting with students, responding to literature, respecting classmates, and assisting classmates with reading and writing projects.

Teachers are the classroom managers: They set expectations and clearly explain to students what is expected of them and what is valued in the classroom. The classroom rules are specific and consistent, and teachers also set limits. For example, students might be allowed to talk quietly with classmates when they are working, but they are not allowed to shout across the classroom or talk when the teacher is talking or when students are making a presentation to the class. Teachers also model classroom rules themselves as they interact with students. According to Sumara and Walker (1991), the process of socialization at the beginning of the school year is planned, deliberate, and crucial to the success of the literacy program.

Not everything can be accomplished during the first 2 weeks, however; teachers continue to reinforce classroom routines and literacy procedures. One way is to have student leaders model the desired routines and behaviors. When this is done, other stu-

Figure 1-3 Ten Characteristics of a Community of Learners

Characteristic	Teacher's Role	Students' Role
Responsibility	Teachers set guidelines and have the expectation that students will be responsible. Teachers also model responsible behavior.	Students are responsible for fully participating in the classroom, including completing assignments, participating in groups, and cooperating with classmates.
Opportunities	Teachers provide opportunities for students to read and write in genuine and meaningful activities, not contrived practice activities.	Students take advantage of learning opportunities provided in class. They read independently during reading workshop, and they share their writing during sharing time.
Engagement	Teachers make it possible for students to be engaged by the literature and activities they provide for students. Also, by planning units with students and allowing them to make choices, they motivate students to complete assignments.	Students are actively involved in reading and writing activities. They are motivated and industrious because they are reading real literature and are involved in activities they find meaningful.
Demonstration	Teachers demonstrate what readers and writers do and use think-alouds to explain their thinking during the demonstrations.	Students observe the teacher's demonstrations of skills and strategies that readers and writers use.
Risk taking	Teachers encourage students to take risks, make guesses, and explore their thinking. They deemphasize students' need to get things "right."	Students explore what they are learning, take risks as they ask questions, and make guesses. They expect not to be laughed at or made fun of. They view learning as a process of exploration.
Instruction	Teachers provide instruction through minilessons. During minilessons, teachers provide information and make connections to the reading and writing in which students are involved.	Students look to the teacher to provide instruction on procedures, concepts, strategies, and skills related to reading and writing. Students participate in minilessons and then apply what they have learned in their own reading and writing.
Response	Teachers provide opportunities for students to share and respond to reading and writing activities.	Students respond to books they are reading in reading logs and grand conversations. They share their writing in writing groups and get feedback from classmates. Students are a supportive audience for classmates.
Choice	Teachers encourage students to choose some of the books they read and some of the writing activities and projects they develop.	Students make choices about some books they read, some writing activities, and some projects they develop within parameters set by the teacher.
Time	Teachers organize the class schedule with large chunks of time for reading and writing activities. They plan units and set deadlines with students.	Students have large chunks of time for reading and writing activities. They work on projects over days and weeks and understand when assignments are due.
Assessment	Teachers set grading plans with students before beginning each unit, meet with students in assessment conferences, and assist students in collecting work for portfolios.	Students understand how they will be assessed and graded, and they participate in their assessment. They collect their work-in-progress in folders and choose which work they will place in portfolios.

dents are likely to follow the lead. Teachers also continue to teach additional literacy procedures as students are involved in new types of activities. The classroom community evolves during the school year, but the foundation is laid during the first 2 weeks.

Teachers develop a predictable classroom environment with familiar routines and literacy procedures. Children feel comfortable, safe, and more willing to take risks and experiment in a predictable classroom environment. This is especially true for students from varied cultures, English learners, and students who struggle.

The classroom community also extends beyond the walls of the classroom to include the entire school and the wider community. Within the school, students become "buddies" with students in other classes and get together to read and write in pairs (Morrice & Simmons, 1991). When parents and other community members come into the school, they demonstrate the value they place on education by working as tutors and aides, sharing their cultures, and demonstrating other types of expertise (Graves, 1995).

Principle 4: Effective Teachers Adopt a Balanced Approach to Literacy Instruction

Visit Chapter 1 on the Companion Website at *www.prenhall.com/ tompkins* to connect to web links related to literacy instruction.

In recent years, we have witnessed a great deal of controversy about the best way to teach reading. On one side are the proponents of a skills-based or phonics approach; on the other side are advocates of a holistic approach. Teachers favoring each side cite research to support their views, and state legislatures have joined the debate by mandating systematic, intensive phonics instruction in the primary grades. Today, many teachers agree with Richard Allington that there is "no quick fix" and no one program to meet the needs of all children (Allington & Walmsley, 1995). Many teachers recognize value in both points of view and recommend a "balance" or combination of holistic and skills approaches (Baumann, Hoffman, Moon, & Duffy-Hester, 1998). That is the perspective taken in this text.

A balanced approach to literacy, according to Spiegel (1998), is a decision-making approach through which teachers make thoughtful and purposeful decisions about how to help students become better readers and writers. A balanced approach "is built on research, views the teacher as an informed decision maker who develops a flexible program, and is constructed around a comprehensive view of literacy" (Spiegel, 1998, p. 117).

Fitzgerald (1999) identified three principles of a balanced literacy approach. First, teachers develop students' skills knowledge, including decoding skills, their strategy knowledge for comprehension and responding to literature, and their affective knowledge, including nurturing students' love of

Scaffolding Struggling Readers

Do struggling students benefit from a balanced approach to literacy instruction?

Sometimes teachers think that students who struggle need a different kind of instructional program, but all students benefit from a balanced instructional program that combines direct instruction on literacy skills and strategies, practice activities, and opportunities to read real literature and write for meaningful purposes. Some adaptations may be necessary, however. It's unrealistic to assume that struggling readers can read instructional materials at their grade level; they need interesting reading materials at their instructional level. Struggling students who have limited knowledge of phonics, spelling, or other skills need additional instruction to bring their knowledge up to grade-level expectations. When students are more than 1 year below grade level, they often benefit from working with a reading specialist in addition to participating in the classroom balanced reading program.

reading. Second, instructional approaches that are sometimes viewed as opposites are used to meet students' learning needs; direct instruction in phonics and reading workshop, for instance, are two very different instructional programs that are used in a balanced literacy approach. Third, students read a variety of reading materials, ranging from trade books to leveled books with controlled vocabulary and basal reading textbooks.

Even though balanced programs vary, they usually embody these characteristics:

- Literacy is viewed comprehensively, as involving both reading and writing.
- Literature is at the heart of the program.
- Skills and strategies are taught both directly and indirectly.
- Reading instruction involves learning word recognition and identification, fluency, vocabulary, and comprehension.
- Writing instruction involves learning to express meaningful ideas and use conventional spelling, grammar, and punctuation to express those ideas.
- Students use reading and writing as tools for learning in the content areas.
- The goal is to develop lifelong readers and writers. (Baumann & Ivey, 1997; McIntyre & Pressley, 1996; Spiegel, 1998; Weaver, 1998)

Miss Paniccia's balanced literacy program, described in the vignette at the beginning of the chapter, exemplifies many of these characteristics.

Figure 1–4 lists 10 components of a balanced literacy program; they embody the characteristics and recommendations from researchers, professional literacy organizations, and state boards of education. These components are addressed in each chapter of this text to show how the topic of that chapter fits into a balanced literacy program.

PRINCIPLE 5: EFFECTIVE TEACHERS SCAFFOLD CHILDREN'S READING AND WRITING EXPERIENCES

Teachers scaffold or support children's reading and writing as they demonstrate, guide, and teach, and they vary the amount of support they provide according to their instructional purpose and the children's needs. Sometimes teachers model how experienced readers read or record children's dictation when the writing is too difficult for children to do on their own. At other times, they guide children as they read a leveled book or proofread their writing. Teachers use five levels of support, moving from the greatest amount to the least as children assume more and more of the responsibility for themselves (Fountas & Pinnell, 1996). Figure 1–5 summarizes these five levels—modeled, shared, interactive, guided, and independent—of reading and writing.

Teachers working with kindergartners through eighth graders use all five levels. For instance, when teachers introduce a new writing form or teach a reading strategy or skill, they use demonstrations or modeling. Or, when teachers want children to practice a strategy or skill they have already taught, they might use a guided or independent literacy activity. The purpose of the activity, not the activity itself, determines which level of support is used. Teachers are less actively involved in directing independent reading and writing, but the quality of instruction that children have received is clearest when children work independently because they are applying what they have learned.

Figure 1-4   Components of a Balanced Literacy Program

Component	Description
Reading	Students participate in a variety of modeled, shared, interactive, guided, and independent reading experiences using trade books, basal reader textbooks, content-area textbooks, and self-selected books.
Phonics and Other Skills	Students learn to use phonics to decode and spell words. In addition, students learn other types of skills that they use in reading and writing, including comprehension, grammar, reference, and study skills.
Strategies	Students use problem-solving and monitoring behaviors called *strategies* as they read and write. Types of strategies include word-identification, comprehension, writing, and spelling strategies.
Vocabulary	Students learn the meanings of words through wide reading as well as by posting key words from books and thematic units on word walls and by participating in vocabulary activities.
Comprehension	Students choose appropriate reading materials; activate background knowledge and vocabulary; consider the structure of the text; make connections to their own lives, to the world, and to other literature; and apply reading strategies to ensure that they understand what they are reading.
Literature	Students read and respond to a variety of fiction and nonfiction texts as part of literature focus units, literature circles, and reading workshop.
Content-Area Study	Students use reading and writing to learn about social studies and science topics in content-area units. They read content-area textbooks as well as stories, informational books, and poetry, learn to conduct research, and prepare projects to apply what they have learned.
Oral Language	Students participate in oral language activities as they work in small groups, participate in grand conversations and instructional conversations, and present oral reports. They also listen to the teacher during read-alouds, minilessons, and other oral presentations.
Writing	Students use informal writing when they write in reading logs and other journals and make graphic organizers, and they use the writing process to write stories, essays, reports, and poems.
Spelling	Students apply phonics, syllabication, and morphemic analysis skills to spell words. They learn to spell high-frequency words first, and then other words that they need for writing through a variety of spelling activities that may include weekly spelling tests.

Modeled Reading and Writing

Teachers provide the greatest amount of support when they demonstrate or model how expert readers read and expert writers write while children observe. When teachers read aloud to children, they are modeling: They read fluently and with expression, and they talk about the strategies they use while they are reading. When they model writing, teachers write a composition on chart paper or using an overhead projector so that all children can see what the teacher does and what is being written. Teachers use this level to demonstrate how to make small books and how to do new writing genres and formats, such as poems and letters. Often teachers talk about or reflect on their reading and writing processes as they read and write to show students the types of decisions they make and the strategies they use. Teachers use modeling to

- demonstrate fluent reading and writing;
- explain how to use comprehension strategies, such as predicting, monitoring, and revising;
- teach the procedure for a new reading or writing activity;
- show how reading and writing conventions and other skills work.

Shared Reading and Writing

At this level, students and the teacher "share" the reading and writing tasks. Teachers use shared reading to read big books with primary-grade children. The teacher does most of the reading, but children join in the reading of familiar and repeated words and phrases. Upper-grade teachers also use shared reading. When students are reading a book that is too difficult for them to read independently, the teacher may read aloud while students follow along, reading silently.

Figure 1–5	**A Continuum of Literacy Instruction**	

Level of Support		Reading	Writing
High	*Modeled*	Teacher reads aloud, modeling how good readers read fluently and with expression. Books too difficult for students to read themselves are used. Examples: reading aloud to students and listening centers.	Teacher writes in front of students, creating the text, doing the writing, and thinking aloud about writing strategies and skills. Example: demonstrations.
	Shared	Teacher and students read books together, with the students following as the teacher reads and then repeating familiar refrains. Books students can't read by themselves are used. Examples: big books, buddy reading.	Teacher and students create the text together; then the teacher does the actual writing. Students may assist by spelling familiar or high-frequency words. Example: Language Experience Approach.
	Interactive	Teacher and students read together and take turns doing the reading. The teacher helps students read fluently and with expression. Instructional-level books are used. Examples: choral reading and readers theatre.	Teacher and students create the text and share the pen to do the writing. Teacher and students talk about writing conventions. Examples: interactive writing and daily news.
	Guided	Teacher plans and teaches reading lessons to small, homogeneous groups using instructional-level books. Focus is on supporting and observing students' use of strategies. Example: guided reading groups.	Teacher plans and teaches lesson on a writing procedure, strategy, or skill, and students participate in supervised practice activities. Example: class collaborations.
Low	*Independent*	Students choose and read self-selected books independently. Teachers conference with students to monitor their progress. Examples: reading workshop and reading centers.	Students use the writing process to write stories, informational books, and other compositions. Teacher monitors students' progress. Examples: writing workshop and writing centers.

Teachers at different grade levels use shared writing in a variety of ways. Primary-grade teachers often use the language experience approach to write children's dictation on paintings and brainstorm lists of words on the chalkboard, for example, and upper-grade teachers may take students' dictation when they make K-W-L charts, draw graphic organizers, and write class collaboration poems.

The most important way that sharing differs from modeling is that students actually participate in the activity rather than simply observe the teacher. In the shared reading activity, students follow along as the teacher reads, and in shared writing, they suggest the words and sentences that the teacher writes. Teachers use shared reading and writing to

- involve students in reading and writing activities that they could not do independently;
- provide opportunities for students to experience success in reading and writing;
- provide practice before students read and write independently.

Interactive Reading and Writing

Students assume an increasingly important role in interactive reading and writing activities. At this level, students no longer observe the teacher read or write, repeat familiar words, or suggest what the teacher will write; instead, students are more actively involved in reading and writing. They support their classmates by sharing the reading and writing responsibilities, and their teacher provides assistance when needed. Choral reading and readers theatre are two examples of interactive reading. In choral reading, students take turns reading lines of a poem, and in readers theatre, they assume the roles of characters and read lines in a script. In both of these interactive reading activities, the students support each other by actively participating and sharing the work. Teachers provide support by helping students with unfamiliar words or reading a sentence with more expression.

Interactive writing is a recently developed writing activity in which students and the teacher create a text and "share the pen" to write the text on chart paper (Button, Johnson, & Furgerson, 1996; Tompkins & Collom, 2004). The text is composed by the group, and the teacher assists students as they write the text word by word on chart paper. Students take turns writing known letters and familiar words, adding punctuation marks, and marking spaces between words. The teacher helps them to spell all words correctly and use written language conventions so that the text can be read easily. All students participate in creating and writing the text on chart paper, and they also write the text on small white boards. After writing, students read and reread the text using shared and independent reading. Teachers use interactive reading and writing to

- practice reading and writing high-frequency words;
- teach and practice phonics and spelling skills;
- read and write texts that students could not do independently;
- have students share their reading and writing expertise with classmates.

Guided Reading and Writing

Teachers continue to support students' reading and writing during guided literacy activities, but the students do the actual reading and writing themselves. In guided reading, small, homogeneous groups of students meet with the teacher to read a book at their instructional level. The teacher introduces the book and guides students as they begin read-

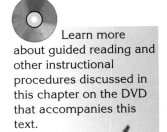
Learn more about guided reading and other instructional procedures discussed in this chapter on the DVD that accompanies this text.

ing. Then students continue reading on their own while the teacher monitors their reading. After reading, students and the teacher discuss the book, and then students often reread the book.

In guided writing, teachers plan structured writing activities and then supervise as students do the writing. For example, when students make pages for a class alphabet book or write formula poems, they are doing guided writing because the teacher has set up the writing activity. Teachers also guide students' writing when they conference with students as they write, participate in

writing groups to help students revise their writing, and proofread with students.

Teachers use guided reading and writing to provide instruction and assistance as students are actually reading and writing. Teachers use guided reading and writing to

- support students' reading in instructional-level materials;
- teach literacy procedures, concepts, skills, and strategies during minilessons;
- introduce different types of writing activities;
- teach students to use the writing process—in particular, how to revise and edit.

Independent Reading and Writing

Students do the reading and writing themselves during independent reading and writing activities. They apply and practice the procedures, concepts, strategies, and skills they have learned. Students may be involved in reading workshop or literature circles. During independent reading, they usually choose the books they read and work at their own pace. Similarly, during independent writing, children may be involved in writing workshop or work at a writing center. They usually choose their own topics for writing and move at their own pace through the stages of the writing process as they develop and refine their writing.

Through independent reading experiences, children learn the joy of reading and, teachers hope, become lifelong readers. In addition, as they write, students come to view themselves as authors. Teachers use independent reading and writing to

- create opportunities for students to practice the reading and writing procedures, concepts, strategies, and skills they have learned;

- provide authentic literacy experiences in which students choose their own topics, purposes, and materials;
- develop lifelong readers and writers.

PRINCIPLE 6: EFFECTIVE TEACHERS ORGANIZE LITERACY INSTRUCTION IN FOUR WAYS

Effective teachers promote literature in their instructional programs, and they combine opportunities for students to read and write with direct instruction on literacy skills and strategies. Teachers choose among four instructional approaches for their reading programs: basal reading programs, literature focus units, literature circles, and reading and writing workshop.

Basal Reading Progams

Commercially produced reading programs are known as basal readers. These programs feature a textbook or anthology of stories and accompanying workbooks, supplemental books, and related instructional materials at each grade level. Phonics, vocabulary, comprehension, grammar, and spelling instruction is coordinated with the reading selections and aligned with grade-level standards. Teacher's manuals provide detailed procedures for teaching the selections and the related skills and strategies. Instruction is typically presented to students together as a class, with reteaching to small groups of struggling students. Testing materials are also included so that teachers can monitor students' progress. The companies tout these books as complete literacy programs, but effective teachers integrate basal reading programs with other instructional approaches.

Literature Focus Units

All students in the class read and respond to the same book, and the teacher supports students' learning through a variety of related activities. Books chosen for literature focus units should be of high quality; teachers often choose books for literature focus units from a district- or state-approved list of books that all students are expected to read at that grade level.

Literature Circles

Teachers select five or six books for a text set. These books range in difficulty to meet the needs of all students in the classroom, and they are often related in theme or written by the same author. Teachers collect five or six copies of each book and give a book talk to introduce the books. Then students choose a book to read from a text set and form a group to read and respond to the book they have chosen.

Reading and Writing Workshop

In reading workshop, students individually select books to read and then read independently and conference with the teacher about their reading. Similarly, in writing workshop, students write books on topics that they choose and the teacher conferences with them about their writing. Usually teachers set aside a time for reading and writing workshop, and all students read and write while the teacher conferences with small groups. Sometimes, however, when the teacher is working with guided reading groups, the remainder of the class works in reading and writing workshop.

These four approaches are used at all grade levels, from kindergarten through eighth grade; effective teachers generally use a combination of them, as Miss Paniccia did in the vignette at the beginning of the chapter. Students need a variety of reading opportunities, and some books that students read are more difficult and require more support from the teacher. Some teachers alternate literature focus units or literature circles with reading and writing workshop and basal readers, whereas others use some components from each approach throughout the school year. Figure 1–6 presents a comparison of the four approaches.

As you continue reading, you will often see the terms *basal reading programs, literature focus units, literature circles,* and *reading and writing workshop* used because they are the instructional approaches presented in this text. In addition, entire chapters are devoted to each of these instructional approaches in Part III, "How Do Teachers Organize Literacy Instruction?"

PRINCIPLE 7: EFFECTIVE TEACHERS CONNECT INSTRUCTION AND ASSESSMENT

Teachers understand that students learn to read and write through a combination of direct instruction on strategies and skills and opportunities to apply what they're learning in real reading and writing activities. This understanding affects the way they assess students: No longer does it seem enough to grade students' vocabulary exercises or ask them to answer multiple-choice comprehension questions on reading passages that have no point beyond the exercise. Similarly, it no longer seems appropriate to measure success in writing by means of spelling and grammar tests. Instead, teachers need assessment information that tells about the complex achievements students are making in reading and writing.

Teachers use assessment procedures that they develop and others that are commercially available to:

- determine students' background knowledge
- identify students' reading levels
- monitor students' learning
- identify strengths and weaknesses in students' reading and writing
- analyze students' spelling development
- document students' learning
- showcase students' best work
- assign grades

Also, teachers use the results of standardized achievement tests as indicators of students' literacy levels and their strengths and weaknesses, as well as to assess the effect of their instruction.

Assessment is more than testing; it is an integral and ongoing part of teaching and learning (Glazer, 1998). Serafini (2000/2001) describes assessment as an inquiry

Figure 1-6   Four Instructional Approaches

	Basal Reading Programs	Literature Focus Units
Description	Students read textbooks containing stories, informational articles, and poems that are sequenced according to grade level. Teachers follow directions in the teacher's guide to teach word identification, vocabulary, comprehension, grammar, and writing lessons. Directions are also provided to meet the special needs of English learners and struggling students. Additional program materials include workbooks, charts, manipulatives, supplemental books, and assessment materials.	Teachers and students read and respond to one text together as a class. They choose texts that are high-quality literature and are appropriate for the grade level and students' interests. The books may be too difficult for some students to read on their own, so teachers may read them aloud or use shared reading. After reading, students explore the text and apply their learning by creating projects.
Strengths	• Textbooks are aligned with grade-level standards. • Students read selections at their grade level. • Teachers teach strategies and skills and provide structured practice opportunities. • Teachers are available to reteach strategies as needed. • The teacher's guide provides detailed instructions. • Assessment materials are included in the program.	• Teachers develop units using the reading process. • Teachers choose picture-book and chapter-book stories or informational books for units. • Teachers scaffold reading instruction as they read with the whole class or small groups. • Teachers teach minilessons on reading skills and strategies. • Students explore vocabulary and literary language. • Students develop projects to extend their reading.
Limitations	• Selections may be too difficult for some students. • Selections may lack the authenticity of good literature. • Programs include many worksheets. • Most of the instruction is presented to the whole class.	• Students all read the same book whether or not they like it and whether or not it is at their reading level. • Many of the activities are teacher directed.

process that teachers use in order to make informed instructional decisions. Figure 1–7 shows the teach-assess cycle. Effective teachers identify their goals and plan their instruction at the same time as they develop their assessment plan. The assessment plan involves three components: preassessing, monitoring, and assessing.

Preassessing

Teachers assess students' background knowledge before reading to determine whether students are familiar with the topic they will read about. They also verify that students are familiar with the genre, vocabulary, skills, and strategies. Then, based on the results of the assessment, teachers either help students develop more background knowledge or move on to the next step of their instructional plan. Here are some preassessment tools:

- creating a K-W-L chart
- quickwriting about a topic
- completing an anticipation guide

Literature Circles	Reading and Writing Workshop
Teachers choose five or six books and collect multiple copies of each book. Students each choose the book they want to read and form groups or "book clubs" to read and respond to the book. They develop a reading and discussion schedule, and teachers often participate in the discussions.	Students choose books and read and respond to them independently during reading workshop and write books on self-selected topics during writing workshop. Teachers monitor students' work through conferences. During a sharing period, students share with classmates the books they read and the books they write.
• Books are available at a variety of reading levels. • Students are more strongly motivated because they choose the books they read. • Students have opportunities to work with their classmates. • Students participate in authentic literacy experiences. • Activities are student directed, and students work at their own pace. • Teachers may participate in discussions to help students clarify misunderstandings and think more deeply about the book.	• Students read books appropriate for their reading levels. • Students are more strongly motivated because they choose the books they read. • Students work through the stages of the writing process during writing workshop. • Teachers teach minilessons on reading skills and strategies. • Activities are student directed, and students work at their own pace. • Teachers have opportunities to work individually with students during conferences.
• Teachers often feel a loss of control because students are reading different books. • To be successful, students must learn to be task oriented and to use time wisely. • Sometimes students choose books that are too difficult or too easy for them.	• Teachers often feel a loss of control because students are reading different books and working at different stages of the writing process. • To be successful, students must learn to be task oriented and to use time wisely.

Monitoring

Teachers often monitor students' progress in reading and writing as they observe students participating in literacy activities: Students might participate in conferences with the teacher, for example, and talk about what they are reading and writing, the strategies and skills they are learning to use, and problem areas. They reflect on what they do well as readers and writers and on what they need to learn next. Here are some monitoring tools:

- listening to students read aloud
- making running records of students' oral reading "miscues" or errors
- conferencing with students during reading and writing workshop
- listening to comments students make during grand and instructional conversations
- reading students' reading log entries and rough drafts of other compositions
- examining students' work-in-progress

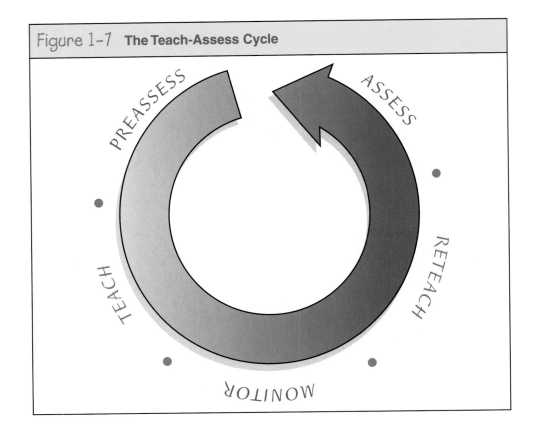

Figure 1-7 **The Teach-Assess Cycle**

PREASSESS

ASSESS

RETEACH

MONITOR

TEACH

Assessing

Teachers document students' learning and showcase their best work as well as grade their learning at the end of a unit. Besides grading students' written assignments, teachers collect other assessment information through the following activities:

- observing students' presentation of oral language projects, such as puppet shows, oral reports, and story retellings
- examining students' art and other visual projects
- analyzing students' comprehension through charts, dioramas, murals, Venn diagrams, and other graphic organizers they have made
- examining all drafts of students' writing to document their use of the writing process
- checking students' use of newly taught vocabulary in their compositions and other projects
- analyzing students' spelling using their compositions

Teachers also have students keep track of their progress using checklists that list assignments and other requirements. Then at the end of the unit, teachers collect and grade students' assignments.

You will learn more about how to monitor, document, and grade student learning in Chapter 9, "Assessing Students' Literacy Development."

PRINCIPLE 8: EFFECTIVE TEACHERS BECOME PARTNERS WITH PARENTS

Effective teachers communicate the importance of parent involvement to parents, view parents as teaching partners, and understand that even parents with limited education or those who do not speak English are valuable resources. They recognize that families from various cultures use literacy in different ways, but that parents from all sociocultural groups value literacy and want their children to succeed in school (Shockley, 1993).

Parents are the most powerful influence on children's literacy development, and when parents are involved in their children's literacy development, children become better readers and writers. Three ways that parents can become involved are as teaching partners in the classroom, as resource people, and as teachers at home (Tinajero & Nagel, 1995).

Teachers are also learning that working with parents of preschoolers and kindergartners can help prevent children's reading problems later on (France & Hager, 1993). Through parent programs, low-income and minority parents can learn how to create a home environment that fosters literacy and how to read aloud to their young children. Parents with limited literacy skills benefit in other ways, too: They develop their own reading and writing abilities through family literacy programs.

Providing Literacy Information to Parents

Today, children are learning to read in new ways, and these instructional methods are often unfamiliar to parents. Not surprisingly, these changes have made many parents anxious about how their children are learning to read and write. Parent information programs are crucial in helping parents to understand why children use trade books as well as textbooks, why children explore meanings of stories they have read through grand conversations, how skills and strategies are taught in minilessons, how writing supports children's reading development, and what invented spelling is. Teachers provide literacy information to parents in a variety of ways:

- back-to-school nights
- newsletters
- conferences with parents
- workshops on strategies for working with young readers and writers
- homework telephone hot lines
- telephone calls and notes conveying good news

In parent workshops and other information-sharing sessions, teachers use videotapes, demonstrations, and guest speakers to provide information about literacy development and the programs in their classrooms. Teachers share some of the books children are reading, especially books representing the cultures of the children in the classroom. Parents can write small books during a writing workshop session, use the computer for literacy activities, and learn how to examine the work their children bring home. Teachers also show parents how to work with their children at home. Without sharing these types of information, parents often feel isolated from the school and are unsure of how to help their children at home.

Patricia Edwards (1995) developed a literacy program for low-income parents in Louisiana, and she reports that parents want to know how to work with their children.

Parents told her that they didn't know reading books aloud to their young children was so important and wished they had known sooner how to support their children's literacy development. In her study, parents were grateful that someone explained and demonstrated to them exactly what teachers expect them to do at home.

Parent Volunteers

Schools need lots of adults to read with children and to conference with them about books they are reading and compositions they are writing. Parents, grandparents, older students, and other community volunteers can be extremely useful.

Volunteer experiences can be beneficial for parents, too, and they learn about the school and the literacy program. Come and Fredericks (1995) report that parents need to be involved in planning the program, and that they are more likely to become involved if they believe the school has their needs and those of their children at heart. Rasinski and Fredericks (1988) recommend five steps for establishing a quality volunteer program:

1. *Recruitment.* Teachers invite parents and others to volunteer to assist in the classroom. Sometimes telephone calls and home visits are necessary to let parents know they are truly welcome and needed.

2. *Training.* Volunteers need to be trained so that they know how to work with children, where things are located in the school, and how to assist teachers.

3. *Variety.* Because volunteers may feel more comfortable helping in one way than in another or because they may have a special talent to share, teachers need to offer parents a variety of ways to be involved in schools.

4. *Recognition.* For a volunteer program to be successful, the volunteers need to know they are appreciated. Often schools plan recognition receptions each spring to publicly thank the volunteers for their dedication and service.

5. *Evaluation.* Teachers evaluate their volunteer programs and make changes based on the feedback they get from the volunteers and students.

In bilingual schools with children from many cultural backgrounds, parents play a key role in their children's education: Monolingual English-speaking teachers rely on parents to develop an environment that is linguistically and culturally relevant for the children. Minority parents also provide a feeling of security and belonging for culturally and linguistically diverse students. Some parents from other cultures feel inadequate to help in schools, either because they speak another language or because they have limited education themselves, so it is the teacher's responsibility to let parents know they are valued (Tinajero & Nagel, 1995).

Supporting Literacy at Home

Parents are children's first and best teachers, and parents can do many things to support their children's literacy development at home. In addition to reading to their children and listening to their children read to them, parents can build children's self-esteem and spend quality time with them.

Families use literacy in many ways. Some read the Bible and other religious publications, and others read the newspaper or novels as entertainment. In some homes, the main reading experience is reading *TV Guide,* and in other homes, families write letters and sign greeting cards. Some parents read to their children each evening, and in other homes, parents are busy catching up on work from the office while children do homework in the evening. Some children and parents communicate with friends and relatives over the Internet. In many homes, parents demonstrate daily living routines, such as making shopping lists, paying bills, and leaving messages for family members that involve reading and writing.

Many teachers assume that children from families with low socioeconomic status have few, if any, literacy events in their homes, but other teachers argue that such children live in homes where people use print for many and varied functions, even though some of those purposes might be different from those of middle-class families. In an interesting study, researchers uncovered great variation in the number and types of uses of reading and writing in low-income families (Purcell-Gates, L'Allier, & Smith, 1995). Included in the study were white, African American, Hispanic American, and Asian American low-income families, and all children spoke English as their primary language. The findings confirm that teachers cannot make generalizations and must look at each child as an individual from a unique family setting. It is not enough to use demographic characteristics such as family income level to make assumptions about a child's literacy environment.

Family Literacy

Schools are designing family literacy programs for minority parents, parents who are not fluent readers and writers, and parents who are learning English as a second language. These programs are intergenerational and are designed to improve the literacy development of both children and their parents. Adults learn to improve their literacy skills as well as how to work with their children to foster their literacy development (Holloway, 2004). Family literacy programs have these components:

- *Parent literacy education.* Parents participate in activities to develop their own reading and writing competencies.

- *Information about how young children become literate.* Parents learn how they can support their young children as they emerge into reading and writing and how they can work with their older children at home.

- *Support groups for parents.* Parents get acquainted with other parents and share ways of working with their children.

- *Planned interactions between parents and children.* Parents and their children participate together in reading and writing activities.

Now family literacy programs are based on the "wealth model," which stresses that all families have literacy patterns within their homes and that family literacy programs should build on these patterns rather than impose mainstream, school-like activities on parents (Morrow, Tracey, & Maxwell, 1995). Cultural differences in reading and writing development and literacy use are now regarded as strengths, not weaknesses. The wealth model has replaced the older deficit model, which assumed that children from minority groups and low-income families lacked the preschool literacy activities necessary for success in school (Auerback, 1989).

Organizations dedicated to family literacy, including The National Center for Family Literacy (NCFL), Reading Is Fundamental (RIF), and the Barbara Bush Foundation for Family Literacy, have been instrumental in promoting family literacy initiatives at the national level. The NCFL, which began in 1989, disseminates information about family literacy and works to implement family literacy programs across the country. The NCFL has trained staff for almost 1,000 family literacy programs and sponsors an annual Family Literacy Conference. RIF was formed in 1966 to promote children's reading. The organization originally provided assistance to local groups in obtaining and distributing low-cost books for children and sponsoring reading-related events, but since 1982, RIF has developed other programs to support parents as children's first teachers. Former First Lady Barbara Bush organized the Barbara Bush Foundation in 1989 to promote family literacy. This foundation provides grants for family literacy programs and published a book describing 10 model family literacy programs in the United States (Barbara Bush Foundation for Family Literacy, 1989).

A variety of local programs have been developed; some programs are collaborations among local agencies, whereas others are run by adult literacy groups. Businesses in many communities, too, are forming partnerships to promote family literacy. Also, schools in multicultural communities are creating literacy programs for parents who are not yet proficient in English so that they can support their children's literacy learning. For example, Shanahan, Mulhern, and Rodriguez-Brown (1995) developed a literacy project in a Chicago Latino neighborhood through which parents learned to speak and read English and became actively involved in their children's education.

Schools also organize writing programs for parents. Susan Akroyd (1995), a principal of a multicultural school in Virginia, developed a weeklong program for her school. She advertised the program in the school's newsletter for parents, and approximately 15 parents from different cultures speaking languages ranging from Korean and Vietnamese to Urdu attended. Many parents spoke very little English, but they came together to write and to learn more about writing. They wrote about memories, their experiences immigrating to the United States, and hopes and dreams for their children. Some parents wrote in English, and others wrote in their native languages. Akroyd brought in translators so that the parents' writing could be shared with the group. At each class meeting, parents wrote, shared their writing in small groups, and then shared selected compositions with the class. At the end of the program, Akroyd published an anthology of the parents' writing. This sort of program can work in diverse communities, even when parents read and write in different languages.

Complete a self-assessment to check your understanding of the concepts presented in this chapter on the Companion Website at *www.prenhall. com/tompkins*

Review: How Effective Teachers Teach Reading and Writing

1. Effective teachers apply learning, language, and literacy theories as they teach reading and writing.
2. Effective teachers support students' use of the four cueing systems.
3. Effective teachers create a community of learners in their classrooms.
4. Effective teachers adopt a balanced approach to literacy instruction.
5. Effective teachers scaffold students' reading and writing experiences.
6. Effective teachers use a combination of modeled, shared, interactive, guided, and independent reading and writing activities.
7. Effective teachers use literature in their instructional programs.
8. Effective teachers organize literacy instruction using basal reading programs, literature focus units, literature circles, and reading and writing workshop.
9. Effective teachers link instruction and assessment using a cycle of preassess, teach, monitor, reteach, and assess.
10. Effective teachers become partners with parents.

Professional References

Akroyd, S. (1995). Forming a parent reading-writing class: Connecting cultures, one pen at a time. *The Reading Teacher, 48,* 580–584.

Allington, R., & Walmsley, S. (Eds.). (1995). *No quick fix: Rethinking literacy programs in America's elementary schools.* New York: Teachers College Press.

Auerbach, E. R. (1989). Toward a social-contextual approach to family literacy. *Harvard Educational Review, 59,* 165–181.

Barbara Bush Foundation for Family Literacy. (1989). *First teachers.* Washington, DC: Author.

Baumann, J. F., Hoffman, J. V., Moon, J., & Duffy-Hester, A. M. (1998). Where are teachers' voices in the phonics/whole language debate? Results from a survey of US. elementary teachers. *The Reading Teacher, 51,* 636–650.

Baumann, J. F., & Ivey, G. (1997). Delicate balances: Striving for curricular and instructional equilibrium in a second-grade, literature/strategy-based classroom. *Reading Research Quarterly, 23,* 244–275.

Bomer, R., & Bomer, K. (2001). *For a better world: Reading and writing for social action.* Portsmouth, NH: Heinemann.

Button, K., Johnson, M. J., & Furgerson, P. (1996). Interactive writing in a primary classroom. *The Reading Teacher, 49,* 446–454.

Cambourne, B., & Turbill, J. (1987). *Coping with chaos.* Rozelle, New South Wales, Australia: Primary English Teaching Association.

Come, B., & Fredericks, A. D. (1995). Family literacy in urban schools: Meeting the needs of at-risk children. *The Reading Teacher, 48,* 556–570.

Dixon-Krauss, L. (1996). *Vygotsky in the classroom.* White Plains, NY: Longman.

Edwards, P. A. (1995). Empowering low-income mothers and fathers to share books with young children. *The Reading Teacher, 48,* 558–564.

Fitzgerald, J. (1999). What is this thing called "balance"? *The Reading Teacher, 53,* 100–107.

Foss, A. (2002). Peeling the onion: Teaching critical literacy with students of privilege. *Language Arts, 79,* 393–403.

Fountas, I. C., & Pinnell, G. S. (1996). *Guided reading: Good first teaching for all children.* Portsmouth, NH: Heinemann.

France, M. G., & Hager, J. M. (1993). Recruit, respect, respond: A model for working with low-income families and their preschoolers. *The Reading Teacher, 46,* 568–572.

Freire, P. (2000). *Pedagogy of the oppressed* (30th anniversary ed.). New York: Continuum.

Freire, P., & Macedo, D. (1987). *Literacy: Reading the word and the world.* South Hadley, MA: Bergin & Garvey.

Giroux, H. (1988). *Teachers as intellectuals: Toward a critical pedagogy of learning.* South Hadley, MA: Bergin & Garvey.

Glazer, S. M. (1998). *Assessment is instruction: Reading, writing, spelling, and phonics for all learners.* Norwood, MA: Christopher-Gordon.

Graves, D. H. (1995). A tour of Segovia School in the year 2005. *Language Arts, 72,* 12–18.

Halliday, M. A. K. (1978). *Language as social semiotic: The social interpretation of language and meaning.* Baltimore: University Park Press.

Harris, T. L., & Hodges, R. E. (Eds.). (1995). *The literacy dictionary: The vocabulary of reading and writing.* Newark, DE: International Reading Association.

Heath, S. B. (1983). Research currents: A lot of talk about nothing. *Language Arts, 60,* 999–1007.

Hirsch, E. D., Jr. (1987). *Cultural literacy: What every American needs to know.* Boston: Houghton Mifflin.

Holloway, J. H. (2004). Family literacy. *Educational Leadership, 61*(6), 88–89.

International Reading Association. (2000). *Honoring children's rights to excellent reading instruction: A position statement of the International Reading Association.* Newark, DE: Author.

International Reading Association and the National Council of Teachers of English. (1989). *Cases in literacy: An agenda for discussion.* Newark, DE: Author.

Lewison, M., Flint, A. S., & Van Sluys, K. (2002). Taking on critical literacy: The journey of newcomers and novices. *Language Arts, 79,* 382–392.

Lindfors, J. W. (1987). *Children's language and learning* (2nd ed.). Englewood Cliffs, NJ: Prentice Hall.

Luke, A., & Freebody, P. (1997). Shaping the social practices of reading. In S. Muspratt, A. Luke, & P. Freebody (Eds.), *Constructing critical literacies* (pp. 185–225). Cresskill, NJ: Hampton.

McDaniel, C. (2004). Critical literacy: A questioning stance and the possibility for change. *The Reading Teacher, 57,* 472–481.

McIntyre, E. & Pressley, M. (Eds.). (1996). *Balanced instruction: Strategies and skills in whole language.* Norwood, MA: Christopher-Gordon.

McLaughlin, M., & De Voogd, G. L. (2004). *Critical literacy: Enhancing students' comprehension of text.* New York: Scholastic.

Morrice, C., & Simmons, M. (1991). Beyond reading buddies: A whole language cross-age program. *The Reading Teacher, 44,* 572–578.

Morrow, L. M., Tracey, D. H., & Maxwell, C. M. (1995). *A survey of family literacy in the United States.* Newark, DE: International Reading Association.

Nagy, W. E. (1988). *Teaching vocabulary to improve reading comprehension.* Urbana, IL: ERIC Clearinghouse on Reading and Communication Skills and the National Council of Teachers of English and the International Reading Association.

Nathenson-Mejia, S. (1989). Writing in a second language: Negotiating meaning through invented spelling. *Language Arts, 66,* 516–526.

O'Donohue, W., & Kitchener, R. F. (Eds.). (1998). *Handbook of behaviorism.* New York: Academic Press.

Piaget, J. (1969). *The psychology of intelligence.* Paterson, NJ: Littlefield, Adams.

Purcell-Gates, V., L'Allier, S., & Smith, D. (1995). Literacy at the Harts' and the Larsons': Diversity among poor, inner city families. *The Reading Teacher, 48,* 572–579.

Rafferty, C. D. (1999). Literacy in the information age. *Educational Leadership, 57,* 22–25.

Rasinski, T. V., & Fredericks, A. D. (1988). Sharing literacy: Guiding principles and practices for parent involvement. *The Reading Teacher, 41,* 508–512.

Reutzel, D. R. (1998/1999). On balanced reading. *The Reading Teacher, 52*, 322–324.

Reutzel, D. R., & Mitchell, J. P. (2003). The best of times and the worst of times: Reading instruction today. *The Reading Teacher, 57*, 6–10.

Rosenblatt, L. (1978). *The reader, the text, the poem: The transactional theory of the literary work.* Carbondale, IL: Southern Illinois University Press.

Rosenblatt, L. (1983). *Literature as exploration* (4th ed.). New York: Modern Language Association.

Rosenblatt, L. (1991). Literature—S.O.S.! *Language Arts, 68*, 444–448.

Rumelhart, D. E. (1977). Toward an interactive model of reading. In S. Dornic (Ed.), *Attention and performance* (Vol. 6). Hillsdale, NJ: Erlbaum.

Serafini, F. (2000/2001). Three paradigms of assessment: Measurement, procedure, and inquiry. *The Reading Teacher, 54*, 384–393.

Shanahan, T., Mulhern, M., & Rodriguez-Brown, F. (1995). Project FLAME: Lessons learned from a family literacy program for linguistic minority families. *The Reading Teacher, 48*, 586–593.

Shannon, P. (1995). *Text, lies, & videotape: Stories about life, literacy, and learning.* Portsmouth, NH: Heinemann.

Shockley, B. (1993). Extending the literate community: Reading and writing with families. *The New Advocate, 6*, 11–24.

Skinner, B. F. (1974). *About behaviorism.* New York: Random House.

Spiegel, D. L. (1998). Silver bullets, babies, and bath water: Literature response groups in a balanced literacy program. *The Reading Teacher, 52*, 114–124.

Stanovich, K. (1980). Toward an interactive-compensatory model of individual differences in the development of reading fluency. *Reading Research Quarterly, 16*, 32–71.

Sumara, D., & Walker, L. (1991). The teacher's role in whole language. *Language Arts, 68*, 276–285.

Teale, B. (1995). Dear readers. *Language Arts, 72*, 8–9.

Tinajero, J. V., & Nagel, C. (1995). "I never knew I was needed until you called!": Promoting parent involvement in schools. *The Reading Teacher, 48*, 614–617.

Tompkins, G. E., & Collom, S. (2004). *Sharing the pen: Interactive writing with young children.* Upper Saddle River, NJ: Merrill/Prentice Hall.

Vasquez, V. (2003). *Getting beyond "I like the book": Creating space for critical literacy in K–6 classrooms.* Newark, DE: International Reading Association.

Vygotsky, L. S. (1978). *Mind in society.* Cambridge, MA: Harvard University Press.

Vygotsky, L. S. (1986). *Thought and language.* Cambridge, MA: MIT Press.

Weaver, C. (Ed.). (1998). *Reconsidering a balanced approach to reading.* Urbana, IL: National Council of Teachers of English.

Wells, G., & Chang-Wells, G. L. (1992). *Constructing knowledge together: Classrooms as centers of inquiry and literacy.* Portsmouth, NH: Heinemann.

Wink, J. (2000). *Critical pedagogy: Notes from the real world* (2nd ed.). New York: Longman.

Children's Book References

Blume, J. (1990). *Fudge-a-mania.* New York: Dell.

Curtis, C. P. (1995). *The Watsons go to Birmingham—1963.* New York: Delacorte.

Dahl, R. (1996). *James and the giant peach.* New York: Knopf.

Ellis, D. (2000). *The breadwinner.* Toronto: Groundwood Books.

Frank, A. (1995). *Anne Frank: The diary of a young girl* (new ed.). New York: Doubleday.

George, J. C. (1988). *My side of the mountain.* New York: Dutton.

Gibbons, G. (1994). *Nature's green umbrella: Tropical rain forests.* New York: Morrow.

Howe, D., & Howe, J. (1979). *Bunnicula: A rabbit-tale of mystery.* New York: Aladdin.

Karr, K. (1998). *The great turkey walk.* New York: Farrar, Straus & Giroux.

MacLachlan, P. (1985). *Sarah, plain and tall.* New York: Harper & Row.

Ryan, P. M. (2000). *Esperanza rising.* New York: Scholastic.

Sachar, L. (1991). *Dogs don't tell jokes.* New York: Random House.

Van Allsburg, C. (1979). *The garden of Abdul Gasazi.* Boston: Houghton Mifflin.

Van Allsburg, C. (1981). *Jumanji.* Boston: Houghton Mifflin.

Van Allsburg, C. (1983). *The wreck of the Zephyr.* Boston: Houghton Mifflin.

Van Allsburg, C. (1984). *The mysteries of Harris Burdick.* Boston: Houghton Mifflin.

Van Allsburg, C. (1985). *The polar express.* Boston: Houghton Mifflin.

Van Allsburg, C. (1986). *The stranger.* Boston: Houghton Mifflin.

Van Allsburg, C. (1988). *Two bad ants.* Boston: Houghton Mifflin.

Van Allsburg, C. (1990). *Just a dream.* Boston: Houghton Mifflin.

Van Allsburg, C. (1991). *The wretched stone.* Boston: Houghton Mifflin.

Van Allsburg, C. (1993). *The sweetest fig.* Boston: Houghton Mifflin.

Van Allsburg, C. (2002). *Zathura.* Boston: Houghton Mifflin.

Whelan, G. (2000). *Homeless bird.* New York: Scholastic.

White, E. B. (2000). *The trumpet of the swans.* New York: HarperCollins.

Wilder, L. I. (2001). *Little house in the big woods.* New York: HarperCollins.

Chapter 2

Teaching the Reading and Writing Processes

Chapter Questions

- What are the stages in the reading process?
- What are the stages in the writing process?
- How are the two processes alike?
- How do teachers use these two processes in teaching reading and writing?

Mrs. Goodman's Seventh Graders Read The Giver

The seventh graders in Mrs. Goodman's class are reading the Newbery Medal–winning book *The Giver* (Lowry, 1993). In this futuristic story, 12-year-old Jonas is selected to become the next Keeper of the Memories, and he discovers the terrible truth about his community. Mrs. Goodman has a class set of paperback copies of the book, and her students use the reading process as they read and explore the book.

To introduce the book, Mrs. Goodman asks her students to get into small groups

to brainstorm lists of all the things they would change about life if they could. Their lists, written on butcher paper, include no more homework, no AIDS, no crime, no gangs, no parents, no taking out the garbage, and being allowed to drive a car at age 10. The groups hang their lists on the chalkboard and then share them. Then Mrs. Goodman puts check marks by many of the items, seeming to agree with the points. Next she explains that the class is going to read a story about life in the future. She explains that *The Giver* takes place in a planned utopian, or "perfect," society with the qualities that she checked on students' brainstormed lists.

She passes out copies of the book and uses shared reading to read the first chapter aloud as students follow along in their books. Then the class talks about the first chapter in a grand conversation and ask a lot of questions: Why were there so many rules? Doesn't anyone drive a car? What does *released* mean? Why are children called a "Seven" or a "Four"? What does it mean that people are "given" spouses—don't they fall in love and get married? Why does Jonas have to tell his feelings? Classmates share their ideas and are eager to continue reading. Mrs. Goodman's reading aloud of the first chapter and the questions that the students raise cause everyone to become interested in the story, even several students who try to remain uninvolved in class activities. The power of this story grabs them all.

They set up a schedule for reading and discussion. Every 3 days, they will come together to talk about the chapters they have read, and over 2 weeks, the class will complete the book. They will also write in reading logs after reading the first chapter and then five more times as they are reading. In these logs, students write reactions to the story. Maria wrote this journal entry after finishing the book:

> Jonas had to do it. He had to save Gabriel's life because the next day Jonas's father was going to release (kill) him. He had it all planned out. That was important. He was very brave to leave his parents and his home. But I guess they weren't his parents really and his home wasn't all that good. I don't know if I could have done it but he did the right thing. He had to get out. He saved himself and he saved little Gabe. I'm glad he took Gabriel. That community was supposed to be safe but it really was dangerous. It was weird to not have colors. I guess that things that at first seem to be good are really bad.

Ron explored some of the themes of the story:

> Starving. He has memories of food. He's still hungry. But he's free. Food is safe. Freedom is surprises. Never saw a bird before. Same-same-same. Before he was starved for colors, memories and choice. Choice. To do what you want. To be who you can be. He won't starve.

Alicia thought about a lesson her mother taught her as she wrote:

> As Jonas fled from the community he lost his memories so that they would go back to the people there. Would they learn from them? Would they remember them? Or would life go on just the same? I think you have to do it yourself if you are going to learn. That's what my mom says. Somebody else can't do it for you. But Jonas did it. He got out with Gabe.

Tomas wrote about the Christmas connection at the end of the story:

> *Jonas and Gabe came to the town at Christmas. Why did Lois Lowry do that? Gabe is like the baby Jesus, I think. It is like a rebirth—being born again. Jonas and his old community didn't go to church. Maybe they didn't believe in God. Now Jonas will be a Christian and the people in the church will welcome them. Gabe won't be released. I think Gabe is like Jesus because people tried to release Jesus.*

Check the Compendium of Instructional Procedures, which follows Chapter 14, for more information on highlighted terms.

During their grand conversations, students talk about many of the same points they raise in their journal entries. The story fascinates the students—at first they think about how simple and safe life would be, but then they think about all the things they take for granted that they would have to give up to live in Jonas's ordered society. They talk about bravery and making choices, and applaud Jonas's decision to flee with Gabriel. They also speculate about Jonas's and Gabe's new lives in Elsewhere: Will they be happy? Will they ever go back to check on their old community? Will other people escape to Elsewhere?

The students collect "important" words from the story for their word wall. After reading chapters 4, 5, and 6, they add these words to the word wall:

leisurely pace	bikeports	regulated
invariably	gravitating	rehabilitation
serene	chastised	rule infraction
the wanting	stirrings	reprieve
relinquish	chastisement	assignment

Sometimes students choose unfamiliar or long words, but they also choose words such as *assignment* that are important to the story. Students refer to the list for words and their spellings for the various activities they are involved in. Later during the unit, Mrs. Goodman teaches a minilesson about root words using some of these words.

As students read the story, Mrs. Goodman teaches a series of minilessons about reading strategies and skills. The day after students read about colors in the story, she teaches a minilesson on the visualization strategy. She begins by rereading excerpts from chapters 7 and 8 about Jonas being selected to be the next Receiver and asks students to try to draw a picture of the scene in their minds. She asks them to focus on the sights, sounds, smells, and feelings, and she talks about the importance of bringing a story to life in their minds as they read. Then students draw pictures of their visualizations and share them in small groups.

To review spelling patterns and phonics rules, Mrs. Goodman does a making words activity. She divides the class into six groups and gives each group a different set of letter cards that can be sorted to spell a word from the word wall: *stirrings, release, memories, receiver, fascinated,* or *ceremony*. She asks the students in each group to arrange the letter cards to spell as many words as they can; letters from *ceremony,* for example, can be used to spell *me, my, on, no, eye, men, more, core, corn, mercy,* and *money*. Then they arrange all of the letters to spell the word-wall word.

Another minilesson is about literary opposites. Mrs. Goodman explains that authors often introduce conflict and develop themes using contrasts or opposites. She asks students to think of opposites in *The Giver;* one example that she suggests is *safe* and *free*. Other opposites that the students suggest include:

alive—released	color—black and white
choice—no choice	conform—do your own thing

rules—anarchy   stirrings—the pill

families—family units   memories—no memories

Mrs. Goodman asks students to think about how the opposites relate to the development of the story and how Lois Lowry made the opposites explicit in *The Giver*. Students talk about how the community seemed safe at the beginning of the story, but chapter by chapter, Lowry uncovered the shortcomings of the community. They also talk about themes of the story reflected in these opposites. Mrs. Goodman ends the minilesson by asking students to look for opposites in other stories they read.

After they finish reading the book, students have a read-around in which they select and read aloud favorite passages to the class. Then students make a quilt to probe the themes in the story: Each student prepares a construction paper quilt square with an illustration and several sentences of text. One quilt square is shown below. The students decide to use white, gray, and black for most of the quilt squares to represent the sameness of Jonas's community, red for the first color Jonas saw, and colors in the center to represent Elsewhere.

Students also choose projects that they will work on individually or in small groups to apply their reading of *The Giver*. One student makes a book box with objects related to the story, and two other students read *Hailstones and Halibut Bones*

One Square for a Quilt on *The Giver*

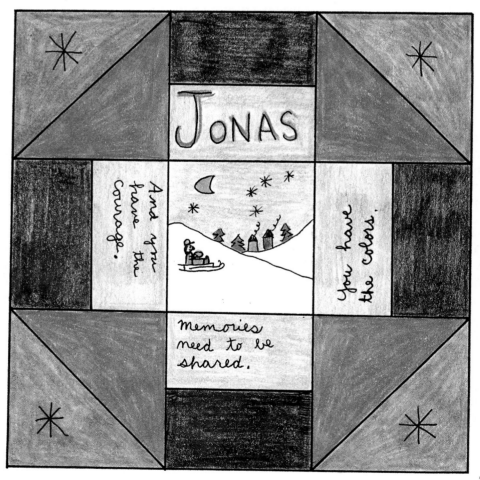

(O'Neill, 1989) and then write their own collection of color poetry. One student makes an open-mind portrait of Jonas to show his thoughts the night he decided to escape with Gabe. Some students read other books with similar themes or other books by Lois Lowry, including *Gathering Blue* (2000), and they share their books with the class during a book talk. Other students write about memories of their own lives. They use the writing process to draft, refine, and publish their writing. They share their published pieces at a class meeting at the end of the unit.

The reading process that Mrs. Goodman uses represents a significant shift in thinking about what people do as they read. Mrs. Goodman understands that readers construct meaning as they negotiate the texts they are reading, and that they use their life and literature experiences and knowledge of written language as they read. She knows that it is quite common for two people to read the same story and come away with different interpretations, and that their understanding of the story will depend on what has happened in their own lives. Meaning does not exist on the pages of the book readers are reading; instead, comprehension is created through the interaction between readers and the texts they are reading.

The reading process involves a series of stages during which readers construct interpretations as they read and respond to the text. The term *text* refers to all reading materials—stories, maps, newspapers, cereal boxes, textbooks, and so on; it is not limited to basal reader textbooks. The writing process is a similar recursive process involving a variety of activities as students gather and organize ideas, draft their compositions, revise and edit the drafts, and, finally, publish their writings.

Reading and writing have been thought of as opposites: Readers decoded or deciphered written language, and writers encoded or produced written language. Then researchers began to note similarities between reading and writing and talked of both of them as processes. Now reading and writing are viewed as parallel processes of meaning construction, and we understand that readers and writers use similar strategies for making meaning with text.

In a balanced literacy program, teachers use the reading and writing processes to organize their instruction and students' reading and writing experiences. The feature on page 47 shows how the reading and writing processes fit into a balanced program. As you continue reading this chapter, you will learn more about the ideas presented in the feature.

Visit Chapter 2 on the Companion Website at *www. prenhall.com/tompkins* to connect to web links related to the reading and writing processes.

THE READING PROCESS

Reading is a process in which readers comprehend and construct meaning. During reading, the meaning does not go from the page to readers. Instead, reading is a complex negotiation among the text, readers, and their purpose for reading that is shaped by many factors:

- Readers' knowledge about the topic
- Readers' knowledge about reading and about written language

How the Reading and Writing Processes Fit Into a Balanced Literacy Program

Component	Description
Reading	Teachers use the five-stage reading process to teach reading.
Phonics and Other Skills	Teachers teach phonics and other skills during the exploring stage of the reading process and during the editing stage of the writing process.
Strategies	Teachers teach strategies during the reading and writing processes, and students apply these strategies as they read and write.
Vocabulary	Students learn vocabulary as they read, and teachers involve students in vocabulary activities during the exploring stage of the reading process.
Comprehension	Making meaning is at the heart of both the reading and writing processes.
Literature	Students use the reading process as they read stories in literature focus units, literature circles, and reading workshop.
Content-Area Study	Students use the reading process as they read informational books and content-area textbooks, and they use the writing process as they create projects during content-area units.
Oral Language	Students use talk in both the reading and writing processes to activate background knowledge, clarify their understanding, and share ideas.
Writing	Teachers use the five-stage writing process to teach students to write narrative, expository, poetic, and persuasive compositions.
Spelling	Students focus on correcting spelling errors in the editing stage of the writing process because they learn that conventional spelling is a courtesy to readers.

- The language community to which readers belong
- The match between readers' language and the language used in the text
- Readers' culturally based expectations about reading
- Readers' expectations about reading based on their previous experiences (Weaver, 1988).

Teachers involve students in a series of activities as they guide and support students' construction of meaning during the reading process. These activities serve different purposes and can be organized into five stages or steps: prereading, reading, responding, exploring, and applying. Figure 2–1 presents an overview of these stages.

Figure 2-1	Key Features of the Reading Process

Stage 1: Prereading
- Set purposes.
- Connect to prior personal experiences.
- Connect to prior literary experiences.
- Connect to thematic units or special interests.
- Make predictions.
- Preview the text.
- Consult the index to locate information.

Stage 2: Reading
- Make predictions.
- Apply skills and strategies.
- Read independently; with a partner; using shared reading or guided reading; or listen to the text read aloud.
- Read the illustrations, charts, and diagrams.
- Read the entire text from beginning to end.
- Read one or more sections of text to learn specific information.
- Take notes.

Stage 3: Responding
- Write in a reading log.
- Participate in a grand conversation or instructional conversation.

Stage 4: Exploring
- Reread and think more deeply about the text.
- Make connections with personal experiences.
- Make connections with other literary experiences.
- Examine the author's craft.
- Identify memorable quotes.
- Learn new vocabulary words.
- Participate in minilessons on reading procedures, concepts, strategies, and skills.

Stage 5: Applying
- Construct projects.
- Use information in thematic units.
- Connect with related books.
- Reflect on their interpretation.
- Value the reading experience.

Stage 1: Prereading

The reading process does not begin as readers open a book and read the first sentence; on the contrary, the first stage is preparing to read. In the vignette, Mrs. Goodman developed her students' background knowledge and stimulated their interest in *The Giver* as they brainstormed lists and talked about how wonderful life would be in a "perfect" world. As readers prepare to read, they activate background knowledge, set purposes, and plan for reading.

Activating Background Knowledge. Readers activate their background knowledge, or schemata, about the text they plan to read. They make connections to personal experiences, to literary experiences, or to thematic units in the classroom. The topic of the book, the title, the author, the genre, an illustration, a comment someone makes about the text, or something else may trigger this activation, but for readers to make meaning with the text, schemata must be activated.

Setting Purposes. The two overarching purposes for reading are pleasure and information: When students read for pleasure or enjoyment, they read aesthetically, to be carried into the world of the text, and when they read to locate information or for directions about how to do something, they read efferently (Rosenblatt, 1978). Often readers use a combination of purposes as they read, but usually one purpose is more important to the reading experience than the other. For example, when students pick up *The Sweetest Fig* (1993), one of Chris Van Allsburg's picture-book fantasies, their primary purpose is enjoyment. They want to experience the story, but at the same time, they search for the white dog, a trademark that Van Allsburg includes in all of his books, and they compare this book with others of his they that have read. As they search for the white dog or make comparisons, they add efferent purposes to their primarily aesthetic reading experience.

Purpose setting is directed by the teacher in basal reading programs and literature focus units, but in reading workshop, students set their own purposes because everyone is reading different self-selected books. For teacher-directed purpose setting, teachers explain how students are expected to read and what they will do after reading. The goal of teacher-directed purpose setting is to help students learn how to set personally relevant purposes when they are reading independently (Blanton, Wood, & Moorman, 1990). Students should always have a purpose for reading, whether they are reading aesthetically or efferently, whether reading a text for the first time or the tenth. Readers are more successful when they have a single purpose for reading the entire selection. A single purpose is more effective than multiple purposes, and sustaining a single purpose is more effective than presenting students with a series of purposes as they read.

When readers have purposes for reading, their comprehension of the selection is enhanced in three ways, whether teachers provide the purpose or students set their own purpose (Blanton et al., 1990). First of all, the purpose guides students' reading. Having a purpose provides motivation and direction for reading, as well as a mechanism for monitoring the reading. As they monitor their reading, students ask themselves whether they are fulfilling their purpose.

Second, setting a purpose activates a plan for readers to use while reading. Purpose setting causes students to draw on background knowledge, consider strategies they might use as they read, and think about the structure of the text they are reading. When students have a purpose for reading, they are better able to identify important information as they read. Teachers direct students' attention to relevant concepts as they set purposes for reading and show them how to connect the concepts they are reading about to their prior knowledge about a topic.

Students read differently depending on the purpose for reading, and the instructional procedures that teachers use also vary according to the purpose for reading. When students are reading stories, teachers might use the Directed Reading-Thinking Activity (DRTA) to help students predict and then read to confirm or reject their predictions, or have students create story maps to focus their attention on plot, characters, or another element of story structure. When students are reading informational books and content-area textbooks, teachers might use an anticipation guide to activate prior knowledge, or use cubing to explore a concept from different viewpoints.

In contrast to teacher-directed purpose setting, students set their own purposes for reading during literature circles, reading workshop, and at other times when they choose their own books to read. Often they choose materials that are intrinsically interesting or that describe something they want to learn more about. As students gain experience in reading, identify favorite authors, and learn about genre, they acquire other criteria to use in choosing books and setting purposes for reading. When teachers conference with students, they often ask them about their purposes for reading and why they choose particular books to read.

Planning for Reading. Students often preview the reading selection during the prereading stage: They look through the selection and check its length, the reading difficulty, and the illustrations to judge the general suitability of the selection for them as readers. Previewing serves an important function as students connect their prior knowledge, identify their purpose for reading, and take their first look at the selection. Teachers set the guidelines by explaining how the book will be read—independently, in small groups, or as a class—and setting the schedule for reading. Setting the schedule is especially important when students are reading a chapter book. Often teachers and students work together to create a 2-, 3-, or 4-week schedule for reading and responding and then write the schedule on a calendar to which students can refer.

Students make other types of plans depending on the type of selection they will read. Those who are preparing to read stories, for instance, make predictions about the characters and events in the story. Students often base their predictions on the title of the selection and the illustration on the cover of the book or on the first page. If they have read other books by the same author or other selections in the same genre, students also use this information in making their predictions. Sometimes students share their predictions as they talk about the selection, and at other times they write and draw their predictions as the first entry in their reading logs.

When students are preparing to read informational books, they preview the selection by flipping through the pages and noting section headings, illustrations, diagrams, and other charts. Sometimes they examine the table of contents to see how the book is organized, or consult the index to locate specific information they want to read. They may also notice unfamiliar terminology and other words they can check in the glossary, ask a classmate or the teacher about, or look up in a dictionary. Teachers also use anticipation guides, prereading plans, and the survey step of the SQ3R study strategy as they introduce informational books and content-area textbooks.

Students often make notes in learning logs as they explore informational books and content-area textbooks. They do quickwrites to activate prior knowledge and explore the concepts to be presented in the selection, write down important terminology, and make graphic organizers they will complete as they read. As they move through the remaining stages in the reading process, students add other information to their learning logs.

Stage 2: Reading

Students read the book or other selection in the reading stage. To understand what they are reading, they use their knowledge of decoding and word identification, high-frequency words, strategies, skills, and vocabulary. Fluent readers are better able to understand what they are reading because they identify most words automatically and use decoding skills when necessary. They also apply their knowledge of the structure of text as they create meaning. They continue reading as long as what they are reading fits the meaning they are constructing. When something doesn't make sense, readers slow down, back up, and reread until they are making meaning again.

Outside of school, readers usually read silently and independently. Sometimes, however, people listen as someone else reads. For example, young children often sit in a parent's lap and look at the illustrations as the parent reads a picture book aloud. Adults also listen to books read aloud on cassette tapes. In the classroom, teachers and students use five types of reading; independent reading, buddy reading, guided reading, shared reading, and reading aloud to students. Teachers choose the amount of scaffolding students need according to the purpose for reading, students' reading levels, and the number of available copies of the text.

Independent Reading. When students read independently, they read silently by themselves, for their own purposes, and at their own pace (Hornsby, Sukarna, & Parry, 1986). For students to read independently, the reading selections must be at their reading level. Primary-grade students often read the featured selection independently during literature focus units, but this is often after they have already read the selection once or twice with assistance from the teacher.

Nurturing English Learners

What should I do if my students can't read the basal reader?

If your EL students can't read the basal reader (or any other book, for that matter), they need a different book—one at their instructional level. Sometimes teachers read a textbook aloud to students when they can't read it themselves, but that isn't effective reading instruction because students need to be doing the reading themselves. Before abandoning the basal reader, however, you should try several things to make a book more accessible: Build students' background knowledge, introduce new vocabulary before reading, do a text walk to preview the reading assignment, or read the first page aloud to get students started. If none of these strategies work, though, it's time to find a more appropriate book for your English learners to read.

In the upper grades, many students read chapter books independently, but less capable readers may not be able to read the featured book independently. Students also independently read related books at varied reading levels from the text set as part of these units.

During reading workshop, students read independently; even first graders can participate by rereading familiar books as well as new books at their reading level. Because students choose the books they want to read, they need to learn how to choose books that are written at an appropriate level of difficulty.

Independent reading is an important part of a balanced reading program because it is the most authentic type of reading. This type of reading is what most people do when they read, and this is the way students develop a love of reading and come to think of themselves as readers. The reading selection, however, must be at an appropriate level of difficulty so that students can read it independently. Otherwise, teachers use one of the other four types of reading to support students and make it possible for them to participate in the reading experience.

Buddy Reading. In buddy reading, students read or reread a selection with a classmate. Sometimes students read with buddies because it is an enjoyable social activity, and sometimes they read together to help each other. Often students can read selections together that neither student could read individually. Buddy reading is a good alternative to independent reading because students can choose books they want to read and then read at their own pace. By working together, they are often able to figure out unfamiliar words and talk out comprehension problems.

As teachers introduce buddy reading, they show students how to read with buddies and how to support each other as they read. Students take turns reading aloud to each other or read in unison. They often stop and help each other identify an unfamiliar word or take a minute or two at the end of each page to talk about what they have read. Buddy reading is a valuable way of providing the practice that beginning readers need to become fluent readers; it is also an effective way to work with students with special learning needs and students who are learning English. However, unless the teacher has explained the approach and taught students how to work collaboratively, buddy reading often deteriorates into the stronger of the two buddies reading aloud to the other student, and that is not the intention of this type of reading.

Guided Reading. Teachers use guided reading to work with groups of four or five students who are reading at the same level (Clay, 1991). They select a book that students can read at their instructional level, with approximately 90–94% accuracy. Teachers support students' reading and their use of reading strategies during guided reading (Depree & Iversen, 1996; Fountas & Pinnell, 1996). Students do the actual reading themselves, although the teacher may read aloud with children to get them started on the first page or two. Young children often murmur the words softly as they read, which helps the teacher keep track of students' reading and the strategies they are using. Older, more fluent readers usually read silently during guided reading.

Guided reading lessons usually last 25 to 30 minutes. When the students arrive for the small-group lesson, they often reread, either individually or with a buddy, familiar books used in previous guided reading lessons. For the new guided reading lesson, students read books that they have not read before. Beginning readers usually read small picture books at one sitting, but older students who are reading longer chapter books take several days to several weeks to read their books.

Teachers observe students as they read during guided reading lessons. They spend a few minutes observing each student, sitting either in front of or beside the student. They watch for evidence of strategy use and confirm the student's attempts to identify words and solve reading problems. Teachers take notes about their observations and use the information in deciding what minilessons to teach and what books to choose for students to read.

Teachers also take running records of one or two students during each guided reading lesson and use this information as part of their assessment. Teachers verify that

Reading Aloud to Students

During a literature focus unit on "The Little Red Hen," this first-grade teacher reads aloud *Cook-a-Doodle-Doo!* (Stevens & Crummel, 1999), the story of Little Red Hen's great-grandson Big Brown Rooster who bakes a strawberry shortcake with his friends. After predicting that Rooster's friends won't help, the students listen intently as their teacher reads. They discover that Rooster's friends are more helpful than Little Red Hen's friends were, but they notice many similarities to the traditional story. After a second reading, they dramatize the story, and later follow the Rooster's recipe to cook a yummy dessert.

the books students are reading are at their instructional level and that they are making expected progress toward increasingly more difficult levels of books.

Shared Reading. Teachers use shared reading to read aloud books and other texts that children can't read independently (Holdaway, 1979). Often primary-grade teachers use big books or texts written on charts so that both small groups and whole-class groups can see the text and read along with the teacher. Teachers model what fluent readers do as they involve students in enjoyable reading activities (Fountas & Pinnell, 1996). After the text is read several times, teachers use it to teach phonics concepts and high-frequency words. Students can also read small versions of the book independently or with partners, and the pattern or structure used in the text can be used for writing activities (Slaughter, 1993).

Shared reading is part of a balanced literacy program for children in the primary grades. Teachers read aloud books that are appropriate for children's interest level but too difficult for them to read for themselves. The books chosen for shared reading are available in both big-book and small-book formats and are close to children's reading level, but still beyond their ability to read independently. As an instructional strategy, shared reading differs from reading aloud to students because students see the text as the teacher reads. Students often join in the reading of predictable refrains and rhyming words, and after listening to the teacher read the text several times, they often remember enough of the text to read along with the teacher.

Shared reading is also used to read novels with older students when the books are too difficult for students to read independently. Teachers distribute copies of the book to all students, and students follow along as the teacher reads aloud. Sometimes students take turns reading sections aloud, but the goal is not for everyone to have a turn reading. Students who want to read and are fluent enough to keep the reading meaningful volunteer to read. Often the teacher begins reading, and when a student wants to take over the reading, he or she begins reading aloud with the teacher. Then the teacher drops off and the student continues reading. After a paragraph or a page, another student joins in and the first student drops off. Many teachers call this technique "popcorn reading."

Reading Aloud to Students. In kindergarten through eighth grade, teachers read aloud to students for a variety of purposes each day. During literature focus units, for example, teachers read aloud featured selections that are appropriate for students' interest level but too difficult for students to read themselves. Sometimes it is also appropriate to read the featured selection aloud before distributing copies of it for students to read with buddies or independently. There are many benefits of reading aloud: introducing vocabulary, modeling comprehension strategies, and increasing students' motivation (Rasinski, 2003).

Reading aloud to students is not the same as "round-robin" reading, a practice that is no longer recommended in which students take turns reading paragraphs aloud as the rest of the class listens. Round-robin reading has been used for reading chapter books aloud, but it is more commonly used for reading chapters in content-area textbooks, even though there are more effective ways to teach content-area information and read textbooks.

Round-robin reading is no longer recommended, for several reasons (Opitz & Rasinski, 1998). First, if students are going to read aloud, they should read fluently. When less capable readers read, their reading is often difficult to listen to and is embarrassing to them personally. Less capable readers need reading practice, but performing in front of the entire class is not the most productive way for them to practice. Better techniques are for them to read with buddies and in small groups during guided

Figure 2-2 **A Comparison of the Five Types of Reading**

Type	Strengths	Limitations
Independent Reading Students read a text on their own. There is no teacher scaffolding when students read independently.	• Develops responsibility and ownership. • Self-selection of texts. • Experience is more authentic.	• Students may need assistance to read the text. • Little teacher involvement and control.
Buddy Reading Two students read or reread a text together.	• Collaboration between students. • Students assist each other. • Use to reread familiar texts. • Develops reading fluency. • Students talk and share interpretations.	• Teacher's involvement is limited. • Less teacher control.
Guided Reading Teacher supports students as they apply reading strategies and skills to read a text.	• Teaches skills and strategies. • Teacher provides direction and scaffolding. • Opportunities to model reading strategies. • Useful with unfamiliar texts.	• Multiple copies of text needed. • Teacher controls the reading experience. • Some students may not be interested in the text.
Shared Reading Teacher reads aloud while students follow along using individual copies of book, a class chart, or a big book.	• Access to books students could not read themselves. • Teacher models fluent reading. • Opportunities to model reading strategies. • Students practice fluent reading. • Develops a community of readers.	• Multiple copies, a class chart, or a big book needed. • Text may not be appropriate for all students. • Students may not be interested in the text.
Reading Aloud to Students Teacher or other fluent reader reads aloud to students. Teacher scaffolding is greatest when reading aloud.	• Access to books students could not read themselves. • Reader models fluent reading. • Opportunities to model reading strategies. • Develops a community of readers. • Useful when only one copy of text is available.	• No opportunity for students themselves to read. • Text may not be appropriate for all students. • Students may not be interested in the text.

reading. Second, if the selection is appropriate for students to read aloud, they should be reading independently. Third, round-robin reading is often tedious and boring, and students lose interest in reading. In fact, students often follow along only just before it is their turn to read.

A comparison of the types of reading is outlined in Figure 2–2. In the vignette at the beginning of this chapter, Mrs. Goodman used a combination of these approaches. She used shared reading as she read the first chapter aloud, with students following in their own copies of *The Giver*. Later, students read together in small groups, with a buddy, or independently. As teachers plan their instructional programs, they include reading aloud to students, teacher-led student reading, and independent reading each day.

Stage 3: Responding

Students respond to what they read and continue to negotiate the meaning. This stage reflects the reader response theory. Two ways that students make tentative and exploratory comments immediately after reading are by writing in reading logs and participating in grand or instructional conversations.

Writing in Reading Logs. Students write and draw their thoughts and feelings about what they have read in reading logs. Rosenblatt (1978) explains that as students write about what they have read, they unravel their thinking and, at the same time, elaborate on and clarify their responses. When students read informational books, they sometimes write in reading logs, as they do after reading stories and poems, but at other times they make notes of important information or draw charts and diagrams to use in thematic units.

Students usually make reading logs by stapling together 10 to 12 sheets of paper at the beginning of a literature focus unit or reading workshop. At the beginning of a thematic unit, students make learning logs to write in during the unit. They decorate the covers, keeping with the theme of the unit, write entries related to their reading, and make notes related to what they are learning in minilessons. Teachers monitor students' entries during the unit, reading and often responding to students' entries. Because these journals are learning tools, teachers rarely correct students' spellings; they focus their responses on the students' ideas, but they expect students to spell the title of the book and the names of characters accurately. At the end of the unit, teachers review students' work and often grade the journals based on whether students completed all the entries and on the quality of the ideas in their entries.

Participating in Discussions. Students also talk about the text with classmates in grand conversations and instructional conversations. Peterson and Eeds (1990) explain that in grand conversations, students share their personal responses and tell what they liked about the text. After sharing personal reactions, they shift the focus to "puzzle over what the author has written and . . . share what it is they find revealed" (p. 61). Often students make connections between the text and their own lives or between the text and other literature they have read. If they are reading a chapter book, they also make predictions about what will happen in the next chapter.

Teachers often share their ideas in grand conversations, but they act as interested participants, not leaders. The talk is primarily among the students, but teachers ask questions regarding things they are genuinely interested in learning more about and share information in response to questions that students ask. In the past, many discussions have been "gentle inquisitions" during which students recited answers to factual questions teachers asked about books that students were reading (Eeds & Wells, 1989); teachers asked these questions to determine whether students read and understood an assignment. Although teachers can still judge whether students have read the assignment, the focus in grand conversations is on clarifying and deepening students' understanding of the story they have read. Teachers and students have similar instructional conversations after reading content-area textbooks and informational books.

These grand conversations can be held with the whole class or in small groups. Young children usually get together as a class, whereas older students often prefer to talk with classmates in small groups. When students meet as a class, there is a shared feeling of community, and the teacher can be part of the group. When students meet in small groups, they have more opportunities to participate in the discussion and share their interpretations, but fewer viewpoints are expressed in each group and teachers must move around, spending only a few minutes with each group. Some teachers compromise and have students begin their discussions in small groups and then come together as a class so that the groups can share what they discussed.

Stage 4: Exploring

Students go back into the text to explore it more analytically in the exploring stage. This stage is more teacher directed than the other stages; it reflects the teacher-centered theory. Students reread the selection, examine the author's craft, and focus on words from the selection. Teachers also present minilessons on procedures, concepts, strategies, and skills.

Rereading the Selection. As students reread the selection, they think again about what they have read. Each time they reread a selection, students benefit in specific ways (Yaden, 1988): They deepen their comprehension and make further connections between the selection and their own lives or between the selection and other literature they have read. Students often reread a basal reader story, a picture book, or excerpts from a chapter book several times. If the teacher used shared reading to read the selection with students in the reading stage, students might reread it with a buddy once or twice, read it with their parents, and, after these experiences, read it independently.

Examining the Author's Craft. Teachers plan exploring activities to focus students' attention on the structure of text and the literary language that authors use. Students notice opposites in the story, use story boards to sequence the events in the story, and make story maps to highlight the plot, characters, and other elements of story structure. Another way students learn about the structure of stories is by writing books based on the selection they have read. In sequels, students tell what happens to the characters after the story ends. Stories such as *Jumanji* (Van Allsburg, 1981), a fantasy about a board game that comes to life, suggest another episode at the end of the story and invite students to create a sequel. Students also write innovations, or new versions, for the selection, in which they follow the same sentence pattern but substitute their own ideas; for example, first graders often write innovations for Bill Martin Jr.'s *Brown Bear, Brown Bear, What Do You See?* (1983) and *Polar Bear, Polar Bear, What Do You Hear?* (1992), and older students write innovations for *Alexander and the Terrible, Horrible, No Good, Very Bad Day* (Viorst, 1977).

Teachers share information about the author of the featured selection and introduce other books by the same author. Sometimes teachers help students make comparisons among several books written by a particular author. They also provide information about the illustrator and the illustration techniques used in the book. To focus on literary language, students often reread favorite excerpts in read-arounds and write memorable quotes on quilts that they create.

Focusing on Words and Sentences. Teachers and students add "important" words to word walls after reading and post these word walls in the classroom. Students refer to the word walls when they write, using these words for a variety of activities during the exploring stage. Students make word clusters and posters to highlight particular words. They also make word chains, do word sorts, create semantic feature analysis charts to analyze related words, and play word games.

Teachers also choose words from word walls to use in minilessons on a variety of concepts. For example, words can be used to teach phonics skills, such as beginning sounds, rhyming words, vowel patterns, *r*-controlled vowels, and syllabication. Other concepts, such as root words and affixes, compound words, contractions, and metaphors, can also be taught using examples from word walls. Teachers may decide to teach a minilesson on a particular concept, such as words with the -*ly* suffix, because five or six words representing the concept are listed on the word wall.

Students also locate "important" sentences in books they read; these sentences might be important because of figurative language, because they express the theme or illustrate a character trait, or simply because students like them. Students often copy the sentences onto sentence strips to display in the classroom and use in other exploring activities. Also, students can copy the sentences in their reading logs.

Teaching Minilessons. Teachers present minilessons on reading procedures, concepts, strategies, and skills during the exploring stage. In a minilesson, teachers introduce the topic and make connections between the topic and examples in the featured selection students have read; in this way, students are better able to connect the information teachers are presenting with their own reading process. In the vignette, Mrs. Goodman presented minilessons on the visualization strategy and on root words and affixes using examples from *The Giver*.

 Learn more about word walls and other instructional procedures discussed in this chapter on the DVD that accompanies this text.

Stage 5: Applying

During the applying stage, readers extend their comprehension, reflect on their understanding, and value the reading experience. Building on the initial and exploratory responses they made immediately after reading, students create projects. These projects can involve reading, writing, talk and drama, art, or research and can take many forms, including murals, readers theatre scripts, and class collaborations and reports, as well as reading other books by the same author. Usually students choose which projects they will do rather than having the entire class do the same project. Sometimes, however, the class decides to work together on a project. In Mrs. Goodman's class, for example, some students wrote color poems, and others read books and wrote about memories. A list of projects is presented in Figure 2–3. The purpose of these activities is for students to expand the ideas they read about, create a personal interpretation, and value the reading experience.

THE WRITING PROCESS

The focus in the writing process is on what students think and do as they write. The five stages are prewriting, drafting, revising, editing, and publishing. The labeling and numbering of the stages do not mean that the writing process is a linear series of neatly packaged categories; rather, research has shown that the process involves recurring cycles, and labeling is simply an aid to identifying and discussing writing activities. In the classroom, the stages merge and recur as students write. The key features of each stage in the writing process are shown in Figure 2–4.

Figure 2-3   Projects Students Develop During the Applying Stage

Visual Projects

- Make a diagram or model using information from a book.
- Create a collage to represent the theme of a book.
- Decorate a coffee can or a potato chip can with scenes from a book and fill it with quotes from the book.
- Construct a shoebox or other miniature scene of an episode for a favorite book (or use a larger box to construct a diorama).
- Make illustrations for each important event in a book.
- Make a map of a book's setting or something related to the book.
- Construct a mobile illustrating a book.
- Make a comic strip to illustrate the sequence of events in a book.
- Prepare bookmarks for a book and distribute them to classmates.
- Prepare illustrations of characters for pocket props to use in retelling the story.
- Prepare illustrations of the events in the story for clothesline props to use in retelling the story.
- Experiment with art techniques related to the mood of a poem.
- Make a mural of the book.
- Make a book box and decorate it with scenes from a book. Collect objects, poems, and illustrations that represent characters, events, or images from the book to add to the box.

Writing Projects

- Write a letter about a book to a classmate, friend, or pen pal.
- Write another episode or a sequel for book.
- Create a newspaper with news stories and advertisements based on characters and episodes from a book.
- Write a simulated letter from one book character to another.
- Copy five "quotable quotes" from a book and arrange them on a poster.
- Make a scrapbook about the book. Label all items in the scrapbook and write a short description of the most interesting ones.
- Write a poem related to the book.
- Write a life line related to a character or the author.
- Write a business letter to a company or organization requesting information on a topic related to the book.
- Keep a simulated journal from the perspective of one character from the book.
- Write a dictionary defining specialized vocabulary in a book.
- Write the story from another point of view.
- Make a class collaboration book.
- Create a PowerPoint presentation about the book.

Stage 1: Prewriting

Prewriting is the "getting ready to write" stage. The traditional notion that writers have a topic completely thought out and ready to flow onto the page is ridiculous: If writers wait for ideas to fully develop, they may wait forever. Instead, writers begin tentatively—talking, reading, writing—to see what they know and in what direction they want to go. Prewriting has probably been the most neglected stage in the writing process; however, it is as crucial to writers as a warm-up is to athletes. Murray (1982) believes that at least 70% of writing time should be spent in prewriting. During the prewriting stage, students choose a topic, consider purpose, audience, and form, and gather and organize ideas for writing. They also learn about the qualities of good writing.

Figure 2-3 (Continued)

Reading Projects
- Read another book by the same author or illustrator.
- Read another book on the same theme.
- Read another book in the same genre.
- Read another book about the same character.
- Read and compare another version of the same story.
- Tape-record a book or an excerpt from it to place in the listening center.
- Read aloud to the class a poem that complements the book.
- Tape-record background music and sound effects to accompany a book.

Drama and Talk Projects
- Give a readers theatre presentation of a book.
- Write a script and present a play about a book.
- Dress as a character from the book and answer questions from classmates.
- Write and present a rap about the book.
- Videotape a commercial for a book.
- Interview someone in the community who is knowledgeable about a topic related to the book.

Literary Analysis Projects
- Make a chart to compare the story with another version or with the film version of the story.
- Make an open-mind portrait to probe the thoughts of one character.
- Make a Venn diagram to compare two characters.
- Make a plot diagram of the book.

Research Projects
- Research the author of the book on the Internet and compile the information on a poster.
- Research a topic related to the book using book and Internet resources and present the information in a report.

Social Action Projects
- Write a letter to the editor of the local newspaper on a topic related to the book.
- Get involved in a community project related to the book.

Choosing a Topic. Choosing a topic for writing can be a stumbling block for students who have become dependent on teachers to supply topics. For years, teachers have supplied topics by suggesting gimmicky story starters and relieving students of the "burden" of topic selection. These "creative" topics often stymied students, who were forced to write on topics they knew little about or were not interested in. Graves (1976) calls this situation "writing welfare." Instead, students need to choose their own writing topics.

If some students complain that they don't know what to write about, teachers can help them brainstorm a list of three, four, or five topics and then identify the one topic they are most interested in and know the most about. Students who feel they cannot generate any writing topics are often surprised that they have so many options available. Then, through prewriting activities, students talk, draw, read, and even write to develop information about their topics.

Asking students to choose their own topics for writing does not mean that teachers never give writing assignments; teachers do provide general guidelines. They may specify the writing form, and at other times they may establish the function, but students should choose their own content.

Considering Purpose. As students prepare to write, they need to think about the purpose of their writing: Are they writing to entertain? to inform? to persuade? Setting the purpose for writing is just as important as setting the purpose for reading, because purpose influences decisions students make about audience and form.

Considering Audience. Students may write primarily for themselves—to express and clarify their own ideas and feelings—or they may write for others. Possible audiences include classmates, younger children, parents, foster grandparents, children's authors, and pen pals. Other audiences are more distant and less well known. For example, students write letters to businesses to request information, articles for the local newspaper, or stories and poems for publication in literary magazines.

Children's writing is influenced by their sense of audience. Britton and his colleagues (1975) define audience awareness as "the manner in which the writer expresses a relationship with the reader in respect to the writer's understanding" (pp. 65–66). Students adapt their writing to fit their audience, just as they vary their speech to meet the needs of the people who are listening to them.

Considering Form. One of the most important considerations is the form the writing will take: a story? a letter? a poem? a journal entry? A writing activity could be handled in any one of these ways. As part of a science unit on hermit crabs, for instance, students could write a story or poem about a hermit crab, write a report on hermit crabs with information about how they obtain shells to live in, or write a

---

Figure 2-4   **Key Features of the Writing Process**

Stage 1: Prewriting
- Write on topics based on personal experiences.
- Engage in rehearsal activities before writing.
- Identify the audience who will read the composition.
- Identify the purpose of the writing activity.
- Choose an appropriate form for the composition based on audience and purpose.

Stage 2: Drafting
- Write a rough draft.
- Emphasize content rather than mechanics.

Stage 3: Revising
- Reread the composition.
- Share writing in writing groups.
- Participate constructively in discussions about classmates' writing.
- Make changes in the composition to reflect the reactions and comments of both teacher and classmates.
- Between the first and final drafts, make substantive rather than only minor changes.

Stage 4: Editing
- Proofread the composition.
- Help proofread classmates' compositions.
- Identify and correct mechanical errors.
- Meet with the teacher for a final editing.

Stage 5: Publishing
- Publish writing in an appropriate form.
- Share the finished writing with an appropriate audience.

description of the pet hermit crabs in the classroom. There is a wide variety of writing forms or genres that children learn to use during the elementary grades; a list of six genres is presented in Figure 2–5. Students need to experiment with a wide variety of writing forms and explore the potential of these functions and formats.

Through reading and writing, students develop a strong sense of these genres and how they are structured. Langer (1985) found that by third grade, students responded in distinctly different ways to story- and report-writing assignments; they organized the writing differently and included varied kinds of information and elaboration. Similarly, Hidi and Hildyard (1983) found that elementary students could differentiate between stories and persuasive essays. Because children are clarifying the distinctions between various writing genres during the elementary grades, it is important that teachers use the correct terminology and not label all children's writing "stories."

Decisions about purpose, audience, and form influence each other. For example, if the purpose is to entertain, an appropriate form might be a story, script, or poem—and these three forms look very different on a piece of paper. Whereas a story is written in the traditional block format, scripts and poems have unique page arrangements. Scripts are written with the character's name and a colon, and the dialogue is set off. Action and dialogue, rather than description, carry the story line in a script. In contrast, poems have unique formatting considerations, and words are used judiciously. Each word and phrase is chosen to convey a maximum amount of information.

Gathering and Organizing Ideas. Students engage in activities to gather and organize ideas for writing. Graves (1983) calls what writers do to prepare for writing "rehearsal" activities. Rehearsal activities take many forms, including reading, talking, and drawing. Through these activities, students develop ideas and collect the words to express them. Sometimes teachers brainstorm words with English learners and other students with limited vocabularies and make a list on the chalkboard that students can refer to as they write.

Teachers also encourage students to draw weblike diagrams called *clusters* or another graphic organizer to visually display how they will format their writing. For a cluster, students write the topic in a center circle and then draw rays out from the circle for each main idea; then they add details and other information on additional rays drawn from each main idea. Clusters work best for descriptive writing; other diagrams with boxes, lines, and circles are suitable for other genres. When students prepare to write a story, for example, it is more effective for them to use a three-part diagram with sections for the beginning, middle, and end of their stories; for a cause-and-effect essay, a two-part diagram with a section for the cause and another for the effect is a good choice. Through many, many writing experiences, students learn to design a graphic that best fits their writing plans.

Stage 2: Drafting

Students write and refine their compositions through a series of drafts. During the drafting stage, they focus on getting their ideas down on paper. Because writers don't begin writing with their pieces already composed in their minds, students begin with tentative ideas developed through prewriting activities. The drafting stage is the time to pour out ideas, with little concern about spelling, punctuation, and other mechanical errors.

Students skip every other line when they write their rough drafts to leave space for revisions. They use arrows to move sections of text, cross-outs to delete sections, and scissors and tape to cut apart and rearrange text, just as adult writers do. They write

Visit Chapter 2 on the Companion Website at *www.prenhall.com/ tompkins* to check into your state's standards for writing instruction.

Figure 2-5   Writing Genres

Genre	Purpose	Activities
Descriptive Writing	Students observe carefully and choose precise language. They take notice of sensory details and create comparisons (metaphors and similes) to make their writing more powerful.	Character sketches Comparisons Descriptive essays Descriptive sentences Five-senses poems Found poems
Expository Writing	Students collect and synthesize information. This writing is objective; reports are the most common type. Students use expository writing to give directions, sequence steps, compare one thing to another, explain causes and effects, or describe problems and solutions.	Alphabet books Autobiographies Biographies Cubes Data charts Directions Posters Reports Simulated journals Summaries
Journals and Letters	Students write to themselves and to specific, known audiences. Their writing is personal and often less formal than other genres. They share news, explore new ideas, and record notes. Students learn the special formatting that letters and envelopes require.	Business letters Courtesy letters Double-entry journals E-mail messages Friendly letters Learning logs Personal journals Postcards Simulated journals
Narrative Writing	Students retell familiar stories, develop sequels for stories they have read, write stories about events in their own lives, and create original stories. They include a beginning, middle, and end in the narratives to develop the plot and characters.	Original short stories Personal narratives Retellings of stories Sequels to stories Story scripts
Persuasive Writing	Persuasion is winning someone to your viewpoint or cause using appeals to logic, moral character, and emotion. Students present their position clearly and support it with examples and evidence.	Advertisements Book and movie reviews Editorials Letters to the editor Persuasive essays Persuasive letters
Poetry Writing	Students create word pictures and play with rhyme and other stylistic devices as they create poems. As students experiment with poetry, they learn that poetic language is vivid and powerful but concise, and they learn that poems can be arranged in different ways on a page.	Acrostic poems Cinquain poems Color poems Diamante poems Free verse Haiku "I wish" poems "If I were . . ." poems Poems for two voices

only on one side of a sheet of paper so it can be cut apart or rearranged. As computers become more available in classrooms, revising, with all its moving, adding, and deleting of text, will be much easier. However, for students who handwrite their compositions, the wide spacing is crucial. Teachers might make small x's on every other line of students' papers as a reminder to skip lines as they draft their compositions.

Students label their drafts by writing *Rough Draft* in ink at the top or by using a ROUGH DRAFT stamp. This label indicates to the writer, other students, parents, and administrators that the composition is a draft in which the emphasis is on content, not mechanics; it also explains why the teacher has not graded the paper or marked mechanical errors.

Instead of writing drafts by hand, students can use computers to compose rough drafts, polish their writing, and print out final copies. There are many benefits of using computers for word processing. For example, students are often more motivated to write, and they tend to write longer pieces. Their writing looks neater, and they can use spellcheck programs to identify and correct misspelled words. Even young children can word-process their compositions using Magic Slate and other programs designed for beginning writers.

During drafting, students may need to modify their earlier decisions about purpose, audience, and, especially, the form their writing will take. For example, a composition that began as a story may be transformed into a report, letter, or poem; the new format allows the student to communicate more effectively. The process of modifying earlier decisions continues into the revising stage.

As students write rough drafts, it is important for teachers not to emphasize correct spelling and neatness. In fact, pointing out mechanical errors during the drafting stage sends students a false message that mechanical correctness is more important than content (Sommers, 1982). Later, during editing, students clean up mechanical errors in publishing, and they put their composition into a new, final form.

Stage 3: Revising

During the revising stage, writers refine ideas in their compositions. Students often break the writing process cycle as soon as they complete a rough draft, believing that once they have jotted down their ideas, the writing task is complete. Experienced writers, however, know they must turn to others for reactions and revise on the basis of these comments. Revision is not just polishing; it is meeting the needs of readers by adding, substituting, deleting, and rearranging material. *Revision* means "seeing again," and in this stage, writers see their compositions again with the help of classmates and the teacher. Revising consists of three activities: rereading the rough draft, sharing the rough draft in a writing group, and revising on the basis of feedback.

Rereading the Rough Draft. After finishing the rough draft, writers need to distance themselves from it for a day or two, then reread it from a fresh perspective, as a reader

Scaffolding Struggling Readers

How can I get my struggling writers to revise?

Struggling writers often think their work is finished after they write a rough draft. They don't realize that to communicate more effectively, they need to revise their writing. The key to enticing struggling writers to revise is helping them develop a sense of audience. Many novice writers write primarily for themselves, but when they want their classmates to understand their message, they begin to recognize the importance of revision. Teachers emphasize audience by encouraging students to share their writing with classmates from the author's chair, and they model the revision process through minilessons when students work together to revise an anonymous piece of writing. Lots of writing and sharing are necessary before students begin to appreciate revision.

might. As they reread, students make changes—adding, substituting, deleting, and moving—and place question marks by sections that need work; it is these trouble spots that students ask for help with in their writing groups.

Sharing in Writing Groups. Students meet in writing groups to share their compositions with classmates. They respond to the writer's rough draft and suggest possible revisions. Writing groups provide a scaffold in which teachers and classmates talk about plans and strategies for writing and revising (Applebee & Langer, 1983; Calkins, 1983).

Writing groups can form spontaneously when several students have completed drafts and are ready to share their compositions, or they can be formal groupings with identified leaders. In some classrooms, writing groups form when four or five students finish writing their rough drafts; students gather around a conference table or in a corner of the classroom and take turns reading their rough drafts aloud. Classmates in the group listen and respond, offering compliments and suggestions for revision. Sometimes the teacher joins the writing group, but if the teacher is involved in something else, students work independently.

In other classrooms, the writing groups are assigned; students get together when all students in the group have completed their rough drafts and are ready to share their writing. Sometimes the teacher participates in these groups, providing feedback along with the students. Or, the writing groups can function independently. For these assigned groups, each cluster is made up of four or five students, and a list of groups and their members is posted in the classroom. The teacher puts a star by one student's name, and that student serves as a group leader. The leader changes every quarter.

Making Revisions. Students make four types of changes to their rough drafts: additions, substitutions, deletions, and moves (Faigley & Witte, 1981). As they revise, students might add words, substitute sentences, delete paragraphs, and move phrases. Students often use a blue or red pen to cross out, draw arrows, and write in the space left between the double-spaced lines of their rough drafts so that revisions will show clearly; that way, teachers can see the types of revisions students make by examining their revised rough drafts. Revisions are another gauge of students' growth as writers.

Revising Centers. Many teachers set up revising centers to give students a variety of revision options: They can talk about the ideas in their rough draft with a classmate, examine the organization of their writing, consider their word choice, or check that they have included all required components in the composition. A list of revising centers is shown in Figure 2–6. Teachers introduce these centers as they teach their students about the writing process and the qualities of good writing, and then students work at these centers before or after participating in a writing group. Teachers usually provide a checklist of center options that students put in their writing folders, and then they check off the centers that they complete. Through these center activities, students develop a repertoire of revising strategies, and they personalize their writing process.

Stage 4: Editing

Editing is putting the piece of writing into its final form. Until this stage, the focus has been primarily on the content of students' writing. Once the focus changes to mechanics, students polish their writing by correcting spelling mistakes and other mechanical errors. The goal here is to make the writing "optimally readable" (Smith, 1982, p. 127). Writers who write for readers understand that if their compositions are not readable, they have written in vain because their ideas will never be read.

Figure 2-6   Revising and Editing Centers

Type	Center	Activities
Revising	Rereading	Students reread their rough drafts with a partner and the partner offers compliments and asks questions.
	Word Choice	Students choose 5–10 words in their rough drafts and look for more specific or more powerful words for them using a thesaurus, word walls in the classroom, or suggestions from classmates.
	Graphic Organizer	Students draw a chart or diagram to illustrate the organization of their compositions, and revise their rough drafts if the organization isn't effective or the writing isn't complete.
	Highlighting	Students use highlighter pens to mark their rough drafts according to the teacher's direction. Depending on the skills being taught, students may mark topic sentences, descriptive language, or sensory details.
	Sentence Combining	Students choose a section of their rough drafts with too many short sentences (often signaled by overuse of *and*) and use sentence combining to improve the flow of the writing.
Editing	Spelling	Students work with a partner to proofread their writing. They locate misspelled words and use a dictionary to correct them. Students may also check for specific errors in their use of recently taught skills, such as contractions or apostrophes.
	Homophones	Students check their rough drafts for homophone errors (e.g., *there–their–they're*), and consulting a chart posted in the center, they correct the errors.
	Punctuation	Students proofread their writing to check for punctuation marks. They make corrections as needed, and then highlight the punctuation marks in their compositions.
	Capitalization	Students check that each sentence begins with a capital letter, the word *I* is capitalized, and proper nouns and adjectives are capitalized. After the errors are corrected, students highlight all capitalized letters in the compositions.
	Sentences	Students analyze the sentences in their rough drafts, and then categorize them as simple, compound, complex, or fragment on a chart. Then they make any necessary changes.

Mechanics are the commonly accepted conventions of written Standard English; they consist of capitalization, punctuation, spelling, sentence structure, usage, and formatting considerations specific to poems, scripts, letters, and other writing genres. The use of these commonly accepted conventions is a courtesy to those who will read the composition.

Students learn mechanical skills best through hands-on editing of their own compositions, not through workbook exercises. When they edit a composition that will be shared with a genuine audience, students are more interested in using mechanical skills correctly so they can communicate effectively. Calkins (1980) compared how teachers in two third-grade classrooms taught punctuation skills. She found that the students in the class who learned punctuation marks as a part of editing could define or explain more marks than the students in the other class, who were taught punctuation skills in a traditional manner, with instruction and practice exercises on each punctuation mark. The results of this research, as well as other studies (Bissex, 1980; Elley,

Barham, Lamb, & Wyllie, 1976; Graves, 1983), suggest that it is more effective to teach mechanical skills as part of the writing process than through practice exercises.

Students move through three activities in the editing stage: getting distance from the composition, proofreading to locate errors, and correcting errors.

Getting Distance. Students are more efficient editors if they set the composition aside for a few days before beginning to edit. After working so closely with a piece of writing during drafting and revising, they are too familiar with it to notice many mechanical errors. With the distance gained by waiting a few days, children are better able to approach editing with a fresh perspective and gather the enthusiasm necessary to finish the writing process by making the paper optimally readable.

Proofreading. Students proofread their compositions to locate and mark possible errors. Proofreading is a unique type of reading in which students read slowly, word by word, hunting for errors rather than reading quickly for meaning (King, 1985). Concentrating on mechanics is difficult because of our natural inclination to read for meaning; even experienced proofreaders often find themselves reading for meaning and thus overlooking errors that do not inhibit meaning. It is important, therefore, to take time to explain proofreading to students and to demonstrate how it differs from regular reading.

To demonstrate proofreading, teachers copy a piece of writing on the chalkboard or display it on an overhead projector. The teacher reads it several times, each time hunting for a particular type of error. During each reading, the teacher reads the composition slowly, softly pronouncing each word and touching it with a pencil or pen to focus attention on it. The teacher marks possible errors as they are located.

Editing checklists help students focus on particular types of errors. Teachers can develop checklists with two to six items appropriate for the grade level. A first-grade checklist, for example, might have only two items—perhaps one about capital letters at the beginning of sentences and a second about periods at the end of sentences. In contrast, a middle-grade checklist might contain items such as using commas in a series, indenting paragraphs, capitalizing proper nouns and adjectives, and spelling homonyms correctly. Teachers revise the checklist during the school year to focus attention on skills that have recently been taught.

A sample third-grade editing checklist is presented in Figure 2–7. The writer and a classmate work as partners to edit their compositions. First, students proofread their own compositions, searching for errors in each category on the checklist, and, after proofreading, check off each item. After completing the checklist, students sign their names and trade checklists and compositions: Now they become editors and complete each other's checklist. Having writer and editor sign the checklist helps them to take the activity seriously.

Correcting Errors. After students proofread their compositions and locate as many errors as they can, they use red pens to correct the errors independently or with an editor's assistance. Some errors are easy to correct, some require use of a dictionary, and others involve instruction from the teacher. It is unrealistic to expect students to locate and correct every mechanical error in their compositions; not even published books are always error-free! Once in a while, students may change a correct spelling or punctuation mark and make it incorrect, but they correct far more errors than they create.

Students also work at editing centers to check for and correct specific types of errors. A list of editing centers is also shown in Figure 2–6. Teachers often vary the activities at the center to reflect the types of errors students are making. Students

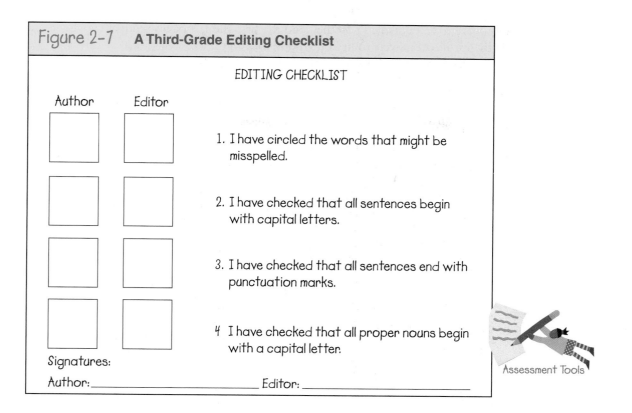

Figure 2-7   A Third-Grade Editing Checklist

EDITING CHECKLIST

Author   Editor

1. I have circled the words that might be misspelled.

2. I have checked that all sentences begin with capital letters.

3. I have checked that all sentences end with punctuation marks.

4 I have checked that all proper nouns begin with a capital letter.

Signatures:

Author: _____   Editor: _____

Assessment Tools

who continue to misspell common words can check for these words using a chart posted in the center. Or, after a series of lessons on contractions or punctuation marks, for example, one or more centers will focus on applying the newly taught skill.

Editing can end after students and their editors correct as many mechanical errors as possible, or after students meet with the teacher in a conference for a final editing conference. When mechanical correctness is crucial, this conference is important. Teachers proofread the composition with the student, and they identify and make the remaining corrections together, or the teacher makes check marks in the margin to note errors for the student to correct independently.

Stage 5: Publishing

In this stage, students bring their compositions to life by writing final copies and by sharing them orally with an appropriate audience. When they share their writing with real audiences of classmates, other students, parents, and the community, students come to think of themselves as authors.

Making Books. One of the most popular ways for children to publish their writing is by making books. Simple booklets can be made by folding a sheet of paper into quarters, like a greeting card. Students write the title on the front and use the three remaining sides for their composition. They can also construct booklets by stapling sheets of writing paper together and adding covers made out of construction paper. Sheets of wallpaper cut from old sample books also make sturdy covers. These stapled booklets can be cut into various shapes, too. Students can make more sophisticated books by covering cardboard covers with contact paper, wallpaper samples, or cloth.

Pages are sewn or stapled together, and the first and last pages (endpapers) are glued to the cardboard covers to hold the book together.

Sharing Writing. Students read their writing to classmates or share it with larger audiences through hardcover books placed in the class or school library, plays performed for classmates, or letters sent to authors, businesses, and other correspondents. Here are some other ways to share students' writing:

- Submit the piece to writing contests
- Display the writing as a mobile
- Contribute to a class anthology
- Contribute to the local newspaper
- Make a shape book
- Record the writing on a cassette tape
- Submit it to a literary magazine
- Read it at a school assembly
- Share it at a read-aloud party
- Share it with parents and siblings
- Display poetry on a "poet-tree"
- Send it to a pen pal
- Display it on a bulletin board

Author's Chair

These fifth graders take turns sitting in the special author's chair to read their published writings aloud to classmates. It's a celebratory activity, and after reading, students take turns asking questions and offering compliments. These students have learned to show interest in their classmates' writing, and to think about the writing so that they can participate in the discussion that follows the reading. Afterward, another student is chosen to share, and the process is repeated. As students sharing their writing from the author's chair, they learn to think of themselves as writers and consider their audience more carefully when they write.

Part 1 What Is a Balanced Approach to Literacy Instruction?

- Make a big book
- Design a poster about the writing
- Read it to foster grandparents
- Share it as a puppet show
- Display it at a public event
- Read it to students in other classes

Through this sharing, students communicate with genuine audiences who respond to their writing in meaningful ways. Sharing writing is a social activity that helps children develop sensitivity to audiences and confidence in themselves as authors. Dyson (1985) advises that teachers consider the social interpretations of sharing—the students' behavior, the teacher's behavior, and the interaction between students and teacher—within the classroom context. Individual students interpret sharing differently. Beyond just providing the opportunity for students to share writing, teachers need to teach students how to respond to their classmates. Teachers themselves serve as a model for responding to students' writing without dominating the sharing.

Qualities of Good Writing

Students learn about the qualities of good writing through minilessons and apply what they are learning as they use the writing process. Spandel (2005) has identified these six qualities, which she calls *traits*:

1. *Ideas.* The ideas are the essence of a piece of writing. Students choose an interesting idea, narrow it, and develop it using main ideas and details. They choose an idea during prewriting and develop it as they draft and revise their writing.

2. *Organization.* The organization is the skeleton of the piece. Students hook the reader in the beginning, identify the purpose, present ideas logically, provide transitions between ideas, and end with a satisfying conclusion so that the important questions are answered. Students organize their writing during prewriting and follow their plans as they draft.

3. *Voice.* The writer's distinctive style is voice; it is what breathes life into a piece of writing. Culham (2003) calls voice "the writer's music coming out through the words" (p. 102). During the drafting and revising stages, students create voice in their writing through the words they use, the sentences they craft, and the tone they adopt.

4. *Word Choice.* Careful word choice makes the meaning clear and the piece more interesting to read. Students learn to choose lively verbs and specific nouns, adjectives, and adverbs; create word pictures; and use idiomatic expressions as they craft their pieces. They focus on word choice as they draft and revise their writing.

5. *Sentence Fluency.* Sentence fluency is the rhythm and flow of language. Students vary the length and structure of their writing so that it has a natural cadence and is easy to read aloud. They develop sentence fluency as they draft, revise, and edit their writing.

6. *Mechanics.* The mechanics are spelling, capitalization, punctuation, and grammar. In the editing stage of the writing process, students proofread their writing and correct spelling and grammatical errors to make their writing easier to read.

Figure 2-8	Teaching the Qualities of Good Writing	
Quality	**Books**	**Ways to Teach**
Ideas	Baylor, B. (1986). *I'm in charge of celebrations.* New York: Aladdin. (P-M-U) Moss, T. (1993). *I want to be.* New York: Penguin. (P-M) Van Allsburg, C. (1984). *The mysteries of Harris Burdick.* Boston: Houghton Mifflin. (M-U) Wyeth, S. D. (1998). *Something beautiful.* New York: Doubleday. (P-M-U)	• Read aloud books with well-developed ideas. • Choose photos, pictures, or objects to write about. • Quickwrite to narrow and develop an idea. • Make clusters to develop an idea.
Organization	Fanelli, S. (1995). *My map book.* New York: HarperCollins. (P-M) Fleischman, P. (1997). *Seedfolks.* New York: HarperCollins. (M) Ryan, P. M. (2001). *Mice and beans.* New York: Scholastic. (P-M) Wysocki, C. (1994). *Heartland.* New York: Artisan. (M-U)	• Analyze the structure of a book using a graphic organizer. • Collect effective leads from books. • Find examples of effective transitions in books. • Collect effective endings from books.
Voice	Fleischman, P. (1993). *Bull Run.* New York: HarperCollins. (U) Hall, D. (1994). *I am the dog, I am the cat.* New York: Dial. (P) Myers, W. D. (2002). *Patrol: An American soldier in Vietnam.* New York: HarperCollins. (U) Yolen, J. (1981). *Sleeping ugly.* New York: Putnam. (M)	• Read aloud books with strong voices. • Have students describe the voice in a text. • Personalize a story by telling it from one character's viewpoint. • Add emotion to a voiceless piece of writing.
Word Choice	Brown, R. (1997). *Toad.* New York: Putnam. (M-U) Curtis, J. L. (1998). *Today I feel silly & other moods that make my day.* New York: HarperCollins. (P) Leedy, L., & Street, P. (2003). *There's a frog in my throat! 440 animal sayings a little bird told me.* New York: Holiday House. (P-M-U) Snicket, L. (1999). *A series of unfortunate events: The bad beginning.* New York: HarperCollins. (U)	• Read aloud books with good word choice. • Collect lively and precise words. • Learn to use a thesaurus. • Craft metaphors and similes.
Sentence Fluency	Aylesworth, J. (1992). *Old black fly.* New York: Henry Holt. (P) Grimes, N. (1999). *My man blue.* New York: Putnam. (M-U) Grossman, B. (1996). *My little sister ate one hare.* New York: Dragonfly Books. (P-M) Locker, T. (1997). *Water dance.* San Diego: Harcourt Brace. (M-U)	• Do choral readings of books with sentence fluency. • Collect favorite sentences on sentence strips. • Practice writing alliterative sentences. • Reread favorite books.
Mechanics	Bunting, E. (1998). *Your move.* San Diego: Harcourt Brace. (U) Pattison, D. (2003). *The journey of Oliver K. Woodman.* San Diego: Harcourt Brace. (M) Pulver, R. (2003). *Punctuation takes a vacation.* New York: Holiday House. (P-M-U) Simont, M. (2001). *The stray dog.* New York: HarperCollins. (P-M)	• Proofread excerpts from books to find mechanical errors that have been added. • Add capital letters to excerpts that have had them removed. • Add punctuation marks to excerpts that have had them removed. • Correct grammatical errors that have been added to excerpts from books.

Adapted from Spandel, 2001, 2005, Culham, 2003.

P = primary grades (K–2); M = middle grades (3–5); U = upper grades (6–8)

Teachers teach series of lessons about each quality. They explain the quality, show examples from children's literature and students' own writing, involve students in activities to investigate and experiment with the quality, and encourage students to apply what they have learned about the quality in their own writing as they move through the stages of the writing process. Figure 2–8 presents a list of books and activities that teachers can use in teaching the qualities of good writing.

As students study the six qualities, they internalize what good writers do. They learn to recognize good writing, develop a vocabulary for talking about writing, become better able to evaluate their own writing, and acquire strategies for improving the quality of their writing.

READING AND WRITING ARE SIMILAR PROCESSES

Reading and writing are both meaning-making processes, and readers and writers are involved in many similar activities. It is important that teachers plan literacy activities so that students can connect reading and writing.

Comparing the Two Processes

The reading and writing processes have comparable activities at each stage (Butler & Turbill, 1984). In both reading and writing, the goal is to construct meaning, and, as shown in Figure 2–9, reading and writing activities at each stage are similar. For example, notice the similarities between the activities listed for the third stage of reading and writing—responding and revising, respectively. Fitzgerald (1989) analyzed these two activities and concluded that they draw on similar processes of author-reader-text interactions. Similar analyses can be made for other activities as well.

Tierney (1983) explains that reading and writing are multidimensional and involve concurrent, complex transactions between writers, between writers as readers, between readers, and between readers as writers. Writers participate in several types of reading activities: They read other authors' works to obtain ideas and to learn about the structure of stories, but they also read and reread their own work in order to problem solve, discover, monitor, and clarify. The quality of these reading experiences seems closely tied to success in writing. Readers as writers is a newer idea, but readers participate in many of the same activities that writers use—generating ideas, organizing, monitoring, problem solving, and revising.

Classroom Connections

Teachers can help students appreciate the similarities between reading and writing in many ways. Tierney explains: "What we need are reading teachers who act as if their students were developing writers and writing teachers who act as if their students were readers" (1983, p. 151). Here are some ways to point out the relationships between reading and writing:

- Help writers assume alternative points of view as potential readers.
- Help readers consider the writer's purpose and viewpoint.
- Point out that reading is much like composing, so that students will view reading as a process, much like the writing process.
- Talk with students about the similarities between the reading and writing processes.
- Talk with students about reading and writing strategies.

Figure 2-9   A Comparison of the Reading and Writing Processes

	What Readers Do	What Writers Do
Stage 1	*Prereading* Readers use knowledge about • the topic • reading • literature • cueing systems Readers' expectations are cued by • previous reading/writing experiences • genre/format of the text • purpose for reading • audience for reading Readers make predictions.	*Prewriting* Writers use knowledge about • the topic • writing • literature • cueing systems Writers' expectations are cued by • previous reading/writing experiences • genre/format of the text • purpose for writing • audience for writing Writers gather and organize ideas.
Stage 2	*Reading* Readers • use word-identification strategies • use comprehension strategies • monitor reading • create meaning	*Drafting* Writers • use transcription strategies • use meaning-making strategies • monitor writing • create meaning
Stage 3	*Responding* Readers • respond to the text • deepen meaning • clarify misunderstandings • expand ideas	*Revising* Writers • respond to the next • deepen meaning • clarify misunderstandings • expand ideas
Stage 4	*Exploring* Readers • examine the impact of words and literary language • explore structural elements • compare the text to others	*Editing* Writers • identify and correct mechanical errors • review paragraph and sentence structure
Stage 5	*Applying* Readers • go beyond the text to extend their interpretations • share projects with classmates • reflect on the reading process • make personal, world, and literary connections • value the text • feel success • want to read again	*Publishing* Writers • make the finished copy of their compositions • share their compositions with genuine audiences • reflect on the writing process • value the composition • feel success • want to write again

Readers and writers use similar strategies for constructing meaning as they interact with print. As readers, we use a variety of problem-solving strategies to make decisions about an author's meaning and to construct meaning for ourselves. As writers, we also use problem-solving strategies to decide what our readers need as we construct meaning for them and for ourselves. Comparing reading to writing, Tierney and Pearson (1983) described reading as a composing process because readers compose and refine meaning through reading much as writers do through writing.

There are practical benefits of connecting reading and writing: Reading contributes to students' writing development, and writing contributes to students' reading development. Shanahan (1988) has outlined seven instructional principles for relating reading and writing so that students develop a clear concept of literacy:

Complete a self-assessment to check your understanding of the concepts presented in this chapter on the Companion Website at *www.prenhall.com/ tompkins*

1. Involve students in reading and writing experiences every day.
2. Introduce the reading and writing processes in kindergarten.
3. Plan instruction that reflects the developmental nature of reading and writing.
4. Make the reading-writing connection explicit to students.
5. Emphasize both the processes and the products of reading and writing.
6. Emphasize the purposes for which students use reading and writing.
7. Teach reading and writing through authentic literacy experiences.

These principles are incorporated into a balanced literacy program in which students read and write books and learn to view themselves as readers and writers.

Review: How Effective Teachers Teach the Reading and Writing Processes

1. Teachers use the five-stage reading process—prereading, reading, responding, exploring, and applying—for a balanced instructional program.
2. Teachers and students set purposes for reading.
3. Teachers incorporate different types of reading activities into their instructional program: independent reading, buddy reading, guided reading, shared reading, and reading aloud to students.
4. Students respond to their reading as they participate in grand conversations and write in reading logs.
5. Students reread the selection, examine the author's craft, and focus on words during the teacher-centered exploring stage.
6. Teachers regularly teach minilessons on strategies and skills during the exploring stage.
7. Teachers provide opportunities for students to complete both class collaboration and self-selected application projects.
8. Teachers teach students how to use the five stages of the writing process—prewriting, drafting, revising, editing, and publishing—to write and refine their compositions.
9. Teachers use a process approach to teach students about the qualities of good writing—ideas, organization, voice, word choice, sentence fluency, and conventions.
10. Teachers understand that the goal of both reading and writing is to construct meaning, and that the two processes involve similar activities at each stage.

Professional References

Applebee, A. N., & Langer, J. A. (1983). Instructional scaffolding: Reading and writing and natural language activities. *Language Arts, 60,* 168–175.

Bissex, G. L. (1980). *Gyns at wrk: A child learns to write and read.* Cambridge: Harvard University Press.

Blanton, W. E., Wood, K. D., & Moorman, G. B. (1990). The role of purpose in reading instruction. *The Reading Teacher, 43,* 486–493.

Britton, J., Burgess, T., Martin, N., McLeod, A., & Rosen, H. (1975). *The development of writing abilities (11–18)*. London: Schools Council Publications.

Butler, A., & Turbill, J. (1984). *Towards a reading-writing classroom*. Portsmouth, NH: Heinemann.

Calkins, L. M. (1980). When children want to punctuate: Basic skills belong in context. *Language Arts, 57,* 567–573.

Calkins, L. M. (1983). *Lessons from a child: On the teaching and learning of writing*. Portsmouth, NH: Heinemann.

Clay, M. M. (1991). *Becoming literate: The construction of inner control*. Portsmouth, NH: Heinemann.

Culham, R. (2003). *6 + 1 traits of writing*. New York: Scholastic.

Depree, H., & Iversen, S. (1996). *Early literacy in the classroom: A new standard for young readers*. Bothell, WA: Wright Group.

Dyson, A. H. (1982). The emergence of visible language: Interrelationships between drawing and early writing. *Visible Language, 6,* 360–381.

Dyson, A. H. (1985). Second graders sharing writing: The multiple social realities of a literacy event. *Written Communication, 2,* 189–215.

Dyson, A. H. (1986). The imaginary worlds of childhood: A multimedia presentation. *Language Arts, 63,* 799–808.

Eeds, M., & Wells, D. (1989). Grand conversations: An exploration of meaning construction in literature study groups. *Research in the Teaching of English, 23,* 4–29.

Elley, W. B., Barham, I. H., Lamb, H., & Wyllie, M. (1976). The role of grammar in a secondary school English curriculum. *Research in the Teaching of English, 10,* 5–21.

Faigley, L., & Witte, S. (1981). Analyzing revision. *College Composition and Communication, 32,* 400–410.

Fitzgerald, J. (1989). Enhancing two related thought processes: Revision in writing and critical thinking. *The Reading Teacher, 43,* 42–48.

Fountas, I. C., & Pinnell, G. S. (1996). *Guided reading: Good first teaching for all children*. Portsmouth, NH: Heinemann.

Graves, D. H. (1976). Let's get rid of the welfare mess in the teaching of writing. *Language Arts, 53,* 645–651.

Graves, D. H. (1983). *Writing: Teachers and children at work*. Exeter, NH: Heinemann.

Hidi, S., & Hildyard, A. (1983). The comparison of oral and written productions in two discourse modes. *Discourse Processes, 6,* 91–105.

Holdaway, D. (1979). *The foundations of literacy*. Portsmouth, NH: Heinemann.

Hornsby, D., Sukarna, D., & Parry, J. (1986). *Read on: A conference approach to reading*. Portsmouth, NH: Heinemann.

King, M. (1985). Proofreading is not reading. *Teaching English in the Two-Year College, 12,* 108–112.

Langer, J. A. (1985). Children's sense of genre. *Written Communication, 2,* 157–187.

Murray, D. H. (1982). *Learning by teaching*. Montclair, NJ: Boynton/Cook.

Opitz, M. F., & Rasinski, T. V. (1998). *Good-bye round robin: 25 effective oral reading strategies*. Portsmouth, NH: Heinemann.

Peterson. R., & Eeds, M. (1990). *Grand conversations: Literature groups in action*. New York: Scholastic.

Rasinski, T. V. (2003). *The fluent reader*. New York: Scholastic.

Rosenblatt, L. (1978). *The reader, the text, the poem: The transactional theory of the literary work*. Carbondale: Southern Illinois University Press.

Shanahan, T. (1988). The reading-writing relationship: Seven instructional principles. *The Reading Teacher, 41,* 636–647.

Slaughter, J. P. (1993). *Beyond storybooks: Young children and the shared book experience*. Newark, DE: International Reading Association.

Smith, F. (1982). *Writing and the writer*. New York: Holt, Rinehart and Winston.

Sommers, N. (1982). Responding to student writing. *College Composition and Communication, 33,* 148–156.

Spandel, V. (2001). *Books, lessons, ideas for teaching the six traits*. Wilmington, MA: Great Source.

Spandel, V. (2005). *Creating writers through 6-trait writing assessment and instruction* (4th ed.). Boston: Allyn & Bacon.

Tierney, R. J. (1983). Writer-reader transactions: Defining the dimensions of negotiation. In P. L. Stock (Ed.), *Forum: Essays on theory and practice in the teaching of writing* (pp. 147–151). Upper Montclair, NJ: Boynton/Cook.

Tierney, R. J., & Pearson, P. D. (1983). Toward a composing model of reading. *Language Arts, 60,* 568–580.

Yaden, D. B., Jr. (1988). Understanding stories through repeated read-alouds: How many does it take? *The Reading Teacher, 41,* 556–560.

Children's Book References

Lowry, L. (1993). *The giver*. Boston: Houghton Mifflin.

Lowry, L. (2000). *Gathering blue*. Boston: Houghton Mifflin.

Martin, B., Jr. (1983). *Brown bear, brown bear, what do you see?* New York: Holt, Rinehart and Winston.

Martin, B., Jr. (1992). *Polar bear, polar bear, what do you hear?* New York: Holt, Rinehart and Winston.

O'Neill, M. (1989). *Hailstones and halibut bones*. New York: Doubleday.

Stevens, J., & Crummel, S. S. (1999). *Cook-a-doodle-doo!* San Diego: Harcourt Brace.

Van Allsburg, C. (1981). *Jumanji*. Boston: Houghton Mifflin.

Van Allsburg, C. (1993). *The sweetest fig*. Boston: Houghton Mifflin.

Viorst, J. (1977). *Alexander and the terrible, horrible, no good, very bad day*. New York: Atheneum.

How Do Children Learn to Read and Write?

Researchers have identified what students need to learn to become successful readers and writers. The five components:

- **Alphabetic Code**
  Students learn about the English sound-symbol system, including phonemic awareness, phonics, and spelling.

- **High-Frequency Words**
  Students learn to read and spell the most common words, such as *the*, *what*, and *said*.

- **Fluency**
  Students develop the ability to read and write effortlessly so that they have cognitive resources available for comprehension.

- **Vocabulary**
  Students acquire a wide vocabulary and develop strategies for unlocking the meaning of unfamiliar words.

- **Comprehension**
  Students learn to use comprehension strategies to direct their reading and similar strategies when they write.

In this photo essay, you'll see how Ms. McCloskey incorporates these components into her balanced literacy program.

These first graders develop phonemic awareness and phonics knowledge as they sing the Jelly Beans song and pick out rhyming words.

Ms. McCloskey teaches students to make predictions, decode unfamiliar words, and monitor their reading as they read books in guided reading groups.

During literacy centers, these two students practice reading high-frequency words at the word wall.

This first grader is developing writing fluency as he writes on self-selected topics during writing workshop.

I am a POLeaSMan

When I am a POLeasman I wil Wher a blue Soot. I wil tace pele to Jail. I wil stop pele So the children can walk by. If pele crash I wil tack them to jail. I wil have a dog to Chas pele. I wil have a car when I am a poleasman. I wil LoCK the pele in jail. Aftr I am a Police man I wil go to bed and shore.

These first graders spend 15 minutes each day reading and rereading books independently or with a classmate.

Ms. McCloskey uses interactive writing to write the daily news report.

After Ms. McCloskey reads a story aloud, students draw questions from the story jar to guide their grand conversation.

Working With Young Readers and Writers

- How does emergent literacy differ from traditional reading readiness?
- What are the three stages of early literacy development?
- What do children learn as they develop as readers and writers?
- How do teachers scaffold young children's literacy learning?

Ms. McCloskey's Students Become Readers and Writers

Kindergarten through third-grade children sit together on the carpet in an open area in the classroom for a shared reading lesson. They watch and listen intently as Ms. McCloskey prepares to read aloud *Make Way for Ducklings* (McCloskey, 1969), the big-book version of an award-winning story about the dangers facing a family of ducks living in the city of Boston. She reads the title and the author's name, and some children recognize that the author's last name is the same as hers, but she points out that they are not related. She reads the first page of the text and asks the children to make predictions about the story. During this first reading of the book, Ms. McCloskey reads each page expressively and tracks the text, word by word, with a pointer as she reads. She clarifies the meaning as she talks about the illustrations on each page. A child helps balance the book on the easel and turn the pages for her. After she finishes reading the book, the children participate in a grand conversation and talk about the story. Some of the English learners are hesitant at first, but others are eager to relate their own experiences to the story and ask questions to clarify misunderstandings and learn more about the story.

The next day, Ms. McCloskey prepares to reread *Make Way for Duck-*

lings. She begins by asking for volunteers to retell the story. Children take turns retelling each page, using the illustrations as clues. Ms. Mc-Closkey includes this oral language activity because many of her students are English learners. The class is multilingual and multicultural: Approximately 45% of the children are Asian Americans who speak Hmong, Khmer, or Lao, 45% are Hispanics who speak Spanish or English at home, and the remaining 10% are African Americans and whites who speak English.

After the children retell the story, Ms. McCloskey rereads it, stopping several times to ask children to think about the characters, make inferences, and reflect on the theme. Her questions include: Why did the police officer help the ducks? What would have happened to the ducks if the police officer didn't help? Do you think that animals should live in cities? What was Robert McCloskey trying to say to us in this story?

On the third day, Ms. McCloskey reads the story again, and the children take turns using the pointer to track the text and join in reading familiar words. After they finish reading the story, the children clap. They're proud of their reading, and rereading the now familiar story provides a sense of accomplishment.

Ms. McCloskey understands that her students are moving through three developmental stages—emergent, beginning, and fluent—as they learn to read and write. She monitors each child's stage of development to provide instruction that meets his or her needs. As she reads the big book aloud, she uses a pointer to show the direction of print, from left to right and top to bottom on the page. She also moves the pointer across the lines of text, word by word, to demonstrate the relationship between the words on the page and the words she is reading aloud. These are concepts that many of the younger, emergent-stage readers are learning.

Other children are beginning readers who are learning to recognize high-frequency words and decode phonetically regular words. One day after rereading the story, Ms. McCloskey turns to one of the pages and asks the children to identify familiar high-frequency words (e.g., *don't, make*) and decode other CVC words (e.g., *run, big*). She also asks children to isolate individual sentences on the page and note the capital letter at the beginning and the punctuation that marks the end of the sentence.

The third group of children are fluent readers. Ms. McCloskey addresses their needs, too, as she rereads a page from the story: She asks several children to identify the words that are adjectives and to notice inflectional endings on verbs. She also rereads the last sentence on the page and asks a child to explain why commas are used in it.

Ms. McCloskey draws the children's attention to the text as a natural part of shared reading. She demonstrates concepts, points out letters, words, and punctuation marks, models strategies, and asks questions. All of the children are usually present for these lessons no matter what their stage of development, and as they think about the words and sentences, watch Ms. McCloskey, and listen to their classmates, they are learning more about literacy.

Check the Compendium of Instructional Procedures, which follows Chapter 14, for more information on highlighted terms.

Ms. McCloskey and her teaching partner, Mrs. Papaleo, share a large classroom and the 38 students; despite the number of children in the classroom, it feels spacious. Children's desks are arranged in clusters around the large, open area in the middle of the classroom where children meet for whole-class activities. An easel to display big books is placed next to the teacher's chair. Several chart racks stand nearby; one rack holds morning messages and other interactive writings that children have written, a second one holds charts with poems that the children have used for choral reading, and a third rack holds a pocket chart with word cards and sentence strips.

On one side of the classroom is a large classroom library with books arranged in crates by topic. One crate has frog books, and others have books about the ocean, plants, and the five senses. Other crates contain books by authors who have been featured in author studies, including Eric Carle, Norman Bridwell, Paul Galdone, and Paula Danziger. Picture books and chapter books are neatly arranged in the crates; children take turns keeping the area neat. Sets of leveled books are arranged above the children's reach for the teachers to use in guided reading instruction. A child-size sofa, a table and chairs, pillows, and rugs make the library area cozy and inviting to children. A listening center is set up at a nearby table with a tape player and headphones that can accommodate up to six children at a time.

A word wall with high-frequency words fills a partition separating sections of the classroom. The word wall is divided into small sections, one for each letter of the alphabet. Arranged on the word wall are nearly 100 words written on small cards cut into the shape of the words. The teachers introduce new words each week and post them on the word wall. The children often practice reading and writing the words as a center activity, and they refer to the word wall to spell words when they are writing.

On another side of the classroom are a bank of computers and a printer. All of the children, even the youngest ones, use the computers. Children who have stronger computer skills help their classmates. They use word processing and publishing software to publish their writing during writing workshop. They monitor their independent reading practice on the computer using the Accelerated Reader® program. At other times during the day, they use the Internet to find information related to topics they are studying in science and social studies and use other computer software to learn typing skills.

Literacy, math, and science center materials are stored in another area. Clear plastic boxes hold sets of magnetic letters, puppets and other props, white boards and dry-erase pens, puzzles and games, flash cards, and other manipulatives. The teachers choose materials from the boxes to use during minilessons and guided reading lessons, and they also set carefully prepared boxes of materials out on the children's desks for them to use during the centers time.

Ms. McCloskey spends the morning teaching reading and writing using a variety of teacher-directed and student-choice activities. Her daily schedule is shown in the box on page 81. After shared reading and a minilesson, the children participate in reading and writing workshop.

Children write books and other compositions during writing workshop. The children pick up their writing folders and write independently at their desks. While most of the children are working, Ms. McCloskey brings together a small group of children for a special activity: She conducts interactive writing lessons with emergent writers and teaches the writing process and revision strategies to more fluent writers. Today she is conferencing with a group of six children who are beginning writers. Because they are writing longer compositions, Ms. McCloskey has decided to introduce revising. After each child reads his or her composition aloud to the group, classmates ask questions and offer compliments, and Ms. McCloskey encourages them to make a change in their writing so that their readers will understand it better. Anthony reads

	Ms. McCloskey's Schedule	
Time	**Activity**	**Explanation**
8:10–8:20	Class Meeting	Children participate in opening activities, including saying the Pledge of Allegiance, marking the calendar, and reading the morning message.
8:20–8:45	Shared Reading	Ms. McCloskey reads and rereads big books and poems written on charts with children. She often uses this activity as a lead-in to the minilesson.
8:45–9:00	Minilesson	Ms. McCloskey teaches a minilesson to a small group or to the whole class on a literacy procedure, concept, strategy, or skill, depending on children's needs.
9:00–9:45	Writing Workshop	Children write stories, books, letters, and other compositions independently while Ms. McCloskey confers with individual children and small groups. She also does interactive writing activities with emergent and beginning writers.
9:45–10:00	Recess	
10:00–11:15	Reading Workshop	Children read self-selected books and reread leveled books independently while Ms. McCloskey does guided reading with small groups of children reading at the same level.
11:15–11:30	Class Meeting	Children meet to review the morning's activities and to share their writing from the author's chair.
11:30–12:10	Lunch	
12:10–12:30	Read Aloud	Ms. McCloskey reads aloud picture books and chapter books, and children discuss the books in grand conversations.

aloud a story about his soccer game, and after a classmate asks a question, he realizes that he needs to add more about how he scored a goal. He moves back to his desk to revise. The group continues with children sharing their writing and beginning to make revisions. At the end of the writing workshop, the teachers bring the children together for author's chair. Each day, three children take turns sitting in a special chair called "the author's chair" to read their writing aloud to their classmates. Classmates clap after each child reads and they offer compliments.

During reading workshop, children read and reread books independently while Ms. McCloskey and her teaching partner conduct guided reading lessons. The children have access to a wide variety of books in the classroom library, including predictable books for emergent readers, decodable books for beginning readers, and easy-to-read chapter books for fluent readers. Ms. McCloskey has taught them how to choose books that they can read successfully so they are able to spend their time reading, either independently or with a buddy. They read library books, reread books they have recently read in guided reading, and read books in the Accelerated Reader® program and take the computer-generated comprehension tests. The children keep lists of the books they read and reread in their workshop folders so that Ms. McCloskey can monitor their progress.

Ms. McCloskey is working with a group of four emergent readers. They will read *Playing* (Prince, 1999), a seven-page predictable book with one line of text on each page that uses the pattern "I like to _____." She begins by asking children what they like to do when they are playing. Der says, "I like to play with my brother, " and Ms. McCloskey writes the sentence on a strip of paper. Some of the children say only a word or two, and she expands the words into a sentence for the child to repeat. Then she writes the expanded sentence and reads it with the child. Next, she introduces the book and reads the title and the author's name. Then Ms. McCloskey does a picture walk with the children, talking about the picture on each page and naming the activity the child is doing—running, jumping, sliding, and so on. She reviews the "I like to _____" pattern, and then the children read the book independently while Ms. McCloskey supervises and provides assistance as needed. The children eagerly reread the book several times, becoming more confident and excited with each reading.

Ms. McCloskey reviews the high-frequency words *I, like*, and *to,* and the children point them out on the classroom word wall. They use magnetic letters to form the words and then write sentences that begin with *I like to . . .* on white boards. Then Ms. McCloskey cuts apart their sentence strips for them to sequence, and the children each put their sentences into an envelope to practice another day. At the end of the group session, Ms. McCloskey suggests that the children might want to write "I like to _____" books during writing workshop the next day.

During the last 30 minutes before lunch, the children work at literacy centers. Ms. McCloskey and Mrs. Papaleo have set out 12 centers in the classroom, and the children are free to work at any centers they choose. They practice phonics at the games center, for example, and reread texts at the interactive chart center and the library center. The children are familiar with the routine and know what is expected of them at each center. The two teachers circulate around the classroom, monitoring children's work and taking advantage of teachable moments to clarify misunderstandings, reinforce previous lessons, and extend children's learning. A list of the literacy centers is presented in the box on the next page.

After lunch, Ms. McCloskey finishes her literacy block by reading aloud picture books and easy-to-read chapter books. Sometimes she reads aloud books by a particular author, such as Marc Brown, Lois Ehlert, and Paula Danziger, but at other times, she reads books related to a social studies or science unit. She uses these read-alouds to teach comprehension strategies, such as predicting, visualizing, and making connections. This week, she is reading award-winning books, and today she reads aloud *The Stray Dog* (Simont, 2001), the story of a homeless dog that is taken in by a loving family. After she reads the book aloud, the children talk about it in a grand conversation, and Ms. McCloskey asks them to make text-to-self, text-to-world, and text-to-text connections. As the children share their connections, the teachers record them on a chart divided into three sections. Most of their comments are text-to-self connections, but several children make other types of connections: Rosario says, "I am thinking of a movie. It was 101 Dalmations. It was about dogs, too." Angelo offers,

Part 2 How Do Children Learn to Read and Write?

The Literacy Centers in Ms. McCloskey's Classroom

Center	Activities
Bag a Story	The teacher places seven objects in a lunch bag. Children use the objects to create a story. They divide a sheet of paper into eight sections, and they introduce the character in the first section and focus on one object in each of the remaining boxes.
Clip Boards	Children search the classroom for words beginning with a particular letter or featuring a particular characteristic. They read books, charts, and signs and consult dictionaries.
Games	Children play alphabet, phonics, opposites, and other literacy card games and board games.
Interactive Chart	The teacher introduces a poetry frame, and children create a poem together as a class. They brainstorm words to fit the frame and the teacher writes the words on cards. The children arrange the cards in a pocket chart to make the poem. Then the materials are placed in the center, and children arrange the word cards to create poems.
Library	Children read books related to a thematic unit. Then they write a sentence or two about the book and draw an illustration in their reading logs.
Listening	Children listen to a tape of a story or informational book while they follow along in copies of the book.
Making Words	The teacher chooses a secret word related to a story children are reading or to a thematic unit and sets magnetic letters spelling the word in a metal pan for children to use to make words. Children use the letters to spell two-, three-, and four-letter words. Then they arrange all of the letters to discover the secret word.
Messages	Children write messages to classmates and to Ms. McCloskey and post them on a special bulletin board titled "Message Center."
Pocket Chart	Children use the high-frequency and thematic word cards displayed in the pocket chart for word sorts.
Reading the Room	Children use pointers to point to and reread big books, charts, signs, and other texts in the classroom.
Research	Children use the Internet, informational books, photos, and realia to learn about the social studies or science topics as part of thematic units.
Story Reenactment	Children use small props, finger puppets, or flannel board figures to reenact stories they have read or listened to the teacher read aloud.

"You got to stay away from stray dogs. They can bite you, and they might have this bad disease—it can kill you. I know that you have to get shots if a dog bites you."

Ms. McCloskey knows her students well. She knows about their families, their language backgrounds, their interests, and their academic abilities. She knows how to monitor progress, facilitate their development, and what to do if they are not progressing. She knows the level of achievement that is expected by the end of the school year according to school district guidelines and state-mandated standards. Ms. McCloskey's literacy program facilitates her instruction and assessment.

Visit Chapter 3 on the Companion Website at *www. prenhall.com/tompkins* to check into your state's literacy standards for kindergarten through third grade.

Literacy is a process that begins well before the elementary grades and continues into adulthood, if not throughout life. It used to be that 5-year-old children came to kindergarten to be "readied" for reading and writing instruction, which would formally begin in first grade. The implication was that there was a point in children's development when it was time to begin teaching them to read and write. For those not ready, a variety of "readiness" activities would prepare them for reading and writing. Since the 1970s, this view has been discredited by the observations of both teachers and researchers (Clay, 1989). The children themselves demonstrated that they could recognize signs and other environmental print, retell stories, scribble letters, invent printlike writing, and listen to stories read aloud. Some children even taught themselves to read.

This perspective on how children become literate—that is, how they learn to read and write—is known as *emergent literacy,* a term that New Zealand educator Marie Clay is credited with coining. Studies from 1966 on have shaped the current outlook (Clay, 1967; Durkin, 1966; Holdaway, 1979; McGee & Richgels, 2003; Morrow & Ashby, 1999; Taylor, 1983; Teale, 1982). Now, researchers are looking at literacy learning from the child's point of view. The age range has been extended to include children as young as 1 or 2 who listen to stories being read aloud, notice labels and signs in their environment, and experiment with pencils. The concept of literacy has been broadened to incorporate the cultural and social aspects of language learning, and children's experiences with and understandings about written language—both reading and writing—are included as part of emergent literacy.

Teale and Sulzby (1989) paint a portrait of young children as literacy learners with these characteristics:

- Children begin to learn to read and write very early in life.
- Young children learn the functions of literacy through observing and participating in real-life settings in which reading and writing are used.
- Young children's reading and writing abilities develop concurrently and interrelatedly through experiences in reading and writing.
- Through active involvement with literacy materials, young children construct their understanding of reading and writing.

In the vignette at the beginning of this chapter, Ms. McCloskey's students exemplified many of these characteristics.

Teale and Sulzby describe young children as active learners who construct their own knowledge about reading and writing with the assistance of parents, teachers, and other literate people. These adults demonstrate literacy as they read and write, supply reading and writing materials, scaffold opportunities for children to be involved in reading and writing, and provide instruction about how written language works. The feature below shows how young children's literacy development fits into a balanced literacy program.

How Young Children's Literacy Development Fits Into a Balanced Literacy Program

Component	Description
Reading	Teachers read aloud to children and use shared reading, guided reading, and the Language Experience Approach to teach reading.
Phonics and Other Skills	Young children learn concepts about print, the letters of the alphabet, phonemic awareness, and phonics and apply these skills as they learn to read and write.
Strategies	Children learn to use the four cueing systems to monitor word identification and spelling as they learn to read and write.
Vocabulary	Children learn vocabulary words as they listen to the teacher read books aloud, and they also post important words on word walls as part of literature focus units and content-area units.
Comprehension	Teachers teach young children to make predictions and then check to see if their predictions are correct. They also teach children to make connections and use other strategies.
Literature	Teachers read aloud picture books—both stories and informational books—every day. They also use predictable books in big-book format for shared reading and leveled books for guided reading.
Content-Area Study	Young children participate in social studies- and science-based thematic units to learn about the world around them.
Oral Language	Children talk informally with classmates as they participate in small-group activities and share their ideas with the whole class in grand conversations and instructional conversations.
Writing	Children participate in interactive writing lessons, make class collaboration charts and books, and write independently at writing centers.
Spelling	Young children use invented spelling that reflects their phonics knowledge; as they learn more phonics, their spelling becomes more conventional.

Fostering Young Children's Interest in Literacy

Children's introduction to written language begins before they come to school. Parents and other caregivers read to young children, and children observe adults reading. They learn to read signs and other environmental print in their community. Children experiment with writing and have their parents write for them; they also observe adults writing. When young children come to kindergarten, their knowledge about written language expands quickly as they participate in meaningful experiences with reading and writing. They learn concepts about print, words, and letters of the alphabet.

Concepts About Print

Through experiences in their homes and communities, young children learn that print carries meaning and that reading and writing are used for a variety of purposes. They read menus in restaurants to know what foods are being served, write and receive letters to communicate with friends and relatives, and read and listen to stories for enjoyment. Children also learn about language purposes as they observe parents and teachers using written language for all these reasons.

Children's understanding about the purposes of reading and writing reflects how written language is used in their community. Although reading and writing are part of daily life for almost every family, families use written language for different purposes in different communities (Heath, 1983). Young children have a wide range of literacy experiences in both middle-class and working-class families, even though those experiences might be different (Taylor, 1983; Taylor & Dorsey-Gaines, 1987). In some communities, written language is used mainly as a tool for practical purposes such as paying bills, whereas in other communities, reading and writing are also used for leisure-time activities. In still other communities, written language serves even wider functions, such as debating social and political issues.

Ms. McCloskey and other primary-grade teachers demonstrate the purposes of written language and provide opportunities for students to experiment with reading and writing in many ways:

posting signs in the classroom

making a list of classroom rules

using reading and writing materials in literacy play centers

exchanging messages with classmates

reading and writing stories

labeling classroom items

drawing and writing in journals

writing morning messages

writing notes to parents

Young children learn other concepts about print through these activities, too: They learn book-orientation concepts, including how to hold a book and turn pages, and that the text, not the illustrations, carries the message. Children also learn directionality concepts—that print is written and read from left to right and from top to bottom on a page. They match voice to print, pointing word by word to the text as it is read aloud. Children also notice punctuation marks and learn their names and purposes (Clay, 1991).

Concepts About Words

At first, young children have only vague notions of language terms, such as *word, letter, sound,* and *sentence,* that teachers use in talking about reading and writing, but children develop an increasingly sophisticated understanding of these terms during the primary grades (Downing & Oliver, 1973–1974). Researchers have investigated children's understanding of a word as a unit of language. Papandropoulou and Sinclair (1974) identified four stages of word consciousness. At first, young children do not differentiate between words and things. At the next level, children describe words as labels for things; they consider words that stand for objects as words, but they do not classify articles and prepositions as words because words such as *the* and *with* cannot be represented with objects. At the third level, children understand that words carry meaning and that stories are built from words. Finally, more fluent readers and writers describe words as autonomous elements having meanings of their own with definite semantic and syntactic relationships. Children might say, "You make words with letters." Also children understand that words have different appearances: They can be spoken, listened to, read, and written. Invernizzi (2003) explains the importance of reaching the fourth level this way: "A concept of word allows children to hold onto the printed word in their mind's eye and scan it from left to right, noting every sound in the beginning, middle, and end" (p. 152).

Children acquire concepts about words through active participation in literacy activities. They watch as teachers point to words in big books during shared reading lessons, and they mimic the teacher and point to words as they reread familiar texts. After many, many shared reading experiences, children notice that word boundaries are marked with spaces, and they pick out familiar words. Through Language Experience Approach activities and interactive writing, young children have additional experiences reading and writing words and marking word boundaries. With experience, children's pointing becomes more exact and they become more proficient at picking out specific words in the text, noticing that words at the beginning of sentences are marked with capital letters and words at the end of sentences are followed with punctuation marks.

Environmental Print. Children move from recognizing environmental print to reading decontextualized words in books. Young children begin reading by recognizing logos on fast-food restaurants, department stores, grocery stores, and commonly used household items within familiar contexts (Harste, Woodward, & Burke, 1984). They recognize the golden arches of McDonald's and say "McDonald's," but when they are shown the word *McDonald's* written on a sheet of paper without the familiar sign and restaurant setting, they cannot read the word. Researchers have found that young emergent readers depend on context to read familiar words and memorized texts (Dyson, 1984; Sulzby, 1985). Slowly, children develop relationships linking form and meaning as they learn concepts about written language and gain more experience reading and writing.

When children begin writing, they use scribbles or single letters to represent complex ideas (Clay, 1975; Schickedanz, 1990). As they learn about letter names and phoneme-grapheme correspondences, they use one, two, or three letters to stand for words. At first, they run their writing together, but they slowly learn to segment words and to leave spaces between words. They sometimes add dots or lines as markers between words or draw circles around words. They also move from capitalizing words randomly to using capital letters at the beginning of sentences and to marking proper nouns and adjectives. Similarly, children move from using a period at the end of each line of writing to marking the ends of sentences with periods. Then they learn about other end-of-sentence markers and, finally, punctuation marks that are embedded in sentences.

Literacy Play Centers. Young children learn about the purposes of reading and writing as they use written language in their play: As they construct block buildings, children write signs and tape them on the buildings; as they play doctor, children write prescriptions on slips of paper; and as they play teacher, children read stories aloud to classmates who are pretending to be students or to doll and stuffed animal "students." Young children use these activities to reenact familiar, everyday activities and to pretend to be someone or something else. Through these literacy play activities, children use reading and writing for a variety of purposes.

Kindergarten teachers adapt play centers and add literacy materials to enhance the value of the centers for literacy learning. Housekeeping centers are probably the most common play centers in kindergarten classrooms, but these centers can be transformed into a grocery store, a post office, or a medical center by changing the props. They become literacy play centers when materials for reading and writing are included: Food packages, price stickers, and money are props in grocery store centers; letters, stamps, and mailboxes are props in post office centers; and appointment books, prescription pads, and folders for patient records are props in medical centers. A variety of literacy play centers can be set up in classrooms, and they can often be coordinated with literature focus units and content-area units.

Concepts About the Alphabet

Young children also develop concepts about the alphabet and how letters are used to represent phonemes. Pinnell and Fountas (1998) have identified these components of letter knowledge:

- The letter's name
- The formation of the letter in upper- and lowercase manuscript handwriting
- The features of the letter that distinguish it from other letters
- The direction the letter must be turned to distinguish it from other letters (e.g., *b* and *d*)
- The use of the letter in known words (e.g., names and common words)
- The sound the letter represents in isolation
- The sound the letter represents in combination with others (e.g., *ch, th*)
- The sound the letter represents in the context of a word

Children use this knowledge to decode unfamiliar words as they read and to create spellings for words as they write.

The most basic information children learn about the alphabet is how to identify and form the letters in handwriting. They notice letters in environmental print, and they often learn to sing the ABC song. By the time children enter kindergarten, they can usually recognize some letters, especially those in their own names, in names of family members and pets, and in common words in their homes and communities. Children can also write some of these familiar letters.

Young children associate letters with meaningful contexts—names, signs, T-shirts, and cereal boxes. Baghban (1984) notes that the letter *M* was the first letter her daughter noticed—she pointed to *M* in the word *K Mart* and called it "McDonald's." Even though the child confused a store and a restaurant, this account demonstrates how young children make associations with letters. Research suggests that children do not learn alphabet letter names in any particular order or by isolating letters from meaningful written language. McGee and Richgels (2001) conclude that learning letters of the alphabet requires many, many experiences with meaningful written language. They recommend that teachers take three steps to encourage children's alphabet learning:

1. *Capitalize on children's interests.* Teachers provide letter activities that children enjoy, and they talk about letters when children are interested in talking about them. Teachers know what features to comment on because they observe children during reading and writing activities to find out which letters or features of letters children are exploring. Children's questions also provide insights into what they are curious about.

2. *Talk about the role of letters in reading and writing.* Teachers talk about how letters represent sounds and how letters combine to spell words, and they point out capital letters and lowercase letters. Teachers often talk about the role of letters as they write with children.

3. *Teach routines and provide a variety of opportunities for alphabet learning.* Teachers use children's names and environmental print in literacy activities, do interactive writing, encourage children to use invented spellings, share alphabet books, and play letter games.

Teachers begin teaching letters of the alphabet using two sources of words—children's own names and environmental print. They also teach the ABC song so that children will have a strategy to use to identify a particular letter. Children learn to sing this song and point to each letter on an alphabet chart until they reach the unfamiliar letter; this is an important strategy because it gives them a real sense of independence in identifying letters. Teachers also provide routines, activities, and games for talking about and manipulating letters. During these familiar, predictable activities, teachers and children say letter names, manipulate magnetic letters, and write letters on white boards. At first, the teacher structures and guides the activities, but with experience, the children internalize the routine and do it independently, often at a literacy center. Figure 3–1 presents 10 routines or activities to teach the letters of the alphabet.

Being able to name the letters of the alphabet is a good predictor of beginning reading achievement, even though knowing the names of the letters does not directly affect a child's ability to read (Adams, 1990; Snow, Burns, & Griffin, 1998). A more likely explanation for this relationship between letter knowledge and reading is that children who have been actively involved in reading and writing activities before entering first grade know the names of the letters, and they are more likely to begin reading quickly. Simply teaching children to name the letters without the accompanying reading and writing experiences does not have this effect.

How Children Develop as Readers and Writers

Young children move through three stages as they learn to read and write: (1) emergent, (2) beginning, and (3) fluent (Juel, 1991). During the emergent stage, young children gain an understanding of the communicative purpose of print, and they move from pretend reading to reading repetitive books and from using scribbles to simulate writing to writing patterned sentences, such as *I see a bird. I see a tree. I see a car.* The focus of the second stage, beginning reading and writing, is to teach children to use phonics to "crack the alphabetic code" in order to decode and spell words. In addition, children learn to read and write many high-frequency words. They also write several sentences to develop a story or other composition. In the fluent stage, children

Visit
Chapter 3 on the
Companion Website at
*www.prenhall.com/
tompkins* to connect to
web links related to
young children's literacy
development.

| Figure 3-1 | Routines to Teach the Letters of the Alphabet |

Environmental Print
Children sort food labels, toy traffic signs, and other environmental print to find examples of a letter being studied.

Alphabet Books
Teachers read aloud alphabet books to build vocabulary, and later children reread the books to find words when making books about a letter.

Magnetic Letters
Children pick all examples of one letter from a collection of magnetic letters or match upper- and lowercase letter forms of magnetic letters. They also arrange the letters in alphabetical order and use the letters to spell familiar words.

Letter Stamps
Children use letter stamps and ink pads to print letters on paper or in booklets. They also use letter-shaped sponges to paint letters and letter-shaped cookie cutters to cut out clay letters.

Alphabet Chart
Children point to letters and pictures on the alphabet chart as they recite the alphabet and the name of the picture, such as "A-airplane, B-baby, C-cat," and so on.

Letter Containers
Teachers collect coffee cans or shoe boxes, one for each letter, and place several familiar objects that represent the letter in each container. Teachers use these containers to introduce the letters, and children use them for sorting and matching activities.

Letter Frames
Teachers make circle-shaped letter frames from tagboard, collect large plastic bracelets, or shape pipe cleaners or Wikki-Stix (pipe cleaners covered in wax) into circles for students to use to highlight particular letters on charts or in big books.

Letter Books and Posters
Children make letter books with pictures of objects beginning with a particular letter on each page. They add letter stamps, stickers, or pictures cut from magazines. For posters, the teacher draws a large letter form on a chart and children add pictures, stickers, and letter stamps.

Letter Sorts
Children sort objects and pictures representing two or more letters and place them in containers marked with the specific letters.

White Boards
Children practice writing upper- and lowercase forms of a letter and familiar words on white boards.

move from slow, word-by-word reading to become automatic, fluent readers, and in writing, they develop good handwriting skills, spell many high-frequency words, and organize their writing into more than one paragraph.

The goal of reading and writing instruction in the primary grades is to ensure that all children reach the fluent stage by the end of third grade. Figure 3–2 summarizes children's accomplishments in reading and writing development at each of the three stages.

Figure 3-2 Young Children's Literacy Development

Stage	Reading	Writing
Emergent	Children: • notice environmental print • show interest in books • pretend to read • use picture cues and predictable patterns in books to retell the story • reread familiar books with predictable patterns • identify some letter names • recognize 5–20 familiar or high-frequency words • make text-to-self connections	Children: • distinguish between writing and drawing • write letters and letterlike forms or scribble randomly on the page • develop an understanding of directionality • show interest in writing • write their first and last names • write 5–20 familiar or high-frequency words • use sentence frames to write a sentence
Beginning	Children: • identify letter names and sounds • match spoken words to written words • recognize 20–100 high-frequency words • use beginning, middle, and ending sounds to decode words • apply knowledge of the cueing systems to monitor reading • self-correct while reading • read slowly, word by word • read orally • point to words when reading • make reasonable predictions • make text-to-self and text-to-world connections	Children: • write from left to right • print the upper- and lowercase letters • write one or more sentences • add a title • spell phonetically • spell 20–50 high-frequency words correctly • write single-draft compositions • use capital letters to begin sentences • use periods, question marks, and exclamation points to mark the end of sentences • can reread their writing
Fluent	Children: • identify most words automatically • read with expression • read at a rate of 100 words per minute or more • prefer to read silently • identify unfamiliar words using the cueing systems • recognize 100–300 high-frequency words • use a variety of strategies effectively • often read independently • use knowledge of text structure and genre to support comprehension • make text-to-self, text-to-world, and text-to-text connections • make inferences	Children: • use the writing process to write drafts and final copies • write compositions of one or more paragraphs in length • indent paragraphs • spell most of the 100 high-frequency words • use sophisticated and technical vocabulary • apply vowel patterns to spell words • add inflectional endings on words • apply capitalization rules • use commas, quotation marks, and other punctuation marks

Emergent Reading and Writing

Children gain an understanding of the communicative purpose of print and develop an interest in reading and writing during the emergent stage. They notice environmental print in the world around them and in the classroom. They develop concepts about print as teachers read and write with them. As children dictate stories for the teacher to record during Language Experience Approach activities, for example, they learn that their speech can be written and they observe how teachers write from left to right and top to bottom.

Children make scribbles to represent writing. The scribbles may appear randomly on a page at first, but with experience, children line up the letters or scribbles from left to right and from top to bottom. Children also begin to "read," or tell what their writing says (Harste et al., 1984; Temple, Nathan, Burris, & Temple, 1988). At first, they can reread their writing only immediately after writing, but with experience, they learn to remember what their writing says, and as their writing becomes more conventional, they are able to read it more easily.

During the emergent stage, children accomplish the following:

- develop an interest in reading and writing
- acquire concepts about print
- develop book-handling skills
- learn to identify the letters of the alphabet
- develop handwriting skills
- learn to read and write some familiar and high-frequency words

Children are usually emergent readers and writers in kindergarten, but some children whose parents have read to them every day and provided a variety of literacy experiences do learn how to read before they come to school (Durkin, 1966).

Emergent readers and writers participate in a variety of literacy activities ranging from modeled and shared reading and writing, during which they watch as teachers read and write, to independent reading and writing that they do themselves. Ms. McCloskey's students, for example, listened to her read aloud books and read big books using shared reading, and they also participated in reading and writing workshop. When working with children at the emergent stage, however, teachers often use modeled and shared reading and writing activities because they are demonstrating what readers and writers do and teaching concepts about print.

One shared literacy activity is morning messages. The teacher begins by talking about the day and upcoming events, and children share their news with the class. Then the children and teacher, working together, compose the morning message (Kawakami-Arakaki, Oshiro, & Farran, 1989). The message includes classroom news that is interesting to the children. Here is a morning message that Ms. McCloskey and her students wrote:

> Today is Friday, March 10. Ms. McCloskey brought 3 frogs and 10 tadpoles for us to observe. They are in the pond.

The teacher writes the morning message on chart paper as children watch. While writing the message, the teacher demonstrates that writing is done from left to right and top to bottom and how to form letters. Then the teacher reads the message aloud, pointing to each word as it is read. The class talks about the meaning of the message, and the teacher uses the message to point out spelling, capitalization, or punctuation skills. Afterward, children are encouraged to reread the message and pick out familiar letters and words. As the school year progresses, the morning message grows longer, and children assume a greater role in reading and writing the message so that the activity becomes interactive writing.

Through the routine of writing morning messages, young children learn a variety of things about written language. Reading and writing are demonstrated as integrated processes, and children learn that written language is used to convey information. They learn about the direction of print, the alphabet, spelling, and other conventions used in writing. Children also learn about appropriate topics for messages and how to organize ideas into sentences.

Beginning Reading and Writing

This stage marks children's growing awareness of the alphabetic principle. Children learn about phoneme-grapheme correspondences and phonics generalizations in *run, hand, this, make, day,* and *road,* and *r*-controlled vowel words, such as *girl* and *farm.* They also apply (and misapply) their developing phonics knowledge to spell words. For example, they spell *night* as NIT and *train* as TRANE. At the same time, they are learning to read and write high-frequency words, many of which can't be sounded out, such as *what, are, there,* and *get.*

Children usually read aloud slowly, in a word-by-word fashion, stopping often to sound out unfamiliar words. They point at each word as they read, but by the end of this stage, their reading becomes smoother and more fluent, and they point at words only when the text is especially challenging.

Although the emphasis in this stage is on decoding and recognizing words, children also learn that reading involves understanding what they are reading. They make predictions to guide their thinking about events in stories they read, and they make connections between what they are reading and their own lives and the world around them as they personalize the reading experience. They practice the cross-checking strategy so that they learn what to do when what they are reading doesn't make sense. They learn to consider phonological, semantic, syntactic, and pragmatic information in the text and make self-corrections (Fountas & Pinnell, 1996). They also learn about story structure, particularly that stories have a beginning, a middle, and an end, and they use this knowledge to guide their retelling of stories.

Children move from writing one or two sentences to developing longer compositions, with five, eight, or more sentences, organized into paragraphs by the end of this stage. Children's writing is better developed, too, because they are acquiring a sense of audience, and they want their classmates to like their writing. Children continue to write single-draft compositions but begin to make a few revisions and editing corrections as they learn about the writing process toward the end of the stage.

Children apply what they are learning about phonics in their spelling, and they correctly spell many of the high-frequency words that they have learned to read. They have learned to spell some of the high-frequency words, and they locate other words on word walls that are posted in the classroom. They learn to use capital letters to mark the beginnings of sentences and punctuation to mark the ends of sentences. Children are more adept at rereading their writing, both immediately after writing and days later, because they are able to read many of the words they have written.

During the beginning stage of reading and writing development, children accomplish the following:

- learn phonics skills
- recognize 20–100 high-frequency words
- make reasonable predictions
- self-correct while reading
- write five or more sentences, sometimes organized into a paragraph
- spell phonetically
- spell 20–50 high-frequency words
- use capital letters to begin sentences
- use punctuation marks to mark the ends of sentences
- reread their writing

Most first and second graders are beginning readers and writers, and with instruction in reading and writing strategies and skills and daily opportunities to read and write, children move through this stage to reach the fluent stage.

Teachers plan activities for children at the beginning stage that range from modeled to independent reading and writing activities, but the emphasis in this stage is on interactive and guided activities. Through interactive writing, choral reading, and guided reading, teachers scaffold children as they read and write and provide strategy and skill instruction. For example, Ms. McCloskey's students were divided into small, homogeneous groups for guided reading lessons. The children met to read leveled books at their reading levels, and Ms. McCloskey introduced new vocabulary words, taught reading strategies, and monitored children's comprehension.

Teachers introduce the writing process to beginning-stage writers once they develop a sense of audience and want to make their writing better so that their classmates will like it. Children don't immediately begin writing rough drafts and final copies or doing both revising and editing: They often begin the writing process by rereading their compositions and adding a word or two, correcting a misspelled word, or changing a lowercase letter to a capital letter. These changes are usually cosmetic, but the idea that the writing process doesn't end after the first draft has been written is established. Next, children show interest in making a final copy that really looks good. They either recopy the composition by hand or word process the composition on a computer and print out the final copy. Once the idea that writing involves a rough draft and a final copy is established, children are ready to learn more about revising and editing, and they usually reach this point at about the same time they become fluent writers.

Fluent Reading and Writing

The third stage is fluent reading and writing. Fluent readers can recognize hundreds and hundreds of words automatically, and they have the tools to identify unfamiliar words when reading. Fluent writers use the writing process to draft, revise, and publish their writing, and they participate in writing groups. They are familiar with a variety of genres and know how to organize their writing. They use conventional spelling and other elements of written language, including capital letters and punctuation marks. By the end of third grade, all students should be fluent readers and writers.

The distinguishing characteristic of fluent readers is that they read words accurately, rapidly, and automatically, and they read with expression. Their reading rate has increased to 100 words or more per minute. They automatically recognize many words and can identify unfamiliar words efficiently.

Most fluent readers prefer to read silently because they can read more quickly than when they read orally. No longer do they point at words as they read. Children actively make predictions as they read and monitor their understanding. They have a range of strategies available and use them to self-correct when the words they are reading do not make sense. Children can read most books independently.

Fluent readers' comprehension is stronger and they think more deeply about their reading than do readers in the previous stages. Researchers speculate that children's comprehension improves at this stage because they have more cognitive energy available for comprehension now that they recognize so many words automatically and can identify unfamiliar words more easily (LaBerge & Samuels, 1976; Perfitti, 1985; Stanovich, 1986); in contrast, beginning readers use much more cognitive energy in identifying words. So, as students become fluent readers, they use less energy for word identification and have more cognitive resources available for comprehending what they read.

When children talk about stories they are reading, they retell story events effectively, share details about the characters, and make connections between the stories and their own lives, between stories and the world, and between books or a book and a film. They also use background knowledge and clues in the text to make inferences. When they read informational books, children can distinguish between big ideas and details, notice information in illustrations and other graphics, and use technical vocabulary from the book.

During the fluent reading stage, children read longer, more sophisticated picture books and chapter books, but they generally prefer chapter books because they enjoy getting into a story. They learn more about the genres of literature and literary devices, such as alliteration, personification, and symbolism. They participate in literature focus units that feature a single author, genre, or book, in small-group literature circles where children all read and discuss the same book, and in author studies where they read and compare several books by the same author and examine that author's writing style. They are able to explain why they liked a particular book, and they make recommendations to classmates.

Fluent readers learn more about comprehension. Through literature discussions and minilessons, they learn to make inferences and to think more deeply about stories they are reading. Teachers encourage children to compare books they have read and make text-to-text connections.

Fluent writers understand that writing is a process, and they use most of the writing process stages—prewriting, drafting, revising, editing, and publishing. They make plans for writing and write both rough drafts and final copies. They reread their rough drafts and make revisions and editing changes that reflect their understanding of writing forms and their purpose for writing. They increasingly share their rough drafts with classmates and turn to their classmates for advice on how to make their writing better.

Children get ideas for writing from books they have read and from television programs and movies they have viewed. They organize their writing into paragraphs, indent paragraphs, and focus on a single idea in each paragraph. They develop ideas more completely and use more sophisticated vocabulary to express their ideas.

Fluent writers are aware of writing genres and organize their writing into stories, reports, letters, and poems. The stories they write have a beginning, middle, and end, and their reports are structured using sequence, comparison, or cause-and-effect structures. Their letters reflect an understanding of the parts of a letter and how the parts are arranged on a page. Their poems incorporate rhyme or other structures to create impressions.

Children's writing looks more conventional. They spell most of the 100 high-frequency words correctly and use phonics to spell other one-syllable words correctly. They add inflectional endings (e.g., *-s, -ed, -ing*) and experiment with two-syllable and longer words. They have learned to capitalize the first word in sentences and names and to use punctuation marks correctly at the ends of sentences, although they are still experimenting with punctuation marks within sentences.

Fluent readers and writers accomplish the following:

- read fluently and with expression
- recognize most one-syllable words automatically and can decode other words efficiently
- use comprehension strategies effectively
- make text-to-self, text-to-world, and text-to-text connections
- write well-developed, multiparagraph compositions
- use the writing process to draft and refine their writing

- write stories, reports, letters, and other genres
- spell most high-frequency and other one-syllable words correctly
- use capital letters and punctuation marks correctly most of the time

Some second graders reach this stage, and all children should be fluent readers and writers by the end of third grade. Reaching this stage is an important milestone because it indicates that children are well prepared for the increased literacy demands of fourth grade, in which students are expected to be able to read longer chapter-book stories, use writing to respond to literature, read content-area textbooks, and write essays and reports.

A list of instructional recommendations for each of the three stages of reading and writing development is shown in Figure 3–3.

INSTRUCTIONAL PRACTICES

Teachers who work with young readers and writers use many of the same instructional practices used with older students, such as teaching phonics lessons, doing guided reading with leveled books, teaching from basal reading textbooks, and providing opportunities for independent reading and writing in reading and writing workshop. Teachers adapt these approaches to provide enough scaffolding so that young children are successful. Other instructional practices have been developed specifically for young children and other novice readers and writers.

Shared Reading

Teachers use shared reading to read aloud books that are appropriate for children's interest level but too difficult for them to read for themselves (Holdaway, 1979; Parkes, 2000). Teachers use the five stages of the reading process in shared reading, as Ms. McCloskey did in the vignette at the beginning of the chapter. The steps in shared reading are presented in Figure 3–4, showing how the activities fit into the five stages of the reading process. Through the reading process, teachers model what fluent readers do as they involve students in enjoyable reading activities (Fountas & Pinnell, 1996). After the text is read several times, teachers use it to teach phonics concepts and high-frequency words. Students can also read small versions of the book with partners or independently, and the pattern or structure found in the text can be used for writing activities (Slaughter, 1993).

The books chosen for shared reading are available as big books and are close to children's reading level, but still beyond their ability to read independently. As an instructional strategy, shared reading differs from reading aloud to students because students see the text as the teacher reads. Also, students often join in the reading of predictable refrains and rhyming words, and after listening to the teacher read the text several times, students often remember enough of the text to read along with the teacher. Through shared reading, teachers also demonstrate how print works, provide opportunities for students to use the prediction strategy, and increase children's confidence in their ability to read.

Big books are greatly enlarged picture books that teachers use in shared reading, most commonly with primary-grade students. In this technique, developed in New Zealand, teachers place an enlarged picture book on an easel or chart stand where all children can see it. Then they read it with small groups of children or the whole class. Trachtenburg and Ferruggia (1989) used big books with their class of transitional first graders and found that making and reading big books dramatically improved

Learn more about shared reading, interactive writing, and other instructional procedures discussed in this chapter on the DVD that accompanies this text.

Figure 3-3	Instructional Recommendations for the Three Stages of Reading and Writing	
Stage	**Reading**	**Writing**
Emergent	• Use environmental print. • Include literacy materials in play centers. • Read aloud to children. • Read big books and poems on charts using shared reading. • Introduce the title and author of books before reading. • Teach directionality and letter and word concepts using big books. • Encourage children to make predictions. • Encourage children to make text-to-self connections. • Have children retell and dramatize stories. • Have children respond to literature through talk and drawing. • Have children manipulate sounds using phonemic awareness activities. • Use alphabet-teaching routines. • Take children's dictation using the Language Experience Approach. • Teach 20–24 high-frequency words. • Post words on a word wall.	• Have children use crayons for drawing and pencils for writing. • Encourage children to use scribble writing or write random letters if they cannot do more conventional writing. • Teach handwriting skills. • Use interactive writing for whole-class and small-group writing projects. • Have children write their names on sign-in sheets each day. • Write morning messages. • Have children write their own names and names of classmates. • Have children inventory words they know how to write. • Have children "write the classroom" by making lists of familiar words they find in the classroom. • Have children use frames such as "I like ____" and "I see a ____" to write sentences. • Encourage children to remember what they write so they can read it.
Beginning	• Read charts of poems and songs using choral reading. • Read leveled books using guided reading. • Provide daily opportunities to read and reread books independently. • Teach phonics skills. • Teach children to cross-check using the cueing systems. • Teach the 100 high-frequency words. • Point out whether texts are stories, informational books, or poems. • Model and teach predicting and other strategies. • Teach the elements of story structure, particularly beginning, middle, and end. • Have children write in reading logs and participate in grand conversations. • Have children make text-to-self and text-to-world connections. • Have children take books home to read with parents.	• Use interactive writing to teach concepts about print and spelling skills. • Provide daily opportunities to write for a variety of purposes and using different forms. • Introduce the writing process. • Teach children to develop a single idea in their compositions. • Teach children to proofread their compositions. • Teach children to spell the 100 high-frequency words. • Teach contractions. • Teach capitalization and punctuation skills. • Have children use computers to publish their writing. • Have children share their writing from the author's chair.
Fluent	• Have children participate in literature circles. • Have children participate in reading workshop. • Teach about genres and literary devices. • Involve children in author studies. • Teach children to make text-to-self, text-to-world, and text-to-text connections. • Respond to literature through talk and writing.	• Have children participate in writing workshop. • Teach children to use the writing process. • Teach children to revise and edit their writing. • Teach paragraphing skills. • Teach spelling generalizations. • Teach homophones. • Teach synonyms. • Teach root words and affixes. • Teach children to use a dictionary and a thesaurus.

> ## Figure 3-4   How a Shared Reading Lesson Fits Into the Reading Process
>
> **1. Prereading**
>   - Activate or build background knowledge on a topic related to the book.
>   - Show the cover of the book and tell the title.
>   - Talk about the author and illustrator.
>   - Talk about the book and have students make predictions.
>
> **2. Reading**
>   - Use a big book or text printed on a chart.
>   - Use a pointer to track during reading.
>   - Read expressively with very few stops during the first reading.
>   - Highlight vocabulary and repetitive patterns.
>   - Reread the book once or twice, and encourage students to join in the reading.
>
> **3. Responding**
>   - Discuss the book in a grand conversation.
>   - Ask inferential and critical level questions, such as "What would happen if . . . ?" and "What did this book make you think of?"
>   - Share the pen to write a sentence interactively about the book.
>   - Have students draw and write in reading logs.
>
> **4. Exploring**
>   - Reread the book using small books.
>   - Add important words to the word wall.
>   - Teach minilessons on skills and strategies.
>   - Present more information about the author and the illustrator.
>   - Provide a text set with other books by the same author and illustrator.
>
> **5. Applying**
>   - Have students write an innovation imitating the pattern used in the book.
>   - Have students create an art project related to the book.

children's reading scores on standardized achievement tests. The teachers reported that children's self-concepts as readers were decidedly improved as well.

With the big book on a chart stand or easel, the teacher reads it aloud, pointing to every word. Before long, students join in the reading, especially in repeating the refrain. Then the teacher rereads the book, inviting students to help with the reading. The next time the book is read, the teacher reads to the point that the text becomes predictable, such as the beginning of a refrain, and the students supply the missing text; having students supply the missing words is important because it leads to independent reading. When students have become familiar with the text, they are invited to read the big book independently (Parkes, 2000).

Predictable Books. The stories and other books that teachers use for shared reading with young children often have repeated words and sentences, rhyme, or other patterns; books that use these patterns are called *predictable books.* For example, in *The Gingerbread Boy* (Galdone, 1975), a cumulative story, the cookie repeats and expands his boast as he meets each character on his run away from the Little Old Man and the Little Old Woman, and in *The Very Hungry Caterpillar* (Carle, 1969), a sequential pattern story, the author uses number and day-of-the-week sequences as the caterpillar eats through an amazing array of foods. Figure 3–5 presents a list of eight types of predictable books and examples of each type. These books are a valuable tool for emergent readers because

Figure 3-5	Types of Predictable Books	
Type	**Description**	**Books**
Rhymes	Rhyming words and refrains are repeated through the book.	Hennessy, B. G. (1992). *Jake baked the cake.* New York: Puffin. Lindbergh, R. (1993). *There's a cow in the road.* New York: Puffin. Martin, B., Jr., & Archambault, J. (1989). *Chicka chicka boom boom.* New York: Simon & Schuster. Seuss, Dr. (1963). *Hop on Pop.* New York: Random House. Shaw, N. (1988). *Sheep in a jeep.* Boston: Houghton Mifflin.
Repetitive Sentences	A sentence is repeated through the book.	Brown, R. (1981). *A dark, dark tale.* New York: Dial Books. Carle, E. (1991). *Have you seen my cat?* New York: Simon & Schuster. Rathmann, P. (2000). *Good night, gorilla.* New York: Puffin. Rosen, M. (2004). *We're going on a bear hunt.* New York: Candlewick.
Sequential Patterns	The book is organized using numbers, days of the week, or other familiar patterns.	Carle, E. (1997). *Today is Monday.* New York: Puffin. Christelow, E. (1998). *Five little monkeys jumping on the bed.* Boston: Houghton Mifflin. Mack, S. (1974). *10 bears in my bed.* New York: Pantheon. Peek, M. (1991). *Roll over: A counting song.* New York: Clarion.
Pattern Stories	Episodes are repeated with new characters or other variations.	Brett, J. (1989). *The mitten.* New York: Putnam. Carle, E. (1987). *A house for hermit crab.* Saxonville, MA: Picture Book Studio. Carle, E. (1977). *Grouchy ladybug.* New York: Crowell. Galdone, P. (1985). *Little red hen.* New York: Clarion. Taback, S. (1997). *There was an old lady who swallowed a fly.* New York: Viking.
Circular Stories	The plot is organized so that the ending leads back to the beginning.	Aardema, V. (1992). *Why mosquitoes buzz in people's ears.* New York: Puffin. Kalan, K. (1993). *Stop, thief.* New York: Greenwillow. Munsch, R. (2002). *Alligator baby.* New York: Scholastic. Numeroff, L. J. (1985). *If you give a mouse a cookie.* New York: HarperCollins. Wood, A. (1984). *The napping house.* San Diego: Harcourt Brace.
Cumulative Stories	As each new episode is introduced, the previous episodes are repeated.	Cole, H. (1997). *Jack's garden.* New York: HarperCollins. Dunphy, M. (1995). *Here is the southwestern desert.* New York: Hyperion. Kimmell, E. A. (1996). *The old woman and her pig.* New York: Holiday House. Taback, S. (2004). *This is the house that Jack built.* New York: Puffin. West, C. (1996). *"Buzz, buzz, buzz," went bumblebee.* New York: Candlewick.
Questions and Answers	A question is repeated again and again through the book.	Guarino, D. (1989). *Is your mama a llama?* New York: Scholastic. Hill, E. (1987). *Where's Spot?* New York: Putnam. Kraus, R. (1970). *Whose mouse are you?* New York: Macmillan. Martin, B., Jr. (1983). *Brown bear, brown bear, what do you see?* New York: Holt, Rinehart and Winston. Martin, B., Jr. (1992). *Polar bear, polar bear, what do you hear?* New York: Holt, Rinehart and Winston.
Songs	Familiar songs with repetitive patterns are presented with one line or verse on each page.	Galdone, P. (1988). *Cat goes fiddle-I-fee.* New York: Clarion. Messenger, J. (1986). *Twinkle, twinkle, little star.* New York: Macmillan. Raffi. (1988). *Wheels on the bus.* New York: Crown. Raffi. (1999). *Down by the bay.* New York: Crown. Westcott, N. B. (1988). *The lady with the alligator purse.* Boston: Little, Brown.

the repeated words and sentences, patterns, and sequences enable children to predict the next sentence or episode in the text (Bridge, 1979; Tompkins & Webeler, 1983).

Traveling Bags of Books. A second way to encourage more shared reading is to involve parents in the program by using traveling bags of books, sets of four or five books that teachers collect on various topics for children to take home and read with their parents (Reutzel & Fawson, 1990). For example, teachers might collect copies of *Hattie and the Fox* (Fox, 1986), *The Gingerbread Boy* (Galdone, 1975), *Flossie and the Fox* (McKissack, 1986), and *Rosie's Walk* (Hutchins, 1968) for a traveling bag of fox stories. Or, for a set of books about the desert, they might collect *Listen to the Desert/Oye al Desierto* (Mora, 1994), *Desert Dog* (Johnson, 2001), *Dig, Wait, Listen: A Desert Toad's Tale* (Sayre, 2001), *In the Desert* (Salzmann, 2001), and *The Seed and the Giant Saguaro* (Ward, 2001). Then children and their parents read one or more of the books and draw or write a response to the books they have read in the reading log that accompanies the books in the traveling bag. Children keep the bag at home for several days, often rereading the books each day with their parents, and then return it to school so that another child can borrow it. Text sets usually combine stories, informational books, and poems. Teachers can also add small toys, stuffed animals or puppets, audiotapes of one or more of the books, or other related objects to the bags.

Teachers often introduce traveling bags at a special parents' meeting at which they explain to parents how to read with their children. It is important that parents understand that their children may not be familiar with the books and that children are not expected to be able to read them independently. Teachers also talk about the responses children and parents write in the reading log and show sample entries from the previous year.

Shared Reading

These kindergartners watch as their teacher reads aloud a big book. On the second and third readings, they will join in and repeat the familiar refrains as their teacher reads. Later the young children will read small-book versions of the big book and participate in a variety of oral language, reading, and writing activities related to the book. Through reading and rereading the big book, children develop concepts about print and about words: They learn that print moves from left to right and top to bottom, and they also learn to recognize individual letters, words, and sentences.

Part 2 How Do Children Learn to Read and Write?

Figure 3-6   One Page From a Kindergarten Class Book About Bears

Polar bears live in
ice and snow.

Jesse

Language Experience Approach

The Language Experience Approach (LEA) is based on children's language and experiences (Ashton-Warner, 1965; Stauffer, 1970). In this approach, teachers do shared writing: Children dictate words and sentences about their experiences, and the teacher writes down what the children say; the text they develop becomes the reading material. Because the language comes from the children themselves and because the content is based on their experiences, they are usually able to read the text easily. Reading and writing are connected, because students are actively involved in reading what they have written.

Using this approach, students create individual booklets. They draw pictures on each page or cut pictures from magazines to glue on each page, and then they dictate the text that the teacher writes beside each illustration. Students can also make class collaborations, where each child creates one page to be added to a class book. For example, as part of the unit on "The Three Bears," a kindergarten class made a collaborative book on bears. Children each chose a fact they knew about bears for their page; they drew an illustration and dictated the text for their teacher to record. One page from this class book is shown in Figure 3–6. The teacher took the students' dictation rather than having the children write the book themselves because she wanted it to be written in conventional spelling so that students could read and reread the book.

When taking dictation, it is a great temptation to change the child's language to the teacher's own, in either word choice or grammar, but editing should be kept to a minimum so that children do not get the impression that their language is inferior or inadequate. Also, as children become familiar with dictating to the teacher, they learn to pace their dictation to the teacher's writing speed. At first, children dictate as they think of ideas, but with experience, they watch as the teacher writes and supply the text word by word. This change also provides evidence of children's developing concept of a word.

The Language Experience Approach is an effective way to help children emerge into reading. Even students who have not been successful with other types of reading activities can read what they have dictated. There is a drawback, however: Teachers provide a "perfect" model when they take children's dictation—they write neatly and spell words correctly. After language experience activities, some young children are not eager to do their own writing; they prefer their teacher's "perfect" writing to their own childlike writing. To avoid this problem, young children should also be doing interactive writing and independent writing at the same time they are participating in language experience activities. This way, they will learn that sometimes they do their own writing and at other times the teacher takes their dictation.

Interactive Writing

In interactive writing, children and the teacher create a text together and "share the pen" as they write the text on chart paper (Button, Johnson, & Furgerson, 1996; McCarrier, Pinnell, & Fountas, 2000). The text is composed by the group, and the teacher guides children as they write the text word by word on chart paper. Children take turns writing known letters and familiar words, adding punctuation marks, and marking spaces between words. All children participate in creating and writing the text on chart paper, and they also write the text on small white boards, on small chalkboards, or on paper as it is written on the chart paper. After writing, children read and reread the text using shared reading and independent reading.

Children use interactive writing to write class news, predictions before reading, retellings of stories, thank-you letters, reports, math story problems, and many other types of group writings (Tompkins & Collom, 2004). Two interactive writing samples are shown in Figure 3–7; the top sample was written by a kindergarten class during a health unit, and the second one is a first-grade class's interactive writing of a math story problem. After writing this story problem, students wrote other subtraction problems individually. The boxes drawn around some of the letters and words represent correction tape that was used to correct misspellings or poorly formed letters. In the kindergarten sample, students took turns writing individual letters; in the first-grade sample, students took turns writing entire words.

Through interactive writing, students learn concepts about print, letter-sound relationships and spelling patterns, handwriting concepts, and capitalization and punctuation skills. Teachers model conventional spelling and use of conventions of print, and students practice segmenting the sounds in words and spelling familiar words. Students use the skills they learn through interactive writing when they write independently.

During interactive writing, teachers help students spell all words conventionally. They teach high-frequency words such as *the* and *of,* assist students in segmenting sounds and syllables in other words, point out unusual spelling patterns such as *pieces* and *germs,* and teach other conventions of print. Whenever students misspell a word or form a letter incorrectly, teachers use correction tape to cover the mistake and help students make the correction. For example, when a child wrote the numeral *8* to spell *ate* in the second sample in Figure 3–7, the teacher explained the *eight–ate* homophone, covered the numeral with correction tape, and helped the child "think out" the spelling of the word, including the silent *e.* Teachers emphasize the importance of using conventional spelling as a courtesy to readers, not that a student made a mistake. In contrast to the emphasis on conventional spelling in interactive writing, students are encouraged to use invented spelling and other spelling strategies when writing independently. They learn to look for familiar words posted on classroom word walls or in books they have read, think about spelling patterns and rimes, or ask

To learn more about rimes and other phonics and spelling concepts, see Chapter 4, " Cracking the Alphabetic Code."

Figure 3-7   **Two Samples of Interactive Writing**

Wash [y]our hands with soap to kill [g]erms.

Luis had 5 pieces of candy but he [a]te 3 [of] them. Th[e]n he gave 1 to his friend Mario. How man[y] does he have now?

a classmate for help. Teachers also talk about purpose and explain that in personal writing and rough drafts, students do use invented spelling. Increasingly, however, students want to use conventional spelling and even ask to use the correction tape to fix errors they make as they write.

Manuscript Handwriting

Children enter kindergarten with different backgrounds of handwriting experience. Some 5-year-olds have never held a pencil, but many others have written cursivelike scribbles or manuscript letterlike lines and circles. Some have learned to print their

Writing Center

These first graders write in journals, make books, and compose notes to classmates at the writing center. This center is stocked with writing supplies, a word wall with high-frequency words is displayed on a dry-erase board, and a message center bulletin board (shown in the upper right-hand part of the photo) is available for children to post their notes. They keep their writing projects in folders stored nearby. Children work at this center while the teacher has guided reading groups. Through this center activity, young children develop the independence they need for writing workshop.

names and even a few other letters. Handwriting instruction in kindergarten typically includes developing children's ability to hold pencils, refining their fine motor control, and focusing on letter formation. Some people might argue that kindergartners are too young to learn handwriting skills, but young children should be encouraged to write from the first day of school. They write letters and words on labels, draw and write stories, keep journals, and write other types of messages. The more they write, the greater their need becomes for instruction in handwriting. Instruction is necessary so that students do not learn bad habits that later must be broken.

To teach children how to form letters, many kindergarten and first-grade teachers create brief directions for forming letters that they sing to a familiar tune; for example, to form a lowercase letter *a*, try "All around and make a tail" sung to the tune of "Row, Row, Row Your Boat." As teachers sing the directions, they model the formation of the letter in the air or on the chalkboard using large arm motions. Then children sing along and practice forming the letter in the air. Later, they practice writing letters using sponge paintbrushes dipped in water at the chalkboard or dry-erase pens on white boards as well as in authentic paper-and-pencil writing activities.

Handwriting research suggests that moving models are much more effective than still models in teaching children how to handwrite. Therefore, worksheets on the letters aren't very useful because children often don't form the letters correctly. Researchers recommend that children watch teachers to see how letters are formed and then practice forming them themselves. Also, teachers supervise students as they write so that they can correct children who form letters incorrectly. It is important that students write circles counterclockwise, starting from 1:00, and form most lines from top to bottom and left to right across the page. When students follow these guidelines, they are less likely to tear the paper they are writing on, and they will have an easier transition to cursive handwriting.

Writing Centers

Writing centers can be set up in kindergarten and first-grade classrooms so that children have a special place where they can go to write. The center should be located at a table with chairs, and a box of supplies, including pencils, crayons, a date stamp, different kinds of paper, journal notebooks, a stapler, blank books, notepaper, and envelopes, should be stored nearby. The alphabet, printed in upper- and lowercase letters, should be available on the table for children to refer to as they write. In addition, there should be a crate where children can file their work. They can also share their completed writings by sending them to classmates or while sitting in a special seat called the "author's chair."

When children come to the writing center, they draw and write in journals, compile books, and write messages to classmates. Teachers should be available to encourage and assist children at the center. They can observe children as they invent spellings and can provide information about letters, words, and sentences as needed. If the teacher cannot be at the writing center, perhaps an aide, a parent volunteer, or an upper-grade student can assist.

Figure 3–8 presents two reading log entries created by kindergartners and first graders at the writing center. The top piece shows a kindergartner's response to *If You Give a Mouse a Cookie* (Numeroff, 1985). The child's writing says, "I love chocolate chip cookies." The bottom piece was written by a first grader after reading *Are You My Mother?* (Eastman, 1960). The child wrote, "The bird said, 'Are you my mother, you big ole Snort?'" After students shared their log entries during a grand conversation, this student added, "The mommy said, 'Here is a worm. I am here. I'm here.'" Notice that the part the mother says is written as though it were coming out of the bird's mouth and going up into the air.

Young children also make books at the writing center based on the books they have read. For example, they can use the same patterns as in *Polar Bear, Polar Bear, What Do You Hear?* (Martin, 1991), *If you Give a Mouse a Cookie* (Numeroff, 1985), and *If the Dinosaurs Came Back* (Most, 1978) to create innovations, or new versions of familiar stories. A first grader's four-page book about a mouse named Jerry, written after reading *If You Give a Mouse a Cookie,* is shown in Figure 3–9. In these writing projects, children often use invented spelling, but they are encouraged to spell familiar words correctly. They also learn to use the books they are reading to check the spelling of characters' names and other words from the story.

Children also write notes and letters to classmates at the writing center. They learn about the form of friendly letters and how to phrase the greeting and the closing. Then they apply what they are learning as they write to classmates to say hello, offer a compliment, share news, trade telephone numbers, and offer birthday wishes. As they write messages, the children practice writing their names, their classmates' names, and the words they are learning to read and spell. The classmates who receive the messages also gain practice reading the messages. Teachers participate, too, by regularly writing brief messages to children. Through their activities, they model how to write messages and how to read and respond to the messages they receive. To facilitate the sharing of these messages, teachers often set up a message bulletin board or individual mailboxes made from milk cartons or shoe boxes. This activity is especially valuable because children discover the social purposes of reading and writing as they write and receive notes and letters, and they often become more interested in other literacy activities.

Complete a self-assessment to check your understanding of the concepts presented in this chapter on the Companion Website at *www.prenhall.com/ tompkins*

Figure 3-8   Two Children's Reading Log Entries

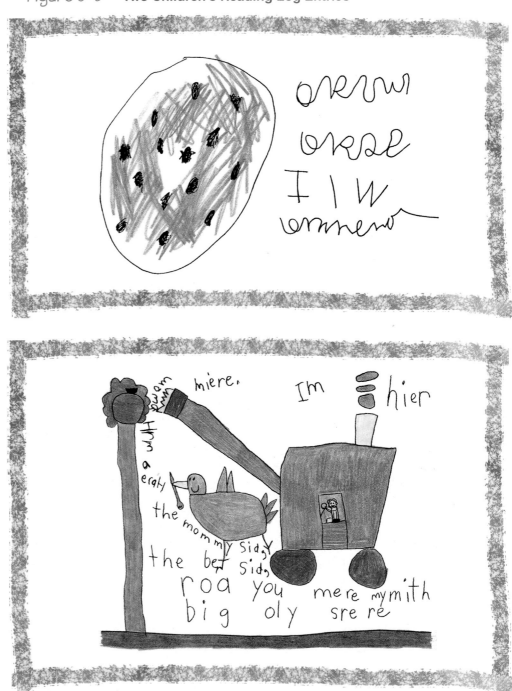

Review: How Effective Teachers Support Young Children's Literacy Development

1. Teachers understand that young children can participate in reading and writing activities.

2. Teachers provide developmentally appropriate reading and writing activities for children beginning on the first day of school.

3. Teachers demonstrate the purposes of written language through a variety of literacy activities.

4. Teachers teach book-orientation concepts as they do shared reading and read aloud to children.

5. Teachers develop children's directionality concepts through shared reading and interactive writing.

6. Teachers help children develop letter and word concepts through minilessons and daily reading and writing experiences.

7. Teachers include literacy materials in play centers.

8. Teachers understand that children move through the emergent, beginning, and fluent stages of reading and writing.

9. Teachers monitor children's literacy development to see that they are moving through the three stages.

10. Teachers match instructional activities to children's stage of reading and writing development.

Professional References

Adams, M. J. (1990). *Beginning to read: Thinking and learning about print.* Cambridge, MA: MIT Press.

Ashton-Warner, S. (1965). *Teacher.* New York: Simon & Schuster.

Baghban, M. J. M. (1984). *Our daughter learns to read and write: A case study from birth to three.* Newark, DE: International Reading Association.

Bridge, C. A. (1979). Predictable materials for beginning readers. *Language Arts, 56,* 503–507.

Button, K., Johnson, M. J., & Furgerson, P. (1996). Interactive writing in a primary classroom. *The Reading Teacher, 49,* 446–454.

Clay, M. M. (1967). The reading behaviour of five year old children. *New Zealand Journal of Educational Studies, 2,* 11–31.

Clay, M. M. (1975). *What did I write? Beginning writing behavior.* Portsmouth, NH: Heinemann.

Clay, M. M. (1989). Foreword. In D. S. Strickland & L. M. Morrow (Eds.)., *Emerging literacy: Young children learn to read and write.* Newark, DE: International Reading Association.

Clay, M. M. (1991). *Becoming literate: The construction of inner control.* Portsmouth, NH: Heinemann.

Downing, J., & Oliver, P. (1973–1974). The child's conception of "a word." *Reading Research Quarterly, 9,* 568–582.

Durkin, D. (1966). *Children who read early.* New York: Teachers College Press.

Dyson, A. H. (1984). "N spell my Grandmama": Fostering early thinking about print. *The Reading Teacher, 38,* 262–271.

Fountas, I. C., & Pinnell, G. S. (1996). *Guided reading: Good first teaching for all children.* Portsmouth, NH: Heinemann.

Harste, J., Woodward, V., & Burke, C. (1984). *Language stories and literacy lessons.* Portsmouth, NH: Heinemann.

Heath, S. B. (1983). *Ways with words.* New York: Oxford University Press.

Holdaway, D. (1979). *The foundations of literacy.* Portsmouth, NH: Heinemann.

Invernizzi, M. (2003). Concepts, sounds, and the ABCs: A diet for a very young reader. In D. M. Barone & L. M. Morrow (Eds.), *Literacy and young children: Research-based practices* (pp. 140–156). New York: Guilford Press.

Juel, C. (1991). Beginning reading. In R. Barr, M. L. Kamil, P. Mosenthal, & P. D. Pearson (Eds.), *Handbook of reading research* (Vol. 2, pp. 759–788). New York: Longman.

Kawakami-Arakaki, A., Oshiro, M., & Farran, S. (1989). Research to practice: Integrating reading and writing in a kindergarten curriculum. In J. Mason (Ed.), *Reading and writing connections* (pp. 199–218). Boston: Allyn & Bacon.

LaBerge, D., & Samuels, S. J. (1976). Toward a theory of automatic information processing in reading. In H. Singer & R. Ruddell (Eds.), *Theoretical models and processes of reading* (pp. 548–579). Newark, DE: International Reading Association.

McCarrier, A., Pinnell, G. S., & Fountas, I. C. (2000). *Interactive writing: How language and literacy come together, K–2.* Portsmouth, NH: Heinemann.

McGee, L. M., & Richgels, D. J. (2001). *Literacy's beginnings: Supporting young readers and writers* (3rd ed.). Boston: Allyn & Bacon.

McGee, L. M., & Richgels, D. J. (2003). *Designing early literacy programs: Strategies for at-risk preschool and kindergarten children.* New York: Guilford Press.

Morrow, L. M., & Ashbury, E. (1999). Best practices for a balanced early literacy program. In L. B. Gambrell, L. M. Morrow, S. B. Neuman, & M. Pressley (Eds.), *Best practices in literacy instruction* (pp. 49–67). New York: Guilford Press.

Papandropoulou, I., & Sinclair, H. (1974). What is a word? Experimental study of children's ideas on grammar. *Human Development, 17,* 241–258.

Parkes, B. (2000). *Read it again! Revisting shared reading.* Portland, ME: Stenhouse.

Perfitti, C. A. (1985). *Reading ability.* New York: Oxford University Press.

Pinnell, G. S., & Fountas, I. C. (1998). *Word matters: Teaching phonics and spelling in the reading/writing classroom.* Portsmouth, NH: Heinemann.

Reutzel, D. R., & Fawson, P. C. (1990). Traveling tales: Connecting parents and children in writing. *The Reading Teacher, 44,* 222–227.

Schickedanz, J. A. (1990). *Adam's righting revolutions: One child's literacy development from infancy through grade one.* Portsmouth, NH: Heinemann.

Slaughter, J. P. (1993). *Beyond storybooks: Young children and the shared book experience.* Newark, DE: International Reading Association.

Snow, C. E., Burns, M. S., & Griffin, P. (Eds.). (1998). *Preventing reading difficulties in young children.* Washington, DC: National Academy Press.

Stanovich, K. E. (1986). Matthew effects in reading: Some consequences of individual differences in the acquisition of literacy. *Reading Research Quarterly, 21,* 360–406.

Stauffer, R. G. (1970). *The language experience approach to the teaching of reading.* New York: Harper & Row.

Sulzby, E. (1985). Kindergartners as readers and writers. In M. Farr (Ed.), *Advances in writing research. Vol. 1: Children's early writing development* (pp. 127–199). Norwood, NJ: Ablex.

Taylor, D. (1983). *Family literacy: Young children learning to read and write.* Exeter, NH: Heinemann.

Taylor, D., & Dorsey-Gaines, C. (1987). *Growing up literate: Learning from inner-city families.* Portsmouth, NH: Heinemann.

Teale, W. H. (1982). Toward a theory of how children learn to read and write. *Language Arts, 59,* 555–570.

Teale, W. H., & Sulzby, E. (1989). Emerging literacy: New perspectives. In D. S. Strickland & L. M. Morrow (Eds.), *Emerging literacy: Young children learn to read and write* (pp. 1–15). Newark, DE: International Reading Association.

Temple, C., Nathan, R., Burris, N., & Temple, F. (1988). *The beginnings of writing*. Boston: Allyn & Bacon.

Tompkins, G. E., & Collom, S. (2004). *Sharing the pen: Interactive writing with young children*. Upper Saddle River, NJ: Merrill/Prentice Hall.

Tompkins, G. E., & Webeler, M. (1983). What will happen next? Using predictable books with young children. *The Reading Teacher, 36,* 498–502.

Trachtenburg, R, & Ferruggia, A. (1989). Big books from little voices: Reaching high risk beginning readers. *The Reading Teacher, 42,* 284–289.

Children's Book References

Carle, E. (1969). *The very hungry caterpillar*. Cleveland: Collins-World.

Eastman, P. D. (1960). *Are you my mother?* New York: Random House.

Fox, M. (1986). *Hattie and the fox*. New York: Bradbury Press.

Galdone, P. (1975). *The gingerbread boy*. New York: Seabury.

Johnson, T. (2001). *Desert dog*. San Francisco: Sierra Club.

Hutchins, P. (1968). *Rosie's walk*. New York: Macmillan.

Martin, B., Jr. (1991). *Polar bear, polar bear, what do you hear?* New York: Henry Holt.

McCloskey, R. (1969). *Make way for ducklings*. New York: Viking.

McKissack, P. C. (1986). *Flossie and the fox*. New York: Dial.

Mora, P. (1994). *Listen to the desert/Oye al desierto*. New York: Clarion Books.

Most, B. (1978). *If the dinosaurs came back*. San Diego: Harcourt Brace.

Numeroff, L. J. (1985). *If you give a mouse a cookie*. New York: Harper & Row.

Prince, S. (1999). *Playing*. Littleton, MA: Sundance.

Salzmann, M. E. (2001). *In the desert*. Edina, MN: Abdo/Sand Castle.

Sayre, A. P. (2001). *Dig, wait, listen: A desert toad's tale*. New York: Greenwillow.

Simont, M. (2001). *The stray dog*. New York: HarperCollins.

Ward, J. (2003). *The seed and the giant saguaro*. New York: Rising Moon/Northland.

Cracking the Alphabetic Code

- What is phonemic awareness?
- Why do children need to become phonemically aware?
- Which phonics concepts are most important for children to learn?
- How do teachers teach phonics?
- What are the stages of spelling development?
- How do teachers teach spelling?

Mrs. Firpo Teaches Phonics Using a Basal Reading Program

It's 8:10 on Thursday morning, and the 19 first graders in Mrs. Firpo's classroom are gathered around her on the carpet for their phonics focus lesson that the teacher calls "word work." This week's topic is the long *i* and long *e* sounds for *y:* For example, in *my* and *multiply,* the *y* is pronounced as long *i,* and in *baby* and *sunny,* the *y* is pronounced as long *e.* She reminds the students of the week's topic and then shows pictures representing words that end with *y: fly, baby, jelly, bunny,* and *sky.* The children

identify each object and say its name slowly so that they can isolate the final sound. Saleena goes first. She picks up the picture of a fly and says, "It's a fly: /f/ /l/ /ī/. It ends with the ī sound." Vincent is confused when it's his turn to identify the long *e* sound at the end of *bunny* so Mrs. Firpo demonstrates how to segment the sounds in the word: /b/ /ŭ/ /n/ /ē/. Then Vincent recognizes the long *e* sound at the end of the word. Next the first graders sort the picture cards according to the final sound and place them in two columns in a nearby pocket chart. They add labels to the columns: *y = ī* and *y = ē.*

Mrs. Firpo begins her phonics lessons with an oral activity because she knows it's important to integrate phonemic awareness with phonics. In the oral activities, students focus on phonemic awareness — segmenting and blending the sounds they hear in words — without worrying about phoneme-grapheme correspondences.

Next, Mrs. Firpo introduces a set of word cards on which she has written words ending in *y* for the students to read and classify. The children take turns using their phonics skills to sound out these words: *funny, my, try, happy, why, fussy, very, sticky, shy,* and *cry.* They add the word cards to the columns on the pocket chart. Then she asks the students to suggest other words they know (or have read this week) that end in *y*; Fernando names *yucky,* Crystal says *crunchy,* and Joel adds *dry.* Mrs. Firpo writes these words on small cards, too, and the students add them to the pocket chart. Then she chooses Austin to use the pointer to point to each card in the pocket chart for the class to read aloud

At the end of this 15-minute lesson, the students return to their desks and get out their dry-erase boards for spelling practice. All eight of this week's spelling words end in *y* pronounced as long *i.* Mrs. Firpo calls out each spelling word, and the students practice writing it three times on their small dry-erase boards. If they need help spelling the word, they check the list of spelling words on the Focus Wall. As they write, Mrs. Firpo circulates around the classroom, modeling how to form letters, reminding Jordan and Kendra to leave a "two-finger" space between words, and checking that their spellings are correct.

Each week, Mrs. Firpo posts on the Focus Wall the strategies and skills she will be teaching. The vocabulary words and spelling words are listed there, too. Mrs. Firpo's Focus Wall is shown in the box on the next page. The vocabulary words are written on cards and displayed in a pocket chart attached to the Focus Wall so that they can be rearranged and used for various activities. Mrs. Firpo uses *Houghton Mifflin Reading* (Cooper & Pikulski, 2003), a basal reading textbook series; each week's topics are identified for her in the teacher's edition of the textbook. The reason why she posts these topics is to emphasize what she is teaching and what students are learning. In addition, Mrs. Firpo has her state's reading and writing standards for first grade listed on a chart next to the wall.

Next, Mrs. Firpo guides students as they complete one, two, or three pages in the Practice Book, the workbook that accompanies the basal reading textbook. Some pages reinforce phonics and spelling skills, and others focus on comprehension, vocabulary, grammar, and writing skills. Today, they begin on page 201. The directions state that students are to examine the illustration at the top of the page and write two sentences about the silly things they see in the picture on the lines at the bottom of the page. The children talk about the illustration, identifying the silly things they see. Felicia says, "I see a bunny reading a book, and I think that's silly." Mrs. Firpo gives Felicia a "thumbs up" to compliment her. And Fernando comments, "I see something else. It's a bear up in a balloon." "Is the balloon up in the sky?" Mrs. Firpo asks because she wants to emphasize the phonics pattern of the week. Fernando agrees

Mrs. Firpo's Focus Wall

Theme 9: Special Friends　　　Week: 1　　　Reading Level: 1.5

PHONICS FOCUS:　Long i and long e sounds for y

WORD PATTERN:　＿＿y

say	day	way	bay	stay	gray
pay	may	lay	ray	pray	spray

SPELLING CONCEPT:　Long i sound at the end of a word spelled with y

COMPREHENSION STRATEGY:　Monitoring

COMPREHENSION SKILL:　Noting Details

GRAMMAR CONCEPT:　is/are

WRITING GENRE:　Friendly Letters

VOCABULARY WORDS

ocean	though	by
dance	talk	my
open	else	cry
ever	around	any
	Grandaddy	

SPELLING WORDS

1. by
2. my
3. fly
4. try
5. cry
6. why
7. pry
8. multiply

---

that it is, and he repeats, "I see a bear up in a balloon in the sky." He, too, gets a "thumbs up."

After students identify five or six silly things, they get ready to write. Mrs. Firpo reminds them to begin their sentences with capital letters and to end them with periods. As they are writing their sentences, Alicia notices that she has written *bunny*—a word that ends in *y* and has an ē sound. Mrs. Firpo congratulates her and encourages other students to point out when they write words that end in *y*. Joel waves his hand in the air, eager to report that he has written *sky*—a word that ends in *y* and has an ī sound.

After they finish page 201, the students move on to page 202. On this page, there is a word bank with words that end in *y* and represent the ī sound at the top and sentences with blank lines at the bottom. The children practice reading aloud the words in the word bank. After reading the words several times, Vincent volunteers, "I get it! Look at these words: They all have *y* and they say ī." Mrs. Firpo is pleased and gives him a "thumbs up." Next, the teacher reads aloud the sentences at the bottom of the page and asks students to supply the missing words from the words listed in the word bank. Then students work independently to reread the sentences and complete them by filling in the missing words. Mrs. Firpo circulates around the classroom, from one group of desks to the next as the children work, monitoring their work and providing assistance as needed.

Each week, the students receive three take-home books that Mrs. Firpo has duplicated, folded, and stapled together; the purpose of these books is to reinforce the phonics focus of the week and the vocabulary introduced in the reading textbook. The first graders read the books at school and use them for a phonics activity, then they take them home to practice reading with their families. Today's book is *I Spy:* It's eight pages long with illustrations and text on each page. Mrs. Firpo introduces the

April 29, 2004

Dear Nanna Isabel,

I am writting you a letter. My birthday is in 35 days!
Did you no that? I wud like to get a
present. I want you to come to my party.
It will be very funny.

Love,

Angelica

book and reads it aloud once while the students follow along in their copies. The students keep the book at their desks to use for a seatwork activity. They put the books from each unit in book bags that they take home each day. Already they have collected more than 75 books!

During the last 40 minutes of the reading period, Mrs. Firpo conducts guided reading groups. Her students' reading levels range from beginning first grade to the middle of second grade with about half the students reading at grade level. She has grouped the first graders into four guided reading groups, and she meets with two groups each day. Children reading below grade level read leveled books, and those reading at and above grade level read easy-to-read chapter books, including Barbara Park's series of funny stories about a kindergartner named Junie B. Jones (e.g., *Junie B. Jones and Her Big Fat Mouth* [1993]) and Mary Pope Osborne's Magic Tree House series of adventure stories (e.g., *Mummies in the Morning* [1993]). She calls this period *differentiated instruction* because students participate in a variety of activities, based on their reading levels.

While Mrs. Firpo works with one group for guided reading, the other students are involved in seatwork and center activities. For the seatwork activity, students read their take-home book and highlight all the words in it ending in *y* pronounced as $\bar{\imath}$; they don't highlight *bunny*, *play*, and other words where the *y* is not pronounced as $\bar{\imath}$. They also work in small groups to cut out pictures and words that end in *y*, sort into $y = \bar{e}$, $y = \bar{\imath}$, and $y = other$ categories, and paste them on a sheet of paper. The pictures and words for the activity include *puppy, city, they, buy, pretty, play, funny, dry, party, fifty, boy, sky, fly, today,* and *yummy*.

The first graders practice their spelling words using magnetic letters at the spelling center, practice the phonics focus and word pattern using letter cards and flip books at the phonics center, make books at the writing center, listen to the take-home books read aloud at the listening center, and practice phonics skills and read books

Check the Compendium of Instructional Procedures, which follows Chapter 14, for more information on highlighted terms.

interactively at the computer center. The centers are arranged around the perimeter of the classroom; students know how to work at centers and understand what they are expected to do at each one.

After a 15-minute recess, students spend the last 55 minutes of literacy instruction in writing workshop. Each week, the class focuses on the genre specified in the basal reading program; this week's focus is on writing personal letters. First, Mrs. Firpo teaches a minilesson and guides students as they complete writing skills pages in their Practice Books. Today, Mrs. Firpo reviews how to use commas in a friendly letter. The students examine several letters the class wrote earlier in the school year using interactive writing; the laminated letters are hanging in the classroom. After the class rereads each letter, Mrs. Firpo asks students to take turns marking the commas used in the letters with Vis-à-Vis pens (so their marks can be cleaned off afterward). Crystal points out that commas are used in the date, Saleena notices that a comma is used at the end of the greeting, and Luis marks the comma used after the closing. Next, students practice adding commas in the sample friendly letters on page 208 in their Practice Books.

Then students spend the remaining 35 minutes of writing workshop working on the letters they are writing to their families and friends this week. Mrs. Firpo brings together five students to work with her on their letters while the other students work independently. At the end of the writing time, Joel and Angelica sit in the author's chair to read their letters aloud to their classmates. Angelica's letter to her grandmother is shown in the box on page 113.

Mrs. Firpo's Weekly Schedule

Activity	Monday	Tuesday	Wednesday	Thursday	Friday
8:00–8:10 Journal Writing					
8:10–10:20 Reading	Word Work	Word Work	Read aloud selection in the anthology and discuss it	Word Work	Grammar
	Read aloud the introductory selection in the Teacher's Edition	Practice spelling words		Practice spelling words	Practice spelling words
		Practice Book	Practice Book	Practice Book	Practice Book
	Introduce strategies and skills for the week listed on the Focus Wall using the introductory selection	Introduce and read take-home book	Introduce and read take-home book	Introduce and read take-home book	Reread take-home books
		Differentiated Instruction • Guided Reading • Seatwork • Centers	Differentiated Instruction • Guided Reading • Seatwork • Centers	Differentiated Instruction • Guided Reading • Seatwork • Centers	Differentiated Instruction • Guided Reading • Seatwork • Centers
	Practice Book				
10:20–10:35 Recess					
10:35–11:30 Writing Workshop	Introduce Spelling Words	Minilesson/ Practice Book	Minilesson/ Practice Book	Minilesson/ Practice Book	Spelling Test
	Independent and Interactive Writing	Independent and Interactive Writing	Independent and Interactive Writing	Independent and Interactive Writing	Independent and Interactive Writing

Mrs. Firpo's students spend 3 1/2 hours each morning involved in literacy activities. Her daily schedule of activities is presented in the box on page 114. Most of the goals, activities, and instructional materials come from the basal reading program, but Mrs. Firpo adapts some activities to meet her students' instructional needs. Through these phonemic awareness, phonics, and spelling activities, these first graders are learning to crack the alphabetic code.

English is an alphabetic code, and children crack this code as they learn about phonemes (sounds), graphemes (letters), and graphophonemic (letter-sound) relationships. They learn about phonemes as they notice rhyming words, segment words into individual sounds, and invent silly words by playing with the sounds, much like Dr. Seuss did. They learn about letters as they sing the ABC song, name letters of the alphabet, and spell their own names. They learn graphophonemic relationships as they match letters and letter combinations to sounds, blend sounds to form words, and decode and spell vowel patterns. By third grade, most students have figured out the alphabetic code, and in fourth through eighth grades, students apply what they have learned to decode and spell multisyllabic words. You may think of all of this as phonics, but students actually develop three separate but related abilities about the alphabetic code:

Visit Chapter 4 on the Companion Website at *www.prenhall.com/ tompkins* to check into your state's standards for phonemic awareness, phonics, and spelling.

- *Phonemic awareness.* The ability to notice and manipulate the sounds of oral language. Children who are phonemically aware understand that spoken words are made up of sounds, and they can segment and blend sounds in spoken words.

- *Phonics.* The ability to convert letters into sounds and blend them to recognize words. Children who have learned phonics understand that there are predictable sound-symbol correspondences in English, and they can use decoding strategies to figure out unfamiliar written words.

- *Spelling.* The ability to segment spoken words into sounds and convert the sounds into letters to spell words. Children who have learned to spell conventionally understand English sound-symbol correspondences and spelling patterns, and they can use spelling strategies to spell unfamiliar words.

In the vignette, Mrs. Firpo incorporated all three areas in her literacy program. She began the word work lesson on the long *e* and long *i* sounds of *y* with an oral phonemic awareness activity; next, she moved to a phonics activity where students read words that ended in *y* and categorized them on a pocket chart. Later, students practiced spelling words that ended with *y* on dry-erase boards.

Teaching these graphophonemic relationships is not a complete reading program, but phonemic awareness, phonics, and spelling are integral to effective literacy instruction, especially for young children (National Reading Panel, 2000). The feature on page 116 shows how phonemic awareness, phonics, and spelling fit into a balanced literacy program.

How Phonemic Awareness, Phonics, and Spelling Fit Into a Balanced Literacy Program

Component	Description
Reading	Students need to crack the alphabetic code so that they can easily decode unfamiliar words and focus on comprehension when they read.
Phonics and Other Skills	Students learn phonemic awareness and phonics skills during the primary grades to decode unfamiliar words.
Strategies	Students learn two phonemic awareness strategies—blending and segmenting—that they use to decode and spell words.
Vocabulary	Knowing the meanings of words is important because familiar words are easier to decode and spell.
Comprehension	Students must be able to quickly decode unfamiliar words in order to read fluently and to comprehend what they are reading.
Literature	Until students develop phonics skills that enable them to decode unfamiliar words, they often listen to the teacher read literature aloud.
Content-Area Study	Students use decoding as they read trade books and content-area textbooks and spelling skills as they write reports and other compositions.
Oral Language	Students orally manipulate sounds as they participate in phonemic awareness training.
Writing	Students apply what they have learned about spelling when they write.
Spelling	Students learn to spell words through direct instruction, word study activities, and wide reading.

PHONEMIC AWARENESS

Phonemic awareness is children's basic understanding that speech is composed of a series of individual sounds, and it provides the foundation for phonics and spelling (Armbruster, Lehr, & Osborn, 2001). When children can choose a duck as the animal whose name begins with /d/ from a collection of toy animals, identify *duck* and *luck* as rhyming words in a song, or blend the sounds /d/ /ŭ/ /k/ to pronounce *duck*, they are phonemically aware. The emphasis is on the sounds of spoken words, not on reading letters or pronouncing letter names. Developing phonemic awareness enables children to use sound-symbol correspondences to read and spell words.

Phonemes are the smallest units of speech, and they are written as graphemes, or letters of the alphabet. In this book, phonemes are marked using diagonal lines (e.g., /d/) and graphemes are italicized (e.g., *d*). Sometimes phonemes (e.g., /k/ in *duck*) are spelled with two graphemes (*ck*).

Understanding that words are composed of smaller units—phonemes—is a significant achievement for young children because phonemes are abstract language units. Phonemes carry no meaning, and children think of words according to their meanings, not their linguistic characteristics (F. Griffith & Olson, 1992). When children think about ducks, for example, they think of feathered animals that swim in ponds, fly through the air, and make noises we describe as "quacks." They don't think of "duck" as a word with three phonemes or four graphemes, as a word beginning with /d/ and rhyming with *luck*. Phonemic awareness requires that children treat speech as an object and that they shift their attention away from the meaning of words to the linguistic features of speech. This focus on phonemes is even more complicated because phonemes are not discrete units in speech: Often they are slurred or clipped in speech—think about the blended initial sound in *tree* and the ending sound in *eating*.

Visit Chapter 4 on the Companion Website at *www.prenhall.com/ tompkins* to connect to web links related to phonemic awareness and phonics.

Components of Phonemic Awareness

Children develop phonemic awareness as they learn to hear and manipulate spoken language in these five ways:

1. *Identify sounds in words.* Children learn to identify a word that begins or ends with a particular sound. For example, when shown a brush, a car, and a doll, they can identify *doll* as the word that ends with /l/.

2. *Categorize sounds in words.* Children learn to recognize the "odd" word in a set of three words; for example, when the teacher says *ring, rabbit,* and *sun*, students recognize that *sun* doesn't belong.

3. *Substitute sounds to make new words.* Children learn to remove a sound form a word and substitute a different sound. Sometimes they substitute the beginning sound, changing *bar* to *car,* for example. Or, students change the middle sound, making *tip* from *top,* or they substitute the ending sound, changing *gate* to *game.*

4. *Blend sounds to form words.* Children learn to blend two, three, or four individual sounds to form a word; the teacher says /b/ /ĭ/ /g/, for example, and the children repeat the sounds, blending them to form the word *big.*

5. *Segment a word into sounds.* Children learn to break a word into its beginning, middle, and ending sounds. For example, children segment the word *feet* into /f/ /ē/ /t/ and *go* into /g/ /ō/.

These five components of phonemic awareness are strategies that children use with phonics to decode and spell words. The two most important of these strategies are blending and segmenting. When children use phonics to sound out a word, for example, they say the sounds represented by each letter and blend them together to read the word. Blending is the phonemic awareness strategy that children use to decode words. Similarly, to spell a word, children say the word slowly to themselves, segmenting the sounds. Then they write the letters representing each sound. Segmenting is the phonemic awareness strategy that children use to spell words.

Teaching Phonemic Awareness

Teachers nurture children's phonemic awareness through the language-rich environments they create in the classroom. As they sing songs, chant rhymes, read aloud wordplay books, and play games, children have many opportunities to orally match, isolate, blend, and substitute sounds and to segment words into sounds (F. Griffith &

Olson, 1992). Teachers often incorporate phonemic awareness components into other oral language and literacy activities, but it is also important to teach lessons that specifically focus on the components of phonemic awareness.

Phonemic awareness instruction should meet three criteria, according to Yopp and Yopp (2000). First, the activities should be appropriate for 4-, 5-, and 6-year-old children. Activities involving songs, nursery rhymes, riddles, and wordplay books are good choices because they are engaging and encourage children's playful experimentation with oral language. Second, the instruction should be planned and purposeful, not just incidental. When teachers have an objective in mind as they are teaching phonemic awareness, they are more likely to be effective in focusing children's attention on the sound structure of oral language. Third, phonemic awareness activities should be one part of a balanced literacy program and integrated with comprehension, decoding, vocabulary, writing, and spelling activities. It is important that children perceive the connection between oral and written language.

Nurturing English Learners

How do I teach phonemic awareness to my EL students?

English learners often need more opportunities to play informally with rhyme and to orally manipulate the sounds in words during small-group activities, and they may need to listen to wordplay books read aloud more times than their English-speaking classmates. They also need to participate in minilessons on specific phonemic awareness strategies. ELs should already be familiar with the words used in these lessons and understand their meanings before they are asked to manipulate them. Try using Elkonin boxes to teach segmenting (see further discussion of Elkonin boxes on p. 123) because they make the lesson more concrete. English learners whose native language uses an alphabetic system, such as Spanish, develop phonemic awareness more easily than students whose native language employs a logographic system of symbols without sound correspondences, such as Chinese.

Many wordplay books are available for young children. A list of wordplay books for young children is presented in Figure 4–1. Books such as *Cock-a-doodle-moo!* (Most, 1996) and *The Baby Uggs Are Hatching* (Prelutsky, 1982) stimulate children to experiment with sounds and to create nonsense words; and teachers focus children's attention on the smaller units of language when they read books with alliterative or assonant patterns, such as *Faint Frogs Feeling Feverish and Other Terrifically Tantalizing Tongue Twisters* (Obligado, 1983). Teachers often read wordplay books aloud more than once. During the first reading, children usually focus on comprehension or what interests them in the book. During a second reading, however, children's attention shifts to the wordplay elements, and teachers help to focus their attention on the way the author manipulated words and sounds by making comments and asking questions—"Did you notice how _____ and _____ rhyme?" "This book is fun because of all the words beginning with the /m/ sound"—and encourage children to make similar comments themselves (Yopp, 1995).

Teachers often incorporate wordplay books, songs, and games into the minilessons they teach. The feature on page 120 presents a kindergarten teacher's minilesson on blending sounds to make a word. The teacher reread Dr. Seuss's *Fox in Socks* (1965) and then asked students to identify words from the book that she pronounced sound by sound. This book is rich in wordplay and teaching opportunities: It could be used to teach rhyming (e.g., *do, you, goo, chew*), initial consonant substitutions (e.g., *trick, brick, chick, quick, slick*), vowel substitution (e.g., *blabber, blibber, blubber*), and alliteration (e.g., *Luke Luck likes lakes*).

Figure 4-1   Wordplay Books to Develop Phonemic Awareness

Ahlberg, J., & Ahlberg, A. (1978). *Each peach pear plum.* New York: Scholastic.

Cameron, P. (1961). *"I can't," said the ant.* New York: Coward-McCann.

Degan, B. (1983). *Jamberry.* New York: Harper & Row.

Deming, A. G. (1994). *Who is tapping at my window?* New York: Penguin.

Downey, L. (2000). *The flea's sneeze.* New York: Henry Holt.

Ehlert, L. (1989). *Eating the alphabet: Fruits and vegetables from A to Z.* San Diego: Harcourt Brace.

Galdone, P. (1968). *Henny Penny.* New York: Scholastic.

Gollub, M. (2000). *The jazz fly.* Santa Rosa, CA: Tortuga Press.

Hillenbrand, W. (2002). *Fiddle-I-fee.* San Diego: Gulliver Books.

Hoberman, M. A. (1998). *Miss Mary Mack.* Boston: Little, Brown.

Hoberman, M. A. (2000).The *eensy-weensy spider.* Boston: Little, Brown.

Hoberman, M. A. (2003). The lady with the alligator purse. Boston: Little, Brown.

Hutchins, P. (1976). *Don't forget the bacon!* New York: Mulberry Books.

Kuskin, K. (1990). *Roar and more.* New York: Harper & Row.

Martin, B., Jr., & Archambault, J. (1987). *Chicka chicka boom boom.* New York: Simon & Schuster.

Most, B. (1990). *The cow that went oink.* San Diego: Harcourt Brace.

Most, B. (1991). *A dinosaur named after me.* San Diego: Harcourt Brace.

Most, B. (1996). *Cock-a-doodle-moo!* San Diego: Harcourt Brace.

Obligado, L. (1983). *Faint frogs feeling feverish and other terrifically tantalizing tongue twisters.* New York: Puffin Books.

Prelutsky, J. (1982). *The baby uggs are hatching.* New York: Mulberry Books.

Prelutsky, J. (1989). *Poems of A. Nonny Mouse.* New York: Knopf. (See also the second volume in the series.)

Raffi. (1987). *Down by the bay.* New York: Crown.

Sendak, M. (1990). *Alligators all around: An alphabet.* New York: Harper & Row.

Seuss, Dr. (1963). *Hop on pop.* New York: Random House. (See also other books by the author.)

Shaw, N. (1986). *Sheep in a jeep.* Boston: Houghton Mifflin. (See also other books in this series.)

Showers, P. (1991). *The listening walk.* New York: Harper & Row.

Slate, J. (1996). *Miss Bindergarten gets ready for kindergarten.* New York: Dutton.

Slepian, J., & Seidler, A. (1967). *The hungry thing.* New York: Scholastic.

Westcott, N. B. (1992). *Peanut butter and jelly: A play rhyme.* New York: Puffin Books.

Westcott, N. B. (2003). *I know an old lady who swallowed a fly.* Boston: Little, Brown.

Wilson, K. (2003). *A frog in a bag.* New York: McElderry.

Winthrop, E. (1986). *Shoes.* New York: Harper & Row.

Sound-Matching Activities. In sound matching, children choose one of several words beginning with a particular sound or say a word that begins with a particular sound (Yopp, 1992). For these games, teachers use familiar objects (e.g., feather, toothbrush, book) and toys (e.g., small plastic animals, toy trucks, artificial fruits and vegetables), as well as pictures of familiar objects.

Teachers can play a sound-matching guessing game (Lewkowicz, 1994). For this game, teachers collect two boxes and pairs of objects to place in the boxes (e.g., forks, mittens, erasers, combs, and books); one item from each pair is placed in each box. After the teacher shows students the objects in the boxes and they name them together, two children play the game. One child selects an object, holds it, and pronounces the initial (or medial or final) sound. The second child chooses the same object from the second box and holds it up. Classmates check to see if the two players are holding the same object.

Children also identify rhyming words as part of sound-matching activities: They name a word that rhymes with a given word and identify rhyming words from familiar songs and stories. As children listen to parents and teachers read Dr. Seuss books, such as *Fox in Socks* (1965) and *Hop on Pop* (1963), and other wordplay books, they refine their understanding of rhyme.

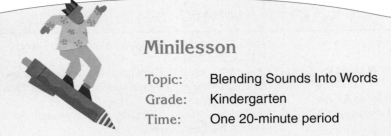

Minilesson

Topic: Blending Sounds Into Words
Grade: Kindergarten
Time: One 20-minute period

Ms. Lewis regularly includes a 20-minute lesson on phonemic awareness in her literacy block. She usually rereads a familiar wordplay book and plays a phonemic awareness game with the kindergartners that emphasizes one of the phonemic awareness strategies.

1. Introduce the Topic
Ms. Lewis brings her 19 kindergartners together on the rug and explains that she's going to reread Dr. Seuss's *Fox in Socks* (1965). It's one of their favorite books, and they clap their pleasure. She explains that after reading, they're going to play a word game.

2. Share Examples
Ms. Lewis reads aloud *Fox in Socks,* showing the pictures on each page as she reads. She encourages the children to read along. Sometimes she stops and invites the children to fill in the last rhyming word in a sentence or to echo read (repeating after her like an echo) the alliterative sentences. After they finish reading, she asks what they like best about the book. Pearl replies, "It's just a really funny book. That's why it is so good."

"What makes it funny?" Ms. Lewis asks. "Everything," answers Pearl. Ms. Lewis asks the question again, and Teri explains, "The words are funny. They make my tongue laugh. You know—*fox-socks-box-Knox.* That's funny on my tongue!" "Oh," Ms. Lewis clarifies, "your tongue likes to say rhyming words. I like to say them, too." Other children recall other rhyming words in the book: *clocks-tocks-blocks-box, noodle-poodle,* and *new-do-blue-goo.*

3. Provide Information
"Let me tell you about our game," Ms. Lewis explains. "I'm going to say some of the words from the book, but I'm going to say them sound by sound and I want you to blend the sounds together and guess the word." "Are they rhyming words?" Teri asks. "Sure," the teacher agrees. "I'll say two words that rhyme, sound by sound, for you to guess." She says the sounds /f/ /ŏ/ /x/ and /b/ /ŏ/ /x/ and the children correctly blend the sounds and say the words *fox* and *box.* She repeats the procedure for *clock-tock, come-dumb, big-pig, new-blue, rose-hose, game-lame,* and *slow-crow.* Ms. Lewis stops and talks about how to "bump" or blend the sounds to figure out the words. She models how she blends the sounds together to form the word. "Make the words harder," several children say, and Ms. Lewis offers several more difficult pairs of rhyming words, including *chick-trick* and *beetle-tweedle.*

4. Guide Practice
Ms. Lewis continues playing the guessing game, but now she segments individual words rather than pairs of rhyming words for the children to guess. As each child correctly identifies a word, that child leaves the group and goes to work with the aide in another part of the classroom. Finally, six children remain who need additional practice blending sounds into words. They continue practicing *do, new,* and other two-sound words and some of the easier three-sound words, including *box, come,* and *like.*

5. Assess Learning
Through the guided practice part of the lesson, Ms. Lewis checks to see which children need more practice blending sounds into words and provides additional practice for them.

Sound-Isolation Activities. Teachers say a word and then children identify the sounds at the beginning, middle, or end of the word, or teachers and children isolate sounds as they sing familiar songs. Yopp (1992) created new verses to the tune of "Old MacDonald Had a Farm":

> What's the sound that starts these words:
> Chicken, chin, and cheek?
> (wait for response)
> /ch/ is the sound that starts these words:
> Chicken, chin, and cheek.
> With a /ch/, /ch/ here, and a /ch/, /ch/ there,
> Here a /ch/, there a /ch/, everywhere a /ch/, /ch/.
> /ch/ is the sound that starts these words:
> Chicken, chin, and cheek. (p. 700)

Teachers change the question at the beginning of the verse to focus on medial and final sounds. For example:

> What's the sound in the middle of these words?
> Whale, game, and rain. (p. 700)

And for final sounds:

> What's the sound at the end of these words?
> Leaf, cough, and beef. (p. 700)

Teachers also set out trays of objects and ask students to choose the one object that doesn't belong because it doesn't begin with the sound. For example, from a tray with a toy pig, a puppet, a teddy bear, and a pen, the teddy bear doesn't belong.

Sound-Blending Activities. Children blend sounds together in order to combine them to form a word. For example, children blend the sounds /d/ /ŭ/ /k/ to form the word *duck.* Teachers play the "What am I thinking of?" guessing game with children by identifying several characteristics of the item and then saying the name of the item, articulating each of the sounds slowly and separately (Yopp, 1992). Then children blend the sounds together and identify the word, using the phonological and semantic information that the teacher provided. For example:

> I'm thinking of a small animal that lives in the pond when it is young. When it is an adult, it lives on land and it is called a /f/ /r/ /ŏ/ /g/. What is it?

The children blend the sounds together to pronounce the word *frog.* Then the teacher can move into phonics and spelling by setting out magnetic letters for students to arrange to spell *frog.* In this example, the teacher connects the game with a thematic unit, thereby making the game more meaningful for students.

Sound-Addition and -Substitution Activities. Students play with words and create nonsense words as they add or substitute sounds in words in songs they sing or in books that are read aloud to them. Teachers read wordplay books such as Pat Hutchins's *Don't Forget the Bacon!* (1976), in which a boy leaves for the store with a mental list of four items to buy. As he walks, he repeats his list, substituting words each time. "A cake for tea" changes to "a cape for me" and then to "a rake for leaves." Children suggest other substitutions, such as "a game for a bee."

Students substitute sounds in refrains of songs (Yopp, 1992). For example, students can change the "Ee-igh, ee-igh, oh!" refrain in "Old MacDonald Had a Farm" to "Bee-bigh, bee-bigh, boh!" to focus on the initial /b/ sound. Teachers can choose one sound, such as /sh/, and have children substitute it for the beginning sound in their names and in words for items in the classroom. For example, *Jimmy* becomes *Shimmy*, *José* becomes *Shosé*, and *clock* becomes *shock*.

Sound-Segmentation Activities. One of the more difficult phonemic awareness activities is segmentation, in which children isolate the sounds in a spoken word (Yopp, 1988). An introductory segmentation activity is to draw out the beginning sound in words. Children enjoy exaggerating the initial sound in their own names and other familiar words. For example, a pet guinea pig named Popsicle lives in Mrs. Firpo's classroom, and the children exaggerate the beginning sound of her name so that it is pronounced as "P-P-P-Popsicle." Children can also pick up objects or pictures of objects and identify the initial sound; a child who picks up a toy tiger says, "This is a tiger and it starts with /t/."

From that beginning, children move to identifying all the sounds in a word. Using a toy tiger again, the child would say, "This is a tiger, /t/ /ī/ /g/ /er/." Yopp (1992) suggests singing a song to the tune of "Twinkle, Twinkle, Little Star" in which children segment entire words. Here is one example:

> Listen, listen
> To my word
> Then tell me all the sounds you heard: coat
> (slowly)
> /k/ is one sound
> /ō/ is two
> /t/ is last in coat
> It's true. (p. 702)

After several repetitions of the verse segmenting other words, the song ends this way:

> Thanks for listening
> To my words
> And telling all the sounds you heard! (p. 702)

Teachers also use Elkonin boxes to teach students to segment words; this activity comes from the work of Russian psychologist D. B. Elkonin (Clay, 1985). As seen in Figure 4–2, the teacher shows an object or picture of an object and draws a row of boxes, with one box for each sound in the name of the object or picture. Then the teacher or a child moves a marker into each box as the sound is pronounced. Children can move small markers onto cards on their desks, or the teacher can draw the boxes on the chalkboard and use tape or small magnets to hold the larger markers in place. Elkonin boxes can also be used for spelling activities: When a child is trying to spell a word, such as *duck*, the teacher can draw three boxes, do the segmentation activity, and then have the child write the letters representing each sound in the boxes.

Children are experimenting with oral language in these activities. They stimulate children's interest in language and provide valuable experiences with books and words. Effective teachers recognize the importance of building this foundation as children are beginning to read and write. Guidelines for phonemic awareness activities are reviewed in the box on page 124.

Figure 4-2 **Ways to Use Elkonin Boxes**

Type	Goal	Steps in the Activity
Phonemic Awareness	Segmenting sounds in a one-syllable word	1. Show children an object or a picture of an object with a one-syllable name, such as a duck, game, bee, or cup. 2. Prepare a diagram with a row of boxes, side-by-side, corresponding to the number of sounds heard in the name of the object. Draw the row of boxes on the chalkboard or on a small white board. For example, draw two boxes to represent the two sounds in *bee* or three boxes for the three sounds in *duck*. 3. Distribute coins or other small items to use as markers. 4. Say the name of the object slowly and move a marker into each box as the sound is pronounced. Then have children repeat the procedure.
	Segmenting syllables in a multisyllabic word	1. Show children an object or picture of an object with a multisyllabic name, such as a butterfly, alligator, cowboy, or umbrella. 2. Prepare a diagram with a row of boxes, corresponding to the number of syllables in the name of the object. For example, draw four boxes to represent the four syllables in *alligator*. 3. Distribute markers. 4. Say the name of the object slowly and move a marker into each box as the syllable is pronounced. Then have children repeat the procedure.
Spelling	Representing sounds with letters	1. Draw a row of boxes corresponding to the number of sounds heard in a word. For example, draw two boxes for *go*, three boxes for *ship*, and four boxes for *frog*. 2. Pronounce the word, pointing to each box as the corresponding sound is pronounced. 3. Have the child write the letter or letters representing the sound in each box.
	Applying spelling patterns	1. Draw a row of boxes corresponding to the number of sounds heard in a word. For example, draw three boxes for the word *duck, game*, or *light*. 2. Pronounce the word, pointing to each box as the corresponding sound is pronounced. 3. Have the child write the letter or letters representing the sound in each box. 4. Pronounce the word again and examine how each sound is spelled. Insert additional unpronounced letters to complete the spelling patterns.

Guidelines for Teaching Phonemic Awareness

Begin with oral activities using objects and pictures, but after children learn to identify the letters of the alphabet, add reading and writing components.

Emphasize experimentation as children sing songs and play word games because these activities are intended to be fun.

Read and reread wordplay books, and encourage children to experiment with rhyming words, alliteration, and other wordplay activities.

Teach minilessons on manipulating words, moving from easier to more complex levels.

Emphasize blending and segmenting because children need these two strategies for phonics and spelling.

Use small-group activities so children can be more actively involved in manipulating language.

Teach phonemic awareness in the context of authentic reading and writing activities.

Spend 20 hours teaching phonemic awareness strategies, but recognize that children develop phonemic awareness at different rates and that some children will need more or less instruction.

Why Is Phonemic Awareness Important?

A clear connection exists between phonemic awareness and learning to read; researchers have concluded that phonemic awareness is a prerequisite for learning to read (Cunningham, 1999; Tunmer & Nesdale, 1985; Yopp, 1985). As they become phonemically aware, children recognize that speech can be segmented into smaller units; this knowledge is very useful as they learn about sound-symbol correspondences and spelling patterns.

Researchers have concluded that children can be explicitly taught to segment and blend speech, and that children who receive approximately 20 hours of training in phonemic awareness do better in both reading and spelling (P. L. Griffith, 1991; Juel, Griffith, & Gough, 1986). Phonemic awareness can also be nurtured in spontaneous ways by providing children with language-rich environments and emphasizing wordplay as teachers read books aloud to children and engage them in singing songs, chanting poems, and telling riddles.

Moreover, phonemic awareness has been shown to be the most powerful predictor of later reading achievement (Juel et al., 1986; Lomax & McGee, 1987; Tunmer & Nesdale, 1985). In a study comparing children's progress in learning to read in whole-language and traditional reading instruction, Klesius, Griffith, and Zielonka (1991) found that children who began first grade with strong phonemic awareness did well regardless of the kind of reading instruction they received. And neither type of instruction was better for children who were low in phonemic awareness at the beginning of first grade.

PHONICS

Phonics is the set of relationships between phonology (the sounds in speech) and orthography (the spelling patterns of written language). The emphasis is on spelling patterns, not individual letters, because there is not a one-to-one correspondence between phonemes and graphemes in English. Sounds are spelled in different ways. There are several reasons for this variety. One reason is that the sounds, especially vowels, vary according to their location in a word (e.g., *go–got*). Adjacent letters often influence how letters are pronounced (e.g., *bed–bead*), as do vowel markers such as the final *e* (e.g., *bit–bite*) (Shefelbine, 1995).

Language origin, or etymology, of words also influences their pronunciation. For example, the *ch* digraph is pronounced in several ways; the three most common are /ch/ as in *chain* (English), /sh/ as in *chauffeur* (French), and /k/ as in *chaos* (Greek). Neither the location of the digraph within the word nor adjacent letters account for these pronunciation differences: In all three words, the *ch* digraph is at the beginning of the word and is followed by two vowels, the first of which is *a*. Some letters in words are not pronounced, either. In words such as *write*, the *w* is no longer pronounced, even though it probably was at one time. The same is true in *knight*, *know*, and *knee*. "Silent" letters in words such as *sign* and *bomb* reflect their parent words *signature* and *bombard* and have been retained for semantic, not phonological, reasons (Venezky, 1999).

Phonics Concepts

Phonics explains the relationships between phonemes and graphemes. There are 44 phonemes in English, and they are represented by the 26 letters. The alphabetic principle suggests that there should be a one-to-one correspondence between phonemes and graphemes, so that each sound is consistently represented by one letter. English, however, is an imperfect phonetic language, and there are more than 500 ways to spell

Phonics

These first graders are reviewing the letters of the alphabet and the sounds they represent. Today, the teacher has a collected a box of small, familiar objects. She sets out letter cards, and students name each letter and the sound it represents. Then the children sort the objects according to beginning sound. For each word, the children pronounce the word slowly to identify the beginning sound and then place the object by the correct letter card. Later this week, the teacher will set this phonics activity out as a center for these students to continue practicing on their own.

the 44 phonemes. The /f/ sound is fairly phonetic, but it can be spelled in four ways: It is often spelled with *f*, as in *father* and *leaf*, but it can also be spelled with *ff* as in *muffin*, *ph* as in *photo*, and *gh* as in *laugh*. Consonants are more consistent and predictable than vowels; long *e*, for instance, is spelled 14 ways in common words! Consider, for example, *me, seat, feet, people, yield, baby,* and *cookie.* How a word is spelled depends on several factors, including the location of the sound in the word and whether the word entered English from another language (Horn, 1957).

Consonants. Phonemes are classified as either consonants or vowels. The consonants are *b, c, d, f, g, h, j, k, l, m, n, p, q, r, s, t, v, w, x, y,* and *z.* Most consonants represent a single sound consistently, but there are some exceptions. *C,* for example, does not represent a sound of its own: When it is followed by *a, o,* or *u,* it is pronounced /k/ (e.g., *castle, coffee, cut*), and when it is followed by *e, i,* or *y,* it is pronounced /s/ (e.g., *cell, city, cycle*). *G* represents two sounds, as the word *garbage* illustrates: It is usually pronounced /g/ (e.g., *glass, go, green, guppy*), but when *g* is followed by *e, i,* or *y,* it is pronounced /j/, as in *giant.* *X* is also pronounced differently according to its location in a word. At the beginning of a word, it is often pronounced /z/, as in *xylophone,* but sometimes the letter name is used, as in *x-ray.* At the end of a word, *x* is pronounced /ks/, as in *box.* The letters *w* and *y* are particularly interesting: At the beginning of a word or a syllable, they are consonants (e.g., *wind, yard*), but when they are in the middle or at the end, they are vowels (e.g., *saw, flown, day, by*).

Two kinds of combination consonants are blends and digraphs. Consonant blends occur when two or three consonants appear next to each other in words and their individual sounds are "blended" together, as in *grass, belt,* and *spring.* Consonant digraphs are letter combinations for single sounds that are not represented by either letter; the four most common are *ch* as in *chair* and *each, sh* as in *shell* and *wish, th* as in *father* and *both,* and *wh* as in *whale.* Another consonant digraph is *ph,* as in *photo* and *graph.*

Vowels. The remaining five letters—*a, e, i, o,* and *u*—represent vowels, and *w* and *y* are vowels when used in the middle and at the end of syllables and words. Vowels often represent several sounds. The two most common are short (marked with the symbol ˘, called a breve) and long sounds (marked with the symbol ¯, called a macron). The short vowel sounds are /ă/ as in *cat,* /ĕ/ as in *bed,* /ĭ/ as in *win,* /ŏ/ as in *hot,* and /ŭ/ as in *cup.* The long vowel sounds—/ā/, /ē/, /ī/, /ō/, and /ū/—are the same as the letter names, and they are illustrated in the words *make, feet, bike, coal,* and *mule.* Long-vowel sounds are usually spelled with two vowels, except when the long vowel is at the end of a one-syllable word or a syllable, as in *she* or *secret* and *try* or *tribal.*

When *y* is a vowel at the end of a word, it is pronounced as long *e* or long *i,* depending on the length of the word. In one-syllable words such as *by* and *cry,* the *y* is pronounced as long *i,* but in longer words such as *baby* and *happy,* the *y* is usually pronounced as long *e.*

Scaffolding Struggling Readers

Why are vowels so difficult for my struggling readers and writers?

Vowels are especially difficult because they are more complicated than consonants: Most consonants represent only one or two sounds, but vowels can be pronounced and spelled in different ways, depending on whether they are short, long, or something else. Spelling patterns vary, too, according to the location of the vowel in the word. Think about the difference in the way the *a* in these words is pronounced: *apron, at, want, laugh, chalk, play, what, game, chart, saw,* and *peach.* On top of that, regional dialects make some vowels, particularly short *e* and *i,* difficult to distinguish. Pronounce *pin* and *pen:* Do the vowels sound different? People in some parts of the United States pronounce these words the same way even though they are spelled differently.

Vowel sounds are more complicated than consonant sounds, and there are many vowel combinations representing long vowels and other vowels sounds. Consider these combinations:

ai as in *nail*

au as in *laugh* and *caught*

aw as in *saw*

ea as in *peach* and *bread*

ew as in *sew* and *few*

ia as in *dial*

ie as in *cookie*

oa as in *soap*

oi as in *oil*

oo as in *cook* and *moon*

ou as in *house* and *through*

ow as in *now* and *snow*

oy as in *toy*

Most vowel combinations are vowel digraphs or diphthongs: When two vowels represent a single sound, the combination is a vowel digraph (e.g., *nail, snow*), and when the two vowels represent a glide from one sound to another, the combination is a diphthong. Two vowel combinations that are consistently diphthongs are *oi* and *oy,* but other combinations, such as *ou* as in *house* (but not in *through*) and *ow* as in *now* (but not in *snow*), are diphthongs when they represent a glided sound. In *through,* the *ou* represents the /ū/ sound as in *moon,* and in *snow,* the *ow* represents the /ō/ sound.

When the letter *r* follows one or more vowels in a word, it influences the pronunciation of the vowel sound, as shown in the words *car, air, are, ear, bear, first, for, more, murder,* and *pure.* Students learn many of these words by sight.

The vowels in the unaccented syllables of multisyllabic words are often softened and pronounced "uh," as in the first syllable of *about* and *machine,* and the final syllable of *pencil, tunnel, zebra,* and *selection.* This vowel sound is called *schwa* and is represented in dictionaries with ə, which looks like an inverted *e.*

Blending Into Words. Readers blend or combine sounds in order to decode words. Even though children may identify each sound in a word, one by one, they must also be able to blend them together into a word. For example, to read the short-vowel word *best,* children identify /b/ /ĕ/ /s/ /t/ and then combine them to form the word. For long-vowel words, children must identify the vowel pattern as well as the surrounding letters. In *pancake,* for example, children identify /p/ /ă/ /n/ /k/ /ā/ /k/ and recognize that the *e* at the end of the word is silent and marks the preceding vowel as long. Shefelbine (1995) emphasizes the importance of blending and suggests that students who have difficulty decoding words usually know the sound-symbol correspondences but cannot blend the sounds together into recognizable words. The ability to blend sounds together into words is part of phonemic awareness, and students who have not had practice blending speech sounds into words are likely to have trouble blending sounds into words in order to decode unfamiliar words.

Rimes and Rhymes. One-syllable words and syllables in longer words can be divided into two parts, the onset and the rime. The onset is the consonant sound, if any, that precedes the vowel, and the rime is the vowel and any consonant sounds that follow it

Figure 4-3   The 37 Rimes and Common Words Using Them

Rime	Examples	Rime	Examples
-ack	black, pack, quack, stack	-ide	bride, hide, ride, side
-ail	mail, nail, sail, tail	-ight	bright, fight, light, might
-ain	brain, chain, plain, rain	-ill	fill, hill, kill, will
-ake	cake, shake, take, wake	-in	chin, grin, pin, win
-ale	male, sale, tale, whale	-ine	fine, line, mine, nine
-ame	came, flame, game, name	-ing	king, sing, thing, wing
-an	can, man, pan, than	-ink	pink, sink, think, wink
-ank	bank, drank, sank, thank	-ip	drip, hip, lip, ship
-ap	cap, clap, map, slap	-ir	birth, dirt, first, girl
-ash	cash, dash, flash, trash	-ock	block, clock, knock, sock
-at	bat, cat, rat, that	-oke	choke, joke, poke, woke
-ate	gate, hate, late, plate	-op	chop, drop, hop, shop
-aw	claw, draw, jaw, saw	-ore	chore, more, shore, store
-ay	day, play, say, way	-or	for, or, short, torn
-eat	beat, heat, meat, wheat	-uck	duck, luck, suck, truck
-ell	bell, sell, shell, well	-ug	bug, drug, hug, rug
-est	best, chest, nest, west	-ump	bump, dump, hump, lump
-ice	ice, mice, nice, rice	-unk	bunk, dunk, junk, sunk
-ick	brick, pick, sick, thick		

(Treiman, 1985). For example, in *show, sh* is the onset and *ow* is the rime, and in *ball, b* is the onset and *all* is the rime. For *at* and *up*, there is no onset; the entire word is the rime. Research has shown that children make more errors decoding and spelling final consonants than initial consonants and that they make more errors on vowels than on consonants (Treiman, 1985). These problem areas correspond to rimes, and educators now speculate that onsets and rimes could provide an important key to word identification.

The terms *onset* and *rime* are not usually introduced to children because they might confuse *rime* and *rhyme*. Instead, teachers call the rhyming words made from a rime "word families." Teachers can focus children's attention on a rime, such as *ay*, and create rhyming words, including *bay, day, lay, may, ray, say*, and *way*. These words can be read and spelled by analogy because the vowel sounds are consistent in rimes. Wylie and Durell (1970) identified 37 rimes that can be used to produce nearly 500 common words; these rimes and some words made from them are presented in Figure 4–3.

Phonics Generalizations. Because English does not have a one-to-one correspondence between sounds and letters, linguists have created generalizations or rules to clarify English spelling patterns. One rule is that *q* is followed by *u* and pronounced /kw/, as in *queen, quick*, and *earthquake;* there are very few, if any, exceptions to this rule. Another generalization that has few exceptions relates to *r*-controlled vowels: *r* influences the preceding vowel so that the vowel is neither long nor short. Examples are *car, market, birth*, and *four*. There are exceptions, however; one example is *fire*.

Many generalizations aren't very useful because there are more exceptions than words that conform to the rule (Clymer, 1963). A good example is this rule for long vowels: When there are two adjacent vowels, the long vowel sound of the first one is pronounced and the second is silent; teachers sometimes call this the "when two vowels go walking, the first one does the talking" rule. Examples of words conforming to this rule are *meat, soap*, and *each*. There are many more exceptions, however, including *food, said, head, chief, bread, look, soup, does, too, again*, and *believe*.

Only a few phonics generalizations have a high degree of utility for readers. The generalizations that work most of the time are the ones that students should learn because they are the most useful (Adams, 1990). Eight high-utility generalizations are listed in Figure 4–4. Even though these rules are fairly reliable, very few of them approach 100% utility. The rule about *r*-controlled vowels just mentioned has been calculated to be useful in 78% of words in which the letter *r* follows the vowel (Adams, 1990). Other commonly taught, useful rules have even lower percentages of utility. The CVC pattern rule—which says that when a one-syllable word has only one vowel and the vowel comes between two consonants, it is usually short, as in *bat, land,* and *cup*—is estimated to work only 62% of the time. Exceptions include *told, fall, fork,* and *birth.* The CVCe pattern rule—which says that when there are two vowels in a one-syllable word and one vowel is an *e* at the end of the word, the first vowel is long and

Pattern	Description	Examples
Two sounds of *c*	The letter *c* can be pronounced as /k/ or /s/. When *c* is followed by *a, o,* or *u,* it is pronounced /k/—the hard *c* sound. When *c* is followed by *e, i,* or *y,* it is pronounced /s/—the soft *c* sound.	cat cough cut cent city cycle
Two sounds of *g*	The sound associated with the letter *g* depends on the letter following it. When *g* is followed by *a, o,* or *u,* it is pronounced as /g/—the hard *g* sound. When *g* is followed by *e, i,* or *y,* it is usually pronounced /j/—the soft *g* sound. Exceptions include *get* and *give.*	gate go guess gentle giant gypsy
CVC pattern	When a one-syllable word has only one vowel and the vowel comes between two consonants, it is usually short. One exception is *told.*	bat cup land
Final *e* or CVCe pattern	When there are two vowels in a one-syllable word and one of them is an *e* at the end of the word, the first vowel is long and the final *e* is silent. Three exceptions are *have, come,* and *love.*	home safe cute
CV pattern	When a vowel follows a consonant in a one-syllable word, the vowel is long. Exceptions include *the, to,* and *do.*	go be
r-controlled vowels	Vowels that are followed by the letter *r* are overpowered and are neither short nor long. One exception is *fire.*	car for birthday
-*igh*	When *gh* follows *i,* the *i* is long and the *gh* is silent. One exception is *neighbor.*	high night
kn- and *wr-*	In words beginning with *kn-* and *wr-,* the first letter is not pronounced.	knee write

Figure 4–4 The Most Useful Phonics Generalizations

Adapted from Clymer, 1963.

the final *e* is silent—is estimated to work in 63% of CVCe words. Examples of conforming words are *came, hole,* and *pipe;* but three very common words, *have, come,* and *love,* are exceptions.

Teaching Phonics

The best way to teach phonics is through a combination of direct instruction and application activities. The National Reading Panel (2000) reviewed the research about phonics instruction and concluded that the most effective programs were systematic; that is, the most useful phonics skills are taught in a predetermined, logical sequence. Shefelbine (1995) agrees; he explains that the phonics program should be "systematic and thorough enough to enable most students to become independent and fluent readers, yet still efficient and streamlined" (p. 2).

Most teachers begin with consonants and then introduce the short vowels so that students can read and spell consonant-vowel-consonant or CVC-pattern words, such as *dig, rat,* and *cup.* Then students learn about consonant blends and diagraphs and long vowels so that they can read and spell consonant-vowel-consonant-*e* or CVCe-pattern words such as *shape, broke,* and *white* and consonant-vowel-vowel-consonant or CVVC-pattern words such as *clean, wheel,* and *snail.* Finally, students learn about the less common vowel diagraphs and diphthongs, such as *claw, bought, shook,* and *boil,* and *r*-controlled vowels, including *square, hard, clear,* and *year.* Figure 4–5 details this sequence of phonics skills.

The second component of phonics instruction is daily opportunities for students to apply the phonics skills they are learning in authentic reading and writing activities (National Reading Panel, 2000). Cunningham and Cunningham (2002) estimate that the ratio of time spent on real reading and writing to time spent on phonics instruction should be 3 to 1. Without this meaningful application of what they are learning, phonics instruction is often ineffective (Cunningham, 2000; Dahl, Scharer, Lawson, & Grogan, 2001; Freppon & Dahl, 1991).

Phonics instruction usually begins in kindergarten when children learn to identify the letter names and connect consonant and short vowel sounds to the letters, and it should be completed by third grade because older students rarely benefit from it (Ivey & Baker, 2004; National Reading Panel, 2000). Guidelines for teaching phonics are presented in the box on page 132.

Direct Instruction. Teachers present minilessons on phonics skills to the whole class or to small groups of students, depending on the students' instructional needs. They follow the minilesson format, explicitly presenting information about the phonics skills, demonstrating how to use the skill, and presenting words for students to use in guided practice, as Mrs. Firpo did in the vignette at the beginning of the chapter. During the minilesson, teachers use these activities to provide guided practice opportunities for students to manipulate sounds and read and write words:

- Sort objects, pictures, and word cards according to a phonics skill.
- Write letters or words on small dry-erase boards.
- Arrange magnetic letters or letter cards to spell words.
- Make class charts of words representing phonics skills, such as the two sounds of *g* or ways to spell long *o.*
- Make a poster or book of words representing a phonics skill.
- Locate other words exemplifying the sound or spelling pattern in books students are reading.

Figure 4-5 Sequence of Phonics Instruction

Grade	Skill	Description	Examples
K	Most common consonant sounds	Students identify consonant sounds, match sounds to letters, isolate sounds in words, and substitute sounds in words.	/b/, /d/, /f/, /m/, /n/, /p/, /s/, /t/
K–1	Less common consonant sounds	Students identify consonant sounds, match sounds to letters, isolate sounds in words, and substitute sounds in words.	/g/, /h/, /j/, /k/, /l/, /q/, /v/, /w/, /x/, /y/, /z/
	Short vowel sounds	Students identify the five short vowel sounds and match them to letters.	/ă/ = cat, /ĕ/ = bed, /ĭ/ = pig, /ŏ/ = hot, /ŭ/ = cut
	CVC vowel pattern	Students read and spell CVC-pattern words.	dad, men, sit, hop, but
1	Consonant blends	Students identify and blend consonant sounds at the beginning and end of words.	/pl/ = play /str/ = string /mp/ = camp
	Onsets and rimes	Students break CVC words into onsets and rimes and substitute onsets and rimes to form new words.	c-at, l-amp, sp-ill cat-rat-sat-hat sand-sing-sock
	Consonant digraphs	Students identify consonant diagraphs, match sounds to letters, and read and spell words with consonant digraphs.	/ch/ = chop /sh/ = wish /th/ = this, bath /wh/ = when, why
	Long vowel sounds	Students identify the five long vowel sounds and match them to letters.	/ā/ = name, /ē/ = bee, /ī/ = ice, /ō/ = soap, /ū/ = use
	CVCe vowel pattern	Students read and spell CVCe-pattern words.	game, ride, bone
	Common long vowel digraphs	Students identify the vowel sound represented by common long vowel digraphs and read and spell words using them.	/ā/ = ai (rain), ay (day) /ē/ = ea (reach), ee (sweet) /ō/ = oa (soap), ow (know)
1–2	w and y as consonants and vowels	Students recognize w and y as consonants at the beginning of words or syllables and as vowels at the end, and identify the sounds they represent.	window, yesterday y = /ī/ (by) y = /ē/ (baby)
	Onsets and rimes	Students divide CVCe and other long-vowel pattern words into onsets and rimes and substitute onsets and rimes to form new words.	ch-ase, m-ile, sm-oke sl-eep, p-each, dr-ain cl-ay, gl-ow, tr-ee, fl-y
	Hard and soft consonant sounds	Students identify the hard and soft sounds represented by c and g, and read and write words using these consonants.	g = girl (hard), gem (soft) c = cat (hard), city (soft)
2	Less common vowel digraphs	Students identify the vowel sounds of less common vowel digraphs and read and write words using them.	/ô/ = al (walk), au (caught), aw (saw), ou (bought) /ā/ = ei (weigh) /ē/ = ey (key), ie (chief) /ī/ = ie (pie) /ŭ/ = oo (good), ou (could) /ū/ = oo (moon), ew (new), ue (blue), ui (fruit)
	Vowel diphthongs	Students identify the vowel diphthongs and read and write words using them.	/oi/ = oi (boil), oy (toy) /ou/ = ou (cloud), ow (down)
	Less common consonant digraphs	Students identify the sounds of less common consonant digraphs and read and write words using them.	ph = phone, graph gh = laugh ng = sing tch = match
	r-controlled vowels	Students identify r-controlled vowel patterns and read and spell words using them.	/âr/ = hair, care, bear, there, their /ar/ = star /er/ = ear, deer, here /or/ = born, more /ûr/ = learn, first, work, burn
	Consonant spelling patterns	Students read and write words with these spelling patterns.	/g/ = girl, ghost /j/ = jet, gem, cage, judge /k/ = cat, key, duck /s/ = sun, city, goose /z/ = zoo, dogs, rose

Guidelines for Teaching Phonics

Teach high-utility phonics skills that are most useful for decoding and spelling unfamiliar words.

Follow a developmental continuum for systematic phonics instruction, beginning with rhyming and ending with phonics generalizations.

Provide direct instruction to teach phonics skills.

Choose words for phonics instruction from books students are reading and other high-frequency words.

Provide opportunities for students to apply what they are learning about phonics through word sorts, making words, interactive writing, and other literacy activities.

Take advantage of teachable moments to clarify misunderstandings and infuse phonics instruction into literacy activities.

Use oral activities to reinforce phonemic awareness skills as students blend and segment written words during phonics and spelling instruction.

Review phonics skills as part of the spelling program in the upper grades.

The minilesson feature on page 133 shows how a first-grade teacher teaches a minilesson on reading and spelling CVC-pattern words using final consonant blends.

Teachable Moments. In addition to direct instruction, teachers often give impromptu phonics lessons as they engage children in authentic literacy activities using children's names, titles of books, and environmental print in the classroom. During these teachable moments, teachers answer students' questions about words, model how to use phonics knowledge to decode and spell words, and have students share the strategies they use for reading and writing (Mills, O'Keefe, & Stephens, 1992).

Teachers also use interactive writing to support children's growing awareness of phonics (McCarrier, Pinnell, & Fountas, 2000; Tompkins & Collom, 2004). Interactive writing is similar to the Language Experience Approach, except that children do as much of the writing themselves as they can. Children segment words into sounds and take turns writing letters and sometimes whole words on the chart. Teachers help children to correct any errors, and they take advantage of teachable moments to review consonant and vowel sounds and spelling patterns, as well as handwriting skills and rules for capitalization and punctuation.

What Is the Role of Phonics in a Balanced Literacy Program?

Phonics is a controversial topic. Some parents and politicians, as well as even a few teachers, believe that most of our educational ills could be solved if children were taught to read using phonics. A few people still argue that phonics is a complete reading program, but that view ignores what we know about the interrelatedness of the four cueing systems. Reading is a complex process, and the phonological system works in conjunction with the semantic, syntactic, and pragmatic systems, not in isolation.

The controversy now centers on how to teach phonics. Marilyn Adams (1990), in her landmark review of the research on phonics instruction, recommends that phonics be taught within a balanced approach that integrates instruction in reading skills

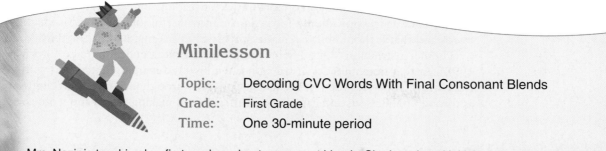

Minilesson

Topic: Decoding CVC Words With Final Consonant Blends
Grade: First Grade
Time: One 30-minute period

Mrs. Nazir is teaching her first graders about consonant blends. She introduced initial consonant blends to the class, and students practiced reading and spelling words, such as *club, drop,* and *swim,* that were chosen from the selection they were reading in their basal readers. Then, in small groups, they completed workbook pages and built words using plastic tiles with onsets and rimes printed on them. For example, using the *-ip* rime, they built *clip, drip, flip, skip,* and *trip.* This is the fifth whole-class lesson in the series. Today, Mrs. Nazir is introducing final consonant blends, and tomorrow, she'll focus on the *-ck* blend. Later, the first graders will practice reading and spelling words with both initial and final blends, such as *stamp, drink,* and *frost.*

1. Introduce the Topic

Mrs. Nazir explains that blends are also used at the end of words. She writes these words on the chalkboard: *best, rang, hand, pink,* and *bump.* Together the students sound them out: They pronounce the initial consonant sound, the short vowel sound, and the final consonants. They blend the final consonants, then they blend the entire word and say it aloud. Children use the words in sentences to ensure that everyone understands the word, and Dillon, T.J., Pauline, Cody, and Brittany circle the blends in the words on the chalkboard. The teacher points out that *st* is a familiar blend also used at the beginning of words, but that the other blends are used only at the end of words.

2. Share Examples

Mrs. Nazir says these words: *must, wing, test, band, hang, sink, bend,* and *bump.* The first graders repeat each word, isolate the blend, and identify it. For example, Carson says, "The word is *must*—/m/ /ŭ/ /s/ /t/—and the blend is *st* at the end." Bryan points out that Ng is his last name, and everyone claps because his name is so special. Several students volunteer additional words: Dillon suggests *blast,* and Henry adds *dump* and *string.* Then the teacher passes out word cards and students read the words, including *just, lamp, went,* and *hang.* They sound out each word carefully, pronouncing the initial consonant, the short vowel, and the final consonant blend. Then they blend the sounds and say the word.

3. Provide Information

Mrs. Nazir posts a piece of chart paper, and labels it *-ink* Words. The students brainstorm these words with the *-ink* rime: *blink, sink, pink, rink, mink, stink,* and *wink,* and they take turns writing the words on the chart. They also suggest *twinkle* and *wrinkle,* and Mrs. Nazir adds them to the chart.

4. Guide Practice

Students create other rime charts using *-and, -ang, -ank, -end, -ent, -est, -ing, -ump,* and *-ust.* Each group brainstorms at least five words and writes them on the chart. Mrs. Nazir monitors students' work and helps them think of additional words and correct spelling errors. Then students post their charts and share them with the class.

5. Assess Learning

Mrs. Nazir observes the first graders as they brainstorm words, blend onsets and rimes, and spell the words. She notices who needs more practice and will call them together for a follow-up lesson.

and strategies with meaningful opportunities for reading and writing. She emphasizes that phonics instruction should focus on the most useful information for identifying words and that it should be systematic, intensive, and completed by the third grade.

Phonics instruction looks different today than it did a generation ago (Strickland, 1998). At that time, phonics instruction often involved marking letters and words on worksheets. Today, however, students learn phonics through reading and writing as well as through minilessons and gamelike activities such as making words and word sorts.

SPELLING

Learning to spell is also part of "cracking the code." As children learn about sound-symbol correspondences, they apply what they are learning through both reading and writing. Children's early spellings reflect what they know about phonics and spelling patterns, and as their knowledge grows, their spelling increasingly approximates conventional spelling.

Students need to learn to spell words conventionally so that they can communicate effectively through writing. Learning phonics during the primary grades is part of spelling instruction, but students also need to learn other strategies and information about English orthography. In the past, weekly spelling tests were the main instructional strategy. Now, they are only one part of a comprehensive spelling program. Guidelines for spelling instruction are presented in the feature below.

Stages of Spelling Development

As young children begin to write, they create unique spellings, called *invented spelling,* based on their knowledge of sound-symbol correspondences and phonics generalizations. Charles Read (1971, 1975, 1986) found that young children use their knowledge of phonology to invent spellings. The children in Read's studies used letter names to spell words, such as U (*you*) and R (*are*), and they used consonant sounds rather consistently: GRL (*girl*), TIGR (*tiger*), and NIT (*night*). They used several unusual but phonetically based spelling patterns to represent affricates; for example, they

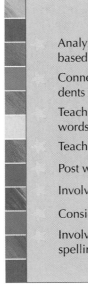

Guidelines for Teaching Spelling

Analyze the errors in students' writing to provide appropriate spelling instruction based on their stage of development.

Connect phonemic awareness, phonics, and spelling during minilessons by having students manipulate words orally and read and spell words.

Teach students to use spelling strategies, including "think it out," to spell unfamiliar words.

Teach students how to use the dictionary to locate the spelling of unfamiliar words.

Post words on word walls and use them for a variety of reading and writing activities.

Involve students in making words, word sorts, and other hands-on spelling activities.

Consider spelling tests as only one part of a spelling program.

Involve students in daily authentic reading and writing activities to develop their spelling knowledge.

replaced *tr* with *chr* (e.g., CHRIBLES for *troubles*) and *dr* with *jr* (e.g., JRAGIN for *dragon*). Words with long vowels were spelled using letter names: MI (*my*), LADE (*lady*), and FEL (*feel*). The children used several ingenious strategies to spell words with short vowels: The preschoolers selected letters to represent short vowels on the basis of place of articulation in the mouth. Short *i* was represented with *e*, as in FES (*fish*), short *e* with *a*, as in LAFFT (*left*), and short *o* with *i*, as in CLIK (*clock*). These spellings may seem odd to adults, but they are based on phonetic relationships.

Based on observations of children's spellings, researchers have identified five stages that children move through on their way to becoming conventional spellers: emergent spelling, letter-name spelling, within-word pattern spelling, syllables and affixes spelling, and derivational relations spelling (Bear, Invernizzi, Templeton, & Johnston, 2004). At each stage, they use different types of strategies and focus on different aspects of spelling. The characteristics of the five stages of spelling development are summarized in Figure 4–6.

Stage 1: Emergent Spelling. Children string scribbles, letters, and letterlike forms together, but they do not associate the marks they make with any specific phonemes. Spelling at this stage represents a natural, early expression of the alphabet and other concepts about writing. Children may write from left to right, right to left, top to bottom, or randomly across the page, but by the end of the stage, they have an understanding of directionality. Some emergent spellers have a large repertoire of letter forms to use in writing, whereas others repeat a small number of letters over and over. They use both upper- and lowercase letters, but they show a distinct preference for uppercase letters. Toward the end of this stage, children are beginning to discover how spelling works and that letters represent sounds in words. This stage is typical of 3- to 5-year-olds. During the emergent stage, children learn:

- the distinction between drawing and writing
- how to make letters
- the direction of writing on a page
- some letter-sound matches

Stage 2: Letter-Name Spelling. Children learn to represent phonemes in words with letters. They develop an understanding of the alphabetic principle, that a link exists between letters and sounds. At first, the spellings are quite abbreviated and represent only the most prominent features in words. Children use only several letters of the alphabet to represent an entire word. Examples of early Stage 2 spelling are D (*dog*) and KE (*cookie*), and children may still be writing mainly with capital letters. Children pronounce slowly the words they want to spell, listening for familiar letter names and sounds.

In the middle of the letter-name stage, students use most beginning and ending consonants and often include a vowel in most syllables; they spell *like* as *lik* and *bed* as *bad*. By the end of the stage, students use consonant blends and digraphs and short-vowel patterns to spell *hat, get,* and *win*, but some students still spell *ship* as *sep*. They can also spell some CVCe words such as *name* correctly. Spellers at this stage are usually 5- to 7-year-olds. During the letter-name stage, students learn:

- the alphabetic principle
- consonant sounds
- short-vowel sounds
- consonant blends and digraphs

Figure 4-6   Stages of Spelling Development

Stage 1: Emergent Spelling

Children string scribbles, letters, and letterlike forms together, but they do not associate the marks they make with any specific phonemes. This stage is typical of 3- to 5-year-olds. Children learn:

- the distinction between drawing and writing
- how to make letters
- the direction of writing on a page
- some letter-sound matches

Stage 2: Letter-Name Spelling

Children learn to represent phonemes in words with letters. At first, their spellings are quite abbreviated, but they learn to use consonant blends and digraphs and short-vowel patterns to spell many short-vowel words. Spellers are 5- to 7-year-olds. Children learn:

- the alphabetic principle
- consonant sounds
- short-vowel sounds
- consonant blends and digraphs

Stage 3: Within-Word Pattern Spelling

Students learn long-vowel patterns and *r*-controlled vowels, but they may confuse spelling patterns and spell *meet* as *mete,* and they reverse the order of letters, such as *form* for *from* and *gril* for *girl.* Spellers are 7- to 9-year-olds, and they learn these concepts:

- long-vowel spelling patterns
- *r*-controlled vowels
- more complex consonant patterns
- diphthongs and other less common vowel patterns

Stage 4: Syllables and Affixes Spelling

Students apply what they have learned about one-syllable words to spell longer, multisyllabic words, and they learn to break words into syllables. They also learn to add inflectional endings (e.g., *-es, -ed, -ing*) and to differentiate between homophones, such as *your–you're.* Spellers are often 9- to 11-year-olds, and they learn these concepts:

- inflectional endings
- rules for adding inflectional endings
- syllabication
- homophones

Stage 5: Derivational Relations Spelling

Students explore the relationship between spelling and meaning and learn that words with related meanings are often related in spelling despite changes in sound (e.g., *wise–wisdom, sign–signal, nation–national*). They also learn about Latin and Greek root words and derivational affixes (e.g., *amphi-, pre-, -able, -tion*). Spellers are 11- to 14-year-olds. Students learn these concepts:

- consonant alternations
- vowel alternations
- Latin affixes and root words
- Greek affixes and root words
- etymologies

Adapted from Bear, Invernizzi, Templeton, & Johnston, 2004.

Stage 3: Within-Word Pattern Spelling. Students begin the within-word pattern stage when they can spell most one-syllable short-vowel words, and during this stage, they learn to spell long-vowel patterns and *r*-controlled vowels (Henderson, 1990). They experiment with long-vowel patterns and learn that words such as *come* and *bread* are exceptions that do not fit the vowel patterns. Students may confuse spelling patterns and spell *meet* as *mete,* and they reverse the order of letters, such as *form* for *from* and *gril* for *girl.* Students also learn about complex consonant sounds, including *-tch* (*match*) and *-dge* (*judge*) and less frequent vowel patterns, such as *oi/oy* (*boy*), *au* (*caught*), *aw* (*saw*), *ew* (*sew, few*), *ou* (*house*), and *ow* (*cow*). Students also become aware of homophones and compare long- and short-vowel combinations (*hope–hop*) as they experiment with vowel patterns. Spellers at this stage are 7- to 9-year-olds, and they learn these spelling concepts:

- long-vowel spelling patterns
- *r*-controlled vowels
- more complex consonant patterns
- diphthongs and other less common vowel patterns

Stage 4: Syllables and Affixes Spelling. The focus is on syllables in this stage. Students apply what they have learned about one-syllable words to longer, multisyllabic words, and they learn to break words into syllables. They learn about inflectional endings (*-s, -es, -ed,* and *-ing*) and rules about consonant doubling, changing the final *y* to *i,* or dropping the final *e* before adding an inflectional suffix. They also learn about homophones and compound words and are introduced to some of the more common prefixes and suffixes. Spellers in this stage are generally 9- to 11-year-olds. Students learn these concepts during the syllables and affixes stage of spelling development:

- inflectional endings (*-s, -es, -ed, -ing*)
- rules for adding inflectional endings
- syllabication
- homophones

Stage 5: Derivational Relations Spelling. Students explore the relationship between spelling and meaning during the derivational relations stage, and they learn that words with related meanings are often related in spelling despite changes in vowel and consonant sounds (e.g., *wise–wisdom, sign–signal, nation–national*) (Templeton, 1983). The focus in this stage is on morphemes, and students learn about Greek and Latin root words and affixes. They also begin to examine etymologies and the role of history in shaping how words are spelled. They learn about eponyms (words from people's names), such as *maverick* and *sandwich.* Spellers at this stage are 11- to 14-year-olds. Students learn these concepts at this stage of spelling development:

- consonant alternations (e.g., *soft–soften, magic–magician*)
- vowel alternations (e.g., *please–pleasant, define–definition, explain–explanation*)
- Greek and Latin affixes and root words
- etymologies

Children's spelling provides evidence of their growing understanding of English orthography. The words they spell correctly show which phonics skills, spelling patterns, and other language features they have learned to apply, and the words they invent and misspell show what they are still learning to use and those features of spelling that they have not noticed or learned about. Invented spelling is sometimes criticized because it may appear that students are learning bad habits by misspelling words, but researchers have confirmed that students grow more quickly in phonemic awareness, phonics, and spelling when they use invented spelling as long as they are also receiving spelling instruction (Snow, Burns, & Griffin, 1998). As students learn more about spelling, their invented spellings become more sophisticated to reflect their new knowledge, even if the words are still spelled incorrectly, and increasingly students spell more and more words correctly as they move through the stages of spelling development.

To learn how to assess a student's stage of spelling development, see Chapter 9, "Assessing Students' Literacy Development."

Teaching Spelling

Perhaps the best-known way to teach spelling is through weekly spelling tests, but spelling tests should never be considered a complete spelling program. To become good spellers, students need to learn about the English orthographic system and move through the stages of spelling development. They develop strategies to use in spelling unknown words and gain experience in using dictionaries and other resources. A complete spelling program:

- teaches spelling strategies
- matches instruction to students' stage of spelling development
- provides instruction on spelling strategies and skills

Interactive Writing

These first graders are writing a story summary using interactive writing. The children take turns writing a word or part of a word on the chart. The teacher guides them to spell the words correctly as she supervises their work. When a child makes an error, the teacher covers it with correction tape and assists the first grader to correct it. At the same time children are taking turns to write on the class chart, they are also writing the text on small dry-erase boards they have in their laps. Everyone is busy writing words and spelling them correctly.

- provides daily reading and writing opportunities
- requires students to learn to spell high-frequency words

Students learn spelling strategies that they can use to figure out the spelling of unfamiliar words. As students move through the stages of spelling development, they become increasingly more sophisticated in their use of phonological, semantic, and historical knowledge to spell words; that is, they become more strategic. Important spelling strategies include:

- segmenting the word and spelling each sound
- predicting the spelling of a word by generating possible spellings and choosing the best alternative
- breaking the word into syllables and spelling each syllable
- applying affixes to root words
- spelling unknown words by analogy to known words
- writing a letter or two as a placeholder for a word they do not know how to spell when they are writing rough drafts
- locating words on word walls and other charts
- proofreading to locate spelling errors in a rough draft
- locating the spelling of unfamiliar words in a dictionary

Instead of giving the traditional "sound it out" advice when students ask how to spell an unfamiliar word, teachers can provide more useful information when they suggest that students use a strategic "think it out" approach. This advice reminds students that spelling involves more than phonological information and encourages them to think about spelling patterns, root words and affixes, and the shape of the word—what it looks like.

Two of the most important ways that students learn to spell are through daily reading and writing activities. Students who are good readers tend to be good spellers, too: As they read, students visualize words—the shape of the word and the configuration of letters within it—and they use this knowledge to spell many words correctly and to recognize when a word they've written doesn't look right. Through writing, of course, students gain valuable practice using the strategies they have learned to spell the words they are writing. And, as teachers work with students to proofread and edit their writing, they learn more about spelling and other writing conventions.

In addition to reading and writing activities, students learn about the English orthographic system through spelling activities and minilessons about phonics, high-frequency words, spelling rules, and spelling strategies. The minilesson feature on p. 140 shows how Mr. Cheng teaches his first graders to spell rhyming -*at* family words. Then in the following sections, you will read about a number of spelling activities that expand students' spelling knowledge and help them move through the stages of spelling development.

Word Walls. Teachers use two types of word walls in their classrooms. One word wall features "important" words from books students are reading or social studies and science thematic units. Words may be written on a large sheet of paper hanging in the classroom or on word cards and placed in a large pocket chart. Then students refer to these word walls when they are writing. Seeing the words posted on word walls and other charts in the classroom and using them in their writing help students learn to spell the words.

The second type of word wall displays high-frequency words. Researchers have identified the most commonly used words and recommend that students learn to spell

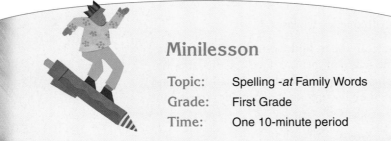

Minilesson

Topic: Spelling *-at* Family Words

Grade: First Grade

Time: One 10-minute period

Mr. Cheng teaches phonics skills during guided reading lessons. He introduces, practices, and reviews phonics concepts using words from selections his first graders are reading. The children decode and spell words using letter and word cards, magnetic letters, and small dry-erase boards and pens.

1. Introduce the Topic

Mr. Cheng holds up a copy of *At Home,* the small paperback level E book the children read yesterday, and asks them to reread the title. Then he asks the children to identify the first word, *at.* After they read the word, he hands a card with the word *at* written on it to each of the six children in the guided reading group. "Who can read this word?" he asks. Several children recognize it immediately, and others carefully sound out the two-letter word.

2. Share Examples

Mr. Cheng asks children to think about rhyming words: "Who knows what rhyming words are?" Mike answers that rhyming words sound alike at the end—for example, *Mike, bike,* and *like.* The teacher explains that there are many words in English that rhyme, and that today, they are going to read and write words that rhyme with *at.* "One rhyming word is *cat,*" he explains. Children name rhyming words, including *hat, fat,* and *bat.* Mr. Cheng helps each child in the guided reading group to name at least three rhyming words.

3. Provide Information

Mr. Cheng explains that children can spell these *at* rhyming words by adding a consonant in front of *at.* For example, he places the foam letter *c* in front of his *at* card, and the children blend *c* to *at* to decode *cat.* Then he repeats the procedure by substituting other foam letters for the *c* to spell *bat, fat, hat, mat, pat, rat,* and *sat.* He continues the activity until all children in the group successfully decode one of the rhyming words.

4. Guide Practice

Mr. Cheng passes out small plastic trays with foam letters to each child and asks them to form each *at* rhyming word by adding one of the letters to their *at* cards to spell the words as he pronounces them. He continues the activity until children have had several opportunities to spell each of the rhyming words, and they can quickly choose the correct initial consonant to spell the word. Then Mr. Cheng collects the *at* cards and trays with foam letters.

5. Assess Learning

Mr. Cheng passes out small dry-erase boards and pens to the children in the group. He asks them to write the rhyming words as he says each one aloud: *cat, hat, mat, pat, rat, sat, bat, fat.* He carefully observes as each child segments the onset and rime to spell the word. The children hold up their boards to show him their spellings. Afterward, children erase the word and repeat the process, writing the next word. After children write all eight words, Mr. Cheng quickly jots a note about which children need additional practice with the *-at* word family before continuing with the guided reading lesson.

100 of these words because of their usefulness. The most frequently used words represent more than 50% of all the words children and adults write (Horn, 1926)! Figure 4–7 lists the 100 most frequently used words.

Making Words. Teachers choose a five- to eight-letter word (or longer words for older students) and prepare sets of letter cards for a making words activity (Cunningham & Cunningham, 1992; Gunning, 1995). Then students use the cards to practice spelling words and to review spelling patterns and rules. They arrange and rearrange the cards to spell one-letter words, two-letter words, three-letter words, and so forth, until they use all the letters to spell the original word. Second graders, for example, can create these words using the letters in *weather: a, at, we, he, the, are, art, ear, eat, hat, her, hear, here, hate, heart, wheat, there,* and *where.*

Learn more about making words and other instructional procedures discussed in this chapter on the DVD that accompanies this text.

Figure 4–7   The 100 Most Frequently Used Words

A		B		C		D E	
a	and	back		came		day	
about	are	be		can		did	
after	around	because		could		didn't	
all	as	but				do	
am	at	by				don't	
an						down	

F G		H		I J		K L	
for		had	his	I	is	know	
from		have	home	if	it	like	
get		he	house	in	just	little	
got		her	how	into			
		him					

M N		O		P Q R		S	
man	no	of	our	people		said	
me	not	on	out	put		saw	
mother	now	one	over			school	
my		or				see	
						she	
						so	
						some	

T		U V		W X		Y Z	
that	think	up		was	when	you	
the	this	us		we	who	your	
them	time	very		well	will		
then	to			went	with		
there	too			were	would		
they	two			what			
things							

Teachers often choose words from thematic units for making words activities. For example, during a unit on the American Revolution, a fifth-grade teacher chose the word *revolutionary,* and the students spelled these words:

1-letter words: I, a

2-letter words: it, in, on, an, at, to

3-letter words: lay, are, not, run, ran, oil, via, toy, tie, lie, urn, lye, rye, our, out, nut, ear, rat, lit, lot, let, vet

4-letter words: rain, tire, year, vote, only, live, love, rule, rely, your, rule, tail, near, earn, liar, turn, tear, rear, note, rate, rein, root, volt, yarn, vary, into, toil

5-letter words: learn, yearn, rerun, royal, relay, you're, early, liter, ultra, ruler, voter, lover, liver, outer, value, untie, until

6-letter words: lotion, nation, ration, turner, return, nearly, lively, tailor, revolt

9-letter words: voluntary

10-letter words: revolution

13-letter words: revolutionary

As students manipulated letter cards to spell the words, the teacher listed the words on a chart, beginning with one-letter words and adding increasingly longer words until students used all of the letters to spell *revolutionary.* The students consulted dictionaries to check the spelling of possible words and to argue (unsuccessfully) that *litter* was spelled *liter* and *volunteer* was spelled *voluntear* so that the words could be added to the chart. They manipulated many spelling patterns in this activity and reviewed prefixes and suffixes, homophones, and rhyming words. Some students were also introduced to new words, including *urn, ration, rye, yearn,* and *volt.*

Word Sorts. Students use word sorts to explore, compare, and contrast word features as they sort a pack of word cards. Teachers prepare word cards for students to sort into two or more categories according to their spelling patterns or other criteria (Bear et al., 2004). Sometimes teachers tell students what categories to use, which makes the sort a closed sort; when students determine the categories themselves, the sort is an open sort. Students can sort word cards and then return them to an envelope for future use, or they can glue the cards onto a sheet of paper. Figure 4–8 shows a word sort for four vowel patterns using words with short *a* and long *a.* In this sort, students worked with partners and sorted the words into four categories (CVC, CVCe, CVVC, and CVV).

Interactive Writing. Teachers use interactive writing to teach spelling concepts as well as other concepts about written language. Because correct spelling and legible handwriting are courtesies for readers, they emphasize correct spelling as students take turns to collaboratively write a message. It is likely that students will misspell a few words as they write, so teachers take advantage of these "teachable moments" to clarify students' misunderstandings. Through interactive writing, students learn to use a variety of resources to correct misspelled words, including classroom word walls, books, classmates, and the dictionary.

Proofreading. Proofreading is a special kind of reading that students use to locate misspelled words and other mechanical errors in rough drafts. As students learn about the writing process, they are introduced to proofreading in the editing stage. More in-depth instruction about how to use proofreading to locate spelling errors and then

Figure 4-8   **A Word Sort of Long- and Short-*a* Words**

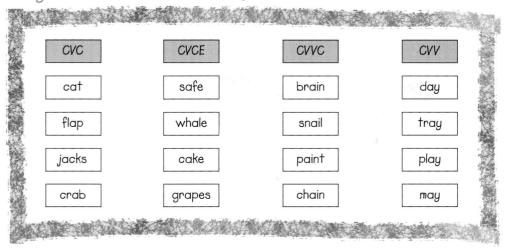

CVC	CVCE	CVVC	CVV
cat	safe	brain	day
flap	whale	snail	tray
jacks	cake	paint	play
crab	grapes	chain	may

correct these misspelled words is part of spelling instruction (Cramer, 1998). Through a series of minilessons, students can learn to proofread sample student papers and mark misspelled words. Then, working in pairs, students can correct the misspelled words.

Proofreading should be introduced in the primary grades. Young children and their teachers proofread collaborative books and dictated stories together, and students can be encouraged to read over their own compositions and make necessary corrections soon after they begin writing. This way, students accept proofreading as a natural part of writing. Proofreading activities are more valuable for teaching spelling than are dictation activities, in which teachers dictate sentences for students to write and correctly capitalize and punctuate. Few people use dictation in their daily lives, but students use proofreading skills every time they polish a piece of writing.

Dictionary Use. Students need to learn to locate the spelling of unfamiliar words in the dictionary. Although it is relatively easy to find a "known" word in the dictionary, it is hard to locate unfamiliar words, and students need to learn what to do when they do not know how to spell a word. One approach is to predict possible spellings for unknown words, then check the most probable spellings in a dictionary.

Students should be encouraged to check the spellings of words in a dictionary as well as to use dictionaries to check multiple meanings of a word or its etymology. Too often, students view consulting a dictionary as punishment; teachers must work to change this view of dictionary use. One way to do this is to appoint some students in the classroom as dictionary checkers: These students keep dictionaries on their desks, and they are consulted whenever questions about spelling, word meaning, and word usage arise.

Spelling Options. In English, there are alternate spellings for many sounds because so many words borrowed from other languages retain their native spellings. There are many more options for vowel sounds than for consonants; Figure 4–9 lists common spelling options for vowels. Even so, there are four spelling options for /f/ (*f, ff, ph, gh*). Spelling options sometimes vary according to the letter's position in the word. For example, *ff* is found in the middle and at the end of words but not at the beginning (e.g., *muffin, cuff*), and *gh* represents /f/ only at the end of a syllable or word (e.g., *cough, laughter*).

Teachers point out spelling options as they write words on word walls and when students ask about the spelling of a word. They also can use a series of minilessons to

Figure 4-9	Spelling Options for Vowels	
Sound	**Spellings**	**Examples**
long *a*	a-e	date
	a	angel
	ai	pail
	ay	day
aw	au	caught
	aw	saw
	al	talk
	ou	bought
short *e*	e	egg
	ea	head
long *e*	ea	peach
	ee	feet
	e	be
	e-e	these
	ea-e	breathe
	ie	field
	y	baby
	ey	key
long *i*	i-e	five
	y	dry
	igh	light
	ie	pie
	i	child
short *o*	o	off
	a	all
	au	author
long *o*	o	go
	o-e	note
	ow	slow
	oa	loaf
oi	oi	boil
	oy	boy
ou	ou	out
	ow	cow
short *u*	u	put
	o	of
	oo	book
	ou	could
long *u*	u	unit
	u-e	rule
	ue	true
	ew	new
	oo	too
	o	to

Figure 4-10 Spelling Options Chart for Long *o*

Spelling	Word	Location in the Syllable		
		Initial	Medial	Final
o	oh, obedient	x		
	go, no, so			x
o-e	home, pole		x	
ow	own	x		
	known		x	
	blow, elbow, yellow			x
oa	oaf, oak, oat	x		
	boat, groan		x	
ew	sew			x
ol	yolk, folk		x	
oe	toe			x
ough	though			x
eau	beau			x
ou	bouquet		x	

teach upper-grade students about these options. During each lesson, students can focus on one phoneme, such as /f/ or /ar/, and as a class or small group they can develop a list of the various ways the sound is spelled, giving examples of each spelling. A sixth-grade chart on long *o* is presented in Figure 4–10.

Weekly Spelling Tests

Many teachers question the usefulness of spelling tests to teach spelling, because research on invented spelling suggests that spelling is best learned through reading and writing (Gentry & Gillet, 1993; Wilde, 1992). In addition, teachers complain that lists of spelling words are unrelated to the words students are reading and writing and that the 30 minutes of valuable instructional time spent each day in completing spelling textbook activities is excessive. Even so, parents and school board members value spelling tests as evidence that spelling is being taught. Weekly spelling tests, when they are used, should be individualized so that children learn to spell the words they need for their writing.

In the individualized approach to spelling instruction, students choose the words they will study, many of which are words they use in their writing projects. Students study 5 to 10 specific words during the week using a study strategy; this approach places more responsibility on students for their own learning. Teachers develop a weekly word list of 20 or more words of varying difficulty from which students select words to study. Words for the master list include high-frequency words, words from the word wall related to literature focus units and thematic units, and words students needed for their writing projects during the previous week. Words from spelling textbooks can also be added to the list.

On Monday, the teacher administers a pretest using the master list of words, and students spell as many of the words as they can. Students correct their own pretests, and from the words they misspell they create individual spelling lists. They make two copies of their study list, using the numbers on the master list to make it easier to take the final test on Friday. Students use one copy of the list for study activities, and the teacher keeps the second copy.

Students spend approximately 5 to 10 minutes studying the words on their study lists each day during the week. Research shows that instead of "busy-work" activities such as using their spelling words in sentences or gluing yarn in the shape of the words, it is more effective for students to use this study strategy:

1. Look at the word and say it to yourself.
2. Say each letter in the word to yourself.
3. Close your eyes and spell the word to yourself.
4. Write the word, and check that you spelled it correctly.
5. Write the word again and check that you spelled it correctly.

This strategy focuses on the whole word rather than on breaking the word apart into sounds or syllables. Teachers explain how to use the strategy during a minilesson at the beginning of the school year and then post a copy of the strategy in the classroom. In addition to this study strategy, sometimes students trade word lists on Wednesday or Thursday and give each other a practice test.

A final test is administered on Friday. The teacher reads the master list, and students write only those words they have practiced during the week. To make it easier to administer the test, students first list the numbers of the words they have practiced from their study lists on their test papers. Any words that students misspell should be included on their lists the following week.

This individualized approach is recommended instead of a textbook approach. Typically, textbooks are arranged in weeklong units, with lists of 10 to 20 words and practice activities that often require at least 30 minutes per day to complete. Research indicates that only 60 to 75 minutes per week should be spent on spelling instruction, because greater periods of time do not result in increased spelling ability (Johnson, Langford, & Quorn, 1981).

What Is the Controversy About Spelling Instruction?

Complete a self-assessment to check your understanding of the concepts presented in this chapter on the Companion Website at *www.prenhall.com/ tompkins*

The press and concerned parent groups periodically raise questions about invented spelling and the importance of weekly spelling tests. There is a misplaced public perception that today's children cannot spell: Researchers who have examined the types of errors students make have noted that the number of misspellings increases in grades 1 through 4, as students write longer compositions, but that the percentage of errors decreases. The percentage continues to decline in the upper grades, although some students continue to make errors (Taylor & Kidder, 1988).

Review: How Effective Teachers Assist Students in "Cracking the Code"

1. Teachers teach students to "crack the code" through phonemic awareness, phonics, and spelling instruction.

2. Teachers understand that phonemic awareness is the foundation for phonics instruction.

3. Teachers develop students' phonemic awareness using songs, rhymes, and wordplay books as well as more structured minilessons.

4. Teachers teach students to segment and blend sounds in words orally and then to apply these strategies in reading and writing.

5. Teachers teach the high-utility phonics concepts, skills, and generalizations.

6. Teachers encourage students to apply what they know about phonics through invented spelling.

7. Teachers analyze students' spelling errors as a measure of their understanding of phonics.

8. Teachers recognize that daily reading and writing experiences contribute to students' spelling development.

9. Teachers teach minilessons on spelling using words from students' reading and writing.

10. Teachers may use spelling tests, but only as part of the spelling program.

Professional References

Adams, M. J. (1990). *Beginning to read: Thinking and learning about print*. Cambridge, MA: MIT Press.

Armbruster, B. B., Lehr, F., & Osborn, J. (2001). *Put reading first: The research building blocks for teaching children to read*. Urbana, IL: Center for the Improvement of Early Reading Achievement.

Bear, D. R., Invernizzi, M., Templeton, S., & Johnston, F. (2004). *Words their way: Word study for phonics, vocabulary, and spelling instruction*. Upper Saddle River, NJ: Merrill/Prentice Hall.

Clay, M. M. (1985). *The early detection of reading difficulties* (3rd ed.). Portsmouth, NH: Heinemann.

Clymer, T. (1963). The utility of phonic generalizations in the primary grades. *The Reading Teacher, 16*, 252–258.

Cooper, J. D., & Pikulski, J. J. (2003). *Houghton Mifflin reading* (California ed.). Boston: Houghton Mifflin.

Cramer, R. L. (1998). *The spelling connection: Integrating reading, writing, and spelling instruction*. New York: Guilford Press.

Cunningham, P. M. (1999). What should we do about phonics? In L. B. Gambrell, L. M. Morrow, S. B. Neuman, & M. Pressley (Eds.), *Best practices in literacy instruction* (pp. 68–89). New York: Guilford Press.

Cunningham, P. M. (2000). *Phonics they use: Words for reading and writing* (3rd ed.). New York: Longman.

Cunningham, P. M., & Cunningham, J. W. (1992). Making words: Enhancing the invented spelling-decoding connection. *The Reading Teacher, 46*, 106–115.

Cunningham, P. M., & Cunningham, J. W. (2002). What we know about how to teach phonics. In A. E. Farstrup & S. J. Samuels (Eds.), *What research has to say about reading instruction* (3rd ed., pp. 87–109). Newark, DE: International Reading Association.

Dahl, K. L., Scharer, P. L., Lawson, L. L., & Grogan, P. R. (2001). *Rethinking phonics: Making the best teaching decisions*. Portsmouth, NH: Heinemann.

Freppon, P. A., & Dahl, K. L. (1991). Learning about phonics in a whole language classroom. *Language Arts, 68*, 190–197.

Gentry, J. R., & Gillet, J. W. (1993). *Teaching kids to spell*. Portsmouth, NH: Heinemann.

Griffith, F., & Olson, M. (1992). Phonemic awareness helps beginning readers break the code. *The Reading Teacher, 45*, 516–523.

Griffith, P. L. (1991). Phonemic awareness helps first graders invent spellings and third graders remember correct spellings. *Journal of Reading Behavior, 23*, 215–232.

Gunning, T. G. (1995). Word building: A strategic approach to the teaching of phonics. *The Reading Teacher, 48*, 484–488.

Hanna, P. R., Hanna, J. S., Hodges, R. E., & Rudorf, E. H. (1966). *Phoneme-grapheme correspondences as cues to spelling improvement*. Washington, DC: US Government Printing Office.

Henderson, E. H. (1990). *Teaching spelling* (2nd ed.). Boston: Houghton Mifflin.

Horn, E. (1926). *A basic writing vocabulary*. Iowa City: University of Iowa Press.

Horn, E. (1957). Phonetics and spelling. *Elementary School Journal, 57*, 233–235, 246.

Ivey, G., & Baker, M. I. (2004). Phonics instruction for older students? Just say no. *Educational Leadership, 61*(6), 35–39.

Johnson, T. D., Langford, K. G., & Quorn, K. C. (1981). Characteristics of an effective spelling program. *Language Arts, 58*, 581–588.

Juel, C., Griffith, P. L., & Gough, P. B. (1986). Acquisition of literacy: A longitudinal study of children in first and second grade. *Journal of Educational Psychology, 78,* 243–255.

Klesius, J. P., Griffith, P. L., & Zielonka, P. (1991). A whole language and traditional instruction comparison: Overall effectiveness and development of the alphabetic principle. *Reading Research and Instruction, 30,* 47–61.

Lewkowicz, N. K. (1994). The bag game: An activity to heighten phonemic awareness. *The Reading Teacher, 47,* 508–509.

Lomax, R. G., & McGee, L. M. (1987). Young children's concepts about print and meaning: Toward a model of word reading acquisition. *Reading Research Quarterly, 22,* 237–256.

McCarrier, A., Pinnell, G. S., & Fountas, I. C. (2000). *Interactive writing: How language and literacy come together, K–2.* Portsmouth, NH: Heinemann.

McGee, L. M., & Richgels, D. J. (1989). "K is Kristen's": Learning the alphabet from a child's perspective. *The Reading Teacher, 43,* 216–225.

Mills, H., O'Keefe, T., & Stephens, D. (1992). *Looking closely: Exploring the role of phonics in one whole language classroom.* Urbana, IL: National Council of Teachers of English.

National Reading Panel. (2000). *Teaching children to read: An evidence-based assessment of the scientific research literature on reading and its implications for reading instruction.* Washington, DC: National Institute of Child Health and Human Development.

Read, C. (1971). Pre-school children's knowledge of English phonology. *Harvard Educational Review, 41,* 1–34.

Read, C. (1975). *Children's categorization of speech sounds in English* (NCTE Research Report No. 17). Urbana, IL: National Council of Teachers of English.

Read, C. (1986). *Children's creative spelling.* London: Routledge & Kegan Paul.

Shefelbine, J. (1995). *Learning and using phonics in beginning reading* (Literacy research paper; volume 10). New York: Scholastic.

Snow, C., Burns, M. W., & Griffin, P. (1998). *Preventing reading difficulties in young children.* Washington, DC: National Academy Press.

Strickland, D. S. (1998). *Teaching phonics today: A primer for educators.* Newark, DE: International Reading Association.

Taylor, K. K., & Kidder, E. B. (1988). The development of spelling skills: From first grade through eighth grade. *Written Communication, 5,* 222–244.

Templeton, S. (1983). Using the spelling/meaning connection to develop word knowledge in older students. *Journal of Reading, 27,* 8–14.

Tompkins, G. E., & Collom, S. (2004). *Sharing the pen: Interactive writing with young children.* Upper Saddle River, NJ: Merrill/Prentice Hall.

Tompkins, G. E., & Yaden, D. B., Jr. (1986). *Answering students' questions about words.* Urbana, IL: ERIC Clearinghouse on Reading and Communication Skills and National Council of Teachers of English.

Treiman, R. (1985). Onsets and rimes as units of spoken syllables: Evidence from children. *Journal of Experimental Child Psychology, 39,* 161–181.

Tunmer, W., & Nesdale, A. (1985). Phonemic segmentation skill and beginning reading. *Journal of Educational Psychology, 77,* 417–427.

Venezky, R. L. (1999). *The American way of spelling: The structure and origins of American English orthography.* New York: Guilford Press.

Wilde, S. (1992). *You kan red this! Spelling and punctuation for whole language classrooms, K–6.* Portsmouth, NH: Heinemann.

Wylie, R. E., & Durrell, D. D. (1970). Teaching vowels through phonograms. *Elementary English, 47,* 787–791.

Yopp, H. K. (1985). Phoneme segmentation ability: A prerequisite for phonics and sight word achievement in beginning reading? In J. Niles & R. Lalik (Eds.), *Issues in literacy: A research perspective* (pp. 330–336). Rochester, NY: National Reading Conference.

Yopp, H. K. (1988). The validity and reliability of phonemic awareness tests. *Reading Research Quarterly, 23,* 159–177.

Yopp, H. K. (1992). Developing phonemic awareness in young children. *The Reading Teacher, 45,* 696–703.

Yopp, H. K. (1995). Read-aloud books for developing phonemic awareness: An annotated bibliography. *The Reading Teacher, 48,* 538–542.

Yopp, H. K., & Yopp, R. H. (2000). Supporting phonemic awareness development in the classroom. *The Reading Teacher, 54,* 130–143.

Children's Book References

Hutchins, P. (1976). *Don't forget the bacon!* New York: Mulberry Books.

Most, B. (1996). *Cock-a-doodle-moo!* San Diego: Harcourt Brace.

Obligado, L. (1983). *Faint frogs feeling feverish and other terrifically tantalizing tongue twisters.* New York: Puffin.

Osborne, M. P. (1993). *Mummies in the morning.* New York: Random House.

Park, B. (1993). *Junie B. Jones and her big fat mouth.* New York: Scholastic.

Prelutsky, J. (1982). *The baby uggs are hatching.* New York: Mulberry Books.

Sendak, M. (1963). *Where the wild things are.* New York: Harper & Row.

Seuss, Dr. (1963). *Hop on pop.* New York: Random House.

Seuss, Dr. (1965). *Fox in socks.* New York: Random House.

Shaw, N. (1986). *Sheep in a jeep.* Boston: Houghton Mifflin.

Developing Fluent Readers and Writers

- Why do students need to learn to read and write high-frequency words?
- What strategies do students learn to use to recognize and spell unfamiliar words?
- How do students become fluent readers?
- How do students become fluent writers?
- Why is fluency important?

Ms. Williams's Students Learn High-Frequency Words

Ms. Williams's second graders are studying hermit crabs and their tide pool environments. A plastic habitat box sits in the center of each grouping of desks, and a hermit crab is living in each box. As students care for their crustaceans, they observe the crabs. They have examined hermit crabs up close using magnifying glasses and identified the body parts. Ms. Williams helped them draw a diagram of a hermit crab on a large chart and label the body parts. They have compared hermit crabs to true crabs and examined their exoskeletons. They have also learned how to feed hermit crabs, how to get them to come out of their shells, and how they molt. And, they've conducted experiments to determine whether hermit crabs prefer wet or dry environments.

These second graders are using reading and writing as tools for learning. Eric Carle's *A House for Hermit Crab* (1987) is the featured book for this unit. Ms. Williams has read it aloud to students several times, and students are rereading it at the listening center. *Moving Day* (Kaplan, 1996), *Pagoo* (Holling, 1990), and other story books and informational books, including *Hermit Crabs* (Pohl, 1987) and *Tide Pool* (Greenaway, 1992), are available on a special shelf in the classroom li-

brary. Ms. Williams has read some of the
books aloud to students, and others they listen to at the listening center or read independently
or with buddies. Students make charts about hermit crabs
that they post in the classroom, and they write about hermit crabs in learning logs.
One log entry is shown on the next page.

Ms. Williams and her students also write many interesting and important vocabulary words related to hermit crabs that they learn about on a word wall made on
a sheet of butcher paper. They write these words on their word wall:

coral	larvae	sea urchins
crustacean	molting	seaweed
eggs	pebbles	shells
enemies	pincers	shrimp
exoskeleton	regeneration	snails
lantern fish	scavenger	starfish
larva	sea anemone	tide pool

Then students refer to these words as they write about hermit crabs, and Ms. Williams
uses them for various reading activities. This word wall will be displayed in the classroom only during the unit on hermit crabs.

Ms. Williams integrates many components of reading instruction, including
word recognition and fluency activities, into the unit on hermit crabs. To develop her
second graders' ability to recognize many high-frequency words, she uses another
word wall. This word wall is different from the hermit crab word wall, which contains only words related to these ocean animals. Her high-frequency word wall is a
brightly colored alphabet quilt with 26 blocks, one for each letter of the alphabet.
The most common words are written on small cards and displayed permanently on
one wall of the classroom.

At the beginning of the school year, Ms. Williams and her students posted on
the word wall the 70 high-frequency words that they were familiar with from first
grade. Then each week, Ms. Williams adds three to five new words. At first, the words
she chose were from her list of the 100 highest-frequency words, and after finishing
that list, she has begun choosing words from a list of the second 100 high-frequency
words. She doesn't introduce the words in the order that they are presented in the
list, but rather chooses words that she can connect to units and words that students
misspell in their writing.

This week, Ms. Williams adds *soon, house, your,* and *you're* to the word wall.
She chooses *soon* and *house* because these words are used in *A House for Hermit
Crab* and several students have recently asked her how to spell *house*. She chooses
the homophones *your* and *you're* because students are confusing and misspelling
these two words. She also has noticed that some students are confused about contractions, so she plans to review contractions, using *you're* as an example.

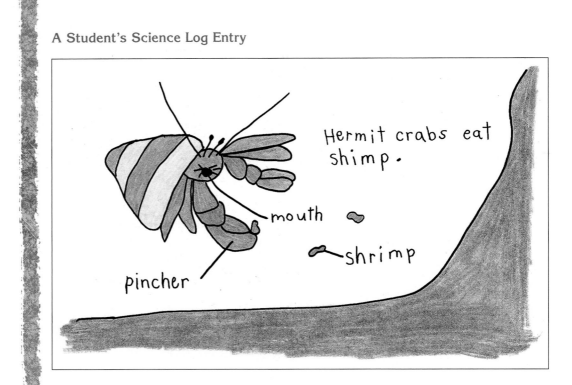

Ms. Williams has her students sit on the floor near the word wall to introduce and post the words on the word wall. She uses a cookie sheet and large magnetic letters to introduce each new word. She explains that two of the new words—*house* and *soon*—are from *A House for Hermit Crab*. She scrambles the letters at the bottom of the cookie sheet and slowly builds the new word at the top of the sheet as students guess the word. She begins with *h*, adds the *ou*, and several children call out "house." Ms. Williams continues adding letters, and when they are all in place, a chorus of voices says, "house." Then Kari places the new word card in the *H* square of the word wall, and students chant and clap as they say the word and spell it. Ms. Williams begins, "House, house, h-o-u-s-e," and students echo her chant. Then she calls on Enrique to begin the chant, and students echo him. Then Ms. Williams repeats the procedure with the three remaining words.

The next day, Ms. Williams and her students use interactive writing to compose sentences using each of the new words. They write:

> *The hermit crab has a good shell for a <u>house</u>. He likes it but <u>soon</u> he will move. "<u>You're</u> too small for me," he says. "I have to move, but I will always be <u>your</u> friend."*

Students take turns writing these sentences on a chart, and after rereading the sentences, they underline the four new words. Each week, the students write sentences using the new word wall words on this chart. Ms. Williams and the students often reread the sentences they've written during previous weeks.

The next day, after students practice the word wall words, Ms. Williams takes a few minutes to review contractions so that the students understand that *you're* is a contraction of *you* and *are* and that the apostrophe indicates that a letter has been omitted. Then students volunteer other contractions. Michael identifies three: *I'm, can't,* and *don't.* The students use interactive writing to make a chart of contractions:

Check the Compendium of Instructional Procedures, which follows Chapter 14, for more information on highlighted terms.

They list the contractions and the two words that make up each one. Ms. Williams explains that she'll put the chart in the word work center and that students can use the information to make books about contractions.

After this practice with high-frequency words, students participate in activities at literacy centers while Ms. Williams meets with guided reading groups. Most of the center activities relate to the unit on hermit crabs and Eric Carle's book *A House for Hermit Crab*, but students also practice reading and writing high-frequency words at two of the centers. The eight literacy centers in Ms. Williams's classroom are described in the box below.

Each morning, a sixth-grade student aide comes to the classroom to monitor students' work at the centers and provide assistance as needed. Ms. Williams worked with two sixth-grade teachers to train 10 students to serve as student aides, and these students come to the classroom once every week or two on a rotating basis.

Ms. Williams's Literacy Centers

1. Retelling Center
Students use pictures and labels with the month of the year to sequence the events in the book and retell the story.

2. Science Center
Children observe a hermit crab and make notes in their learning logs about its physical characteristics and eating habits.

3. Word Work Center
Children use magnetic letters to spell the four high-frequency words—*house, soon, your,* and *you're*—and the words from the last 2 weeks. They also make a book of contractions with picture and sentence examples.

4. Listening Center
Children use headphones to listen to an informational book on hermit crabs read aloud.

5. Word Wall Center
Children practice reading the word wall using pointers. Then they take a clipboard and a sheet of paper divided into 10 sections; the letters spelling h-e-r-m-i-t c-r-a-b have been written in the sections. Then children choose two words from the word wall beginning with each letter to write in each section on their papers.

6. Writing Center
Children write "I Am a Hermit Crab" poems following the model posted at the center. They also write and illustrate other books about hermit crabs.

7. Word Sort Center
Children sort vocabulary words from *A House for Hermit Crab* according to category. For example, months of the year are put in one category and ocean animals and plants in another.

8. Library Center
Children practice reading leveled books at their individual levels and other books about hermit crabs and the ocean that are placed on a special shelf in the classroom library. Ms. Williams includes *Moving Day* (Kaplan, 1996) (Level 7), *Hermit Crab* (Randell, 1994) (Level 8), and *Hermit's Shiny Shell* (Tuchman, 1997) (Level 10), three familiar books about hermit crabs, for students to reread.

The second graders keep track of their work in centers using small booklets with eight sheets of paper that Ms. Williams calls their "center passports." The student aide marks their passports with stickers or stamps at each center after they finish the assignment, and students leave their written work in a basket at the center.

As a culminating activity, Ms. Williams and her students write a retelling of *A House for Hermit Crab.* The students compose the text, and Ms. Williams uses the Language Experience Approach to write their rough draft on chart paper so that everyone can see it. Students learn revision strategies as they fine-tune their retelling, and then Ms. Williams types the text on five sheets of paper, duplicates copies, and compiles a booklet for each student. Students each receive a copy of the booklet to read. They also add illustrations. Later they will take their booklets home to read to their families.

Ms. Williams reads their retelling aloud as students follow along, and then students join in the reading. Children do choral reading as they read in small groups, with classmates sitting at the same grouping of desks. The numbers on the left side indicate which group of students reads each sentence. As students read and reread the text aloud, they become increasingly fluent readers. Here is the last section of the class's retelling:

1	*Soon it was January.*
2	*Hermit Crab moved out of his house and the little crab moved in.*
3	*"Goodbye," said Hermit Crab.*
	"Be good to my friends."
4	*Soon Hermit Crab saw the perfect house.*
5	*It was a big, empty shell.*
1	*It looked a little plain but Hermit Crab didn't care.*
2	*He will decorate it*
3	*with sea urchins,*
4	*with sea anemones,*
5	*with coral,*
1	*with starfish,*
2	*with snails.*
ALL	*So many possibilities!*

The underlined words are high-frequency words that are posted on the word wall in Ms. Williams's classroom. Of the 68 words in this excerpt, 37 are high-frequency words! Also, two of the new words for this week, *soon* and *house,* are used twice.

Visit Chapter 5 on the Companion Website at *www.prenhall.com/ tompkins* to check into your state's standards for word identification and fluency.

As students learn to read, they move from word-by-word reading with little or no expression to fluent reading. Fluency is the ability to read quickly and with expression, and to read fluently, students must be able to recognize many, many words automatically. By third grade, most students have moved from word-by-word reading into fluent reading, but 10–15% have difficulty learning to recognize words, and their learning to read is slowed (Allington, 1998). Fluency is an important component of reading instruction, especially in the primary grades, because fluent readers are more successful than less fluent readers (National Reading Panel, 2000). The difference is that fluent readers have more cognitive resources available for com-

How Fluency Fits Into a Balanced Literacy Program

Component	Description
Reading	Students need to become fluent readers by third grade; that is, they need to be able to recognize words automatically and to read quickly and with expression.
Phonics and Other Skills	Phonics is an important word-identification strategy because most words can be at least partly sounded out.
Strategies	Students learn to use four word-identification strategies—phonic analysis, analogies, syllabic analysis, and morphemic analysis.
Vocabulary	Students learn to read high-frequency words and use word-identification strategies to identify unfamiliar vocabulary.
Comprehension	Fluent readers are better able to comprehend what they read because they can identify words easily.
Literature	As students read literature, their focus should be on comprehending and responding, but that is possible only when they are fluent readers.
Content-Area Study	As students read content-area textbooks and informational books, their focus should be on remembering big ideas and making connections, but that is possible only when they are fluent readers.
Oral Language	Talking and listening are not important components of fluency.
Writing	Students become fluent writers so that they can express ideas quickly and easily.
Spelling	Students learn to spell high-frequency words and use word-identification strategies to spell other words.

prehension. The feature on this page shows the role of fluency in a balanced literacy program.

Students become fluent readers through a combination of instruction and lots of reading experience. Through systematic phonics instruction, students learn how to identify unfamiliar words; as they read and reread hundreds of books during the primary grades, these words become familiar and students learn to recognize them automatically. They also learn increasingly sophisticated strategies for identifying the unfamiliar words, including syllabic and morphemic analysis, in which they break words into syllables and into root words and affixes.

At the same time students are becoming fluent readers, they are also becoming fluent writers. Through phonics instruction and lots of writing practice, students learn to spell many words automatically, apply capitalization and punctuation rules, and develop writing speed. They also develop strategies for spelling longer, multisyllabic words. Developing fluency is just as important for writers because both readers and writers must be able to focus on meaning, not identifying and spelling words.

TEACHING STUDENTS TO READ AND WRITE WORDS

Teachers have two goals as they teach students to read and write words. The first is to teach students to instantly recognize a group of several hundred high-frequency words. Students need to be able to read and write these words automatically, a goal they usually accomplish by second or third grade. The second is to equip students with strategies such as syllabic analysis that they can use to identify unfamiliar words—often longer, multisyllabic words they come across during reading and need to spell during writing. Students learn and refine their use of these strategies between kindergarten and eigth grade.

Word Recognition

Students need to develop a large stock of words that they recognize instantly and automatically because it is impossible for them to analyze every word that they encounter when reading or want to spell when writing; these recognizable words are called *sight words*. Through repeated reading and writing experiences, students develop automaticity, the ability to quickly recognize words they read and know how to spell words they are writing (LaBerge & Samuels, 1976). The vital element in word recognition is learning each word's unique letter sequence; this knowledge about the sequence of letters is useful as students learn to spell. At the same time they are becoming fluent readers, students are also becoming fluent writers and are learning to spell the words they write most often. Hitchcock (1989) found that by third grade, most students spell 90% of the words they use correctly.

High-Frequency Words. The most common words that readers and writers use again and again are high-frequency words. There have been numerous attempts to identify specific lists of these words and to calculate their frequency in reading materials. Pinnell and Fountas (1998, p. 89) identified these 24 common words that kindergartners need to learn to recognize:

a	at	he	it	no	the
am	can	I	like	see	to
an	do	in	me	she	up
and	go	is	my	so	we

For a list of the 100 high-frequency words, see Chapter 4, "Cracking the Alphabetic Code." Children learn to both read and spell these words during the primary grades.

The 24 words are part of the 100 most commonly used words, which account for more than half of the words children read and write. Children learn the rest of these 100 words in first grade. Eldredge (2005) has identified the 300 highest-frequency words used in first-grade basal readers and trade books found in first-grade classrooms; these 300 words account for 72% of the words that beginning readers read. Figure 5–1 presents Eldredge's list of 300 high-frequency words; the 100 most commonly used words are marked with an asterisk.

It is essential that children learn to read and write high-frequency words, but many of these words are difficult to learn because they cannot be easily decoded (Cunningham, 2000): Try sounding out *to, what,* and *could* and you will see why they are called *sight words.* Because these words can't be decoded easily, it is crucial that children learn to recognize them instantly and automatically. A further complication is that many of

Figure 5-1 The 300 High-Frequency Words

*a	children	great	looking	ran	through
*about	city	green	made	read	*time
*after	come	grow	make	red	*to
again	*could	*had	*man	ride	toad
*all	couldn't	hand	many	right	together
along	cried	happy	may	road	told
always	dad	has	maybe	room	*too
*am	dark	hat	*me	run	took
*an	*day	*have	mom	*said	top
*and	*did	*he	more	sat	tree
animals	*didn't	head	morning	*saw	truck
another	*do	hear	*mother	say	try
any	does	heard	mouse	*school	*two
*are	dog	help	Mr.	sea	under
*around	*don't	hen	Mrs.	*see	until
*as	door	*her	much	*she	*up
asked	*down	here	must	show	*us
*at	each	hill	*my	sister	*very
ate	eat	*him	name	sky	wait
away	end	*his	need	sleep	walk
baby	even	*home	never	small	walked
*back	ever	*house	new	*so	want
bad	every	*how	next	*some	wanted
ball	everyone	*I	nice	something	*was
*be	eyes	I'll	night	soon	water
bear	far	I'm	*no	started	way
*because	fast	*if	*not	stay	*we
bed	father	*in	nothing	still	*well
been	find	inside	*now	stop	*went
before	fine	*into	*of	stories	*were
began	first	*is	off	story	*what
behind	fish	*it	oh	sun	*when
best	fly	it's	old	take	where
better	*for	its	*on	tell	while
big	found	jump	once	than	*who
bird	fox	jumped	*one	*that	why
birds	friend	*just	only	that's	*will
blue	friends	keep	*or	*the	wind
book	frog	king	other	their	witch
books	*from	*know	*our	*them	*with
box	fun	last	*out	*then	wizard
boy	garden	left	*over	*there	woman
brown	gave	let	*people	these	words
*but	*get	let's	picture	*they	work
*by	girl	*like	pig	thing	*would
called	give	*little	place	*things	write
*came	go	live	play	*think	yes
*can	going	long	pulled	*this	*you
can't	good	look	*put	thought	you're
cat	*got	looked	rabbit	three	*your

From *Teach Decoding: How and Why* (2nd ed., pp. 119–120), by J. L. Eldredge, © 2005. Adapted by permission of Prentice Hall, Inc., Upper Saddle River, NJ.

*The first 100 most frequently used words, as shown in Figure 4–7 on p. 141.

these words are function words in sentences and don't carry much meaning. Children find it much easier to learn to recognize *whale* than *what*, because *whale* conjures up the image of the aquatic mammal, whereas *what* is abstract. However, *what* is used much more frequently, and children need to learn to recognize it.

Children who recognize many high-frequency words are able to read more fluently than students who do not, and fluent readers are better able to understand what they are reading. Once children can read many of these words, they gain confidence in themselves as readers and begin reading books independently. Similarly, students who can spell these words are more successful writers.

Word Walls. Primary-grade teachers create word walls in their classrooms to display the high-frequency words their students are learning (Cunningham, 2000), as Ms. Williams did in the vignette at the beginning of the chapter. Some teachers use butcher paper or squares of construction paper for the word wall, and others use large pocket charts that they divide into sections for each letter of the alphabet. Word walls should be placed in a large, accessible location in the classroom so that new words can be added easily and all students can see the words.

Teachers prepare word walls at the beginning of the school year and then add words to them each week. Kindergarten teachers often begin the year by listing students' names on the word wall and then add the 24 highest-frequency words, one or two words per week, during the school year. First-grade teachers often begin with the 24 highest-frequency words already on the word wall at the beginning of the year, and then add two to five words each week during the school year. Figure 5–2 presents a first-grade word wall with just over 100 words that were added during the school year. In second grade, teachers often begin the year with the easier half of the high-frequency words already on the word wall, and they add 50 to 75 more words during the school year. Third-grade teachers often test their students' knowledge of the 100 high-frequency words at the beginning of the year, add to the word wall those words that students cannot read and write, and then continue with words from the next 200 high-frequency words.

Teachers can create word walls for older students, too. To assist struggling readers, teachers can post the 100 high-frequency words or some of the 300 high-frequency words on a word wall in the classroom, or they can make individual word walls for these students. Teachers can type up a list of words in alphabetical order and duplicate copies to cut into bookmarks, to glue on a file folder, or to make personal dictionaries. Teachers who work with students who read and write on grade level can also make word walls to display more difficult common words. Figure 5–3 presents a list of 100 common words that fourth- through eighth-grade students need to learn. Some of the words, such as *himself, finally,* and *remember,* are more appropriate for fourth and fifth graders, and others, such as *independent, foreign,* and *throughout,* are more appropriate for sixth through eighth graders. These are commonly used words that students often misspell or confuse with other words.

Teachers carefully select the words they introduce each week. They choose words that students are familiar with and use in conversation. The selected words should have appeared in books students are reading or been introduced in guided reading lessons, or they should be words that students have misspelled in interactive writing activities or in other writing activities. Even though the words are listed alphabetically in Figures 5–2 and 5–3, they should not be taught in that order; in the vignette, for example, Ms. Williams chose *soon* and *house* from *A House for Hermit Crab* and the homophones *your* and *you're,* which students were confusing in their writing.

Teaching high-frequency words is not easy, because most of the words are functional words. Many words are abstract and have little or no meaning when they are

Learn more about word walls and other instructional procedures discussed in this chapter on the DVD that accompanies this text.

Figure 5–2   A First-Grade Word Wall

A	B	C	D	E
a are	be	call	did	each
about as	been	called	didn't	eat
after at	boy	can	do	
all	but	can't	does	
am	by	come	don't	
and		could	down	

F	G	H	I	J K
find	get	had him	I	just
first	go	has his	if	know
for	good	have how	in	
from		he	into	
		her	is	
		here	it	

L	M	N	O	P Q R
like	made must	no	of other	people
little	make my	not	on our	pretty
long	may	now	one out	
look	me		only over	
	more		or	

S	T	U V	W	X Y Z
said	than there	up	was where	you
saw	that these	us	water which	your
see	the they	very	way who	
she	their this		we will	
so	them to		were with	
some	then two		what words	
should			when would	

read or written in isolation. Cunningham (2000) recommends this procedure for practicing the words being placed on the word wall:

1. ***Introduce the word or words in context.*** The words can be presented in the context of a book students are familiar with or by using pictures or objects. For example, to introduce the words *for* and *from*, teachers might bring in a box gift wrapped and tied with a bow, and with an attached gift tag labeled "for" and "from." Then teachers pass out extra gift tags they have made, and students read the words *for* and *from* and briefly talk about gifts they have given and received. Teachers also clarify that *for* is not the number *four* and show students where the number *four* is written on the number chart posted in the classroom.

2. ***Have students chant and clap the spelling of the words.*** Teachers introduce the new word cards that will be placed on the word wall and read the words. Then they begin a chant, "For, for, f-o-r," and clap their hands. Then students repeat the

Figure 5-3   100 High-Frequency Words for Older Students

A	B	C	D	E
a lot	beautiful	caught	decided	either
again	because	certain	desert-dessert	embarrassed
all right	belief	close-clothes	different	enough
although	believe	committee	discussed	especially
another	beneath	complete	doesn't	etc.
anything	between			everything
around	board-bored			everywhere
	breathe			excellent
	brought			experience

F G	H	I J	K	L
familiar	hear-here	immediately	knew-new	language
favorite	heard-herd	interesting	know-no	lying
field	height	it's-its	knowledge	
finally	herself			
foreign	himself			
friends	humorous			
frighten	hungry			

M	N	O	P	Q R
maybe	necessary	once	particular	quiet-quite
	neighbor	ourselves	people	really
			piece-peace	receive
			please	recommend
			possible	remember
			probably	restaurant
				right-write

S	T	U V	W	X Y Z
safety	their-there-they're	until	weight	your-you're
school	themselves	usually	were	
separate	though		we're	
serious	thought		where	
since	threw-through		whether	
special	throughout		whole-hole	
something	to-two-too			
success	together			

chant. After several repetitions, teachers begin a second chant, "From, from, f-r-o-m," and the students repeat the chant and clap their hands as they chant. Students practice chanting and clapping the words each day that week.

3.   *Have students practice reading and spelling the words in a word work center.* Students use white boards and magnetic letters to practice spelling the

These first graders participate in daily word wall activities. In this teacher-directed activity, the children read the high-frequency words posted on the word wall and write them on dry-erase boards. They apply phonics skills as they make up riddles about words for their classmates to guess. For example: "What word begins with /g/ and rhymes with *pet*?" Students take turns creating riddles and sharing them. One child solves the riddle, and everyone writes it on dry-erase boards. Then they hold their boards up so the teacher can check their work.

words. For practice reading the words, they can also sort word cards. For example, the words *for, from, four, fun, fish, fast, free, from, for, four, free*, and *fun* are written on cards, and students sort them into three piles: one pile for *for*, a second pile for *from*, and a third pile for all other words.

4. ***Have students apply the words they are learning in reading and writing activities.*** Because these are high-frequency words, it is likely that students will read and write them often. Teachers can also create writing opportunities through interactive writing activities.

Through this procedure, teachers make the high-frequency words more concrete, and easily confused words are clarified and practiced. Also, students have many opportunities to practice reading and writing the words.

Teaching and Assessing Word Recognition. Activities involving word walls are important ways that teachers teach word recognition; reading and writing practice are two other ways. Children develop rapid word recognition by reading words. They read words in the context of

Nurturing English Learners

Why are high-frequency words so difficult for English learners?

High-frequency words, such as *of, very*, and *do*, are difficult because they aren't meaningful. By contrast, words such as *eat* and *tree* are much easier to learn because they are more meaningful. It is usually more effective to teach high-frequency words in sentences so students can understand how the words are used in English. First, work with students to read the words in sentences taken from literature or written about the students or classroom activities, and then focus their attention on the words in isolation. Have students practice reading and writing them using magnetic letters or dry-erase boards. Finally, have students write and then read new sentences using the words. With teacher-directed practice plus independent reading and writing opportunities, students can learn high-frequency words.

stories and other books, and they read them on word lists and on word cards. Practice makes students more fluent readers and even has an impact on their comprehension. Research is inconclusive about whether it is better to have students practice reading words in context or in isolation, but most teachers prefer to have students read words in the context of stories or other books because the activity is much more authentic (I. W. Gaskins, Ehri, Cress, O'Hara, & Donnelly, 1996/1997).

A minilesson showing how a first-grade teacher focuses her students' attention on high-frequency words is presented in the feature on page 163. These first graders learn high-frequency words that come from big books they are reading. The teacher uses a whole-part-whole approach (Flood & Lapp, 1994; Trachtenburg, 1990): The students meet the words in their reading (the whole), then they study three of the high-frequency words through word work activities (the part), and then they apply what they have learned in other reading and writing activities (the whole again). The value of the whole-part-whole approach is that students understand that what they are learning will be useful in authentic literacy activities.

Students also practice word recognition through writing because they write high-frequency words again and again. For example, when first graders were studying animals, they wrote riddle books. One first grader wrote this riddle book, entitled "What Is It?":

Page 1: _It is a bird._
Page 2: _It can't fly but it can swim._
Page 3: _It is black and white._
Page 4: _It eats fish._
Page 5: _What is it?_
Page 6: _A penguin._

Of the words that the child wrote, more than half are among the 24 highest-frequency words already listed! (These words are underlined.) Students can refer to the word wall when they are writing so that they can write fluently.

Because word recognition is so important in beginning reading, children's developing word recognition should be monitored and assessed on a regular basis (Snow, Burns, & Griffin, 1998). Teachers can ask students individually to read the words posted on the word wall or read high-frequency words on word cards. Kindergartners might be tested on the list of 24 words, first graders on the list of 100 words, and second and third graders on the list of 300 words. Teachers can also monitor students' use of the high-frequency words in their writing.

Word Identification

Beginning readers encounter many words that they don't recognize immediately, and even more fluent readers come upon words that they don't recognize at once. Students use word-identification strategies to identify these unfamiliar words. Young children often depend on phonics to identify unfamiliar words, but older students develop a repertoire of strategies that use phonological information as well as semantic, syntactic, and pragmatic cues to identify words. Here are four word-identification strategies:

- Phonic analysis
- Analogies
- Syllabic analysis
- Morphemic analysis

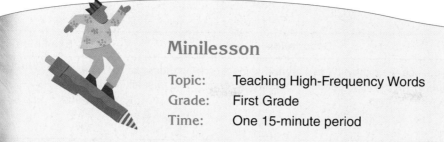

Minilesson

Topic:	Teaching High-Frequency Words
Grade:	First Grade
Time:	One 15-minute period

Miss Shapiro teaches first grade, and her goal is for her first graders to be able to read at least 75 of the 100 highest-frequency words. She has a large word wall on one wall of the classroom that is divided into sections for each letter of the alphabet. Each week, she introduces three new high-frequency words and adds them to the word wall. She chooses words from the big book she is using for shared reading. On Monday, she introduces the new words and over the next 4 days, she focuses on the new words and reviews those she has introduced previously. To make the word study more authentic, the children often hunt for the word in reading materials available in the classroom; sometimes they look in familiar big books, in small books they are rereading, on charts of familiar poems and songs, or on language experience and interactive writing charts. On other days, the children create sentences using the words, which she writes on sentence strips and displays in the classroom.

1. Introduce the Topic

"Let's read the D words on the word wall," Miss Shapiro says. As she points to the words, the class reads them aloud. "Which word is a new word this week?" she asks. The children respond, "do." Next, they read the H words and identify *here* as a new word, and then the M words and identify *my* as a new word. She asks individual children to reread the D, H, and M words on the word wall.

2. Share Examples

"Who can come up and point to our three new words for this week?" Miss Shapiro asks. Aaron eagerly comes to the word wall to point out *do, here*, and *my*. As he points to each word, Miss Shapiro writes it on the chalkboard, pronounces it, and spells it aloud. She and Aaron lead the class as they chant and clap the spelling of the three words: "Do, do, d-o, do!" "Here, here, h-e-r-e, here!" "My, my, m-y, my!"

3. Provide Information

"Let's look for *do, here*, and *my* in these books," Miss Shapiro suggests as she passes out a familiar big book to the children at each table. In each group, the students reread the book, pointing out *do, here*, and *my* each time they occur. The teacher circulates around the classroom, checking that the children notice the words.

4. Guide Practice

Miss Shapiro asks Aaron to choose three classmates to come to the chalkboard to spell the words with large magnetic letters; Daniel, Elizabeth, and Wills spell the words and read them aloud. Then Aaron passes out plastic bags with small magnetic letters and word cards to each pair of students. They read the word cards and spell the three words at their desks.

5. Assess Learning

On Friday, Miss Shapiro works with the first graders in small groups, asking them to locate the words in sentences they have written and to read the words individually on word cards.

Figure 5-4 Word-Identification Strategies

Strategy	Description	Examples
Phonic Analysis	Students use their knowledge of sound-symbol correspondences and spelling patterns to decode words when reading and to spell words when writing.	*flat* *peach* *spring* *blaze* *chin*
Analogies	Students use their knowledge of rhyming words to deduce the pronunciation or spelling of an unfamiliar word.	*creep* from *sheep* *think* from *pink* *include* from *dude*
Syllabic Analysis	Students break multisyllabic words into syllables and then use phonics and analogies to decode the word, syllable by syllable.	*cul-prit* *tem-po-rar-y* *vic-to-ry* *neg-a-tive* *sea-weed* *bi-o-de-grad-a-ble*
Morphemic Analysis	Students apply their knowledge of root words and affixes (prefixes at the beginning of the word and suffixes at the end) to identify an unfamiliar word. First they "peel off" any prefixes or suffixes and identify the root word, then they add the affixes.	*trans-port* *astro-naut* *bi-cycle* *centi-pede* *pseudo-nym* *tele-scope*

Writers use these same strategies to spell words as they write. As with reading, young children depend on phonics to spell many, many words, but as they learn more about words, they apply more of these strategies to spelling. The word-identification strategies are summarized in Figure 5–4.

Eldredge (2005) calls these strategies "interim strategies" because students use them only until they learn to recognize words automatically. For example, fourth graders may break the word *disruption* into syllables to identify the word the first time they encounter it, but with practice, they learn to recognize it automatically. And seventh graders writing a report need to spell the word *bibliography*, which they learn to spell using their knowledge of word parts: *Biblio-* is a Greek word part meaning *books*, and *-graphy*, also a Greek word part, means *writing*. In time, they will write *bibliography* without breaking it into word parts or thinking about the meaning: They will write it automatically.

Phonic Analysis. Students use what they have learned about phoneme-grapheme correspondences, phonic generalizations, and spelling patterns to decode words when they are reading and to spell words when they are writing. Even though English is not a perfectly phonetic language, phonic analysis is a very useful strategy because almost every word has some phonetically regular parts. The words *have* and *come*, for example, are considered irregular words because the vowel sounds are not predictable; however, the initial and final consonant sounds in both words are regular.

Beginning readers often try to identify words based on a partial word analysis (Gough, Juel, & Griffith, 1992): They may guess at a word using the beginning sound or look at the overall shape of the word as a clue to word identification. However, these are not effective techniques. Through phonics instruction, students learn to focus on the letter sequences in words so that they examine the entire word as they identify it (Adams, 1990).

Researchers report that the big difference between students who identify words effectively and those who do not is whether they survey the letters in the word and analyze the interior components (Stanovich, 1992; Vellutino & Scanlon, 1987). Capable readers notice all or almost all letters in a word, whereas less capable readers do not completely analyze the letter sequences of words. Struggling readers with limited phonics skills often try to decode words by sounding out the beginning sound and then making a wild guess at the word without using the cueing systems to verify their guesses (I. W. Gaskins et al., 1996/1997). And, as you might imagine, their guesses are usually wrong. Sometimes they don't even make sense in the context of the sentence.

Once students know some letter-sound sequences, the focus of phonics instruction should become using phonic analysis to decode and spell words. Here are the steps students follow in decoding an unfamiliar one-syllable word:

1. Determine the vowel sound in the word, and isolate that sound.
2. Blend all of the consonant sounds in front of the vowel sound with the vowel sound.
3. Isolate the consonant sound(s) after the vowel sound.
4. Blend the two parts of the word together so the word can be identified. (Eldredge, 2005, p. 134)

For students to use this strategy, they need to be able to identify vowels and vowel patterns in words. They also need to be able to blend sounds together to form recognizable words. For multisyllabic words, students break the word into syllables and then use the same procedure to decode each syllable. Because the location of stress in words varies, sometimes students have to try accenting different syllables to pronounce a recognizable word.

Analogies. Students identify some words by associating them with words they already know; this procedure is known as decoding by analogy (Cunningham, 1975–1976; R. W. Gaskins, Gaskins, & Gaskins, 1991). For example, when readers come to an unfamiliar word such as *lend*, they might think of *send* and figure the word out by analogy; for *cart*, they might notice the word *art* and use that to figure the word out. Students use analogy to figure out the spelling of unfamiliar words as well; students might use *cat* to help them spell *that*, for example. This strategy accounts for students' common misspelling of *they* as *thay*, because *they* rhymes with *day* and *say*.

This word-identification strategy is dependent on students' phonological knowledge. Students who can break words into onsets and rimes and substitute sounds in words are more successful than those who cannot. Moreover, researchers have found that only students who know many sight words can use this strategy because they must be able to identify patterns in familiar words to associate with those in unfamiliar words (Ehri & Robbins, 1992).

Teachers introduce this strategy when they have students read and write "word families" or rimes. Using the *-ill* family, for example, students can read or write *bill*, *chill*, *fill*, *hill*, *kill*, *mill*, *pill*, *quill*, *spill*, *still*, and *will*. Students can add inflectional endings to create even more words, including *filling*, *hills*, and *spilled*. Two-syllable words can also be created using these words: *killer*, *chilly*, and *hilltop*. Students read word cards, write the words using interactive writing, use magnetic letters to spell the words, and make rhyming word books during the primary grades to learn more about substituting beginning sounds, breaking words into parts, and spelling word parts. It is a big step, however, for students to move from these structured activities to using this strategy independently to identify unfamiliar words.

Syllabic Analysis. During the middle grades, students learn to divide words into syllables in order to read and write multisyllabic words such as *biodegradable*, *admonition*, and *unforgettable*. Once a word is divided into syllables, students use phonic analysis and analogy to pronounce or spell the word. Identifying syllable boundaries is important, because these affect the pronunciation of the vowel sound. For example, compare the vowel sound in the first syllables of *cabin* and *cable*. For *cabin*, the syllable boundary is after the *b*, whereas for *cable*, the division is before the *b*. We can predict that the *a* in *cabin* will be short because the syllable follows the CVC pattern, and that the *a* in *cable* will be long because the syllable follows the CV pattern.

The most basic rule about syllabication is that there is one vowel sound in each syllable. Consider the words *bit* and *bite*. *Bit* is a one-syllable word because there is one vowel letter representing one vowel sound. *Bite* is a one-syllable word, too, because even though there are two vowels in the word, they represent one vowel sound. *Magic* and *curfew* are two-syllable words; there is one vowel letter and sound in each syllable in *magic*, but in the second syllable of *curfew*, the two vowels *ew* represent one vowel sound. Let's try a longer word: How many syllables are in *inconvenience?* There are six vowel letters representing four sounds in four syllables.

Syllabication rules are useful in teaching students how to divide words into syllables. Five of the most useful rules are listed in Figure 5–5. These 12 two-syllable words are from *A House for Hermit Crab* (Carle, 1987), the book Ms. Williams read in the vignette at the beginning of the chapter, and they illustrate all but one of the rules:

a-round	prom-ise	her-mit
pret-ty	ur-chin	nee-dles
slow-ly	o-cean	ti-dy
with-out	cor-al	com-plain

The first two rules focus on consonants, and the last three focus on vowels. The first rule, to divide between two consonants, is the most common rule; examples from the list include *her-mit* and *pret-ty*. The second rule deals with words where three consonants appear together in a word, such as *com-plain*: The word is divided between the *m* and the *p* in order to preserve the *pl* blend. The third and fourth rules involve the VCV pattern. Usually the syllable boundary comes after the first vowel, as in *ti-dy, o-cean,* and *a-round;* however, the division comes after the consonant in *cor-al* because dividing the word *co-ral* does not produce a recognizable word. The syllable boundary comes after the consonant in *without*, too, but this compound word has easily recognizable word parts. According to the fifth rule, words such as *qui-et* are divided between the two vowels because the vowels do not represent a vowel digraph or diphthong. This rule is the least common, and there were no examples of it in the story.

Teachers use minilessons to introduce the concept of syllabication and the sylabication rules. During additional minilessons, students and teachers choose words from books students are reading and from thematic units for guided practice breaking words into syllables. After identifying syllable boundaries, students pronounce and spell the words, syllable by syllable. Teachers also mark syllable boundaries on multisyllabic words on word walls in the classroom and create center activities in which students

Figure 5–5 Syllabication Rules

Rules	Examples
1. When two consonants come between two vowels in a word, divide syllables between the consonants.	cof-fee bor-der hec-tic plas-tic jour-ney
2. When there are more than two consonants together in a word, divide syllables keeping the blends together.	em-ploy mon-ster lob-ster en-trance bank-rupt
3. When there is one consonant between two vowels in a word, divide syllables after the first vowel.	ca-jole bo-nus fau-cet plu-ral gla-cier
4. If following the third rule does not make a recognizable word, divide syllables after the consonant that comes between the vowels.	doz-en dam-age ech-o meth-od cour-age
5. When there are two vowels together that do not represent a long-vowel sound or a diphthong, divide syllables between the vowels.	cli-ent du-et po-em cha-os li-on qui-et

practice dividing words into syllables and building words using word parts. For example, after the word *compromise* came up in a social studies unit, a sixth-grade teacher developed a center activity in which students created two- and three-syllable words beginning with *com-* using syllable cards. Students created these words:

comic	compliment	common
companion	complex	computer
complete	commitment	complain
compromise	comment	compartment

After building these words, students brainstormed a list of additional words beginning with *com-* including *complement, commuter, company, communicate, compass,* and *committee.* Through this activity, students become more familiar with syllables in words and the vowel patterns in syllables.

Morphemic Analysis. Students examine the root word and affixes of longer unfamiliar words in order to identify the words. A root word is a morpheme, the basic part of a word to which affixes are added. Many words are developed from a single root word; for example, the Latin words *portare* (to carry), *portus* (harbor), and *porta* (gate) are the sources of at least 12 words: *deport*, *export*, *exporter*, *import*, *port*, *portable*, *porter*, *report*, *reporter*, *support*, *transport*, and *transportation*. Latin is the most common source of English root words; Greek and English are two other sources.

Some root words are whole words, and others are parts of words. Some root words have become free morphemes and can be used as separate words, but others cannot. For instance, the word *cent* comes from the Latin root word *cent*, meaning "hundred." English treats the word as a root word that can be used independently and in combination with affixes, as in *century*, *bicentennial*, and *centipede*. The words *cosmopolitan*, *cosmic*, and *microcosm* come from the Greek root word *cosmo*, meaning "universe"; it is not an independent root word in English. A list of Latin and Greek root words appears in Figure 5–6. English words such as *eye*, *tree*, and *water* are root words, too. New words are formed through compounding—for example, *eyelash*, *treetop*, and *waterfall*—but other English root words, such as *read*, combine with affixes, as in *reader* and *unreadable*.

Affixes are bound morphemes that are added to words and root words: Prefixes are added to the beginning of words, as in *replay*, and suffixes are added to the end of words, as in *playing*, *playful*, and *player*. Like root words, some affixes are English and others come from Latin and Greek. Affixes often change a word's meaning, such as adding *un-* to *happy* to form *unhappy*. Sometimes they change the part of speech, too; for example, when *-tion* is added to *attract* to form *attraction*, the verb *attract* becomes a noun.

There are two types of suffixes: inflectional and derivational. Inflectional suffixes are endings that indicate verb tense and person, plurals, possession, and comparison;

Root Words

This sixth-grade teacher teaches a minilesson on adding the suffixes *-able* and *-ible* to root words. The students learn that *-able* usually is added to root words that stand alone, such as *agreeable*, whereas *-ible* is added to root words that can't stand alone, such as *credible*. Next, they collect more words, including *legible* and *laughable*, from books they are reading and sort them according to suffix. Later, they'll make posters about these suffixes to hang in the classroom. These sixth graders are learning more about how the English language works, expanding their vocabularies, and practicing spelling rules.

Figure 5-6 Latin and Greek Root Words

Root	Language	Meaning	Sample Words
ann/enn	Latin	year	anniversary, annual, centennial, millennium, perennial, semiannual
arch	Greek	ruler	anarchy, archbishop, architecture, hierarchy, monarchy, patriarch
astro	Greek	star	aster, asterisk, astrology, astronaut, astronomy, disaster
auto	Greek	self	autobiography, automatic, automobile, autopsy, semiautomatic
bio	Greek	life	biography, biohazard, biology, biodegradable, bionic, biosphere
capit/capt	Latin	head	capital, capitalize, Capitol, captain, caption, decapitate, per capita
cent	Latin	hundred	bicentennial, cent, centennial, centigrade, centipede, century, percent
circ	Latin	around	circle, circular, circus, circumspect, circuit, circumference, circumstance
cosmo	Greek	universe	cosmic, cosmopolitan, microcosm
cred	Latin	believe	credit, creed, creditable, discredit, incredulity
cycl	Greek	wheel	bicycle, cycle, cyclist, cyclone, recycle, tricycle
dict	Latin	speak	contradict, dictate, dictator, prediction, verdict
graph	Greek	write	autobiography, biographer, cryptograph, epigraph, graphic, paragraph
gram	Greek	letter	cardiogram, diagram, grammar, monogram, telegram
jus/jud/jur	Latin	law	injury, injustice, judge, juror, jury, justice, justify, prejudice
lum/lus/luc	Latin	light	illuminate, lucid, luminous, luster
man	Latin	hand	manacle, maneuver, manicure, manipulate, manual, manufacture
mar/mer	Latin	sea	aquamarine, marine, maritime, marshy, mermaid, submarine
meter	Greek	measure	centimeter, diameter, seismometer, speedometer, thermometer
mini	Latin	small	miniature, minibus, minimize, minor, minimum, minuscule, minute
mort	Latin	death	immortal, mortality, mortuary, postmortem
ped	Latin	foot	biped, pedal, pedestrian, pedicure
phono	Greek	sound	earphone, microphone, phonics, phonograph, saxophone, symphony
photo	Greek	light	photograph, photographer, photosensitive, photosynthesis
pod/pus	Greek	foot	octopus, podiatry, podium, tripod
port	Latin	carry	exporter, import, port, portable, porter, reporter, support, transportation
quer/ques/quis	Latin	seek	query, quest, question, inquisitive
scope	Latin	see	horoscope, kaleidoscope, microscope, periscope, telescope
scrib/scrip	Latin	write	describe, inscription, postscript, prescribe, scribble, scribe, script
sphere	Greek	ball	atmosphere, atmospheric, hemisphere, sphere, stratosphere
struct	Latin	build	construct, construction, destruction, indestructible, instruct, reconstruct
tele	Greek	far	telecast, telegram, telegraph, telephone, telescope, telethon, television
terr	Latin	land	subterranean, terrace, terrain, terrarium, terrier, territory
vers/vert	Latin	turn	advertise, anniversary, controversial, divert, reversible, versus
vict/vinc	Latin	conquer	convince, convict, evict, invincible, victim, victor, victory
vis/vid	Latin	see	improvise, invisible, revise, supervisor, television, video, vision, visitor
viv/vit	Latin	live	revive, survive, vital, vitamin, vivacious, vivid, viviparous
volv	Latin	roll	convolutions, evolve, evolution, involve, revolutionary, revolver, volume

these suffixes are English. They influence the syntax of sentences. Following are some examples:

the -*ed* in *walked*	the -*es* in *beaches*
the -*ing* in *singing*	the -*'s* in *girl's*
the -*s* in *asks*	the -*er* in *faster*
the -*s* in *dogs*	the -*est* in *sunniest*

In contrast, derivational suffixes show the relationship of the word to its root word. Consider, for example, these words containing the root word *friend: friendly, friendship,* and *friendless.*

When a word's affix is "peeled off," the remaining word is usually a real word. For example, when the prefix *pre-* is removed from *preview* or the suffix -*er* is removed from *viewer,* the word *view* can stand alone. Some words include letter sequences that might be affixes, but because the remaining word cannot stand alone, they are not affixes. For example, the *in-* at the beginning of *include* is not a prefix because *clude* is not a word. Similarly, the -*ic* at the end of *magic* is not a suffix because *mag* cannot stand alone as a word. Sometimes, however, Latin and Greek root words cannot stand alone. One example is *legible:* The -*ible* is a suffix, and *leg* is the root word even though it cannot stand alone. Of course, *leg*—meaning part of the body—is a word, but the root word *leg-* from *legible* is not: It is a Latin root word, meaning "to read."

A list of English, Greek, and Latin prefixes and suffixes is presented in Figure 5–7. Not surprisingly, most affixes are from Latin, as are 50–60% of words in English. White, Sowell, and Yanagihara (1989) researched affixes and identified the most common ones; these are marked with an asterisk in Figure 5–7. White and his colleagues recommend that the commonly used affixes be taught to middle- and upper-grade students because of their usefulness. Some of the most commonly used prefixes can be confusing because they have more than one meaning; the prefix *un-,* for example, can mean *not* (e.g., *unclear*) or it can reverse the meaning of a word (e.g., *tie–untie*).

Teaching and Assessing Word Identification. Word-level learning is an essential part of a balanced literacy program (Hiebert, 1991), and teaching minilessons about analogies and phonic, syllabic, and morphemic analysis is a useful way to help students focus on words. Minilessons grow out of meaningful literature experiences or thematic units, and teachers choose words for minilessons from books students are reading, as Ms. Williams did in the vignette. The minilesson feature on page 172 shows how Mr. Morales teaches his sixth graders about morphemic analysis as part of a social studies unit on ancient civilizations.

Delpit (1987) and Reyes (1991) have argued that learning words implicitly through reading and writing experiences assumes that students have existing literacy and language proficiencies and that the same sort of instruction works equally well for everyone. They point out that not all students have a rich background of literacy experiences before coming to school. Some students, especially those from nonmainstream cultural and linguistic groups, may not have been read to as preschoolers. They may not have recited nursery rhymes to develop phonemic awareness, or experimented with writing by writing letters to grandparents. Perhaps even more important, they may not be familiar with the routines of school—sitting quietly and listening while the teacher reads, working cooperatively on group projects, answering questions and talking about books, and imitating the teacher's literacy behaviors. Delpit and Reyes conclude that explicit instruction is crucial for nonmainstream students who do not have the same literacy background as middle-class students.

Figure 5-7 **English, Greek, and Latin Affixes**

Language	Prefixes	Suffixes
English	***over-** (too much): overflow **self-** (by oneself): self-employed ***un-** (not): unhappy ***un-** (reversal): untie **under-** (beneath): underground	**-ed** (past tense): played **-ful** (full of): hopeful **-ing** (participle): eating, building **-ish** (like): reddish **-less** (without): hopeless **-ling** (young): duckling ***-ly** (in the manner of): slowly ***-ness** (state or quality): kindness **-s/-es** (plural): cats, boxes **-ship** (state of, art, or skill): friendship, seamanship **-ster** (one who): gangster **-ward** (direction): homeward ***-y** (full of): sleepy
Greek	**a-/an-** (not): atheist, anaerobic **amphi-** (both): amphibian **anti-** (against): antiseptic **di-** (two): dioxide **hemi-** (half): hemisphere **hyper-** (over): hyperactive **hypo-** (under): hypodermic **micro-** (small): microfilm **mono-** (one): monarch **omni-** (all): omnivorous **poly-** (many): polygon **sym-/syn-/sys-** (together): synonym	**-ism** (doctrine of): communism **-ist** (one who): artist **-logy** (the study of): zoology
Latin	**bi-** (two, twice): bifocal, biannual **contra-** (against): contradict **de-** (away): detract ***dis-** (not): disapprove ***dis-** (reversal): disinfect **ex-** (out): export ***il-/im-/in-/ir-** (not): illegible, impolite, inexpensive, irrational ***in-** (in, into): indoor **inter-** (between): intermission **mille-** (thousand): millennium ***mis-** (wrong): mistake **multi-** (many): multimillionaire **non-** (not): nonsense **post-** (after): postwar **pre-** (before): precede **quad-/quart-** (four): quadruple, quarter **re-** (again): repay ***re-/retro-** (back): replace, retroactive ***sub-** (under): submarine **super-** (above): supermarket **trans-** (across): transport **tri-** (three): triangle	**-able/-ible** (worthy of, can be): lovable, audible ***-al/-ial** (action, process): arrival, denial **-ance/-ence** (state or quality): annoyance, absence **-ant** (one who): servant **-ary/-ory** (person, place): secretary, laboratory **-cule** (very small): molecule **-ee** (one who is): trustee ***-er/-or/-ar** (one who): teacher, actor, liar **-ic** (characterized by): angelic **-ify** (to make): simplify **-ment** (state or quality): enjoyment **-ous** (full of): nervous ***-sion/-tion** (state or quality): tension, attraction **-ure** (state or quality): failure

The * indicates the most commonly used affixes (White, Sowell, & Yanagihara, 1989).

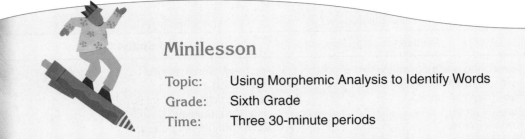

Minilesson

Topic: Using Morphemic Analysis to Identify Words
Grade: Sixth Grade
Time: Three 30-minute periods

As part of a social studies unit on ancient civilizations, Mr. Morales introduces the concepts *democracy*, *monarchy*, *oligarchy*, and *theocracy* to his sixth graders and adds the words to the social studies word wall; however, he notices that many of his students have difficulty pronouncing the words and remembering what they mean even though they have read about them in the social studies textbook.

1. Introduce the Topic
Mr. Morales reads over the word wall for the social studies unit on ancient civilizations and reads aloud these words: *democracy*, *monarchy*, *oligarchy*, and *theocracy*. Marcos volunteers that he thinks that the words have something to do with kings or rulers, but he's not sure.

2. Share Examples
The teacher writes the words on the chalkboard, dividing them into syllables so that the sixth graders can pronounce them more easily. The students practice saying the words several times, but they are puzzled about their meanings even though they learned about the words when they listed them on the word wall.

3. Provide Information
Mr. Morales tells the class that he can help them figure out the meaning of the words. "The words are Greek," he says, "and they have two word parts. If you know the meaning of the word parts, you will be able to figure out the meaning of the words." He writes the four words from the word wall and the word parts this way:

democracy = *demo* + *cracy*   *monarchy* = *mono* + *archy*

oligarchy = *olig* + *archy*   *theocracy* = *theo* + *cracy*

Then he explains that Marcos was right—the words have to do with kings and rulers: They describe different kinds of government. *Cracy* means *government* and *archy* means *leader*. The first word part tells more about the kind of government; one of them means *gods*, and the others mean *one*, *people*, and *few*. The students work in small groups to figure out that *democracy* means government by the people, *monarchy* means one leader, *oligarchy* means rule by a few leaders, and *theocracy* means government by the gods.

4. Guide Practice
The next day, Mr. Morales divides the class into four groups, and each group makes a poster to describe one of the four types of government. On each poster, students write the word, the two Greek word parts, and a definition. They also create an illustration based on what they have learned about this type of government. Afterward, students share their posters with the class and display them in the classroom.

5. Assess Learning
On the third day, Mr. Morales passes out a list of six sentences about the different types of government taken from the social studies textbook and asks them to identify the type of government. He encourages the sixth graders to refer to the posters the class made as they complete the assignment. Afterward, he reviews students' papers to determine which students understand the four types of government and can use the words correctly.

Fluent readers develop a large repertoire of sight words and use word-identification strategies to decode unfamiliar words. Less capable readers, in contrast, cannot read as many sight words and do not use as many strategies for decoding words. Researchers have concluded again and again that students who do not become fluent readers depend on explicit instruction to learn how to identify words (Calfee & Drum, 1986; R. W. Gaskins et al., 1991; Johnson & Baumann, 1984).

Many fourth-grade teachers notice that their students seem to stand still or lose ground in their reading development. It has been assumed that the increased demands for reading informational books with unfamiliar, multisyllabic words caused this phenomenon. Now researchers are suggesting that lack of instruction in word-identification strategies might be the cause of the "fourth-grade slump" (Chall, Jacobs, & Baldwin, 1990). Perhaps more minilessons on identifying multisyllabic words will help eliminate this difficulty. The guidelines for teaching word identification are summarized in the feature below.

Teachers informally assess students' ability to use word-identification strategies as they observe students reading and writing and monitor their use of the strategies. They can also assess students' use of word-identification strategies by asking them to read or write a list of grade-level-appropriate words or by asking them to think aloud and explain how they decoded or spelled a particular word. It is also important that teachers check to see that students use these strategies on an "interim basis" and that through practice, students learn to read and write words automatically.

WHAT IS FLUENCY?

Fluency is the ability to read effectively, and it involves three components: reading speed, word recognition, and prosody (Rasinski, 2000, 2004; Richards, 2000). Reading speed refers to the rate at which students read; to read fluently, students need to read at least 100 words per minute. Most students reach this reading speed by third grade. Students' reading speed continues to grow, and by the time they are adults, they will read from 250 to 300 words per minute. Of course, both children and adults vary

Visit Chapter 5 on the Companion Website at *www.prenhall.com/ tompkins* to connect to web links related to fluency.

Guidelines for Teaching Students to Identify Words

Post high-frequency words on word walls.

Teach high-frequency words in minilessons.

Practice reading and writing high-frequency words through reading and writing workshop and other literacy activities.

Introduce key words before reading, and teach other words during and after reading.

Model word-identification strategies during read-alouds and shared reading.

Teach students through minilessons to use phonic analysis, analogies, syllabic analysis, and morphemic analysis word-identification strategies.

Use words from reading selections as examples in minilessons on word-identification strategies.

Encourage students to apply word-identification strategies to both reading and spelling.

their reading speed depending on the difficulty of what they are reading and their purpose for reading, but excessively slow reading is often a characteristic of unsuccessful readers.

Word recognition is the second component of fluency. To read fluently, students need to instantly and automatically recognize most of the words they are reading. They need to know the 100 high-frequency words and other common words and have sounded out phonetically regular words so many times that these words, too, have become automatic. They also need to recognize many of the specialized words contained in the reading selection—names of characters in stories or technical terms in informational texts. Students usually encounter a few words that they do not know, but they use word-identification strategies to quickly identify those words and continue reading. When students have to stop and decode words in every sentence, their reading will not be fluent. It is an indication that the selection is too difficult for them.

The third component, prosody, is the ability to orally read sentences expressively, with appropriate phrasing and intonation. Dowhower (1991) describes prosody as "the ability to read in expressive rhythmic and melodic patterns" (p. 166). Students move from word-by-word reading with little or no expression to chunking words into phrases, attending to punctuation, and applying appropriate syntactic emphases. Fluent readers' oral reading approximates talking, and for their reading to be expressive, they have to read quickly and recognize automatically most of the words they are reading.

Fluent readers are better able to comprehend what they read because they can identify words easily (LaBerge & Samuels, 1976; Perfitti, 1985; Stanovich, 1986). Students who are not fluent readers often read hesitantly, in a word-by-word fashion and with great effort. These less competent readers spend too much mental energy in identifying words, leaving little energy to focus on comprehension. Readers do not have an unlimited amount of mental energy to use when they read, and they cannot focus on word recognition and comprehension at the same time. So, as students become fluent readers, they use less energy for word recognition and focus more energy on comprehending what they read.

By third grade, most students have become fluent readers. They have acquired a large stock of high-frequency words that they can read automatically, and they have developed word-identification strategies, including phonic analysis and syllabic analysis, to use to figure out unfamiliar words. But some students continue to read slowly, in a halting manner and without expression. They do not read fluently, and they exemplify some of these characteristics:

- Students read slowly.
- Students cannot decode individual words.
- Students try to sound our phonetically irregular words.
- Students guess at words based on the beginning sound.
- Students do not remember a word the second or third time it is used in a passage.
- Students do not break multisyllabic words into syllables to decode them.
- Students do not break multisyllabic words into root words and affixes to decode them.
- Students point at words as they read.
- Students repeat words and phrases.
- Students read without expression.
- Students read word-by-word.

Part 2 How Do Children Learn to Read and Write?

- Students ignore punctuation marks.
- Students do not remember or understand what they read.

Writing fluency is similar to reading fluency: Students need to be able to write quickly and easily so that their hands and arms do not hurt. Slow, laborious hand-writing interferes with the expression of ideas. In addition, students must be able to spell words automatically so that they can take notes, write journal entries, and handle other writing assignments.

Promoting Reading Fluency

Nonfluent readers can learn to read fluently (Allington, 1983). These readers may need to work on their reading speed, word recognition, prosody, or on all three components of fluency. They may also need more reading practice—more opportunities to read books at their reading levels to develop reading stamina.

Improving Reading Speed. The best approach to improve students' reading speed is repeated readings (Samuels, 1979), in which students practice rereading a book or an excerpt from a book three to five times, striving to improve their reading speed and decrease the number of errors they make. Teachers often time students' reading and plot their speed on a graph so that improvements can be noted. Repeated readings also enhance students' ability to chunk words into meaningful phrases and read with more expression (Dowhower, 1987). Researchers have also found that through repeated readings, students deepen their comprehension of the books they reread (Yaden, 1988).

Teachers often incorporate repeated readings as part of guided reading when they want to assist students in rereading. Sometimes the teacher reads the passage aloud while students follow along or use echo reading in which they repeat each phrase or sentence after the teacher reads it. Then students reread the passage using choral reading. After several repetitions, students can read the passage one more time, this time independently. Teachers can also set up rereading opportunities at a listening center. If students are timing their reading, then a stopwatch or other timing device can be added to the center. Teachers also use paired repeated readings in which students work together to read, reread, and evaluate their reading (Koskinen & Blum, 1986).

Enhancing Word Recognition. To become fluent readers, students learn to instantly and automatically recognize two kinds of words during the primary grades—high-frequency words that often cannot be sounded out and phonetically regular words. Students who are not fluent may need instruction in one or both types of words, depending on which words they can read. To teach high-frequency words, teachers present minilessons on the words and post them on a word wall in the classroom, and to teach phonetically regular words, teachers present minilessons on phonics skills. Then students need daily opportunities to practice the words they are learning in reading and writing activities.

Teaching Prosody. Schreider (1980) recommends teaching students how to phrase or chunk together parts of sentences in order to read with expression. Fluent readers seem to understand how to chunk parts of sentences into meaningful units, perhaps because they have been read to or have had many reading experiences themselves, but many struggling readers do not have this ability. Consider this sentence from *Sarah, Plain and Tall* (MacLachlan, 1985): "A few raindrops came, gentle at first, then stronger and louder, so that Caleb and I covered our ears and stared at each other without speaking" (p. 47). This sentence comes from the chapter describing a terrible storm that the pioneer family endured, huddled with their animals in their sturdy barn. Three commas help students read the first part of this sentence, but then they must decide how to chunk the second part.

Teachers can work with nonfluent readers to have them practice breaking sentences into chunks and then reading the sentences with expression. Teachers can make copies of a page from a book students are reading so that they can use a pencil to mark pauses in longer sentences. Or, teachers can choose a sentence to write on the chalkboard, chunking it into phrases like this:

A few raindrops came,

gentle at first,

then stronger and louder,

so that Caleb and I

covered our ears

and stared at each other

without speaking.

After chunking, students practice reading the sentence in chunks with classmates and individually. After working with one sentence, students can choose another sentence to chunk and practice reading. Students who don't chunk words into phrases when they read aloud need many opportunities to practice chunking and rereading sentences.

Reading activities such as choral reading also help students improve their phrasing. In choral reading, students and the teacher take turns reading the text, as Ms. Williams and her students did in the vignette at the beginning of the chapter. Students provide support for each other because they are reading in small groups, and they learn to phrase sentences as they read along with classmates. Choral reading also improves students' reading speed because they read along with classmates.

One variation of choral reading is unison reading, in which the teacher and students read a text together (Reutzel & Cooter, 2000). The teacher is the leader and reads loudly enough to be heard above the group. Another variation is echo reading, in which the teacher reads a sentence with good phrasing and intonation, and then students read the same material again. If the students read confidently, the teacher moves to the next sentence. However, if students struggle to read the sentence, the teacher repeats the first sentence. These activities are especially useful for helping English learners to develop appropriate prosody.

Reading Practice. Students need many opportunities to practice reading and rereading books in order to develop fluency (Rasinski, 2003). The best books for reading practice are ones that students are interested in reading and that are written at a level just below their instructional level; books for fluency practice should be neither too easy nor too difficult. Students should automatically recognize most words in the book, but if the book is extremely easy, it provides no challenge. And, when students read books that are too difficult, they read slowly because they stop again and again to identify unfamiliar words. This constant stopping reinforces nonfluent readers' already choppy reading style.

For reading practice, students often choose "pop" literature that is fun to read but rather ordinary. These books are often more effective than some high-quality literature selections in helping children develop fluency because the vocabulary is more controlled, which allows students to be more successful. Children like them because the stories are humorous or fantastic, or because they relate to their own lives. Series books such as *Junie B. Jones and the Stupid Smelly Bus* (Park, 1992) and *Night of the Ninjas* (Osborne, 1995) are written at the first- and second-grade level, and *The Teacher From the Black Lagoon* (Thaler, 1989) and *The Adventures of Captain Underpants* (Pilkey, 1997) are written at the third- and fourth-grade level. A list of picture-book and chapter-book series written at the first- through fourth-grade levels is presented in Figure 5–8. More and more easy-to-read picture books and chapter books are becoming available each year, and many of these books appeal to boys.

Teachers provide two types of daily opportunities for children to practice reading and rereading familiar stories and other books; some activities provide assisted practice, and others provide students with opportunities to read independently, without assistance. In assisted practice, students have a model to follow as they read or reread. Choral reading, and readers theatre are two examples. In readers theatre, students practice reading story scripts to develop fluency before reading the script to an audience of classmates. In a recent study, Martinez, Roser, and Strecker (1998/1999) found that practice reading using readers theatre scripts resulted in significant improvement in second graders' reading fluency.

Middle- and upper-grade students often participate in read-arounds. In this activity, students choose a favorite sentence or paragraph from a book or other reading assignment they have already read and practice reading the passage several times. Then students take turns reading their passages aloud. They read in any order they want, and usually several students will read the same passage aloud. Teachers often plan this activity to bring closure to a book students have read or to review information presented in a content-area textbook.

Developing Reading Stamina. Once students become fluent readers, the focus shifts to helping them develop reading stamina or the strength to read silently for increasingly longer periods of time. Students develop this stamina through daily opportunities to read independently for extended periods. When students' reading is limited to reading basal reader selections, single chapters in novels, or magazine articles that can be completed in 15 or 20 minutes, they may not develop the endurance they need. Many teachers find that by sixth and seventh grades, their students can't read for more than 15 or 20 minutes at a time, or students complain about how tired they are or how hard reading is when they are asked to read for longer periods. It's crucial that students learn to read for longer periods of time so that they can handle novels and other chapter books and the lengthy texts they are asked to read on standardized tests.

Students develop this endurance through reading books at their independent level. Teachers typically include extended opportunities each day for independent reading of self-selected texts through reading workshop or Sustained Silent Reading at all grade levels. Kindergartners read for 5 to 10 minutes; in first grade, students begin by reading and rereading books for 10 to 15 minutes, and reach 20 minutes or more by

---

Scaffolding Struggling Readers

How can I help my struggling fifth-grade readers who don't read fluently?

There are three things you can do to help your struggling readers. First, teach them to read the high-frequency words. Test them on the 300 high-frequency words, and teach the ones they don't know. Post these words on a word wall that students can see, and teach them to use it. Second, teach students to use word-identification strategies. Have them practice decoding one-syllable words using phonics and analogies and breaking longer words into syllables before decoding them. Third, provide daily opportunities for students to read and reread books at a level just below their instructional reading level. Explain the importance of fluency, and monitor your students' reading carefully to ensure that they actually are reading and are trying to read quickly and smoothly. One way to do this is to use the repeated readings procedure.

Figure 5–8   Popular Series of Picture Books and Chapter Books

Reading Level	Series	Description
1	Amelia Bedelia, by Peggy Parish	Comical stories about a housekeeper who takes instructions literally.
	Fox and Friends, by Edward and James Marshall	Stories about Fox, who likes to have everything his way.
	Pinky and Rex, by James Howe	Chapter-book stories about two best friends, a boy named Pinky and a girl named Rex.
1–2	Arthur, by Marc Brown	Picture-book stories about Arthur the Aardvark.
	Henry and Mudge, by Cynthia Rylant	Chapter-book stories about Henry and his lovable 180-pound dog, Mudge.
	Junie B. Jones, by Barbara Park	Chapter-book stories about a delightful kindergartner who is always getting in trouble.
	Magic Tree House, by Mary Pope Osborne	Chapter-book stories about a magical tree house that transports children back in time.
	Third-Grade Detectives, by George F. Stanley	Adventures of two clever third graders, Todd and Noelle.
2	Cam Jansen, by David A. Adler	Funny chapter books about a girl detective named Cam Jansen.
	Jigsaw Jones Mysteries, by James Preller	Stories about private eye Jigsaw Jones and his partner, Mila Yeh.
	Franklin, by Paulette Bourgeois	Picture-book stories featuring a gentle turtle-hero named Franklin.
	George and Martha, by James Marshall	Picture-book stories about two hippo friends named George and Martha.
	Horrible Harry, by Suzy Kline	Hilarious chapter-book stories about a second-grade prankster named Harry.
	The Kids in Ms. Colman's Class, by Ann M. Martin	Chapter-book stories about the second graders in Ms. Colman's class.
2–3	Black Lagoon, by Mike Thaler	Picture-book series dealing with children's fears of the unknown.
	Marvin Redpost, by Louis Sachar	Funny stories about third-grade Marvin Redpost.
	The Zack Files, by Dan Greenburg	Time-travel stories featuring fifth-grade Zack.
	A to Z Mysteries, by Ron Roy	Alphabetical collection of mysteries to solve.
3	Adventures of the Bailey School Kids, by Debbie Dadey and Marcia Thornton Jones	Chapter-book stories about the adventures of a diverse third-grade class.
	Hank the Cowdog, by John R. Erickson	Fantastic chapter-book stories told by a cowdog named Hank.
	The Magic School Bus chapter books, by Joanna Cole	More of Ms. Frizzle's adventures in her magic school bus.
	The Secrets of the Droon, by Tony Abbott	Fantasy adventures set in the magical world of Droon.
	Geronimo Stilton, by Scholastic	Adventures of a mouse named Geronimo Stilton, who runs *The Rodent's Gazette*.
3–4	Amber Brown, by Paula Danziger	Chapter-book stories about a spunky girl with a colorful name.
	Captain Underpants, by Dav Pilkey	Hilarious chapter-book series about the superhero Captain Underpants.
	Time Warp Trio, by Jon Scieszka	Three friends travel back in time for adventure in this chapter-book series.

the end of the school year. The time students spend reading gradually increases to at least 30 minutes a day in second and third grades, and students shift from oral to silent reading as they become fluent readers. In fourth and fifth grades, students' independent reading time increases to 40 or 45 minutes, and in sixth, seventh, and eighth grades, students spend 45 to 60 minutes a day reading. Students also benefit from doing additional independent reading at home.

Another way of looking at how students develop stamina is by the number of words they are expected to read. Many school districts now call for students to read 500,000 words in fourth grade and gradually increase the number of words until they read one million words in eighth grade. You may wonder how the number of words translates to books: Students in fourth, fifth, and sixth grades often read novels that are approximately 200 pages long, and these books typically have approximately 35,000 words; for example: *Esperanza Rising* (Ryan, 2000), *Poppy* (Avi, 1995), *Loser* (Spinelli, 2002), and *Homeless Bird* (Whelan, 2000); therefore, students need to read approximately 14 books to reach 500,000 words. Students who read two novels each month will reach the 500,000-word mark.

Students in seventh and eighth grades usually read longer books with 250 pages or more. Books with 250 pages contain at least 50,000 words; for example: *Bud, Not Buddy* (Curtis, 1999), *Holes* (Sachar, 1998), and *Crispin: The Cross of Lead* (Avi, 2002). Books containing more than 300 pages, such as *Harry Potter and the Chamber of Secrets* (Rowling, 1999), range from 75,000 to 100,000 words. Students need to read 10 to 20 books, depending on length, to reach one million words. So, students who read two books with 250 to 350 pages each month will reach the one million–word mark.

Why Is Round-Robin Reading No Longer Recommended? Round-robin reading is an outmoded oral reading activity in which the teacher calls on children to read aloud, one after the other. Some teachers used round-robin reading in small groups and others used the procedure with the whole class, but neither version is advocated today. According to Opitz and Rasinski (1998), many problems are associated with round-robin reading. First of all, students may develop an inaccurate view of reading because they are expected to read aloud to the class without having opportunities to rehearse. Next, they may develop inefficient reading habits because they alter their silent reading speed to match the various speeds of classmates when they read aloud. Students signal their inattention and boredom by misbehaving as classmates read aloud. In addition to these problems for students who are listening, round-robin reading causes problems for some students when they are called upon to read: Struggling readers are often anxious or embarrassed when they read aloud.

Most teachers now agree that round robin reading wastes valuable classroom time that could be spent on more meaningful reading activities. Instead of round-robin reading, students should read the text independently if it is at their reading level. If it is too difficult, students can read with buddies, participate in shared reading, or listen to the teacher or another fluent reader read aloud. Also, they might listen to the teacher read the material aloud and then try reading it with a buddy or independently.

Developing Writing Fluency

To become fluent writers, students must be able to rapidly form letters and spell words automatically. Just as nonfluent readers read word-by-word and have to stop and decode many words, nonfluent writers write slowly, word-by-word, and have to stop and check the spelling of many words. In fact, some nonfluent writers write so slowly that they forget the sentence they are writing! Through varied, daily writing activities, students develop the muscular control to form letters quickly and legibly. They write high-frequency words again and again until they can spell them automatically. Being able to write fluently usually coincides with being able to read fluently because reading and writing practice are mutually beneficial (Shanahan, 1988; Tierney, 1983).

Students become fluent writers as they practice writing, and they need opportunities for both assisted and unassisted practice. Writing on white boards during interactive writing lessons is one example of assisted writing practice (Tompkins, 2004). The teacher and classmates provide support for students.

Quickwriting. Peter Elbow (1973, 1981) recommends using quickwriting to develop writing fluency. In quickwriting, students write rapidly and without stopping as they explore an idea. As part of the unit on hermit crabs, Ms. Williams asked the second-grade students to do a quickwrite listing what they had learned about hermit crabs. Here is Arlette's quickwrite:

> *Hermit crabs live in tide pools. They have pincers and 10 legs in all. They can pinch you very hard. Ouch! They are crabs and they molt to grow and grow. They have to buro (borrow) shells to live in becus (because) other anmels (animals) will eat them. They like to eat fish and shrimp. Sea enomes (anemones) like to live on ther (their) shells.*

Arlette listed a great deal of information that she had learned about hermit crabs. She misspelled five words, and the correct spellings are given in parentheses. Arlette was able to write such a long quickwrite and to misspell very few words because she is already a fluent writer. While she was writing, she checked the hermit crab word wall and the high-frequency word wall in the classroom in order to spell *pincers, shrimp,* and *other.* The other words she knew how to spell and wrote them automatically.

In contrast, Jeremy is not yet a fluent writer. Here is his quickwrite:

> *The hermit crab liv (lives) in a hues (house) he eat (eats) shimp (shrimp).*

Jeremy writes slowly and laboriously. He stops to think of an idea before writing each sentence and starts each sentence on a new line. He rarely refers to the word walls in the classroom, and he spells most words phonetically. Even though Jeremy's writing is not as fluent as Arlette's, quickwriting is a useful activity for him because he will become more fluent through practice.

Ms. Williams has her students quickwrite several times each week. They quickwrite to respond to a story she has read aloud or to write about what they are learning in science or another content area. She reads and responds to the quickwrites, and she writes the correct form of misspelled words at the bottom of the page so that students will notice the correct spelling. Once in a while, she has students revise and edit their quickwrites and make a final, published copy, but her goal is to develop writing fluency, not to develop finished, polished compositions.

Why Is Copying From the Chalkboard No Longer Recommended? Some teachers write sentences and poems on the chalkboard for students to copy in hopes that this activity will develop writing fluency. Copying isn't a very effective instructional strategy, though, because students are passively copying letters, not actively creating sentences, breaking the sentences into words, and spelling the words. In fact, sometimes students are copying sentences they cannot read, so the activity becomes little more than handwriting practice. It is much more worthwhile for students to write sentences to express their own ideas and to practice spelling words.

Assessing Students' Reading and Writing Fluency

Primary-grade teachers monitor students' developing reading and writing fluency by observing students as they read and write. Teachers assess students' reading fluency by listening to them read aloud. As they listen, teachers consider these four components of reading fluency:

1. *Speed.* Do students read hesitantly, or do they read quickly enough to understand what they are reading?

2. *Automaticity.* Do students have to decode many words, or do they read most words automatically?

3. *Phrasing.* Do students read word-by-word, or do they chunk words into phrases?

4. *Prosody.* Do students read in a monotone, or do they read with expression in a manner that approximates talking?

By third grade, students should be fluent readers. If students have difficulty with any of the four components, teachers should provide instruction in that area in addition to reading practice to improve their fluency.

Teachers assess students' writing fluency in a similar manner. They observe students as they write and consider these components:

1. *Ideas.* Do students have trouble thinking of something to write, or do they readily think of ideas for writing?

2. *Speed.* Do students write slowly, or do they write quickly enough to complete the writing task?

3. *Automaticity.* Do students have to sound out or locate the spelling of most words, or do they spell most words automatically?

4. *Ease.* Do students write laboriously or easily?

Students should be fluent writers by third grade. If students have difficulty with any of the four components, teachers should provide instruction in that area plus lots of writing practice to improve their fluency.

Complete a self-assessment to check your understanding of the concepts presented in this chapter on the Companion Website at *www.prenhall.com/ tompkins*

Review: How Effective Teachers Develop Fluent Readers and Writers

1. Teachers teach students to read and spell the high-frequency words because they are the most useful for them.

2. Teachers post high-frequency words on word walls in the classroom.

3. Teachers provide daily opportunities for students to practice word recognition through word work centers and reading and writing practice.

4. Teachers teach four decoding strategies and related skills—phonic analysis, analogies, syllabic analysis, and morphemic analysis.

5. Teachers encourage students to look at every letter in a word and to decode as much of the word as possible, not just to guess at the word using initial consonants as a clue.

6. Teachers involve students in repeated reading, choral reading, readers theatre, and other reading activities to develop their reading fluency.

7. Teachers have students choose books written at levels just below their instructional level for fluency-building activities.

8. Teachers involve students in interactive writing, quickwriting, and other writing activities to develop their writing fluency.

9. Teachers observe students as they read and write to determine whether they are becoming fluent.

10. Teachers ensure that students become fluent readers and writers by third grade.

Professional References

Adams, M. J. (1990). *Beginning to read: Thinking and learning about print.* Cambridge, MA: MIT Press.

Allington, R. L. (1983). Fluency: The neglected reading goal. *The Reading Teacher, 33,* 556–561.

Allington, R. L. (Ed.). (1998). *Teaching struggling readers.* Newark, DE: International Reading Association.

Calfee, R., & Drum, P. (1986). Research on teaching reading. In M. W. Wittrock (Ed.), *Handbook of research on teaching* (3rd ed.) (pp. 804–849). New York: Macmillan.

Chall, J. S., Jacobs, V. A., & Baldwin, L. E. (1990). *The reading crisis: Why poor children fall behind.* Cambridge, MA: Harvard University Press.

Cunningham, P. M. (1975–1976). Investigating a synthesized theory of mediated word identification. *Reading Research Quarterly, 11,* 127–143.

Cunningham, P. M. (2000). *Phonics they use: Words for reading and writing* (3rd ed.). New York: HarperCollins.

Delpit, L. (1987). The silenced dialogue: Power and pedagogy in educating other people's children. *Harvard Educational Review, 58,* 280–298.

Dowhower, S. L. (1987). Effects of repeated reading on second-grade transitional readers' fluency and comprehension. *Reading Research Quarterly, 22,* 389–406.

Dowhower, S. L. (1991). Speaking of prosody: Fluency's unattended bedfellow. *Theory Into Practice, 30,* 165–173.

Ehri, L., C., & Robbins, C. (1992). Beginners need some decoding skill to read words by analogy. *Reading Research Quarterly, 27,* 13–26.

Elbow, P. (1973). *Writing without teachers.* Oxford: Oxford University Press.

Elbow, P. (1981). *Writing with power.* Oxford: Oxford University Press.

Eldredge, J. L. (2005). *Teach decoding: How and why* (2nd ed.). Upper Saddle River, NJ: Merrill/Prentice Hall.

Flood, J., & Lapp, D. (1994). Developing literary appreciation and literacy skills: A blueprint for success. *The Reading Teacher, 48,* 76–79.

Gaskins, I. W., Ehri, L. C., Cress, C., O'Hara, C., & Donnelly, K. (1996/1997). Procedures for word learning: Making discoveries about words. *The Reading Teacher, 50,* 312–326.

Gaskins, R. W., Gaskins, J. W., & Gaskins, I. W. (1991). A decoding program for poor readers—and the rest of the class, too! *Language Arts, 68,* 213–225.

Gough, P. B., Juel, C., & Griffith, P. L. (1992). Reading, spelling, and the orthographic cipher. In P. B. Gough, L. C. Ehri, & R. Treiman (Eds.), *Reading acquisition* (pp. 35–48). Hillsdale, NJ: Erlbaum.

Hiebert, E. H. (1991). The development of word-level strategies in authentic literacy tasks. *Language Arts, 68,* 234–240.

Hitchcock, M. E. (1989). *Elementary students' invented spellings at the correct stage of spelling development.* Unpublished doctoral dissertation, Norman, University of Oklahoma.

Johnson, D. D., & Baumann, J. F. (1984). Word identification. In P. D. Pearson (Ed.), *Handbook of reading research* (pp. 583–608). New York: Longman.

Koskinen, P. S., & Blum, I. H. (1986). Paired repeated reading: A classroom strategy for developing fluent reading. *The Reading Teacher, 40,* 70–75.

LaBerge, D., & Samuels, S. J. (1976). Toward a theory of automatic information processing in reading. In H. Singer & R. Ruddell (Eds.), *Theoretical models and processes of reading* (pp. 548–579). Newark, DE: International Reading Association.

Martinez, M., Roser, N. L., & Strecker, S. (1998/1999). "I never thought I could be a star": A readers theatre ticket to fluency. *The Reading Teacher, 52,* 326–334.

National Reading Panel. (2000). *Teaching children to read: An evidence-based assessment of the scientific research literature on reading and its implications for reading instruction.* Washington, DC: National Institute of Child Health and Human Development.

Opitz, M. F., & Rasinski, T. V. (1998). *Good-bye round robin: Twenty-five effective oral reading strategies.* Portsmouth, NH: Heinemann.

Perfitti, C. A. (1985). *Reading ability.* New York: Oxford University Press.

Pinnell, G. S., & Fountas, I. C. (1998). *Word matters: Teaching phonics and spelling in the reading/writing classroom.* Portsmouth, NH: Heinemann.

Rasinski, T. V. (2000). Speed does matter in reading. *The Reading Teacher, 54,* 146–151.

Rasinski, T. V. (2003). *The fluent reader.* New York: Scholastic.

Rasinski, T. V. (2004). Creating fluent readers. *Educational Leadership, 61*(6), 146–51.

Reutzel, D. R., & Cooter, R. B. (2000). *Teaching children to read: From basals to books* (3rd ed.). Upper Saddle River, NJ: Merrill/Prentice Hall.

Reyes, M. de la Luz. (1991). A process approach to literacy using dialogue journals and literature logs with second language learners. *Research in the Teaching of English, 25,* 291–313.

Richards, M. (2000). Be a good detective: Solve the case of oral reading fluency. *The Reading Teacher, 53,* 534–539.

Samuels, S. J. (1979). The method of repeated readings. *The Reading Teacher, 32,* 403–408.

Schreider, P. A. (1980). On the acquisition of reading fluency. *Journal of Reading Behavior, 12,* 177–186.

Shanahan, T. (1988). The reading-writing relationship: Seven instructional principles. *The Reading Teacher, 41,* 636–647.

Snow, C. E., Burns, M. S., & Griffin, P. (Eds.). (1998). *Preventing reading difficulties in young children.* Washington, DC: National Academy Press.

Stanovich, K. E. (1986). Matthew effects in reading: Some consequences of individual differences in the acquisition of literacy. *Reading Research Quarterly, 21,* 360–406.

Stanovich, K. E. (1992). Speculations on the causes and consequences of individual differences in early reading acquisition. In P. B. Gough, L. C. Ehri, & R. Treiman (Eds.), *Reading acquisition* (pp. 307–342). Hillsdale, NJ: Erlbaum.

Tierney, R. J. (1983). Writer-reader transactions: Defining the dimensions of negotiation. In P. L. Stock (Ed.), *Forum: Essays on theory and practice in the teaching of writing* (pp. 147–151). Upper Montclair, NJ: Boynton/Cook.

Tompkins, G. E. (2004). *Teaching writing: Balancing process and product* (4th ed.). Upper Saddle River, NJ: Merrill/Prentice Hall.

Trachtenburg, P. (1990). Using children's literature to enhance phonics instruction. *The Reading Teacher, 43,* 648–654.

Vellutino, F. R., & Scanlon, D. M. (1987). Phonological coding, phonological awareness, and reading ability: Evidence from a longitudinal and experimental study. *Merrill-Palmer Quarterly, 33,* 321–363.

White, T. G., Sowell, J., & Yanagihara, A. (1989). Teaching elementary students to use word-part clues. *The Reading Teacher, 42,* 302–308.

Yaden, D. B., Jr. (1988). Understanding stories through repeated read-alouds: How many does it take? *The Reading Teacher, 41,* 556–560.

Children's Book References

Avi. (1995). *Poppy.* New York: Orchard Books.

Avi. (2002). *Crispin: The cross of lead.* New York: Hyperion Books.

Carle, E. (1987). *A house for hermit crab.* Saxonville, MA: Picture Book Studio.

Curtis, C. P. (1999). *Bud, not Buddy.* New York: Delacorte.

Greenaway, F. (1992). *Tide pool.* New York: DK Publishing.

Holling, H. C. (1990). *Pagoo.* Boston: Houghton Mifflin.

Kaplan, R. (1996). *Moving day.* New York: Greenwillow.

MacLachlan, P. (1985). *Sarah, plain and tall.* New York: Harper & Row.

Osborne, M. P. (1995). *Night of the ninjas.* New York: Random House.

Park, B. (1992). *Junie B. Jones and the stupid smelly bus.* New York: Random House.

Pilkey, D. (1997). *The adventures of Captain Underpants.* New York: Scholastic.

Pohl, K. (1987). *Hermit crabs.* Milwaukee: Raintree.

Randell, B. (1994). *Hermit crab.* Crystal Lake, IL: Rigby Books.

Rowling, J. K. (1999). *Harry Potter and the chamber of secrets.* New York: Scholastic.

Ryan, P. M. (2000). *Esperanza rising.* New York: Scholastic.

Sachar, L. (1998). *Holes.* New York: Farrar, Straus & Giroux.

Spinelli, J. (2002). *Loser.* New York: HarperCollins.

Thaler, M. (1989). *The teacher from the black lagoon.* New York: Scholastic.

Tuchman, G. (1997). *Hermit's shiny shell.* New York: Macmillan/McGraw-Hill.

Whelan, G. (2000). *Homeless bird.* New York: HarperCollins.

Expanding Students' Knowledge of Words

Chapter Questions

- How do students learn vocabulary words?
- What is the relationship between vocabulary knowledge and reading?
- How do teachers teach vocabulary?
- What are the components of word study?

Mrs. Sanom's Word Wizards Club

Mrs. Sanom is the resource teacher at John Muir Elementary School, and she sponsors an after-school Word Wizards Club for fifth and sixth graders; the club meets for an hour on Wednesday afternoons. Nineteen students are club members this year, and many of them are English learners. Mrs. Sanom teaches vocabulary lessons during the club meetings using costumes, books, and hands-on activities. She focuses on a different word study topic each week; the topics include writing alliterations, choosing synonyms carefully, applying context clues to figure out unfamiliar words, using a dictionary and a thesaurus, understanding multiple meanings of words, choosing between homophones, adding prefixes and suffixes to words, and studying root words.

She devised this club because many of the students at John Muir Elementary School have limited vocabularies, which affects their reading achievement. She has two banners displayed in her classroom that say "Expanding your vocabulary leads to school success" and "Knowing words makes you powerful." In the letters that the Word Wizards club members write to Mrs. Sanom at the end of the school year, they display a new sense of how important vocabulary is in life. They find themselves paying more attention to words an author uses, and

they are more successful in figuring out the meaning of unfamiliar words using context clues. Most important, the students say that participation in the Word Wizards Club gives them an appreciation for words that will last a lifetime. Rosie writes:

I love being a Word Wizard. I learned lots of new words and that makes me smart. I have a favorite word that is hypothesis. Did you know that I am always looking for more new words to learn? My Tio Mario gave me a dictionary because I wanted it real bad. I like looking for words in the dictionary and I like words with lots of syllables the best. I want to be in the club next year in 6th grade. Ok?

At the first meeting of the Word Wizards Club, Mrs. Sanom read aloud *Miss Alaineus: A Vocabulary Disaster* (Frasier, 2000), an outrageous and touching story of a girl named Sage who loves words. In the story, Sage misunderstands the meaning of *miscellaneous*, but what begins as embarrassment turns into victory when she wins an award for her costume in the school's annual vocabulary parade. The students talked about the story in a grand conversation, and they decided that they want to dress in costumes and have a vocabulary parade themselves, just as Mrs. Sanom knew they would. They decided that they will have a vocabulary parade at the end of the year, and they will invite their classmates and teachers to participate, too. "I like to dress in vocabulary costumes," Mrs. Sanom explained. "I plan to dress up in clothes or a hat that represents a vocabulary word at each club meeting." With that introduction, she reached into a shopping bag and pulled out an oversized, wrinkled shirt and put it on over her clothes. "Here is my costume," she announced. "Can you guess the word?" She modeled the shirt, trying to smooth the wrinkles, until a student guessed the word *wrinkled*.

The students talked about *wrinkle*, forms of the word (*wrinkled, unwrinkled,* and *wrinkling*), and the meanings. They checked the definitions of *wrinkle* in the dictionary. They understood the first meaning, "a crease or fold in clothes or skin," but the second meaning—"a clever idea or trick"—was more difficult. Mrs. Sanom called their idea to have a vocabulary parade "a new wrinkle" in her plans for the club, and then the students began to grasp the meaning.

The borders of each page in *Miss Alaineus* are decorated with words beginning with a specific letter of the alphabet; the first page has words beginning with A, the second page B, and so on through the story. To immerse students in words, Mrs. Sanom asked them each to choose a letter from a box of plastic alphabet letters, turn to that page in the book, and then choose a word beginning with that letter from the border to use in an activity. The words they chose included *awesome, berserk, catastrophe,* and *dwindle.* Students wrote the word on the first page of their Word Wizard Notebooks (small, spiral-bound notebooks that Mrs. Sanom purchased for them), checked its meaning in a dictionary and wrote it beside the word, and then drew a picture to illustrate the meaning. While they

Check the Compendium of Instructional Procedures, which follows Chapter 14, for more information on highlighted terms.

worked, Mrs. Sanom wrote the words on the alphabetized word wall she has posted in the classroom. Afterward, the students shared their words and illustrations with the other club members using a tea party activity.

Mrs. Sanom has a collection of vocabulary books in her classroom library, and she gives brief book talks to introduce the books to the Word Wizards Club members. Her library includes alphabet books, wordplay books, books about the history of English, and novels that range from second- to sixth-grade reading levels. A list of some of her books is presented in the box below. She explains that the very best way to learn lots of words is to read every day, and she encourages students to choose a vocabulary book or other book from her library each week to read between club meetings. At the end of each meeting, she allows a few minutes for students to choose a book to take home to read.

At today's club meeting, Mrs. Sanom is wearing a broad-rimmed hat with two wrecked cars and a stop sign attached. The students check out Mrs. Sanom's cos-

---

Mrs. Sanom's Collection of Books About Words

Agee, J. (2000). *Elvis lives!: And other anagrams*. New York: Farrar, Straus & Giroux.
Amato, M. (2000). *The word eater*. New York: Scholastic.
Brook, D. (1998). *The journey of English*. New York: Clarion.
Brown, R. (1996). *Toad*. New York: Puffin Books.
Cheney, L. (2002). *America: A patriotic primer*. New York: Simon & Schuster.
Clements, A. (1996). *Frindle*. New York: Simon & Schuster.
Edwards, P. D. (1996). *Some smug slug*. New York: HarperCollins.
Edwards, P. D. (2001). *Slop goes the soup: A noisy warthog word book*. New York: Hyperion.
Fakih, K. O. (1995). *Off the clock: A lexicon of time words and expressions*. New York: Ticknor.
Frasier, D. (2000). *Miss Alaineus: A vocabulary disaster*. San Diego: Harcourt Brace.
Graham, J. B. (1999). *Flicker flash*. Boston: Houghton Mifflin.
Gwynne, F. (1970). *The king who rained*. New York: Windmill Books.
Gwynne, F. (1976). *A chocolate moose for dinner*. New York: Windmill Books.
Gwynne, F. (1980). *The sixteen hand horse*. New York: Prentice Hall.
Gwynne, F. (1988). *A little pigeon toad*. New York: Simon & Schuster.
Heller, R. (1987). *A cache of jewels and other collective nouns*. New York: Grosset & Dunlap.
Janeczko, P. (Sel.). (2001). *A poke in the I: A collection of concrete poems*. Cambridge, MA: Candlewick Press.
Kalman, B., & Lewis, J. (2000). *Pioneer dictionary*. New York: Crabtree.
Mammano, J. (2001). *Rhinos who play soccer*. San Francisco: Chronicle Books. (And others in the Rhino series.)
Presson, L. (1996). *What in the world is a homophone?* New York: Barron's.
Scieszka, J. (2001). *Baloney (Henry P.)*. New York: Viking.
Scillian, D. (2001). *A is for America*. Chelsea, MI: Sleeping Bear Press.
Terban, M. (1983). *In a pickle and other funny idioms*. New York: Clarion.
Terban, M. (1987). *Mad as a wet hen! And other funny idioms*. New York: Clarion.
Terban, M. (1988). *Guppies in tuxedos: Funny eponyms*. New York: Clarion.
Terban, M. (1989). *Superdupers: Really funny real words*. New York: Clarion.
Terban, M. (1990). *Punching the clock: Funny action idioms*. New York: Clarion.
Terban, M. (1991). *Hey, hay! A wagonload of funny homonym riddles*. New York: Clarion.
Terban, M. (1992). *The dove dove: Funny homograph riddles*. New York: Clarion.
Terban, M. (1996). *Scholastic dictionary of idioms: More than 600 phrases, sayings, and expressions*. New York: Scholastic.

tume because they know it represents a word—and that word is the topic of today's meeting. They quickly begin guessing words: "Is it *crash*?" Oscar asks. "I think the word is *accident*. My dad had a car accident last week," says Danielle. Ramon suggests, "Those cars are *wrecked*. Is that the word?" Mrs. Sanom commends the club members for their good guesses and says that they're on the right track. To provide a little help, she draws a row of nine letter boxes on the chalkboard and fills in the first letter and the last four letters. Then Martha guesses it—*collision*. Mrs. Sanom begins a cluster on the chalkboard with the word *collision* written in the middle circle and related words on each ray. The students compare the noun *collision* and the verb *collide*. They also check the dictionary and a thesaurus for more information and write *crash, accident, wreck, hit, smashup,* and *collide* on the rays to complete the cluster. They talk about how and when to use *collide* and *collision*. Ramon offers, "I know a sentence: On 9-11, the terrorists' airplanes collided with the World Trade Center."

Mrs. Sanom explains that ships can be involved in collisions, too. A ship can hit another ship or it can collide with something else in the water—an iceberg, for example. Several students know about the *Titanic,* and they share what they know about that ship's fateful ocean crossing. Mrs. Sanom selects *Story of the Titanic* (Kentley, 2001) from her text set of books about the *Titanic* and shows photos and drawings of the ship to provide more background information. They make a K-W-L chart, listing what they know in the K column and questions they want to find answers for in the W column. The students also make individual charts in their Word Wizard Notebooks.

Next, Mrs. Sanom presents a list of words using an overhead projector—some about the *Titanic* article they will read and some not—for an exclusion brainstorming activity; the words include *unsinkable, crew, liner, passengers, voyage, airplane, catastrophe, ship, mountain, lifeboat,* and *general.* The students predict which words relate to the article and which do not. The word *general* stumps them because they think of it as an adjective meaning "having to do with the whole, not specific." A student checks the dictionary to learn about the second meaning—a high-ranking military officer (noun). The students are still confused, but after reading the article, they realize that the word *general* is not related: The officer in charge of the *Titanic* (or any ship, for that matter) is called a *captain.*

Mrs. Sanom passes out copies of the one-page article and reads it aloud while students follow along. They discuss the article, talking and asking more questions about the needless tragedy. Then they complete the L section of the K-W-L chart and the exclusion brainstorming activity. Because the students are very interested in learning more about the disaster, Mrs. Sanom introduces her text set of narrative and informational books about the *Titanic,* including *Inside the Titanic* (Brewster, 1997), *Polar, the Titanic Bear* (Spedden, 1994), *Tonight on the Titanic* (Osborne & Osborne, 1995), *Titanic: A Nonfiction Companion to Tonight on the Titanic* (Osborne & Osborne, 2002), *On Board the Titanic: What It Was Like When the Great Liner Sank* (Tanaka, 1996), and *Voyage on the Great Titanic: The Diary of Margaret Ann Brady* (White, 1998). She invites the students to spend the last few minutes of the club meeting choosing a book from the text set to take home to read before the next club meeting.

Mrs. Sanom wears a different costume or hat each week. Ten of her favorite costumes are:

Bejeweled:	A silky shirt with "jewels" glued across the front
Champion:	Racing shorts, tee shirt, and a medal on a ribbon worn around her neck
Hocus-pocus:	A black top hat with a stuffed rabbit stuck inside, white gloves, and a magic wand

International:	A dress decorated with the flags of many countries and a globe cut in half for a hat
Mercury:	A white sheet worn toga style with a baseball cap with wings on each side
Myriad:	A dress made of fabric with thousands of tiny stars printed on it and other stars attached to a headband
Porous:	A necklace with small strainer hanging on it and a colander for a hat
Slick:	A black leather jacket, sunglasses, and hair slicked back with mousse
Transparent:	A clear plastic raincoat, clear plastic gloves, and a clear shower cap
Vacant:	A bird cage with a "for rent" sign worn as a hat with an artificial bird sitting on her shoulder

One week, however, Mrs. Sanom forgets to bring a costume, so after a bit of quick thinking, she decides to feature the word *ordinary,* and she wears her everyday clothes as her costume!

For their 17th weekly club meeting, Mrs. Sanom dressed as a queen with a flowing purple robe and a tiara on her head. The focus of the week was words beginning with Q, the 17th letter of the alphabet. They began by talking about queens—both historical queens such as Queen Isabella of Spain, who financed Christopher Columbus's voyage to the New World, and queens who are alive today. Next, Mrs. Sanom began a list of Q words with *queen,* and then the students added words to the list. They checked the Q page in alphabet books and examined dictionary entries for Q words. They chose interesting words, including *quadruped, quadruplet, qualify, quest, quarantine, quintet, quiver, quench,* and *quotation.* After they had more than 20 words on their list, Mrs. Sanom asked each student to choose a Q word, study it, and make a square poster to share what they learned about the word. Afterward, Mrs. Sanom collected the posters, made a quilt, and hung it on the wall outside the classroom. One student's square about *quadruped* is presented in the box on page 189, and it documents the student's understanding of root words.

Last week's topic was homographs, two or more words that are spelled alike but pronounced differently, such as *record, bow, read,* and *dove.* Mrs. Sanom was dressed with a big red ribbon bow tied around her waist and smaller red bows tied on pigtails. At the beginning of the club meeting, she retied the bow at her waist and then she bowed to the students. Ramon quickly guessed that the word was *bow,* but the concept of homographs is new to him and the other club members. Mrs. Sanom introduced the word *homograph,* explained the definition, and offered examples. Then she shared several homograph riddles from *The Dove Dove: Funny Homograph Riddles* (Terban, 1992), including "The nurse *wrapped* the bandage around the *injury.*" The students solve the riddle by identifying the homograph that can replace the two highlighted words; for this riddle, the answer is *wound.*

Next, Mrs. Sanom divided the students into small groups, and she gave each group a different homograph riddle from Terban's book to solve. Then they shared the riddles with the whole group. As they got more practice with homographs, the students became more confident at solving the riddles, but some of the students were confused about homophones and homographs. Mrs. Sanom explained that homophones are words that sound alike but are spelled differently, such as *wood–would* and *there–their–they're.* The students used the last 10 minutes of the club meeting to write about homographs in their Word Wizard Notebooks. They also chose new books to take home to read before the next club meeting.

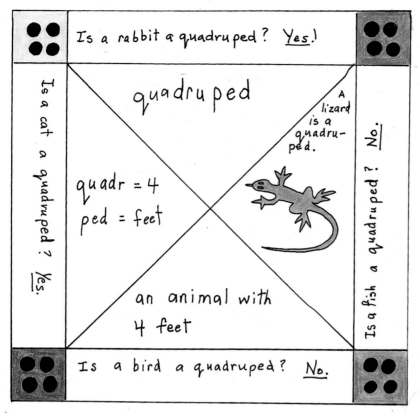

The Word Wizards make and wear word bracelets to highlight special words; in October, for example, the students make word bracelets that spell the word they've chosen to describe or represent themselves, such as *genius, ornery,* or *sincere.* Mrs. Sanom's word is *sassy,* and she demonstrates how to make a bracelet using small alphabet beads strung on an elastic string. Then the students follow her steps as they make their own bracelets, which they proudly wear to school and show off to their classmates. In February, they study patriotic words, such as *allegiance, citizen, equality, independence,* and *republic,* and choose a word for a second bracelet. They choose words after reading books with patriotic themes, such as Lynne Cheney's *America: A Patriotic Primer* (2002) and *A is for America: An American Alphabet* (Scillian, 2001). For their third word bracelet, they choose the most interesting word from all the words they've collected on the word wall and in their Word Wizard Notebooks. Some of the words that the club members choose for their third bracelets are *valiant, awesome, phenomenon, plethora, incredulous, cryptic, guffaw, mischievous,* and *razzle-dazzle.*

The vocabulary parade is the highlight of the year. Every club member creates a costume and participates in the parade. Mrs. Sanom dresses as a wizard—a word wizard, that is—and she leads the parade from classroom to classroom in the intermediate wing of the school. The students dress as *camouflage, victory, shimmer, monarch, liberty, uncomfortable, fortune, emerald,* and *twilight,* for example, and they carry word cards so that everyone will know the words they represent. As they tour each classroom, Mrs. Sanom and the students talk about their words and what they are learning. The club members' parents come to school to view the parade, and a local television station videotapes the parade for the evening news.

Children learn vocabulary by being immersed in words, and Mrs. Sanom engaged her fifth and sixth graders with words as they participated in Word Wizards Club activities. Researchers have reported again and again that reading is the best way for students to learn words. As they read, students learn many, many words incidentally, and teachers reinforce students' learning by directly teaching some difficult words that are significant to the story or important for general knowledge (Stahl, 1999).

Unfamiliar words are not equally hard or easy to learn; the degree of difficulty depends on what students already know about the word. Graves (1985) identifies four possible situations for unfamiliar words:

1. *New written word.* Students recognize the word and know what it means when they hear someone say it; they can use it orally, but they don't recognize its written form.

How Vocabulary Fits Into a Balanced Literacy Program

Component	Description
Reading	Reading is the most important way that students learn words.
Phonics and Other Skills	Vocabulary skills include recognizing synonyms, antonyms, and homophones; understanding idioms; using the dictionary; and applying root words and affixes.
Strategies	Students learn strategies for using context clues, identifying multiple meanings of words, examining etymological information in dictionaries, and studying words.
Vocabulary	Students learn an average of 3,000 words a year through a combination of reading and direct instruction.
Comprehension	Knowing the meaning of words students are reading is a prerequisite for comprehension.
Literature	Teachers post words on word walls and involve students in vocabulary activities and direct instruction lessons to teach important words.
Content-Area Study	Teachers post word walls as part of content-area units and involve students in word study activities using these words.
Oral Language	Students use the words they are learning orally as they talk about books they are reading, in content-area study, and through direct instruction activities.
Writing	Students apply their knowledge of vocabulary when they use words in writing.
Spelling	Students apply knowledge about words in spelling homophones and other words.

2. *New word.* Students have a concept related to the word, but they are not familiar with the word, either orally or in written form.

3. *New concept.* Students have little or no background knowledge about the concept underlying the word, and they don't recognize the word itself.

4. *New meaning.* Students know the word, but they are unfamiliar with the way the word is used and its meaning in this situation.

Of the four categories of word learning, the most difficult one for students is the one involving new concepts because they must first learn the concept and then attach a word label and learn the definition.

In a balanced literacy program, students meet unfamiliar words every day through literature and content-area study. Teachers recognize that they need to assist students in different ways, depending on whether the unfamiliar words are new written words, new words, new concepts, or new meanings. Sometimes simply pronouncing a new word is all that is needed, and sometimes relating a new meaning to a familiar one will be enough, but sometimes teaching a direct instruction lesson is necessary for students to learn a difficult new word or concept. The feature on page 190 shows how vocabulary fits into a balanced literacy program. As you continue reading this chapter, you will learn more about the ideas presented in the feature.

HOW DO STUDENTS LEARN VOCABULARY WORDS?

Students' vocabularies grow at an astonishing rate—about 3,000 words a year, or roughly 7 to 10 new words every day (Nagy & Herman, 1985). By the time students graduate from high school, their vocabularies may reach 25,000 words or more. It seems obvious that to learn words at such a prolific rate, students learn words both in school and outside of school, and they learn most words incidentally, not through explicit instruction. Reading has the largest impact on children's vocabulary development, but other activities are important, too. For example, students learn words through family activities, hobbies, and trips. Television can also have a significant impact on children's vocabularies, especially when children view educational programs and limit the amount of time they spend watching television each day. Teachers often assume that students learn words primarily through the lessons they teach, but students actually learn many more words in other ways.

Visit Chapter 6 on the Companion Website at *www.prenhall.com/ tompkins* to connect to web links related to vocabulary instruction.

Levels of Word Knowledge

Students develop knowledge about a word slowly, through repeated exposure to the word. They move from not knowing the word at all to recognizing that they have seen the word before, and then to a level of partial knowledge where they have a general sense of the word or know one meaning. Finally, students know the word fully: They know multiple meanings of the word and can use it in a variety of ways (Dale & O'Rourke, 1986; Nagy, 1988). Here are the four levels or degrees of word knowledge:

1. *Unknown word.* I don't know this word.

2. *Initial recognition.* I have seen or heard this word or I can pronounce it, but I don't know the meaning.

3. *Partial word knowledge.* I know one meaning of this word and can use it in a sentence.

4. *Full word knowledge.* I know more than one meaning or several ways to use this word. (Allen, 1999)

Once students reach the third level of word knowledge, they can usually understand the word in context and use it in their writing. Students do not reach the fourth level with all the words they learn. Stahl (1999) describes full word knowledge as "flexible": Students understand the core meaning of a word and how it changes in different contexts.

Incidental Word Learning

Students learn words incidentally, without explicit instruction all the time, and because students learn so many words this way, teachers know that they do not have to teach the meaning of every unfamiliar word in a text. Students learn words from many sources, but researchers report that reading is the single largest source of vocabulary growth for students after third grade (Beck & McKeown, 1991; Nagy, 1988). In addition, the amount of time children spend reading independently is the best predictor of vocabulary growth between second and fifth grades.

Students need daily opportunities for independent reading in order to learn vocabulary words, and they need to read books that are appropriate for their reading levels. If they read books that are too easy or too hard, students will learn very few new words. Two of the best ways to provide opportunities for independent reading are reading workshop and literature circles. Through both of these activities, students have opportunities to read self-selected books that interest them and to learn words in context.

A third way teachers provide for incidental learning of vocabulary is by reading books aloud to students at every grade level, kindergarten through eighth grade. Teachers should read stories and informational books to students every day, whether during

Independent Reading

These girls spend 35 minutes each day reading books they select from the classroom library. The books are interesting and appropriate for their reading level. Their teacher calls this independent reading activity DEAR time; it also goes by other names, such as Sustained Silent Reading. So far this year, these students have read 17 books each! As they read, they gain reading stamina, increase background knowledge, apply what they have learned about using context clues, and expand their vocabulary. Again and again, reading researchers have concluded that reading is the most important way students learn new words.

"story time" or as part of literature focus units, reading workshop, or thematic units. Although reading aloud is important for all students, it is an especially important experience for struggling readers who typically read fewer books themselves, and because the books at their reading level have less sophisticated vocabulary words. In fact, researchers report that students learn as many words incidentally while listening to teachers read aloud as they do by reading themselves (Stahl, Richek, & Vandevier, 1991).

Context Clues

Students learn many words from context as they read books (Nagy, Anderson, & Herman, 1987; Nagy, Herman, & Anderson, 1985). Six types of context clues are definition, example-illustration, contrast, logic, root words and affixes, and grammar. The surrounding words and sentences offer context clues; some clues provide information about the meaning of the word, and others provide information about the part of speech and how the unfamiliar word is used in a sentence. This contextual information helps students figure out the meaning of the word. Illustrations also provide contextual information that helps readers identify words. Figure 6–1 lists six types of context clues that readers use to figure out unfamiliar words as they read sentences and paragraphs.

The six types of context clues do not operate in isolation; two or three types of contextual information are often included in the same sentence. Also, readers' differing levels of background knowledge affect the types of word-identification strategies they can use effectively.

Consider how context clues might help students figure out the italicized words in these four sentences from *The Magic School Bus and the Electric Field Trip* (Cole, 1997):

We must have an unbroken *circuit*—circle—of wire. (p. 12)

Never use appliances with *frayed*, torn, or damaged insulation. (p. 42)

Figure 6–1	**Six Types of Context Clues**	
Clue	**Description**	**Sample Sentence**
Definition	Readers use the definition in the sentence to understand the unknown word.	Some spiders spin silk with tiny organs called *spinnerets*.
Example-Illustration	Readers use an example or illustration to understand the unknown word.	Toads, frogs, and some birds are *predators* that hunt and eat spiders.
Contrast	Readers understand the unknown word because it is compared or contrasted with another word in the sentence.	Most spiders live for about one year, but *tarantulas* sometimes live for 20 years or more!
Logic	Readers think about the rest of the sentence to understand the unknown word.	An *exoskeleton* acts like a suit of armor to protect the spider.
Root Words and Affixes	Readers use their knowledge of root words and affixes to figure out the unknown word.	People who are terrified of spiders have *arachnophobia*.
Grammar	Readers use the word's function in the sentence or its part of speech to figure out the unknown word.	Most spiders *molt* five to ten times.

Steam is an invisible gas made of water molecules—the tiniest bits of water. (p. 20)

The *switch* pulled the contacts together, and the electric path was complete again. (p. 41)

Which sentences provided sufficient context clues to figure out the meaning of the italicized words? Which types of context clues did the author use in these sentences? In the first sentence, for example, *circle*—a synonym for *circuit*—provides useful information, but it may not provide enough information for students who do not understand concepts related to electricity.

Unfortunately, context clues rarely provide enough information in a sentence to help students learn a word. The clues may seem to be useful to someone who already knows a word, but context clues often provide only partial information, and the information can be misleading. In the third sentence, for example, the definition of *steam* leaves out important information—that steam is dangerously hot! Researchers have concluded that context clues are relatively ineffective unless they provide definitions (Baumann & Kameenui, 1991; Nagy, 1988). Nonetheless, researchers recommend that students be taught how to use context clues because some clues are useful, and they do help students develop word-learning strategies to use on their own (Nagy, 1988).

Nagy, Anderson, and Herman (1987) found that students who read books at their grade level had a 1 in 20 chance of learning the meaning of any word from context. Although that chance might seem insignificant, if students read 20,000 words a year, and if they learn 1 of every 20 words from context, they would learn 1,000 words, or one-third of the average child's annual vocabulary growth. How much time does it take for students to read 20,000 words? Nagy (1988) has estimated that if elementary teachers provide 30 minutes of daily reading time, students will learn an additional 1,000 words a year!

The best way to teach students about context clues is by modeling. When teachers read aloud, they should stop at a difficult word and talk with students about how they can use context clues to figure out the meaning of the word. When the context provides enough information, teachers use the information and continue reading, but when the rest of the sentence or paragraph does not provide enough information, teachers model other strategies (such as looking up the word in the dictionary) to learn the meaning of the word.

It is interesting to note that capable and less capable readers learn from context at about the same rate (Stahl, 1999). Researchers have speculated that the difference in vocabulary growth is due to differences in the amount of words that students read, not the differences in their reading achievement.

Word-Learning Strategies

Capable readers use a variety of effective strategies to figure out the meaning of unknown words as they read. For instance, they might check the definition of a word in a dictionary or ask a teacher, classmate, or parent about a word. Sometimes they can use context clues to figure out the meaning of the unknown word. They also figure out a probable meaning by thinking about possible synonyms that make sense in the context of the sentence. Allen (1999) lists these ways students can figure out the meaning of unknown words:

Look at the word in relation to the sentence.

Look up the word in the dictionary and see if any meanings fit the sentence.

Ask the teacher.

Sound it out.

Read the sentence again.

Look at the beginning of the sentence again.

Look for other key words in the sentence that might tell you the meaning.

Think what makes sense.

Ask a friend to read the sentence to you.

Read around the word and then go back again.

Look at the picture, if there is one.

Skip the word if you don't need it. (p. 23)

Less capable readers, in contrast, have fewer strategies for figuring out the meaning of unfamiliar words: They often depend on just one or two strategies, such as sounding out the word or skipping it.

Why Is Vocabulary Knowledge Important?

Vocabulary knowledge and reading achievement are closely related: Students with larger vocabularies are more capable readers, and they have a wider repertoire of strategies for figuring out the meanings of unfamiliar words than less capable readers do (McKeown, 1985). Reading widely is the best way students develop their vocabularies, and that is one reason why capable readers have larger vocabularies (Nagy, 1988; Stahl, 1999): They simply do more reading, both in school and out of school (Anderson, Wilson, & Fielding, 1986).

The idea that capable readers learn more vocabulary because they read more is an example of the Matthew effect (Stanovich, 1986), which suggests that "the rich get richer and the poor get poorer" in vocabulary development and other aspects of reading. Capable readers become better readers because they read more, and the books they read are more challenging and have sophisticated vocabulary words. The gulf between more capable and less capable readers grows larger because less capable readers read less and the books they do read are less challenging.

TEACHING STUDENTS TO UNLOCK WORD MEANINGS

Vocabulary instruction plays an important role in balanced literacy classrooms (Rupley, Logan, & Nichols, 1998/1999). Teachers highlight important vocabulary words related to literature focus units and thematic units and teach minilessons about multiple meanings of words, etymologies, idioms, dictionary use, and other word-study skills. These lessons focus on words that students are reading and teach students how to figure out the meaning of unfamiliar words (Blachowicz & Lee, 1991). They are even more important to English learners, because these students rely more heavily on explicit instruction than native speakers do. The feature on the next page lists guidelines for teaching vocabulary.

Characteristics of Effective Instruction

The goal of vocabulary instruction is for students to learn how to learn new words. According to Carr and Wixon (1986), Nagy (1988), and Allen (1999), effective vocabulary instruction exemplifies these characteristics:

Visit Chapter 6 on the Companion Website at *www.prenhall.com/tompkins* to check into your state's standards for vocabulary.

- *Connections to background knowledge.* For vocabulary instruction to be effective, students must relate new words to their background knowledge. Because learning words in isolation is rarely effective, teachers should teach words in concept clusters whenever possible.

- *Repetition.* Students need to read, write, or say words 8 to 10 times or more before they recognize them automatically. Repetition helps students remember the words they are learning.

- *Higher-level word knowledge.* The focus of instruction should be to help students develop higher-level word knowledge; just having students memorize definitions or learn synonyms will not lead to full word knowledge.

- *Strategy learning.* Not only are students learning the meanings of particular words through vocabulary lessons, they are developing knowledge and strategies for learning new words independently.

- *Meaningful use.* Students need to be actively involved in word-study activities and opportunities to use the words in projects related to literature focus units and thematic units.

Teachers apply these five characteristics when they teach minilessons about vocabulary. Too often, vocabulary instruction has emphasized looking up definitions of words in a dictionary, but this is not a particularly effective activity, at least not as it has been used in the past.

Minilessons. Teachers present minilessons to teach key words, vocabulary concepts, and strategies for unlocking word meanings. These lessons should focus on words that students are reading and writing and involve students in meaningful activities. Students make predictions about the meaning of unfamiliar words as they read, using a combination of context clues, morphemic analysis, and their own prior knowledge (Blachowicz, 1993). Later, teachers often ask students to return to important words after reading to check their understanding of the words. The minilesson on page 198 shows how one teacher introduces vocabulary before reading a chapter in a content-area textbook.

Using Dictionaries. In traditional classrooms, the most common vocabulary activities involved listing new words on the chalkboard and directing students to write the words and copy the definitions from a dictionary or use the words in sentences. These activities are not effective for developing in-depth understanding and are no longer recommended (Stahl, 1999).

Looking words up in the dictionary generally isn't very effective because definitions do not provide enough useful information for students or because the words used in the definition are forms of the word being defined (Allen, 1999; Stahl, 1999). Sometimes the definition that students choose—usually the first one—is the wrong one. Or, the definition they find may not make sense to them. In addition, many entries don't provide examples of how the word is used in sentences. For example, the word *pollution* is usually defined as "the act of polluting"; this is not a useful definition. Students could look for an entry for *polluting,* but they won't find one. If they continue looking, they might notice an entry for *pollute,* where the first definition is "to make impure." The second definition is "to make unclean, especially with man-made waste," but even this definition provides very little useful information. On-line dictionaries may be more useful to students because the entries often provide more information about words and related words.

Although parents and teachers urge students to look up unknown words in a dictionary, dictionary definitions are most useful after a person already knows the meaning of a word. Therefore, teachers play an important role in dictionary work: They contextualize the definitions that students locate by explaining the meaning of the word in more detail, providing sample sentences, and comparing the word to related words and opposites.

Components of Word Study

Word knowledge involves more than learning definitions. Word study involves eight components:

1. Concepts and word meanings
2. Multiple meanings
3. Morphemic analysis
4. Synonyms
5. Antonyms
6. Homonyms
7. Etymologies
8. Figurative meanings

Students learn a wide range of information about words and make connections between words and concepts. They learn one or more meanings for a word and synonyms and antonyms to compare and contrast meanings. Sometimes they confuse words they

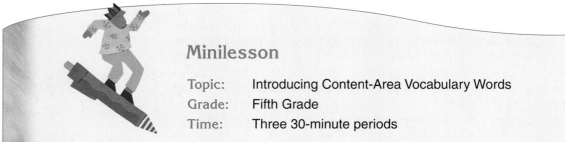

Minilesson

Topic: Introducing Content-Area Vocabulary Words
Grade: Fifth Grade
Time: Three 30-minute periods

Mrs. Cramer's fifth-grade class is involved in a social studies unit on immigration. The class has already created a K-W-L chart on immigration to develop and activate students' background knowledge, and students have written about how and when their families came to the United States. They have also marked their countries of origin on a world map in the classroom. In this 3-day minilesson, Mrs. Cramer introduces six key vocabulary words before students read a chapter in their social studies textbook. Many of her students are English learners, so she takes more time to practice vocabulary before reading the chapter.

1. Introduce the Topic

Mrs. Cramer explains to her class of fifth graders that after a week of studying immigration, they are now getting ready to read the chapter about immigration in the social studies text. She places these six words and phrases written on word cards in a pocket chart and reads each one aloud: *culture, descendant, ethnic custom, immigrant, prejudice,* and *pluralism.* She tells the students that these words are used in the chapter and that it is important to be familiar with them before reading.

2. Share Examples

Mrs. Cramer distributes anticipation guides for students to rate their knowledge of the new words. The guide has four columns; the six new words are listed in the left column, and the other three columns have these headings: I know the word well, I have heard of it, I don't know this word. For each word, the students put a check mark in the appropriate column. At the end of the unit, students will again rate their knowledge of the words and then compare the two ratings to assess their learning.

3. Provide Information

Mrs. Cramer divides the students into small groups for a word sort. Each group receives a pack of 12 cards; the new vocabulary words are written on six of the cards and their definitions on the other six cards. The students work together to match the words and definitions. Then Mrs. Cramer reviews the meaning of each word.

4. Guide Practice

The next day, the students repeat the word sort activity to review the meaning of each word. Next, they work with partners to complete a cloze activity: Mrs. Cramer has prepared a list of sentences taken from the chapter in which she has omitted the new vocabulary words; the students write the correct word in each blank. Then the teacher reviews the sentences with the students, explaining any words students use incorrectly.

5. Assess Learning

On the third day, Mrs. Cramer adds the six new words to the alphabetized word wall on immigration displayed on a wall in the classroom. Next she models writing a quickwrite using the new words and other "immigration" words from the word wall. Then the students write quickwrites following the teacher's model and using at least three of the new words and three other words from the word wall. After they finish writing, the students use highlighters to mark the "immigration" words they have incorporated in their writings. Later, Mrs. Cramer reads the quickwrites and uses them to assess the students' vocabulary knowledge.

Figure 6-2   A Seventh Grader's Investigation of *Vaporize*

Morphemic Analysis	Root Word	Suffix
vapor + ize	vapor	ize
		It is used to change a noun into a verb.

VAPORIZE

To change from a solid into a vapor (gas) (verb)

Word History	Related Words	Figurative Use
It became a word in the 1600's. It came from the Latin word "steam".	evaporate vaporizer vaporous	The boy's thoughts vaporized and he couldn't remember the answer.

are learning with homonyms that sound or are spelled the same as the word they are learning. Students also learn that prefixes and suffixes change the meaning of a word. And, they learn about idioms and figurative sayings involving the word they are learning. A seventh grader's investigation of the word *vaporize* is shown in Figure 6–2.

Concepts and Word Meanings. Students use words to label concepts, and they learn words best when they are related to a concept. It is always easier to learn a group of words relating to a concept than to learn unrelated words. Consider the words *axle, groundwater, buffalo chips, wagon train, ford, fur trader, dysentery, outpost, guide, mountain men, oxen, Bowie knife, snag, cut-off, cholera, winch,* and *prairie dog,* which all relate to pioneers traveling west on the Oregon Trail. When students read a book about the Oregon Trail, for example, or during a social studies unit on the westward movement, they learn many of these words by connecting them to their Oregon Trail schema or concept.

Multiple Meanings of Words. Many words have more than one meaning. For some words, multiple meanings develop for the noun and verb forms of the word, but sometimes meanings develop in other ways. The word *bank,* for example, has the following meanings:

a piled-up mass of snow or clouds

the slope of land beside a lake or river

the slope of a road on a turn

the lateral tilting of an airplane in a turn

to cover a fire with ashes for slow burning

a business establishment that receives and lends money

a container in which money is saved

a supply for use in emergencies (e.g., a blood bank)

a place for storage (e.g., a computer's memory bank)

to count on

similar things arranged in a row (e.g., a bank of elevators)

to arrange things in a row

You may be surprised that there are at least a dozen meanings for the common word *bank*. Some are nouns and others are verbs, but grammatical form alone does not account for so many meanings.

The meanings of *bank* come from three sources. The first five meanings come from a Viking word, and they are related because they all deal with something slanted or making a slanted motion. The next five meanings come from the Italian word *banca*, a money changer's table. All these meanings deal with financial banking except for the tenth meaning, "to count on," which requires a bit more thought. We use the saying "to bank on" figuratively to mean "to depend on," but it began more literally from the actual counting of money on a table. The last two meanings come from the French word *banc*, meaning "bench." Words have acquired multiple meanings as society became more complex and finer shades of meaning were necessary; for example, the meanings of *bank* as an emergency supply and a storage place are fairly new. As with many words with multiple meanings, it is just a linguistic accident that three original words from three languages with related meanings came to be spelled the same way (Tompkins & Yaden, 1986). A list of other common words with more than five meanings is shown in Figure 6–3.

Students gradually acquire additional meanings for words, and they usually learn these new meanings through reading. When a familiar word is used in a new way, students often notice the new application and may be curious enough to check the meaning in a dictionary.

Morphemic Analysis. Students use their knowledge of affixes to unlock many multisyllabic words. For example, *omnivorous, carnivorous,* and *herbivorous* relate to the foods that animals eat. *Omni* means "all," *carno* means "flesh," and *herb* means "vegetation." The common word part *vorous* comes from the Latin *vorare*, meaning "to swallow up." When students know *carnivorous* or *carnivore*, they can use their knowledge of prefixes to figure out the other words.

Many English words are compound words whose meanings are usually clear from the word parts and the context in which each word or phrase is used, as in the words *toothbrush, breakneck, earthquake,* and *anteater.* The word *fire* is used in a variety of compound words and phrases, such as *fire hydrant, firebomb, fireproof, fireplace, firearm, fire drill, under fire, set the world on fire, fire away,* and *open fire.*

Students can examine words developed from a common root, such as these words from the Latin roots *-ann* and *-enn*, which mean "year": *annual, biennial, perennial, centennial, bicentennial, millennium,* and *sesquicentennial.* Students figure out the meaning of the words by locating the root and identifying prefixes and suffixes. Then they work together to make a cluster to highlight the words and their meanings.

Synonyms: Words With the Same Meaning. Words that have nearly the same meaning as other words are synonyms. English has so many synonyms because so many words have been borrowed from other languages. Synonyms are useful because they

Figure 6-3　Common Words With More Than Five Meanings

act	drive	lay	place	set	strike
air	dry	leave	plant	sharp	stroke
away	dull	line	plate	shine	strong
bad	eye	low	play	shoot	stuff
bar	face	make	point	short	sweep
base	fail	man	post	side	sweet
black	fair	mark	print	sight	swing
blow	fall	mind	quiet	sign	take
boat	fast	mine	rain	sing	thick
break	fire	natural	raise	sink	thing
carry	fly	new	range	slip	think
case	good	nose	rear	small	throw
catch	green	note	rest	sound	tie
change	hand	now	return	spin	tight
charge	have	off	rich	spread	time
check	head	open	ride	spring	touch
clear	heel	out	right	square	tough
color	high	paper	ring	stamp	train
count	hold	part	rise	star	trip
cover	hot	pass	roll	stay	turn
crack	house	pay	rule	step	under
cross	keep	pick	run	stick	up
crown	key	picture	scale	stiff	watch
cut	knock	piece	score	stock	way
draw	know	pitch	serve	stop	wear

provide options, allowing writers to be more precise. Think of all the synonyms for the word *cold: cool, chilly, frigid, icy, frosty,* and *freezing.* Each word has a different shade of meaning: *Cool* means moderately cold; *chilly* is uncomfortably cold; *frigid* is intensely cold; *icy* means very cold; *frosty* means covered with frost; and *freezing* is so cold that water changes into ice. Our language would be limited if we had only the word *cold.*

Teachers should be careful to articulate the differences among synonyms. Nagy (1988) emphasizes that teachers should focus on teaching concepts and related words, not just provide single-word definitions using synonyms. For example, to tell a child that *frigid* means *cold* provides only limited information. And, when a child says, "I want my sweater because it's frigid in here," it shows that the child does not understand the different degrees of cold; there's a big difference between *chilly* and *frigid.*

Antonyms: Words That Mean the Opposite. Words that express opposite meanings are antonyms. Antonyms for the word *loud,* for example, are *soft, subdued, quiet, silent, inaudible, sedate, somber, dull,* and *colorless.* These words express shades of meaning just as synonyms do, and some opposites are more appropriate for one meaning of *loud* than for another. When *loud* means *gaudy,* for instance, opposites are *somber, dull,* and *colorless;* when *loud* means *noisy,* the opposites are *quiet, silent,* and *inaudible.*

Students learn to use a thesaurus to locate both synonyms and antonyms. *A First Thesaurus* (Wittels & Greisman, 1985), *Scholastic Children's Thesaurus* (Bollard, 1998), and *The American Heritage Children's Thesaurus* (Hellweg, 1997) are three excellent thesauri designed for children. Students need to learn how to use these handy reference books to locate more effective words when revising their writing and for word-study activities.

Homophones: Words That Confuse. Homophones, also known as homonyms, are words that sound alike but are spelled differently, such as *right and write, to, too*, and *two*, and *there, their*, and *they're*. A list of homophones is presented in Figure 6–4. Sometimes students confuse the meanings of these words, but more often they confuse their spellings.

Most homophones are linguistic accidents, but *stationary* and *stationery* share an interesting history: *Stationery*, meaning paper and books, developed from *stationary*. In medieval England, merchants traveled from town to town selling their wares. The merchant who sold paper goods was the first to set up shop in one town. His shop was "stationary" because it did not move, and he came to be called the "stationer." The spelling difference between the two words signifies the semantic difference.

There are many books of homophones for children, including Gwynne's *The King Who Rained* (1970), *A Chocolate Moose for Dinner* (1976), *The Sixteen Hand Horse* (1980), and *A Little Pigeon Toad* (1988); Maestro's *What's a Frank Frank? Tasty Homograph Riddles* (1984); *What in the World Is a Homophone?* (Presson, 1996); and *Eight Ate: A Feast of Homonym Riddles* (Terban, 1982).

Figure 6–4	**Homophones, Words That Sound Alike But Are Spelled Differently**			
air–heir	creak–creek	knead–need	peak–peek–pique	shoot–chute
allowed–aloud	days–daze	knew–new	peal–peel	side–sighed
ant–aunt	dear–deer	knight–night	pedal–peddle	slay–sleigh
ate–eight	dew–do–due	knot–not	plain–plane	soar–sore
ball–bawl	die–dye	know–no	pleas–please	soared–sword
bare–bear	doe–dough	lead–led	pole–poll	sole–soul
be–bee	ewe–you	leak–leek	pore–pour	some–sum
beat–beet	eye–I	lie–lye	praise–prays–preys	son–sun
berry–bury	fair–fare	loan–lone	presence–presents	stairs–stares
billed–build	feat–feet	made–maid	pride–pried	stake–steak
blew–blue	fined–find	mail–male	prince–prints	stationary–stationery
boar–bore	fir–fur	main–mane	principal–principle	steal–steel
board–bored	flea–flee	manner–manor	profit–prophet	straight–strait
bough–bow	flew–flu	marshal–martial	quarts–quartz	suite–sweet
brake–break	flour–flower	meat–meet–mete	rain–rein–reign	tail–tale
brews–bruise	for–fore–four	medal–meddle–metal	raise–rays–raze	taught–taut
bridal–bridle	forth–fourth	might–mite	rap–wrap	tear–tier
brows–browse	foul–fowl	mind–mined	red–read	their–there–they're
buy–by–bye	gorilla–guerrilla	miner–minor	reed–read	threw–through
capital–capitol	grate–great	missed–mist	right–rite–write	throne–thrown
ceiling–sealing	grill–grille	moan–mown	ring–wring	tide–tied
cell–sell	groan–grown	morning–mourning	road–rode–rowed	to–too–two
cellar–seller	guessed–guest	muscle–mussel	role–roll	toad–toed–towed
cent–scent–sent	hair–hare	naval–navel	root–route	toe–tow
chews–choose	hall–haul	none–nun	rose–rows	troop–troupe
chic–sheik	hay–hey	oar–or–ore	rung–wrung	vain–vane–vein
chili–chilly	heal–heel	one–won	sail–sale	wade–weighed
choral–coral	hear–here	pail–pale	scene–seen	waist–waste
chord–cord–cored	heard–herd	pain–pane	sea–see	wait–weight
cite–sight–site	hi–high	pair–pare–pear	sealing–ceiling	wares–wears
close–clothes	hoarse–horse	passed–past	seam–seem	way–weigh
coarse–course	hole–whole	patience–patients	serf–surf	weak–week
colonel–kernel	hour–our	peace–piece	sew–so–sow	wood–would

Teachers in the primary grades introduce the concept of homophones and teach the easier pairs, including *see–sea, I–eye, right–write,* and *dear–deer.* In the upper grades, teachers focus on the homophones that students continue to confuse, such as *there–their–they're* and the more sophisticated pairs, including *morning–mourning, flair–flare,* and *complement–compliment.*

Intensive study is necessary because homophones are confusing to many students. The words sound alike and the spellings are often very similar—sometimes only one letter varies or one letter is added: *pray–prey, hole–whole.* And sometimes the words have the same letters, but they vary in sequence: *bear–bare* and *great–grate.*

Teachers teach minilessons to explain the concept of homophones and make charts of the homophone pairs and triplets; calling children's attention to the differences in spelling and meaning helps to clarify the words. Students can also make homophone posters, as shown in Figure 6–5. On the posters, students draw pictures and write sentences to contrast the homophones. Displaying these posters in the classroom reminds students of the differences between the words.

Etymologies: The History of the English Language. Glimpses into the history of the English language provide interesting information about word meanings and spellings (Tompkins & Yaden, 1986; Venezky, 1999). The English language began in 447 A.D. when the Angles, Saxons, and other Germanic tribes invaded England. This Anglo-Saxon English was first written down by Latin missionaries in approximately 750 A.D. The English of the period from 450 to 1100 is known as Old English. During this time, English was a very phonetic language and followed many German syntactic patterns. Many loan words, including *ugly, window, egg, they, sky,* and *husband,* were contributed by the marauding Vikings who plundered villages along the English coast.

The English of the second period of development, Middle English (1100–1500), began with the Norman Conquest in 1066. William, Duke of Normandy, invaded England and became the English king. William, his lords, and the royals who followed him spoke French for nearly 200 years, so French was the official language of England. Many French loan words were added to the language, and French spellings were substituted for Old English spellings. For example, *night* was spelled *niht* and *queen* was spelled *cwen* in Old English to reflect how they were pronounced; their modern spellings reflect changes made by French scribes. Loan words from Dutch, Latin, and other languages were added to English during this period, too.

The invention of the printing press marks the transition from Middle English to the Modern English period (1500–present). William Caxton brought the first printing press to England in 1476, and soon books and pamphlets were being mass-produced. Spelling became standardized as Samuel Johnson and other lexicographers compiled dictionaries, even though English pronunciation of words continued to evolve. Loan words continued to flow into English from almost every language in the world. Exploration and colonization in North America and around the world accounted for many of the loan words. For example, *canoe* and *moccasin* are from Native American languages; *bonanza, chocolate,* and *ranch* are from Mexican Spanish; and *cafeteria, prairie,* and *teenager* are American English. Other loan words include *zero* (Arabic), *tattoo* (Polynesian), *robot* (Czech), *yogurt* (Turkish), *restaurant* (French), *dollar* (German), *jungle* (Hindi), and *umbrella* (Italian). Some words, such as *electric, democracy,* and *astronaut,* were created using Greek word parts. New words are added to English every year, and the new words reflect new inventions and cultural practices. Many new words today, such as *e-mail,* relate to the Internet. The word *Internet* is a recent word, too; it is less than 25 years old!

Figure 6–5   **A Sixth Grader's Homophone Poster**

Students use etymological information in dictionaries and other books about word histories to learn how particular words developed and what the words mean. Etymological information is included in brackets at the beginning or end of dictionary entries. Here is the etymological information for three words and elaboration of the information:

democracy [1576, < MF < LL < Gr demokratia, demos (people) + kratia (cracy = strength, power)]

The word *democracy* entered English in 1576 through French, and the French word came from Latin and the Latin word from Greek. In Greek, the word *demokratia* means "power to the people."

house [bef. 900, ME hous, OE hus]

House is an Old English word that entered English before 900. It was spelled *hus* in Old English and *hous* in Middle English.

moose [1603, < Algonquin, "he who strips bark"]

The word *moose* is Native American—from an Algonquin tribe in the northeastern part of the United States—and entered English in 1603. It comes from the Algonquin word for "he who strips bark."

Even though words have entered English from around the world, the three main sources of words are English, Latin, and Greek. Upper-grade students can learn to identify the languages that these words came from; knowing the language backgrounds helps students to predict the spellings and meanings (Venezky, 1999).

English words are usually one- or two-syllable common, familiar words that may or may not be phonetically regular, such as *fox, arm, Monday, house, match, eleven, of, come, week, horse, brother,* and *dumb*. Words with *ch* (pronounced as /ch/), *sh, th,* and *wh* digraphs are usually English, as in *church, shell, bath,* and *what*. Many English words are compound words or use comparative and superlative forms, such as *starfish, toothache, fireplace, happier, fastest*.

Many words from Latin are similar to comparable words in French, Spanish, or Italian, such as *ancient, judicial, impossible,* and *officer*. Latin words have related words or derivatives, such as *courage, courageous, encourage, discourage,* and *encouragement*. Also, many Latin words have *-tion/-sion* suffixes: *imitation, corruption, attention, extension,* and *possession*.

Greek words are the most unusual. Many are long words, and their spellings seem unfamiliar. The letters *ph* are pronounced /f/, and the letters *ch* are pronounced /k/ in Greek loan words, as in *autograph, chaos,* and *architect*. Longer words with *th,* such as *thermometer* and *arithmetic,* are Greek. The suffix *-ology* is Greek, as in the words *biology, psychology,* and *geology*. The letter *y* is used in place of *i* in the middle of some words, such as *bicycle* and *myth*. Many Greek words are composed of two parts: *bibliotherapy, microscope, biosphere, hypodermic,* and *telephone*. Figure 6–6 presents lists of words from English, Latin, and Greek that teachers can use for word sorts and other vocabulary activities.

Related words have developed from English, Latin, and Greek sources. Consider the words *tooth, dentist,* and *orthodontist. Tooth* is an English word, which explains its irregular plural form, *teeth. Dentist* is a Latin word; *dent* means "tooth" in Latin, and the suffix *-ist* means "one who does." The word *orthodontist* is Greek. *Ortho* means "straighten" and *dont* means "tooth"; therefore, *orthodontist* means "one who straightens teeth." Other related triplets include:

book: bookstore (E), bibliography (Gr), library (L)

eye: eyelash (E), optical (Gr), binoculars (L)

foot: foot-dragging (E), tripod (Gr), pedestrian (L)

great: greatest (E), megaphone (Gr), magnificent (L)

see: foresee (E), microscope (Gr), invisible (L)

star: starry (E), astronaut (Gr), constellation (L)

time: time-tested (E), chronological (Gr), contemporary (L)

water: watermelon (E), hydrate (Gr), aquarium (L)

When students understand English, Latin, and Greek root words, they appreciate the relationships among words and their meanings.

Figurative Meanings of Words. Many words have both literal and figurative meanings: Literal meanings are the explicit, dictionary meanings, and figurative meanings are metaphorical or use figures of speech. For example, to describe *winter* as the coldest season of the year is literal, but to say that "winter has icy breath" is figurative. Two types of figurative language are idioms and comparisons.

Idioms are groups of words, such as "in hot water," that have a special meaning. Idioms can be confusing to students because they must be interpreted figuratively rather than literally. "In hot water" is an old expression meaning to be in trouble. Cox (1980) explains that hundreds of years ago, there were no police officers and people had to protect themselves from robbers. When a robber tried to break into a house, the homeowner might pour boiling water from a second-floor window onto the head of the robber, who would then be "in hot water." There are hundreds of idioms in English, and we use them every day to create word pictures that make language more colorful. Some examples are "out in left field," "a skeleton in the closet," "raining cats and dogs," "stick your neck out," "a chip off the old block," and "don't cry over spilled milk."

Four excellent books of idioms for students are *Put Your Foot in Your Mouth and Other Silly Sayings* (Cox, 1980), *Scholastic Dictionary of Idioms: More Than 600 Phrases, Sayings, and Expressions* (Terban, 1996), *Punching the Clock: Funny Action Idioms* (Terban, 1990), and *In a Pickle and Other Funny Idioms* (Terban, 1983). Because idioms are figurative sayings, many children—and especially those who are English learners—have difficulty learning them. It is crucial that children move beyond the literal meanings and become flexible in using language. One way for students to learn flexibility is to create idiom posters showing both literal and figurative meanings, as illustrated in Figure 6–7.

Metaphors and similes are comparisons that liken something to something else. A simile is a comparison signaled by the use of *like* or *as:* "The crowd was as rowdy as a bunch of marauding monkeys" and "My apartment was like an oven after the air-

Figure 6-6	Words From English, Latin, and Greek	
English	**Latin**	**Greek**
apple	addiction	ache
between	administer	arithmetic
bumblebee	advantage	astronomy
child	beautiful	atomic
cry	capital	biology
cuff	confession	chaos
earth	continent	chemical
fireplace	delicate	democracy
fourteen	discourage	disaster
freedom	erupt	elephant
Friday	explosion	geography
get	fraction	gymnastics
have	fragile	helicopter
horse	frequently	hemisphere
knight	heir	hieroglyphics
know	honest	kaleidoscope
ladybug	identify	myth
lamb	January	octopus
lip	journal	phenomenal
lock	junior	photosynthesis
mouth	nation	pseudonym
out	occupy	rhinoceros
quickly	organize	rhythm
ride	principal	sympathy
silly	procession	telescope
this	salute	theater
twin	special	thermometer
weather	uniform	trophy
whisper	vacation	zodiac
wild	vegetable	zoo

Figure 6–7 **A Sixth Grader's Idiom Poster for "In Hot Water"**

conditioning broke last summer" are two examples. In contrast, a metaphor compares two things by implying that one is the other, without using *like* or *as*: "The children were frisky puppies playing in the yard" is an example. Metaphors are stronger comparisons, as these examples show:

> She's as cool as a cucumber.
> She's a cool cucumber.
>
> In the moonlight, the dead tree looked like a skeleton.
> In the moonlight, the dead tree was a skeleton.

Differentiating between the terms *simile* and *metaphor* is less important than understanding the meaning of comparisons in books students read and having students use comparisons to make their writing more vivid. For example, a sixth-grade student compared anger to a thunderstorm using a simile. She wrote, "Anger is like a thunderstorm, screaming with thunder-feelings and lightning-words." Another student compared anger to a volcano. Using a metaphor, he wrote, "Anger is a volcano, erupting with poisonous words and hot-lava actions."

Students begin by learning traditional comparisons such as "happy as a clam" and "high as a kite," and then they learn to notice and invent fresh, unexpected comparisons. To introduce traditional comparisons to primary-grade students, teachers can

Why is the vocabulary in content-area texts so difficult for my struggling readers?

Vocabulary in social studies and science is dependent on concept knowledge and often is more technical than the vocabulary in literature. Moreover, students may be able to get by with only a superficial understanding of a word to keep reading a story, but when they are learning about historical and scientific concepts, they need more in-depth knowledge. To help your struggling readers, focus on concepts when you teach vocabulary, and teach related words together. Be sure to emphasize the relationships among the words. Because you usually can't teach all the words that struggling students need to learn, focus on those that are most crucial to understanding the big ideas. Memorizing definitions isn't very effective for these students, so use real experiences, artifacts, videos, and dramatizations to expand their understanding.

use Audrey Wood's *Quick as a Cricket* (1982). Middle- and upper-grade students can invent new comparisons for stale expressions such as "butterflies in your stomach." In *Anastasia Krupnik*, for example, Lois Lowry (1979) substituted "ginger ale in her knees" for the trite "butterflies in her stomach" to describe how nervous Anastasia was when she had to stand up in class to read her poem.

Choosing Words to Study

Teachers choose the most important words from books to teach. Important words include those that are essential to understanding the text, words that may confuse students, and general utility words students will use as they read other books (Allen, 1999). Teachers should avoid words that are unrelated to the central concept of the book or unit or words that are too conceptually difficult for students. As teachers choose words to highlight and for word-study activities, they consider their students, the book being read, and the instructional context. For example, during a theme on bears, first graders listened to their teacher read these books:

The Three Bears (Galdone, 1972)

Somebody and the Three Blairs (Tolhurst, 1990)

Brown Bear, Brown Bear, What Do You See? (Martin, 1983)

Polar Bear, Polar Bear, What Do You Hear? (Martin, 1991)

Alaska's Three Bears (Cartwright, 1990)

These words were highlighted:

shaggy	fur	dangerous
meat-eating	polar bear	grizzly bear
claws	hind legs	hibernate
cubs	tame	brown bear
den	black bear	sharp teeth

These are vocabulary words—content-related words—not high-frequency words such as *who* and *this*.

Students do not have to know all of the words in a book to read and comprehend it or listen to it read aloud. Researchers estimate that students can tolerate books with as many as 15% unfamiliar words (Freebody & Anderson, 1983). Of course, students vary in the percentage of unfamiliar words they can tolerate, depending on the topic of the book, their purpose for reading, and the role of the unfamiliar words. It is unrealistic for teachers to expect students to learn every word in a book or expect to have to teach every word.

This third grader writes an unfamiliar word beginning with *f* on the word wall in his classroom. When students need to know how to spell an unfamiliar word, they ask the teacher, and together the teacher and student figure out the spelling and write the word on a small sticky note. The student takes the note to his or her desk and uses it in the writing project. Later, the teacher invites students who have sticky notes to add their words to the class word wall. Word walls are not only vocabulary tools, but also useful resources for writers.

Spotlighting Words on Word Walls

Teachers post word walls in the classroom; usually they're made from large sheets of butcher paper and divided into sections for each letter of the alphabet. Students and the teacher write interesting, confusing, and important words on the word wall. Usually students choose the words to write on the word wall and may even do the writing themselves. Teachers add other important words that students have not chosen. Words are added to the word wall as they come up in books students are reading or during a thematic unit, not in advance. Students use the word wall to locate a word they want to use during a grand conversation or to check the spelling of a word they are writing, and teachers use the words listed on the word wall for word-study activities.

Some teachers use pocket charts and word cards instead of butcher paper for their word walls. This way, the word cards can easily be used for word-study activities, and they can be sorted and rearranged on the pocket chart. After the book or unit is completed, teachers punch holes in one end of the cards and hang them on a ring. Then the collection of word cards can be placed in the writing center for students to use in writing activities.

Word walls play an important role in vocabulary learning. The words are posted in the classroom so that they are visible to all students, and because they are so visible, students will read them more often and refer to the chart when writing. Their availability will also remind teachers to use the words for word-study activities. If the words aren't large enough for everyone to see, teachers encourage students to walk over to the word wall to check a word.

Students also make individual word walls by dividing a sheet of paper into 20–24 boxes, labeling the boxes with the letters of the alphabet; they put several letters together in one box. Then students write important words and phrases in the boxes as they read and discuss the book. Figure 6–8 shows a sixth grader's word wall for *Hatchet* (1987), a wilderness survival story by Gary Paulsen.

Sometimes teachers categorize words in other ways. Middle- and upper-grade teachers often integrate grammar instruction with vocabulary and organize the words according to part of speech. Because many words can represent more than one part of speech depending on how they are used in the sentences, students often need to carefully analyze how the word is used. For example, consider how the word *glowing* is used in *The crew watched the glowing stone for hours* and *The stone was glowing brighter each day:* In the first sentence, *glowing* is an adjective but in the second sentence, it is a verb. Figure 6–9 shows a fifth-grade class word wall organized by parts of speech using words from Chris Van Allsburg's *The Wretched Stone* (1991), a story about a strange glowing stone picked up on a sea voyage that captivates a ship's crew and has a terrible transforming effect on them. After students read and discussed the book, they reread it to locate and classify the words. They organized the word wall with

---

Figure 6–8   A Sixth Grader's Alphabetized Word Wall for *Hatchet*

A	B	C	D
alone	bush plane	Canadian wilderness	divorce
absolutely terrified	Brian Robeson	controls	desperation
arrows	bruised	cockpit	destroyed
aluminum cookset	bow & arrow	crash	disappointment
		careless	devastating
		campsite	

E	F	G	H
engine	fire	gut cherries	hatchet
emergency	fuselage	get food	heart attack
emptiness	fish		hunger
exhaustion	foolbirds		hope
	foodshelf		
	54 days		

I J	K L	M N	O P Q
instruments	lake	memory	pilot
insane		mosquitoes	panic
incredible wealth		mistakes	painful
		matches	porcupine quills
		mental journal	patience
		moose	

R	S T	U V	W X Y Z
rudder pedals	stranded	visitation rights	wilderness
rescue	secret	viciously thirsty	windbreaker
radio	survival pack	valuable asset	wreck
relative comfort	search	vicious whine	woodpile
raspberries	sleeping bag	unbelievable riches	wolf
roaring bonfire	shelter		
raft	starved		

Nouns	Adjectives	Verbs	Adverbs
crew	wretched	abandon	approximately
voyage	grave	scuttle	roughly
danger	horrifying	lock	unbelievably
island	glowing	believe	well
stone	alert	read	apparently
sailors	unnatural	play	steadily
shrieks	peculiar	fascinate	away
omen	clumsy	sail	unfortunately
rescue	feverish	write	quickly
vessel	hairy	glowing	slightly
cargo	clever	sing	too
boredom	strange	swing	quite
quarters	lush	fade	perfectly
apes	overpowering	grinning	soon
rock	powerful	staring	so

nouns and adjectives side by side because adjectives modify nouns and verbs and adverbs side by side because adverbs modify verbs.

Even though 25, 50, or more words may be added to the word wall, not all of them will be directly taught to students. As they plan, teachers create lists of words that will probably be written on word walls during the lesson. From this list, teachers choose the key words—the ones that are critical to understanding the book or the unit—and these are the words they include in minilessons.

Activities for Exploring Words

Word-study activities provide opportunities for students to explore the meaning of words listed on word walls, other words related to books they are reading, and words they are learning during social studies and science units. Through these activities, students develop concepts, learn the meanings of words, and make associations among words. None of these activities require students to simply write words and their definitions or to use the words in sentences or a contrived story.

1.   *Word posters.* Students choose a word from the word wall and write it on a small poster. Then they draw and color a picture to illustrate the word. They also use the word in a sentence on the poster. This is one way that students can visualize the meaning of a word.

2.   *Word maps.* Word maps are another way to visualize a word's meaning (Duffelmeyer & Banwart, 1992–1993; Schwartz & Raphael, 1985). Students draw a cluster on a small card or a sheet of paper with a word from the word wall in the center circle. Then they draw rays from the center and write on each ray important information about the word to make connections between the word and what they are reading or studying. Three kinds of information are included in a word map: a category for the word, examples, and characteristics or associations. Figure 6–10

Figure 6–10 **A Word Map**

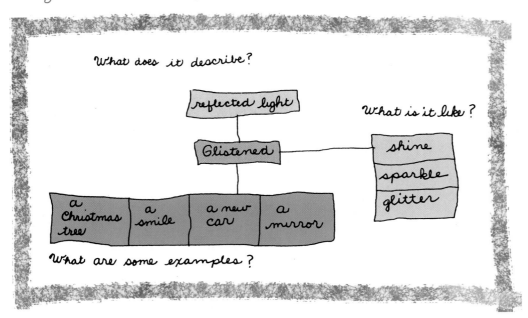

shows a word map made by a fifth grader reading *Bunnicula: A Rabbit-Tale of Mystery* (Howe & Howe, 1979).

3. ***Dramatizing words.*** Students each choose a word from the word wall and dramatize it for classmates, who then try to guess it. Sometimes an action is a more effective way to explain a word than a verbal definition. For example, a teacher teaching a literature focus unit on *Chrysanthemum* (Henkes, 1991), the story of a little girl who didn't like her name, dramatized the word *wilted* for her second graders when they didn't understand how a girl could wilt. Other words in *Chrysanthemum* that can easily be acted out include *humorous, sprouted, dainty,* and *wildly.* Dramatization is an especially effective activity for students who are English learners.

Learn more about word sorts, word walls, and other instructional procedures discussed in this chapter on the DVD that accompanies this text.

4. ***Word sorts.*** Students sort a collection of words taken from the word wall into two or more categories in a word sort (Bear, Invernizzi, Templeton, & Johnston, 2004). Usually students choose the categories they will use for the sort, but sometimes the teacher chooses them. For example, words from a story might be sorted by character, or words from a thematic unit on machines might be sorted according to type of machine. The words can be written on cards, and then students sort a pack of word cards into piles. Or, students can cut apart a list of words, sort them into categories, and then paste the grouped words together.

5. ***Word chains.*** Students choose a word from the word wall and then identify three or four words to sequence before or after the word to make a chain. For example, the word *tadpole* can be chained this way: *egg, tadpole, frog;* and the word *aggravate* can be chained like this: *irritate, bother, aggravate, annoy.* Students can draw and write their chains on a sheet of paper, or they can make a chain out of construction paper and write the words on each link.

6. ***Semantic feature analysis.*** Students learn the meanings of words that are conceptually related by examining their characteristics in a semantic feature analysis. Teachers select a group of related words, such as animals and plants in the

rain forest or planets in the solar system, and then make a grid to classify them according to distinguishing characteristics (Heimlich & Pittelman, 1986). Students analyze each word, characteristic by characteristic, and they put check marks, circles, and question marks in each cell to indicate whether the word represents that characteristic. For example, on a semantic feature analysis about the rain forest, animals, plants, and people who live in the rain forest are listed on one side of the grid and characteristics on the other. For the word *sloth*, students would add check marks in the grid to indicate that it is a mammal, lives in the canopy, goes to the forest floor, and has camouflage. They would add circles to indicate that a sloth is not colorful, not dangerous to people, not a plant, and not a bird or insect. If they aren't sure whether sloths are used to make medicine, they would add a question mark.

Complete a self-assessment to check your understanding of the concepts presented in this chapter on the Companion Website at *www.prenhall.com/ tompkins*

Review: How Effective Teachers Expand Students' Knowledge of Words

1. Teachers provide opportunities for students to read stories and informational books daily because students learn many new words through reading.

2. Teachers read aloud to students every day because students learn many new words as they listen to books read aloud.

3. Teachers support students as they develop full word knowledge and learn to use words flexibly in a variety of contexts.

4. Teachers help students to develop a repertoire of word-learning strategies in order to learn words incidentally.

5. Teachers demonstrate how to use context clues to figure out the meaning of unknown words when reading independently.

6. Teachers post vocabulary words on word walls.

7. Teachers choose the most useful words from the word wall for vocabulary activities.

8. Teachers teach minilessons on individual words, vocabulary concepts, and word-learning strategies.

9. Teachers teach many concepts about words, including multiple meanings, morphemic analysis, synonyms, antonyms, homophones, etymologies, and figurative meanings.

10. Teachers involve students in meaningful word-study activities, such as word maps, dramatizing words, word sorts, and semantic feature analysis, that are related to books students are reading and units they are studying.

Professional References

Allen, J. (1999). *Words, words, words.* Portsmouth, NH: Heinemann.

Anderson, R. C., Wilson, P. T., & Fielding, L. G. (1986). *Growth in reading and how children spend their time outside of school* (Technical Report No. 389). Urbana: University of Illinois, Center for the Study of Reading.

Baumann, J. F., & Kameenui, E. J. (1991). Research on vocabulary instruction: Ode to Voltaire. In J. Flood, J. M. Jensen, D. Lapp, & J. R. Squire (Eds.), *Handbook on teaching the English language arts* (pp. 604–632). New York: Macmillan.

Bear, D. R., Invernizzi, M., Templeton, S., & Johnston, F. (2004). *Words their way: Word study for phonics, vocabulary,* *and spelling instruction.* Upper Saddle River, NJ: Merrill/ Prentice Hall.

Beck, I., & McKeown, M. (1991). Conditions of vocabulary acquisition. In R. Barr, M. Kamil, P. Mosenthal, & P. D. Pearson (Eds.), *Handbook of reading research* (Vol. 2, pp. 789–814). White Plains, NY: Longman.

Blachowicz, C. L. Z. (1993). C(2)QU: Modeling context use in the classroom. *The Reading Teacher, 47,* 268–269.

Blachowicz, C. L. Z., & Lee, J. J. (1991). Vocabulary development in the whole literacy classroom. *The Reading Teacher, 45,* 188–195.

Carr, E., & Wixon, K. K. (1986). Guidelines for evaluating vocabulary instruction. *Journal of Reading, 29,* 588–595.

Dale, E., & O'Rourke, J. (1986). *Vocabulary building.* Columbus, OH: Zaner-Bloser.

Duffelmeyer, F. A., & Banwart, B. H. (1992–1993). Word maps for adjectives and verbs. *The Reading Teacher, 46,* 351–353.

Freebody, P., & Anderson, R. C. (1983). Effects of vocabulary difficulty, text cohesion, and schema availability on reading comprehension. *Reading Research Quarterly, 18,* 277–294.

Graves, M. (1985). *A word is a word . . . or is it?* Portsmouth, NH: Heinemann.

Heimlich, J. E., & Pittelman, S. D. (1986). *Semantic mapping: Classroom applications.* Newark, DE: International Reading Association.

McKeown, M. G. (1985). The acquisition of word meaning from context by children of high and low ability. *Reading Research Quarterly, 20,* 482–496.

Nagy, W. E. (1988). *Teaching vocabulary to improve reading comprehension.* Urbana, IL: ERIC Clearinghouse on Reading and Communication Skills and the National Council of Teachers of English and the International Reading Association.

Nagy, W. E., Anderson, R. C., & Herman, P. A. (1987). Learning word meanings from context during normal reading. *American Educational Research Journal, 24,* 237–270.

Nagy, W. E., & Herman, P. (1985). Incidental vs. instructional approaches to increasing reading vocabulary. *Educational Perspectives, 23,* 16–21.

Nagy, W. E., Herman, P. A., & Anderson, R. C. (1985). Learning words from context. *Reading Research Quarterly, 20,* 172–193.

Rupley, W. H., Logan, J. W., & Nichols, W. D. (1998/ 1999). Vocabulary instruction in balanced reading programs. *The Reading Teacher, 52,* 336–346.

Schwartz, R., & Raphael, T. (1985). Concept of definition: A key to improving students' vocabulary. *The Reading Teacher, 39,* 198–205.

Stahl, S. A. (1999). *Vocabulary development.* Cambridge, MA: Brookline Books.

Stahl, S. A., Richek, M. G., & Vandevier, R. (1991). Learning word meanings through listening: A sixth grade replication. In J. Zutell & S. McCormick (Eds.), *Learning factors/teacher factors: Issues in literacy research. Fortieth yearbook of the National Reading Conference* (pp. 185–192). Chicago: National Reading Conference.

Stanovich, K. E. (1986). Matthew effects in reading: Some consequences of individual differences in the acquisition of literacy. *Reading Research Quarterly, 21,* 360–406.

Tompkins, G. E., & Yaden, D. B., Jr. (1986). *Answering students' questions about words.* Urbana, IL: ERIC Clearinghouse on Reading and Communication Skills and the National Council of Teachers of English.

Venezky, R. L. (1999). *The American way of spelling: The structure and origins of American English orthography.* New York: Guilford Press.

Children's Book References

Bollard, J. K. (1998). *Scholastic children's thesaurus.* New York: Scholastic.

Brewster, H. (1997). *Inside the Titanic.* Boston: Little, Brown.

Cartwright, S. (1990). *Alaska's three bears.* Homer, AK: Paws IV Publishing Company.

Cheney, L. (2002). *America: A patriotic primer.* New York: Simon & Schuster.

Cole, J. (1997). *The magic school bus and the electric field trip.* New York: Scholastic.

Cox, J. A. (1980). *Put your foot in your mouth and other silly sayings.* New York: Random House.

Frasier, D. (2000). *Miss Alaineus: A vocabulary disaster.* San Diego, CA: Harcourt Brace.

Galdone, P. (1972). *The three bears.* New York: Clarion Books.

Gwynne, F. (1970). *The king who rained.* New York: Windmill Books.

Gwynne, F. (1976). *A chocolate moose for dinner.* New York: Windmill Books.

Gwynne, F. (1980). *The sixteen hand horse.* New York: Prentice Hall.

Gwynne, F. (1988). *A little pigeon toad.* New York: Simon & Schuster.

Hellweg, P. (1997). *The American Heritage children's thesaurus.* Boston: Houghton Mifflin.

Henkes, K. (1991). *Chrysanthemum.* New York: Greenwillow.

Howe, D., & Howe, J. (1979). *Bunnicula: A rabbit-tale of mystery.* New York: Atheneum.

Kentley, E. (2001). *Story of the Titanic.* London: Dorling Kindersley.

Lowry, L. (1979). *Anastasia Krupnik.* Boston: Houghton Mifflin.

Maestro, G. (1984). *What's a frank Frank? Tasty homograph riddles.* New York: Clarion Books.

Martin, B., Jr. (1983). *Brown bear, brown bear, what do you see?* New York: Holt, Rinehart and Winston.

Martin, B., Jr. (1991). *Polar bear, polar bear, what do you hear?* New York: Henry Holt.

Osborne, W., & Osborne, M. P. (1995). *Tonight on the Titanic.* New York: Random House.

Osborne, W., & Osborne, M. P. (2002). *Titanic: A nonfiction companion to Tonight on the Titanic.* New York: Random House.

Pallotta, J. (1988). *The flower alphabet book.* Watertown, MA: Charlesbridge.

Paulsen, G. (1987). *Hatchet.* New York: Simon & Schuster.

Presson, L. (1996). *What in the world is a homophone?* New York: Barron's.

Scillian, D. (2001). *A is for America.* Chelsea, MI: Sleeping Bear Press.

Spedden, D. C. S. (1994). *Polar, the Titanic bear.* Boston: Little, Brown.

Tanaka, S. (1996). *On board the Titanic: What it was like when the great liner sank.* New York: Hyperion Books.

Terban, M. (1982). *Eight ate: A feast of homonym riddles.* New York: Clarion Books.

Terban, M. (1983). *In a pickle and other funny idioms.* New York: Clarion Books.

Terban, M. (1990). *Punching the clock: Funny action idioms.* New York: Clarion Books.

Terban, M. (1992). *The dove dove: Funny homograph riddles.* New York: Clarion Books.

Terban, M. (1996). *Scholastic dictionary of idioms: More than 600 phrases, sayings, and expressions.* New York: Scholastic.

Tolhurst, M. (1990). *Somebody and the three Blairs.* New York: Orchard Books.

Van Allsburg, C. (1991). *The wretched stone.* Boston: Houghton Mifflin.

White, E. E. (1998). *Voyage on the great Titanic: The diary of Margaret Ann Brady.* New York: Scholastic.

Wittels, H., & Greisman, J. (1985). *A first thesaurus.* New York: Golden Books.

Wood, A. (1982). *Quick as a cricket.* London: Child's Play.

Facilitating Students' Comprehension:
Reader Factors

Chapter Questions

- What is comprehension?
- Which factors affect students' comprehension?
- Which comprehension strategies do readers and writers learn?
- How do capable and less capable readers and writers differ?
- How do teachers teach comprehension?

Mrs. Donnelly Teaches Comprehension Strategies

Posters about each of the eight comprehension strategies—predicting, connecting, visualizing, questioning, identifying big ideas, summarizing, monitoring, and evaluating—hang on the wall in Mrs. Donnelly's classroom. Mrs. Donnelly introduced the idea of comprehension strategies by explaining that sixth graders think while they read and that predicting is one of the eight kinds of thinking they do. Her students made the posters as they reviewed each strategy. Tanner, Vincente, and Ashante's poster for monitoring is shown in the box on the next page.

Mrs. Donnelly began with the predicting strategy, and even though her students were familiar with it, they didn't know why they were using it. She explained that the predictions they make before and while reading direct their thinking as they read. Together they made a chart about the strategy and practiced making predictions as Mrs. Donnelly read *The Garden of Abdul Gasazi* (Van Allsburg, 1979), the story of an evil magician who hates dogs, and *La Mariposa* (Jiménez, 1998), an autobiographical picture-book story of a migrant child and his exceptional artistic skills. The students made predictions about *The Garden of Abdul Gasazi* based on the title and the cover illustration, but making predictions got harder in the middle of the surrealistic story because they didn't know whether the dog would escape the magician's garden after he was turned into a duck. Mrs. Donnelly emphasized the importance of continuing to think about the story and to make predictions when it gets confusing. She stopped reading and talked first about why the dog was likely to be successful and then why he wouldn't be. Only about two thirds of the students predicted he would make it home safely, but he did.

The next day, they read *La Mariposa*. The title, which means "the butterfly," and the illustration on the cover of a boy flying toward the sun didn't provide enough information on which to base a prediction, so the students learned that sometimes they have to read a few pages before they can make useful predictions. After reading several pages about Spanish-speaking Francisco's difficult first day of school in an English-only classroom, Norma figured out that the caterpillar the boy is watching in the classroom will become a butterfly, and that the boy on the front cover is flying like a butterfly, but she didn't know why that connection was important. Several students pointed out that the butterfly might represent freedom. Moises predicted that the boy will be rescued from the migrant tent city where he and his family live, and Lizette suggested that he will move to a bilingual classroom where his teacher will understand him and he will make friends. Even though those

---

Sixth Graders' Monitoring Poster

Monitoring

What is it?	It is checking that you are understanding what you are reading.
Why use it?	Monitoring helps you solve problems so you can be successful.
When?	You should use this strategy while you are reading.
What do you do?	1 Keep asking: Does this make sense? If you are understanding, keep reading, but if it doesn't make sense, take action to solve the problem.
	2 Try these solutions:
	• Go back several pages or to the beginning of the chapter and reread.
	• Keep reading one or two more pages.
	• Reread the last prediction, connection, or summary you wrote.
	• Talk to a friend about the problem.
	• Write a quickwrite about the problem.
	• Talk to Mrs. Donnelly.

predictions were wrong, the students became engaged in the story and were eager for their teacher to continue reading.

Mrs. Donnelly wrote their predictions on small sticky notes and attached them to the edge of the pages as she read. She modeled how to use these sticky notes because she wanted to make their thinking more visible, and she explained that she wants them to use sticky notes, too: "I want you to show me your thinking."

Next, she taught the connecting strategy using *A Day's Work* (Bunting, 1994), a story about a young Mexican American boy who goes with his grandfather to find work; *Baseball Saved Us* (Mochizuki, 1993), the story of boys playing baseball at a Japanese relocation camp during World War II; and *So Far From the Sea* (Bunting, 1998), another story about life at a Japanese relocation camp. She explained that readers make three kinds of connections—text-to-self, text-to-world, and text-to-text. As she read each book aloud, she modeled making connections and encouraged the sixth graders to share their connections. Each time they made a connection, Mrs. Donnelly wrote it on a small sticky note; after she finished reading the book, she collected the notes, had the students sort them according to the kind of connection, and posted them in text-to-self, text-to-world, and text-to-text columns on a chart. The chart for *So Far From the Sea* is shown in the box on page 219.

After that, Mrs. Donnelly repeated the procedure to teach visualizing and the remaining strategies; the picture books she used are listed in the box on page 220. Even though she chose a book to practice a specific strategy, each would have been appropriate for other strategies as well. In fact, the students often mentioned that they were using some of the other strategies as she read each book aloud.

Over several weeks, Mrs. Donnelly reviewed the eight comprehension strategies and considered it was time well spent because she wanted the sixth graders to be familiar with all of them. Next, she introduced *Joey Pigza Loses Control*, a Newbery Honor book by Jack Gantos (2000), so that students could practice integrating the use of all eight comprehension strategies in an authentic reading experience. Mrs. Donnelly explained that readers rarely use only one strategy; instead, they use many of them at the same time.

Mrs. Donnelly introduced the book: "This is a story about a boy named Joey who is about your age. His parents are divorced, and he's going to spend the summer with his dad. Joey is ADHD. His mother says he's 'wired,' and he uses medicine patches to control his behavior. He doesn't know his dad very well, so he doesn't know what to expect. His mom tells him not to expect too much." She asks the sixth graders to think about what they know about divorced parents, summer vacations, and ADHD kids. They talk about what they know about each topic, and then they brainstorm these questions:

What is Joey's dad like?

Will they have fun together?

Will Joey be in the way?

Does he hope they'll get back together?

Does Joey's dad love him?

Will Joey's dad disappoint him?

Will Joey disappoint his dad?

Will Joey's medicine work or will he be hyper?

Will Joey's mom be lonely without him?

Will Joey stay with his dad all summer or come back home sooner?

The Connections Chart About *So Far From the Sea*

Text-to-Self	Text-to-World	Text-to-Text
My grandmother takes flowers when she goes to the cemetery because one of her husbands died.	I know that in World War II, Americans were fighting the Japanese because of Pearl Harbor, and they were fighting Hitler and the Germans, too.	This story is like <u>The Bracelet</u>. That girl and her family were taken to a camp in the desert. It was miserable there and she didn't deserve to have to go.
When my family is eating dinner, we look out the window at the mountains, too. I wonder if they are the same mountains that Laura's Dad's family saw from the relocation center?	In the book it's World War II, but I'm thinking about our war in Iraq.	Another book I know is <u>Journey to Topaz</u>. Topaz was another war relocation center and it was a terrible prison, too.
My Dad told me about this. My great-granddad had to go too, and it wasn't fair because he was a loyal American, but his parents were from Japan.		I've heard about a book called <u>Anne Frank</u>. She was Jewish and this sorta happened to her in Germany and she died, too.
I know how to make origami birds. My cousin and I learned last summer.		
We have an American flag on our car so everyone knows we love America.		

Mrs. Donnelly passes out copies of the book and stacks of small sticky notes for students to use to record their thinking as they read. They read the first chapter together, and then students continue to read on their own or with a partner. The book is contemporary realism, and easy for most students in the class to read. Its reading level is between fourth and fifth grade; Mrs. Donnelly chose it because it would be interesting but easy for students to read, so they would have the cognitive resources available to concentrate on their strategy use.

After reading the first chapter, the students come together to talk about the chapter in a grand conversation and their use of comprehension strategies as they read. The students begin by talking about what they remember from the chapter, and then Mrs. Donnelly reads the sentence from page 10 where Joey says this to his mom about the dad he doesn't know very well: "I just want him to love me as much as I already love him." She asks, "How do parents show that they love their children?" She hangs

Check the Compendium of Instructional Procedures, which follows Chapter 14, for more information on highlighted terms.

Books Mrs. Donnelly Uses to Teach the Comprehension Strategies	
Predicting	Jiménez, F. (1998). *La mariposa*. Boston: Houghton Mifflin. Van Allsburg, C. (1979). *The garden of Abdul Gasazi*. Boston: Houghton Mifflin.
Connecting	Bunting, E. (1998). *So far from the sea*. Boston: Houghton Mifflin. Bunting, E. (1994). *A day's work*. New York: Clarion Books. Mochizuki, K. (1993). *Baseball saved us*. New York: Lee & Low.
Visualizing	Say, A. (1995). *Stranger in the mirror*. Boston: Houghton Mifflin.
Questioning	Tsuchiya, Y. (1988). *Faithful elephants: A true story of animals, people, and war*. Boston: Houghton Mifflin. Van Allsburg, C. (1991). *The wretched stone*. Boston: Houghton Mifflin.
Identifying Big Ideas	Garland, S. (1993). *The lotus seed*. San Diego: Harcourt Brace. Hopkinson, D. (1993). *Sweet Clara and the freedom quilt*. New York: Knopf.
Summarizing	Bunting, E. (1994). *Smoky night*. San Diego: Harcourt Brace. Yolen, J. (1992). *Encounter*. San Diego: Harcourt Brace.
Monitoring	Louie, A. (1982). *Yeh Shen: A Cinderella story from China*. New York: Philomel.
Evaluating	Alexander, L. (1992). *The fortune-tellers*. New York: Puffin Books.

up a sheet of chart paper, divides it into two columns, and writes the question at the top of the first column. The students suggest a number of ways, including giving them presents, taking care of them, spending time with them, taking them to church, keeping them safe, and having dinner with them. Mrs. Donnelly writes their ideas under the question in the first column of the chart. Then she narrows the question and asks, "What do you think Joey is looking for from his dad?" Ashante says, "He wants his dad to pay attention to him." Leticia suggests, "He wants him to say 'I love you, son,' tell him he's missed him, and play basketball with him." Students continue to offer ideas, which Mrs. Donnelly adds to the chart. Then she asks, "How do kids show love to their parents?" and she writes the question at the top of the second column. The students suggest that children show their love by behaving, making their parents proud, being responsible, and doing their chores; she writes these answers under the question in the second column. Finally, Mrs. Donnelly asks, "What is Joey's dad expecting from his son?" It's much harder for the students to put themselves in this role. Henry offers, "I think he just wants to have him live with him every day." The sixth graders also talk about their strategy use. Several students talk about predictions they made, and others talk about how they monitored their reading and made connections while they were reading.

After reading and discussing each chapter, the students collect the small sticky notes they've used to keep track of their thinking and write about the strategies they've used in a double-entry journal. Normally, double-entry journals have two columns, but Mrs. Donnelly asks the students to include three columns—she's calling it a triple-entry journal: They write what was happening in the text or copy a quote from the text in the first column, explain their thinking in the second column, and identify the strategy they used in the third column. Excerpts from Tanner's triple-entry thinking journal are shown in the box on page 222.

The students continue to read, discuss, and write about their strategy use as they read *Joey Pigza Loses Control*. After they have read half the book, Mrs. Donnelly brings the class together for a minilesson. She explains that she's reviewed their thinking journals and has noticed that students aren't using summarizing very much. They talk about the summarizing strategy, how and when to use the strategy, and why they should use it. Mrs. Donnelly models how to summarize as she reads the beginning of the next chapter aloud, and then she encourages students to try to use the strategy as they read the next chapter or two.

After they finish reading the book, the students have another grand conversation. They talk about how Joey's mom rescues him and how disillusioned Joey is about his dad. Next, they return to the list of questions they brainstormed before they began reading and talk about the questions and answers. Jake answers the question "Does Joey's dad love him?" this way: "I think his dad does love him but it's a strange kind of love because his dad is selfish. He loves him as much as he can, but it's not very good love." Lizette answers these two questions: "Will Joey's dad disappoint him?" and "Will Joey disappoint his dad?" She says, "I'm positive that Joey's dad disappointed him. His dad wasn't a good dad. The second question is harder to answer. I know Joey tried to be a good son, but it's impossible to satisfy his dad. His dad made him hyper and then got mad at him for being hyper."

Then they reread the chart they began after reading the first chapter about parents showing their love for their children and children showing their love for their parents. They talk about the things they now know that Joey wanted from his dad: for this dad to listen to him, to take care of him, to be responsible for him. They also talk about what Joey's dad wanted from him. Dillan explains, "I think Joey's dad wanted Joey to be his friend and to take care of him. I think Joey would be a better dad than his dad was." Then Mrs. Donnelly asks about Joey's mom: "Does Joey's mom love him?" Everyone agrees that she does, and they name many ways that she shows her love, including giving him money so he can call her, listening to him, worrying about him, hugging him, and telling him she loves him. They complete the chart by adding the new suggestions and then circling the behaviors that his dad exemplified in blue, his mom's in green, and Joey's in red. Later, students will use the information on this chart as they write an essay during writing workshop about how parents and children show their love for one another.

As they reflect on their strategy use, the students are amazed at how much they remember from the story and how well they understand it. Jake says, "I was thinking all the time in this story. I guess that's why I know so much about it. This thinking is a good idea." Richard agrees, saying, "I don't even have to remember to use strategies now. I just naturally think that way." Mrs. Donnelly smiles at Richard's comment. Her goal is for her students to use comprehension strategies independently. She'll continue to emphasize strategies and remind the sixth graders to use sticky notes to track their thinking for several more months, but she'll gradually remove this scaffold once she sees that they've become strategic readers.

Excerpts From Tanner's Triple-Entry Thinking Journal

Chapter	The Text	Your Thinking	The Strategy
1	Joey's mom warns him that his dad is wired like he is.	I'm thinking that this book is about a kid who doesn't know his dad and he's going to be disappointed by him. His Mom doesn't think it's going to be a good vacation.	Identifying big ideas
	Joey is going to spend the summer with his dad.	I'm going to think about how I would feel and what I'd do if I was Joey when I'm reading. It would be strange to see your dad after such a long time.	Monitoring
4	Joey's dad doesn't act like a dad and his Grandma doesn't act like a grandma.	My stomach feels queasy. Joey doesn't belong with these people. His dad doesn't stop talking to listen to him and his grandma doesn't even like him. I predict bad things are going to happen.	Predicting
p. 39	"Just know that he hasn't turned into the squeaky-clean Boy Scout he says he is . . ."	That's what grandma tells Joey about his dad. Now I know that things are going to turn out bad. Joey's dad is bad news.	Summarizing
7	Joey is part good and part bad at baseball. He's a super pitcher and a lousy batter.	I can see the whole baseball game. He's throwing strike balls, and everyone's scared of him, but he won't leave the mound. He hates to bat. His dad is out of control, yelling and stuff.	Visualizing
	After the game they go to the mall to see Leezy.	My mind is asking questions. Why would Carter let Joey drive the car to the mall? Why would his dad tell him it's OK to steal money out of the wishing pond? Is the author trying to show us what a terrible dad he is? We already know that.	Questioning
8	His dad thinks Joey doesn't need the patches and he won't let him have them.	What is wrong with his dad? The patch is medicine that he needs. I am so mad at his dad. That's all I can think. I'm glad my parents take good care of me.	Connecting
14	Joey calls his mom to come get him at the mall.	I think Joey is really a smart kid. He knows how to save himself. He calls his mom and she comes to get him. Joey is right to call his dad a J-E-R-K because that's what he is. The visit was a fiasco just like I predicted. This is a really great book and I want to read it all over again.	Evaluating

Comprehension is the goal of reading instruction. Decoding the words is relatively easy compared to the challenge of constructing meaning after the words have been recognized (Sweet & Snow, 2003). Students must comprehend what they are reading to learn from the experience; they must make sense of their reading to maintain interest; and they must derive pleasure from reading to become lifelong readers. Students who don't understand what they are reading don't find reading pleasurable, and they won't continue reading.

Comprehension is crucial for writers, too. Both readers and writers use similar processes and strategies to make meaning. As they write, students craft well-organized stories and clearly state big ideas and relevant supporting details in informational books and essays. The reason why writers write is to share their ideas with readers, but when readers can't understand what writers have written, comprehension has failed and the compositions are unsuccessful.

Because of the importance of comprehension to both reading and writing, you might say that comprehension permeates almost everything teachers do, from building background knowledge about a topic to teaching minilessons on revising to encouraging students to ask questions to guide their reading. The feature on page 224 shows the role of comprehension in a balanced literacy program.

WHAT IS COMPREHENSION?

Comprehension is a thinking process. It is a creative, multifaceted process in which students engage with the text (Tierney, 1990). You've read about the word *process* before—both reading and writing also have been described as processes. A process is more complicated than a single action: It involves a series of behaviors that occur over time. The comprehension process begins during prereading as students activate their background knowledge and preview the text, and it continues to develop as students read, respond, explore, and apply their reading. Readers construct a mental "picture" or representation of the text and its interpretation through the comprehension process (Van Den Broek & Kremer, 2000).

Judith Irwin (1991) defines comprehension as the reader's process of using prior experiences and the author's text to construct meaning that is useful to that reader for a specific purpose. This definition emphasizes that comprehension depends on two factors: the reader and the text that is being read. Whether comprehension is successful, according to Anne Sweet and Catherine Snow (2003), depends on the interaction of reader factors and text factors.

Reader and Text Factors

Readers are actively engaged with the text; they think about many things as they read in order to comprehend the text. For example, they:

activate prior knowledge

examine the text to determine the length, structure, and important parts

make predictions

determine big ideas

make connections to their own experiences

create mental images

Visit Chapter 7 on the Companion Website at *www.prenhall.com/ tompkins* to check into your state's standards for comprehension.

How the Reader Factors of Comprehension Fit Into a Balanced Literacy Program

Component	Description
Reading	Students who read fluently have more cognitive energy available for comprehension.
Phonics and Other Skills	Comprehension skills include sequencing, categorizing, separating facts from opinions, and recognizing literary genres.
Strategies	Students use comprehension strategies to activate background knowledge, make connections, monitor their understanding, and reflect on their reading.
Vocabulary	Understanding the meaning of words students are reading and being able to relate them to background knowledge are prerequisites for comprehension.
Comprehension	The goal of reading is comprehension, and students apply reader factors to construct meaning.
Literature	As students read picture-book stories and novels, they are involved in a variety of comprehension activities throughout the reading process.
Content-Area Study	As students read informational books and content-area textbooks, they are involved in a variety of comprehension activities throughout the reading process.
Oral Language	It is often more effective to teach comprehension by reading literature and content-area materials aloud so that students can focus on the meaning rather than on word identification.
Writing	The goal of writing is to produce comprehensible text, and students apply reader factors when they write.
Spelling	Spelling is not an important component of comprehension.

monitor their understanding

generate summaries

evaluate the text

These activities can be categorized as reader and text factors (National Reading Panel, 2000). Reader factors include the background knowledge that readers bring to the reading process as well as their purpose and motivation and the strategies they know to use while reading. Text factors include the author's ideas, the words the author uses to express those ideas, and how the ideas are organized and presented. Both reader factors and text factors affect comprehension. Figure 7–1 presents an overview of these two factors. This chapter focuses on reader factors, and Chapter 8 covers text factors.

Readers use the reader factors—activating background knowledge, setting purposes, reading fluently, applying comprehension strategies, making inferences, and being motivated and attentive—as they read and think about the text. These factors determine whether readers will be successful. If students don't have a purpose for reading, can't read the text fluently, or aren't interested in the text, they are less likely to be successful. Readers have limited cognitive resources available for comprehension, and if they use too many of these resources to decode difficult text or to compensate for limited background knowledge, they may not remember much of what they read. When students use the reader factors effectively, they are more likely to comprehend because they can devote their cognitive resources to thinking about what they are reading.

Background Knowledge

As students get ready to read, they activate their background knowledge about a topic. They have both world knowledge and literary knowledge that they have gained

Figure 7–1		Overview of Comprehension Factors
Type	**Factor**	**Role in Comprehension**
Reader	Background Knowledge	Students activate their world knowledge and literary knowledge to be better prepared to understand what they are reading.
	Purpose	Students are more actively involved in the reading process and they direct their attention to the big ideas when they read with a purpose.
	Fluency	Students have adequate cognitive resources available to understand what they are reading when they read quickly, expressively, and with little effort.
	Comprehension Strategies	Students actively direct their reading when they use strategies such as predicting, visualizing, questioning, and monitoring.
	Making Inferences	Students understand nonexplicitly stated ideas by making inferences based on their background knowledge and the clues they notice in the text.
	Motivation	Students who like to read expect to be successful, become more engaged in reading, and are more likely to comprehend successfully.
Text	Structure	The organization of the text provides a skeleton for comprehension, and students who recognize this structure use it to scaffold their understanding.
	Genres	Genres, such as myths and biographies, have unique characteristics and features, and when students are familiar with a genre, this knowledge provides a scaffold for comprehension.
	Content and Vocabulary	Topics involve specific content information and technical vocabulary, and students draw on their background knowledge of content and vocabulary as they read.

through prior experiences and information learned at school. As you read in Chapter 1, this knowledge is stored in schemata (or categories) and is linked to other knowledge through a complex network of interrelationships. Students continue to add new information to their schemata and expand their networks as they learn. World knowledge includes concepts and vocabulary, and literary knowledge includes familiarity with genres, text structures, and authors. For example, if second or third graders are activating background knowledge as they prepare to read *Mummies in the Morning* (Osborne, 1993), a time-warp story set in ancient Egypt, and its companion research guide, *Mummies and Pyramids* (Osborne & Osborne, 2001), they think about what they already know about ancient Egypt. If they are good readers, they will expect the story to be different from the research guide because they understand the difference between stories and informational books. These two books are part of the popular Magic Tree House series; if students are familiar with the series, they can predict that the story will begin with a time-warp. If they don't understand this literary device, comprehending the story will be more difficult, and if they don't know much about ancient Egypt, comprehending gets much more difficult. Good readers also expect to find an index in the research guide and may use it to learn more about something mentioned in the story. They will read the story from beginning to end, but they will read sections in the research guide in any order as they want to learn more about a topic.

Having adequate background knowledge is a prerequisite for comprehension. When students have both world knowledge and literary knowledge, it provides a bridge to a new text (Pearson & Johnson, 1978). In contrast, without adequate world and literary knowledge, students are less likely to comprehend what they are reading.

Teachers help students activate their background knowledge before they begin reading; when students don't have adequate background knowledge, teachers determine whether students need more world or literary knowledge and provide experiences and information to develop that knowledge. Teachers use a combination of experiences, visual representations, and talk to build the knowledge. Involving students in experiences such as taking field trips, participating in dramatizations, and manipulating artifacts is the best way to build background knowledge, but teachers also can use photos and pictures, picture books, videos, and other visual representations to build background knowledge. Talk is often the least effective way, especially for English learners, but sometimes explaining a concept, introducing vocabulary, or listing the characteristics of a genre can provide enough information.

Background knowledge plays an important role throughout the reading process. Students think back to prior experiences as they make personal connections with the text and compare the book to others they have read. They also use their background knowledge when they make inferences or analyze the structure of the text or genre.

Purpose

When we do something, it is usually with a purpose in mind. Purpose provides direction for our activities. For example, we go grocery shopping to get food to cook for dinner, and we watch a movie or play a video game to be entertained. Reading is no different: We read for a purpose or to achieve some end. It's important that students have a purpose when they read, even though it might change as they read, because readers vary the way they read and what they remember according to their purpose: We read differently to cook a recipe, enjoy a letter from an old friend, understand the opinion expressed in an editorial, or escape in a novel.

Purpose setting facilitates comprehension in several ways (Blanton, Wood, & Moorman, 1990). Setting a purpose activates a mental blueprint to use while reading. It aids in determining how readers focus their attention and how they sort relevant from irrelevant information as they read. In addition, readers actively monitor their comprehension as they read to determine whether their purposes are being met, and if they aren't, they take action to get their comprehension back on track (Sweet & Snow, 2003).

When students read, their purpose can either be internally generated or externally imposed by a teacher. The research on motivation suggests that when students set their own purposes, they are more interested in reading than when teachers set the purpose, but students often need to accept the purpose that the teacher sets. Not surprisingly, if readers don't understand or accept a mandated purpose, they aren't likely to understand what they're reading.

Readers always need purposes when they read, and a single purpose is more effective than multiple purposes (Blanton, Wood, & Moorman, 1990). When students are setting their own purposes, they can ask themselves these questions:

Why am I going to read this text?

What purpose should I have?

What am I supposed to learn?

At other times, teachers identify a purpose, such as "read to see what happened to . . . " or "read to find the three ways to . . . " and students read to find the answer. When teachers set the purpose, they should be teaching students how to set purposes so that they can learn to direct their reading themselves.

Fluency

Fluent readers read quickly and efficiently. Because they recognize most words automatically, their cognitive resources are not consumed by decoding unfamiliar words and they can devote their attention to comprehension. Fluency is another prerequisite for comprehension (Pressley, 2002a).

In the primary grades, developing reading fluency is an important component of comprehension instruction because students need to learn to recognize words automatically so that they can concentrate their attention on comprehending what they are reading (Samuels, 2002). For many struggling readers, their lack of fluency severely affects their ability to understand what they read. Teachers can help older struggling readers who aren't fluent readers by teaching or reteaching word-identification strategies, having students do repeated readings, and providing students with books at their instructional levels so that they can be successful. When teachers are using grade-level texts that are too difficult for struggling students, they should read them aloud so that struggling students can comprehend and participate in related activities.

Comprehension Strategies

Comprehension strategies are thoughtful behaviors that students use to facilitate their understanding as they read (McLaughlin & Allen, 2002). They apply these strategies to determine whether they are comprehending and to solve comprehension problems as they arise. Some strategies are cognitive—they involve thinking or cognition; others are metacognitive—students reflect on their thinking. For example, readers make predictions about a story when they begin reading: They wonder what will happen to the characters and whether they'll enjoy the story. Predicting is a cognitive strategy because it involves thinking. Readers also monitor their reading, and monitoring is a metacognitive strategy. They notice whether they are understanding; and if they get confused, they take action to solve the problem. For example, they may go back and reread or talk to a classmate to clarify their confusion. Students are being metacognitive when they are alert to the possibility that they might get confused, and they know several ways to solve the problem (Pressley, 2002b).

Students learn to use a variety of comprehension strategies; eight of the most important ones are predicting, connecting, visualizing, questioning, identifying big ideas, summarizing, monitoring, and evaluating. Students use these comprehension strategies not only to understand what they are reading, but also for understanding while they are listening and when they are writing. For example, students identify the big ideas when they are listening or reading, and when they are writing, they identify and write the big ideas so that their readers also will recognize them. Figure 7–2 presents an overview of the eight comprehension strategies.

Predicting. Readers make thoughtful "guesses" or predictions about what will happen in the book they are reading. As they make predictions, students often become more interested in reading because the prediction gives them a purpose for reading. These guesses are based on what students already know about the topic and genre or on what they have read thus far. Students often make a prediction before beginning to read and several others at key points in the story or at the beginning of each chapter when reading longer books. As they read, students either confirm or revise their predictions. Before beginning to read an informational book or a content-area textbook, students often preview the text in order to make predictions. Predictions about nonfiction are different than for stories; here students are generating questions about the topic that they would like to find answers to or are trying to determine the big ideas.

Teachers often use the Directed Reading-Thinking Activity (DRTA) (Stauffer, 1975) to teach students to make predictions. It's important that teachers ask students to make predictions at pivotal points in the story—when characters have to make decisions or when the outcome of the story is unclear.

Connecting. Readers personalize what they are reading by connecting it to their own lives: They recall similar experiences or compare the characters to themselves or people they know, or they connect the book they are reading to other literature they have read. Readers often make connections among several books written by one author or between two versions of the same story. They make three types of connections: text-to-self, text-to-world, and text-to-text connections (Fountas & Pinnell, 2001). In text-to-self connections, students link the ideas they are reading about to events in their own lives; these are personal connections. A story event or character may remind them of something or someone in their own lives, and information in a nonfiction book may remind them of a past experience. If students are reading *Snakes* (Wexo, 1990) in the Zoo Books series, for example, they might connect the information they are reading about how a snake sheds its skin to a time when they found a snakeskin or when a classmate brought one to school.

Figure 7-2 Overview of the Eight Comprehension Strategies

Strategy	What Readers Do	How the Strategy Helps Readers to Comprehend a Text
Predicting	Readers make thoughtful "guesses" about what will happen and then read to confirm or revise their predictions.	Readers set a purpose for reading and become more engaged in the reading experience.
Connecting	Readers activate their background knowledge to make text-to-self, text-to-world, and text-to-text links.	Readers personalize their reading by relating what they are reading to their background knowledge.
Visualizing	Readers create mental images of what they are reading.	Readers use the mental images to make the text more memorable.
Questioning	Readers ask themselves literal and inferential questions about the text.	Readers use questions to direct their reading, clarify confusions, and make inferences.
Identifying the Big Ideas	Readers notice the important information in the text.	Readers focus on the big ideas so they don't become overwhelmed with details.
Summarizing	Readers combine the big ideas to create a concise statement.	Readers have better recall of their reading when they summarize.
Monitoring	Readers supervise their reading experience, checking that they are comprehending and taking action if they become confused.	Readers expect that the text they are reading will make sense, and they know what to do if it doesn't.
Evaluating	Readers evaluate both the text itself and their reading experience.	Readers assume responsibility for their own strategy use.

In text-to-world connections, students move beyond personal experience to relate what they are reading to the "world" knowledge they have learned both in and out of school. If they are reading *If You Traveled on the Underground Railroad* (Levine, 1993), for example, readers make connections to their knowledge about slavery, the Big Dipper constellation, or Harriet Tubman, who helped hundreds of slaves to escape. In addition, they make connections with what they know about railroad trains in order to compare them with the Underground Railroad.

When students make text-to-text connections, they link the text itself or an element of it to another text they have read or to a familiar film, video, or television program. Students often compare different versions of familiar folktales, novels and their sequels, and sets of books by the same author. Text-to-text connections are difficult for many students, especially those who have done less reading or who know less about literature.

During the responding stage of the reading process, students make all three types of connections as they participate in grand conversations and write in reading logs. Teachers make connection charts with three columns labeled *text-to-self*, *text-to-world*, and *text-to-text* and have students write their connections on small sticky notes and post them in the correct column of the chart, as Mrs. Donnelly did in the vignette at the beginning of the chapter. Students can also make connection charts in their reading logs and write one or more connections in each column. During the exploring and applying stages, students continue to make connections as they assume the role of a character and create open-mind portraits, reenact the story, write simulated journals from the viewpoint of a character, make quilts, and develop other projects.

Projects

These third graders are sharing the project they developed after reading a book during reading workshop. The boys made a story jar and drew pictures and collected objects to represent the big ideas in the story. They put the items in the jar, and now they are taking each one out and explaining its importance to the story to a small group of classmates. In this way, students are demonstrating their comprehension and are interesting their classmates in the book as well as gaining valuable presentation skills. The teacher monitors this sharing to check students' comprehension.

Visualizing. Readers create mental images of what they are reading. They often place themselves in the images they create, becoming a character in the story they are reading, traveling to that setting, or facing the conflict situations the characters themselves face. Teachers sometimes ask students to close their eyes to help visualize the story or to draw pictures of the scenes and characters they visualize. How well students use visualization often becomes clear when they view film versions of books they have read: Students who are good visualizers are often disappointed with the film version and the actors who perform as the characters, whereas students who don't visualize are often amazed by the film and prefer it to the book.

Questioning. Readers ask themselves questions about the text as they read (Duke & Pearson, 2002). They ask self-questions out of curiosity, and as they use this strategy, they become engaged with the text and want to keep reading to find answers to their questions. These questions often lead to making predictions and drawing inferences. Students also ask themselves questions to clarify misunderstandings as they read. Students use this strategy throughout the reading process—to activate background knowledge and make predictions before reading, to engage with the text and clarify confusions during reading, and to evaluate and reflect on the text and the characters' experiences after reading.

Traditionally, teachers have been the question-askers and students have been the question-answerers, but when students learn to generate questions about the text, their comprehension improves. In fact, students comprehend better when they generate their own questions than when teachers ask questions (Duke & Pearson, 2002).

Many students don't know how to ask questions to guide their reading, so it is important that teachers teach students to ask questions. They model generating questions and then encourage students to do the same. Tovani (2000) suggests having students brainstorm a list of "I wonder" questions on a topic because students need to learn how to generate questions; in the vignette at the beginning of the chapter, for example, Mrs. Donnelly's sixth graders brainstormed questions before they began to read *Joey Pigza Loses Control* (Gantos, 2000).

The questions students ask shape their comprehension: If they ask themselves literal "what" and "who" questions, their comprehension will be more literal, but if students generate inferential "how" and "why" questions, their comprehension will be higher-level. Question-Answer Relationships (QARs) (Raphael & McKinney, 1983) is an effective way to teach students about the different types of questions they can ask about a text. QARs was developed for analyzing the end-of-chapter questions in content-area textbooks, but it is also useful for teaching students to categorize questions and ultimately to ask higher-level questions.

Identifying the Big Ideas. Readers sift through the text to identify and remember the important ideas as they read because it isn't possible to remember everything. Students learn the difference between the big ideas and the details and to recognize the more important ideas as they read and talk about the books and other texts they've read. This comprehension strategy is important because students need to be able to identify the big ideas in order to summarize.

Teachers often direct students toward the big ideas when they set purposes before reading or encourage students to make predictions. The way they introduce the text also influences students' thinking. Mrs. Donnelly's introduction of *Joey Pigza Loses Control* (Gantos, 2000), for instance, directed her sixth graders' thinking about the story and its theme.

Students also use graphic organizers to highlight the big ideas they're reading. When students read stories, they make diagrams about the plot, characters, and setting, and these graphic organizers emphasize the big ideas. Similarly, students make diagrams that reflect the structure of the text when they read informational articles and books and chapters in content-area textbooks. Sometimes teachers provide the diagrams with the big ideas highlighted, and sometimes students analyze the text to determine its structure and then develop their own graphic organizers.

Summarizing. Readers synthesize the important ideas to create a summary that stands for the original and can be remembered (Dole, Duffy, Roehler, & Pearson, 1991). They begin by identifying the big ideas and deleting details and less important information, and then they combine the big ideas to create a summary statement. Because readers can't remember everything they read, they focus on the big ideas and summarize them. It's important that students recognize which ideas are the most important because if they focus on tangential ideas or details, their comprehension is compromised.

Knowing the structure of the text helps students to recognize the big ideas and see how they are related. Students divide stories, for example, into the beginning, middle, and end and understand that the problem is the unifying element—they look for the problem in the beginning, note how it gets worse in the middle, and read the solution in the end. In nonfiction texts, in contrast, they look for compare-and-contrast, cause-and-effect, or other expository text structures, and then use the structure in determining the big ideas. Teachers often have students make graphic organizers to help them focus on the structure in order to identify the big ideas.

Summarizing is a difficult task, but instruction and practice improve not only students' ability to summarize but their overall comprehension as well (Duke & Pearson, 2002). Teachers often use instructional procedures such as GIST (Cunningham, 1982) to teach students how to write summaries, but students can also develop oral summaries after reading chapters in novels or sections in a content-area textbook.

Monitoring. Readers monitor their understanding as they read, although they may be aware that they are using this strategy only when their comprehension breaks down and they have to take action to solve their problem. Monitoring involves regulating reader and text factors at the same time. Readers often ask themselves these questions:

- Do I need to activate background knowledge?
- Am I sticking to my purpose for reading?
- Is this book too difficult for me to read on my own?
- Do I need to read the entire book or only parts of it?
- What is special about the genre of this book?
- How does the author use text structure?
- What is the author's viewpoint?
- What does this book remind me of?
- What are the big ideas?
- Do I understand the meaning of the words I'm reading? (Pressley, 2002b)

Once students detect a comprehension problem, they shift into problem-solving mode to figure out the meaning of an unfamiliar word, learn more about a topic related to the text, pinpoint a confusing part, reread the text, or decide to ask a classmate or a teacher for assistance. These solutions are often called fix-up strategies.

Evaluating. Readers reflect on their reading experience and evaluate the text and what they are learning (Owocki, 2003). As with the other comprehension strategies, students use the evaluating strategy throughout the reading process. They monitor their interest in the text and predict whether they like it from the moment they pick up the book, and they evaluate their success in solving reading problems each time a problem arises. They evaluate their reading experience, including these aspects:

- their ease in reading the text
- the adequacy of their background knowledge
- whether they met their purpose for reading
- their use of comprehension strategies
- how they solved reading problems
- their interest and attention in the text

They also consider the text:

- whether they like the text
- their opinions about the author
- the world knowledge they gain
- how they will use what they're learning

Students usually write about their reflections in reading log entries and talk about their evaluations in conferences with their teachers. Through this evaluation, students learn to take more responsibility for their own learning.

Making Inferences

Readers seem to read between the lines to make inferences, but what they actually do is synthesize their background knowledge with the author's clues to ask questions that point toward inferences or conclusions. Readers make both unconscious and conscious inferences about characters in a story and its theme, the big ideas in a newspaper, magazine article, or informational book, and the author's purpose (Pressley, 2002a). In fact, you may not even be aware much of the time that you are making inferences, but when you wonder about what you're reading and why the author included this or omitted that information, you probably are.

Students often have to reread a story or a chapter of a novel in order to make inferences because during the first reading, they were focusing on literal comprehension, which has to come first. Very capable students seem to make inferences on their own as they read, but other students may not notice opportunities to make them. Sometimes students do make inferences when prompted by the teacher, but it is important to teach students how to make inferences so that they can think more deeply about their reading when they read independently.

Teachers begin by explaining what inferences are, how they differ from literal thinking, and why this kind of comprehension is important. Then they teach students these four steps in making inferences:

1. Think of background knowledge about topics related to the story.
2. Look for the author's clues in the story.
3. Ask questions tying together background knowledge and the author's clues.
4. Make inferences by answering the questions.

Through these four steps, students think more deeply about their reading and become more actively involved in thinking about what they are reading.

Teachers can create inference charts to make the steps more visible as students practice making inferences. Figure 7–3 shows an inference chart developed by a seventh-grade class as they read and analyzed *The Wretched Stone* (Van Allsburg, 1991). The story, told in diary format, is about a ship's crew that picks up a strange, glowing stone on a sea voyage. The stone captivates the sailors and has a terrible transforming effect on them. After reading the story and talking about what they understood and what confused them, students began making the chart. First, they completed the "background knowledge" column. The students thought about what they needed to know about to understand the story: the meaning of the word *wretched*, sailors, the author/illustrator Chris Van Allsburg, and the fantasy genre because fantasies are different from other types of stories. Then they reread the story, searching for clues that might affect the meaning. They noticed that the ship captain's name was Hope, the island was uncharted, and the sailors who could read recovered faster, and they wrote these clues in the second column. Next, they thought about questions they have about the story and wrote them in the third column of the chart. Finally, the teacher reread the book one more time; this time, students listened more confidently, recognizing clues and understanding the inferences they had missed earlier. Finally, they completed the last column of the chart with their inferences.

Students can also make their own versions of the inference chart to answer an inferential question. For example, after reading and discussing another of Chris Van Allsburg's books, *The Garden of Abdul Gasazi* (1979), the story of a magician who turns a misbehaving dog into a duck, students worked in pairs to complete a four-part inference chart to answer the question: What happened to the dog? A completed chart is shown in Figure 7–4. By thinking about their background knowledge, looking for clues in the story, and asking questions, the students figured out that the magician changed the dog into a duck but concluded that the spell didn't last a long time, and soon after the duck flew home, it changed back into a dog.

Figure 7-3 The Seventh Graders' Inference Chart About *The Wretched Stone*

Background Knowledge	Clues in the Story	Questions	Inferences
• The word *wretched* means "causing misery." • The people who work on a ship are called sailors or the crew. Usually they are hard workers but not readers and musicians. • Chris Van Allsburg writes and illustrates fantasy picture books. He has brown hair and a beard. He wears glasses. • In fantasies, magic and other impossible things can happen.	• The captain's last name is Hope. • The crew is clever. They can read, play music, and tell stories. • It is odd that the island is not on any maps. • The odor on the island seems sweet at first, but then it stinks. • The crew sit and stare at the glowing stone. They lose interest in reading, playing music, and telling stories. They stop working, too. • The crew change into monkeys because they keep watching the stone. • Capt. Hope looks just like Chris Van Allsburg. • The sailors who could read recovered the quickest.	• Why did Chris Van Allsburg make himself the captain? • Was it a real island or was it magic? • What is the wretched stone? • Why did the sailors turn into monkeys? • Why did the sailors who could read get well faster?	• Chris Van Allsburg wrote this book with hope for kids. • The wretched stone is television. • This book is a warning that watching too much TV is bad for you. • He wants kids to spend more time reading books because reading is good for you. • He wants kids to spend less time watching television. • Watching television is like the odor on the island. It is sweet and you like it at first, but too much of it stinks and is not good for you.

Motivation and Attention

Motivation is intrinsic, the innate curiosity within each of us that makes us want to figure things out. It involves feeling self-confident, believing you will succeed, and viewing the activity as pleasurable (Cunningham & Cunningham, 2002). Motivation is social, too: We want to socialize, share ideas, and participate in group activities. Motivation is more than one characteristic, however; it is a network of interacting factors (Alderman, 1999). Often students' motivation to become better readers and writers diminishes as they reach the middle grades, and struggling students demonstrate less enthusiasm for reading and writing than other students do.

Many factors contribute to students' engagement or involvement in reading and writing. Some focus on teachers—what they believe and do—and others focus on students (Pressley, Dolezal, Raphael, Mohan, Roehrig, & Bogner, 2003; Unrau, 2004). Figure 7–5 summarizes the factors affecting students' engagement in literacy activities and what teachers can do to nurture students' interest.

Teacher Factors. Everything teachers do affects their students' interest and engagement with literacy, but four of the most important factors are teachers' attitude or excitement, the community teachers create in their classrooms, the instructional approaches teachers use, and the reward systems they use.

1. **Attitude.** It seems obvious that when teachers show that they care about their students and exhibit excitement and enthusiasm for learning, students are more likely to become engaged. Effective teachers also stimulate students' curiosity and encourage them to explore ideas. They emphasize intrinsic over extrinsic motivation because they understand that students' intrinsic desire to learn is more powerful than grades and other extrinsic motivators.

2. **Community.** Students are more likely to engage in reading and writing when their classroom is a learning community that respects and nurtures all students. Students and the teacher show respect for each other, and students learn how to work well with classmates in small groups. In a community of learners, students enjoy social interaction and feel connected to their classmates and their teacher.

3. **Instruction.** The types of literacy activities in which students are involved affect their interest and motivation. Turner and Paris (1995) compared authentic literacy activities such as reading and writing workshop with skills-based reading programs and concluded that students' motivation was determined by the daily classroom activities. They found that open-ended activities and projects in which

Figure 7-4   **Two Students' Inference Chart About** *The Garden of Abdul Gasazi*

Title **The Garden of Abdul Gasazi** Author **Chris Van Allsburg**

BACKGROUND KNOWLEDGE	QUESTIONS
Magicians do tricks. This story is a fantasy so magic can happen. Sometimes dogs don't behave.	Did the magician do it? How did Fritz get home? Why was Alan's hat in Miss Hester's yard?

CLUES FROM THE STORY	INFERENCES
Only time can change Fritz back into a dog. The duck was like Fritz because he took Alan's hat. Fritz the dog has Alan's hat at the end.	The magician did cast a spell and make the dog into a duck. The spell didn't last very long.

Figure 7-5   Factors Affecting Students' Motivation

	Factors	What Teachers Should Do
Teacher Factors	Attitude	• Show students that you care about them. • Show excitement and enthusiasm about what you're teaching. • Stimulate students' curiosity and desire to learn.
	Community	• Create a nurturing and inclusive classroom community. • Insist that students treat classmates with respect.
	Instruction	• Focus on students' long-term learning. • Teach students to be strategic readers and writers. • Engage students in authentic activities. • Offer students choices of activities and reading materials.
	Rewards	• Use specific praise and positive feedback. • Use external rewards only when students' interest is very low.
Student Factors	Expectations	• Expect students to be successful. • Teach students to set realistic goals.
	Collaboration	• Encourage students to work collaboratively. • Minimize competition. • Allow students to participate in making plans and choices.
	Reading and Writing Competence	• Teach students to use reading and writing strategies. • Provide guided reading lessons for struggling readers. • Use interactive writing to teach writing skills to struggling writers. • Provide daily reading and writing opportunities.
	Choices	• Use interest inventories to identify students' interests. • Teach students to choose interesting books at their reading levels. • Encourage students to write about topics that interest them.

students were in control of the processes they used and the products they created were the most successful.

4. ***Rewards.*** Many teachers consider using rewards to encourage students to do more reading and writing, but Alfie Kohn (1993) and others believe that extrinsic incentives are harmful because they undermine students' intrinsic motivation. Incentives such as pizzas, free time, or "money" to spend in a classroom "store" are most effective when students' interest is very low and they are reluctant to participate in literacy activities. Once students become more interested, teachers withdraw these incentives and use less tangible ones, including positive feedback and praise (Stipek, 1993).

Student Factors. Intrinsic motivation is not something that teachers or parents can force on students; rather, it is an innate desire that students must develop themselves. They are more likely to become engaged with reading and writing when they expect to be successful, when they work collaboratively with classmates, when they are capable readers and writers, and when they have opportunities to make choices and develop ownership of their work.

1. ***Expectations.*** Students who feel they have little hope of success are unlikely to become engaged in literacy activities. Teachers play a big role in shaping students' ex-

pectations, and teacher expectations are often self-fulfilling (Good & Brophy, 2000): If teachers believe that their students can be successful, it is more likely that they will be. Stipek (1993) found that in classrooms where teachers take a personal interest in their students and expect that all of them can learn, the students are more successful.

2. *Collaboration.* When students work with classmates in pairs and in small groups, they are often more interested and engaged in activities than when they read and write alone. Collaborative groups support students because they have opportunities to share ideas, learn from each other, and enjoy the collegiality of their classmates. Competition, in contrast, does not develop intrinsic motivation; instead, it decreases many students' interest in learning.

3. *Reading and writing competence.* Not surprisingly, students' competence in reading and writing affects their motivation: Students who read well are more likely to be motivated to read than those who read less well, and the same is true for writers. Teaching students how to read and write is an essential factor in developing students' motivation. Teachers find that once struggling readers and writers improve their reading and writing abilities, they become more interested.

4. *Choices.* Students want to have a say in which books they read and which topics they write about. By making choices, students develop more responsibility for their work and ownership of their accomplishments. Reading and writing workshop are instructional approaches that honor students' choices: In reading workshop, students choose books they are interested in reading and that are written at their reading level, and in writing workshop, students write about topics that interest them.

Oldfather (1995) conducted a 4-year study to examine the factors influencing students' motivation. She found that students were more highly motivated when they had opportunities for authentic self-expression as part of literacy activities. The students she interviewed reported that they were more highly motivated when they had ownership of the learning activities. Specific activities they mentioned included opportunities to:

- express their own ideas and opinions
- choose topics for writing and books for reading
- talk about books they are reading
- share their writing with classmates
- pursue authentic activities—not worksheets—using reading, writing, listening, and talking

Ivey and Broaddus (2001) reported similar conclusions from their study of the factors that influence sixth graders' desire to read. Three of their conclusions are noteworthy. First, students are more interested in reading when their teachers make them feel confident and successful; a nurturing classroom community is an important factor. Second, students are more intrinsically motivated when they have ownership of their literacy learning. Students place great value on being allowed to choose interesting books and other reading materials. Third, students become more engaged with books when they have time for independent reading and opportunities to listen to the teacher read aloud. Students reported that they enjoy listening to teachers read aloud because teachers make books more comprehensible and more interesting through the background knowledge they provide.

Some students are not strongly motivated to learn to read and write, and they adopt strategies for avoiding failure rather than strategies for making meaning; these strategies are defensive tactics (Dweck, 1986; Paris, Wasik, & Turner, 1991). Unmotivated readers give up or remain passive, uninvolved in reading (Johnston & Winograd, 1985). Some students feign interest or pretend to be involved even though they are not. Others don't think reading is important, and they choose to focus on other curricular areas—math or sports, for instance. Some students complain about feeling ill or that other students are bothering them. They place the blame anywhere but on themselves.

There are other students who avoid reading and writing entirely; they just don't do it. Still other students read books that are too easy for them or write short pieces so that they don't have to exert much effort. Even though these strategies are self-serving, students use them because they lead to short-term success. The long-term result, however, is devastating because these students fail to learn to read and write well. Because it takes quite a bit of effort to read and write strategically, it is especially important that students experience personal ownership of the literacy activities going on in their classrooms and know how to manage their own reading and writing behaviors.

Comparing Capable and Less Capable Readers and Writers

Researchers have compared students who are capable readers and writers with other students who are less successful and have found some striking differences (Baker & Brown, 1984; Faigley, Cherry, Jolliffe, & Skinner, 1985; Paris, Wasik, & Turner, 1991). The researchers have found that more capable readers:

- read fluently
- view reading as a process of creating meaning
- decode rapidly
- have large vocabularies
- understand the organization of stories, plays, informational books, poems, and other texts
- use comprehension strategies
- monitor their understanding as they read

Similarly, capable writers:

- vary how they write depending on the purpose for writing and the audience that will read the composition
- use the writing process flexibly
- focus on developing ideas and communicating effectively
- turn to classmates for feedback on how they are communicating
- monitor how well they are communicating in the piece of writing
- use formats and structures for stories, poems, letters, and other texts
- apply comprehension strategies
- postpone attention to mechanical correctness until the end of the writing process

All of these characteristics of capable readers and writers relate to comprehension, and because these students know and use them, they are better readers and writers than students who do not use them.

A comparison of the characteristics of capable and less capable readers and writers is presented in Figure 7–6. Young children who are learning to read and write often

Figure 7-6   Capable and Less Capable Readers and Writers

Categories	Reader Characteristics	Writer Characteristics
Belief Systems	Capable readers view reading as a comprehending process, but less capable readers view reading as a decoding process.	Capable writers view writing as communicating ideas, whereas less capable writers see writing as putting words on paper.
Purpose	Capable readers adjust their reading according to purpose, whereas less capable readers approach all reading tasks the same way.	Capable writers adapt their writing to meet demands of audience, purpose, and form, but less capable writers do not.
Fluency	Capable readers read fluently, whereas less capable readers read word by word, do not chunk words into phrases, and sometimes point at words as they read.	Capable writers sustain their writing for longer periods of time and pause as they draft to think and reread what they have written, whereas less capable writers write less and without pausing.
Background Knowledge	Capable readers relate what they are reading to their background knowledge, whereas less capable readers do not make this connection.	Capable writers gather and organize ideas before writing, but less capable writers do not plan before beginning to write.
Decoding/ Spelling	Capable readers identify unfamiliar words efficiently, whereas less capable readers make nonsensical guesses or skip over unfamiliar words and invent what they think is a reasonable text when they are reading.	Capable writers spell many words conventionally and use the dictionary to spell unfamiliar words, but less capable writers cannot spell many high-frequency words and depend on phonics to spell unfamiliar words.
Vocabulary	Capable readers have larger vocabularies than less capable readers do.	Capable writers use more sophisticated words and figurative language than less capable writers do.
Strategies	Capable readers use a variety of strategies as they read, whereas less capable readers use fewer strategies.	Capable writers use many strategies effectively, but less capable writers use fewer strategies.
Monitoring	Capable readers monitor their comprehension, but less capable readers do not realize or take action when they don't understand.	Capable writers monitor that their writing makes sense, and they turn to classmates for revising suggestions, but less capable writers do not.

Adapted from Faigley, Cherry, Jolliffe, & Skinner, 1985; Paris, Wasik, & Turner, 1991.

exemplify many of the characteristics of less capable readers and writers, but older students who are less successful readers and writers also exemplify them.

Less successful readers exemplify few of the characteristics of capable readers or behave differently when they are reading and writing. Perhaps the most remarkable difference is that more capable readers view reading as a process of comprehending or creating meaning, whereas less capable readers focus on decoding. In writing, less capable writers make cosmetic changes when they revise, rather than changes to communicate meaning more effectively. These important differences indicate that capable students focus on comprehension and the strategies readers and writers use to understand what they read and to make sure that what they write will be comprehensible to others.

Another important difference between capable and less capable readers and writers is that those who are less successful are not strategic. They are naive. They seem reluctant to use unfamiliar strategies or those that require much effort. They do not seem to be motivated or to expect that they will be successful. Less capable readers and writers don't understand or use all stages of the reading and writing processes effectively. They don't monitor their reading and writing (Garner, 1987; Keene & Zimmermann, 1997). Or, if they do use strategies, they remain dependent on primitive ones. For example, as they read, less successful readers seldom look ahead or back into the text to clarify misunderstandings or make plans. Or, when they come to an unfamiliar word, they often stop reading, unsure of what to do. They may try to sound out an unfamiliar word, but if that is unsuccessful, they give up. In contrast, capable readers know several strategies, and if one strategy isn't successful, they try another.

Less capable writers move through the writing process in a lockstep, linear approach. They use a limited number of strategies, most often a "knowledge-telling" strategy in which they list everything they know about a topic with little thought to choosing information to meet the needs of their readers or to organize the information to put related ideas together (Faigley et al., 1985). In contrast, capable writers understand the recursive nature of the writing process and turn to classmates for feedback about how well they are communicating. They are more responsive to the needs of the audience that will read their writing, and they work to organize their writing in a cohesive manner.

This research on capable and less capable readers and writers has focused on comprehension differences and students' use of strategies. It is noteworthy that all research comparing readers and writers focuses on how students use reading and writing strategies, not on differences in the use of skills.

TEACHING COMPREHENSION

Comprehension instruction involves teaching students about comprehension and providing opportunities for them to practice what they are learning through reading and writing. The three components are explicit instruction, reading, and writing (Duke & Pearson, 2002). Teachers teach students how to activate background knowledge, set purposes, use comprehension strategies, and make inferences, and then students practice what they are learning as they read and write.

Researchers emphasize the need to establish the expectation that the books students read and the compositions they write will make sense (Blachowicz & Ogle, 2001; Duke & Pearson, 2002; Owocki, 2003). Teachers create an expectation of comprehension when they:

- Involve students in authentic reading and writing activities every day
- Provide students access to well-stocked classroom libraries
- Teach students to use comprehension strategies
- Have students read and write in a variety of genres
- Ensure that students are fluent readers and writers
- Teach students about genres and the structure of texts
- Provide opportunities for students to talk about the books they read and the compositions they write
- Teach students to make inferences
- Link vocabulary instruction to underlying concepts

Through these activities, students develop an understanding of comprehension and what readers and writers do to be successful.

Visit Chapter 7 on the Companion Website at *www.prenhall. com/tompkins* to connect to web links related to comprehension.

Explicit Comprehension Instruction

The fact that comprehension is an invisible mental process makes it difficult to teach; however, through explicit instruction, teachers make comprehension more visible. They explain what comprehension is and why it's important, and they model how they do it, by thinking aloud. Next, teachers encourage students to direct their thinking as they read, gradually releasing responsibility to students through guided and independent practice. Finally, they move students from focusing on a single comprehension strategy or other component of comprehension to integrating several components in routines, such as reciprocal teaching. Mrs. Donnelly demonstrated the concept of gradual release in the vignette at the beginning of the chapter as she reviewed each comprehension strategy and had the students practice it as they read picture books; then she had them apply all eight strategies as the read *Joey Pigza Loses Control* (Gantos, 2000).

Teaching Comprehension Strategies. Teachers teach individual comprehension strategies and then show students how to integrate several strategies simultaneously. They introduce each comprehension strategy in a minilesson. Teachers describe the strategy, model it for students as they read a text aloud, use it collaboratively with students, and then provide opportunities for guided and then independent practice (Duke & Pearson, 2002). The independent practice is important because it motivates students. The minilesson feature on page 242 shows how Mrs. Macadangdang teaches her third graders to use the questioning strategy.

 Learn more about grand conversations and other instructional procedures discussed in this chapter on the DVD that accompanies this text.

Through a minilesson about a comprehension strategy, students need to learn three things:

- Declarative knowledge—what the strategy does
- Procedural knowledge—how to use the strategy
- Conditional knowledge—when to use the strategy (Baker & Brown, 1984)

Teachers use a combination of explaining, modeling, and thinking aloud to present this information. In the vignette at the beginning of the chapter, Mrs. Donnelly emphasized these three kinds of knowledge in the posters her students made.

Teachers use think-alouds to demonstrate the thought processes they go through as they read (Baumann & Schmitt, 1986; Davey, 1983; Wade, 1990). They say what they are thinking while they are reading so that students become more aware of the thinking that capable readers use; in the process, students also learn to think aloud about their use of strategies. Think-alouds are valuable both when teachers model them for students and when students engage in them themselves. When students use think-alouds, they become more thoughtful, strategic readers (Bereiter & Bird, 1985); they also improve their ability to monitor

Scaffolding Struggling Readers

How can I teach my struggling readers to use comprehension strategies when the books they read are so simple?

Don't postpone strategy instruction until your students can read grade-level books because students must learn to think about their reading no matter what their reading level is. Kindergartners and first graders, for instance, learn to use predicting and connecting very effectively. Struggling readers often benefit from two approaches to strategy instruction: guided reading and literature focus units. In guided reading groups, teachers teach students how to use strategies one at a time and have them practice using them as they read books at their instructional level. During literature focus units, teachers often read aloud the featured book and model what good readers do—asking questions, summarizing, and using other strategies. Students also practice using the strategy as they listen, and when they're listening, they have more cognitive resources available for comprehension.

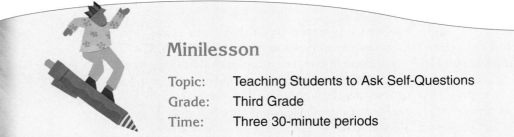

Minilesson

Topic: Teaching Students to Ask Self-Questions

Grade: Third Grade

Time: Three 30-minute periods

Mrs. Macadangdang (the students call her Mrs. Mac) introduced questioning by talking about why people ask questions and by asking questions about stories they were reading. She encouraged the third graders to ask questions, too. They made a list of questions for each chapter of *Chang's Paper Pony* (Coerr, 1988), a story set in the California gold rush era, as she read it aloud, and then they evaluated their questions, choosing the ones that focus on the big ideas and helped them understand the story better. Now all of her students can generate questions, so she's ready to introduce the asking questions strategy.

1. Introduce the Topic

Mrs. Mac reads the list of comprehension strategies posted in the classroom that they've learned to use and explains, "Today, we're going to learn a new thinking strategy—asking questions. Readers ask themselves questions while they're reading to help them think about the book." She adds "Asking Questions" to the list.

2. Share Examples

The teacher introduces *The Josefina Story Quilt* (Coerr, 1986), the story of a pioneer family going to California in a covered wagon. She reads aloud the first chapter, thinking aloud and generating questions about the story. Each time she says a question, she places in a pocket chart a sentence strip on which the question has already been written. Here are the questions: Why is Faith excited? Why are they going in a covered wagon? Who is Josefina? Can a chicken be a pet? Can Josefina do anything useful? Why is Faith crying?

3. Provide Information

Mrs. Mac explains, "Questions really turn your thinking on! I know it's important to think while I'm reading because it helps me understand. I like to ask questions about things I think are important and things that don't make sense to me." They reread the questions in the pocket chart and talk about the most helpful questions. Many students thought the question about the covered wagon was important, but as they continue reading, they'll learn that Josefina does indeed do something useful—she turns out to be a "humdinger of a watch dog" (p. 54)! Then Mrs. Mac reads aloud the second chapter, stopping often for students to generate questions. The students write their questions on sentence strips and add them to the pocket chart.

4. Guide Practice

The following day, Mrs. Mac reviews the questioning strategy and students reread the questions for chapters 1 and 2. Then the students form pairs, get copies of the book, and read the next two chapters of *The Josefina Story Quilt* together, generating questions as they read. They write their questions on small sticky notes and place them in the book. Mrs. Mac monitors students, noticing which ones need additional practice. Then the class comes together to share their questions and talk about the chapters they've read. On the third day, they read the last two chapters and generate more questions.

5. Assess Learning

As she monitored the students, Mrs. Mac made a list of students who needed more practice generating questions, and she will work with them as they read another book together.

Guidelines for Strategy Instruction

- Teach strategies in minilessons using a combination of explanations, demonstrations, think-alouds, and practice activities.
- Provide step-by-step explanations and modeling so that students understand what the strategy does, and how and when to use it.
- Provide both guided and independent practice opportunities so that students learn to apply the strategy in new situations.
- Have students apply the strategy in content-area activities as well as in literacy activities.
- Teach groups of strategies in routines so that students learn to orchestrate the use of multiple strategies.
- Ask students to reflect on their use of single strategies and strategy routines.
- Hang charts in the classroom of strategies and strategy routines students are learning and encourage students to refer to them when reading and writing.
- Differentiate between strategies and skills so that students understand that strategies are problem-solving tactics and skills are automatic behaviors.

their comprehension (Baumann, Seifert-Kessel, & Jones, 1992). The feature on this page presents a list of guidelines for strategy instruction.

Teachers also support students' learning about comprehension strategies in other ways: Figure 7–7 reviews several activities to emphasize each strategy. Second graders practice questioning by asking questions instead of giving answers during a grand conversation, for example, and sixth graders practice connecting when they write favorite quotes in one column of a double-entry journal and then explain in the second column why each quote is meaningful. When teachers involve students in these activities, it is important that they explain that students will be practicing a particular strategy as they complete an activity so that they think about what they are doing and how it is helping them to comprehend better.

Teaching Comprehension Routines. Once students know how to use individual strategies, they need to learn how to use routines or combinations of strategies because capable readers rarely use comprehension strategies one at a time (Duke & Pearson, 2002). In the vignette at the beginning of the chapter, for example, Mrs. Donnelly was teaching her sixth graders to use multiple strategies as they were reading *Joey Pigza Loses Control* (Gantos, 2000) and reflecting on their strategy use in their thinking logs.

One of the most effective comprehension routines is reciprocal teaching (Palincsar & Brown, 1984, 1986). Students use predicting, questioning, clarifying, and summarizing strategies to figure out the meaning of a text, paragraph by paragraph. Teachers can use this instructional procedure with the whole class when students are reading chapters in content-area textbooks or in small groups, such as literature circles when students are reading novels (Oczkus, 2003).

Developing Comprehension Through Reading

Students need to spend lots of time reading authentic texts independently and talking about their reading with classmates and teachers. Having students read interesting books written at their reading level is the best way for them to apply comprehension strategies. As they read and discuss their reading, students are practicing what they are learning about comprehension. Reading a selection in a basal textbook each week is not enough; instead, students need to read many, many books representing a range of genres during reading workshop or Sustained Silent Reading (SSR).

In addition to providing opportunities for students to read independently, teachers read books aloud to young children who are not yet fluent readers and to struggling readers who cannot read age-appropriate books themselves. When teachers do the reading, students have the cognitive resources available to focus on comprehension. Teachers often read books aloud when they introduce comprehension strategies or teach students to make inferences so that they can model procedures and scaffold students' thinking.

Students also develop their comprehension abilities when they discuss the stories they are reading in grand conversations and informational books and chapters in content-area textbooks in instructional conversations. As students and their teachers talk about their reading, make inferences, ask questions to clarify confusions, and

Figure 7–7	Instructional Procedures for Teaching Comprehension Strategies
Strategy	**Instructional Procedures**
Predicting	Using DRTA to make predictions Doing an anticipation guide to generate ideas for predictions Writing a double-entry journal with predictions in one column and summaries in the other
Connecting	Making a connections chart Writing connections in reading log entries Writing a double-entry journal with quotes and students' reflections on the quotes
Questioning	Brainstorming a list of questions before or after reading Asking questions in grand conversations and instructional conversations Analyzing questions using QARs
Visualizing	Drawing pictures of scenes, characters, or other information Dramatizing scenes Writing a description in reading log entries Making an open-mind portrait
Identifying Big Ideas	Creating graphic organizers Making posters highlighting the big ideas
Summarizing	Using the GIST procedure Creating graphic organizers Writing summaries in reading log entries
Monitoring	Doing think-alouds to demonstrate monitoring Writing about strategy use in reading log entries
Evaluating	Writing reflections and evaluations in reading log entries Conferencing with students about the books they read

These students have gathered together for a grand conversation to talk about chapters 6, 7, and 8 in a novel they are reading. The sixth graders share ideas, ask questions, and read and comment on excerpts from the book. Without raising their hands to be called on, the students take turns making comments. The teacher participates in the conversation to share her insights, ask questions, and clarify misconceptions. Later in the discussion, she will focus on story elements and draw students' attention to the characters and talk about the similarities and differences among them.

reflect on their use of the comprehension strategies, they elaborate and refine their comprehension.

Developing Comprehension Through Writing

Reading is so much like writing: Both reading and writing are processes of making meaning with similar stages, and they depend on the same reader and text factors. It's not surprising that both readers and writers activate background knowledge and set purposes, but they also use the same comprehension strategies. Think about the identifying big ideas strategy: Readers use this comprehension strategy to remember what they read, but writers also have to focus on the big ideas so that readers will comprehend. Figure 7–8 shows that both readers and writers use the reader and text factors similarly. Duke and Pearson (2002) emphasize that it's important that teachers emphasize the connections between reading and writing and "develop students' abilities to write like a reader and read like a writer" (p. 208).

Students also apply their knowledge of text factors for both reading and writing. Teachers often have students create a piece of writing by modeling something they have read. In first grade, for example, they might write a new version of a predictable book, such as *Brown Bear, Brown Bear, What Do You See?* (Martin, 1992); in third grade, they might write a poem following the pattern of a poem they've read; in fifth grade, they might write their own question-and-answer books following the style of *If You Were There When They Signed the Constitution* (Levy, 1992); and in seventh grade, they might write a prequel or sequel for a novel they've read. Whenever students write an innovation on a story, informational book, or poem, they are applying their knowledge of comprehension.

Complete a self-assessment to check your understanding of the concepts presented in this chapter on the Companion Website at *www.prenhall.com/ tompkins*

Factors	What Readers Do	What Writers Do
Background Knowledge	Readers use their world knowledge and literary knowledge to make sense of what they are reading.	Writers draw on both their world knowledge and their literary knowledge as they plan, draft, and revise their compositions.
Purpose	Readers set purposes to direct their reading, and they are more likely to remember what they read when they have a purpose in mind.	Writers produce more comprehensible text when they have a purpose in mind and when their main ideas reflect their purpose.
Fluency	Fluent readers have more cognitive energy available to focus on comprehension.	Fluent writers have more cognitive energy available to focus on producing comprehensible text.
Comprehension Strategies	Readers engage with the text they are reading when they use comprehension strategies to monitor, personalize, and evaluate their reading.	Students apply strategies and monitor their strategy use as they plan, draft, revise, and proofread their writing.
Making Inferences	Readers activate background knowledge, notice clues, and ask questions to make inferences and draw conclusions.	Writers choose what to state explicitly and what to leave unsaid in their writing, and they add clues for readers to use in making inferences.
Motivation and Attention	Motivated students are attentive and engaged during reading and are more likely to comprehend successfully.	Students who like to write believe that they are capable writers and expect to be successful.
Structure	Readers recognize the structure of the text they are reading and use it as a skeleton to scaffold their understanding.	Writers provide a structure to their writing so that readers will be able to use it to increase comprehension.
Genres	Readers use their knowledge of genres to scaffold their comprehension of books they are reading.	Students incorporate the characteristics of a genre when they write so that readers will recognize it and understand what they are reading.
Content and Vocabulary	Students draw on their world knowledge and vocabulary to understand what they are reading.	Students apply their knowledge about a concept and its related vocabulary when they write.

Figure 7–8 **Comprehension Connections Between Reading and Writing**

Review: How Effective Teachers Facilitate Students' Comprehension

1. Teachers understand that comprehension is a process involving reader factors and text factors.

2. Teachers build students' world and literary knowledge and scaffold them to activate their background knowledge before reading.

3. Teachers assist students in setting purposes and using the purposes to guide their reading.

4. Teachers teach students to make inferences and draw conclusions.

5. Teachers nurture students' motivation and interest in literacy activities.

6. Teachers use their knowledge of the differences between capable and less capable readers and writers to teach their less capable students to be more successful.

7. Teachers establish a classroom environment that fosters the idea that reading and writing are meaningful processes.

8. Teachers teach comprehension explicitly, including how, when, and why to use strategies and routines of strategies.

9. Teachers provide daily opportunities for students to practice comprehension strategies as they read and talk about books.

10. Teachers emphasize the reading-writing connection by providing daily opportunities for writing.

Professional References

Alderman, M. K. (1999). *Motivation for achievement: Possibilities for teaching and learning*. Mahwah, NJ: Erlbaum.

Baker, L., & Brown, A. (1984). Metacognitive skills of reading. In P. D. Pearson, M. Kamil, P. Mosenthal, & R. Barr (Eds.), *Handbook of reading research* (pp. 353–394). New York: Longman.

Baumann, J. F., & Schmitt, M. C. (1986). The what, why, how, and when of comprehension instruction. *The Reading Teacher, 39*, 640–647.

Baumann, J. F., Seifert-Kessel, N., & Jones, L. A. (1992). Effect of think-aloud instruction on elementary students' comprehension monitoring abilities. *Journal of Reading Behavior, 24*, 143–172.

Bereiter, C., & Bird, M. (1985). Use of thinking aloud in identification and teaching of reading comprehension strategies. *Cognition and Instruction, 2*, 131–156.

Blachowicz, C., & Ogle, D. (2001). *Reading comprehension: Strategies for independent learners*. New York: Guilford Press.

Blanton, W. E., Wood, K. D., & Moorman, G. B. (1990). The role of purpose in reading instruction. *The Reading Teacher, 43*, 486–493.

Cunningham, J. W. (1982). Generating interactions between schemata and text. In J. A. Niles & L. A. Harris (Eds.), *New inquiries in reading research and instruction* (pp. 42–47). Rochester, NY: National Reading Conference.

Cunningham, P. M., & Cunningham, J. W. (2002). What we know about how to teach phonics. In A. E. Farstrup & S. J. Samuels (Eds.), *What research has to say about reading instruction* (3rd ed., pp. 87–109). Newark, DE: International Reading Association.

Davey, B. (1983). Think-aloud—Modelling the cognitive processes of reading comprehension. *Journal of Reading, 27*, 44–47.

Dole, J. A., Duffy, G. G., Roehler, L. R., & Pearson, P. D. (1991). Moving from the old to the new: Research on reading comprehension instruction. *Review of Educational Research, 61*, 239–264.

Duke, N. K., & Pearson, P. D. (2002). Effective practices for developing reading comprehension. In A. E. Farstrup & S. J. Samuels (Eds.), *What research has to say about reading instruction* (3rd ed., pp. 205–242). Newark, DE: International Reading Association.

Dweck, C. S. (1986). Motivating processes affecting learning. *American Psychologist, 41*, 1040–1048.

Faigley, L., Cherry, R. D., Jolliffe, D. A., & Skinner, A. M. (1985). *Assessing writers' knowledge and processes of composing*. Norwood, NJ: Ablex.

Fountas, I. C., & Pinnell, G. S. (2001). *Guiding readers and writers grades 3–6: Teaching comprehension, genre, and content literacy*. Portsmouth, NH: Heinemann.

Garner, R. (1987). *Metacognition and reading comprehension*. Norwood, NJ: Ablex.

Good, T., & Brophy, J. E. (2000). *Looking in classrooms* (2nd ed.). New York: Longman.

Irwin, J. W. (1991). *Teaching reading comprehension processes* (2nd ed.). Boston: Allyn & Bacon.

Ivey, G., & Broaddus, K. (2001). "Just plain reading": A survey of what makes students want to read in middle school classrooms. *Reading Research Quarterly, 36*, 350–377.

Johnson, P., & Winograd, P. (1985). Passive failure in reading. *Journal of Reading Behavior, 17*, 279–301.

Keene, E. O., & Zimmermann, S. (1997). *Mosaic of thought: Teaching comprehension in a reader's workshop.* Portsmouth, NH: Heinemann.

Kohn, A. (1993). *Punished by rewards: The trouble with gold stars, incentive plans, A's, praise, and other bribes.* Boston: Houghton Mifflin.

McLaughlin, M., & Allen, M. B. (2002). *Guided comprehension: A teaching model for grades 3–8.* Newark, DE: International Reading Association.

National Reading Panel. (2000). *Teaching children to read: An evidence-based assessment of the scientific research literature on reading and its implications for reading instruction.* Washington, DC: National Institute of Child Health and Human Development.

Oczkus, L. D. (2003). *Reciprocal teaching at work: Strategies for improving reading comprehension.* Newark, DE: International Reading Association.

Oldfather, P. (1995). Commentary: What's needed to maintain and extend motivation for literacy in the middle grades. *Journal of Reading, 38,* 420–422.

Owocki, G. (2003). *Comprehension: Strategic instruction for K–3 students.* Portsmouth, NH: Heinemann.

Palincsar, A. S., & Brown, A. L. (1984). Reciprocal teaching of comprehension fostering and monitoring activities. *Cognition and Instruction, 1,* 117–175.

Palincsar, A. S., & Brown, A. L. (1986). Interactive teaching to promote independent learning from text. *The Reading Teacher, 39,* 771–777.

Paris, S. G., Wasik, B. A., & Turner, J. C. (1991). The development of strategic readers. In R. Barr, M. L. Kamil, P. B. Mosenthal, & P. D. Pearson (Eds.), *Handbook of reading research* (Vol. 2, pp. 609–640). New York: Longman.

Pearson, P. D., & Johnson, D. (1978). *Teaching reading comprehension.* New York: Holt, Rinehart and Winston.

Pressley, M. (2002a). Comprehension strategies instruction: A turn-of-the-century status report. In C. C. Block & M. Pressley (Eds.), *Comprehension instruction: Research-based best practices* (pp. 11–27). New York: Guilford Press.

Pressley, M. (2002b). Metacognition and self-regulated comprehension. In A. E. Farstrup & S. J. Samuels (Eds.), *What research has to say about reading instruction* (3rd ed., pp. 291–309). Newark, DE: International Reading Association.

Pressley, M., Dolezal, S. E., Raphael, L. M., Mohan, L., Roehrig, A. D., & Bogner, K. (2003). *Motivating primary-grade students.* New York: Guilford Press.

Raphael, T. E., & McKinney, J. (1983). An examination of fifth- and eighth-grade children's question answering behavior: An instructional study in metacognition. *Journal of Reading Behavior, 15,* 67–86.

Samuels, S. J. (2002). Reading fluency: Its development and assessment. In A. E. Farstrup & S. J. Samuels (Eds.), *What research has to say about reading instruction* (3rd ed., pp. 166–185). Newark, DE: International Reading Association.

Stauffer, R. G. (1975). *Directing the reading-thinking process.* New York: Harper & Row.

Stipek, D. J. (1993). *Motivation to learn: From theory to practice* (2nd ed.). Boston: Allyn & Bacon.

Sweet, A. P., & Snow, C. E. (2003). Reading for comprehension. In A. P. Sweet & C. E. Snow (Eds.), *Rethinking reading comprehension* (pp. 1–11). New York: Guilford Press.

Tierney, R. J. (1990). Redefining reading comprehension. *Educational Leadership, 47,* 37–42.

Tovani, C. (2000). *I read it, but I don't get it: Comprehension strategies for adolescent readers.* Portland, ME: Stenhouse.

Turner, J., & Paris, S. G. (1995). How literacy tasks influence children's motivation for literacy. *The Reading Teacher, 48,* 662–673.

Unrau, N. (2004). *Content area reading and writing: Fostering literacies in middle and high school cultures.* Upper Saddle River, NJ: Merrill/Prentice Hall.

Van Den Broek, P., & Kremer, K. E. (2000). The mind in action: What it means to comprehend during reading. In B. M. Taylor, M. F. Graves, & P. Van Den Broek (Eds.), *Reading for meaning: Fostering comprehension in the middle grades* (pp. 1–31). New York: Teachers College Press.

Wade, S. E. (1990). Using think alouds to assess comprehension. *The Reading Teacher, 43,* 422–453.

Children's Book References

Bunting, E. (1994). *A day's work.* New York: Clarion Books.

Bunting, E. (1998). *So far from the sea.* Boston: Houghton Mifflin.

Coerr, E. (1986). *The Josefina story quilt.* New York: HarperCollins.

Coerr, E. (1988). *Chang's paper pony.* New York: HarperCollins.

Cohen, B. (1998). *Molly's pilgrim.* New York: HarperCollins.

Gantos, J. (2000). *Joey Pigza loses control.* New York: HarperCollins.

Jiménez, F. (1998). *La mariposa.* Boston: Houghton Mifflin.

Levine, E. (1993). *If you traveled on the underground railroad.* New York: Scholastic.

Levy, E. (1992). *If you were there when they signed the Constitution.* New York: Scholastic.

Martin, B., Jr. (1992). *Brown bear, brown bear, what do you see?* New York: Henry Holt.

Mochizuki, K. (1993). *Baseball saved us.* New York: Lee & Low.

Osborne, M. P. (1993). *Mummies in the morning.* New York: Random House.

Osborne, W., & Osborne, M. P. (2001). *Mummies and pyramids.* New York: Random House.

Van Allsburg, C. (1979). *The garden of Abdul Gasazi.* Boston: Houghton Mifflin.

Van Allsburg, C. (1991). *The wretched stone.* Boston: Houghton Mifflin.

Waber, B. (1975). *Ira sleeps over.* Boston: Houghton Mifflin.

Wexo, J. B. (1990). *Snakes.* Mankato, MN: Zoo Books.

Facilitating Students' Comprehension:
Text Factors

Chapter Questions

- How are stories organized?
- How are informational books organized?
- How are poems structured?
- How does students' knowledge of text structure affect their reading and writing?

Mr. Abrams's Fourth Graders Learn About Frogs

The fourth graders in Mr. Abrams's class are studying frogs. They began by making a class K-W-L chart (Ogle, 1986), listing what they already know about frogs in the "K: What We Know" column and things they want to learn in the "W: What We Wonder" column. At the end of the unit, students will finish the chart by listing what they have learned in the "L: What We Have Learned" column. The fourth graders want to know how frogs and toads are different and if it is true that you get warts from frogs. Mr. Abrams assures them that they will learn the answers to many of their questions and makes a mental note to find the answer to their question about warts.

Aquariums with frogs and frog spawn are arranged in one area in the classroom. Mr. Abrams has brought in five aquariums and filled them with frogs he collected in his backyard and others he "rented" from a local pet store, and he has also brought in frog spawn from a nearby pond. The fourth graders are observing the frogs and frog spawn daily and drawing diagrams and making notes in their learning logs.

A word wall is posted on one side of the classroom, and students are writing important theme-related words in alphabetized boxes on the chart. They add small pictures to illustrate more difficult words. The words include

amphibian, camouflage, cold blooded, endangered, froglet, gills, hibernation, lungs, metamorphosis, predators, skin, spawn, tadpoles, tongue, and *tympanum.* The students refer to the word wall and use the words as they make notes in their learning logs and participate in other writing activities related to the unit. Mr. Abrams also uses these words for minilessons on syllables, parts of speech, and other skills.

Mr. Abrams sets out a text set with three types of books about frogs—stories, informational books, and poetry books—on a special shelf in the classroom library. Mr. Abrams reads many of the books aloud to the class. When he begins, he reads the title and shows students several pages and asks them whether the book is a story, an informational book, or a poem. After they determine the genre, they talk about their purpose for listening. For an informational book, he writes a question or two on the chalkboard to give students a purpose for listening. During their instructional conversation after reading, the students answer the questions as part of their discussion. Students also read and reread many of these books during an independent reading time, which Mr. Abrams calls DEAR (Drop Everything And Read) time. (DEAR time is similar to Sustained Silent Reading ([SSR]).)

Mr. Abrams also has a class set of *Amazing Frogs and Toads* (Clarke, 1990), an informational book published by Dorling Kindersley with striking photograph illustrations and well-organized presentations of information. Mr. Abrams reads it once with the whole class using shared reading, and they discuss the interesting information in the book in an instructional conversation. He divides the class into nine small groups, and each group chooses a question about frogs to research in the book. Students reread the book, hunting for the answer to their question. Mr. Abrams has already taught the students to use the table of contents and the index to locate facts in an informational book. After they locate and reread the information, they use the writing process to develop a poster to answer the question and share what they have learned. He meets with each group to help them organize their posters and revise and edit their writing.

From the vast amount of information in *Amazing Frogs and Toads*, Mr. Abrams chooses nine questions, which he designs to address some of the questions on the "W: What We Wonder" section of the K-W-L chart, to highlight important information in the text, and to focus on the five expository text structures, the patterns used for nonfiction texts that students read and write. Mr. Abrams is teaching the fourth graders that informational books, like stories, have special organizational elements. Here are his nine questions organized according to the expository structures:

1. What are amphibians? (Description)
2. What do frogs look like? (Description)
3. What is the life cycle of a frog? (Sequence)
4. How do frogs eat? (Sequence)
5. How are frogs and toads alike and different? (Comparison)

6. Why do frogs hibernate? (Cause and Effect)
7. How do frogs croak? (Cause and Effect)
8. How do frogs use their eyes and eyelids? (Problem and Solution)
9. How do frogs escape from their enemies? (Problem and Solution)

After the students complete their posters, they share them with the class through brief presentations, and the posters are displayed in the classroom. Two of the students' posters are shown on page 253; the life cycle poster emphasizes the sequence structure, and the "Frogs Have Big Eyes" poster explains that the frog's eyes help it solve problems—finding food, hiding from enemies, and seeing underwater.

Mr. Abrams's students use the information in the posters to write books about frogs. Students choose three posters and write one- to three-paragraph chapters to report the information from the poster. Students meet in writing groups to revise their rough drafts and then edit with a classmate and with Mr. Abrams. Finally, students word process their final copies and add illustrations, a title page, and a table of contents. Then they compile their books and "publish" them by sharing them with classmates from the author's chair.

Armin wrote this chapter on "Hibernation" in his book:

> *Hibernation means that an animal sleeps all winter long. Frogs hibernate because they are cold blooded and they might freeze to death if they didn't. They find a good place to sleep like a hole in the ground, or in a log, or under some leaves. They go to sleep and they do not eat, or drink, or go to the bathroom. They sleep all winter and when they wake up it is spring. They are very, very hungry and they want to eat a lot of food. Their blood warms up when it is spring because the temperature warms up and when they are warm they want to be awake and eat. They are awake in the spring and in the summer, and then in the fall they start to think about hibernating again.*

Jessica wrote this chapter on "The Differences Between Frogs and Toads" in her book:

> *You might think that frogs and toads are the same but you would be wrong. They are really different but they are both amphibians. I am going to tell you three ways they are different.*
>
> *First of all, frogs really love water so they stay in the water or pretty close to it. Toads don't love water. They usually live where it is dry. This is a big difference between frogs and toads.*
>
> *Second, you should look at frogs and toads. They look different. Frogs are slender and thin but toads are fat. Their skin is different, too. Frogs have smooth skin and toads have bumpy skin. I would say that toads are not pretty to look at.*
>
> *Third, frogs have long legs but toads have short legs. That probably is the reason why frogs are wonderful jumpers and toads can't. They move slowly. They just hop. When you watch them move, you can tell that they are very different.*
>
> *Frogs and toads are different kinds of amphibians. They live in different places, they look different, and they move in different ways. You can see these differences when you look at them and it is very interesting to study them.*

See the Compendium of Instructional Procedures, which follows Chapter 14, for more information on the highlighted terms.

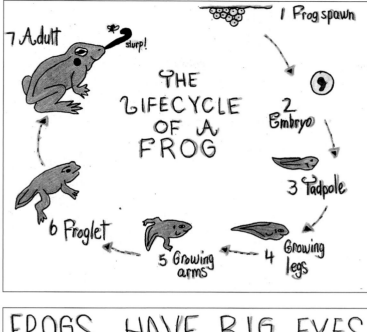

Mr. Abrams and his students develop a rubric to assess students' books. The rubric addresses the following points about the chapters:

- The chapter title describes the chapter.
- The information in each chapter is presented clearly.
- Vocabulary from the word wall is used in each chapter.
- The information in each chapter is written in one or more indented paragraphs.

- The information in each chapter has very few spelling, capitalization, and punctuation errors.
- There is a useful illustration in each chapter.

Other points on the rubric consider the book as a whole:

- The title page lists the title and the author's name.
- All pages in the book are numbered.
- The table of contents lists the chapters and the pages for each chapter.
- The title is written on the cover of the book.
- The illustrations on the cover of the book relate to frogs.

The students evaluate their books using a 4-point scale; Mr. Abrams also uses the rubric to assess students' writing. He conferences with students and shares his scoring with them. Also, he helps the students set goals for their next writing project.

To end the unit, Mr. Abrams asks his students to finish the K-W-L chart. In the third column, "L: What We Have Learned," students list some of the information they have learned, including:

Frogs are amphibians that hibernate in the winter.
There are 3,000 kinds of frogs.
Leopard frogs are the most common kind of frog.
Tadpoles breathe through gills but frogs breathe through lungs.
Tadpoles are vegetarians but frogs eat worms and insects.
Snakes, rats, birds, and foxes are the frogs' enemies.
Some frogs in the rainforest are brightly colored and poisonous, too.
Some frogs are hard to see because they have camouflage coloring.
Male frogs puff up their air sacs to croak and make sounds.
Frogs have teeth but they swallow their food whole.
The largest American frog is the bullfrog.
Frogs have two sets of eyelids and one set is clear so frogs can see when they are underwater.
Frogs can jump ten times their body length but toads can't—they're hoppers.
Frogs live near water and toads live on land.

Mr. Abrams stands back to reread the fourth graders' comments. "I can tell how much you've learned when I read the detailed information you've added in the L column," he remarks with a smile. He knows that one reason why his students are successful is because he teaches them to use text structure as a tool for learning.

What readers know and do during reading has a tremendous impact on how well they comprehend, but comprehension involves more than just reader factors: It also involves text factors. Stories, informational books, and poems can be easier or more difficult to read depending on factors that are inherent in them. When students know how authors organize and present their ideas in texts, this knowledge serves as a scaffold, making comprehension easier. Here are three text factors:

- Text structure or the organization of ideas
- Genres or categories of literature
- The content of a text and its technical vocabulary

Text structure refers to the way authors organize ideas in stories, informational books, and poems. Texts are easier to read when they are well organized and more difficult when they are poorly constructed or when important information or connections between big ideas are missing. Effective text structure emphasizes the most important ideas so that students can identify and remember them more easily (Meyer & Poon, 2004; Sweet & Snow, 2003). Genres play a similar role: When students understand the unique characteristics of genres, they are better equipped to anticipate the structure of the text and comprehend the big ideas more easily.

The content or ideas presented in the text and the vocabulary used to express these ideas also are important. Students who have more background knowledge about the topic and are familiar with the related, and often technical, vocabulary comprehend more easily than students who don't, but the way the information is presented in a text can help to ameliorate the problem of inadequate background knowledge because effective organization highlights the big ideas and clarifies the relationships among them (Duke & Pearson, 2002).

Students apply their knowledge of text factors to writing, too. De Ford (1981) and Eckhoff (1983) found that when primary-grade students read basal reading textbooks, the stories they write reflect the short, choppy linguistic style of the readers, but when students read picture-book stories and novels, their writing reflects the more sophisticated language structures and literary style of these books. Dressel (1990) also found that the quality of fifth graders' writing depended on the quality of the stories they read and listened to read aloud, regardless of the students' reading levels. Similarly, students apply their knowledge of structure of informational books and content-area textbooks in their writing (Flood, Lapp, & Farnan, 1986; McGee & Richgels, 1985; Piccolo, 1987).

For more than a quarter century, researchers have documented that teaching students about text factors aids comprehension (Kintsch & Van Dijk, 1978; Meyer, 1975). The first step is to introduce the text factors to students, but it's not enough that they are familiar with them and notice them when they read; students need to learn how to use text factors to organize and connect the big ideas when they read and write. Graphic organizers are one way to help students visualize the big ideas and the technical vocabulary used in explaining them. In the vignette at the beginning of the chapter, Mr. Abrams used text factors to scaffold his students' learning about frogs. He taught them about the unique characteristics of informational books, emphasized text structures in the questions he asked, used graphic organizers to help students visualize big ideas, and had them write about the big ideas they were learning.

Teachers like Mr. Abrams consider the text factors of the content-area textbooks and trade books they use, and they plan their instruction to facilitate their students' learning. In addition, they teach their students how to use text structures and genres to enhance their comprehension. The feature on the next page shows the role that text factors play in a balanced literacy program.

STORIES

Stories give meaning to the human experience, and they are a powerful way of knowing and learning. When preschoolers listen to family members tell stories and read stories aloud, they develop an understanding or concept about stories by the time they

How the Text Factors of Comprehension Fit Into a Balanced Literacy Program

Component	Description
Reading	Students need to recognize the text structures and genres in books they are reading.
Phonics and Other Skills	Students use comprehension skills when they recognize text structures and genres and examine text features in content-area textbooks.
Strategies	When students know about text structure and recognize genres, they are better able to apply comprehension strategies.
Vocabulary	Vocabulary and content knowledge affect how well students comprehend the texts they are reading.
Comprehension	Both reader factors and text factors play an important role in students' comprehension.
Literature	Students apply their knowledge of story elements, literary devices, and other text factors when they read picture-book stories and novels.
Content-Area Study	Students apply their knowledge of expository text structures and text features when they read informational books and content-area textbooks.
Oral Language	Students use their knowledge of text factors as they listen to the teacher read aloud.
Writing	Students apply their knowledge of text factors when they write stories, reports, poems, and other compositions.
Spelling	Spelling is not an important component of comprehension.

Visit Chapter 8 on the Companion Website at *www.prenhall.com/ tompkins* to connect to web links related to children's literature.

come to school. Students use and refine this knowledge as they read and write stories. Many educators, including Jerome Bruner (1986), recommend using stories as a way into literacy.

Stories are available in picture-book and chapter-book formats. Picture books have brief texts, usually spread over 32 pages, in which text and illustrations combine to tell a story. The text is minimal, and the illustrations supplement the sparse text. The illustrations in many picture books are striking. Many picture books, such as *Rosie's Walk* (Hutchins, 1968), about a clever hen who outwits a fox, are for primary-grade students, but others, such as *Pink and Say* (Polacco, 1994), about two Civil War soldiers, one Black and one White, were written with middle-grade students in mind. Fairy tales have also been retold as picture books; Trina Schart Hyman's *The Sleeping Beauty* (1977) is an especially beautiful picture book. Another type of picture book is wordless picture books, such as *Tuesday* (Wiesner, 1991) and *Good Dog, Carl* (Day, 1985), in which the story is told entirely through the illustrations.

Novels are longer stories written in a chapter format. Most are written for older students, but Dan Greenburg's adventure series, The Zack Files, including *Never Trust a*

Cat Who Wears Earrings (1997), is for students reading at the second- and third-grade levels. Chapter books for middle-grade students include *Charlotte's Web* (White, 1952) and *Bunnicula: A Rabbit-Tale of Mystery* (Howe & Howe, 1979). Complex stories such as *The Giver* (Lowry, 1993) are more suitable for upper-grade students. Chapter books have few illustrations, if any, and the illustrations do not play an integral role in the book.

Narrative Genres

Stories can be categorized in different ways, one of which is according to genres or types of stories (Buss & Karnowski, 2000). Three broad genrel categories are folklore, fantasies, and realistic fiction.

Folklore. Stories that began hundreds of years ago and were passed down from generation to generation by storytellers before being written down are folk literature. These stories, including fables, folktales, and myths, are an important part of our cultural heritage. Fables are brief narratives designed to teach a moral. The story format makes the lesson easier to understand, and the moral is usually stated at the end. Here are the characteristics of fables:

- They are short, often less than a page long.
- The characters are usually animals.
- The characters are one-dimensional, strong or weak, wise or foolish.
- The setting is barely sketched; the stories could take place anywhere.
- The theme is usually stated as a moral at the end of the story.

Our best-known fables, including "The Hare and the Tortoise" and "The Ant and the Grasshopper," are believed to have been written by a Greek slave named Aesop in the 6th century B.C. Individual fables hare been retold as picture-book stories, including *The Hare and the Tortoise* (Ward, 1999) and *The Lion and the Rat* (Jones, 1997).

Folktales began as oral stories, told and retold by medieval storytellers as they traveled from town to town. The problem in a folktale usually revolves around one of four situations: a journey from home to perform a task, a journey to confront a monster, the miraculous change from a harsh home to a secure home, or a confrontation between a wise beast and a foolish beast. Other characteristics:

- The story often begins with the phrase "Once upon a time . . . "
- The setting is generalized and could be located anywhere.
- The plot structure is simple and straightforward.
- Characters are one-dimensional, good or bad, stupid or clever, industrious or lazy.
- The end is happy, and everyone lives "happily ever after."

Some folktales are cumulative tales, such as *Henny Penny* (Galdone, 1968) and *The Gingerbread Boy* (Galdone, 1975); these stories are built around the repetition of words and events. Others are talking animal stories; in these stories, such as *The Three Little Pigs* (Zemach, 1988), animals act and talk like humans. The best-known folktales, however, are fairy tales. These stories have motifs or small recurring elements, including magical powers, transformations, enchantments, magical objects, trickery, and wishes that are granted, and they feature witches, giants, fairy godmothers, and other fantastic characters. Well-known examples are *Cinderella* (Sanderson, 2002), *The Sleeping Beauty* (Yolen, 1986), and *Jack and the Beanstalk* (Howe, 1989).

Today, many folktales have three, four, or even more variations. Some versions came about as storytellers personalized the stories, and others reflect geographic and cultural diversity. In addition to the traditional versions of "Cinderella" retold by Ruth Sanderson (2002) and Paul Galdone (1978) and *Ella Enchanted* (Levine, 1997), a novel-length Cinderella story, there are many others, including:

Abadeha: The Philippine Cinderella (de la Paz, 2001)

Adelita: A Mexican Cinderella Story (dePaola, 2002)

Cendrillon: A Caribbean Cinderella (San Souci, 1998)

Jouanah: A Hmong Cinderella (Coburn, 1996)

Moss Gown (Hooks, 1987)

Mufaro's Beautiful Daughters: An African Tale (Steptoe, 1987)

The Golden Sandal: A Middle Eastern Cinderella Story (Hickox, 1998)

The Rough-Face Girl (Martin, 1992)

The Turkey Girl: A Zuni Cinderella Story (Pollock, 1996)

The Way Meat Loves Salt: A Cinderella Tale From the Jewish Tradition (Jaffe, 1998)

Yeh-Shen: A Cinderella Story From China (Louie, 1982)

As you might imagine, the story varies somewhat from version to version: The glass slipper is missing from some versions or it has been transformed into a sandal or something else, but the conflict between kind and selfish remains, and at the end, the Cinderella character is rewarded for her goodness.

People around the world have created myths to explain natural phenomena. Some myths explain the origin of the world and how human beings were brought into existence; some explain the seasons, the sun and moon, and the constellations; and others explain the mountains and other physical features of the earth. Ancient peoples used myths to explain many things that have since been explained by scientific theories and investigations. Characteristics of myths:

- Myths explain creations.
- Characters are often heroes with supernatural powers.
- The setting is barely sketched.
- Magical powers are required.

Picture-book retellings of myths from various cultures are available for children. For example, the Greek myth *Persephone* (Hutton, 1994) tells how spring originated, and the Native American myth *The Legend of the Bluebonnet* (dePaola, 1983) recounts how these flowers came to beautify the countryside. Other myths tell how animals came to be or why they look the way they do, including *Iktomi and the Boulder* (Goble, 1988) and *The Story of Jumping Mouse* (Steptoe, 1984).

Legends are myths about heroes and heroines who have done something important enough to be remembered in a story; they are thought to have some basis in history but are not verifiable. Stories about Robin Hood and King Arthur, for example, are legends. American legends are tall tales; three of the best known are available as picture books written and illustrated by Steven Kellogg: *Paul Bunyan* (1984), *Johnny Appleseed* (1988), and *Pecos Bill* (1986).

Fantasies. Fantasies are stories that could not really take place. Authors create new worlds for their characters, but these worlds must be based in reality so that readers will believe they exist. Two well-known examples are *Charlotte's Web* (White, 1952) and *Harry Potter and the Sorcerer's Stone* (Rowling, 1997). Four types of fantasies are modern literary tales, fantastic stories, science fiction, and high fantasy.

Modern literary tales are related to folktales and fairy tales because they often incorporate many characteristics and conventions of traditional literature, but they have been written more recently and have identifiable authors. The best-known author of modern literary tales is Hans Christian Andersen, a Danish writer of the 1800s who wrote *The Emperor's New Clothes* (Westcott, 1984) and *The Ugly Duckling* (Pinkney, 1999). Other examples of modern literary tales include *Alexander and the Wind-up Mouse* (Lionni, 1969), *The Wolf's Chicken Stew* (Kasza, 1987), and *The Principal's New Clothes* (Calmenson, 1989).

Fantastic stories are realistic in most details, but some events require readers to suspend disbelief. Following are characteristics of fantasies:

- The events in the story are extraordinary; things that could not happen in today's world.
- The setting is realistic.
- Main characters are people or personified animals.
- Themes often deal with the conflict between good and evil.

Some fantastic stories are animal fantasies, such as *Charlotte's Web* (White, 1952). In these stories, the main characters are animals endowed with human traits. Students often realize that the animals symbolize human beings and that these stories explore human relationships. Some fantasies are toy fantasies, such as *Winnie-the-Pooh* (Milne, 1961). Toy fantasies are similar to animal fantasies except that the main characters are talking toys, usually stuffed animals or dolls. Other fantasies involve enchanted journeys during which wondrous things happen. The journey must have a purpose, but it is usually overshadowed by the thrill and delight of the fantastic world. Examples include *Alice's Adventures in Wonderland* (Carroll, 1984) and *Charlie and the Chocolate Factory* (Dahl, 1964).

In science fiction stories, authors create a world in which science interacts with every area of society (Norton & Norton, 2003). Many stories involve traveling through space to distant galaxies or meeting alien societies. Authors hypothesize scientific advancements and imagine technology of the future to create the plot. Characteristics of science fiction:

- The story is set in the future.
- Conflict is usually between the characters and natural or mechanical forces, such as robots.
- The characters believe in the advanced technology.
- A detailed description of scientific facts is provided.

Time-warp stories in which the characters move forward and back in time are also classified as science fiction. Jon Scieszka's Time Warp Trio stories, including *Knights of the Kitchen Table* (1991), are popular with middle-grade students.

In high fantasy, heroes and heroines confront evil for the good of humanity. The primary characteristic is the focus on the conflict between good and evil, as in C. S. Lewis's *The Lion, the Witch and the Wardrobe* (1994) and J. K. Rowling's Harry Potter stories. High fantasy is related to folk literature in that it is characterized by motifs and themes. Most stories include magical kingdoms, quests, tests of courage, magical powers, and fantastic characters.

Realistic Fiction. These stories are lifelike and believable, without magic or supernatural powers. The outcome is reasonable, and the story is a representation of action that seems truthful. Realistic fiction helps children discover that their problems and desires are not unique and that they are not alone in experiencing certain feelings and situations. Realistic fiction also broadens children's horizons and allows them to experience new adventures. Two types of realistic fiction are contemporary stories and historical stories.

When children read contemporary stories, they identify with characters who are their own age and have similar interests and problems. In *Ramona Quimby, Age 8* (Cleary, 1981), for example, children read about Ramona and her typical family tensions. Characteristics of contemporary fiction:

- Characters act like real people or like real animals.
- The setting is in the world as we know it today.
- Stories deal with everyday occurrences or "relevant subjects."

Other contemporary stories include *Granny Torrelli Makes Soup* (Creech, 2003), *Joey Pigza Loses Control* (Gantos, 2000), and *Loser* (Spinelli, 2002).

Historical stories are set in the past. Details about food, clothing, and transportation must be typical of the era in which the story is set because the setting influences the plot. Characteristics of this genre:

- The setting is historically accurate.
- Conflict is often between characters or between a character and society.
- The language is appropriate to the setting.
- Themes are universal, both to the historical period of the book and for today.

Examples of historical fiction include *Number the Stars* (Lowry, 1989), *Witness* (Hesse, 2001), and *Molly's Pilgrim* (Cohen, 1983). Through historical fiction, children are immersed in historical events, appreciate the contributions of people who have lived before them, and understand human relationships.

Figure 8–1 reviews the folklore, fantasy, and realistic fiction genres and lists additional examples of stories.

Elements of Story Structure

Stories have unique structural elements that distinguish them from other forms of literature. Five story elements are plot, characters, setting, point of view, and theme. These elements work together to structure a story, and authors manipulate them to make their stories hold readers' attention.

Plot. Plot is the sequence of events involving characters in conflict situations. A story's plot is based on the goals of one or more characters and the processes they go through to attain them (Lukens, 2002). The main characters want to achieve a goal, and other characters are introduced to oppose the main characters or prevent them from being successful. The story events are set in motion by characters as they attempt to overcome conflict, reach their goals, and solve their problems.

The most basic aspect of plot is the division of the main events of a story into three parts: beginning, middle, and end. In *The Tale of Peter Rabbit* (Potter, 1902), for instance, the three story parts are easy to pick out. As the story begins, Mrs. Rabbit sends her children out to play after warning them not to go into Mr. McGregor's garden. In the middle, Peter goes to Mr. McGregor's garden and is almost caught. Then Peter finds his way out of the garden and gets home safely—the end of the story. Students can make a story map of the beginning-middle-end of a story using words and pictures, as the story map for *The Tale of Peter Rabbit* in Figure 8–2 shows.

	Figure 8-1	**Narrative Genres**
Category	**Genre**	**Description**
Folklore	Fables	Brief tales told to point out a moral. For example: *Town Mouse, Country Mouse* (Brett, 1994) and *Aesop's Fables* (Pinkney, 2000).
	Folktales	Stories in which heroes and heroines demonstrate virtues to triumph over adversity. For example: *Rumpelstiltskin* (Zelinsky, 1986) and *One Grain of Rice: A Mathematical Folktale* (Demi, 1997).
	Myths	Stories created by ancient peoples to explain natural phenomena. For example: *Why Mosquitoes Buzz in People's Ears* (Aardema, 1975) and *Iktomi and the Boulder* (Goble, 1988).
	Legends	Stories, including hero tales and tall tales, that recount the courageous deeds of people as they struggled against each other or against gods and monsters. For example: *The Sword and the Circle: King Arthur and the Knights of the Round Table* (Sutcliff, 1994) and *Paul Bunyan: A Tall Tale* (Kellogg, 1984).
Fantasy	Modern Literary Tales	Stories written by modern authors that exemplify the characteristics of folktales. For example: *The Ugly Duckling* (Pinkney, 1999) and *Sylvester and the Magic Pebble* (Steig, 1988).
	Fantastic Stories	Imaginative stories that explore alternate realities and contain one or more elements not found in the natural world. For example: *Jeremy Thatcher, Dragon Hatcher* (Coville, 1991) and *Charlotte's Web* (White, 1952).
	Science Fiction	Stories explore scientific possibilities. For example: *The Giver* (Lowry, 1993), and *Stinker From Space* (Service, 1988).
	High Fantasy	These stories focus on the conflict between good and evil and often involve quests. For example: *The Lion, the Witch and the Wardrobe* (Lewis, 1994) and the Harry Potter series.
Realistic Fiction	Contemporary Stories	Stories that portray the real world and contemporary society. For example: *Hatchet* (Paulsen, 1987) and *Surviving the Applewhites* (Tolan, 2002).
	Historical Stories	Realistic stories set in the past. For example: *The Watsons Go to Birmingham—1963* (Curtis, 1995) and *Sarah, Plain and Tall* (MacLachlan, 1985).

Figure 8–2 A Beginning-Middle-End Story Map for *The Tale of Peter Rabbit*

Specific types of information are included in each of the three story parts. In the beginning, the author introduces the characters, describes the setting, and presents a problem. Together, the characters, setting, and events develop the plot and sustain the theme through the story. In the middle, the plot unfolds, with each event preparing readers for what will follow. Conflict heightens as the characters face roadblocks that keep them from solving their problems; how the characters tackle these problems adds suspense to keep readers interested. In the end, all is reconciled, and readers learn whether the characters' struggles are successful.

Conflict is the tension or opposition between forces in the plot, and it is what interests readers enough to continue reading the story. Conflict usually occurs

- between a character and nature
- between a character and society
- between characters
- within a character (Lukens, 2002)

Conflict between a character and nature occurs in stories in which severe weather plays an important role, as in *Julie of the Wolves* (George, 1972), and in stories set in isolated geographic locations, such as *Holes* (Sachar, 1998), in which Stanley struggles to survive at Camp Green Lake, a boys' juvenile detention center.

In some stories, a character's activities and beliefs differ from those of other members of the society, and the differences cause conflict between that character and the local society. One example of this type of conflict is *The Witch of Blackbird Pond* (Speare, 1972), in which Kit Tyler is accused of being a witch because she continues activities in a New England Puritan community that were acceptable in the Caribbean community where she grew up but are not acceptable in her new home. Conflict between characters is common in children's literature. In *Tales of a Fourth Grade Nothing* (Blume, 1972), for instance, the never-ending conflict between Peter and his little brother Fudge is what makes the story interesting. The fourth type of conflict is conflict within a character. In *Esperanza Rising* (Ryan, 2000), the title character must come to terms with her new life as a migrant worker after her father dies and she must leave her family's ranch in Mexico.

The plot is developed through conflict that is introduced at the beginning of a story, expanded in the middle, and finally resolved at the end. Plot development involves four components:

1. *A problem.* A problem that introduces conflict is presented at the beginning of the story.

2. *Roadblocks.* Characters face roadblocks in attempting to solve the problem in the middle of the story.

3. *The high point.* The high point in the action occurs when the problem is about to be solved. This high point separates the middle and end of the story.

4. *The solution.* The problem is solved and the roadblocks are overcome at the end of the story.

Figure 8–3 presents a list of stories with well-developed plots.

Figure 8–4 (p. 265) presents a plot diagram shaped like a mountain that incorporates these four components, which fifth graders completed after reading *Esperanza Rising* (Ryan, 2000). The problem is introduced in the beginning of the story, and the characters are faced with trying to solve it; the problem determines the conflict. The problem in *Esperanza Rising,* for example, is that Esperanza and her mother must create a new life for themselves; they can't remain at their ranch home because her uncles want it for themselves. Certainly, there's conflict between characters here and conflict with society, too, but even more important is Esperanza's conflict within herself as she leaves her comfortable life in Mexico to become a migrant laborer in California.

Dramatizing Stories

These second graders use stuffed animals and other props to reenact *The Mitten,* a story about a series of increasingly larger animals that climb into a mitten until it finally pops. They divide the story into three parts—the beginning, middle, and end—and sequence the events. The students holding the bear, rabbit, hedgehog, mouse, and other animals line up in the order that the animals climb into the mitten as they retell the story. They will read and compare two versions of *The Mitten;* this dramatizing activity makes the comparison easier because it enables the second graders to understand each version better.

After introducing the problem, authors use conflict to throw roadblocks in the way of an easy solution. As characters remove one roadblock, the author devises another to further thwart them. Postponing the solution by introducing roadblocks is the core of plot development. Stories may contain any number of roadblocks, but many children's stories contain three, four, or five.

Esperanza and her mother face many roadblocks in California. They become farm laborers, but the work is very difficult and they earn very little money. Esperanza is homesick and wants to bring her beloved grandmother to join them, but they don't have enough money for her travel expenses. Then Esperanza's mother becomes ill and is hospitalized for many months. Esperanza takes over her mother's work and worries

---

Figure 8-3 Stories Illustrating the Elements of Story Structure

Plot

Brett, J. (1989). *The mitten.* New York: Putnam. (P)
Fleming, D. (2003). *Buster.* New York: Henry Holt. (P)
Gantos, J. (1998). *Joey Pigza swallowed the key.* New York: Farrar, Straus & Giroux. (M–U)
Paulsen, G. (1987). *Hatchet.* New York: Bradbury Press. (U)
Sachar, L. (1998). *Holes.* New York: Farrar, Straus & Giroux. (U)
Steig, W. (1998). *Sylvester and the magic pebble.* New York: Simon & Schuster. (P–M)

Characters

Cushman, K. (1994). *Catherine, called Birdy.* New York: HarperCollins. (U)
Henkes, K. (1991). *Chrysanthemum.* New York: Greenwillow. (P)
Lowry, L. (1993). *The giver.* Boston: Houghton Mifflin. (U)
MacLachlan, P. (1985). *Sarah, plain and tall.* New York: HarperCollins. (M)
Naylor, P. R. (1991). *Shiloh.* New York: Atheneum. (M)
Waber, B. (1972). *Ira sleeps over.* Boston: Houghton Mifflin. (P)

Setting

Curtis, C. P. (1995). *The Watsons go to Birmingham—1963.* New York: Delacorte. (M–U)
Ryan, P. M. (2000). *Esperanza rising.* New York: Scholastic. (M)
Speare, E. (1983). *The sign of the beaver.* Boston: Houghton Mifflin. (M)
Steig, W. (1987). *Brave Irene.* New York: Farrar, Straus & Giroux. (P–M)
Uchida, Y. (1993). *The bracelet.* New York: Philomel. (P–M)

Point of View

Creech, S. (2000). *The wanderer.* New York: HarperCollins. (U)
Hesse, K. (2001). *Witness.* New York: Scholastic. (U)
Howe, D., & Howe, J. (1979). *Bunnicula: A rabbit-tale of mystery.* New York: Atheneum. (M–U)
Lewis, C. S. (1994). *The lion, the witch and the wardrobe.* New York: HarperCollins. (U)
Meddaugh, S. (1995). *Hog-eye.* Boston: Houghton Mifflin. (P–M)

Theme

Babbitt, N. (1975). *Tuck everlasting.* New York: Farrar, Straus & Giroux. (U)
Bunting, E. (1994). *Smoky night.* San Diego: Harcourt Brace. (M–U)
Cohen, N. (1983). *Molly's pilgrim.* New York: Morrow. (M)
Lowry, L. (1989). *Number the stars.* New York: Atheneum. (M–U)
Soto, G. (1993). *Too many tamales.* New York: Putnam. (P–M)
White, E. B. (1952). *Charlotte's web.* New York: Harper & Row. (M)

P = primary grades (K–2); M = middle grades (3–5); U = upper grades (6–8)

Figure 8-4   **A Plot Diagram for *Esperanza Rising***

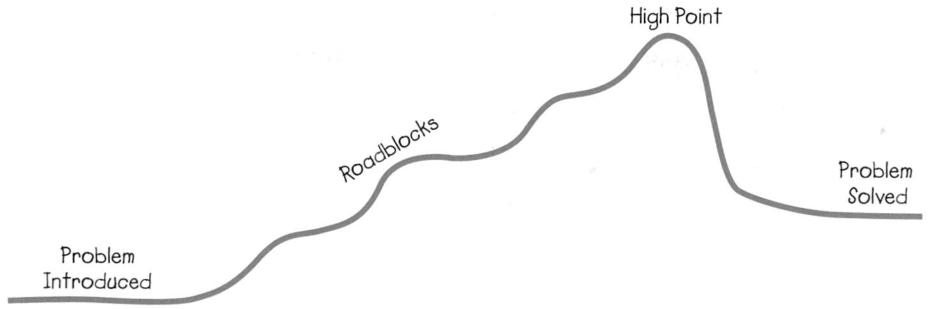

High Point

Roadblocks

Problem
Solved

Problem
Introduced

Beginning	Middle	End
Esperanza has a wonderful childhood as a rich, pampered child in Mexico, but then her father dies and their ranch burns down. She and her mama leave Mexico to begin a new and different life in California.	Esperanza and her mama work as farm laborers but her mama gets very sick and is hospitalized for many months. Esperanza takes over her mama's work and she worries that her mother might die. She misses her Abuelita (grandmother) so she saves all the money she can so she can send for her. Then her money disappears.	Esperanza's mother gets well enough to leave the hospital and she learns that her friend Miguel used her money to bring her Abuelita to join them in California. Now Esperanza has adjusted to her new life.
Problem: Esperanza and her mother must flee Mexico and make a new life in California.	Roadblocks: 1. The work is very hard, there is very little money, and Esperanza is homesick. 2. Mama gets sick. 3. Some of the other workers want to strike. 4. Esperanza's money is missing.	High Point: Mama gets well enough to leave the hospital and Abuelita arrives.

that her mother might die. Finally, Esperanza saves enough money to bring her grandmother to California, but her money disappears.

The high point of the action occurs when the solution to the problem hangs in the balance. Tension is high, and readers continue reading to learn whether the main characters solve the problem. In *Esperanza Rising,* the girl's mother is finally well enough to return to the farm labor camp, and it turns out that her money wasn't stolen after all: Esperanza's friend Miguel used it to bring her grandmother to California.

As the story ends, the problem is solved and the goal is achieved: Esperanza adjusts to her new life in California with her mother and grandmother. *Esperanza* means "hope" in Spanish, and readers have reason to be optimistic that the girl and her family will create a good life for themselves.

Students can chart the plot of a story using a plot profile to track the tension or excitement (Johnson & Louis, 1987). Figure 8–5 presents a plot profile for *Stone Fox*

Figure 8–5   **A Plot Profile for _Stone Fox_**

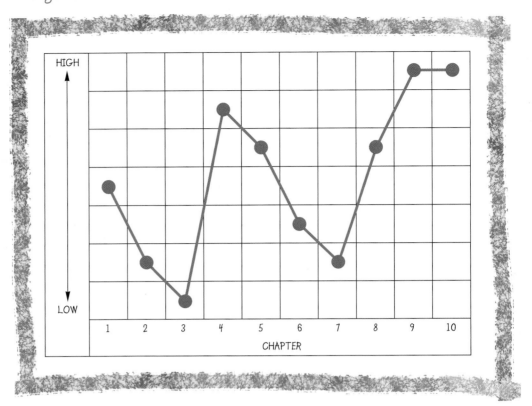

(Gardiner, 1980), a story about a boy who wins a dogsled race to save his grandfather's farm. A class of fourth graders met in small groups to talk about each chapter, and after these discussions, the whole class came together to decide how to mark the chart. At the end of the story, students analyzed the chart and rationalized the tension dips in chapters 3 and 7: They decided that the story would be too stressful without these dips.

Characters. Characters are the people or personified animals who are involved in the story. Characters are often the most important structural element because the story is centered on a character or group of characters. Usually, one or two fully rounded characters and several supporting characters are included. Fully developed main characters have many character traits, both good and bad; that is to say, they have all the characteristics of real people. Inferring a character's traits is an important part of reading: Through character traits, we get to know a character well, and the character seems to come to life. A list of stories with fully developed main characters is included in Figure 8–3.

Characters are developed in four ways: through appearance, action, dialogue, and monologue. Some description of the characters' physical appearance is usually included when they are introduced. Readers learn about characters by the description of their facial features, body shapes, habits of dress, mannerisms, and gestures. On the first page of _Tacky the Penguin_ (Lester, 1988), the illustration of Tacky wearing a bright floral shirt and a purple-and-white tie suggests to readers that Tacky is an "odd bird"! Lester confirms this impression as she describes how Tacky behaves.

The second way—and often the best way—to learn about characters is through their actions. In Van Allsburg's _The Stranger_ (1986), readers deduce that the stranger is Jack Frost because of what he does: He watches geese flying south for the winter, blows a cold wind, labors long hours without becoming tired, has an unusual rapport with wild animals, and is unfamiliar with modern conveniences.

Dialogue is the third way characters are developed. What characters say is important, but so is how they speak. The register of a character's language is determined by the social situation: A character might speak less formally with friends than with respected elders or characters in positions of authority. The geographic location of the story and the characters' socioeconomic status also determine how characters speak. In *Roll of Thunder, Hear My Cry* (Taylor, 1976), for example, Cassie and her family speak Black English, a dialect.

Authors also provide insight into characters by revealing their thoughts, or internal monologue. In *Sylvester and the Magic Pebble* (Steig, 1988), thoughts and wishes are central to the story. Sylvester, a donkey, foolishly wishes to become a rock, and he spends a miserable winter that way. Steig shares the donkey's thinking with us: He thinks about his parents, who are frantic with worry, and we learn how Sylvester feels in the spring when his parents picnic on the rock he has become.

Setting. In some stories, the setting is barely sketched; these are called *backdrop settings.* The setting in many folktales, for example, is relatively unimportant, and the convention "Once upon a time . . ." is enough to set the stage. In other stories, the setting is elaborated and essential to the story's effectiveness; these settings are called *integral settings* (Lukens, 2002). Stories with integral settings also are listed in Figure 8–3. The setting in these stories is specific, and authors take care to ensure the authenticity of the historical period or geographic location in which the story is set.

Four dimensions of setting are location, weather, time period, and time. Location is an important dimension in many stories. For instance, the Boston Commons in *Make Way for Ducklings* (McCloskey, 1969) and the Alaskan North Slope in *Julie of the Wolves* (George, 1972) are integral to those stories' effectiveness. The settings are artfully described and add something unique to the story. In contrast, many stories take place in predictable settings that do not contribute to the story's effectiveness.

Weather is a second dimension of setting and, like location, is crucial in some stories. A rainstorm is essential to the plot development in *Bridge to Terabithia* (Paterson, 1977), but in other books, weather is not mentioned because it does not affect the outcome of the story. Many stories take place on warm, sunny days.

The third dimension of setting is the time period, an important element in stories set in the past or future. If *The Witch of Blackbird Pond* (Speare, 1972) and *Number the Stars* (Lowry, 1989) were set in different eras, for example, they would lose much of their impact. Today, few people would believe that Kit Tyler is a witch or that Jewish people are the focus of government persecution. In stories that take place in the future, such as *A Wrinkle in Time* (L'Engle, 1962), things are possible that are not possible today.

The fourth dimension, time, involves both time of day and the passage of time. Most stories ignore time of day, except for scary stories that take place after dark. In stories such as *The Ghost-Eye Tree* (Martin & Archambault, 1985), in which two children must walk past a scary tree at night to get a pail of milk, time is a more important dimension than in stories that take place during the day, because night makes things more scary.

Many short stories span a brief period of time—often less than a day, and sometimes less than an hour. In *Jumanji* (Van Allsburg, 1981), Peter and Judy's bizarre adventure, during which their house is overtaken by exotic jungle creatures, lasts only several hours. *Hatchet* (Paulsen, 1987) takes place in less than 2 months. Other stories, such as *The Ugly Duckling* (Pinkney, 1999), span a long enough period for the main character to grow to maturity.

Figure 8–6 **A Story Map for *Number the Stars***

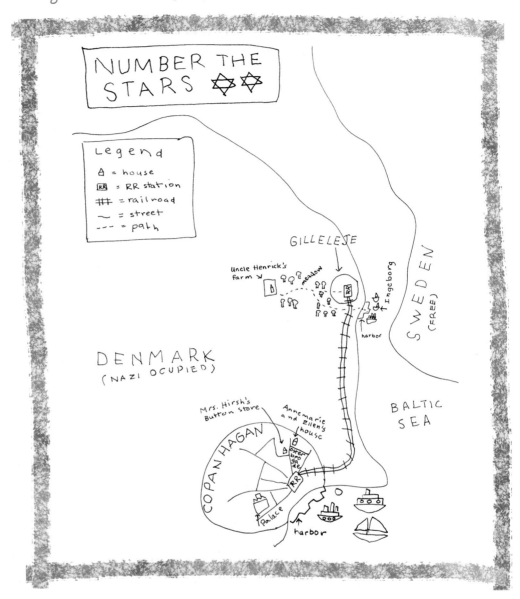

Students can draw maps to show the setting of a story; these maps might show the path a character traveled or the passage of time in a story. Figure 8–6 shows a map for *Number the Stars* (Lowry, 1989). In this chapter book set in Denmark during World War II, a Christian girl and her family help a Jewish family flee to safety in Sweden. The map shows the families' homes in Copenhagen, their trip to a fishing village, and the ship they hid away on to escape to Sweden.

Point of View. Stories are written from a particular viewpoint, and this perspective determines to a great extent readers' understanding of the characters and events of the story. The four points of view are first-person viewpoint, omniscient viewpoint, limited omniscient viewpoint, and objective viewpoint (Lukens, 2002). Stories written from different viewpoints are presented in Figure 8–3.

The first-person viewpoint is used to tell a story through the eyes of one character using the first-person pronoun "I." In this point of view, the reader experiences the story as the narrator tells it. The narrator, usually the main character, speaks as an eyewitness and a participant in the events. For example, in *Alexander and the Terrible, Horrible, No Good, Very Bad Day* (Viorst, 1977), Alexander tells about a day everything seemed to go wrong for him. One limitation of this viewpoint is that the narrator must remain an eyewitness.

In the omniscient viewpoint, the author is godlike, seeing and knowing all. The author tells readers about the thought processes of each character without worrying about how the information is obtained. *Doctor De Soto* (Steig, 1982), a story about a mouse dentist who outwits a fox with a toothache, is told from the omniscient viewpoint. Steig lets readers know that the fox wants to eat the dentist as soon as his toothache is cured and that the mouse dentist is aware of the fox's thoughts and plans a clever trick.

Nurturing English Learners

How important is it to teach ELs about text factors?

You might think that text factors are a low priority for English learners, but you'd be wrong. Oftentimes, these students haven't read or listened to their parents read aloud as many books as their English-speaking classmates have, and typically they are not as familiar with genres and text structure. This lack of knowledge about text factors is a problem because students have a limited amount of cognitive energy available for comprehension, and it is needed to activate background knowledge, set purposes, use strategies, and monitor comprehension. The energy runs short for students who have limited background knowledge, who aren't fluent readers, and who don't know the meaning of many words. When students are familiar with text factors, this knowledge provides a scaffold for them so they have more cognitive energy available to focus on comprehension.

The limited omniscient viewpoint is used so that readers know the thoughts of one character. The story is told in third person, and the author concentrates on the thoughts, feelings, and experiences of the main character or another important character. Gary Paulsen used this viewpoint for *Hatchet* (1987) to be able to explore both Brain's thoughts as he struggled to survive in the wilderness and his coming to terms with his parents' divorce. And Lois Lowry used the limited omniscient viewpoint in *Number the Stars* (1989), so that Annemarie, the Christian girl, can reveal her thoughts about the lies she tells to the Nazi soldiers in this World War II story.

In the objective viewpoint, readers are eyewitnesses to the story and confined to the immediate scene. They learn only what is visible and audible and are not aware of what any characters think. Most fairy tales, such as *The Little Red Hen* (Zemach, 1983), are told from the objective viewpoint. The focus is on recounting events, not on developing the personalities of the characters.

Most teachers postpone introducing the four viewpoints until the upper grades, but younger children can experiment with point of view to understand how the author's viewpoint affects a story. One way to demonstrate point of view is to contrast *The Three Little Pigs* (Galdone, 1970), the traditional version of the story told from an objective viewpoint, with *The True Story of the 3 Little Pigs!* (Scieszka, 1989), a self-serving narrative told by Mr. A. Wolf from a first-person viewpoint. In this satirical retelling, the wolf tries to explain away his bad image. Even first graders are struck by how different the two versions are and how the narrator filters the information.

Theme. Theme is the underlying meaning of a story, and it embodies general truths about human nature (Lehr, 1991; Lukens, 2002). Theme usually deals with the characters' emotions and values. Themes can be stated either explicitly or implicitly: Explicit themes are stated openly and clearly in the story, whereas implicit themes must be inferred from the story. Themes are developed as the characters attempt to overcome the obstacles that prevent them from reaching their goals. In a fable, the theme is often stated explicitly at the end, but in most stories, the theme emerges through the thoughts, speech, and actions of the characters as they seek to resolve their conflicts. In *A Chair for My Mother* (Williams, 1982), for example, a young girl demonstrates the importance of sacrificing personal wants for her family's welfare as she and her mother collect money to buy a new chair after they lose all of their belongings in a fire.

Stories usually have more than one theme, and their themes usually cannot be articulated with a single word. *Charlotte's Web* (White, 1952) has several "friendship" themes, one explicitly stated and others inferred from the text. Friendship is a multidimensional theme—qualities of a good friend, unlikely friends, and sacrificing for a friend, for instance. Teachers can probe students' thinking as they work to construct a theme and move beyond one-word labels (Au, 1992).

The minilesson featured on page 271 demonstrates how Mrs. Miller, a seventh-grade teacher, reviewed the concept of theme. After the minilesson, her students analyzed the theme of books they were reading in literature circles.

Literary Devices

In addition to the five elements of story structure, authors use literary devices to make their writing more vivid and memorable; without these literary devices, writing can be dull (Lukens, 2002). A list of six literary devices that children learn about is presented in Figure 8–7. Imagery is probably the most commonly used literary device; many authors use imagery as they paint rich word pictures that bring their characters and settings to life. Authors use metaphors and similes to compare one thing to another, personification to endow animals and objects with human qualities, and hyperbole to exaggerate or stretch the truth. They also create symbols as they use one thing to represent something else. In Chris Van Allsburg's *The Wretched Stone* (1991), for example, the glowing stone that distracts the crew from reading, from spending time with their friends, and from doing their jobs symbolizes television or, perhaps, computers. For students to understand the theme of a story, they need to recognize symbols. The author's style conveys the tone or overall feeling in a story. Some stories are humorous, some are uplifting celebrations of life, and others are sobering commentaries on society.

Young children focus on events and characters as they read and discuss a story, but in fourth through eighth grades, students become more sophisticated readers: They learn to notice both what the author says and how he or she says it. Teachers facilitate students' growth in reading and evaluating stories by directing their attention to literary devices and the author's style during the responding and exploring stages of the reading process.

INFORMATIONAL BOOKS

Stories have been the principal genre for reading and writing instruction in the primary grades because it has been assumed that constructing stories in the mind is a fundamental way of learning (Wells, 1986). Research, however, suggests that children may prefer to read informational books and are able to understand them as well as they do stories (Pappas, 1993). Certainly, children are interested in learning about their world—about the difference between dolphins and whales, how a road is built, threats to the environment of Antarctica, or Amelia Earhart's ill-fated flight around the world—and informational books provide this knowledge. Even young children read informational books to learn about the world around them.

Students often assume an efferent stance as they read informational books to locate facts, but they do not always use efferent reading (Rosenblatt, 1978). Many times, students pick up an informational book to check a fact and then continue reading—

Visit Chapter 8 on the Companion Website at *www.prenhall.com/ tompkins* to check into your state's standards for comprehension instruction.

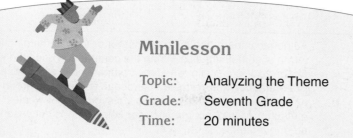

Minilesson

Topic: Analyzing the Theme
Grade: Seventh Grade
Time: 20 minutes

Mrs. Miller's seventh graders are studying the middle ages and are reading novels set in that period, such as *Catherine, Called Birdy* (Cushman, 1994), in literature circles. Mrs. Miller brings the class together to teach a minilesson on theme before asking the students in each literature circle to analyze the theme of the book they are reading.

1. Introduce Topic

"It's time to talk about theme because most of you are getting toward the end of the book you're reading," Mrs. Miller begins. "Before, I asked you to focus on the setting to learn more about medieval life as you were reading and discussing the book. Now, I want you to think about your book in a different way: I want you to think about the theme. Let's review: Theme is the universal message in the book. It might be about friendship, courage, acceptance, determination, or some other important quality."

2. Share Examples

Mrs. Miller uses *Hatchet* (Paulsen, 1987), a survival story that students read in September, as an example. "Did Brian save himself?" the teacher asks. Everyone agrees that he did. "So what is the theme of the story?" Mrs. Miller asks. Students identify survival as the theme, and Mrs. Miller asks them to explain it in a sentence. Jared suggests, "Sometimes you have to do a lot of disgusting things if you want to survive." Mrs. Miller agrees. Carole offers, "I think the theme is that you may not think that you have the guts and the brains to survive, but if you get trapped in the wilderness, you will find that you do." Again she agrees. Jo-Jo expresses the theme another way: "It's like in the movie *Castaway.* Brain has to get mad—really mad and a little crazy, too, but he gets mad enough to survive. You have to stand up and prove to yourself that you can survive." Again she agrees. Mrs. Miller draws a cluster on the chalkboard and writes *survival* in the center circle. Then she draws out rays and writes on them the sentenes that the students offered.

3. Provide Information

"Theme isn't obvious the way plot, characters, and setting are," Mrs. Miller explains. She tells the class that in order to uncover the theme, they need to think about the conflicts facing the character and the way the character goes about solving the problem. "Then you have to answer the question: 'What is the author trying to tell me about life?'" she concludes.

4. Guide Practice

The minilesson ends as the students return to their literature circles to talk about the theme of their book. Mrs. Miller asks them to think of one or more one-word qualities and then to draw out at least three possible sentence-long themes. As they analyze the theme, they draw clusters on chart paper.

5. Assess Learning

Mrs. Miller moves from group to group, talking with students about theme. She checks their clusters and helps them draw out additional themes to add to the cluster.

Figure 8-7   Literary Devices

Comparison	Authors compare one thing to another or view something in terms of something else. When the comparison uses the word *like* or *as,* it is a simile; when the comparison is stated directly, it is a metaphor. For example, "the ocean is like a playground for whales" is a simile; "the ocean is a playground for whales" is a metaphor. Metaphors are stronger comparisons because they are more direct.
Hyperbole	Authors use hyperbole when they overstate or stretch the truth to make obvious and intentional exaggerations for a special effect. "It's raining cats and dogs" and "my feet are killing me" are two examples of hyperbole. American tall tales also have rich examples of hyperbole.
Imagery	Authors use descriptive or sensory words and phrases to create imagery or a picture in the reader's mind. Sensory language stirs the reader's imagination. Instead of saying "the kitchen smelled good as grandmother cooked Thanksgiving dinner," authors create imagery when they write "the aroma of turkey roasting in the oven filled grandmother's kitchen on Thanksgiving."
Personification	Authors use personification when they attribute human characteristics to animals or objects. For example, "the moss crept across the sidewalk" is personification.
Symbolism	Authors often use a person, place, or thing as a symbol to represent something else. For example, a dove symbolizes peace, the Statue of Liberty symbolizes freedom, and books symbolize knowledge.
Tone	Authors create an overall feeling or effect in the story through their choice of words and use of other literary devices. For example, *Bunnicula: A Rabbit-Tale of Mystery* (Howe & Howe, 1979) and *Catherine, Called Birdy* (Cushman, 1994) are humorous stories, and *Babe the Gallant Pig* (King-Smith, 1995) and *Sarah, Plain and Tall* (MacLachlan, 1985) are uplifting, feel-good stories.

aesthetically—because they are fascinated by what they are reading. They get carried away in the presentation of information, just as they do when reading stories. At other times, students read books about topics they are interested in, and they read aesthetically, engaging in the lived-through experience of reading and connecting what they are reading to their own lives and prior reading experiences.

Russell Freedman, who won the 1988 Newbery Award for *Lincoln: A Photobiography* (1987), talks about the purpose of informational books and explains that it is not enough for an informational book to provide information: "[An informational book] must create a vivid and believable world that the reader will enter willingly and leave only with reluctance. . . . It should be just as compelling as a good story" (1992, p. 3). High-quality informational books like Freedman's encourage students to read aesthetically because they engage readers and tap their curiosity. There is a new wave of engaging and artistic informational books being published today, and these books show increased respect for children. Peter Roop (1992) explains that for years, informational books were the "ugly duckling" of children's literature, but now they have grown into a beautiful swan.

Four qualities of informational books are accuracy, organization, design, and style (Vardell, 1991). First and foremost, the facts must be current and complete. They must be well researched, and, when appropriate, varying points of view should be presented. Stereotypes are to be avoided, and details in both the text and the illustrations must be authentic. Second, information should be presented clearly and logically, using organizational patterns to increase the book's readability. Third, the book's design should be eye-catching and should enhance its usability. Illustrations should complement the text, and explanations should accompany each illustration. Last, the style should be lively and stimulating so as to engage readers' curiosity and wonder.

Nonfiction Genres

Informational books are available today on topics ranging from biological sciences, physical sciences, and social sciences to arts and biographies. *Cactus Hotel* (Guiberson, 1991) is a fine informational book about the desert ecosystem; in it, the author discusses the life cycle of a giant saguaro cactus and describes its role as a home for desert creatures. Other books, such as *Whales* (Simon, 1989), illustrated with striking full-page color photos, and *Antarctica* (Cowcher, 1990), illustrated with dramatic double-page paintings, are socially responsible and emphasize the threats people pose to animals and the earth.

Other books present historical and geographic concepts. *A Street Through Time* (Millard, 1998), for instance, traces the evolution of one street from the Stone Age to the present day, and *Knights* (Steele, 1998) tells about the lives of knights during medieval times. These books have lavish illustrations and detailed text that provide an enriching reading experience for students.

Some informational books focus on letters and numbers. Although many alphabet and counting books with pictures of familiar objects are designed for young children, others provide a wealth of information on various topics. In his alphabet book *Illuminations* (1989), Jonathan Hunt presents detailed information about medieval life, and in *The Underwater Alphabet Book* (1991), Jerry Pallotta provides information about 26 types of fish and other sea creatures. Muriel and Tom Feelings present information about Africa in *Moja Means One: Swahili Counting Book* (1971), and Ann Herbert Scott presents information about cowboys in *One Good Horse: A Cowpuncher's Counting Book* (1990). In some of these books, new terms are introduced and illustrated, and in others, the term is explained in a sentence or a paragraph. Other informational books focus on mathematical concepts (Whitin & Wilde, 1992): Tana Hoban's *26 Letters and 99 Cents* (1987) presents concepts about money, *What Comes in 2's, 3's and 4's?* (Aker, 1990) introduces multiplication, and *If You Made a Million* (Schwartz, 1989) focuses on big numbers.

Biographies also are informational books, and the biographies that students are reading today are more realistic than those of the past, presenting well-known personalities warts and all. Jean Fritz's portraits of Revolutionary War figures, such as *Will You Sign Here, John Hancock?* (1976), are among the best known, but she has also written comprehensive biographies, including *The Great Little Madison* (1989). Fritz and other authors often include notes in the back of their books to explain how the details were researched and to provide additional information. Only a few autobiographies are available to students, but more are being published each year. Autobiographies about authors and illustrators, such as Cynthia Rylant's *Best Wishes* (1992), are also popular.

Other books present information within a story context. Some combination informational/story books are imaginative fantasies. The Magic School Bus series is

Figure 8-8 The Five Expository Text Structures

Pattern	Description	Graphic Organizer	Sample Passage
Description	The author describes a topic by listing characteristics, features, and examples. Cue words include *for example* and *characteristics are.*		The Olympic symbol consists of five interlocking rings. The rings represent the five continents from which athletes come to compete in the games. The rings are colored black, blue, green, red, and yellow. At least one of these colors is found in the flag of every country sending athletes to compete in the Olympic games.
Sequence	The author lists items or events in numerical or chronological order. Cue words include *first, second, third, next, then,* and *finally.*	1. _____ 2. _____ 3. _____ 4. _____ 5. _____	The Olympic games began as athletic festivals to honor the Greek gods. The most important festival was held in the valley of Olympia to honor Zeus, the king of the gods. This festival became the Olympic games in 776 B.C. They were ended in A.D. 394. No Olympic games were held for more than 1,500 years. Then the modern Olympics began in 1896. Almost 300 male athletes competed in the first modern Olympics. In the 1900 games, female athletes were allowed to compete. The games have continued every four years since 1896 except during World War II.
Comparison	The author explains how two or more things are alike and/or how they are different. Cue words include *different, in contrast, alike, same as,* and *on the other hand.*		The modern Olympics is very unlike the ancient Olympic games. While there were no swimming races in the ancient games, for example, there were chariot races. There were no female contestants, and all athletes competed in the nude. Of course, the ancient and modern Olympics are also alike in many ways. Some events, such as the javelin and discus throws, are the same. Some people say that cheating, professionalism, and nationalism in the modern games are a disgrace to the Olympic tradition. But according to the ancient Greek writers, there were many cases of cheating, nationalism, and professionalism in their Olympics, too.

perhaps the best known. In *The Magic School Bus Inside a Beehive* (Cole, 1996), for example, Ms. Frizzle and her class study bees and take a field trip on the magic school bus into a beehive to learn about the life cycle of honeybees, how honey is made, and bee society. The page layout is innovative, with charts and reports containing factual information presented at the outside edges of most pages.

Expository Text Structures

Informational books are organized in particular ways called *expository text structures.* Five of the most common organizational patterns are description, sequence, comparison, cause and effect, and problem and solution (Meyer & Freedle, 1984; Niles, 1974). Figure 8–8 describes these patterns, presents sample passages and cue words that signal use of each pattern, and suggests an appropriate graphic organizer for each structure. When readers are aware of these patterns, they understand better what they are reading, and when writers use these structures to organize their writing, it is more easily understood by readers. Sometimes the pattern is signaled clearly by means of titles, topic sentences, and cue words, and sometimes it is not.

Figure 8-8 (Continued)

Pattern	Description	Graphic Organizer	Sample Passage
Cause and Effect	The author lists one or more causes and the resulting effect or effects. Cue words include *reasons why, if . . . then, as a result, therefore,* and *because.*	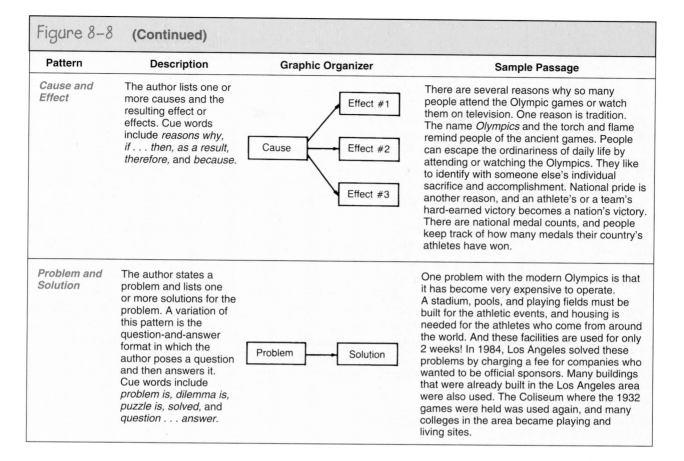	There are several reasons why so many people attend the Olympic games or watch them on television. One reason is tradition. The name *Olympics* and the torch and flame remind people of the ancient games. People can escape the ordinariness of daily life by attending or watching the Olympics. They like to identify with someone else's individual sacrifice and accomplishment. National pride is another reason, and an athlete's or a team's hard-earned victory becomes a nation's victory. There are national medal counts, and people keep track of how many medals their country's athletes have won.
Problem and Solution	The author states a problem and lists one or more solutions for the problem. A variation of this pattern is the question-and-answer format in which the author poses a question and then answers it. Cue words include *problem is, dilemma is, puzzle is, solved,* and *question . . . answer.*	Problem → Solution	One problem with the modern Olympics is that it has become very expensive to operate. A stadium, pools, and playing fields must be built for the athletic events, and housing is needed for the athletes who come from around the world. And these facilities are used for only 2 weeks! In 1984, Los Angeles solved these problems by charging a fee for companies who wanted to be official sponsors. Many buildings that were already built in the Los Angeles area were also used. The Coliseum where the 1932 games were held was used again, and many colleges in the area became playing and living sites.

Description. The author describes a topic by listing characteristics, features, and examples. Phrases such as *for example* and *characteristics are* cue this structure. Examples of books using description include *Grizzly Bears* (Gibbons, 2003) and *Spiders* (Simon, 2003), in which the authors describe many facets of their topic. When students delineate any topic, such as the Mississippi River, eagles, or Alaska, they use description.

Sequence. The author lists or explains items or events in numerical or chronological order. Cue words for sequence include *first, second, third, next, then,* and *finally.* Caroline Arnold describes the steps in creating a museum display in *Dinosaurs All Around: An Artist's View of the Prehistoric World* (1993), Ruth Swain explains the history of candy in *How Sweet It Is (and Was): The History of Candy* (2003), and David Macaulay describes how a castle is built in *Castle* (1977). Students use the sequence pattern to write directions for completing a math problem or for the stages in an animal's life cycle. The events in a biography are often written in the sequence pattern.

Comparison. The author compares two or more things. *Different, in contrast, alike,* and

Scaffolding Struggling Readers

How can I help my struggling readers read nonfiction?

Struggling students often read informational books the same way they read stories, so it's important that they figure out how fiction and nonfiction differ. Have them study a text set of books on the same topic so that they can compare genres, text structures, and text features. Students also need to learn about the five expository text structures and how to use this knowledge as they read: When they notice the structure of text, it will help them to identify big ideas and to summarize and remember what they have read. There are other benefits, too. For example, when students apply their knowledge of text factors when they write, their writing will improve—it will be easier to understand and will score higher on rubrics.

on the other hand are cue words and phrases that signal this structure. In *Horns, Antlers, Fangs, and Tusks* (Rauzon, 1993), for example, the author compares animals with distinctive types of headgear. When students compare and contrast book and movie versions of a story, reptiles and amphibians, or life in ancient Greece with life in ancient Egypt, they use this organizational pattern.

Cause and Effect. The author explains one or more causes and the resulting effect or effects. *Reasons why, if . . . then, as a result, therefore,* and *because* are words and phrases that cue this structure. Explanations of why dinosaurs became extinct, the effects of pollution on the environment, or the causes of the Civil War are written using this pattern. *How Do Apples Grow?* (Maestro, 1992) and *Flick a Switch: How Electricity Gets to Your Home* (Seuling, 2003) are two books that exemplify this structure.

Problem and Solution. The author states a problem and offers one or more solutions. In *Man and Mustang* (Ancona, 1992), for example, the author describes the problem of wild mustangs and explains how they are rescued. A variation is the question-and-answer format, in which the writer poses a question and then answers it. One question-and-answer book is . . . *If You Traveled West in a Covered Wagon* (Levine, 1986). Cue words and phrases include *the problem is, the puzzle is, solve,* and *question . . . answer.* Students use this structure when they write about why money was invented, why endangered animals should be saved, or why dams are needed to ensure a permanent water supply. They often use the problem-solution pattern in writing advertisements and other persuasive writing as well. Figure 8–9 lists additional books that illustrate each of the five expository text structures.

Text Features

Many picture-book and chapter-book informational books have unique text features that stories and books of poetry normally don't have, including:

- Headings and subheadings to direct readers' attention to the big ideas
- Photographs and drawings to illustrate the big ideas
- Figures, maps, and tables to provide diagrams and detailed information visually
- Margin notes that provide supplemental information or direct readers to additional information on a topic
- Highlighted vocabulary words to identify key terms
- An index to assist readers in locating specific information
- A glossary to assist readers in pronouncing and defining key terms
- Review sections or charts at the end of chapters or the entire book

The purpose of these text features is to make the book easier to read. It's important that students understand them because they can use them to make their reading more effective and to improve their comprehension (Harvey & Goudvis, 2000).

POETRY

Poetry "brings sound and sense together in words and lines," according to Donald Graves, "ordering them on the page in such a way that both the writer and reader get a different view of life" (1992, p. 3). Poetry surrounds us; children chant jump-rope rhymes on the playground and dance in response to songs and their lyrics. Larrick

Figure 8–9 Informational Books Representing the Expository Text Structures

Description

Horvatic, A. (1989). *Simple machines*. New York: Dutton. (M)

Lauber, P. (1998). *Painters of the caves*. Washington, DC: National Geographic Society. (U)

Morris, A. (1989). *Hats, hats, hats*. New York: Mulberry Books. (P)

Pfeffer, W. (2003). *Dolphin talk: Whistles, clicks, and clapping jaws*. New York: HarperCollins. (P–M)

Simon, S. (2000). *Gorillas*. New York: HarperCollins. (M–U)

Sequence

Aliki. (1992). *Milk from cow to carton*. New York: HarperCollins. (P–M)

Cole, J. (1991). *My puppy is born*. New York: Morrow. (P–M)

Provensen, A. (1990). *The buck stops here*. New York: HarperCollins. (M–U)

Schanzer, R. (1997). *How we crossed the west: The adventures of Lewis and Clark*. Washington, DC: National Geographic Society. (U)

Thomas, V. M. (1997) *Lest we forget: The passage from Africa to slavery and emancipation*. New York: Crown. (U)

Comparison

Gibbons, G. (1984). *Fire! Fire!* New York: Harper & Row. (P–M)

Lasker, J. (1976). *Merry ever after: The story of two medieval weddings*. New York: Viking. (M–U)

Markle, S. (1993). *Outside and inside trees*. New York: Bradbury Press. (M)

Munro, R. (1987). *The inside-outside book of Washington, DC*. New York: Dutton. (M–U)

Spier, P. (1987). *We the people*. New York: Doubleday. (M–U)

Cause and Effect

Branley, F. M. (1985a). *Flash, crash, rumble, and roll*. New York: Harper & Row. (P–M)

Branley, F. M. (1985b). *Volcanoes*. New York: Harper & Row. (P–M)

Branley, F. M. (1986). *What makes day and night?* New York: Harper & Row. (P–M)

Heller, R. (1983). *The reason for a flower*. New York: Grosset & Dunlap. (M)

Showers, P. (1985). *What happens to a hamburger?* New York: Harper & Row. (P–M)

Problem and Solution

Cole, J. (1983). *Cars and how they go*. New York: Harper & Row. (P–M)

George, J. C. (2000). *How to talk to your dog*. New York: HarperCollins. (M)

Lauber, P. (1990). *How we learned the earth is round*. New York: Crowell. (P–M)

Showers, P. (1980). *No measles, no mumps for me*. New York: Crowell. (P–M)

Wollard, K. (1999). *How come? Planet earth*. New York: Workman. (M–U)

Combination

Aliki. (1981). *Digging up dinosaurs*. New York: Harper & Row. (M)

Armstrong, J. (1998). *Shipwreck at the bottom of the world: The extraordinary true story of Shackleton and the Endurance*. New York: Crown. (M–U)

Guiberson, B. Z. (1991). *Cactus hotel*. New York: Henry Holt. (P–M)

Hoyt-Goldsmith, D. (1992). *Hoang Anh: A Vietnamese-American boy*. New York: Holiday House. (M)

Venutra, P., & Ceserani, G. P. (1985). *In search of Tutankhamun*. Morristown, NJ: Silver Burdett. (U)

(1991) believes that we enjoy poetry because of the physical involvement that the words evoke. Also, people play with language as they invent rhymes and ditties, create new words, and craft powerful comparisons.

Today, more poets are writing for children, and more books of poems for children are being published than ever before. No longer is poetry confined to rhyming verse about daffodils, clouds, and love; recently published poems about dinosaurs, Halloween, chocolate, baseball, and insects are very popular. Children choose to read poetry and share favorite poems with classmates. They read and respond to poems containing beautiful language and written on topics that are meaningful to them.

Types of Poetry Books

Three types of poetry books are published for children. First, a number of picture-book versions of single poems in which each line or stanza is illustrated on a page are available, such as *The Midnight Ride of Paul Revere* (Longfellow, 2001). Other books are specialized collections of poems, either written by a single poet or related to a single theme, such as dinosaurs. Comprehensive anthologies are the third type of poetry books for children, and they feature 50 to 500 or more poems arranged by category. One of the best anthologies is Jack Prelutsky's *The Random House Book of Poetry for Children* (2000). A list of poetry books that includes examples of each of the three types is presented in Figure 8–10.

Poetic Forms

Poems for children assume many forms, including rhymed verse, narrative poems, haiku, and free verse. Children also use a variety of other structured forms when they write poems.

Figure 8–10 **Collections of Poetry Written for Children**

Picture Book Versions of Single Poems

Carroll, L. (2003). *Jabberwocky* (J. Stewart, Illus.). Cambridge, MA: Candlewick Press. (M–U)

Frost, R. (2001). *Stopping by woods on a snowy evening* (S. Jeffers, Illus.). New York: Dutton. (M–U)

Lear, E. (1986). *The owl and the pussycat* (L. B. Cauley, Illus.). New York: Putnam. (P–M)

Sandburg, C. (1993). *Arithmetic.* New York: Harcourt Brace. (P–M)

Westcott, N. B. (1988). *The lady with the alligator purse.* Boston: Little, Brown. (P–M)

Specialized Collections

Fleischman, P. (1988). *Joyful noise: Poems for two voices.* New York: Harper & Row. (M–U)

George, K. O. (1998). *Old elm speaks: Tree poems.* New York: Clarion Books. (P–M)

Greenfield, E. (1988). *Under the Sunday tree.* New York: Harper & Row. (M)

Hoberman, M. A. (1998). *The llama who had no pajama: 100 favorite poems.* New York: Browndeer Press. (P–M)

Hopkins, L. B. (1987). *Click, rumble, roar: Poems about machines.* New York: Crowell. (M)

Janeczko, P. B. (Sel.) (1993). *Looking for your name: A collection of contemporary poems.* New York: Orchard Books. (U)

Jones, H. (Ed.). (1993). *The trees stand shining: Poetry of the North American Indians.* New York: Dial Books. (M–U)

Kuskin, K. (2003). *Moon, have you met my mother? The collected poems of Karla Kuskin.* New York: HarperCollins. (P–M–U)

Lansky, B. (2002). *My dog ate my homework: A collection of funny poems.* New York: Meadowbrooke Press. (M–U)

Livingston, M. C. (1986). *Earth songs.* New York: Holiday House. (See also *Sea songs* and *Space songs.*) (M–U)

McCord, D. (1974). *One at a time.* Boston: Little, Brown. (M–U)

Prelutsky, J. (1981). *It's Christmas.* New York: Scholastic. (Collections for other holidays, too.) (P–M)

Prelutsky, J. (1984). *The new kid on the block.* New York: Greenwillow. (P–M)

Prelutsky, J. (1989). *Poems of A. Nonny Mouse.* New York: Knopf. (P–M)

Prelutsky, J. (1996). *A pizza the size of the sun.* New York: Greenwillow. (P–M–U)

Prelutsky, J. (2000). *It's raining pigs and noodles.* New York: Greenwillow. (P–M–U)

Sierra, J. (1998). *Antarctic antics: A book of penguin poems.* San Diego: Gulliver. (P–M)

Silverstein, S. (1974). *Where the sidewalk ends.* New York: Harper & Row. (P–M–U)

Stevenson, J. (1998). *Popcorn.* New York: Greenwillow. (M–U)

Wong, J. S. (1994). *Good luck gold and other poems.* New York: McElderry. (M–U)

Yolen, J. (1990). *Bird watch: A book of poetry.* New York: Philomel. (M–U)

Comprehensive Anthologies

dePaola, T. (Sel.). (1988). *Tomie dePaola's book of poems.* New York: Putnam. (P–M)

de Regniers, B. S., Moore, E., White, M. M., & Carr, J. (Sels.). (1988). *Sing a song of popcorn: Every child's book of poems.* New York: Scholastic. (P–M–U)

Kennedy, X. J., & Kennedy, D. M. (Sels.). (1982). *Knock at a star: A child's introduction to poetry.* Boston: Little, Brown. (P–M–U)

Prelutsky, J. (Sel.). (1999). *The 20th century children's poetry treasury.* New York: Knopf. (P–M–U)

Prelutsky, J. (Sel.). (2000). *The Random House book of poetry for children.* New York: Random House. (P–M–U)

Rhymed Verse. The most common type of poetry is rhymed verse, as in *Hailstones and Halibut Bones* (O'Neill, 1989), *My Parents Think I'm Sleeping* (Prelutsky, 1985), and *Sierra* (Siebert, 1991). Poets use various rhyme schemes, and the effect of the rhyming words is a poem that is pleasurable to read and listen to when it is read aloud. Children should savor the rhyming words but not be expected to pick out the rhyme scheme.

Rhyme is the sticking point for many would-be poets. In searching for a rhyming word, children often create inane verse; for example:

> I see a funny little goat
> Wearing a blue sailor's coat
> Sitting in an old motorboat.

Certainly children should not be forbidden to write rhyming poetry, but rhyme should never be imposed as a criterion for acceptable poetry. Children may use rhyme when it fits naturally into their writing. When children write poetry, they are searching for their own voices, and they need freedom to do that. Freed from the pressure to create rhyming poetry and from other constraints, children create sensitive word pictures, vivid images, and unique comparisons.

One type of rhymed verse—limericks—can be used effectively with older students. A limerick is a short verse form popularized by Edward Lear that incorporates both rhyme and rhythm. The poem consists of five lines; the first, second, and fifth lines rhyme, and the third and fourth lines rhyme with each other and are shorter than the other three. The rhyme scheme is a-a-b-b-a. The last line often contains a funny or surprise ending, as in this limerick written by an eighth grader.

> There once was a frog named Pete
> Who did nothing but sit and eat.
> He examined each fly
> With so careful an eye
> And then said, "You're dead meat."

Poet X. J. Kennedy (1982) suggests introducing students to limericks by reading aloud some of Lear's verses so that students can appreciate their rhythm. One collection of Lear's limericks for children is *There Was an Old Man: A Gallery of Nonsense Rhymes* (Lear, 1994). Younger children especially enjoy *AnimaLimericks* (Driver, 1994), which feature animals instead of people. Arnold Lobel has also written a book of unique pig limericks, *Pigericks* (1983). After reading Lobel's pigericks, students will want to write "fishericks." Writing limericks can be a challenging assignment, but students can write them successfully if they write class collaboration poems.

Narrative Poems. Poems that tell a story are narrative poems. Perhaps our best-known narrative poem is Clement Moore's classic, "The Night Before Christmas." Other narrative poems include Longfellow's *The Midnight Ride of Paul Revere* (2001), illustrated by Christopher Bing; Alfred Noyes's *The Highwayman* (1983), illustrated by Charles Mikolaycak; and Jeanette Winter's *Follow the Drinking Gourd* (1988), which is about the Underground Railroad.

Haiku and Related Forms. Haiku is a Japanese poetic form that contains just 17 syllables arranged in three lines of 5, 7, and 5 syllables. Haiku poems deal with nature and present a single clear image. Haiku is a concise form, much like a telegram. Because of

Poetry Unit

These fifth graders are studying Jack Prelutsky and reading his poems. They especially enjoy his CD-ROM of *The New Kid on the Block*. The students pick favorite poems and copy them on chart paper. Next they choose a familiar tune, such as "Twinkle, Twinkle, Little Star" or "I've Been Working on the Railroad," that fits the cadence of the poem and sing the poem to that tune. Singing poems is a favorite daily activity. They're also writing their own verses collaboratively using Prelutsky's poetic forms, such as "My Fish Can Ride a Bicycle," that they will make into class books.

its brevity, it has been considered an appropriate form of poetry for children to read and write. A fourth grader wrote this haiku about a spider web she saw one morning.

Spider web shining
Tangled on the grass with dew
Waiting quietly.

Books of haiku to share with students include *Shadow Play: Night Haiku* (Harter, 1994) and *Cool Melons—Turn to Frogs! The Life and Poems of Issa* (Gollub, 1998). The artwork in these picture books may give students ideas for illustrating their haiku poems.

A poetic form similar to haiku is the cinquain, a five-line poem containing 22 syllables in a 2-4-6-8-2 syllable pattern. Cinquains often describe something, but they may also tell a story. Have students ask themselves what their subject looks like, smells like, sounds like, and tastes like, and record their ideas using a five-senses cluster. The formula is as follows:

Line 1: a one-word subject with two syllables

Line 2: four syllables describing the subject

Line 3: six syllables showing action

Line 4: eight syllables expressing a feeling or observation about the subject

Line 5: two syllables describing or renaming the subject

Students in a fourth-grade class wrote cinquains as part of a thematic unit on westward movement. One student wrote this cinquain about the transcontinental railroad:

> *Railroads*
> *One crazy guy's*
> *Transcontinental dream . . .*
> *With a golden spike it came true.*
> *Iron horse*

Another student wrote about the gold rush:

> *Gold rush*
> *Forty-niners*
> *were sure to strike it rich*
> *Homesickness, pork and beans, so tired.*
> *Panning*

Another related form is the diamante (Tiedt, 1970), a seven-line contrast poem written in the shape of a diamond. This poetic form helps students apply their knowledge of opposites and parts of speech. Here is the formula:

Line 1: one noun as the subject

Line 2: two adjectives describing the subject

Line 3: three participles (ending in -*ing*) telling about the subject

Line 4: four nouns (the first two related to the subject and the last two related to the opposite)

Line 5: three participles telling about the opposite

Line 6: two adjectives describing the opposite

Line 7: one noun that is the opposite of the subject

A third-grade class wrote this diamante poem about the stages of life:

> *Baby*
> *wrinkled tiny*
> *crying wetting sleeping*
> *rattles diapers money house*
> *caring working loving*
> *smart helpful*
> *Adult*

Notice that the students created a contrast between *baby,* the subject represented by the noun in the first line, and *adult,* the opposite in the last line. This contrast gives students the opportunity to play with words and apply their understanding of opposites. The third word in the fourth line, *money,* begins the transition from *baby* to its opposite, *adult.*

Free Verse. Unrhymed poetry is free verse. Word choice and visual images take on greater importance in free verse, and rhythm is less important than in other types of poetry. *Nathaniel Talking* (Greenfield, 1988) and *Neighborhood Odes* (Soto, 1992) are two collections of free verse. In *Nathaniel Talking,* Eloise Greenfield writes from the viewpoint of a young African American child who has lost his mother but not his spirit. Most of the poems are free verse, but one is a rap and several others rhyme. Greenfield uses few capital letters or punctuation marks. In *Neighborhood Odes,* Gary Soto writes about his childhood as a Mexican American child living in Fresno, California. Soto adds a few Spanish words to his poems to sharpen the pictures the poems paint of life in his neighborhood.

In free verse, children choose words to describe something and put them together to express a thought or tell a story, without concern for rhyme or other arrangements. The number of words per line and use of punctuation vary. In the following poem, an eighth grader poignantly describes "Loneliness" using only 15 well-chosen words.

> *A lifetime*
> *Of broken dreams*
> *And promises*
> *Lost love*
> *Hurt*
> *My heart*
> *Cries*
> *In silence*

Students can use several methods for writing free verse. They can select words and phrases from brainstormed lists and clusters to create the poem, or they can write a paragraph and then "unwrite" it to create the poem by deleting unnecessary words. They arrange the remaining words to look like a poem.

During a literature focus unit on MacLachlan's *Sarah, Plain and Tall* (1985), a third-grade class wrote this free-form poem after discussing the two kinds of dunes in the story:

> *Dunes of sand*
> *on the beach.*
> *Sarah walks on them*
> *and watches the ocean.*
> *Dunes of hay*
> *beside the barn.*
> *Papa makes them for Sarah*
> *because she misses Maine.*

Poems for two voices are unique, written in two columns, side by side, and the columns are read together by two readers. The two best-known books of poems for two voices are Paul Fleischman's *I Am Phoenix* (1985), which is about birds, and the Newbery Award–winning *Joyful Noise* (1988), which is about insects.

A small group of fifth graders wrote this poem for two voices as a project after reading *Number the Stars* (Lowry, 1989), the story of the friendship of two girls, a Christian and a Jew, set in Denmark during World War II.

> *I am Annemarie, a Christian.*
>
> > *I am Ellen, a Jew.*
>
> *I hate this war.*   *I hate this war.*
>
> > *The Nazis want to kill me.*
>
> *The Nazis want to kill my friend.*
> *Why?*   *Why?*

I want to help my friend.	
	Can you help me?
My mother will take you to her brother, my uncle. He is a fisherman.	
	Your uncle is a fisherman?
He will hide you on his ship.	
	He will hide me on his ship?
He will take you to Sweden. To freedom. I am Annemarie, a Christian.	To freedom.
	I am Ellen, a Jew.
I want to help my friend.	
	I need the help of my friends or I will die.
I hate this war.	I hate this war.

Found poems are another type of free verse. Students create found poems by culling words from various sources, such as newspaper articles, stories, and informational books. Found poems give students the opportunity to manipulate words and sentence structures they don't normally use themselves. A small group of third graders composed the following found poem, "This Is My Day," after reading *Sarah Morton's Day: A Day in the Life of a Pilgrim Girl* (Waters, 1989):

> Good day.
> I must get up and be about my chores.
> The fire is mine to tend.
> I lay the table.
> I muck the garden.
> I pound the spices.
> I draw vinegar to polish the brass.
> I practice my lessons.
> I feed the fire again.
> I milk the goats.
> I eat dinner.
> I say the verses I am learning.
> My father is pleased with my learning.
> I fetch the water for tomorrow.
> I bid my parents good night.
> I say my prayers.
> Fare thee well.
> God be with thee.

To compose the found poem, the students collected their favorite words and sentences from the book and organized them sequentially to describe the pilgrim girl's day.

Other Poetic Forms. Students use a variety of other forms when they write poems, even though few adults use them. These forms provide a scaffold or skeleton for students' poems. After collecting words, images, and comparisons, students craft their poems, choosing words and arranging them to create a message. Meaning is always most important, and form follows the search for meaning. Poet Kenneth Koch (2000), working with third through sixth graders, developed some simple formulas that make it easy for nearly every child to become a successful poet. These formulas call for students to begin every line the same way or to insert a particular kind of word in every line. The formulas use repetition, a stylistic device that is more effective for young poets than rhyme. Some forms may seem more like sentences than poems, but the dividing line between poetry and prose is a blurry one, and these poetry experiences help children move toward poetic expression.

For "I Wish . . ." poems, children begin each line of their poems with the words "I wish" and complete the line with a wish (Koch, 2000). In this second-grade class collaboration poem, children simply listed their wishes:

Our Wishes

I wish I had all the money in the world.
I wish I was a star fallen down from Mars.
I wish I were a butterfly.
I wish I were a teddy bear.
I wish I had a cat.
I wish I were a pink rose.
I wish it wouldn't rain today.
I wish I didn't have to wash a dish.
I wish I had a flying carpet.
I wish I could go to Disney World.
I wish school was out.
I wish I could go outside and play.

After this experience, students can choose one of their wishes and expand on the idea in another poem. Brandi expanded her wish this way:

I wish I were a teddy bear
Who sat on a beautiful bed
Who got a hug every night
By a little girl or boy
Maybe tonight I'll get my wish
And wake up on a little girl's bed
And then I'll be as happy as can be.

In color poems, students begin each line of their poems with a color. They can repeat a color in each line or choose a different color (Koch, 2000). In this example, a class of seventh graders writes about yellow:

Yellow is shiny galoshes
splashing through mud puddles.
Yellow is a street lamp
beaming through a dark, black night.

Yellow is the egg yolk
bubbling in a frying pan.
Yellow is the lemon cake
that makes you pucker your lips.
Yellow is the sunset
and the warm summer breeze.
Yellow is the tingling in your mouth
after a lemon drop melts.

Students can also write more complex poems by expanding each idea into a stanza, as this poem about black illustrates.

Black

Black is a deep hole
sitting in the ground
waiting for animals
that live inside.
Black is a beautiful horse
standing on a high hill
with the wind
swirling its mane.
Black is a winter night sky
without stars
to keep it
company.
Black is a panther
creeping around a jungle
searching for
its prey.

Hailstones and Halibut Bones (O'Neill, 1989) is another source of color poems; however, O'Neill uses rhyme as a poetic device, and it is important to emphasize that students' poems need not rhyme.

Acrostic poems are another poetic form. Students begin an acrostic poem by writing a word vertically. They then write a word or phrase beginning with each letter to complete the poem. As part of literature focus units, for example, students can write about a book title or a character's name. This acrostic poem about *Jumanji* (Van Allsburg, 1981) was written by a fourth grader:

Jungle adventure game and
fUn for a while.
Monkeys ransacking kitchens
And boa constrictors slithering past.
No way out until the game is done—
Just reach the city of Jumanji.
I don't want to play!

In five-senses poems, students write about a topic using each of the five senses. Sense poems are usually five lines long, with one line for each sense, but sometimes an extra line is added, as this poem written by a sixth grader demonstrates:

Being Heartbroken

Sounds like thunder and lightning
Looks like a carrot going through a blender
Tastes like sour milk
Feels like a splinter in your finger
Smells like a dead fish
It must be horrible!

It is often helpful to have students develop a five-senses cluster and collect ideas for each sense. Students select from the cluster the most vivid or strongest idea for each sense to use in a line of the poem.

For "If I were . . ." poems, children write about how they would feel and what they would do if they were something else—a dinosaur, a hamburger, sunshine (Koch, 2000). They begin each poem with "If I were" and tell what it would be like to be that thing. In this example, 7-year-old Robbie wrote about what he would do if he were a dinosaur:

If I were a Tyrannosaurus Rex
I would terrorize other dinosaurs
And eat them up for supper.

In composing "If I were . . ." poems, students use personification, explore ideas and feelings, and consider the world from a different vantage point.

Finally, in writing preposition poems, students experiment with prepositional phrases. They begin each line of a preposition poem with a preposition, and a delightful poetic rewording of lines often results from the attempt. A seventh grader wrote this preposition poem about a movie superhero:

Superman

Within the city
In a phone booth
Into his clothes
Like a bird
In the sky
Through the walls
Until the crime
Among us
is defeated!

Complete a self-assessment to check your understanding of the concepts presented in this chapter on the Companion Website at *www.prenhall.com/ tompkins*

It is helpful for children to brainstorm a list of prepositions to refer to when they write preposition poems. Students may find that they need to ignore the formula for a line or two to give the content of their poems top priority, or they may mistakenly begin a line with an infinitive (e.g., "to say") rather than a preposition. These forms provide a structure or skeleton for students' writing that should be adapted as necessary.

Review: How Effective Teachers Focus on Text Factors

1. Teachers understand the important role text factors play in comprehension.

2. Teachers teach students about narrative genres and provide opportunities for students to read books representing each one.

3. Teachers teach students about story elements—plot, characters, setting, point of view, and theme—in stories they are reading.

4. Teachers teach students about literary devices—comparison, hyperbole, imagery, personification, symbolism, and tone—and encourage them to note examples in the books they read of how authors use these devices.

5. Teachers have students examine the expository text structures—description, sequence, comparison, cause and effect, and problem and solution—in informational books they are reading.

6. Teachers have students make graphic organizers to emphasize the structure of stories and informational books.

7. Teachers encourage students to use text features when reading informational books.

8. Teachers have students read a wide variety of single-poem books, specialized anthologies, and comprehensive anthologies.

9. Teachers have students examine the patterns authors use to write poems and then write their own poems using the same patterns.

10. Teachers encourage students to apply their knowledge of text structure and genres when writing stories, informational books, and poems.

Professional References

Au, K. H. (1992). Constructing the theme of a story. *Language Arts, 69,* 106–111.

Bruner, J. (1986). *Actual minds, possible worlds.* Cambridge, MA: Harvard University Press.

Buss, K., & Karnowski, L. (2000). *Reading and writing literary genres.* Newark, DE: International Reading Association.

De Ford, D. (1981). Literacy: Reading, writing, and other essentials. *Language Arts, 58,* 652–658.

Dressel, J. H. (1990). The effects of listening to and discussing different qualities of children's literature on the narrative writing of fifth graders. *Research in the Teaching of English, 24,* 397–414.

Duke, N. K., & Pearson, P. D. (2002). Effective practices for developing reading comprehension. In A. E. Farstrup & S. J. Samuels (Eds.), *What research has to say about reading instruction* (3rd ed., pp. 205–242). Newark, DE: International Reading Association.

Eckhoff, B. (1983). How reading affects children's writing. *Language Arts, 60,* 607–616.

Flood, J., Lapp, D., & Farnan, N. (1986). A reading-writing procedure that teaches expository paragraph structure. *The Reading Teacher, 39,* 556–562.

Freedman, R. (1992). Fact or fiction? In E. B. Freeman & D. G. Person (Eds.), *Using nonfiction tradebooks in the elementary classroom: From ants to zeppelins* (pp. 2–10). Urbana, IL: National Council of Teachers of English.

Graves, D. H. (1992). *Explore poetry.* Portsmouth, NH: Heinemann.

Harvey, S., & Goudvis, A. (2000). *Strategies that work: Teaching comprehension to enhance understanding.* York, ME: Stenhouse.

Johnson, T. D., & Louis, D. R. (1987). *Literacy through literature.* Portsmouth, NH: Heinemann.

Kintsch, W., & Van Dijk, T. A. (1978). Toward a model of text comprehension and production. *Psychological Review, 85,* 363–394.

Koch, K. (2000). *Wishes, lies, and dreams: Teaching children to write poetry.* New York: HarperPerennial.

Larrick, N. (1991). *Let's do a poem! Introducing poetry to children.* New York: Delacorte.

Lehr, S. S. (1991). *The child's developing sense of theme: Responses to literature.* New York: Teachers College Press.

Lukens, R. J. (2002). *A critical handbook of children's literature* (7th ed.). Boston: Allyn & Bacon.

McGee, L. M., & Richgels, D. J. (1985). Teaching expository text structures to elementary students. *The Reading Teacher, 38,* 739–745.

Meyer, B. J. F. (1975). *The organization of prose and its effects on memory.* Amsterdam: North-Holland.

Meyer, B. J. F., & Freedle, R. O. (1984). Effects of discourse type on recall. *American Educational Research Journal, 21,* 121–143.

Meyer, B. J. F., & Poon, L. W. (2004). Effects of structure strategy training and signaling on recall of text. In R. B. Ruddell & N. J. Unrau (Eds.), *Theoretical models and processes of reading* (5th ed., pp. 810–850). Newark, DE: International Reading Association.

Niles, O. S. (1974). Organization perceived. In H. L. Herber (Ed.), *Perspectives in reading: Developing study skills in secondary schools*. Newark, DE: International Reading Association.

Norton, D. E., & Norton, S. (2003). *Through the eyes of a child* (6th ed.). Upper Saddle River, NJ: Merrill/Prentice Hall.

Ogle, D. M. (1986). K-W-L: A teaching model that develops active reading of expository text. *The Reading Teacher, 39,* 564–570.

Pappas, C. (1993). Is narrative "primary"? Some insights from kindergartners' pretend readings of stories and information books. *Journal of Reading Behavior, 25,* 97–129.

Piccolo, J. A. (1987). Expository text structures: Teaching and learning strategies. *The Reading Teacher, 40,* 838–847.

Roop, P. (1992). Nonfiction books in the primary classroom: Soaring with the swans. In E. B. Freeman & D. G. Person (Eds.), *Using nonfiction tradebooks in the elementary classroom: From ants to zeppelins* (pp. 106–112). Urbana, IL: National Council of Teachers of English.

Rosenblatt, L. (1978). *The reader, the text, the poem: The transactional theory of the literary work*. Carbondale: Southern Illinois University Press.

Sweet, A. P., & Snow, C. E. (2003). Reading for comprehension. In C. E. Snow & A. P. Sweet (Eds.), *Rethinking reading comprehension* (pp. 1–11). New York: Guilford Press.

Tiedt, I. (1970). Exploring poetry patterns. *Elementary English, 45,* 1082–1084.

Vardell, S. (1991). A new "picture of the world": The NCTE Orbis Pictus Award for outstanding nonfiction for children. *Language Arts, 68,* 474–479.

Wells, G. (1986). *The meaning makers: Children learning language and using language to learn*. Portsmouth, NH: Heinemann.

Whitin, D. J., & Wilde, S. (1992). *Read any good math lately? Children's books for mathematical learning, K–6*. Portsmouth, NH: Heinemann.

Children's Book References

Aardema, V. (1975). *Why mosquitoes buzz in people's ears*. New York: Dial Books.

Aker, S. (1990). *What comes in 2's, 3's, and 4's?* New York: Simon & Schuster.

Ancona, G. (1992). *Man and mustang*. New York: Macmillan.

Arnold, C. (1993). *Dinosaurs all around: An artist's view of the prehistoric world*. New York: Clarion.

Blume, J. (1972). *Tales of a fourth grade nothing*. New York: Dutton.

Brett, J. (1994). *Town mouse, country mouse*. New York: Putnam.

Calmenson, S. (1989). *The principal's new clothes*. New York: Scholastic.

Carroll. L. (1984). *Alice's adventures in Wonderland*. New York: Knopf.

Clarke, B. (1990). *Amazing frogs and toads*. New York: Knopf.

Cleary, B. (1981). *Ramona Quimby, age 8*. New York: Morrow.

Coburn, J. R. (1996). *Jouanah: A Hmong Cinderella*. Arcadia, CA: Shen's Books.

Cohen, B. (1983). *Molly's pilgrim*. New York: Lothrop, Lee & Shepard.

Cole, J. (1996). *The magic school bus inside a beehive*. New York: Scholastic.

Coville, B. (1991). *Jeremy Thatcher, dragon hatcher*. San Diego: Harcourt Brace.

Cowcher, H. (1990). *Antarctica*. New York: Farrar, Straus & Giroux.

Creech, S. (2003). *Granny Torrelli makes soup*. New York: HarperCollins.

Curtis, C. P. (1995). *The Watsons go to Birmingham—1963*. New York: Delacorte.

Cushman, K. (1994). *Catherine, called Birdy*. New York: HarperCollins.

Dahl, R. (1964). *Charlie and the chocolate factory*. New York: Knopf.

Day, A. (1985). *Good dog, Carl*. New York: Green Tiger Press.

de la Paz, M. J. (2001). *Abadeha: The Philippine Cinderella*. Arcadia, CA: Shen's Books.

Demi. (1997). *One grain of rice: A mathematical folktale*. New York: Scholastic.

dePaola, T. (1983). *The legend of the bluebonnet*. New York: Putnam.

dePaola, T. (2002). *Adelita: A Mexican Cinderella story*. New York: Putnam.

Driver, R. (1994). *AnimaLimericks*. New York: Half Moon Books.

Feelings, M., & Feelings, T. (1971). *Moja means one: Swahili counting book*. New York: Dial Books.

Fleischman, P. (1985). *I am phoenix: Poems for two voices*. New York: Harper & Row.

Fleischman, P. (1988). *Joyful noise: Poems for two voices*. New York: Harper & Row.

Fleming, D. (2003). *Buster*. New York: Henry Holt.

Freedman, R. (1987). *Lincoln: A photobiography*. New York: Clarion Books.

Fritz, J. (1976). *Will you sign here, John Hancock?* New York: Coward-McCann.

Fritz, J. (1989). *The great little Madison*. New York: Putnam.

Galdone, P. (1968). *Henny Penny*. New York: Seabury.

Galdone, P. (1970). *The three little pigs*. New York: Seabury.

Galdone, P. (1978). *Cinderella*. New York: McGraw-Hill.

Galdone, P. (1985). *The gingerbread boy*. New York: Seabury.

Gantos, J. (2000). *Joey Pigza loses control*. New York: HarperCollins.

Gardiner, J. R. (1980). *Stone Fox*. New York: Harper & Row.

George, J. C. (1972). *Julie of the wolves*. New York: Harper & Row.

Gibbons, G. (2003). *Grizzly bears*. New York: Holiday House.

Goble, P. (1988). *Iktomi and the boulder: A Plains Indian story*. New York: Orchard Books.

Gollub, M. (1998). *Cool melons—turn to frogs! The life and poems of Issa*. New York: Lee & Low.

Greenburg, D. (1997). *Never trust a cat who wears earrings*. New York: Grosset & Dunlap.

Greenfield, E. (1988). *Nathaniel talking*. New York: Black Butterfly Children's Books.

Guiberson, B. Z. (1991). *Cactus hotel*. New York: Henry Holt.

Harter, P. (1994). *Shadow play: Night haiku*. New York: Simon & Schuster.

Hesse, K. (2001). *Witness*. New York: Scholastic.

Hickox, R. (1998). *The golden sandal: A Middle Eastern Cinderella story*. New York: Holiday House.

Hoban, T. (1987). *26 letters and 99 cents*. New York: Greenwillow.

Hooks, W. H. (1987). *Moss gown*. New York: Clarion Books.

Howe, D., & Howe, J. (1979). *Bunnicula: A rabbit-tale of mystery*. New York: Atheneum.

Howe, J. (1989). *Jack and the beanstalk*. Boston: Little, Brown.

Hunt, J. (1989). *Illuminations*. New York: Bradbury Press.

Hutchins, P. (1968). *Rosie's walk*. New York: Macmillan.

Hutton, W. (1994). *Persephone*. New York: McElderry.

Hyman, T. S. (1977). *The sleeping beauty*. New York: Holiday House.

Jaffe, N. (1998). *The way meat loves salt: A Cinderella tale from the Jewish tradition*. New York: Henry Holt.

Jones, C. (1997). *The lion and the rat*. Boston: Houghton Mifflin.

Kasza, K. (1987). *The wolf's chicken stew*. New York: Putnam.

Kellogg, S. (1984). *Paul Bunyan: A tall tale*. New York: Morrow.

Kellogg, S. (1986). *Pecos Bill: A tall tale*. New York: Morrow.

Kellogg, S. (1988). *Johnny Appleseed: A tall tale*. New York: Morrow.

Kennedy, X. J. (1982). *Knock at a star: A child's introduction to poetry*. Boston: Little, Brown.

King-Smith, D. (1995). *Babe the gallant pig*. New York: Random House.

Lear, E. (1994). *There was an old man: A gallery of nonsense rhymes*. New York: Morrow.

L'Engle, M. (1962). *A wrinkle in time*. New York: Farrar, Straus & Giroux.

Lester, H. (1988). *Tacky the penguin*. Boston: Houghton Mifflin.

Levine, E. (1986). *. . . If you traveled west in a covered wagon*. New York: Scholastic.

Levine, G. C. (1997). *Ella enchanted*. New York: Harper-Collins.

Lewis, C. S. (1994). *The lion, the witch and the wardrobe*. New York: HarperCollins.

Lionni, L. (1969). *Alexander and the wind-up mouse*. New York: Pantheon.

Lobel, A. (1983). *Pigericks: A book of pig limericks*. New York: Harper & Row.

Longfellow, H. W. (2001). *The midnight ride of Paul Revere* (C. Bing, Illus.). Brooklyn, NY: Handprint Books.

Louie, A. L. (1982). *Yeh-Shen: A Cinderella story from China*. New York: Philomel.

Lowry, L. (1989). *Number the stars*. Boston: Houghton Mifflin.

Lowry, L. (1993). *The giver*. Boston: Houghton Mifflin.

Macaulay, D. (1977). *Castle*. Boston: Houghton Mifflin.

MacLachlan, P. (1985). *Sarah, plain and tall*. New York: Harper & Row.

Maestro, B. (1992). *How do apples grow?* New York: HarperCollins.

Martin, B., Jr., & Archambault, J. (1985). *The ghost-eye tree*. New York: Holt, Rinehart and Winston.

Martin, R. (1992). *The rough-face girl*. New York: Putnam.

McCloskey, R. (1969). *Make way for ducklings*. New York: Viking.

Millard, A. (1998). *A street through time*. New York: DK Publishing.

Milner, A. A. (1961). *Winnie-the-pooh*. New York: Dutton.

Noyes, A. (1983). *The highwayman*. New York: Lothrop, Lee & Shepard.

O'Neill, M. (1989). *Hailstones and halibut bones*. New York: Doubleday.

Pallotta, J. (1991). *The underwater alphabet book*. Watertown, MA: Charlesbridge.

Paterson, K. (1977). *Bridge to Terabithia*. New York: Crowell.

Paulsen, G. (1987). *Hatchet*. New York: Viking.

Pinkney, J. (1999). *The ugly duckling*. New York: Morrow.

Pinkney, J. (2000). *Aesop's fables*. San Francisco: SeaStar Books.

Polacco, P. (1994). *Pink and Say*. New York: Putnam.

Pollock, P. (1996). *The turkey girl: A Zuni Cinderella story*. Boston: Little, Brown.

Potter, B. (1902). *The tale of Peter Rabbit*. New York: Warne.

Prelutsky, J. (Sel.). (2000). *The Random House book of poetry for children*. New York: Random House.

Prelutsky, J. (1985). *My parents think I'm sleeping*. New York: Greenwillow.

Rauzon, M. J. (1993). *Horns, antlers, fangs, and tusks*. New York: Lothrop, Lee & Shepard.

Rowling, J. K. (1997). *Harry Potter and the sorcerer's stone*. New York: Levine.

Ryan, P. M. (2000). *Esperanza rising*. New York: Scholastic.

Rylant, C. (1992). *Best wishes*. Katonwah, NY: Richard C. Owen.

Sachar, L. (1998). *Holes*. New York: Farrar, Straus & Giroux.

Sanderson, R. (2002). *Cinderella*. Boston: Little, Brown.

San Souci, R. D. (1998). *Cendrillon: A Caribbean Cinderella*. New York: Aladdin Books.

Schwartz, D. (1989). *If you made a million*. New York: Lothrop, Lee & Shepard.

Scieszka, J. (1989). *The true story of the 3 little pigs!* New York: Viking.

Scieszka, J. (1991). *Knights of the kitchen table*. New York: Viking.

Scott, A. H. (1990). *One good horse: A cowpuncher's counting book*. New York: Greenwillow.

Service, R. (1988). *Stinker from space*. New York: Scribner.

Seuling, B. (2003). *Flick a switch: How electricity gets to your home*. New York: Holiday House.

Siebert, D. (1991). *Sierra*. New York: HarperCollins.

Simon, S. (1989). *Whales*. New York: Crowell.

Simon, S. (2003). *Spiders*. New York: HarperCollins.

Soto, G. (1992). *Neighborhood odes*. San Diego: Harcourt Brace.

Speare, E. G. (1972). *The witch of Blackbird Pond*. Boston: Houghton Mifflin.

Spinelli, J. (2002). *Loser*. New York: HarperCollins.

Steele, P. (1998). *Knights*. New York: Kingfisher.

Steig, W. (1982). *Doctor De Soto*. New York: Farrar, Straus & Giroux.

Steig, W. (1988). *Sylvester and the magic pebble*. New York: Simon & Schuster.

Steptoe, J. (1984). *The story of Jumping Mouse: A Native American legend*. New York: Lothrop, Lee & Shepard.

Steptoe, J. (1987). *Mufaro's beautiful daughters: An African tale*. New York: Lothrop, Lee & Shepard.

Sutcliff, R. (1994). *The sword and the circle: King Arthur and the knights of the round table*. New York: Penguin.

Swain, R. F. (2003). *How sweet it is (and was): The history of candy*. New York: Holiday House.

Taylor, M. D. (1976). *Roll of thunder, hear my cry*. New York: Dial Books.

Tolan, S. S. (2002). *Surviving the Applewhites*. New York: HarperCollins.

Van Allsburg, C. (1981). *Jumanji*. Boston: Houghton Mifflin.

Van Allsburg, C. (1986). *The stranger*. Boston: Houghton Mifflin.

Van Allsburg, C. (1991). *The wretched stone*. Boston: Houghton Mifflin.

Viorst, J. (1977). *Alexander and the terrible, horrible, no good, very bad day*. New York: Atheneum.

Ward, C. (1999). *The hare and the tortoise*. New York: Millbrook.

Waters, K. (1989). *Sarah Morton's day: A day in the life of a pilgrim girl*. New York: Scholastic.

Westcott, N. B. (1984). *The emperor's new clothes*. Boston: Little, Brown.

White, E. B. (1952). *Charlotte's web*. New York: Harper & Row.

Wiesner, D. (1991). *Tuesday*. New York: Clarion Books.

Williams, V. B. (1982). *A chair for my mother*. New York: Mulberry Books.

Winter, J. (1988). *Follow the drinking gourd*. New York: Knopf.

Yolen, J. (1986). *The sleeping beauty*. New York: Random House.

Zelinsky, P. O. (1986). *Rumpelstiltskin*. New York: Dutton.

Zemach, M. (1983). *The little red hen*. New York: Farrar, Straus & Giroux.

Zemach, M. (1988). *The three little pigs*. New York: Farrar, Straus & Giroux.

Chapter 9

Assessing Students' Literacy Development

- Which tools do teachers use to assess students' learning in the classroom?
- How do teachers determine children's reading levels?
- How do teachers use student portfolios for authentic assessment?
- How do teachers assign grades?

Mrs. McNeal Conducts Second-Quarter Assessments

The end of the second quarter is approaching, and Mrs. McNeal is assessing her first-grade students. She collects four types of assessment data about her students' reading, writing, and spelling development. Then she uses the data to document children's achievement, verify that children are meeting district standards, determine report card grades, write narratives to accompany the grades, and make instructional plans for the next quarter.

Today, Mrs. McNeal assesses Seth, who is 6½ years old. He's a quiet, well-behaved child who regularly completes his work. She has a collection of Seth's writing and other papers he has done, but she wants to assess his current reading level. At the beginning of the school year, Mrs. McNeal considered him an average student, but in the past month, his reading progress has accelerated. She is anxious to see how much progress he has made since the end of the first quarter.

Assessment 1: Determining Seth's Instructional Reading Level. Mrs. McNeal regularly takes running records as she listens to children reread books they are familiar with in order to monitor their ability to recognize familiar and high-frequency words, decode unfamiliar words, and use strategic

reading behaviors. In addition, Mrs. Mc-
Neal assesses each child's instructional reading level at the beginning of the school year and at
the end of each quarter. She uses the *Developmental Read-
ing Assessment* (DRA) (Beaver, 2001), an assessment kit designed for kindergarten
through third grade, which includes 44 small paperback books arranged from kindergarten to fifth-grade reading levels.

To determine a child's instructional reading level, Mrs. McNeal chooses a book
that the child has not read before and introduces it to the child by reading the title,
examining the picture on the cover, and talking about the story. The child does a picture walk, looking through the book and talking about what is happening on each
page, using the illustrations as clues. Next, the child reads the book aloud as Mrs.
McNeal takes a running record, checking the words the child reads correctly and noting those read incorrectly. Then the child retells the story, and the teacher prompts with
questions, if necessary, to assess his or her understanding. Afterward, Mrs. McNeal
scores the running record to determine the child's instructional reading level.

At the beginning of the school year, most of Mrs. McNeal's first graders were
reading at level 4; by midyear, they are reading at level 8; and by the end of the
school year, they should be reading at levels 18 to 20. At the beginning of the school
year, Seth was reading at level 4, like many of his classmates, and at the end of the
first quarter, he was already reading at level 8. Mrs. McNeal decides to test him at
level 16 because he is reading a level 16 book in his guided reading group.

Seth reads *The Pot of Gold* (2001), a level 16 book in the DRA assessment kit.
The book is an Irish folktale about a mean man named Grumble who makes an elf
show him where his pot of gold is hidden. Grumble marks the spot by tying a scarf
around a nearby tree branch while he goes to get a shovel with which to dig up the
gold. Grumble admonishes the elf not to move the scarf, and he doesn't. Instead he
ties many other scarves on nearby trees so that Grumble can't find the elf's gold. Mrs.
McNeal takes a running record while Seth reads; it is shown in the box on page 294.

As indicated on the running record sheet, there are 266 words in the book. Seth
makes 17 errors but self-corrects 5 of them; his accuracy rate is 95%. Mrs. McNeal
analyzes Seth's errors and concludes that he overdepends on visual (or phonological) cues while ignoring semantic cues. Of the 12 errors, only one—*Grumply* for
Grumble—makes sense in the sentence. When Seth retells the story, he shows that
he understands the big idea, but his retelling is not especially strong. He retells the
beginning and end of the story, but he leaves out the setting and important details in
the middle; however, he does make interesting connections between the story and
his own life. Mrs. McNeal concludes that level 16 is his instructional level and that
his ability to read words is stronger than his comprehension.

Mrs. McNeal makes notes about Seth's instructional priorities for the next quarter. Comprehension will be her focus for Seth. She will teach Seth more about the
structure of stories, including plot and setting, and help him use semantic cues to support his use of visual cues. She will encourage him to structure his oral and written
retellings in three parts—beginning, middle, and end—and include more details in his

A Running Record Scoring Sheet

Name **Seth**   Date **Jan. 18**

Level **16**   Title **The Pot of Gold**   Easy   (Instructional)   Hard

Running Record	E	SC	E	SC

Row 2:
✓✓✓✓✓✓✓✓
✓ grumply/Grumble |T ✓✓✓✓✓✓   1 | | m s (v)
✓✓✓ always |T ^A |T   1
✓✓✓✓✓✓✓✓

Row 3:
✓✓✓✓✓✓✓✓
✓✓✓✓✓✓ did not/didn't | 1 | | (m)(s)v
✓✓
✓✓✓✓✓✓✓✓
✓✓✓✓✓✓✓✓
✓✓

Row 4:
✓✓✓✓✓✓
✓✓✓✓✓✓✓✓
✓✓✓

Row 5:
✓✓✓✓✓✓✓✓
✓✓✓✓✓✓ I/I'll | make/move | ✓✓   1 / 1 | | (m)(s)(v) / m s (v)
✓✓✓✓✓✓✓
safr/scarf | ✓✓✓✓✓ or/of | ✓✓   1 / 1 | | m s (v) / m s (v)

Row 6:
✓✓✓✓✓✓ me/my |sc self/scarf | | 1 | m s (v) / m s (v)   (m)(s)(v)
✓✓✓   1
✓✓✓✓
✓✓✓✓

Row 7:
✓✓✓✓✓✓
✓✓✓✓✓✓✓
✓✓✓✓✓

Row 8:
✓✓✓✓✓✓✓
✓✓

Row 9:
✓✓✓ take/taken | ✓ scafer/scarf | ✓✓✓   1 / 1 | | (m)s(v) / m s (v)
✓✓✓✓✓✓✓✓✓

Row 10:
✓✓✓✓✓✓✓ | 1 | m s (v)   (m)(s)(v)
✓✓✓ they/that |sc ^R ✓| ✓✓✓✓✓✓
✓✓✓ maybe/may | sit/still | ✓✓   1 / 1 | | m s (v) / m s (v)

Scoring 12/266 95% accuracy	Picture Walk Gets gist of story
Types of Errors: M S (V) overdependent on v cues	Oral Reading Reads fluently
Self-correction Rate 1:5	Retelling/Questions Tells BME but middle is brief

retellings. She also decides to introduce Seth to easy chapter books, including Jane Yolen's Henry and Mudge series about a boy named Henry and the adventures he has with his dog, named Mudge (e.g., *Henry and Mudge and the Best Day of All*, 1995).

Assessment 2: Testing Seth's Knowledge of High-Frequency Words. Mrs. McNeal's goal is for her first graders to be able to read at least 75 of the 100 high-frequency words. At the beginning of the year, most children could read 12 or more of the words; Seth read 16 of the words correctly. Mrs. McNeal has a high-frequency word wall posted in the classroom with more than 50 of the words displayed in alphabetized boxes. At the beginning of the year, she reviewed the 12 most common words introduced in kindergarten (e.g., *the, I, is*) and added them to the word wall, and she began adding 2 or 3 new words each week.

Today, Mrs. McNeal asks Seth to read the list of 100 high-frequency words again, which is arranged in order of difficulty. She expects that he will be able to read 50 or 60 of the words and when he misses 5 in a row, she will stop the test, but Seth surprises her and reads the entire list! He misses only these 6 words: *don't, how, there, very, were,* and *would.* Seth's high score on this assessment reinforces his results on the running record: He is a very good word reader.

Assessment 3: Checking Seth's Ability to Write and Spell Words. Several days ago, Mrs. McNeal administered the "Words I Know" Test to the whole class. She asked the children to write as many words as they could in 10 minutes without copying from charts posted in the classroom. At the beginning of the school year, most of the children could write and spell correctly 15 to 20 words; Mrs. McNeal's goal is that they can write 50 words by the end of the school year. Seth wrote 22 words in August, and on the recent test he wrote 50 words that were spelled correctly. Seth's "Words I Know" test is shown in the box below.

Mrs. McNeal reviews the list of words that Seth wrote and notices that most are one-syllable words with short vowels, such as *cat, pig,* and *fin,* but that he is beginning to write words with irregular or more complex spellings, such as *what, snow, come,* and *night,* words with inflectional endings, such as *trees* and *going,* and two-syllable words, such as *cowboys.* She concludes that Seth is making very good

See the Compendium of Instructional Procedures, which follows Chapter 14, for more information on the highlighted terms.

Seth's "Words I Know" Test

the im a can eat look took she Play so he
man what han hat bat zadl got god cat
red in meat pig pi n see need ds and
night fight Dog come from sun run
ran going lettle fin will hill rat
srach ring ua fel tnees snow fun
cowBoys stop get no yes hors you

LatSmi I cap wachgup. My dad Sept with me then I fli fast a sep Then dad Went ot bed.

All about Planis.

There are difer planis in Space like Juqiter and Saturn neptune But the hots one is the sun.

progress, both in terms of the number of words he is writing and the complexity of the spelling patterns he is using.

Assessment 4: Scoring Seth's Compositions. Mrs. McNeal looks through Seth's journal and chooses two representative samples written in the past 3 weeks to score; they are shown above. The top one, which we'll call "Sleeping," is about a personal experience. The text (with conventional spelling and punctuation) reads:

> Last night I kept waking up. My dad slept with me. Then I fell fast asleep. Then dad went to bed.

The second entry is entitled "All About Planets" and demonstrates Seth's interest in the thematic unit. The text reads:

> There are different planets in space like Jupiter and Saturn [and] Neptune. But the hottest one is the sun.

Using the school district's 6-point rubric, Mrs. McNeal scores the compositions as a 4. A score of 5 is considered grade-level at the end of the school year, and Mrs. McNeal feels that Seth will reach that level before then. She notes that Seth is writing two to four sentences in an entry, even though he often omits punctuation at the ends of sentences. He draws illustrations to support his compositions, and his sentences can be read. He is beginning to add titles to his entries, as shown in the "All About Planets" entry. Seth writes fluently, but he sometimes omits a word or two. Mrs. McNeal plans to talk to Seth about the importance of rereading his writing to catch any omissions, add punctuation marks, and correct misspelled words.

Seth correctly spells more than two-thirds of the words he writes, and he uses invented spelling that usually represents beginning, middle, or ending sounds. In the "Sleeping" entry, Seth wrote 21 words, spelling 13 of them correctly; in the "Planets" entry, Seth again wrote 21 words, spelling 17 of them correctly. This means that Seth spelled 71% of the words in his compositions correctly. He reversed the order of letters in three words in the "Sleeping" entry (*lats* for *last, fli* for *fell, ot* for *to*) but did not make any letter-order reversals in the "All About Planets" entry. Mrs. McNeal recognizes that many first graders form letters backward and make letter-order reversals; she isn't concerned about Seth's reversals because she thinks that with more writing practice, he'll outgrow them.

Assessment 5: Measuring Seth's Phonics and Spelling Knowledge. Each week, Mrs. McNeal and the first graders craft two sentences to use for a dictation test. On Monday, they create the sentences and write them on a piece of chart paper that is displayed in the classroom for the week. Often the sentences are about current events, books Mrs. McNeal reads aloud, or the thematic unit they are studying. During the week, the children practice writing the sentences on small white boards, and Mrs. McNeal uses the text for minilessons during which she draws children's attention to high-frequency words they have studied, the phonetic features of various words, and capitalization and punctuation rules applied in the sentences. At the beginning of the school year, they wrote one sentence each week, but for the past 6 weeks, they have been writing two sentences. Last week's sentences focused on the class's thematic unit on the solar system and *The Magic School Bus Lost in the Solar System* (Cole, 1993), a book Mrs. McNeal read aloud to the class:

> Their bus turned into a rocket ship. They wanted to visit all of the planets.

After practicing the sentences all week, Mrs. McNeal dictates the sentences for the students to write on Friday. She tells them to spell as many words correctly as they can and to write all the sounds they hear in the words they don't know how to spell. Seth wrote:

> *The bus turd into a rocket ship they wande to vist all of the planis.*

Seth spelled 10 of the 15 words correctly and included 46 of 51 sounds in his writing. In addition, he omitted the period at the end of the first sentence and did not capitalize the first word in the second sentence.

Mrs. McNeal uses this test to check the students' phonics knowledge and ability to spell high-frequency words. Seth spelled most of the high-frequency words correctly, except that he wrote *the* for *their*. In the other four misspellings, Seth's errors involved the second syllable of the word or an inflectional ending. Mrs. McNeal concludes that Seth is making good progress in learning to spell high-frequency words and that he is ready to learn more about two-syllable words and inflectional endings.

Grading Seth's Reading, Writing, and Spelling Achievement. Having collected these data, Mrs. McNeal is ready to complete Seth's report card. Seth and his classmates receive separate number grades in reading, writing, and spelling: The grades range from 1, not meeting grade-level standards, to 4, exceeding grade-level standards. Seth will receive a 3 in reading, writing, and spelling. A score of 3 means that Seth is meeting grade-level standards in all three areas. Even though his reading level is higher than average, his dependence on visual cues when decoding unfamiliar words and his weakness in comprehension keep him at level 3 in reading.

Mrs. McNeal writes narratives to explain each student's progress in reading and writing and to offer suggestions to parents about how they can help their children at home. She sends the narrative home along with the report card. Here is what Mrs. McNeal wrote about Seth's progress in reading and writing:

Reading progress: Seth is reading at level 16. He uses a variety of strategies and is a fluent reader. He is beginning to retell the beginning, middle, and end of stories, but he needs to use more details.

Writing and spelling progress: Seth writes two to four sentences about a subject. He still uses a lot of invented spellings, especially in two-syllable words, although his sight word memory has grown from 26 to 50 words. He often forgets to put in ending punctuation marks.

Visit Chapter 9 on the Companion Website at *www.prenhall.com/ tompkins* to connect to web links related to assessment.

Assessment goes hand in hand with teaching (Flippo, 2003). It is an ongoing process that informs and guides instruction, as Mrs. McNeal demonstrated in the vignette. Reading researchers explain that "a system of frequent assessment, coupled with strong content standards and effective reading instruction helps ensure that teachers' . . . approaches are appropriate to each student's needs" (Kame'enui, Simmons, & Cornachione, 2000, p. 1). Teachers use the assessment cycle described in Chapter 1 to integrate assessment with instruction: They preassess, monitor, and assess students' learning no matter whether they teach reading and writing using basal reader programs, literature focus units, literature circles, or reading and writing workshop.

The purpose of reading and writing assessment is to collect meaningful information or data about what students know and are able to do, and it takes many forms (Kuhs, Johnson, Agruso, & Monrad, 2001). Probably the best-known assessments are tests, such as state-mandated standardized achievement tests, basal reading textbook unit tests, and districtwide and statewide writing assessments. These traditional forms of assessment measure how well students are achieving compared to national norms or grade-level expectations.

The focus in this chapter is not on administering standardized tests; instead, it is on classroom assessment tools that teachers use in balanced literacy programs—the informal assessments that teachers use every day to determine students' reading levels, to plan for instruction, and to monitor students' progress. The box on the next page explains the role of assessment in a balanced literacy program. As you continue reading this chapter, you will learn more about the ideas presented in the box.

How Assessment Fits Into a Balanced Literacy Program

Component	Description
Reading	Teachers use assessment tools to regularly monitor students' reading development and plan for instruction. Informal reading inventories (IRIs) are used to determine students' reading levels.
Phonics and Other Skills	Teachers use phonemic awareness tests and Clay's Observational Survey to assess young children's knowledge of phonics and The Names Test to assess older, struggling readers' decoding ability. They also use running records to analyze students' word-identification errors.
Strategies	Teachers use observation to monitor students' use of reading and writing strategies.
Vocabulary	Teachers monitor students' use of vocabulary through classroom activities, including grand conversations and reading logs.
Comprehension	Teachers ask questions and listen to students' comments in grand conversations and read their reading log entries to assess students' comprehension. They also administer an IRI to determine students' reading levels.
Literature	Teachers assess students' literature experiences through response to literature activities, such as grand conversations, reading logs, and projects.
Content-Area Study	Teachers assess students' learning in content-area units through learning logs, classroom activities, and projects.
Oral Language	Teachers use an IRI to determine whether students can understand grade-level books that teachers read aloud.
Writing	Teachers assess students' writing using rubrics, which students also can use to assess their own writing.
Spelling	Teachers assess students' stage of spelling development by categorizing the spelling errors they make in their writing. Many teachers also use weekly spelling tests to monitor students' growth in spelling.

LITERACY ASSESSMENT TOOLS

Teachers use a variety of literacy assessment tools and procedures to monitor, document, and evaluate students' reading and writing development. These tools examine students' ability to identify words, read fluently, comprehend what they are reading, use the writing process, and spell words. Many are informal and are created by teachers, but others have been developed, standardized, and published by researchers. Teachers also use assessment tools to diagnose struggling students' reading and writing problems. Many of these assessments are used with individual students, and even though it takes time to administer individual assessments, the information the teacher gains is useful and valuable. Giving a paper-and-pencil test to the entire class rarely provides much useful information about students; teachers learn much more as they listen to individual students read, watch individual students write, and talk with individual students about their reading and writing. The feature on this page presents guidelines for using assessment tools to assess students' literacy development.

Assessing Students' Concepts About Print

Young children learn concepts about print as they observe written language in their environment, listen to parents and teachers read books aloud, and experiment with reading and writing themselves. They learn basic concepts about letters, words, writing, and reading, and they demonstrate this knowledge when they turn the pages in a book, participate in interactive writing activities, and identify letters, words, and sentences on classroom charts.

Marie Clay (1985) developed the Concepts About Print Test (CAP Test) to more formally assess young children's understanding of written language concepts. The test has 24 items, and it is administered individually in 10 minutes. As the teacher reads the story aloud, the child looks at a test booklet with a story that has a picture on one facing page and text on the other. The child is asked to open the book, turn pages, and point out particular features of the text, including letters, words, sentences, and punctuation marks, as the story is read.

Teachers can also create their own versions of the CAP Test to use with any story they are reading with a child. As with the CAP Test, teachers' adaptations examine

Guidelines for Classroom Assessment

Use a teach-assess cycle to link assessment with instruction.

Identify students' reading levels to match students to appropriate reading materials.

Select appropriate tools based on your purposes for assessment.

Examine what students can do, not just what they can't do.

Assess students' literacy development in a variety of contexts because students often do better in one type of activity than in another.

Document students' learning by examining both the processes students use as they read and write and their finished products.

Make time to observe, conference with, and assess individual students to develop clear understandings of the student's literacy development.

Involve students in self-assessment activities so they can reflect on their progress and take responsibility for their own learning.

Concepts About Print

Marie Clay developed the Concepts About Print Test (CAP Test) to assess young children's understanding of concepts about print. These three types of concepts are assessed:

Book-orientation concepts
Directionality concepts
Letter and word concepts

Four forms of the CAP Test booklet are available: *Sand* (Clay, 1972), *Stones* (Clay, 1979), *Follow Me, Moon* (Clay, 2000a), and *No Shoes* (Clay, 2000b), as well as a Spanish version. Teachers use the CAP Test booklets or an interesting picture book. They administer the test by reading a book to the child and asking him or her to point to the first page of the story, show the direction of print, and point to letters, words, and punctuation marks. Teachers carefully observe children as they respond, and then mark their responses on a scoring sheet.

children's understanding that print carries the meaning, directionality of print, tracking of print, and letter, word, and sentence representation.

As they read any big book or small book with a child, teachers ask the child to show book-orientation concepts, directionality concepts, and letter and word concepts. Teachers can use the CAP Test scoring sheet shown in Figure 9–1 or develop one of their own to monitor children's growing understanding of these concepts.

Assessing Students' Phonemic Awareness and Phonics

Students learn about the alphabetic principle (that letters represent sounds) in the primary grades. Through phonemic awareness instruction, students learn strategies for segmenting, blending, and substituting sounds in words, and through phonics instruction, they learn about consonant and vowel sounds and phonics generalizations. Teachers often monitor students' learning as they participate in phonemic awareness and phonics activities in the classroom: When they sort picture cards according to beginning sounds or identify rhyming words in a familiar song, students are demonstrating their knowledge of phonemic awareness; similarly, when students use magnetic letters to spell words ending in -*at*, such as *bat, cat, hat, mat, rat,* and *sat,* they are demonstrating their phonics knowledge.

Phonics instruction is usually completed in the primary grades, but some older students who are struggling readers may not have acquired all of the phonics skills. Cunningham (1990) developed The Names Test: A Quick Assessment of Decoding Ability to measure older students' ability to decode unfamiliar words. She created a list of 50 first and last names, including both one-syllable and multisyllabic names representing many common phonics elements. Duffelmeyer, Kruse, Merkley, and Fyfe (1994) expanded the test to 70 names in order to increase its validity. Teachers administer this test individually. They ask students to read the list of names, and they mark which names students read correctly and which they mispronounce. Then teachers analyze students' errors to determine which phonics elements students have not acquired in order to plan for future instruction.

To learn more about phonemic awareness and phonics, see Chapter 4, "Cracking the Alphabetic Code."

Figure 9–1   Scoring Sheet for Concepts About Print Test

CAP Test Scoring Sheet

Name _____   Date _____

Title of Book _____

Check the items that the child demonstrates.

1. Book-Orientation Concepts
   - ☐ Shows the front of a book.
   - ☐ Turns to the first page of the story.
   - ☐ Shows where to start reading on a page.

2. Directionality Concepts
   - ☐ Shows the direction of print across a line of text.
   - ☐ Shows the direction of print on a page with more than one line of print.
   - ☐ Points to track words as the teacher reads.

3. Letter and Word Concepts
   - ☐ Points to any letter on a page.
   - ☐ Points to a particular letter on a page.
   - ☐ Puts fingers around any word on a page.
   - ☐ Puts fingers around a particular word on a page.
   - ☐ Puts fingers around any sentence on a page.
   - ☐ Points to the first and last letters of a word.
   - ☐ Points to a period or other punctuation mark.
   - ☐ Points to a capital letter.

Summary Comments:

Assessment Tools

Assessing Students' Word Identification and Fluency

The goal of word identification is for students to read words accurately, rapidly, and automatically. Teachers listen to students read aloud to determine whether they can read words automatically and have strategies for unlocking unfamiliar words. Children in the primary grades learn to read high-frequency sight words, such as *said* and *what,* and apply phonics skills to "sound out" other unfamiliar words. Older students extend this knowledge by learning how to break multisyllabic words into syllables to facilitate pronunciation.

Students who read fluently are better able to comprehend what they read because they have the mental energy to focus on what they are reading. Teachers monitor students' fluency as they listen to students read aloud. They check to see that students read with appropriate speed, intonation, and pausing.

Teachers often take running records of students' oral reading to assess their word identification and reading fluency (Clay, 1985). With a running record, teachers calculate the percentage of words the student reads correctly and then analyze the miscues or errors. They make a series of check marks on a sheet of paper as the child reads each word correctly and use other marks to indicate words that the student substitutes, repeats, mispronounces, or doesn't know, as Mrs. McNeal did in the vignette at the

See Chapter 5, "Developing Fluent Readers and Writers," to read more about word identification.

Assessment Tools

Phonemic Awareness and Phonics

Teachers in kindergarten and first grade monitor students' growing phonemic awareness by using classroom activities and these test instruments:

Phonemic Awareness in Young Children (Adams, Foorman, Lundberg & Beeler, 1997)
Test of Phonological Awareness (Torgesen & Bryant, 1994)
Yopp-Singer Test of Phonemic Segmentation (Yopp, 1995)

Teachers use these assessments from Clay's *Observational Survey* (1993) to assess young children's knowledge of letters of the alphabet, phonics, and words:

Letter Identification
Word Test
Dictation Task

Teachers in kindergarten through second grade can also use the Tile Test (Norman & Calfee, 2004) to assess students' knowledge of phonics, and in grades 3 through 8, teachers use The Names Test: A Quick Assessment of Decoding Ability (Cunningham, 1990; Duffelmeyer et al., 1994) to assess students' knowledge of phonics.

beginning of the chapter. Although teachers can take the running record on a blank sheet of paper, it is much easier to make a copy of the page or pages the student will read and take the running record next to or on top of the actual text. Using a copy of the text is especially important when assessing middle- and upper-grade students who read more complex texts and read them more quickly than younger students do.

Running Records

The teacher is taking a running record to assess the first grader's reading. The student reads aloud at his reading level while the teacher makes a word-by-word record of the student's reading—including errors and corrections he makes. Afterward, they will talk about the student's reading strengths and weaknesses it reveals. Running records are a quick and efficient way to gather information about the strategies and skills children use to decode and comprehend texts they read orally. Teachers use this information to group students, choose instructional materials, and monitor students' strategy knowledge.

After identifying the words the student misread, teachers calculate the percentage of words the student read correctly. Teachers use the percentage of words read correctly to determine whether the book or other reading material is too easy, too difficult, or appropriate for the student at this time. If the student reads 95% or more of the words correctly, the book is easy or at the independent reading level for that child. If the student reads 90–94% of the words correctly, the book is at the student's instructional level. If the student reads fewer than 90% of the words correctly, the book is too difficult for the student to read: It is at the student's frustration level.

Teachers can categorize miscues or errors according to the semantic, graphophonic, and syntactic cueing systems in order to examine what word-identification

Figure 9–2   Miscue Analysis of Seth's Errors

Child ___ Seth ___ Date ___ Jan. 18 ___

Text ___ The Pot of Gold (Level 16) ___

WORDS			MEANING	VISUAL	SYNTAX
Text	Child	Self-corrected?	Similar meaning?	Graphophonic similarity?	Grammatically acceptable?
Grumble	Grumply			✓	
always	–				
didn't	did not		✓	✓	✓
I'll	I		✓	✓	✓
move	make			✓	✓
scarf	safr			✓	
of	or			✓	
my	me	✓		✓	
scarf	self			✓	
taken	take		✓	✓	
scarf	scafer			✓	
that	they	✓		✓	
may	maybe			✓	
still	sit			✓	

Analysis: Seth overrelies on visual cues and rarely self-corrects errors.

Assessment Tools

Word Identification and Fluency

Being able to rapidly identify words without having to use word-analysis skills is an important part of becoming a fluent reader. Teachers often have students read lists of high-frequency words or word cards with the high-frequency words written on them. Students individually read the lists of words and teachers mark which words students can read correctly. By third grade, students should be able to read the 100 most frequently used words (see page 141). Teachers can also use Fry's New Instant Word Lists (1980) or another graded word list of high-frequency words to assess students' word-identification skills. Teachers also use The Names Test: A Quick Assessment of Decoding Ability (Cunningham, 1990) to monitor older, struggling students' word-identification skills.

Teachers take running records (Clay, 1993) to monitor students' oral reading, and assess their fluency. They categorize students' miscues or errors according to the semantic, graphophonic, and syntactic cueing systems in order to examine what word-identification strategies students are using.

strategies students are using. As they categorize the miscues, teachers should ask themselves these questions:

- Does the reader self-correct the miscue?
- Does the miscue change the meaning of the sentence?
- Is the miscue phonologically similar to the word in the text?
- Is the miscue acceptable within the syntax (or structure) of the sentence?

The errors that interfere with meaning and those that are syntactically unacceptable are the most serious because the student doesn't realize that reading should make sense. Errors can be classified and charted; Figure 9–2 shows the miscue analysis of the errors that Seth made on the running record in the vignette at the beginning of the chapter. Only words that students mispronounce or substitute can be analyzed; repetitions and omissions are not calculated.

Running records are an effective assessment tool because they are authentic (Shea, 2000). Students demonstrate how they read using their regular reading materials as teachers make a detailed account of their ability to read a book. Teachers collect valuable information about the strategies and skills students use to decode words and construct meaning. Check the box above for more information about word-identification and fluency assessment tools.

Determining Students' Instructional Reading Level

Thousands and thousands of books are available for children, and effective teachers match students with books written at appropriate difficulty levels. Children need books written at an appropriate level of difficulty because they are more likely to be successful reading books that are neither too hard nor too easy, and research has shown that children who do the most reading make the greatest gains in reading. Even though many books seem to be of similar difficulty because of the size of print, length of the book, or number of illustrations, they are not necessarily at the same reading level.

Traditional Readability Formulas. For the past 40 years or more, teachers have used readability formulas to estimate the difficulty level of trade books and textbooks. Readability levels serve as rough gauges of text difficulty and are reported as grade-level scores. If a book has a readability score of fifth grade, for example, teachers can assume that many average fifth-grade readers will be able to read it. Sometimes readability scores are marked with *RL* and a grade level, such as *RL 5,* on the back covers of paperback trade books.

Traditional readability scores are usually determined using vocabulary difficulty and sentence complexity, as measured by word and sentence length. However, the formulas don't take into account the experience and knowledge that readers bring to their reading, their cognitive and linguistic backgrounds, or their motivation or purpose for reading.

One fairly quick and simple readability formula is the Fry Readability Graph, developed by Edward Fry (1968); Figure 9–3 presents the Fry Readability Graph and lists the steps in using the formula to predict the reading-level score for a text, ranging from first grade through college level. Teachers should always consider using a readability formula as an aid in evaluating textbook and trade book selections for classroom use, but they cannot assume that materials rated as appropriate for a particular grade level will be appropriate for all students at that grade level. Teachers need to recognize the effectiveness of readability formulas as a tool but remember that these formulas have limitations.

Many reading selections that might seem very different actually score at the same level. For example, *Sarah, Plain and Tall* (MacLachlan, 1985), *Tales of a Fourth Grade Nothing* (Blume, 1972), *Bunnicula: A Rabbit-Tale of Mystery* (Howe & Howe, 1979), and *The Hundred Penny Box* (Mathis, 1975) all score at the third-grade reading level according to Fry's Readability Graph, even though their lengths, illustrations, topics, and type sizes differ significantly.

Leveled Books. Basal readers have traditionally been leveled according to grade levels, but grade-level designations, especially in first grade, are too broad. Reading Recovery teachers have developed a text gradient to match children to books that are neither too hard nor too easy for them (Fountas & Pinnell, 1996). Barbara Peterson (2001) examined reading materials for young children to determine the characteristics of texts that support beginning readers. She identified five criteria:

1. *Placement of text.* Books with consistent placement of text on the page are easier for children to read than books with varied placement; and books with only one line of text on a page are easier to read than books with two or more lines of text.

2. *Repetition.* Text that is highly predictable, with one or two patterns and few word changes, is easier to read than less predictable text with varied sentence patterns.

3. *Language structures.* Books in which the text is similar to the children's oral language patterns are easier to read than text using written language or "book" structures.

4. *Content.* Books about familiar objects and experiences are easier to read than books about unfamiliar topics or those using unfamiliar, specialized vocabulary.

5. *Illustrations.* Pictures in which the meaning of the text is visually illustrated are more supportive than illustrations that are minimally related to the text.

Using these criteria, Reading Recovery teachers identified 26 levels for kindergarten through sixth grade. A sample trade book for each level is shown in Figure 9–4;

Figure 9-3   The Fry Readability Graph

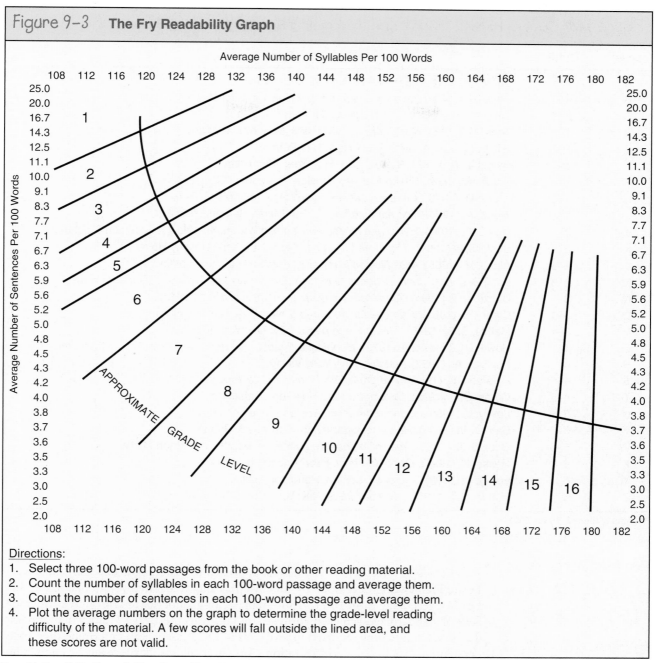

Directions:
1. Select three 100-word passages from the book or other reading material.
2. Count the number of syllables in each 100-word passage and average them.
3. Count the number of sentences in each 100-word passage and average them.
4. Plot the average numbers on the graph to determine the grade-level reading difficulty of the material. A few scores will fall outside the lined area, and these scores are not valid.

From "A Readability Formula That Saves Time," by E. Fry, 1968, *Journal of Reading, 11,* p. 587.

8,500 other leveled books are listed in *Matching Books to Readers: Using Leveled Books in Guided Reading, K–3* (Fountas & Pinnell, 1999) and *Guiding Readers and Writers Grades 3–6* (Fountas & Pinnell, 2001). Teachers are using the same criteria to level books for use in their classrooms. After they level the books, teachers code them with letters written on colored circles and place all books at the same level together in baskets or boxes.

Figure 9-4 Books Ranked According to the Reading Recovery Leveling System

Level	Grade	Book
A	K	Burningham, J. (1985). *Colors.* New York: Crown.
B	K–1	Carle, E. (1987). *Have you seen my cat?* New York: Scholastic.
C	K–1	Williams, S. (1989). *I went walking.* Orlando, FL: Harcourt Brace.
D	1	Peek, M. (1985). *Mary wore her red dress.* New York: Clarion.
E	1	Hill, E. (1980). *Where's Spot?* New York: Putnam.
F	1	Hutchins, P. (1968). *Rosie's walk.* New York: Macmillan.
G	1	Shaw, N. (1986). *Sheep in a jeep.* Boston: Houghton Mifflin.
H	1–2	Kraus, R. (1970). *Whose mouse are you?* New York: Macmillan.
I	1–2	Wood, A. (1984). *The napping house.* San Diego: Harcourt Brace.
J	2	Rylant, C. (1991). *Henry and Mudge and the bedtime thumps.* New York: Simon & Schuster.
K	2	Stevens, J. (1992). *The three billy goats Gruff.* New York: Holiday House.
L	2–3	Allard, H. (1985). *Miss Nelson is missing!* Boston: Houghton Mifflin.
M	2–3	Park, B. (1992). *Junie B. Jones and the stupid smelly bus.* New York: Random House.
N	3	Danziger, P. (1994). *Amber Brown is not a crayon.* New York: Viking.
O	3–4	Cleary, B. (1981). *Ramona Quimby, age 8.* New York: HarperCollins.
P	3–4	Mathis, S. B. (1975). *The hundred penny box.* New York: Viking.
Q	4	Howe, D., & Howe, J. (1979). *Bunnicula: A rabbit-tale of mystery.* New York: Atheneum.
R	4	Paulsen, G. (1987). *Hatchet.* New York: Viking.
S	4–5	Paterson, K. (1984). *The great Gilly Hopkins.* New York: Crowell.
T	4–5	Curtis, C. P. (1999). *Bud, not Buddy.* New York: Delacorte.
U	5	Lowry, L. (1989). *Number the stars.* Boston: Houghton Mifflin.
V	5–6	Sachar, L. (1999). *Holes.* New York: Farrar, Straus & Giroux.
W	5–6	Choi, S. N. (1991). *Year of impossible goodbyes.* Boston: Houghton Mifflin.
X	6	Hesse, K. (1997). *Out of the dust.* New York: Scholastic.
Y	6	Lowry, L. (1993). *The giver.* Boston: Houghton Mifflin.
Z	6	Hinton, S. E. (1967). *The outsiders.* New York: Puffin/Penguin.

Fountas & Pinnell, 1999, 2001.

The Lexile Framework. The newest approach to matching books to readers is the Lexile Framework, developed by MetaMetrics and available through Scholastic, Inc. Lexile levels range from 100 to 1300, representing kindergarten through 12th grade. Several standardized achievement tests are linked to the Lexile Framework, and students' scores are now reported in lexile levels. Or, students can determine their independent, instructional, and frustration scores according to lexile levels by completing the Scholastic Reading Inventory, a computerized reading test in which they silently read text passages and answer comprehension questions.

Many trade books are designated by lexile levels so that teachers can help students choose appropriate books according to their lexile levels. The sixth-grade level, for example, ranges from lexile levels 850 to 1000; trade books that have been leveled in the sixth-grade range according to the Lexile Framework include *Shiloh* (Naylor, 1991), *The Lion, the Witch and the Wardrobe* (Lewis, 1994), and *The Black Pearl* (O'Dell, 1967). Whether these particular books are appropriate for students reading at the sixth-grade level depends on the topics of the books, authors' writing styles, and students' interests. However, the lexile levels provide assistance in matching students to books. Figure 9–5 presents a list of trade books ranging from 100–1300.

Kits With Leveled Books

Teachers use assessment kits with leveled books to monitor and assess children's reading development over time. These assessments identify children's instructional reading levels and document how well children use the cueing systems and demonstrate specific reading behaviors. Here are three popular assessment kits with collections of leveled texts ranging from kindergarten to fifth-grade reading levels:

Beaver, J. (2001). *Developmental reading assessment.* Glenview, IL: Celebration Press/Addison-Wesley.

On-the-mark assessment of reading behavior. (2001). Bothell, WA: Wright Group/McGraw-Hill.

Nelley, E. & Smith, A. (2000). *Rigby PM benchmark kit: A reading assessment resource for grades K–5.* Crystal Lake, IL: Rigby.

These assessment kits have collections of leveled books ranging from kindergarten to fifth grade, scoring sheets, and a variety of other assessments including phonemic awareness and phonics tests and lists of high-frequency words.

Teachers work individually with children. The teacher selects a text for a child to read. After the teacher introduces the book, the child reads it and the teacher takes a running record of the child's reading. Then the child retells the text and answers comprehension questions. The teacher scores the reading and analyzes the results, and testing continues until the teacher determines the child's instructional level.

The Lexile Framework appears to be a promising program, because the wide range of possible scores allows teachers at all grade levels to more closely match students and books. As more and more books are leveled using the Lexile Framework, it seems likely that lexile levels will become increasingly important in reading instruction; however, matching students to books is often more complicated because students' background knowledge, motivation, and other individual factors influence reading success.

Assessing Students' Comprehension

Comprehension is the goal of reading, and students demonstrate their comprehension in many ways. The comments they write in reading logs and make during grand conversations and instructional conversations provide evidence. Children's interest in a book is sometimes an indicator, too: When children dismiss a book as "boring," they may really mean that it is confusing.

Story retelling and the cloze procedure are two informal assessment activities. In a story retelling, teachers ask students to retell the story in their own words; this approach is especially useful with emergent readers (Gambrell, Pfeiffer, & Wilson, 1985; Morrow, 1985). In the cloze procedure, teachers choose an excerpt of 100 to 300 words from a selection students have read, delete every fifth word from the passage, and replace the deleted words with blanks. Then students read the passage and write the missing words in the blanks. Students use their knowledge of the topic, narrative or expository structure, English word order, and the meaning of the words in the sentences to guess the missing words.

To read more about comprehension, see Chapter 7, "Facilitating Students' Comprehension: Reader Factors," and Chapter 8, "Facilitating Students' Comprehension: Text Factors."

Level	Grade	Book
100–149	K	Carle, E. (1989). *The very busy spider.* New York: Philomel.
150–199	K–1	Ziefert, H. (1999). *Turnip.* New York: HarperCollins.
200–249	1	Bridwell, N. (1985). *Clifford the big red dog.* New York: Scholastic.
250–299	1	McDermott, G. (1987). *Anansi the spider.* New York: Holt.
300–349	1–2	Allard, H. (1977). *Miss Nelson is missing!* Boston: Houghton Mifflin.
350–399	2	Thaler, M. (1989). *The teacher from the black lagoon.* New York: Scholastic.
400–449	2	Coerr, E. (1986). *The Josefina story quilt.* New York: HarperCollins.
450–499	2–3	Henkes, K. (1991). *Chrysanthemum.* New York: Morrow.
500–549	3	Rathmann, P. (1995). *Officer Buckle and Gloria.* New York: Putnam.
550–599	3–4	Sobol, D. (1982). *Encyclopedia Brown saves the day.* New York: Dell.
600–649	3–4	Cole, J. (1992). *The magic school bus on the ocean floor.* New York: Scholastic.
650–699	4	Lowry, L. (1989). *Number the stars.* Boston: Houghton Mifflin.
700–749	4	Howe, D., & Howe, J. (1979). *Bunnicula: A rabbit-tale of mystery.* New York: Atheneum.
750–799	4–5	Creech, S. (1994). *Walk two moons.* New York: HarperCollins.
800–849	5	Dahl, R. (1964). *Charlie and the chocolate factory.* New York: Knopf.
850–899	5–6	Naylor, P. (1991). *Shiloh.* New York: Simon & Schuster.
900–949	6–7	Lewis, C. S. (1994). *The lion, the witch and the wardrobe.* New York: HarperCollins.
950–999	7	O'Dell, S. (1967). *The black pearl.* Boston: Houghton Mifflin.
1000–1049	8	Philbrick, R. (1993). *Freak the mighty.* New York: Scholastic.
1050–1099	9–10	Tolkien, J. R. R. (1973). *The hobbit.* Boston: Houghton Mifflin.
1100–1149	10–11	Macaulay, D. (1975). *Pyramid.* Boston: Houghton Mifflin.
1150–1199	11–12	Brooks, B. (1984). *The moves make the man.* New York: HarperCollins.
1200–1300	12	Alcott, L. M. (1968). *Little women.* Boston: Little, Brown.

Figure 9–5   **Books Ranked According to the Lexile Framework**

Teachers use commercial tests called informal reading inventories (IRIs) to determine students' reading levels. The reading levels are expressed as grade-level scores—second-grade level or sixth-grade level, for example. The IRI is an individually administered reading test and is typically composed of graded word lists, graded passages from stories and informational books, and comprehension questions. This inventory can also be used to assess students' reading strengths and weaknesses.

The graded word lists consist of 10 to 20 words at each grade level, from first grade through eighth. Students read the lists of words until they reach a point when the words become too difficult for them; this indicates an approximate level for students to begin reading the graded reading passages. In addition, teachers can note the decoding skills that students use to identify words presented in isolation.

Scaffolding Struggling Readers

How can my struggling readers choose books they can really read?

Stock your classroom library with books written at your students' reading levels, not just grade-level books, and teach them how to choose books. Have students choose a book that interests them and then read a page aloud to check the reading level. If they read it fluently, chunking the words into phrases, and with good intonation and high word recognition (missing three words or less), the book is probably suitable. Too often, struggling readers choose books that are too difficult for them, but when they attempt to read these "too hard" books, they give up in frustration. In contrast, when students read easier books—books at their independent reading level—they are more successful and view reading more positively.

Comprehension

The traditional way to check students' comprehension is to ask literal, inferential, and evaluative questions after reading, but there are better ways to assess comprehension. Teachers can examine students' entries in reading logs, note students' comments during grand conversations, and consider how students apply what they have learned in the projects they develop after reading. Two informal assessments are story retellings and cloze procedure.

Teachers use informal reading inventories (IRIs) to diagnose students' reading levels. A variety of commercially published IRIs are available, including the following:

Analytical Reading Inventory (Woods & Moe, 2003)
Critical Reading Inventory (Applegate, Quinn & Applegate, 2003)
Developmental Reading Assessment (Beaver, 2001)
Flynt-Cooter Reading Inventory for the Classroom (Flynt & Cooter, 2004)
Qualitative Reading Inventory - 3 (Leslie & Caldwell, 2000)

Other IRIs accompany basal reading series, and teachers can construct their own using textbooks or trade books written at each reading level.

The graded reading passages are series of narrative and expository passages, ranging in difficulty. Students read these passages orally or silently and then answer a series of comprehension questions. The questions are designed to focus on big ideas, inferences, and vocabulary. Teachers use scoring sheets to record students' performance, and they analyze the results to see how readers use strategies in context, how they identify unknown words, and how they comprehend what they read.

Students' scores on the IRI can be used to calculate their independent, instructional, and frustration reading levels. At the independent level, students can read the text comfortably and without assistance; students read books at this level for pleasure and during reading workshop. At the instructional level, students can read textbooks and trade books successfully with teacher guidance; books selected for literature focus units and literature circles book clubs should be at students' instructional levels. At the frustration level, the reading materials are too difficult for students to read, so students often don't understand what they are reading. As the name implies, students become very frustrated when they attempt to read trade books and textbooks at this level. When books featured in literature focus units are too difficult for some students to read, teachers need to make provisions for these students; they can use shared reading, buddy reading, or reading aloud to students.

IRIs are also used to identify students' listening capacity levels. Teachers read aloud passages written at or above students' frustration levels and ask the comprehension questions. If students can answer the questions, they understand the passage. Teachers then know that students can comprehend books and texts at that level when they are read aloud and that students have the potential to improve their reading comprehension to this level. The assessment tools box shown above provides more information on IRIs.

Assessing Students' Vocabulary

Students need to understand the meaning of words they read; otherwise, they have problems decoding words and understanding what they are reading. Students learn

To learn more about vocabulary, see Chapter 6, "Expanding Students' Knowledge of Words."

the meanings of 3,000 or more words each year, or 8–10 new words every day, and they learn most of them informally or without direct instruction (Stahl, 1999).

Teachers monitor students' use of new vocabulary as they talk and write about books they are reading for content-area units. In addition to determining whether students know the meaning of specific words, teachers consider whether students can differentiate among related words, such as *grumpy, surly, crabby, stern, rude, discourteous, snarling, grouchy,* and *waspish.* Another way to examine vocabulary knowledge is to ask students to name synonyms or antonyms of words. Teachers also monitor students' knowledge about root words and affixes; for example, if students know that *legible* means "readable," can they figure out what *illegible* means?

There are very few vocabulary tests available, so teachers often depend on informal measures of students' vocabulary knowledge. Some of the comprehension questions on informal reading inventories focus on the meanings of words, and students' answers to these items provide one indication of their vocabulary knowledge.

Assessing Students' Writing

Teachers assess both the process students use as they write and the quality of their compositions. They observe as students use the writing process to develop their compositions, and they conference with students as they revise and edit their writing. Teachers notice, for example, whether students use writing strategies to gather and organize ideas for writing, whether they take into account feedback from classmates in revising their writing, and whether they think about their audience when they write. They also have students keep all drafts of their compositions in writing folders so that they can document their writing processes.

Teachers develop rubrics, or scoring guides, to assess the quality of students' writing (Farr & Tone, 1994). Rubrics make the analysis of writing simpler and the assessment process more reliable and consistent. Rubrics may have 4, 5, or 6 levels, with descriptors related to ideas, organization, language, and mechanics at each level. Some rubrics are general and are appropriate for almost any writing assignment, whereas others are designed for a specific writing assignment. Figure 9–6 presents a second-grade rubric.

Assessment Tools

Writing

Teachers use rubrics to assess the quality of students' compositions. Some rubrics are general and can be used for almost any writing assignment, whereas others are designed for a specific writing assignment. Sometimes teachers use rubrics developed by school districts; at other times, they develop their own rubrics to assess the specific components and qualities they have stressed in their classrooms. Rubrics should have 4 to 6 achievement levels and address ideas, organization, language, and mechanics. Search the Internet for writing rubrics. Many examples of rubrics are available that have been developed by teachers, school districts, state departments of education, and publishers of educational materials.

In addition, kindergarten and first-grade teachers can administer Clay's Writing Vocabulary Test, part of the *Observational Survey* (1993), to examine how many words young children can write in 10 minutes.

Figure 9-6   **Second-Grade Rubric for Stories**

5	Writing has an original title. Story shows originality, sense of humor, or cleverness. Writer uses paragraphs to organize ideas. Writing contains few spelling, capitalization, or punctuation errors. Writer varies sentence structure and word choice. Writer shows a sense of audience.
4	Writing has an appropriate title. Beginning, middle, and end of the story are well developed. A problem or goal is identified in the story. Writing includes details that support plot, characters, and setting. Writing is organized into paragraphs. Writing contains few capitalization and punctuation errors. Writer spells most high-frequency words correctly and spells unfamiliar words phonetically.
3	Writing may have a title. Writing has at least two of the three parts of a story (beginning, middle, and end). Writing shows a sequence of events. Writing is not organized into paragraphs. Spelling, grammar, capitalization, or punctuation errors may interfere with meaning.
2	Writing has at least one of the three parts of a story (beginning, middle, and end). Writing may show a partial sequence of events. Writing is brief and underdeveloped. Writing has spelling, grammar, capitalization, and punctuation errors that interfere with meaning.
1	Writing lacks a sense of story. An illustration may suggest a story. Writing is brief and may support the illustration. Some words may be recognizable, but the writing is difficult to read.

Assessment Tools

Teachers use rubrics to assess writing. They read the composition and highlight words and phrases in the rubric that best describe it. Usually words and phrases in more than one level are marked, so the score is determined by examining the highlighted words and phrases and noting which level has the most highlighted words.

Students, too, can learn to create rubrics to assess the quality of their writing. To be successful, they need to examine examples of other students' writing and determine the qualities that demonstrate strong, average, and weak papers; teachers need to model how to address the qualities at each level in the rubric. Skillings and Ferrell (2000) taught second and third graders to develop the criteria for evaluating their writing, and the students moved from using the rubrics their teachers prepared to creating their own 3-point rubrics, which they labeled as the very best level, the okay level, and the not so good level. Perhaps the most important outcome of teaching students to develop rubrics, according to Skillings and Ferrell, is that students develop metacognitive strategies and the ability to think about themselves as writers.

Figure 9-7	Steps in Determining a Student's Stage of Spelling Development

1. **Choose Writing Samples**
   Teachers choose one or more writing samples written by a single student to analyze. In the primary grades, the samples should total at least 50 words, in the middle grades at least 100 words, and in the upper grades at least 200 words. Teachers must be able to decipher most words in the sample in order to analyze it.

2. **Identify Misspelled Words**
   Teachers read the writing samples and then note the misspelled words and identify the words the student was trying to spell. When necessary, teachers check with the student who wrote the composition to determine the intended word.

3. **Make a Spelling Analysis Chart**
   Teachers draw a chart with five columns, one for each of the stages of spelling development, at the bottom of the student's writing sample or on another sheet of paper.

4. **Categorize the Student's Misspelled Words**
   Teachers classify the student's spelling errors according to the stage of development. They list each spelling error in one of the stages, ignoring proper nouns, capitalization errors, and grammar errors. Teachers often ignore poorly formed letters or reversed letter forms in kindergarten and first grade, but these are significant errors when they are made by older students. They write both the student's spelling and the correct spelling in parentheses to make the analysis easier.

5. **Tally the Errors**
   Teachers count the number of errors in each column to determine the stage with the most errors, which indicates the student's current stage of spelling development.

6. **Identify Topics for Instruction**
   Teachers examine the misspelled words to identify spelling concepts for instruction, such as vowel patterns, possessives, homophones, syllabication, and cursive handwriting skills.

Assessment Tools

Assessing Students' Spelling

For more information on children's spelling development, see Chapter 4, "Cracking the Alphabetic Code."

The choices students make as they spell words are important indicators of their knowledge of both phonics and spelling. For example, a student who spells phonetically might spell *money as mune,* and other students who are experimenting with long vowels might spell the word as *monye* or *monie.* No matter how they spell the word, students are demonstrating what they know about phonics and spelling. Teachers classify and analyze the words students misspell in their writing to gauge students' level of spelling development and to plan for instruction. The steps in determining a students's stage of spelling development are explained in Figure 9–7. An analysis of a first grader's spelling development is shown in Figure 9–8.

Teachers can analyze the errors in students' compositions, analyze students' errors on weekly spelling tests, or administer diagnostic tests such as Bear's Elementary Qualitative

Figure 9–8 An Analysis of a First Grader's Spelling Development

Writing Sample

To bay a perezun at home kob
uz anb seb that a bome wuz in
or skuwl anb mab uz go at zib
anb makbe uz wat a haf uf
a awr anb it mab uz wazt or
time on loren ee ing.

THE eNb

Translation

Today a person at home called us and said that a bomb was in our school and made us go outside and made us wait a half of an hour and it made us waste our time on learning. The end.

Spelling Analysis Chart

Emergent	Letter Name	Within-Word Patterns	Syllables and Affixes	Derivational Relations
	kod (called)	bome (bomb)	peresun (person)	
	sed (said)	or (our)	loreneeing (learning)	
	wus (was)	skuwl (school)		
	mad (made)	makde (made)		
	at (out)	uf (of)		
	sid (side)	awr (hour)		
	wat (wait)	or (our)		
	haf (half)			
	mad (made)			
	wazt (waste)			

Conclusion

Marc spelled 56% of the words correctly, and most of his spelling errors were in the Letter Name and Within-Word Patterns stages, which is typical of first graders' spelling.

Topics for Instruction

high-frequency words
CVCe vowel pattern
-ed inflectional ending

Spelling

Teachers monitor students' spelling development by examining misspelled words in the compositions that students write. They can classify students' spelling according to the five stages of spelling development and plan instruction on the basis of this analysis. Teachers also examine students' misspellings in weekly spelling tests and in diagnostic tests, including the following:

Developmental Spelling Analysis (Ganske, 2000)
Elementary Qualitative Spelling Inventory (Grades K–6) (Bear et al., 2004)
Upper Level Qualitative Spelling Inventory (Grades 6–8) (Bear et al., 2004)
Qualitative Inventory of Spelling Development (Henderson, 1990)
Spelling Knowledge Inventory (Fresch & Wheaton, 2002)

After teachers mark spellings on the tests as correct or incorrect, they analyze students' errors to determine which skills they use correctly, which skills they are using but confusing, and which skills they are not yet using. Then teachers plan instruction based on the test results.

Spelling Inventory for grades K–6 and his Upper Level Qualitative Spelling Inventory for grades 6–8 (Bear, Invernizzi, Templeton, & Johnston, 2004). These tests include 20–25 spelling words listed according to difficulty and can easily be administered to small groups or whole classes. Other spelling tests are available to provide grade-level scores.

Assessing Students' Attitudes and Motivation

Students' attitude and motivation affect their success in learning to read and write (Gambrell, 2001; Walberg & Tsai, 1985). Students who are motivated are likely to have positive attitudes about reading. Those students who view themselves as successful readers and writers are more likely to be successful, and students whose families value literacy are more likely to be motivated to read and write.

Teachers conference with students and parents to understand students' reading and writing habits at home, their interests and hobbies, and their view of themselves as readers and writers. When they know more about students and their interests, teachers can help them select more interesting books, and they can get parents more involved in reading activities at home.

Researchers have developed several survey instruments with which teachers can assess students' attitudes about reading and writing. Two surveys designed for third through sixth

Nurturing English Learners

How can I help my EL students who are "stalled"?

Not all students are eager to learn English: Some see learning English as a repudiation of their families and home cultures, and others don't understand the opportunities that are available to them only if they are fluent in English. During the primary grades, students may learn to converse in English, but in the middle grades, their English development seems to "stall," and they don't learn the academic language necessary to be successful in school. Check your English learners' attitudes toward English and their English-speaking classmates as well as their motivation to learn to speak, read, and write English using an attitude and motivation survey. Try adapting some of the questions to probe your students' feelings in order to find ways to help them.

Attitudes and Motivation

Students' attitudes, values, and motivation play a significant role in their literacy learning. Teachers monitor students' attitudes informally as they talk with them about books they are reading and compositions they are writing.

Researchers have developed instruments that measure students' perceptions of themselves as readers and writers. They probe students' past literacy successes, their comparison of themselves with their peers, input the students have received from teachers and classmates, and feelings students experience during reading and writing. Here are five surveys:

Elementary Reading Attitude Survey (McKenna & Kear, 1990)
Motivation to Read Profile (Gambrell, Palmer, Codling, & Mazzoni, 1996)
Reader Self-Perception Scale (Henk & Melnick, 1995)
Writer Self-Perception Scale (Bottomley et al., 1997/1998)
Writing Attitude Survey (Kear, Coffman, McKenna, & Ambrosio, 2000)

All five instruments are readily available because they have been published in *The Reading Teacher*.

graders are the Reader Self-Perception Scale (Henk & Melnick, 1995) and the Writer Self-Perception Scale (Bottomley, Henk, & Melnick, 1997/1998). On these surveys, students respond to statements such as "I think I am a good reader" and "I write better than my classmates do" using a 5-level Likert scale (responses range from "strongly agree" to "strongly disagree"). Then teachers score students' responses and interpret the results to determine both overall and specific attitude levels.

McKenna and Kear (1990) developed the Elementary Reading Attitude Survey to assess first- through sixth-grade students' attitudes toward reading in school and reading for fun. The test consists of 20 questions about reading that begin with the stem "How do you feel . . . ?" Students respond by marking one of four pictures of Garfield, the cartoon cat; each picture depicts a different emotional state, ranging from positive to negative. This survey enables teachers to quickly estimate students' attitudes toward reading.

Monitoring Students' Progress

Teachers monitor students' learning day by day, and they use the results of their monitoring to make instructional decisions (Baskwill & Whitman, 1988; Winograd & Arrington, 1999). As they monitor students' learning, teachers learn about their students, about themselves as teachers, and about the impact of the instructional program. Following are four ways to monitor students' progress:

1. *Observe students as they read and write.* Effective teachers are "kid watchers," a term Yetta Goodman (1978) coined and defined as "direct and informal observation of students" (p. 37). To be effective kid watchers, teachers must understand how children learn to read and write. Some observation times should be planned when the teacher focuses on particular students and makes anecdotal notes about the students' involvement in literacy events. The focus is on what students do as they read or write, not on whether they are behaving properly or

working quietly. Of course, little learning can occur in disruptive situations, but during these observations, the focus is on literacy, not behavior.

2. *Take anecdotal notes of literacy events.* Teachers write brief notes as they observe students; the most useful notes describe specific events, report rather than evaluate, and relate the events to other information about the student (Rhodes & Nathenson-Mejia, 1992). Teachers make notes about students' reading and writing activities, the questions students ask, and the strategies and skills they use fluently or indicate confusion about. These records document students' growth and pinpoint problem areas for future minilessons or conferences. A teacher's anecdotal notes about sixth-grade students in the literature circle reading *Bunnicula: A Rabbit-Tale of Mystery* (Howe & Howe, 1979) appear in Figure 9–9.

Figure 9-9   **Anecdotal Notes About a Literature Circle**

March 7
Met with the *Bunnicula* literature circle as they started reading the book. They have their reading, writing, and discussion schedule set. Sari questioned how a dog could write the book. We reread the Editor's Note. She asked if Harold really wrote the book. She's the only one confused in the group. Is she always so literal? Mario pointed out that you have to know that Harold supposedly wrote the book to understand the first-person viewpoint of the book. Talked to Sari about fantasy. Told her she'll be laughing out loud as she reads this book. She doubts it.

March 8
Returned to *Bunnicula* literature circle for first grand conversation, especially to check on Sari. Annie, Mario, Ted, Rod, Laurie, and Belinda talked about their pets and imagine them taking over their homes. Sari is not getting into the book. She doesn't have any pets and can't imagine the pets doing these things. I asked if she wanted to change groups. Perhaps a realistic book would be better. She says no. Is that because Ted is in the group?

March 10
The group is reading chapters 4 and 5 today. Laurie asks questions about white vegetables and vampires. Rod goes to get an encyclopedia to find out about vampires. Mario asks about DDT. Everyone—even Sari—involved in reading.

March 13
During a grand conversation, students compare the characters Harold and Chester. The group plans to make a Venn diagram comparing the characters for the sharing on Friday. Students decide that character is the most important element, but Ted argues that humor is the most important element in the story. Other students say humor isn't an element. I asked what humor is a reaction to—characters or plot? I checked journals and all are up to date.

March 15
The group has finished reading the book. I share sequels from the class library. Sari grabs one to read. She's glad she stayed with the book. Ted wants to write his own sequel in writing workshop. Mario plans to write a letter to James Howe.

March 17
Ted and Sari talk about *Bunnicula* and share related books. Rod and Mario share the Venn diagram of characters. Annie reads her favorite part, and Laurie shows her collection of rabbits. Belinda hangs back. I wonder if she has been involved. I need to talk to her.

---

3. ***Conference with students.*** Teachers talk with students to monitor their progress in reading and writing activities as well as to set goals and help students solve problems. Following are seven types of conferences that teachers have with students:

- ***On-the-spot conferences.*** The teacher visits briefly with students at their desks to monitor some aspect of the students' work or to check on progress. These conferences are brief; the teacher may spend less than a minute at each student's desk.

- ***Prereading or prewriting conferences.*** The teacher and student make plans for reading or writing at the conference. At a prereading conference, they may talk about information related to the book, difficult concepts or vocabulary words related to the reading, or the reading log the student will keep. At a prewriting conference, they may discuss possible writing topics or how to narrow down a broad topic.

- ***Revising conferences.*** A small group of students meets with the teacher to get specific suggestions about revising their compositions. These conferences offer student writers an audience to provide feedback on how well they have communicated.

- ***Book discussion conferences.*** Students meet with the teacher to discuss the book they have read. They may share reading log entries, discuss plot or characters, compare the story to others they have read, or make plans to extend their reading.

- ***Editing conferences.*** The teacher reviews students' proofread compositions and helps them correct spelling, punctuation, capitalization, and other mechanical errors.

- ***Minilesson conferences.*** The teacher meets with students to explain a procedure, strategy, or skill (e.g., writing a table of contents, using the visualization strategy when reading, capitalizing proper nouns).

- ***Assessment conferences.*** The teacher meets with students after they have completed an assignment or project to talk about their growth as readers or writers. Students reflect on their competencies and set goals.

Often these conferences are brief and impromptu, held at students' desks as the teacher moves around the classroom. At other times, the conferences are planned, and students meet with the teacher at a designated conference table.

4. ***Collect students' work samples.*** Teachers have students collect their work in folders to document learning. Work samples might include reading logs, audiotapes of students' reading, photos of projects, videotapes of puppet shows and oral presentations, and books students have written. Students often choose some of these work samples to place in their portfolios.

IMPLEMENTING PORTFOLIOS IN THE CLASSROOM

Portfolios are systematic and meaningful collections of artifacts documenting students' literacy development over a period of time (Graves & Sunstein, 1992; Porter & Cleland, 1995; Tierney, Carter, & Desai, 1991). These collections are dynamic and reflect students' day-to-day reading and writing activities as well as across-the-curriculum activities. Students' work samples provide "windows" on the strategies they use as readers and writers. Not only do students select pieces to be placed in their portfolios, they also learn to establish criteria for their selections. Because of students' involvement in selecting pieces for their portfolios and reflecting on them, portfolio assessment respects students and their abilities. Portfolios help students, teachers, and parents see patterns of growth from one literacy milestone to another in ways that are not possible with other types of assessment.

Why Are Portfolio Programs Worthwhile?

There are many reasons why portfolio programs complement balanced reading programs. The most important one is that students become more involved in the assessment of their work and more reflective about the quality of their reading and writing. Other benefits include the following:

- Students feel ownership of their work.
- Students become more responsible about their work.
- Students set goals and are motivated to work toward accomplishing them.
- Students reflect on their accomplishments.
- Students make connections between learning and assessing.
- Students' self-esteem is enhanced.
- Students recognize the connection between process and product.
- Portfolios eliminate the need to grade all student work.
- Portfolios are used in student and parent conferences.
- Portfolios complement the information provided in report cards.

Rolling Valley Elementary School in Springfield, Virginia, implemented a portfolio program schoolwide, and the students overwhelmingly reported that by using portfolios, they were better able to show their parents what they were learning and also better able to set goals for themselves (Clemmons, Laase, Cooper, Areglado, & Dill, 1993). The teachers also reported that portfolios enabled them to assess their students more thoroughly, and their students were better able to see their own progress.

Nurturing English Learners

How can I make my EL students' assessment more meaningful?

Too often, students' achievement is equated with a test score, but teachers understand that a single number—17th percentile, for example—does not adequately describe what a student can do or the growth the student has made during a school year. Portfolios are especially effective for English learners because the artifacts document students' learning in ways that tests cannot. In addition to the work samples that all students keep in portfolios, teachers can document EL students' growth in other ways. For example, students can demonstrate their ability to read fluently on audiotapes and their knowledge of English conventions with writing samples. Students work with the teacher to chart their growth on graphs or checklists using data from the samples in their portfolios.

Collecting Work in Portfolios

Portfolios are folders, large envelopes, or boxes that hold students' work. Teachers often have students label and decorate large folders and then store them in plastic crates or large cardboard boxes. Students date and label items as they place them in their portfolios, and they often attach notes to the items to explain the context for the activity and why they selected this particular item. Students' portfolios should be stored in the classroom in a place where they are readily accessible; students like to review their portfolios periodically and add new pieces to them.

Students usually choose the items to place in their portfolios within the guidelines the teacher provides. Some students submit the original piece of work; others want to keep the original, so they place a copy in the portfolio instead. In addition to the reading and writing samples that can go directly into portfolios, students can record oral language and drama samples on audiotapes and videotapes to place in their portfolios. Large-size art and writing projects can be photographed, and the photographs can be placed in the portfolio. Student work might include books, choral readings on audiotapes, reading logs and learning logs, graphic organizers and other charts, multigenre projects, lists of books read, and compositions. This variety of work samples reflects the students' literacy programs. Samples from literature focus units, literature circles, reading and writing workshop, basal reading programs, and content-area units should be included.

One piece of writing from a third grader's portfolio is shown in Figure 9–10. This sample is a simulated letter written to Peter Rabbit from Mr. McGregor as a project during a literature focus unit on *The Tale of Peter Rabbit* (Potter, 1902). The student's teacher taught a minilesson on persuasive writing, and this student applied what he had learned in his letter. He placed it in his portfolio because he thought it "looked good" and because his classmates had really liked it when he shared it with them. His prewriting, the rough draft, and a scoring rubric were attached to the final copy shown in the figure. The scoring rubric also is shown.

The student and teacher scored the letter together using the rubric and rated it a 4 out of a possible 5 points. First, the child used the friendly letter format, so a check mark was placed on that line. Second, he applied in the letter what he had learned about persuasion: He suggested a deal to Peter and made a threat about what will happen if the rabbit comes back into the garden. A check mark was also placed on the second line. Next, he used character names and other information from the story in the

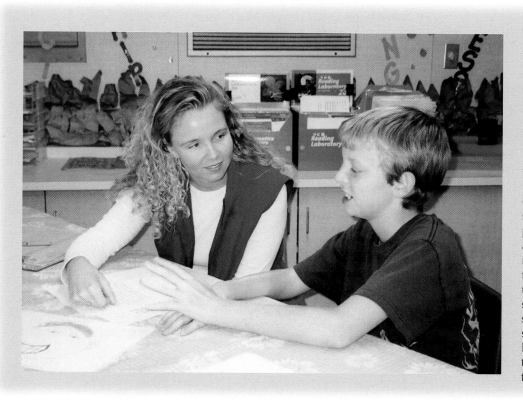

Conferences

This fourth grader meets with his teacher for 15 to 20 minutes to talk about his achievement at the end of the second grading period. Even though it is time-consuming, this teacher meets with each student at the end of every grading period to talk about the student's progress, identify standards-based accomplishments, select pieces to add to the portfolio, determine grades, and set goals for the next quarter. Through this process, teachers involve students in assessment, and students become more responsible for their own learning as they self-evaluate their progress and set goals for themselves.

Figure 9–10   **A Third Grader's Simulated Letter and Scoring Guide**

Dear Peter,

      I wish you would stop stesling my vegetables! I'll tell you what, I'll make a deal. I'll leave some vegetbles out once a week. **OK?** But if you go in my garden one more time with out permission then I will put you in my **Pie!** OH and....ammm.... thanks for the clothes. and rember all you have to do is **tell me** that you want some vegtables.

SiND BY Mr. McGregor

Rubric for Scoring Peter Rabbit Letters

_✓_ Uses the friendly letter format
_✓_ Is persuasive
_✓_ Uses information from the story
_____ Uses mostly correct spelling and other mechanics
_✓_ Paper is neat

Comments:

Very persuasive! I like the way you highlighted the important words. I hear Mr. McGregor's voice clearly in your letter.

Scoring guide:

4 or 5 ✓ = A
3 ✓   = B
2 ✓   = C
1 ✓   = D

Assessment Tools

persuasive argument, so the third item was checked, too. Fourth, the student and teacher looked at the spelling and other conventions. The teacher pointed out five misspelled words (*stesling–stealing, vegetbles–vegetables, rember–remember, vegtables–vegetables*, and *sind–signed*) and checked to see if they had been corrected on the rough draft during editing. All but one had, but the student had failed to use the corrected spellings in his final draft. After some consideration, the student and his teacher decided not to add a check mark on this item, even though the errors were minor and did not interfere with reading the letter. The student recognized that he needed to be more careful when he made his final copy. Finally, the paper was neat, so the fifth item was checked. In addition, the teacher commended this student for his lively writing style and the way he highlighted important words in his letter.

Many teachers collect students' work in folders, and they assume portfolios are basically the same as work folders; however, the two types of collections differ in several important ways. Perhaps the most important difference is that portfolios are student oriented, whereas work folders are usually teachers' collections—students choose which samples will be placed in portfolios, but teachers often place all completed assignments in work folders (Clemmons et al., 1993). Next, portfolios focus on students' strengths, not their weaknesses. Because students choose items for portfolios, they choose samples that best represent their literacy development. Another difference is that portfolios involve reflection (D'Aoust, 1992). Through reflection, students pause and become aware of their strengths as readers and writers. They also use their work samples to identify the literacy procedures, concepts, skills, and strategies they already know and the ones they need to focus on.

Involving Students in Self-Assessment

A portfolio is not just a collection of work samples; instead, it is a vehicle for engaging students in self-evaluation and goal setting (Clemmons et al., 1993). Students can learn to reflect on and assess their own reading and writing activities and their development as readers and writers (Stires, 1991). Teachers begin by asking students to think about their reading and writing in terms of contrasts. For reading, students identify the books they have read that they liked most and least, and ask themselves what these choices suggest about themselves as readers. They also identify what they do well in reading and what they need to improve about their reading. In writing, students make similar contrasts: They identify the compositions they thought were their best and others that were not so good, and they think about what they do well when they write and what they need to improve. By making these comparisons, students begin to reflect on their literacy development.

Teachers use minilessons and conferences to talk with students about the characteristics of good readers and writers. In particular, they discuss:

- what fluent reading is
- what reading skills and strategies students use
- how students demonstrate their comprehension
- how students value books they have read
- what makes a good project to extend reading
- what makes an effective piece of writing
- what writing skills and strategies students use
- how to use writing rubrics
- how the effective use of mechanical skills is a courtesy to readers

As students learn about what it means to be effective readers and writers, they acquire the tools they need to reflect on and evaluate their own reading and writing. They learn how to think about themselves as readers and writers and acquire the vocabulary to use in their reflections, such as "goal," "strategy," and "rubric."

Students write notes on items they choose to put into their portfolios. In these self-assessments, students explain the reasons for their choices and identify strengths and accomplishments in their work. In some classrooms, students write their reflections and other comments on index cards, and in other classrooms, they design special comment sheets that they attach to the items in their portfolios.

Clemmons et al. (1993) recommend collecting baseline reading and writing samples at the beginning of the school year and then conducting portfolio review conferences with students at the end of each grading period. At these conferences, the teacher and student talk about the items placed in the portfolio and the self-assessments the student has written. Together they also set goals for the next grading period. Students talk about what they want to improve or what they want to accomplish during the next grading period, and these points become their goals.

Self-assessment can also be used for an assessment at the end of the school year. Coughlan (1988) asked his seventh-grade students to "show me what you have learned about writing this year" and "explain how you have grown as a written language user, comparing what you knew in September to what you know now" (p. 375). These upper-grade students used a process approach to develop and refine their compositions, and they submitted all drafts with their final copies. Coughlan examined both the content of students' compositions and the strategies they used in thinking through the assignment and writing their responses. He found this "test" to be a very worthwhile project because it "forced the students to look within themselves . . . to realize just how much they had learned" (p. 378). Moreover, students' compositions verified what they had learned about writing and that they could articulate that learning.

Showcasing Students' Portfolios

At the end of the school year, many teachers organize "Portfolio Share Days" to celebrate students' accomplishments and to provide an opportunity for students to share their portfolios with classmates and the wider community (Porter & Cleland, 1995). Often family members, local businesspeople, school administrators, local politicians, college students, and others are invited to attend. Students and community members form small groups, and students share their portfolios, pointing out their accomplishments and strengths. This activity is especially useful in involving community members in the school and showing them the types of literacy activities in which students are involved as well as how students are becoming effective readers and writers.

These sharing days also help students accept responsibility for their own learning—especially those students who have not been as motivated as their classmates. When less-motivated students listen to their classmates talk about their work and how they have grown as readers and writers, they often decide to work harder the next year.

ASSIGNING GRADES

Assigning grades is one of the most difficult responsibilities placed on teachers. "Grading is a fact of life," according to Donald Graves (1983, p. 93), but he adds that teachers should use grades to encourage students, not to hinder their achievement. The assessment procedures described in this chapter encourage students because they document what students can do as they read and write. Reviewing and translating this documentation into grades is the difficult part, but unit assignment sheets make the job easier.

Unit Assignment Sheets

One way for teachers to monitor students' progress and grade their achievements is to use assignment sheets. Teachers create the assignment sheet as they plan the unit, make copies for each student, and then distribute them at the beginning of the unit. All assignments are listed on the sheet along with how they will be graded. These sheets can be developed for any type of unit—literature focus units, literature circles, reading and writing workshop, and content-area units. Teachers can also create assignment sheets to use with literacy centers.

An assignment sheet for a fifth-grade unit on *The Sign of the Beaver* (Speare, 1983) is shown in Figure 9–11. Students receive a copy of the assignment sheet at the beginning of the unit and keep it in their unit folders. Then, as they complete

---

Figure 9–11   An Assignment Sheet for a Literature Focus Unit

Checklist for <u>The Sign of the Beaver</u>

Name _____   Date _____

Student's Check		Teacher's Grade
_____	1. Read <u>The Sign of the Beaver</u>.	_____
_____	2. Make a map of Matt's journey in 1768. (10)	_____
_____	3. Keep a simulated journal as Matt or Attean. (20)	_____
_____	4. Do a word sort by characters. (5)	_____
_____	5. Listen to Elizabeth George Speare's taped interview and do a quickwrite about her. (5)	_____
_____	6. Do an open-mind portrait about one of the characters. (10)	_____
_____	7. Make a Venn diagram to compare/contrast Matt or Attean with yourself. (10)	_____
_____	8. Contribute to a model of the Indian village or the clearing.	_____
_____	9. Write a sequel or do another project. (20) My project is _____	_____
_____	10. Read other books from the text set. (10) _____ _____ _____	_____
_____	11. Write a self-assessment about your work, behavior, and effort in this unit. (10)	_____

TOTAL POINTS _____

Assessment Tools

the assignments, they check them off, so it is easy for the teacher to make periodic checks to monitor students' progress. At the end of the unit, the teacher collects the unit folders and grades the work.

Assignments can be graded as "done" or "not done," or they can be graded for quality. Teachers of middle- and upper-grade students often assign points to each activity on the assignment sheet so that the total point value for the unit is 100 points. Activities that involve more time and effort earn more points. The maximum number of points possible for each assignment is listed in parentheses in Figure 9–11.

Checklists have the power to enhance student learning and simplify assessment (Kuhs, Johnson, Agruso, & Monrad, 2001). Students tend to be more successful when they understand what is expected of them, and when teachers develop and distribute assignment sheets and other checklists at the beginning of a unit, students are much more likely to understand what is expected of them. Later, when teachers grade the students' assignments, the grading is easier because teachers have already identified the criteria for grading. Grading is fairer, too, because teachers use the same criteria to grade all students' assignments.

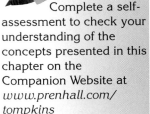

Complete a self-assessment to check your understanding of the concepts presented in this chapter on the Companion Website at *www.prenhall.com/ tompkins*

Review: How Effective Teachers Assess Students' Literacy Development

1. Teachers use assessment as an essential part of teaching.
2. Teachers use a variety of informal and formal assessment tools to assess students' literacy development.
3. Teachers take running records to assess students' reading fluency.
4. Teachers use informal reading inventories to determine students' comprehension levels.
5. Teachers examine both the students' reading and writing processes and the artifacts they produce.
6. Teachers use rubrics to assess the ideas, organization, vocabulary, style, and mechanics in students' compositions.
7. Teachers analyze students' spellings to determine the stage of development and plan for instruction based on students' developmental levels.
8. Teachers monitor students' learning using observation and anecdotal notes, conferences, checklists, and collections of students' work samples.
9. Teachers have students choose work samples to document their literacy development for portfolios.
10. Teachers encourage students to self-assess their work samples and set goals for future learning.

Professional References

Adams, M., Foorman, B., Lundberg, I., & Beeler, C. (1997). *Phonemic awareness in young children.* Baltimore: Paul H. Brookes.

Applegate, M. D., Quinn, K. B., & Applegate, A. J. (2003). *The critical reading inventory: Assessing students' reading and thinking.* Upper Saddle River, NJ: Merrill/Prentice Hall.

Baskwill, J., & Whitman, P. (1988). *Evaluation: Whole language, whole child.* New York: Scholastic.

Bear, D. R., Invernizzi, M., Templeton, S., & Johnston, F. (2004). *Words their way: Word study for phonics, vocabulary,* *and spelling instruction* (3rd ed.). Upper Saddle River, NJ: Merrill/Prentice Hall.

Beaver, J. (2001). *Developmental reading assessment.* Glenview, IL: Celebration Press/Addison-Wesley.

Bottomley, D. M., Henk, W. A., & Melnick, S. A. (1997/1998). Assessing children's views about themselves as writers using the Writer Self-Perception Scale. *The Reading Teacher, 51,* 286–296.

Clay, M. M. (1972). *Sand—the concepts about print test.* Portsmouth, NH: Heinemann.

Clay, M. M. (1979). *Stones—the concepts about print test.* Portsmouth, NH: Heinemann.

Clay, M. M. (1985). *The early detection of reading difficulties: A diagnostic survey with recovery procedures.* Portsmouth, NH: Heinemann.

Clay, M. M. (1991). *Becoming literate: The construction of inner control.* Portsmouth, NH: Heinemann.

Clay, M. M. (1993). *An observational survey of early literacy assessment.* Portsmouth, NH: Heinemann.

Clay, M. M. (2000a). *Follow me, moon.* Portsmouth, NH: Heinemann.

Clay, M. M. (2000b). *No shoes.* Portsmouth, NH: Heinemann.

Clemmons, J., Laase, L., Cooper, D., Areglado, N., & Dill, M. (1993). *Portfolios in the classroom: A teacher's sourcebook.* New York: Scholastic.

Coughlan, M. (1988). Let the students show us what they know. *Language Arts, 65,* 375–378.

Cunningham, P. (1990). The Names Test: A quick assessment of decoding ability. *The Reading Teacher, 44,* 124–129.

D'Aoust, C. (1992). Portfolios: Process for students and teachers. In K. B. Yancy (Ed.), *Portfolios in the writing classroom* (pp. 39–48). Urbana, IL: National Council of Teachers of English.

Duffelmeyer, F. A., Kruse, A. E., Merkley, D. J., & Fyfe, S. A. (1994). Further validation and enhancement of the Names Test. *The Reading Teacher, 48,* 118–128.

Farr, R., & Tone, B. (1994). *Portfolio and performance assessment.* Orlando: Harcourt Brace.

Flippo, R. F. (2003). *Assessing readers: Qualitative diagnosis and instruction.* Portsmouth, NH: Heinemann.

Flynt, E. S., & Cooter, R. B., Jr. (2004). *Flynt-Cooter reading inventory for the classroom.* Upper Saddle River, NJ: Merrill/Prentice Hall.

Fountas, I. C., & Pinnell, G. S. (1996). *Guided reading: Good first teaching for all children.* Portsmouth, NH: Heinemann.

Fountas, I. C., & Pinnell, G. S. (1999). *Matching books to readers: Using leveled books in guided reading, K–3.* Portsmouth, NH: Heinemann.

Fountas, I. C., & Pinnell, G. S. (2001). *Guiding readers and writers grades 3–6: Teaching comprehension, genre, and content literacy.* Portsmouth, NH: Heinemann.

Fresch, M. J., & Wheaton, A. (2002). *Teaching and assessing spelling.* New York: Scholastic.

Fry, E. (1968). A readability formula that saves time. *Journal of Reading, 11,* 587.

Fry, E. B. (1980). The new instant word lists. *The Reading Teacher, 34,* 284–289.

Gambrell, L. B. (2001). What we know about motivation to read. In R. F. Flippo (Ed.), *Reading researchers in search of common ground* (pp. 129–143). Newark, DE: International Reading Association.

Gambrell, L. B., Palmer, B. M., Codling, R. M., & Mazzoni, S. A. (1996). Assessing motivation to read. *The Reading Teacher, 49,* 518–533.

Gambrell, L. B., Pfeiffer, W., & Wilson, R. (1985). The effects of retelling upon reading comprehension and recall of text information. *Journal of Educational Research, 78,* 216–220.

Ganske, K. (2000). *Word journeys: Assessment-guided phonics, spelling, and vocabulary instruction.* New York: Guilford Press.

Goodman, K. S. (1976). Behind the eye: What happens in reading. In H. Singer & R. B. Ruddell (Eds.), *Theoretical models and processes of reading* (2nd ed., pp. 470–496). Newark, DE: International Reading Association.

Goodman, Y. M. (1978). Kid watching: An alternative to testing. *The National Elementary Principal, 57,* 41–45.

Graves, D. H. (1983). *Writing: Teachers and students at work.* Portsmouth, NH: Heinemann.

Graves, D. H., & Sunstein, B. S. (Eds.). (1992). *Portfolio portraits.* Portsmouth, NH: Heinemann.

Henderson, E. (1990). *Teaching spelling.* Boston: Houghton Mifflin.

Henk, W. A., & Melnick, S. A. (1995). The Reader Self-Perception Scale (RSPS): A new tool for measuring how children feel about themselves as readers. *The Reading Teacher, 48,* 470–482.

Kame'enui, E., Simmons, D., & Cornachione, C. (2000). *A practical guide to reading assessments.* Newark, DE: International Reading Association.

Kear, D. J., Coffman, G. A., McKenna, M. C., & Ambrosio, A. L. (2000). Measuring attitude toward writing: A new tool for teachers. *The Reading Teacher, 54,* 10–23.

Kuhs, T. M., Johnson, R. L., Agruso, S. A., & Monrad, D. M. (2001). *Put to the test: Tools and techniques for classroom assessment.* Portsmouth, NH: Heinemann.

Leslie, L., & Caldwell, J. (2000). *Qualitative reading inventory-3* (3rd ed.). Boston: Allyn & Bacon.

McKenna, M. C., & Kear, D. J. (1990). Measuring attitudes toward reading: A new tool for teachers. *The Reading Teacher, 43,* 626–639.

Morrow, L. M. (1985). Retelling stories: A strategy for improving children's comprehension, concept of story structure, and oral language complexity. *Elementary School Journal, 85,* 647–661.

Norman, K. A., & Calfee, R. C. (2004). Tile Test: A hands-on approach for assessing phonics in the early grades. *The Reading Teacher, 58,* 42–52.

Peterson, B. (2001). *Literary pathways: Selecting books to support new readers.* Portsmouth, NH: Heinemann.

Porter, C., & Cleland, J. (1995). *The portfolio as a learning strategy.* Portsmouth, NH: Heinemann.

Rhodes, L. K., & Nathenson-Mejia, S. (1992). Anecdotal records: A powerful tool for ongoing literacy assessment. *The Reading Teacher, 45,* 502–511.

Shea, M. (2000). *Taking running records.* New York: Scholastic.

Skillings, M. J., & Ferrell, R. (2000). Student-generated rubrics: Bringing students into the assessment process. *The Reading Teacher, 53,* 452–455.

Stahl, S. A. (1999). *Vocabulary development.* Cambridge, MA: Brookline Books.

Stires, S. (1991). Thinking through the process: Self-evaluation in writing. In B. M. Power & R. Hubbard (Eds.), *The Heinemann reader: Literacy in process* (pp. 295–310). Portsmouth, NH: Heinemann.

Tierney, R., Carter, M., & Desai, L. (1991). *Portfolio assessment in the reading-writing classroom.* Norwood, MA: Christopher-Gordon.

Torgesen, J. K., & Bryant, B. R. (1994). *Test of phonological awareness*. Austin, TX: Pro-Ed.

Walberg, H. J., & Tsai, S. (1985). Correlates of reading achievement and attitude: A national assessment study. *Journal of Educational Research, 78,* 159–167.

Winograd, P., & Arrington, H. J. (1999). Best practices in literacy assessment. In L. B. Gambrell, L. M. Morrow, S. B. Neuman, & M. Pressley (Eds.), *Best practices in literacy instruction* (pp. 210–241). New York: Guilford Press.

Woods, M. L., & Moe, A. J. (2003). *Analytical reading inventory* (7th ed.). Upper Saddle River, NJ: Merrill/Prentice Hall.

Yopp, H. K. (1995). A test for assessing phonemic awareness in young children. *The Reading Teacher, 40,* 20–28.

Children's Book References

Blume, J. (1972). *Tales of a fourth grade nothing.* New York: Dutton.

Cole, J. (1993). *The magic school bus lost in the solar system.* New York: Scholastic.

George, J. C. (1972). *Julie of the wolves.* New York: Harper & Row.

Howe, D., & Howe, J. (1979). *Bunnicula: A rabbit-tale of mystery.* Boston: Atheneum.

Lewis, C. S. (1994). *The lion, the witch and the wardrobe.* New York: HarperCollins.

MacLachlan, P. (1985). *Sarah, plain and tall.* New York: Harper & Row.

Mathis, S. B. (1975). *The hundred penny box.* New York: Viking.

Naylor, P. R. (1991). *Shiloh.* New York: Atheneum.

Paulsen, G. (1987). *Hatchet.* New York: Viking.

Potter, B. (1902). *The tale of Peter Rabbit.* New York: Warne.

Speare, E. G. (1983). *The sign of the beaver.* Boston: Houghton Mifflin.

The pot of gold (an Irish folk tale). (2001). Glenview, IL: Celebration Press/Addison-Wesley.

Yolen, J. (1995). *Henry and Mudge and the best day of all.* New York: Scholastic.

How Do Teachers Organize Literacy Instruction?

Teachers choose from five instructional approaches as they teach reading and writing:

- Basal Reading Programs
- Literature Focus Units
- Literature Circles
- Reading and Writing Workshop
- Content-Area Units

These approaches differ in significant ways. Probably the most important difference is their theoretical orientation. First, for example, basal reading programs represent behavioral learning theory; literature circles, however, reflect reader response and sociolinguistic theories. Second, the role of the teacher and students varies: Basal reading programs are teacher centered, and writing workshop is student centered. Third, the instructional materials vary. Textbooks are used in basal reading programs; trade books are used in the other approaches; and both are used in content-area units. Teachers use a combination of approaches, depending on their school district expectations, their beliefs about how children learn, and the available materials.

In this photo essay, you'll see how Ms. Boland teaches a content-area unit on the Middle Ages. Her seventh graders read a historical novel set in the period, along with their content-area textbook. Then they study a topic that interests them and apply what they learn in an interactive museum display.

This student is reading Karen Cushman's *Catherine, Called Birdy* (1994), a novel written in diary form. Catherine, the author of the diary, is a young noblewoman in the year 1290, and she provides fascinating details about life in the Middle Ages. The book's humorous tone makes it very popular.

Students meet in small groups to discuss the novel, and Ms. Boland sits in to help students focus on both the events in the story and the historical information they are learning.

Students work in groups to read about the Middle Ages in their social studies textbook. Then they create graphic organizers about the big ideas in each chapter and present the information to the class.

To showcase their learning, the students create an interactive museum about medieval life. Students working in small groups create displays on cathedrals, the life of a knight, and other topics.

Group Roles

As they work, students assume roles in the group, including:

★ Facilitator, who keeps the group on task and solves problems.

★ Research coordinator, who makes sure group members know their research topics.

★ Internet troubleshooter, who assists group members using the Internet.

★ Harmonizer, who helps the group work together smoothly.

★ Supply person, who gets needed materials from Ms. Boland.

These two boys develop a PowerPoint presentation about the life of a knight, which they will use as part of the display.

Research Rubric

5-Excellent	4-Very Good	3-Good	2-Poor	1-Failing
More than four sources of information, including the Internet, were used. Notes are written in your own words.Time and effort clearly demonstrated in note taking. Bibliography is correct.	Four sources of information, including the Internet, were used. Notes are mostly written in your own words. Above average time and effort used in note taking. Bibliography has very few errors.	Three sources of information, including the Internet, were used. Notes are mostly written in your own words. Average amount of time and effort used in note taking. Bibliography has some errors.	Two sources of information, including the Internet, were used. Notes are mostly copied from sources. Little time and effort used in note taking. Bibliography has many errors.	One source of information was used. Notes are copied from sources. Little or no effort used in note taking. There is no bibliography or only part of a bibliography.

The seventh graders create displays to engage museum visitors. Other students at the school, parents, and school board members visit the museum. The presentations take many forms, including labeled artifacts, demonstrations, and PowerPoint presentations. In addition, students dress as "moving statues" on museum day and explain their displays to the visitors.

Teaching With Basal Reading Textbooks

- What is a basal reading program?
- How do teachers teach with basal reading programs?
- How do teachers apply the reading process in this instructional approach?
- Why do teachers use this instructional approach?
- How do teachers differentiate instruction?
- How do teachers use guided reading?

Mrs. Ohashi Teaches Reading Using Basal Readers

Mrs. Ohashi's third graders are reading "The Great Kapok Tree," a selection in their basal reading program. This story, which is set in the Amazon rain forest, was originally published as a trade book for children by Lynne Cherry in 1990. In the basal reader version, the text is unabridged from the original book, but because text from several pages has been printed on a single page, some illustrations from the original book version have been deleted.

The students spend 1 week reading "The Great Kapok Tree" and participating in a variety of related literacy activities. Mrs. Ohashi's language arts block lasts 2½ hours

each morning. During the first hour, she works with reading groups while other students work independently at centers. During the second hour, she teaches spelling, grammar, and writing. The last half hour is an independent reading time when students read self-selected books from the classroom library or the reading center.

The skills that Mrs. Ohashi teaches each week are set by the basal reading program. This week, she focuses on cause and effect as students read and think about the selection. The vocabulary words she highlights in the selection are *community, depend, environment, generations, hesitated, ruins, silent,* and *squawking.* Students learn about persuasive writing, and they write a persuasive letter to their parents. Mrs. Ohashi teaches minilessons on irregular past-tense verbs, and students study the list of spelling words provided by the basal reading program.

Mrs. Ohashi's class is divided into four reading groups, and the students in all of the groups, except one group reading at the first-grade level, can read the basal reader with her support. Her district's policy is that in addition to reading books at their instructional level, all children should be exposed to the grade-level textbooks. Mrs. Ohashi involves all students in most instructional activities, but she reads the story to the students in the lowest group and then they read leveled books at their level.

To choose names for the groups at the beginning of the school year, Mrs. Ohashi put crayons into a basket; a student from each group chose a crayon, and the crayon's name became the name of the group. The students who read at or almost at grade level are heterogeneously grouped into the Wild Watermelon, Electric Lime, and Blizzard Blue groups. The six remaining students form the Atomic Tangerine group.

On Monday, Mrs. Ohashi builds students' background knowledge about the rain forest by reading aloud *Nature's Green Umbrella* (Gibbons, 1994). Students talk about rain forests and together compile a list of information they have learned, including the fact that each year, over 200 inches of rain fall in the rain forest. Next she introduces the selection of the week, and students "text walk" through the story, looking at the illustrations, connecting with what they already know about rain forests, and predicting events in the story. Mrs. Ohashi reads aloud the first two pages to the class, and then most students read the story with buddies, but the Atomic Tangerine group reads the selection with Mrs. Ohashi. These students join Mrs. Ohashi at the reading group table, and she reads the story aloud while students follow along in their books. She stops periodically to explain a word, make predictions, clarify any confusions, and think aloud about the story.

After everyone finishes reading the selection, students come together to talk about the story. Students talk about why the rain forests must be preserved. Ashley explains, "I know why the author wrote the story. On page 71 it tells about her. Her name is Lynne Cherry and it says that she wants to 'try to make the world a better place.' That's the message of this story." Then Katrina compares this story to *Miss Rumphius* (Cooney, 1982), the selection they read several weeks ago: "I think this story is just like the one we read before. It was about making the world more beautiful with flowers, and that's almost the same."

Then Mrs. Ohashi focuses on cause and effect, the skill the teacher's guide advises her to emphasize this week. She asks what would happen if there were no more rain forests. Students mention that animals in the rain forest might become extinct because they wouldn't have homes and that there would be more air pollution because the trees wouldn't be able to clean the air. Then Mrs. Ohashi introduces a basket of foods, spices, and other products that come from the rain forest, including chocolate, coffee, tea, bananas, cashews, cinnamon, ginger, vanilla, bamboo, and rubber. Her students are amazed at the variety of things they and their parents use every day that come from the rain forest.

Next, Mrs. Ohashi turns to spelling. She explains that this week's words end with *-ild* as in *mild*, *-ind* as in *find*, and *-ound* as in *found*. She administers the pretest using 15 words plus 5 challenge words provided in the basal reading program. Students take the pretest on page 83 of their Spelling Activity Book and correct their own pretests. They take these papers home and use them to practice their spelling words during the week.

Then Mrs. Ohashi introduces the grammar skill of the week: the past-tense forms of irregular verbs. She has prepared a series of 10 sentence strips with sentences about "The Great Kapok Tree," leaving blanks for the past-tense verbs, as suggested in the teacher's guide for the basal reading program. On separate cards, she has written correct and incorrect verb forms on each side; for example, *The birds comed/came down from their trees.* She puts the sentence strips and verb cards in a pocket chart. She begins by talking about the past-tense form of regular verbs. The students understand that *-ed* marks the past tense of many verbs, as in this sentence: *The man walked into the rain forest.* Other verbs, she explains, have different forms for present and past tense. For example, *The man sleeps/slept in the rain forest.* Then students read the sentences in the pocket chart and choose the correct form of the irregular verb.

Next, she explains that many irregular verbs have three forms—present tense, past tense, and past tense using *have, has,* or *had*—as in *sing–sang–sung.* She puts word cards with these 10 present-tense forms in another pocket chart: *go, give, come, begin, run, do, eat, grow, see,* and *sing.* Then she passes out additional word cards listing the two past-tense forms of each verb. As they talk about each verb, students holding word cards with the past-tense forms add them to the pocket chart.

During the week, students will continue to practice these irregular verbs at centers, using worksheets from the Grammar Practice Book that is part of the basal reading program, and through other minilessons.

During the last 20 minutes of the language arts block, Mrs. Ohashi introduces the 10 centers where students will work during the week; these centers are described in the box on the next page. The centers are arranged next to bulletin boards, at tables, or in corners of the classroom, and students follow Mrs. Ohashi as she explains each one.

The rest of the week, Mrs. Ohashi meets with reading groups in the first hour of the language arts block while other students work independently at centers to complete grammar worksheets, practice spelling words, and participate in other literacy activities. She meets with the below-grade-level readers in the Atomic Tangerine group each day and students in the other groups twice to reread the selection. She also teaches vocabulary and comprehension lessons as directed in the teacher's guide.

Mrs. Ohashi likes to begin with the Atomic Tangerine group each morning because she feels that it gets them off to a more successful start. She uses guided reading with these students. They begin by rereading several familiar leveled books, and Mrs. Ohashi listens to the students as they read. Next, she reviews one- and two-syllable words with *ar*, and they decode these words: *car, carpet, mark, bookmark, sharp, sharpest,* and *sharks.* Mrs. Ohashi introduces their new book, *Hungry, Hungry Sharks* (Cole, 1986). Students text walk through the first 11 pages, looking at illustrations and making predictions. They put a bookmark at page 11 to remember where to stop reading. Mrs. Ohashi asks students to read to find out if sharks are dinosaurs, and they eagerly begin. Students mumble-read so that Mrs. Ohashi can hear them as they read. When students don't know a word (such as *creatures, dragons,* and *hundred*), Mrs. Ohashi helps them sound it out or, if necessary, pronounces it for them. She writes the words on word cards to review after students finish reading. As soon as they finish reading, students discuss possible answers to her question. Several believe that sharks were dinosaurs, but others disagree. So, Mrs.

Check the Compendium of Instructional Procedures, which follows Chapter 14, for more information on highlighted terms.

The Literacy Centers in Mrs. Ohashi's Classroom

Center	Description
Vocabulary	Students sort rain forest word cards into several categories. Also, students make word maps for three of these words from the story: *community, depend, environment, generations, hesitated, ruins, silent, squawking.* They use the glossaries in their textbooks to check the definitions.
Comprehension	Students examine the cause-and-effect relationships using two activities. First, they match a set of pictures of the animals from the story to their reasons why the kapok tree should not be cut down. For example, the monkey's reason was that if the kapok tree is cut down, the roots will die and the soil will wash away. Mrs. Ohashi has also placed a poster in the center with the question, "What do you think would have happened if the man had chopped down the tree?" and students are encouraged to write their predictions on it. Second, they complete the worksheet on page 108 in the Practice Book by answering eight comprehension questions.
Sentences	Students choose a favorite sentence from the story, write it on a sentence strip, and post it on the bulletin board near the center.
Reading and Rereading	Students read books from the text set on rain forests and supplemental books from the basal reading program. Mrs. Ohashi also has a 1-minute timer at the center, and students practice rereading copies of page 68 from "The Great Kapok Tree" to see how many words they can read in a minute. They read the page once for practice, then read the page and mark how many words they read in a minute. Then they read the page again and mark how many words they read this time. Students work to improve their reading speed because all third graders are expected to reach a reading speed of at least 100 words per minute.
Grammar	Students practice irregular past-tense verbs through several activities. They read sentences about the story written on sentence strips and paper clip word cards with the correct form of verb to the sentence strip. Students sort verb cards and put present, past, and past participle forms of the same verb together, such as *go–went–gone.* Students also complete page 71 of the Grammar Practice Book.
Listening	Students listen to audiotapes of "The Great Kapok Tree" or "The Mahogany Tree," and afterward they write and/or draw a response in listening logs that are kept at the center.
Spelling	Students participate in a variety of activities to practice their spelling words. Lists of words are available at the center, and students build the words using linking letters. They sort spelling word cards according to spelling patterns. They complete Spelling Activity Book page 86 by identifying the correct spelling of each word. And, they write each spelling word three times in their spelling notebooks that are kept at the center.
Writing	Students write a rain forest book with information about plants and animals in the rain forest and the products we use that come from the rain forest.
Chart	Students mark the rain forest on world maps using information from pages 72–73 of their basal readers. They also add labels with names of the countries, rivers, and continents.
Computers	Students use a phonics program to review *r*-controlled vowels and do word processing for writing activities.

Ohashi rereads page 10, which says, "There are no more dinosaurs left on earth. But there are plenty of sharks." After they agree that sharks are not dinosaurs, the students practice reading the word cards that Mrs. Ohashi prepared while they were reading.

Next, the students compose this sentence about sharks using interactive writing: *There are more than three hundred kinds of sharks today.* Students write on individual white boards as they take turns writing on chart paper. Then they reread the five sentences they wrote last week. During the rest of the week, students in the Atomic Tangerine group will continue reading *Hungry, Hungry Sharks* and participating in phonics, spelling, vocabulary, and writing activities with Mrs. Ohashi.

Mrs. Ohashi meets next with the Wild Watermelon group to reread "The Great Kapok Tree." The students read silently, but Mrs. Ohashi asks individual students to read a page aloud so that she can conduct running records to check their fluency. After they finish reading, Mrs. Ohashi asks the students to talk about what the man might have been thinking as he walked away from the kapok tree on the last page of the story.

Next, she examines the students' understanding of cause and effect in the story. She asks the students what is causing a problem in the story, and they respond that cutting down the rain forest is the problem. When she asks what the effects of cutting down the trees might be, students mention several, including air pollution and destroying animal habitats. Then she passes out cards, each with a picture of an animal from the story, and asks students to scan the story to find the effect that that animal mentioned to the sleeping man. Students reread and then share what they found.

Then Mrs. Ohashi repeats the same activities with the other two reading groups. On the fourth and fifth days, she meets with the three reading groups that are on grade level to review vocabulary words from the selection.

In the second hour, Mrs. Ohashi begins a persuasive writing project. She explains that people read and write for three purposes—to entertain, to inform, and to persuade. "Which purpose," she asks, "do you think Lynne Cherry had for writing 'The Great Kapok Tree'?" The students respond that she had all three purposes, but that perhaps the most important purpose was to persuade. Then Mrs. Ohashi explains that in persuasive writing, authors use cause and effect: They explain a problem and then tell how to solve it. They also give reasons why it must be solved and tell what will happen if it isn't solved.

The students talk about environmental problems in their community and decide to write letters to their parents and grandparents urging them to recycle and take good care of the environment. The format they will use is:

Sentence 1: Urge their parents to conserve and recycle.

Sentence 2: Tell how to conserve and recycle.

Sentence 3: Tell another way.

Sentence 4: Tell why it is important.

Sentence 5: Urge their parents to conserve and recycle.

Mrs. Ohashi and the students brainstorm many ideas and words on the chalkboard before students begin writing their rough drafts. Then on Wednesday and Thursday, they revise and edit their letters, and Mrs. Ohashi meets with students to work on their letters. By Friday, most students are writing their final copies and addressing envelopes so their letters can be mailed. Before they begin recopying, Mrs. Ohashi reviews the friendly letter form so students will be sure to format the letter correctly. Rachel's letter to her grandparents is shown in the box on the next page.

Dear Nana and Pappa,

I want you to take very good care of the earth and it a more beautiful place. I want you to recyle paper. Like old newspapper and cardboard and bags from Savemart. You shuold put it in the blue RECYCLE can and it will be made into new paper. Don't burn it!! That means more air pollution. I love you and you love me so help me to have a good life on a healthy planet.

Love,
Rachel

Mrs. Ohashi ends the language arts block on Friday by showing the video version of "The Great Kapok Tree," which appeared on PBS's Reading Rainbow series, and by having students read their favorite sentences from the story in a read-around.

Commercial reading programs, commonly called basal readers, have been a staple in reading instruction for at least 60 years. In the past 25 years, however, basal readers have been criticized for their controlled vocabulary, for their emphasis on isolated skills, and for stories that lack conflict or authentic situations. In the past, the stories in these textbooks have been excerpted from children's literature and rewritten, often substituting simpler or more decodable words for the author's original language (Goodman, Shannon, Freeman, & Murphy, 1988). Educators have demanded more authentic texts—selections that have not been edited or abridged—and publishers of commercial reading programs have redesigned their programs to bring them more in line with the balanced reading movement. Now some basal readers, like the series Mrs. Ohashi used in the vignette, include authentic, unabridged literature in their programs.

McCarthey and Hoffman (1995) compared newer first-grade-level basal readers with older editions and found that the newer editions were very different from the older ones. They examined five characteristics of basal readers and reported their findings:

1. ***Word and sentence difficulty.*** The total number of words is smaller in the new programs, but the newer basal readers contain more unique words. The vocabulary is much less controlled and there is less repetition of words in the new programs.

2. ***Literary characteristics.*** The new editions incorporate different formats. Reading materials are packaged in a variety of ways—as big books, in trade books, and in anthologies. The new editions include a wider variety of genres and fewer adaptations of children's literature.

3. ***Literacy features.*** The selections have more complex plots, more highly developed characters, and more idiomatic and metaphorical language, and are more engaging than the older basal selections.

4. ***Predictability.*** More than half of the selections in the new basal readers have predictable features, including repeated patterns, rhyme, and rhythm. In contrast, less than 20% of the stories in the older editions had predictable features.

5. ***Decodability.*** The new basal readers place much higher decoding demands on students than the older ones did.

McCarthey and Hoffman concluded that skills are still prevalent in newer reading textbooks, but they are slightly more integrated. They noted that assessment tools broadened from a testing-only mentality to include portfolios and other innovative assessment strategies. Based on their findings, McCarthey and Hoffman recommend that teachers become decision makers and use the textbooks judiciously.

Basal reading programs reflect behaviorism, a teacher-centered learning theory, because teachers provide direct instruction using the lesson plans and materials provided by the commercial programs. Most of the instruction is whole-class, but the textbooks do provide suggestions for assisting struggling readers and for challenging high-achieving students. Students usually read independently, with teachers providing guidance about how to decode unfamiliar words and use comprehension strategies, but when students cannot read the textbook themselves, teachers often read aloud to them and then have them try to do the reading themselves. These programs provide detailed information in the teacher's guides about teaching strategies and skills, and charts show how the activities in the lessons meet state or national literacy standards.

Basal reading programs are one of four instructional approaches, and although textbook publishers claim that basal readers are complete instructional programs, effective teachers generally use guided reading, reading and writing workshop, or other approaches in conjunction with basal readers to differentiate instruction and to provide students with books at their reading levels or more opportunities to read literature. The box on the next page shows how basal reading programs fit into a balanced literacy program.

TEACHING WITH BASAL READING TEXTBOOKS

Publishers of basal reading textbooks tout their programs as complete literacy programs containing all the materials needed for students to become successful readers. The accessibility of reading materials is clearly one advantage of textbooks: Teachers have copies of grade-level textbooks for every student, and most textbook programs contain award-winning and unabridged literature. An overview of basal reading programs is presented in the box on page 340.

It is unrealistic, however, to assume that a commercial reading program could be a complete literacy program for all students. Teachers who have students reading below grade level need reading materials at their students' level, as do teachers working with students who read above grade level. These teachers have to supplement their program with appropriate reading materials, as Mrs. Ohashi did in the vignette. In

Visit Chapter 10 on the Companion Website at *www.prenhall. com/tompkins* to connect to web links related to basal reading programs.

How Basal Reading Programs Fit Into a Balanced Literacy Program

Component	Description
Reading	Students read selections in grade-level textbooks while teachers reinforce students' use of word-identification skills and comprehension strategies. When the selection is too difficult, teachers read it aloud to students before students read it themselves.
Phonics and Other Skills	Skills are organized sequentially at each grade level, and directions for teaching phonemic awareness, phonics, grammar, and spelling skills are included in each lesson. Students also complete workbook pages to practice skills.
Strategies	Teachers introduce, practice, and reinforce predicting, monitoring, summarizing, and other strategies as students read selections and complete workbook assignments.
Vocabulary	Vocabulary is controlled in basal readers. Teachers introduce new words before reading the selection, and students complete workbook pages to practice vocabulary.
Comprehension	Teachers teach comprehension strategies and ask questions to guide students' understanding, and students complete workbook pages to reinforce comprehension.
Literature	Stories, informational articles, and poems are included in basal readers, and many selections are multicultural. Some were written specifically for the textbook to reinforce phonics skills, but others were originally published as trade books.
Content-Area Study	Textbooks are organized into units and many have links to science, social studies, and math.
Oral Language	Except at the kindergarten level, oral language is not an important component of basal reading programs.
Writing	Writing activities accompany each selection, with an emphasis on genres and practicing writing and grammar skills using accompanying workbook pages.
Spelling	Spelling words based on phonics skills are included with each selection, and workbook pages provide opportunities to practice words.

some schools, teachers share basal reading textbooks with teachers in other grades; at other schools, teachers locate sets of leveled books to use with below- and above-grade-level readers. In addition, students need many more opportunities to read and reread books than are provided in a basal reading program, so teachers stock their classroom libraries with books and provide daily time for independent reading.

Basal Reading Programs

Topic	Description
Purpose	To teach the skills and strategies that successful readers need using an organized program that includes grade-level reading selections, workbook practice assignments, and frequent testing.
Components	Basal reading programs involve five components: reading the selections in the grade-level textbook, instruction in strategies and skills, workbook assignments, independent reading opportunities, and a management plan that includes flexible grouping and regular assessment.
Theory Base	Basal reading programs are based on behaviorism because teachers provide direct instruction and students are passive rather than active learners.
Applications	Basal reading programs organize instruction into weekly lessons with reading, strategy and skill instruction, and workbook activities. Basal readers should be used in conjunction with other instructional approaches to ensure that students read books at their instructional levels and have opportunities to read and respond to literature.
Strengths	• Textbooks are aligned with grade-level standards. • Students read selections at their grade level. • Teachers teach strategies and skills in a sequential program, and students practice them through reading and workbook assignments. • The teacher's guide provides detailed instructions for teaching reading. • Assessment materials are included in the program.
Limitations	• Selections may be too difficult for some students and too easy for others. • Selections may lack the authenticity of good literature. • Programs include many workbook assignments. • Most of the instruction is presented to the whole class.

Components of Basal Reading Programs

Even though there are a number of commercial programs available today, most include these five components:

- Selections in grade-level textbooks
- Instruction in skills and strategies
- Workbook assignments
- Independent reading opportunities
- A management plan

Basal readers are probably best known for their strong skills component: Teachers teach skills, and students apply what they are learning in the textbook selections they read and the workbook assignments they complete.

Selections in Grade-Level Textbooks. Basal reading programs are organized into units on topics such as challenges, folktales, and school. Each unit includes four to six weeklong lessons, each with a featured selection, often a story such as "The Great Kapok Tree" that Mrs. Ohashi's class read in the vignette at the beginning of the chapter. The selections in the kindergarten and first-grade textbooks contain decodable text so that students can apply the phonics skills they are learning, but as students develop stronger word-identification skills and a bank of familiar high-frequency words, the textbooks transition to literature selections that were originally published as trade books.

All students in the classroom read the same selections in the grade-level textbook each week, no matter what their reading level is. These commercial programs argue that it is important to expose all students to instruction at their grade level because some students, especially minority students, have been denied equal access to instruction; the teacher's guide provides suggestions for meeting the needs of struggling readers and students who are learning English. Many programs also provide video, audio, and Internet resources to accompany the selections. Some of the most useful resources are the audiotapes of the selections, which teachers often play as students follow along in their copies of the textbook. After this shared reading experience, some less successful readers can then read the selection, but many teachers complain that a few students cannot read the selections no matter how much support they provide.

Instruction in Skills and Strategies. Teachers use basal reading programs to deliver explicit and systematic instruction that is aligned with state literacy standards. Most textbooks include instruction in phonemic awareness, phonics, high-frequency words, word-identification skills, spelling, grammar, and writing mechanics (capitalization and punctuation). The programs also emphasize comprehension strategies, including predicting, visualizing, monitoring, questioning, summarizing, and evaluating.

The teacher's guide provides detailed lesson plans for teaching skills and strategies with each selection. Teachers explain the skills and strategies and model their use as they read with students, then students apply the skills and strategies as they read selections and complete workbook pages. Scope-and-sequence charts for each grade level that are included in the teacher's guide show the order for teaching skills and strategies and explain how skills and strategies are introduced at one grade level and reinforced and expanded at the next level. These programs claim that it is their explicit, systematic instruction that ensures success.

Nurturing English Learners

How can I use the basal reader to develop my first-grade English learners' language?

Basal reader selections provide opportunities for many worthwhile English language activities. Teachers often build EL students' concept knowledge and vocabulary on topics related to each basal reader selection using artifacts, picture books, and videos. They teach standard English syntactic patterns using big books and other selections with predictable text, and they have students practice the patterns by rereading the texts and creating their own books. Teachers often ask students to expand their comments and questions into complete sentences as they talk about the selection. They also dramatize selections and retell them using puppets or illustrations taken from the selection. The grammar concepts presented in the textbook provide additional teaching opportunities. English learners can practice the grammar skills orally and by completing workbook pages. Teachers also encourage language development whenever students work with partners or in small groups to complete activities.

Workbooks

This first grader is completing a phonics worksheet. He cuts apart a list of words, sorts them according to vowel sound, and then pastes them on a worksheet. Having students complete workbook pages and other worksheets is an important part of basal reading programs because they provide opportunities for students to practice phonics, vocabulary, comprehension, spelling, and grammar skills that the teacher has taught. Sometimes students do workbook assignments together as a class, but often students do them while other students participate in guided reading groups with the teacher.

Workbook Assignments. Students complete workbook pages before, during, and after reading each selection to reinforce instruction; 10 to 12 workbook pages that focus on phonics, vocabulary, comprehension, grammar, spelling, and writing accompany each selection. On these pages, students write words, letters, or sentences, match words and sentences, or make graphic organizers.

Teachers vary how they use the workbook pages. Once students know how to complete a workbook page, such as the pages that focus on practicing spelling words, they work independently or with partners. However, for more challenging assignments, such as those dealing with comprehension strategies or newly introduced skills, teachers have the whole class do the assignment together, and they direct students as they work. Teachers also devise various approaches for monitoring students' completion of workbook assignments: They may have students check their own work, or they may collect the workbooks and grade the assignments themselves.

Independent Reading Opportunities. Most basal reading programs include a collection of easy, on-grade-level, and challenging paperback books for students to read independently. There are multiple copies of each book, and teachers set these some of these books out for students to read along with each selection. Some of these books, especially in the primary grades, have been written to reinforce phonics skills and vocabulary words, but others are trade books. The goal is for the collection to meet the needs of all students, but sometimes teachers must supplement with much easier books for English learners or struggling readers.

Students can read these books at school during an independent reading time, either Sustained Silent Reading or reading workshop, or they read them at home. Basal reading programs emphasize the need for students to spend time reading every day.

A Management Plan. Basal reading programs provide a management plan with daily and weekly lesson plans, suggestions for pacing for each unit, ideas for flexible grouping, and regular assessment activities; this information is provided in the teacher's guide. There are letters to send home to parents at the beginning of each unit, usually available in several languages, as well as a variety of assessment materials, including phonics tests, end-of-lesson and end-of-unit tests, writing rubrics, and observation guidelines. Teachers are encouraged to assess students' learning regularly to monitor their progress and to evaluate the effectiveness of their instructional program.

Figure 10–1	How Teachers Use the Reading Process With Basal Reading Programs

Stage	Activity
Prereading	Teachers follow directions in the teacher's guide to activate students' background knowledge, introduce vocabulary, teach a strategy, and preview the selection before reading. They also have students complete workbook assignments.
Reading	Students read the selection independently in basal readers, but if the selection is too difficult for students to read, teachers read it aloud or play an audiotape before asking them to read it.
Responding	Teachers follow directions in the teacher's guide to enhance students' comprehension. They ask questions about the author's purpose, model think-alouds, encourage students to make inferences, and summarize the selection. Students also complete workbook assignments that focus on comprehension.
Exploring	Teachers teach phonics, word analysis, spelling, and grammar skills, and students practice the skills by completing workbook assignments. They also teach students about genres, text structure, and authors and illustrators.
Applying	Students read related selections in the basal reader or in other books that accompany the program and participate in writing activities related to the selection or genre being studied.

When teachers implement basal reading programs, they move through the five stages of the reading process as they introduce and read selections in the basal reader, assign workbook pages, and provide instruction on skills and strategies. Figure 10–1 shows how teachers use the reading process in this instructional approach.

Materials Included in Basal Reading Programs

At the center of a basal reading program is the student textbook or anthology. In the primary grades, there are two or more books at each grade level, and in fourth through sixth grades, there is usually one book. Most basal reading programs end in sixth grade because seventh and eighth graders read trade books. Basal readers are colorful and inviting books, often featuring pictures of children and animals on the covers of primary-level books and exciting adventures and fanciful locations on the covers of books for grades 4 through 6. The selections in each textbook are grouped into units, and each unit includes stories, poems, and informational articles. Many multicultural selections have been added, and usually illustrations feature ethnically diverse people. Information about authors and illustrators is given for many selections. The textbooks contain a table of contents and a glossary.

Commercial reading programs provide a wide variety of materials to support student learning. Consumable workbooks are probably the best-known support material. Students write letters, words, and sentences in these books to practice phonics, comprehension, and vocabulary skills. In addition, transparencies and black-line masters of additional worksheets are available for teachers to use in teaching skills and strategies. Big books and kits with letter and word cards, wall charts, and manipulatives are available for kindergarten and first-grade programs. Black-line masters of parent letters are also available.

Some multimedia materials, including audiocassettes, CD-ROMs, and videos, are included with the programs, which teachers can use at listening centers and computer centers. Collections of trade books are available for each grade level to provide supplemental reading materials. In the primary grades, many books have decodable text to provide practice on phonics skills and high-frequency words; in the upper grades, the books are related to unit themes.

Basal reading programs also offer a variety of assessment tools. Teachers use placement evaluations or informal reading inventories to determine students' reading levels and for placement in reading groups. They use running records to informally monitor students' reading. There are also selection and unit tests to determine students' phonics, vocabulary, and comprehension achievement. Information is also provided on how to administer the assessments and analyze the results.

A teacher's instructional guidebook is provided at each grade level. This oversize handbook provides comprehensive information about how to plan lessons, teach the selections, and assess students' progress. The selections are shown in reduced size in the guidebook, and each page includes background information about the selection, instructions for reading the selections, and ideas for coordinating skill and strategy instruction. In addition, information is presented about which supplemental books to use with each selection and how to assess students' learning.

Figure 10–2 summarizes the materials provided in most basal reading programs.

Benefits of Using Basal Reading Programs

Commercial publishers tout basal reading programs as complete literacy programs, but most teachers adapt them to meet their students' needs and use them in conjunction with other instructional approaches. Nonetheless, most of the instructional program is packaged and provided for teachers. When teachers use a basal program, many of the decisions they typically have to make are done for them: The reading materials are selected, the skills and strategies to be taught are sequenced, the questions they will ask about the selection are provided, and workbook pages are available for students to complete. Some teachers, especially beginning teachers and those unfamiliar with grade-level expectations, value having so much of the work done for them, but other teachers feel constrained by textbook materials.

DIFFERENTIATING INSTRUCTION

Teachers know that their students vary—their interests and motivation, their background knowledge and prior experiences, and their culture and language proficiency as well as their reading and writing capabilities—so it's important to allow for these differences as they plan for instruction. According to Carol Ann Tomlinson (2001), differentiating instruction "means 'shaking up' what goes on in the classroom so that students have multiple options for taking information, making sense of ideas, and expressing what they learn" (p. 1). Differentiating instruction is especially important for struggling students who haven't been successful and who cannot read grade-level textbooks. In the vignette, for example, Mrs. Ohashi adapted her instruction to meet her students' needs and provided options for students so that they could be successful.

It is crucial that students who struggle get help. Juel (1988) found that there is a 90% chance that students who are struggling readers at the end of first grade will continue to be struggling readers in fourth grade. Successful early-intervention programs,

Figure 10-2 Materials in Basal Reading Programs

Materials	Description
Textbook or Anthology	The student's book of reading selections. The selections are organized thematically and include literature from trade books. Often the textbook is available in a series of soft-cover books or a single hardcover book.
Big Books	Enlarged copies of books for shared reading. These books are used in kindergarten and first grade.
Supplemental Books	Collections of trade books for each grade level. Kindergarten-level books often feature familiar songs and wordless stories. First- and second-grade books often include decodable words for practicing phonics skills and high-frequency words. In grades 3 to 6, books are often related to unit themes.
Workbooks	Consumable books of phonics, comprehension, vocabulary, spelling, and grammar worksheets.
Transparencies	Color transparencies to use in teaching skills and strategies.
Black-Line Masters	Worksheets that teachers duplicate and use to teach skills and provide additional reading practice.
Kits	Alphabet cards, letter cards, word cards, and other instructional materials. These kits are used in kindergarten through second grade.
Teacher's Guide	An oversize book that presents comprehensive information about how to teach reading using the basal reading program. The selections are shown in reduced size, and background information about the selection, instructions for teaching the selections, and instructions on coordinating skill and strategy instruction are given on each page. In addition, information is presented about which supplemental books to use with each selection and how to assess students' learning.
Parent Materials	Black-line masters that teachers can duplicate and send home to parents. Information about the reading program and lists of ways parents can work with their children at home are included. Often these materials are available in English, Spanish, and several other languages.
Assessment Materials	A variety of assessments, including selection and unit assessments, running records, placement evaluations, and phonics inventories, are available along with teacher's guides.
Multimedia	Audiocassettes of some selections, CD-ROMs of some selections that include interactive components, related videos, and website connections are provided.

including Reading Recovery, can provide insight about how to work with struggling students in regular classrooms. Here are six guidelines:

- Provide more time for reading and writing instruction during the school day.
- Meet with students for a second reading lesson each day to review what was presented to the whole class.
- Group students flexibly so that instruction can match students' needs.
- Have a variety of literacy materials available for students that match their reading levels and interests.
- Provide direct instruction together with opportunities for application.
- Establish home support networks. (Strickland, Ganske, & Monroe, 2002)

In the vignette at the beginning of the chapter, Mrs. Ohashi provided three kinds of support for her struggling students. First, she read aloud the basal reader story because some students could not read it themselves. Second, she adapted lessons so that her struggling students could get additional instruction. Third, she included guided reading lessons using books at the students' reading levels.

Guided Reading

Teachers use guided reading to work with small groups of students who are reading books at their instructional level, with approximately 90–94% accuracy (Clay, 1991). During guided reading, teachers use the reading process to support students' reading and their use of reading strategies (Depree & Iversen, 1996; Fountas & Pinnell, 1996, 2001). Students do the actual reading themselves, although the teacher may read aloud with children to get them started on the first page or two. Beginning readers often mumble the words softly as they read, which helps the teacher keep track of students' reading and the strategies they are using. Older students who are more fluent readers usually read silently during guided reading. Guided reading is not round-robin reading, in which students take turns reading pages aloud to the group.

Teachers choose the books that students read during guided reading; the books are carefully chosen to reflect the students' reading levels and their knowledge of and ability to use reading strategies. Teachers read the book in preparation for the lesson and plan how they will teach it. They consider how to develop students' background knowledge and which big ideas to develop before reading. They choose a strategy to teach, prepare for word work activities, and plan other after-reading activities. Many teachers use little sticky notes to mark teaching points in the book.

Guided reading lessons usually last approximately 30 minutes. Over a day or two, primary-grade students move through all five stages of the reading process. When older students are reading chapter books, the reading process takes longer, often a week or more to complete a book. As with other types of reading lessons, teachers follow the five stages of the reading process for guided reading, allowing some variations for primary- and middle-grade readers.

Scaffolding Struggling Readers

What can I do when my struggling students still can't read the story after I read it aloud to them?

Many teachers are told that they must have all their students use the basal reading program, but when struggling readers can't read the textbook with the teacher's support after having their background knowledge built, being introduced to key vocabulary, and listening to it read aloud, the book is simply too difficult and is not appropriate for these students. Teachers may continue to read weekly selections aloud to these students and involve them in other whole-class activities, but struggling readers need instruction using books at their instructional level and daily opportunities to read books that they can actually read independently. Making these changes is differentiating instruction. Teachers assess students' instructional reading levels through running records or IRIs and then choose appropriate instructional materials—often leveled books—for guided reading lessons.

1. *Prereading.* Teachers introduce the new book and prepare students to read. They often begin by activating or building background knowledge on a topic related to the book. They introduce the book by showing the cover, reading the title and the author's name, and talking about the problem in the story or one or two big ideas in an informational book or article. With older students, teachers often discuss the genre or type of literature, too. They set the purpose for reading, and students often make predictions. They continue with a book walk to present an overview of the selection, but they do not read it aloud to students. During the book walk, teachers point out format considerations

or diagrams and other special features. They introduce vocabulary words that are essential to the meaning of the text and teach or review a strategy that students should use while reading.

2. ***Reading.*** Teachers guide students through one or more readings of the selection; young children who read brief picture books often read the text more than once, but middle-grade students who are reading longer books read the book only once. Sometimes students and the teacher read the first page or two of the book together to get off to a successful start. Then students read the rest of the selection independently, reading aloud softly to themselves or silently, depending on their reading level. Teachers monitor students as they read, prompting for strategies and word identification as needed. They move from student to student, listening in as the student reads aloud. Many teachers do a running record as students read aloud. After younger children finish reading the selection, teachers often invite them to reread it to build fluency and to practice reading new vocabulary. Older students often do a brief writing assignment after they finish reading and while they wait for classmates to finish.

3. ***Responding.*** Students discuss with the teacher the book they have just finished reading in a grand conversation. Teachers move from literal questions to higher-level inferential and critical questions to lead students to think more deeply about the selection. Higher-level questions include:

What would happen if . . . ?

Why did . . . ?

If . . . , what might have happened next?

If you were . . . , what would you . . . ?

What did . . . make you think of?

What did you like best about this book?

Through the discussion, students make text-to-self, text-to-world, and text-to-text connections with the book. Afterward, teachers often have primary-grade students create a summary sentence about the book and then use interactive writing to write it on a chart. This activity gives teachers the opportunity to review concepts about print, phonics, and spelling skills. More capable writers sometimes write in reading logs or share what they wrote earlier.

4. ***Exploring.*** Teachers involve students in three types of instruction. First, teachers review and reinforce the comprehension strategy that students used as they read the book. Sometimes teachers model how they used the strategy or ask students to reread a page from the book and think aloud about their strategy use. The second type of instruction is literary analysis: Teachers explain genres, present information about story elements or other text structures, and locate examples of literary devices in the selection. Sometimes students create story maps or other graphic organizers. Third, through word work activities, teachers focus students' attention on words from the selection. Primary-grade teachers review high-frequency words and have students practice writing several words from the book using magnetic letters and small white boards. Teachers also write sentences on sentence strips and cut the strips apart; then students sequence the words to re-create the sentence. Middle-grade teachers review vocabulary words from the selection and teach students word-identification skills, such as breaking words into syllables and identifying root words and affixes.

Figure 10-3 Steps in a Guided Reading Lesson

Stage	Primary Grades	Middle Grades
Prereading	• Activate or build background knowledge about a topic related to the book. • Show the cover of the book and read the title and author's name. • Introduce big ideas, key vocabulary, and unfamiliar high-frequency words in the text. • Do a picture walk to overview the book, but do not read it. • Point out predictable language patterns. • Set a purpose for reading, and have students make predictions. • Teach a comprehension strategy for students to use during reading.	• Activate or build background knowledge about a topic related to the book. • Show the cover of the book and read the title and author's name. • Talk about the genre and special structural elements in the book. • Introduce big ideas and key vocabulary. • Do a book walk to overview the book, but do not read it. • Set a purpose for reading, and have students make predictions. • Teach a comprehension strategy for students to use during reading.
Reading	• Read the first page aloud to students. • Have students read the book independently, reading aloud softly to themselves. • Prompt for strategies and word identification, as needed. • Move from student to student to listen in as they read. • Do a running record as the student reads aloud. • Have students reread the book twice, once with the teacher and once with a partner or independently.	• Have students read the book independently, reading silently. • Prompt for strategies and word identification, as needed. • Move from student to student to listen in as they read. • Have students do an informal writing assignment while classmates finish reading.
Responding	• Have a grand conversation to discuss the book. • Encourage students to make text-to-self, text-to-world, and text-to-text connections. • Ask inferential and critical-level questions, such as "What would happen if . . . ?" • Use interactive writing to write a summary sentence.	• Have a grand conversation to discuss the book. • Encourage students to make text-to-self, text-to-world, and text-to-text connections. • Ask inferential and critical-level questions, such as "What would happen if . . . ?" • Ask students to find evidence in the book to support their answers. • Have students write in reading logs or share what they wrote earlier.
Exploring	• Review the comprehension strategy. • Reinforce phonics skills. • Practice high-frequency words. • Review vocabulary words from the book. • Use sentence strips to manipulate sentences from the book.	• Review the comprehension strategy. • Teach about genre, text structure, or literary devices. • Review vocabulary words from the book. • Teach word-identification skills, including syllabication and root words and affixes.
Applying	• Apply strategies and practice vocabulary and high-frequency words by rereading the book and other familiar books.	• Apply strategies in independent reading during reading workshop or Sustained Silent Reading.

5. *Applying.* Students apply the strategies they are learning in independent reading activities. Primary-grade students often keep on their desks baskets of books they have already read during guided reading to reread during Sustained Silent Reading, or they go to the reading center and locate other books at their level to read independently or with an aide. Older students often read independently during reading workshop or in preparation for literature circle discussions.

The activities in a guided reading lesson for primary- and middle-grade students are summarized in Figure 10–3.

Literacy Centers

Literacy centers contain meaningful literacy activities that students work at in small groups. For example, students practice phonics skills at the phonics center, sort word cards at the vocabulary center, or listen to books related to a book they are reading at the listening center. Centers are usually organized in special places in the classroom or at groups of tables (Fountas & Pinnell, 1996). Figure 10–4 describes 20 literacy centers.

Literacy centers are usually associated with primary classrooms, but they can be used effectively at all grade levels, even in seventh and eighth grades. In some classrooms, all students work at centers at the same time; in other classrooms, most students work at centers while the teacher works with a small group of students.

Literacy Centers

This second grader works at the center on high-frequency words that accompanies the basal reading program. She completes three activities to practice *would, should,* and *could*—three high-frequency words. First, she reads the words on cards and uses magnetic letters to spell them. Next, she completes a worksheet by writing the words in blanks to complete sentences. Later, she will write the words on a dry-erase board as a classmate dictates them. The teacher updates the literacy center each week with new activities to reinforce high-frequency words addressed that week.

Figure 10-4	**Twenty Literacy Centers**
Center	**Description**
Author	Students examine information about an author they are studying and write letters to the author.
Class Collaborations	Students write pages to be added to the class book, which the teacher later compiles and binds.
Computers	Students use computers with word processing and drawing programs, interactive books on CD-ROM, and other computer programs at this center.
Data Charts	Students compile information for class or individual data charts as part of social studies and science units. They consult informational books and reference books at the center.
Dramatic Play	Young children use literacy materials (e.g., newspapers) and environmental print (e.g., food packages) in play centers.
Library	Students choose books at their reading level to read and reread from a wide variety of books and other reading materials available in the classroom library.
Listening	Students use a tape player and headphones to listen to stories and other texts read aloud. Often copies of the texts are available so students can read along as they listen.
Making Words	Students work with letter cards, magnetic letters, and white boards to spell and write words; they often create words that follow a spelling pattern or sort letters to spell two-, three-, four-, or five-letter words.
Message	Students write notes to classmates, and a message board or a mailbox is set up so they can send their messages.
Phonics	Students practice phonics concepts that teachers have introduced using a variety of small objects, picture cards, magnetic letters, letter cards, and small white boards.
Pocket Charts	Students arrange sentence strips or word cards for a familiar song or poem in the pocket chart, and then they read the poem or sing the song. They also can create new versions and write variations on extra sentence strips and word cards.
Poetry	Students write formula poems, referring to charts describing various poetic forms posted in this center.
Proofreading	Students use spellcheckers, word walls, and dictionaries at this center to proofread compositions they have written.
Puppets	Students work with puppets and puppet stages and small manipulative materials related to books they are reading to retell stories and create sequels.
Reading and Writing the Classroom	Students use reading wands (wooden dowel rods with eraser tips) as they walk around the classroom, reading words and sentences. They also write familiar words and sentences posted in the classroom using small clipboards and pens.
Sequencing	Students sequence sets of pictures about the story or story boards (made by cutting apart two copies of a picture book and backing each page with poster board). Students can also make story boards at this center.
Skills	Students practice phonics, spelling, and grammar skills teachers have taught in minilessons. Students sort word cards, write additional examples on charts, and manipulate other materials used in the minilesson.
Spelling	Students practice spelling words on white boards and with magnetic letters.
Word Sorts	Students sort word cards into categories according to meaning or structural form.
Writing	Students use writing materials, including pens, papers, blank books, postcards, dictionaries, and word walls, in a variety of activities.

The activities in these literacy centers relate to stories students are reading and skills and strategies recently presented in minilessons. Students often manipulate objects, sort word cards, reread books, write responses to stories, and practice skills in centers. Some literacy centers, such as reading and writing centers, are permanent, but others change according to the books students are reading and the activities planned.

In some classrooms, students flow freely from center to center according to their interests; in other classrooms, students are assigned to centers or required to work at some "assigned" centers and choose among other "choice" centers. Students can sign attendance sheets when they work at each literacy center or mark off their names on a class list tacked to each center. Rarely do students move from center to center in a lock-step approach every 15 to 30 minutes; instead, they move from one center to another when they finish what they are doing.

Figure 10–5 shows the checklist Mrs. Ohashi's students used as they worked at literacy centers. They check the box beside the name of each center when they finish work there. Students keep their checklists in their center folders, and they add to their folders any worksheets or papers they do at a center. The P beside some centers on the center checklist in Figure 10–5 indicates that students are to complete a paper at that center and add it to their center folders. Mrs. Ohashi monitors students' progress each day, and at the end of the week, she collects their folders and checks their work. Having a checklist or another approach to monitor students' progress helps them develop responsibility for completing their assignments.

Complete a self-assessment to check your under-standing of the concepts presented in this chapter on the Companion Website at *www.prenhall.com/ tompkins*

Figure 10–5 Mrs. Ohashi's Literacy Centers Checklist

"The Great Kapok Tree" Centers

Name _____

☐ Vocabulary Center

☐ Comprehension Center

☐ Sentences Center

☐ Reading and Rereading Center   P

☐ Grammar Center   P

☐ Listening Center

☐ Spelling Center   P

☐ Writing Center   P

☐ Chart Center   P

☐ Computer Center

Assessment Tools

P = complete a paper at this center

Review: How Effective Teachers Use Basal Reading Textbooks

1. Teachers recognize that basal reading programs are not complete literacy programs and need to be supplemented with other approaches.

2. Teachers use the reading process to teach reading with basal readers.

3. Teachers follow detailed lesson plans in the teacher's guide for teaching skills and strategies.

4. Teachers value that instruction in basal reading programs is aligned with state literacy standards.

5. Teachers use the management system that is part of basal reading programs to monitor and assess students' progress and adapt instruction to meet students' needs.

6. Teachers provide daily opportunities for independent reading.

7. Teachers differentiate instruction to meet all students' needs.

8. Teachers use guided reading to provide instruction using books at students' instructional levels.

9. Teachers teach skills and strategies during guided reading lessons.

10. Teachers provide opportunities for students to practice skills and strategies at literacy centers.

Professional References

Clay, M. M. (1991). *Becoming literate: The construction of inner control.* Portsmouth, NH: Heinemann.

Depree, H., & Iversen, S. (1996). *Early literacy in the classroom: A new standard for young readers.* Bothell, WA: Wright Group.

Fountas, I. C., & Pinnell, G. S. (1996). *Guided reading: Good first teaching for all children.* Portsmouth, NH: Heinemann.

Fountas, I. C., & Pinnell, G. S. (2001). *Guiding readers and writers grades 3–6: Teaching comprehension, genre, and content literacy.* Portsmouth, NH: Heinemann.

Goodman, K. S., Shannon, P., Freeman, V. W., & Murphy, S. (1988). *Report on basal readers.* Katonah, NY: Richard C. Owen.

Juel, C. (1988). Learning to read and write: A longitudinal study of 54 children from first through fourth grade. Paper presented at the annual meeting of the American Educational Research Association, New Orleans, LA.

McCarthey, S. J., & Hoffman, J. V. (1995). The new basals: How are they different? *The Reading Teacher, 49,* 72–75.

Strickland, D. S., Ganske, K., & Monroe, J. K. (2002). *Supporting struggling readers and writers: Strategies for classroom interventions 3–6.* York, ME: Stenhouse.

Tomlinson, C. A. (2001). *How to differentiate instruction in mixed-ability classrooms* (2nd ed.). Alexandria, VA: Association for Supervision and Curriculum Development.

Children's Book References

Cherry, L. (1990). *The great kapok tree.* San Diego: Harcourt Brace.

Cole, J. (1986). *Hungry, hungry sharks.* New York: Random House.

Cooney, B. (1982). *Miss Rumphius.* New York: Viking.

Gibbons, G. (1994). *Nature's green umbrella.* New York: Morrow.

Chapter 11

Teaching Literature Focus Units

- What is a literature focus unit?
- Why do teachers use this instructional approach?
- How do teachers develop literature focus units?
- How do teachers apply the reading process in this instructional approach?
- How do teachers assess students' work?
- What kinds of units do teachers develop?

Mrs. Dillon's Students Read "The Three Little Pigs"

"Who knows the story of 'The Three Little Pigs'?" Mrs. Dillon asks her second-grade class as she holds up a double-sided doll with the faces of two of the pigs on one side and the face of the third pig and a wolf on the other side. The students talk about pigs who build houses of straw, brick, and "something else that isn't very good." They remember the nasty wolf who blows down the houses not made of bricks. Mrs. Dillon tells the students that "The Three Little Pigs" is a folktale and that most folktales have threes in them. "Sometimes there are three characters," she says; "there might be three events, a character might have three objects, or a character does something three times." Then she asks her students to listen for threes as she reads aloud James Marshall's *The Three Little Pigs* (1989).

After she finishes reading, students move into a circle to participate in a grand conversation about the book. Maria begins: "That wolf deserved to die. I'm glad the third pig cooked him up and ate him up." Angela says, "The first little pig and the second little pig were pretty dumb. Their houses weren't very strong." Several children agree that the third little pig was the smart one. Jim remembers that the second building material was sticks, and several children identify threes in the story: three pigs, three houses, three visits by the wolf,

three tricks planned by the wolf and foiled by the third little pig.

Then Mrs. Dillon passes out paperback copies of *The Three Little Pigs* and invites the students to reread the story with partners. Each pair of students has a pad of small sticky notes, which Mrs. Dillon asks them to use to highlight important words in the story as they reread. Her students understand that important words in a story describe characters and events and are essential to comprehending the story. Afterward, students suggest words for the class word wall. The word wall is a large sheet of butcher paper, divided into nine sections and labeled with the letters in alphabetical order. Students take turns writing the important words in their best handwriting on the word wall. Their completed word wall is shown in the box on page 356.

Mrs. Dillon's second graders spend 2 weeks reading and comparing versions of the familiar folktale "The Three Little Pigs." A list of the versions of the story is shown in the box on page 357. She has 15 paperback copies of James Marshall's *The Three Little Pigs*, as well as one or two copies of eight other versions of the folktale, written at varying levels of difficulty. She also has many other stories and informational books about pigs that students can read independently. Mrs. Dillon has arranged the books on one shelf of the classroom library, and she introduces the books to her students during a book talk.

During the first week of the 2-week unit, Mrs. Dillon's students read the story several times—they read the story independently to themselves, the class reads the book together as a readers theatre, and each child reads a favorite excerpt to Mrs. Dillon. They reread the story for other purposes, too: They sequence the events using story boards and choose a favorite quote to use in making a quilt of the story. Mrs. Dillon teaches a minilesson on quotation marks, and then students make a booklet with dialogue among the characters in the story.

Mrs. Dillon teaches a series of minilessons on the spelling of /k/ at the end of short-vowel words such as *brick* and *stick* and at the end of long-vowel words such as *make* and *steak*; she chooses this minilesson because the words *brick* and *stick* are used in this story. During the minilesson, students hunt for words ending with /k/, and Mrs. Dillon writes them on the chalkboard. Then the students sort the words into two columns: words spelled with *ck* and words spelled with *k*. Together they deduce that most short-vowel words are spelled *ck* (exceptions include *pink* and *thank*), and long-vowel words are spelled *k*. In a follow-up lesson, students practice spelling *ck* and *k* words on small dry-erase boards.

Students continue to add important words to the word wall. One day, they divide into four groups: first little pig, second little pig, third little pig, and big bad wolf. Each group makes a vocabulary mobile: Students draw and color a picture of the character and then add words and phrases from the word wall related to that character on word cards hanging below their picture. The second little pig mobile, for example, included "sticks," "build a house," "not by the hair of my chinny chin chin," "ha ha ha," and "gobbled up."

"The Three Pigs" Word Wall		
ABC blew chinny chin chin blue in the face butter churn annoyed bricks	**DEF** dazzling smile frightened displeasure	**GH** house huff and puff gobbled up hungry
IJK iron pot	**LMN** lean mean loitering	**OPQ** pig
RS sow sturdy shimmied solid scrumptious straw sticks splendid	**TUV** turnips	**WXYZ** wolf

Mrs. Dillon reads a version of "The Three Little Pigs" each day, and students compare them. They add information to a comparison chart they are compiling, as shown in the box on page 358. Although several of the versions are very similar, others are unique. In Hooks's Appalachian version (1989), the third little pig, Hamlet, is a girl, and she saves her brothers. In this version, Hamlet builds the only house using rocks. In Lowell's southwestern version (1992), the pigs are javelinas and are pursued by a coyote, not a wolf. This story also ends happily as all three javelina brothers live together in a strong adobe house.

During the second week, students read a variety of pig books independently and work on projects that extend their interpretation of "The Three Little Pigs" stories. The projects they choose include:

- making puppets of pigs and wolf
- writing several poems
- drawing a story map
- making a Venn diagram comparing pigs and wolves
- making houses out of straw, sticks, and bricks
- writing a retelling of the story

Versions of "The Three Little Pigs"

Asch, F. (2001). *Ziggy Piggy and the three little pigs.* Toronto: Kids Can Press.
There's a fourth little pig named Ziggy in this version who saves the day after the wolf blows down the homes of the three pigs.

Bishop, G. (1989). *The three little pigs.* New York: Scholastic.
A traditional retelling of the tale with contemporary illustrations.

Galdone, P. (1970). *The three little pigs.* New York: Seabury.
The classic retelling of this folktale in which the pigs build homes of straw, sticks, and bricks and are threatened by the big, bad wolf.

Hooks, W. H. (1989). *The three little pigs and the fox.* New York: Macmillan.
An Appalachian version of the story in which Hamlet, the youngest pig, rescues her two greedy brothers from the fox.

Kellogg, S. (2002). *The three little pigs.* New York: HarperCollins.
In this contemporary retelling, Searfina Sow who runs a waffle business and her three sons defeat a thuggish, leather-jacketed wolf named Tempesto.

Laird, D. (1990). *Three little Hawaiian pigs and the magic shark.* Honolulu: Barnaby Books.
A shark takes over the wolf's role in this Hawaiian version.

Lowell, S. (1992). *The three little javelinas.* Flagstaff, AZ: Rising Moon Books.
The pigs are transformed into swinelike creatures called javelinas and the wolf becomes a coyote in this southwestern version.

Marshall, J. (1989). *The three little pigs.* New York: Dial Books.
An appealing retelling of the tale in the style of Paul Galdone with exuberant cartoon illustrations.

Moser, B. (2001). *The three little pigs.* Boston: Little, Brown.
The author expands the final confrontation between the clever pig and the scrawny wolf in this cleverly illustrated, classic retelling of the tale.

Scieszka, J. (1989). *The true story of the 3 little pigs!* New York: Viking.
A hilarious parody of the story, told very persuasively by the wolf who claims he was framed.

Trivizas, E. (1993). *The three little wolves and the big bad pig.* New York: McElderry.
Three wolves are threatened by the big bad pig in this version, but they learn to live together.

Whatley, B. (2001). *Wait! No paint!* New York: HarperCollins.
In this twist on the traditional tale, the illustrator repeatedly steps into the story, interrupting it and exasperating the characters.

Wiesner, D. (2001). *The three little pigs.* New York: Clarion Books.
In this Caldecott Medal book with fanciful illustrations, the three pigs escape the wolf by traveling to the world of fairy tales and enlisting the help of a dragon.

Zemach, M. (1988). *The three little pigs.* New York: Farrar, Straus & Giroux.
A traditional retelling of the story enriched with illustrations by Caldecott Medalist Margot Zemach.

Ziefert, H. (1999). *The three little pigs.* Minneapolis: Sagebrush.
An easy-to-read version of the traditional story.

The second graders work on projects individually or in pairs or small groups, and then they share their projects during the last 2 days of the unit.

Mrs. Dillon continues reading versions of "The Three Little Pigs" to the class this week, and they complete the comparison chart. After reading all of the versions, students

A Chart Comparing Versions of "The Three Little Pigs"

Book	Who Are the Three Main Characters?	Who Is the Bad Character?	What Kinds of Houses?	What Happens to the Three Characters?	What Happens to the Bad Character?
The Three Little Pigs James Marshall	3 boy pigs	wolf	1. straw 2. sticks 3. bricks	#1 eaten #2 eaten #3 lives happily	He is cooked and eaten.
The Three Little Pigs Gavin Bishop	3 boy pigs	cool fox	1. straw 2. sticks 3. bricks	#1 eaten #2 eaten #3 lives happily	He is cooked and eaten.
The Three Little Pigs Paul Galdone	3 boy pigs	wolf	1. straw 2. sticks 3. bricks	#1 eaten #2 eaten #3 lives happily	He is cooked and eaten.
The Three Little Javelinas Susan Lowell	2 boy javelinas 1 girl javelina	coyote	1. tumbleweeds 2. cactus 3. adobe	#1 escapes #2 escapes #3 lives safely with her brothers	He is burned up and becomes smoke.
The Three Little Pigs and the Fox William Hooks	Rooter–boy pig Oinky–boy pig Hamlet–girl pig	fox	Only Hamlet builds a rock house.	#1 caught by fox #2 caught by fox #3 catches fox	He is stuffed in a churn and floats down the river.
The Three Little Wolves and the Big Bad Pig Eugene Trivizas	3 boy wolves	big, bad pig	1. brick 2. concrete 3. armor–plated	#1 escaped #2 escaped #3 escaped	He becomes a good pig and lives with the wolves.
The Three Little Pigs Margot Zemach	3 boy pigs	wolf	1. straw 2. sticks 3. bricks	#1 eaten #2 eaten #3 lives happily	He is cooked and eaten.
The Three Pigs David Wiesner	3 pigs and a dragon	wolf	1. straw 2. sticks 3. bricks	#1 escaped #2 escaped #3 escaped	He never gets the pigs.
The True Story of the 3 Little Pigs! Jon Scieszka	The wolf is the good character. He was framed.	the 3 pigs	1. straw 2. sticks 3. bricks	#1 eaten #2 eaten #3 lives happily	The "good" wolf goes to jail.

vote on their favorite and create a graph to show the results. Not surprisingly, Scieszka's *The True Story of the 3 Little Pigs!* (1989), a story told from the wolf's viewpoint, is the class's favorite; the style of this spirited version and its surrealistic illustrations make it popular with students.

Literature focus units are one of the four ways that teachers organize for literacy instruction. Teachers choose a trade book and build a literature focus unit around the featured selection, as Mrs. Dillon did in the vignette. Her featured book was James Marshall's *The Three Little Pigs* (1989), and she developed a 2-week unit around that book. Literature focus units include these components:

- a featured selection
- a text set of related reading materials
- multiple opportunities to read and reread the featured book as well as the text set
- opportunities to comprehend and respond to the featured book
- vocabulary activities
- minilessons on strategies, skills, and procedures
- projects in which students apply what they have learned

Literature focus units represent a transition between teacher-centered and student-centered approaches: Teachers guide and direct students as they read and respond to a book, but the emphasis in this instructional approach is on teaching students about literature and developing lifelong readers. This approach reflects these four theories: interactive, sociolinguistics, reader response, and critical literacy. Teachers apply the interactive theory throughout the reading process as they activate and build students' background knowledge before reading, read the book aloud if students cannot read it themselves to ensure fluency, and emphasize comprehension using grand conversations, reading logs, and minilessons about genres, story structure, and literary devices. They also focus on vocabulary by posting important words on word walls and involving students in other vocabulary activities, as Mrs. Dillon did in the vignette.

Teachers emphasize sociolinguistic theory in this approach because they scaffold students' reading. They direct students' reading and guide their exploration of the books through grand conversations, reading logs, and other activities. Teachers apply reader response theory because they understand that students create meaning gradually as they read and participate in response activities. Teachers provide opportunities for students to think critically about social issues as they read and discuss high-quality books and develop projects to address these issues.

Literature focus units are one way of creating a balanced literacy program, as the box on page 360 shows. High-quality books of children's literature provide the basis for the literacy program, and reading, writing, oral language, and strategy and skills lessons are drawn from the books. As you read this chapter, you'll learn how to implement literature focus units in kindergarten through eighth-grade classrooms.

Check the Compendium of Instructional Procedures, which follows Chapter 14, for more information on highlighted terms.

How Literature Focus Units Fit Into a Balanced Literacy Program

Component	Description
Reading	Students read the featured book independently, or the teacher reads it aloud or uses shared reading if the book is too difficult for students to read it themselves.
Phonics and Other Skills	Teachers teach minilessons on phonics and other skills during the exploring stage of the reading process.
Strategies	Teachers teach minilessons on comprehension strategies and model strategy use as they read aloud and participate in grand conversations.
Vocabulary	Teachers post words on word walls and involve students in a variety of vocabulary activities during literature focus units.
Comprehension	Teachers guide students' literal, inferential, and critical comprehension through activities at each stage of the reading process.
Literature	Teachers select high-quality, grade-appropriate literature, including multicultural literature, usually from district-approved lists for literature focus units.
Content-Area Study	Books of fiction are often selected for literature focus units, but informational books that connect with content-area units can also be used.
Oral Language	Students participate in grand conversations to talk about the featured book, and they often create projects involving oral language, such as puppet shows, dramatizations, and oral reports.
Writing	Students write in reading logs and often use the writing process as they write reports, stories, poems, and other projects.
Spelling	Spelling is not an important component in literature focus units.

CHOOSING LITERATURE FOR UNITS

Teachers choose high-quality trade books as the featured selections for literature focus units. Sometimes the books have been identified as *core books* that must be taught at their grade level, or teachers choose other high-quality books that are appropriate for students at their grade level. Teachers consider both the interest level and the reading level of the books they choose for literature focus units: The books must be interesting to children, and they must be at the appropriate reading level.

In the vignette, Mrs. Dillon was familiar with the wide range of books available for children today. Because she was knowledgeable about literature, she was able to make wise choices and connect language arts and literature. She chose one version of "The Three Little Pigs" as her main selection. Beginning with multiple copies of that book, she added other versions of the folktale and related books to create a text set.

Teachers need to consider the types of books they choose and the impact of their choices on their students. Researchers who have examined teachers' choices have found that they suggest an unconscious gender or racial bias because few books that are chosen feature the experiences of females or of ethnic minorities, and even fewer were written by people from these groups (Jipson & Paley, 1991; Shannon, 1986; Traxel, 1983). These researchers call this pattern the "selective tradition," and they worry about this practice because books reflect and convey sociocultural values, beliefs, and attitudes to readers. It is important that teachers be aware of the ideas their selection patterns convey and become more reflective about the books they choose for classroom use.

The Best of the Best

Visit Chapter 11 on the Companion Website at *www.prenhall.com/ tompkins* to connect to web links related to children's literature.

Teachers who use literature as the basis for their reading programs must be knowledgeable about children's literature. The first step in becoming knowledgeable is to read many of the stories, informational books, and books of poetry available for children today. Many of the stories in basal readers today are also available as trade books or are excerpted from chapter books; teachers need to locate the complete versions of basal reader selections to share with their students. Children's librarians and the salespeople in children's bookstores are very helpful and willing to suggest books for teachers.

As they read and make selections for classroom use, teachers should keep in mind guidelines for selecting literature, the most important of which is that teachers should choose books that they like themselves. Teachers are rarely, if ever, successful in teaching books they don't like—the message that they don't like the book comes across loud and clear, even when they try to hide their feelings.

Each year, a number of books written for children are recognized for excellence and receive awards. The two best-known awards are the Caldecott Medal for excellence in illustration and the Newbery Medal for excellence in writing; lists of the Caldecott and Newbery Medal and Honor Books are presented on the Companion Website. Teachers should be familiar with many of these award-winning books and consider selecting one or more of them to use in their classrooms as featured selections in literature focus units.

Multicultural Literature

Multicultural literature is "literature about racial or ethnic minority groups that are culturally and socially different from the white Anglo-Saxon majority in the United States, whose largely middle-class values and customs are most represented in American literature" (Norton & Norton, 2003, p. 457). Stories such as Faith Ringgold's *Tar Beach* (1991), about how an African American child spends a hot summer evening on the roof of her New York City apartment house, and Gary Soto's *Too Many Tamales* (1993), about a Mexican American child who loses her mother's diamond ring in a batch of tamales she is making, provide glimpses of contemporary life in two cultural groups. Other books tell the history of various cultural and ethnic groups. *So Far From the Sea* (Bunting, 1998), for instance, tells how Japanese Americans were interned in desolate camps during World War II, and *Anthony Burns: The Defeat and Triumph of a Fugitive Slave* (Hamilton, 1988) describes how slaves risked their lives to be free.

Educators recommend selecting multicultural literature that is "culturally conscious" (Sims, 1982)—that is to say, literature that accurately reflects a group's culture, language, history, and values without perpetuating stereotypes. Such literature often deals with issues of prejudice, discrimination, and human dignity. According to Yokota (1993), these books should be rich in cultural details, use authentic dialogue, and present cultural issues in enough depth that readers can think and talk about them. Inclusion of cultural group members should be purposeful. They should be distinct individuals whose lives are rooted in the culture; they should never be included simply to fulfill a quota.

Multicultural literature must meet the criteria for good literature as well as for cultural consciousness. One example is *The Watsons Go to Birmingham—1963* (Curtis, 1995), an award-winning story about an African American family living in Flint, Michigan, and the harsh realities of racial discrimination that the family encounters on a trip to Birmingham, Alabama, during the hate-filled summer of 1963. This well-written story is both historically and culturally accurate. Other examples of good multicultural literature are presented in Figure 11–1.

Why Use Multicultural Literature? There are many reasons to use multicultural literature in literature focus units and other instructional approaches, whether students represent diverse cultures or not. First of all, multicultural literature is good literature. Students enjoy reading stories, informational books, and poems, and through reading, they learn more about what it means to be human and that people of all cultural groups have similar emotions, needs, and dreams (Bishop, 1992). Allen Say's *El Chino* (1990), for example, tells about a Chinese American who achieves his dream of becoming a great athlete, and the book provides a model for children and adults of all ethnic groups.

Second, through multicultural books, students learn about the wealth of diversity in the United States and develop sensitivity to and respect for people of other cultural groups (Walker-Dalhouse, 1992). *Teammates* (Golenbock, 1990), for example, tells about the friendship of baseball greats Jackie Robinson and Pee Wee Reese, and it teaches a valuable lesson in tolerance and respect. Multicultural literature also challenges racial and ethnic stereotypes by providing an inside view of a culture.

Third, students broaden their knowledge of geography and learn different views of history through multicultural literature. They read about the countries that minority groups left as they immigrated to America, and often students gain nonmainstream perspectives about historical events. For example, Yoshiko Uchida tells of her experiences in Japanese American internment camps in the United States during World War II in *The Bracelet* (1993) and *Journey to Topaz* (1971). As they read and respond to multicultural books, students challenge traditional assumptions and gain a more critical view of historical events and the contributions of people from various cultural groups. They learn that traditional historical accounts have emphasized the contributions of European Americans, particularly those made by men.

Fourth, multicultural literature raises issues of social injustice—prejudice, racism, discrimination, segregation, colonization, anti-Semitism, and genocide. Two books that describe the discrimination and mistreatment of Chinese Americans during the 1800s are *Chang's Paper Pony* (Coerr, 1988), a story set during the California gold rush, and *Ten Mile Day and the Building of the Transcontinental Railroad* (Fraser, 1993), a factual account of the race to complete the construction of the first railroad across North America.

Using multicultural literature has additional benefits for nonmainstream students. When students read books about their own cultural group, they develop pride in their cultural heritage and learn that their culture has made important contributions to the

Figure 11–1 Multicultural Books

Primary Grades

Aliki. (1976). *Corn is maize: The gift of the Indians.* New York: Crowell. (Native American)

Bunting, E. (2001). *Jin Woo.* New York: Clarion Books. (Asian American)

Cazet, D. (1993). *Born in the gravy.* New York: Orchard Books. (Hispanic)

Crews, D. (1991). *Bigmama's.* New York: Greenwillow. (African American)

dePaola, T. (1983). *The legend of the bluebonnet.* New York: Putnam. (Native American)

Dooley, N. (1991). *Everybody cooks rice.* Minneapolis: Carolrhoda. (all)

Dorros, A. (1991). *Abuela.* New York: Dutton. (Hispanic)

Greenfield, E. (1991). *Night on Neighborhood Street.* New York: Dial Books. (African American)

Hoffman, M. (1991). *Amazing Grace.* New York: Dial Books. (African American)

Lin, G. (2001). *Dim sum for everyone!* New York: Knopf. (Asian American)

Martin, B., & Archambault, J. (1987). *Knots on a counting rope.* New York: Holt, Rinehart and Winston. (Native American)

Pak, S. (2003). *Sumi's first day of school ever.* New York: Viking. (Asian American)

Ringgold, F. (1991). *Tar beach.* New York: Crown. (African American)

Smothers, E. F. (2003). *The hard-times jar.* New York: Farrar, Straus & Giroux. (Hispanic)

Soto, G. (1993). *Too many tamales.* New York: Putnam. (Hispanic)

Towle, W. (1993). *The real McCoy: The life of an African-American inventor.* New York: Scholastic. (African American)

Winter, J. (2003). *Niño's mask.* New York: Dial Books. (Hispanic)

Middle Grades

Ancona, G. (1993). *Powwow.* Orlando: Harcourt Brace. (Native American)

Anzaldua, G. (1993). *Friends from the other side/Amigos del otro lado.* San Francisco: Children's Book Press. (Hispanic)

Bunting, E. (1998). *So far from the sea.* New York: Clarion Books. (Asian American)

Golenbock, P. (1990). *Teammates.* San Diego: Harcourt Brace. (African American)

Hamilton, V. (1985). *The people could fly: American Black folktales.* New York: Knopf. (African American)

Hewett, J. (1990). *Hector lives in the United States now: The story of a Mexican-American child.* New York: Lippincott. (Hispanic)

Jones, H. (1993). *The trees standing shining: Poetry of the North American Indians.* New York: Dial Books. (Native American)

Mathis, S. B. (1975). *The hundred penny box.* New York: Viking. (African American)

Mead, A. (1995). *Junebug.* New York: Farrar, Straus & Giroux. (African American)

Mochizuki, K. (1993). *Baseball saved us.* New York: Lee & Low. (Asian American)

Mohr, N. (1979). *Felita.* New York: Dial Books. (Hispanic)

Ryan, P. M. (2000). *Esperanza rising.* New York: Scholastic. (Hispanic)

Secakuku, S. (2003). *Meet Mindy: A native girl from the southwest.* Hillsboro, OR: Beyond Words. (Native American)

Soto, G. (1992). *The skirt.* New York: Delacorte. (Hispanic)

Tayac, G. (2002). *Meet Naiche: A native boy from the Chesapeake Bay area.* Hillsboro, OR: Beyond Words. (Native American)

Whelan, G. (1992). *Goodbye, Vietnam.* New York: Knopf. (Asian American)

Winter, J. (1988). *Follow the drinking gourd.* New York: Knopf. (African American)

Upper Grades

Armstrong, W. H. (1969). *Sounder.* New York: Harper & Row. (African American)

Cisneros, S. (1983). *The house on Mango Street.* New York: Vintage Books. (Hispanic)

Curtis, C. P. (1999). *Bud, not Buddy.* New York: Delacorte. (African American)

Denenberg, B. (1999). *The journal of Ben Uchida.* New York: Scholastic. (Asian American)

Hesse, K. (2001). *Witness.* New York: Scholastic. (African American)

Jiménez, F. (1997). *The circuit.* Albuquerque: University of New Mexico Press. (Hispanic)

Martin, A. (2001). *Belle Teal.* New York: Scholastic. (African American)

Myers, W. D. (1988). *Scorpions.* New York: Harper-Collins. (African American)

Paulsen, G. (1993). *Nightjohn.* New York: Delacorte. (African American)

Rice, D. (2001). *Crazy loco.* New York: Dial Books. (Hispanic)

Soto, G. (1992). *Neighborhood odes.* Orlando: Harcourt Brace. (Hispanic)

Uchida, Y. (1971). *Journey to Topaz.* Berkeley, CA: Creative Arts. (Asian American)

Woodson, J. (2003). *Locomotion.* New York: Putnam. (African American)

Yep, L. (1975). *Dragonwings.* New York: HarperCollins. (Asian American)

United States and to the world (Harris, 1992a, 1992b). In addition, these students often become more interested in reading because they are able to better identify with the characters and with the events in those characters' lives.

Teachers' choices of books for instruction and for inclusion in the classroom library influence students in other ways, too. Students tend to choose familiar books and those that reflect their own cultures for reading workshop and other independent reading activities. If teachers read aloud culturally conscious books, include them in literature focus units, and display them in the classroom library, these books become familiar and are more likely to be picked up and read independently by students.

FRAMEWORK FOR A LITERATURE FOCUS UNIT

Visit Chapter 11 on the Companion Website at *www.prenhall. com/tompkins* to connect to web links related to literature focus units.

Teachers plan literature focus units featuring popular and award-winning stories for children and adolescents. Some literature focus units feature a single book, either a picture book or a chapter book, whereas others feature a text set of books for a genre unit or an author study unit. Figure 11–2 presents a list of trade books, genres, and authors recommended for literature focus units for kindergarten through eighth grade. An overview of this instructional approach is shown in the box on page 367.

Steps in Developing a Unit

Teachers develop a literature focus unit through a six-step series of activities, beginning with choosing the literature for the unit and setting goals, then identifying and scheduling activities, and finally deciding how to assess students' learning. Whether teachers are using trade books or basal reader selections, they develop a unit using these steps. An overview of the six steps in developing a literature focus unit is presented in Figure 11–3. Effective teachers do not simply follow directions in basal reader teacher's manuals and literature focus unit planning guides that are available for purchase in school supply stories; rather, they need to make the plans themselves because they are the ones most knowledgeable about their students, the literature books they have available, the time available for the unit, the skills and strategies they want to teach, and the activities they want to develop.

Usually literature focus units featuring a picture book are completed in 1 week, and units featuring a chapter book are completed in 2, 3, or 4 weeks. Genre and author units may last 2, 3, or 4 weeks. Rarely, if ever, do literature focus units continue for more than a month. When teachers drag out a unit for 6 weeks or longer, they risk killing students' interest in that particular book or, worse yet, their love of literature or reading.

Step 1: Select the Literature. Teachers begin by selecting the reading material for the literature focus unit. The featured selection may be a story in a picture-book format, a chapter book, or a story selected from a basal reading textbook. Teachers collect multiple copies of the book or books for the literature focus unit. When teachers use trade books, they have to collect class sets of the books for the unit. Many school districts have class sets of selected books available for loan to teachers; however, in other school districts, teachers have to request that administrators purchase multiple copies of books or buy them themselves through book clubs. When teachers use picture books, students can share books so only half as many books as students are needed.

Figure 11–2 Topics for Literature Focus Units

Books	Genres	Authors and Illustrators
Primary Grades (K–2)		
Allard, H. (1977). *Miss Nelson is missing!* Boston: Houghton Mifflin.	Folk and fairy tales Realistic fiction	Jan Brett Eric Carle
Blume, J. (1971). *Freckle juice.* New York: Bradbury Press.		Tomie dePaola Lois Ehlert
Brett, J. (1989). *The mitten.* New York: Putnam.		Mem Fox
Carle, E. (1970). *The very hungry caterpillar.* New York: Viking.		Kevin Henkes Steven Kellogg
Dorros, A. (1991). *Abuela.* New York: Dutton.		James Marshall
Fleming, D. (2003). *Buster.* New York: Henry Holt.		Bill Martin and John Archambault
Galdone, P. (1972). *The three bears.* New York: Clarion Books.		Patricia and Frederick McKissack Bernard Most
Henkes, K. (1991). *Chrysanthemum.* New York: Greenwillow.		Dr. Seuss Bernard Waber
Hutchins, P. (1968). *Rosie's walk.* New York: Macmillan.		Audrey and Don Wood
Lester, H. (1988). *Tacky the penguin.* Boston: Houghton Mifflin.		
Martin, B. Jr. (1983). *Brown bear, brown bear, what do you see?* New York: Holt, Rinehart and Winston.		
Meddaugh, S. (1995). *Hog-eye.* Boston: Houghton Mifflin.		
Most, B. (1978). *If the dinosaurs came back.* San Diego: Harcourt Brace.		
Numeroff, L. (1985). *If you give a mouse a cookie.* New York: Harper & Row.		
Rylant, C. (1985). *The relatives came.* New York: Bradbury Press.		
Stevens, J., & Crummel, S. S. (1999). *Cook-a-doodle-doo!* San Diego: Harcourt Brace.		
Middle Grades (3–5)		Byrd Baylor
Blume, J. (1972). *Tales of a fourth grade nothing.* New York: Dutton.	Realistic fiction Biography	Eve Bunting Beverly Cleary
Bunting, E. (1994). *Smoky night.* San Diego: Harcourt Brace.	Fables Poetry	Joanna Cole Paula Danziger
Cherry, L. (1990). *The great kapok tree.* Orlando, FL: Harcourt Brace.	Tall tales Fantasies	Jean Fritz Paul Goble
Cleary, B. (1981). *Ramona Quimby, age 8.* New York: Morrow.	Historical fiction	Eloise Greenfield Patricia MacLachlan
Coerr, E. (1977). *Sadako and the thousand paper cranes.* New York: Putnam.		Ann Martin Patricia Polacco
Cohen, B. (1983). *Molly's pilgrim.* New York: Morrow.		Jack Prelutsky
Danziger, P. (1994). *Amber Brown is not a crayon.* New York: Putnam.		Cynthia Rylant William Steig
Gardiner, J. R. (1980). *Stone Fox.* New York: Harper & Row.		R. L. Stine Marvin Terban
Lowry, L. (1989). *Number the stars.* Boston: Houghton Mifflin.		

Figure 11–2 (Continued)

Books	Genres	Authors and Illustrators
Middle Grades (continued)		
MacLachlan, P. (1985). *Sarah, plain and tall.* New York: Harper & Row.		Chris Van Allsburg
Naylor, P. R. (1991). *Shiloh.* New York: Macmillan.		Jane Yolen
Paterson, K. (1977). *Bridge to Terabithia.* New York: Crowell.		
Ryan, P. M. (2000). *Esperanza rising.* New York: Scholastic.		
Speare, E. G. (1983). *The sign of the beaver.* Boston: Houghton Mifflin.		
Steig, W. (1969). *Sylvester and the magic pebble.* New York: Simon & Schuster.		
White, E. B. (1952). *Charlotte's web.* New York: Harper & Row.		
Upper Grades (6–8)		
Avi. (1991). *Nothing but the truth.* New York: Orchard Books.	Science fiction	Avi
Babbitt, N. (1975). *Tuck everlasting.* New York: Farrar, Straus & Giroux.	Myths	Karen Cushman
Curtis, C. P. (1995). *The Watsons go to Birmingham—1963.* New York: Delacorte.	Poetry	Russell Freedman
Cushman, K. (1994). *Catherine, called Birdy.* New York: HarperCollins.	Historical fiction	Virginia Hamilton
George, J. C. (1972). *Julie of the wolves.* New York: Harper & Row.	Biography	Lois Lowry
Hinton, S. E. (1967). *The outsiders.* New York: Viking.		David Macaulay
Howe, D., & Howe, J. (1979). *Bunnicula: A rabbit-tale of mystery.* New York: Atheneum.		Walter Dean Myers
L'Engle, M. (1962). *A wrinkle in time.* New York: Farrar, Straus & Giroux.		Scott O'Dell
Lewis, C. S. (1994). *The lion, the witch and the wardrobe.* New York: HarperCollins.		Katherine Paterson
Lowry, L. (1993). *The giver.* Boston: Houghton Mifflin.		Gary Paulsen
Paulsen, G. (1987). *Hatchet.* New York: Viking.		Richard Peck
Philbrick, R. (1993). *Freak the mighty.* New York: Scholastic.		J. K. Rowling
Taylor, M. (1976). *Roll of thunder, hear my cry.* New York: Dial Books.		Jerry Spinelli
Uchida, Y. (1971). *Journey to Topaz.* Berkeley, CA: Creative Arts.		Yoshiko Uchida
Whelan, G. (2000). *Homeless bird.* New York: Scholastic.		Laurence Yep

Once the book (or books) is selected, teachers collect additional related books for the text set. Books for the text set include:

- other versions of the same story
- other books written by the same author

Literature Focus Units

Topic	Description
Purpose	To teach reading through literature, using high quality, grade-appropriate picture books and novels.
Components	Teachers involve students in three activities: Students read and respond to a trade book together as a class; the teacher teaches minilessons on phonics, vocabulary, and comprehension using the book they are reading; and students create projects to extend their interpretation of the book.
Theory Base	Literature focus units are more teacher directed than other student-centered approaches because the teacher guides students as they read and discuss books. This approach reflects interactive theory because teachers develop students' background knowledge, read aloud if students cannot read the book fluently, and teach vocabulary and comprehension. It also reflects reader response theory because students participate in grand conversations and write in reading logs to personalize and enhance their comprehension, and critical literacy theory because issues of social justice often arise in the trade books.
Applications	Teachers teach units featuring a picture book or a novel, generally using books on a district-approved list, or units featuring a genre or author/illustrator. Literature focus units are taught in conjunction with another instructional approaches where students read books at their own reading levels.
Strengths	• Teachers select award-winning literature for these units. • Teachers scaffold students' comprehension as they read with the whole class or small groups. • Teachers teach minilessons on reading strategies and skills. • Students learn vocabulary through word walls and other activities. • Students learn about genres, story structure, and literary devices.
Limitations	• Students all read the same book whether or not they like it and whether or not it is written at their reading level. • Many activities are teacher directed.

- other books illustrated by the same artist
- books with the same theme
- books with similar geographic or historical settings
- books in the same genre

Figure 11-3 Steps in Developing a Literature Focus Unit

1. Select the Literature

- Identify the featured selection for the unit.
- Collect multiple copies of the featured selection for students to read individually, with partners, or in small groups.
- Collect related books for the text set, including stories, informational books, and poems.
- Identify supplemental materials, including puppets, information about the author and illustrator, and multimedia resources.

2. Set Goals

- Identify four or five broad goals or learning outcomes for the unit.
- Address district, state, or national literacy standards.
- Choose skills and strategies to teach.
- Expect to refine these goals as the unit is developed.

3. Develop a Unit Plan

- Read or reread the featured selection.
- Think about the focus for the unit and the goals or learning outcomes.
- Plan activities for each of the five stages of the reading process.

4. Coordinate Grouping Patterns With Activities

- Decide how to incorporate whole-class, small-group, partner, and individual activities.
- Double-check that all four types of grouping are used during the unit.

5. Create a Time Schedule

- Include activities representing all five stages of the reading process in the schedule for the literature focus unit.
- Incorporate minilessons to teach reading and writing procedures, concepts, skills, and strategies.
- Write weekly lesson plans.

6. Manage Record Keeping and Assessment

- Use unit folders in which students keep all assignments.
- Develop assignment checklists for students to use to keep track of their work during the unit.
- Monitor students' learning using observations, anecdotal notes, conferences, and work samples.

- informational books on a related topic
- books of poetry on a related topic

Teachers collect one or two copies of 10, 20, 30, or more books for the text set and add these to the classroom library during the focus unit. Books for the text set are placed on a special shelf or in a crate in the library center. At the beginning of the unit, teachers do a book talk to introduce the books in the text set, and then students read them during independent reading time.

Teachers also identify and collect supplemental materials related to the featured selection, including puppets, stuffed animals, and toys; charts and diagrams; book boxes of materials to use in introducing the book; and information about the author and illustrator. For many picture books, big book versions are also available that can be used in introducing the featured selection. Teachers also locate multimedia resources, including videotapes of the featured selection, multimedia materials to provide background knowledge on the topic, and videotapes and Internet sites about the author and illustrator.

Step 2: Set Goals. Teachers set goals for the literature focus unit: They decide what they want their students to learn during the unit, the skills and strategies they plan to teach, and the types of activities they want students to do, and then they connect their goals with district, state, or national literacy standards. Teachers identify three or four broad goals for the unit and then refine them as they develop the unit.

Step 3: Develop a Unit Plan. Teachers read or reread the selected book or books and then think about the focus they will use for the unit. Sometimes teachers focus on an element of story structure, the historical setting, wordplay, the author or genre, or a topic related to the book, such as weather or life in the desert. In the vignette at the beginning of this chapter, Mrs. Dillon selected Marshall's *The Three Little Pigs* and read it with her students to introduce a genre unit.

After determining the focus, teachers think about which activities they will use at each of the five stages of the reading process. For each stage, teachers ask themselves these questions:

1. *Prereading*
    - What background knowledge do students need before reading?
    - What key concepts and vocabulary should I teach before reading?
    - How will I introduce the story and stimulate students' interest for reading?

2. *Reading*
    - How will students read this story?
    - What reading strategies will I model or ask students to use?
    - How can I make the story more accessible for less able readers?

3. *Responding*
    - Will students write in reading logs? How often?
    - Will students participate in grand conversations? How often?

4. *Exploring*
    - Which words will be added to the word wall?
    - Which vocabulary activities will be used?

Nurturing English Learners

Should my English learners participate in grand conversations?

It can be difficult for English learners to participate in grand conversations, but it is important to include them so they can grapple with big ideas from the story, increase their motivation, and be part of the learning community. Less fluent ELs may need extra time to translate classmates' comments into their native language and convert their thoughts into English. You may need to step in more often to slow down the tempo of the conversation and remind students to give their EL classmates opportunities to join the conversation. You may also call on students; for example, you might say, "Ka, what do you think?" or "Juan, do you agree with Hernan?" Before asking EL students to participate, giving them a chance to listen to their classmates' ideas and how they incorporate new vocabulary words and string words together to express ideas also is helpful.

Minilessons

This teacher is teaching a minilesson to her third-grade class as part of a literature focus unit featuring Native American legends. The students gather around her on the floor to learn about regular and irregular plural forms, one of the third-grade literacy standards the teacher is required to teach. The students listen to her explanation about forming plurals and then look for examples in the books they are reading. In a follow-up minilesson, students will sort nouns according to their plural forms; the charts they make will remain on the classroom wall so students can refer to them.

- Will students reread the story?
- What skill and strategy minilessons will be taught?
- What word-study or wordplay activities will be used?
- How will books from the text set be used?
- What writing, drama, and other reading activities will be used?
- What can I share about the author, illustrator, or genre?

5. *Applying*
   - What projects might students choose to pursue?
   - How will books from the text set be used?
   - How will students share projects?

Teachers often jot notes on a chart divided into sections for each stage, then they use the ideas they have brainstormed as they plan the unit. Generally, not all of the brainstormed activities will be used in the literature focus unit, but teachers select the most important ones according to their focus and the time available. Teachers do not omit any of the reading process stages, however, in an attempt to make more time available for activities during any one stage.

Step 4: Coordinate Grouping Patterns With Activities. Teachers think about how to incorporate whole-class, small-group, partner, and individual activities into their unit plans. It is important that students have opportunities to read and write independently as well as to work with small groups and to come together as a class. If the featured selection that students are reading will be read together as a class, then students need opportunities to reread it with a buddy or independently or to read related books independently. These grouping patterns should be alternated during various activities in the unit. Teachers often go back to their planning sheet and highlight activities with colored markers according to grouping patterns.

Step 5: Create a Time Schedule. Teachers create a schedule that provides sufficient time for students to move through the five stages of the reading process and to complete the activities planned for the literature focus unit. They also plan minilessons to teach reading and writing procedures, concepts, skills, and strategies identified in their goals and those needed for students to complete the unit activities. Of course, teachers also present impromptu minilessons when students ask questions or need to know how to use a procedure, skill, or strategy, but many minilessons are planned. Sometimes teachers have a set time for minilessons in their weekly schedule, and sometimes they arrange their schedules so that they teach minilessons just before they introduce related activities or assignments.

Step 6: Manage Record Keeping and Assessment. Teachers often distribute unit folders in which students keep all work, reading logs, reading materials, and related materials. Then at the end of the unit, students turn in their completed folders for teachers to evaluate. Keeping all the materials together makes the unit easier for both students and teachers to manage.

Teachers also plan ways to document students' learning and assign grades. One type of record keeping is an assignment checklist, which is developed with students and distributed at the beginning of the literature focus unit. Students keep track of their work during the unit and sometimes negotiate to change the sheet as the unit evolves. Students keep the lists in their unit folders, and they mark off each item as it is completed. At the end of the unit, students turn in their assignment checklist and other completed work. A copy of an assignment checklist for Mrs. Dillon's literature

Guidelines for Using Literature Focus Units

Choose high-quality literature, including multicultural books, for literature focus units.

Use shared reading or read aloud, if necessary, to ensure that all students can comprehend the featured book.

Incorporate activities into literature focus units representing the five stages of the reading process.

Teach students about genres, story structure, and literary devices during literature focus units.

Demonstrate how capable readers use strategies and skills while reading authentic literature.

Teach phonics, vocabulary, and strategies and skills using examples from the featured book.

Include at least one genre unit and one author/illustrator unit during the school year.

Provide daily opportunities for students to read others books at their reading levels, if the featured book is too difficult for them.

Three Little Pigs Unit

Name _____

_____ 1. Read The Three Little Pigs.

_____

_____

_____ 2. Read to Mrs. Dillon.

_____ 3. Make a vocabulary mobile.

_____ 4. Make a quotes book.

_____ 5. Make a square for the quilt.

_____ 6. Read four pig books.

_____

_____

_____

_____

_____ 7. Do a project.

What is your project? _____

_____ 8. Write a letter to Mrs. Dillon.

_____ 9. Write in your journal.

☐ draw pigs

☐ draw wolves

☐ write about the three pigs

☐ write about the wolf

Assessment Tools

unit on "The Three Little Pigs" is presented in Figure 11–4. Although this list does not include every activity students were involved in, it does list the activities and other assignments Mrs. Dillon holds the students accountable for. Students complete the checklist on the left side of the sheet and add titles of books and other requested information.

Teachers also monitor students' learning as they observe students reading, writing, and working in small groups. Students and teachers also meet in brief conferences during literature focus units to talk about the featured selection and other books in the text set students are reading, projects students do during the applying stage of the reading process, and other assignments. These conferences often are brief, but they give teachers insight into students' learning. Teachers make anecdotal notes of their observations and conferences, and they also examine students' work samples to monitor learning.

Guidelines for using literature focus units are presented in the feature on page 371.

Units Featuring a Picture Book

In literature focus units featuring picture books, younger children read predictable picture books or books with very little text, such as *Rosie's Walk* (Hutchins, 1968), and older students read more sophisticated picture books with more text, such as *Pink and Say* (Polacco, 1994) or *A Day's Work* (Bunting, 1994). Teachers use the same six-step approach for developing units featuring a picture book for younger and older students. Second graders, for example, might spend a week reading *Tacky the Penguin* (Lester, 1988), a popular story about an oddball penguin who saves all the penguins from some hunters. During the unit, students read the story several times, share their responses to the story, participate in a variety of exploring activities, and do projects to extend their interpretations. A weeklong plan for teaching a unit on *Tacky the Penguin* is presented in Figure 11–5.

Several types of exploring activities are included in this plan. One type focuses on vocabulary: On Monday, students list words from the story on a word wall; the next day, they reread the words and sort them according to the character they refer to; and on Thursday, the teacher teaches a minilesson about peeling off the *-ly* suffix to learn the "main" word (root word). It's not typical to teach a lesson on derivational suffixes in second grade, but second graders notice that many of the words on the word wall have *-ly* at the end of them and often ask about the suffix.

Another activity examines character: The teacher gives a minilesson on characters on Tuesday, and then students make a character cluster about Tacky and draw open minds to show what Tacky is thinking. To make an open-mind portrait, students draw a portrait of the penguin, cut around the head so that it will flip open, and draw or write what Tacky is thinking on another sheet of paper that has been attached behind the paper with the portrait.

Units Featuring a Chapter Book

Teachers develop literature focus units using chapter books, such as *Bunnicula: A Rabbit-Tale of Mystery* (Howe & Howe, 1979), *Sarah, Plain and Tall* (MacLachlan, 1985), *The Sign of the Beaver* (Speare, 1983), and *Number the Stars* (Lowry, 1989). The biggest difference between picture books and chapter books is their length, and when teachers plan literature focus units featuring a chapter book, they need to decide how to schedule the reading of the book. Will students read one or two chapters each day? How often will they respond in reading logs or grand conversations? It is important that teachers reread the book to note the length of chapters and identify key points in the book where students will want time to explore and respond to the ideas presented there.

Figure 11–6 presents a 4-week lesson plan for Lois Lowry's *Number the Stars*, a story of friendship and courage set in Nazi-occupied Denmark during World War II. The daily routine during the first 2 weeks is as follows:

1. **Reading.** Students and the teacher read two chapters using shared reading.

2. **Responding to the reading.** Students participate in a grand conversation about the chapters they have read, write in reading logs, and add important words from the chapters to the class word wall.

Scaffolding Struggling Readers

How can I help my struggling students who don't understand the featured story when I read it aloud?

Many students who can't read a story themselves can understand it when it is read aloud, but others cannot. Before you decide that the book is entirely too difficult, try several things. Bring your struggling readers together before reading each chapter aloud to review the story and make predictions about what will happen in the next chapter. When students have a purpose for listening, they are more likely to get involved in the listening experience. Then immediately after reading, bring this small group back together to talk about the story to ensure that they understand the big ideas before they write in reading logs or participate in a grand conversation. If these suggestions don't help, try telling the story to the struggling readers. Stop before the climax and encourage students to predict how the story will end. Knowing most of the story should make read-alouds less confusing, and students may develop more confidence, which leads to success.

Figure 11–5 A Weeklong Lesson Plan for *Tacky the Penguin*

	Monday	Tuesday	Wednesday	Thursday	Friday
8:45	Talk about penguins Begin K-W-L chart Begin word wall	Have students share reading log entries in small groups Reread word wall	Have students make open-mind portraits of Tacky	Reread <u>Tacky</u> in small groups while other students work on projects	Finish projects
9:15	Read <u>Tacky the Penguin</u> using guided reading Have grand conversation Ask: Is Tacky an "odd" bird?	Reread story with reading buddies	Discuss possible projects		Sequence story boards with students who are done with their projects
9:45	Break				
10:00	Add words to word wall Have students write in reading logs	Sort words: 1. Tacky words 2. Other penguin words 3. Hunter words	Begin work on projects	ML: Suffix –ly. Show students how to peel off suffix	Share projects
10:30	Introduce text set Read aloud <u>Three Cheers for Tacky</u>	ML: Character development Make a character cluster for Tacky	Add to K-W-L chart Read <u>A Penguin Year</u> aloud	Read aloud two other books by Helen Lester: <u>Me First</u> <u>A Porcupine Named Fluffy</u>	
11:00	Reading Workshop/ Guided Reading Groups				Add favorite story quotes and interesting penguin facts to penguin bulletin board to make a quilt

Figure 11–6 **A 4-Week Lesson Plan for *Number the Stars***

	Monday	Tuesday	Wednesday	Thursday	Friday
Week 1	Build background on World War II The Resistance movement ML: Reading maps of Nazi-occupied Europe Read aloud The Lily Cupboard	Introduce NTS Begin word wall Read Ch. 1 & 2 Grand conversation Reading log Add to word wall Book talk on text set	Read Ch. 3 & 4 Grand conversation Reading log Word wall ML: Connecting with a character Read text set books	Read Ch. 5 Grand conversation Reading log Word wall ML: Visualizing Nazis in apartment (use drama)	Read Ch. 6 & 7 Grand conversation Reading log Word wall ML: Information about the author and why she wrote the book
Week 2	Read Ch. 8 & 9 Grand conversation Reading log Word wall ML: Compare home front and war front Read text set books →	Read Ch. 10 & 11 Grand conversation Reading log Word wall ML: Visualizing the wake (use drama) →	Read Ch. 12 & 13 Grand conversation Reading log Word wall ML: Compare characters – make Venn diagram →	Read Ch. 14 & 15 Grand conversation Reading log Word wall ML: Make word maps of key words →	Finish book Grand conversation Reading log Word wall ML: Theme of book →
Week 3	Plan class interview project Choose individual projects Independent reading/ projects →	Activities at Centers: 1. Story map 2. Word sort 3. Plot profile 4. Quilt →	→	→	→
Week 4	Revise interviews Independent reading/ projects →	→	Edit interviews Share projects →	Make final copies →	Compile interview book →

3. ***Minilesson.*** The teacher teaches a minilesson on a reading strategy or presents information about World War II or about the author.

4. ***More reading.*** Students read related books from the text set independently.

The schedule for the last 2 weeks is different. During the third week, students choose a class project (interviewing people who were alive during World War II) and individual projects. They work in teams on activities related to the book and continue to read other books about the war. During the final week, students finish the class interview project and share their completed individual projects.

Units Featuring a Genre

During a genre unit, students learn about a particular genre or category of literature, such as folktales or science fiction. Students read stories illustrating the genre and then participate in a variety of activities to deepen their knowledge about the genre. In these units, students participate in the following activities:

- reading several stories illustrating a genre
- learning the characteristics of the genre
- reading other stories illustrating the genre
- responding to and exploring the genre stories
- writing or rewriting stories exemplifying the genre

Genre studies about traditional literature, including fables, folktales, legends, and myths, are very appropriate for kindergarten through eighth-grade students. A list of recommended genre units also was included in Figure 11–2.

Units Featuring an Author or Illustrator

Students learn about authors and illustrators who write and illustrate the books they read as part of literature focus units. They need to develop concepts of author and illustrator so that they think of them as real people—real people who eat breakfast, ride bikes, and take out the garbage, just as they do. When students think of them as real people, they view reading and literature in a different, more personal way. The concepts of author and illustrator also carry over to children's writing: As they learn about authors and illustrators, students realize that they too can write and illustrate books. They can learn about the writing process from these authors, and from illustrators they can learn about using illustrations to extend the meaning of their text. Students need to be familiar with authors and illustrators so that they can have favorites and compare them.

In kindergarten or first grade, for example, many children read Eric Carle's books and experiment with his illustration techniques, and middle-grade students focus on Beverly Cleary as they read her chapter books about Ramona and her family. Many students write letters to Beverly Cleary, and she is faithful about writing back. Older students often read Chris Van Allsburg's fantasy picture books, hunt for the picture of the white dog that Van Allsburg includes in every book, and write their own fantasy stories based on *The Mysteries of Harris Burdick* (Van Allsburg, 1984). Gary Paulsen and Lois Lowry are two other contemporary authors that upper-grade students enjoy learning about. A list of recommended authors and illustrators for units also was included in Figure 11–2.

One of the best ways to interest students in learning about authors and illustrators is to teach a unit focusing on a favorite author or illustrator. In these units, students learn about the author's life and read many of his or her books. They also examine the author's

or illustrator's style. Studying authors is easier than ever today, because many authors have written autobiographies, appeared in videos, and put websites on the Internet.

To plan for a unit on an author or illustrator, teachers collect books written by a particular author or illustrated by a particular illustrator, as well as related materials about the author's or illustrator's life. Following are seven types of material:

- A collection of books written by the author or illustrated by the illustrator
- Audiotape or videotape versions of the books
- Posters about the books, author, or illustrator provided by publishers or made by students
- Wwebsites about the author or illustrator
- Autobiographies, biographical brochures and pamphlets, and other information about the author or illustrator
- Letters written by the author or illustrator to the teacher or former students
- Audiotapes and videotapes featuring the author or illustrator

Teachers can locate a variety of materials about authors and illustrators, if they are willing to do a little extra work. For example, they can check publishers' websites and authors' and illustrators' websites for photographs and information. Authors and illustrators have written autobiographical books for children, such as Patricia Polacco's *Firetalking* (1994) and Laura Numeroff's *If You Give an Author a Pencil* (2003). Each year, more and more of these books are published; these personal glimpses into authors' and illustrators' lives are very popular with students. Teachers also can check professional journals and magazines, including *Book Links, Language Arts, Horn Book,* and *The Reading Teacher,* for articles about authors and illustrators.

All types of literature focus units include activities incorporating the five stages of the reading process. Teachers involve students in prereading activities to build and activate their background knowledge. Next, students read the featured selection and respond in grand conversations and entries in reading logs. Students participate in exploring activities as they learn vocabulary, study literature concepts, and participate in minilessons. Last, students apply their learning as they create projects and share them with their classmates at the end of the unit. Through these activities, teachers guide students as they read and respond to high-quality literature.

Benefits of Literature Focus Units

Literature focus units are successful because students read and respond to award-winning stories and other high-quality books. They connect what they are reading to their own lives, and they think about themes such as bravery, friendship, cleverness, and loyalty. The featured selection also provides an authentic context for instruction. Students learn vocabulary words and expressions from the selection through reading, responding, and exploring activities, and they have many opportunities to examine the sentence structure that the author used. Instruction is authentic and meaningful because teachers tie strategy and skills instruction to the selection. In this way, students are able to apply what they are learning to their reading and writing.

Literature focus units are somewhat teacher directed, and teachers play several important roles. They share their love of literature, direct students' attention to genres, elements of story structure, and literary devices, and help students analyze a story. They model the strategies that capable readers use and guide students to read more strategically. They also scaffold students, providing support and guidance so that students can be successful. Through this instruction and support, students learn about reading and literature, and they apply what they have learned as they participate in literature circles and reading workshop, two more student-centered approaches.

Complete a self-assessment to check your understanding of the concepts presented in this chapter on the Companion Website at *www.prenhall.com/ tompkins*

Review: How Effective Teachers Use Literature Focus Units

1. Teachers choose high-quality literature for literature focus units.
2. Teachers introduce students to Caldecott and Newbery Medal books.
3. Teachers select multicultural books for featured selections and for text sets.
4. Teachers determine the difficulty level of books they use for literature focus units.
5. Teachers find ways to make difficult books accessible for students.
6. Teachers provide daily opportunities for students to choose and read books at their own reading levels from text sets.
7. Teachers carefully develop literature focus units using the six-step approach described in this chapter.
8. Teachers spend approximately 1 week on a picture book unit and no longer than a month on other types of units.
9. Teachers use four types of literature focus units: picture book units, chapter book units, genre units, and author or illustrator units.
10. Teachers incorporate activities from all five stages of the reading process in literature focus units.

Professional References

Bishop, R. S. (1992). Multicultural literature for children: Making informed choices. In V. J. Harris (Ed.), *Teaching multicultural literature in grades K–8* (pp. 37–54). Norwood, MA: Christopher-Gordon.

Harris, V. J. (1992a). Multiethnic children's literature. In K. D. Wood & A. Moss (Eds.), *Exploring literature in the classroom: Content and methods* (pp. 169–201). Norwood, MA: Christopher-Gordon.

Harris, V. J. (Ed.). (1992b). *Teaching multicultural literature in grades K–8*. Norwood, MA: Christopher-Gordon.

Jipson, J., & Paley, N. (1991). The selective tradition in teachers' choice of children's literature: Does it exist in the elementary classroom? *English Education, 23,* 148–159.

Norton, D. E., & Norton, S. E. (2003). *Through the eyes of a child: An introduction to children's literature* (6th ed.). Upper Saddle River, NJ: Merrill/Prentice Hall.

Shannon, P. (1986). Hidden within the pages: A study of social perspective in young children's favorite books. *The Reading Teacher, 39,* 656–661.

Sims, R. (1982). *Shadow and substance*. Urbana, IL: National Council of Teachers of English.

Traxel, J. (1983). The American Revolution in children's fiction. *Research in the Teaching of English, 17,* 61–83.

Walker-Dalhouse, D. (1992). Using African-American literature to increase ethnic understanding. *The Reading Teacher, 45,* 416–422.

Yokota, J. (1993). Issues in selecting multicultural children's literature. *Language Arts, 70,* 156–167.

Children's Book References

Bishop, G. (1989). *The three little pigs*. New York: Scholastic.

Bunting, E. (1994). *A day's work*. New York: Clarion.

Bunting, E. (1998). *So far from the sea*. New York: Clarion.

Coerr, E. (1988). *Chang's paper pony*. New York: Harper & Row.

Curtis, C. P. (1995). *The Watsons go to Birmingham—1963*. New York: Delacorte.

Fraser, M. A. (1993). *Ten mile day and the building of the transcontinental railroad*. New York: Henry Holt.

Golenbock, P. (1990). *Teammates*. San Diego: Harcourt Brace.

Hamilton, V. (1988). *Anthony Burns: The defeat and triumph of a fugitive slave*. New York: Knopf.

Hooks, W. H. (1989). *The three little pigs and the fox*. New York: Macmillan.

Howe, D., & Howe, J. (1979). *Bunnicula: A rabbit-tale of mystery*. New York: Atheneum.

Hutchins, P. (1968). *Rosie's walk*. New York: Macmillan.

Lester, H. (1988). *Tacky the penguin*. Boston: Houghton Mifflin.

Lowell, S. (1992). *The three little javelinas*. Flagstaff, AZ: Northland.

Lowry, L. (1989). *Number the stars*. Boston: Houghton Mifflin.

MacLachlan, P. (1985). *Sarah, plain and tall*. New York: Harper & Row.

Marshall, J. (1989). *The three little pigs*. New York: Dial Books.

Numeroff, L. (2003). *If you give an author a pencil*. Katonah, NY: Richard C. Owen.

Polacco, P. (1994a). *Firetalking*. Katonah, NY: Richard C. Owen.

Polacco, P. (1994b). *Pink and Say*. New York: Philomel.

Ringgold, F. (1991). *Tar beach*. New York: Crown.

Say, A. (1990). *El Chino*. Boston: Houghton Mifflin.

Scieszka, J. (1989). *The true story of the 3 little pigs!* New York: Viking.

Soto, G. (1993). *Too many tamales*. New York: Putnam.

Speare, E. G. (1983). *The sign of the beaver*. Boston: Houghton Mifflin.

Uchida, Y. (1971). *Journey to Topaz*. Berkeley, CA: Creative Arts.

Uchida, Y. (1993). *The bracelet*. New York: Philomel.

Van Allsburg, C. (1979). *The garden of Abdul Gasazi*. Boston: Houghton Mifflin.

Van Allsburg, C. (1984). *The mysteries of Harris Burdick*. Boston: Houghton Mifflin.

Chapter 12

Orchestrating Literature Circles

Chapter Questions

- What is a literature circle?
- How do teachers apply the reading process in this instructional approach?
- How do teachers implement literature circles?
- Why do teachers use this instructional approach?

Mrs. Donnelly's Students Read in Book Clubs

The students in Mrs. Donnelly's fourth/fifth-grade classroom have divided into six small-group literature circles that they call "book clubs" to read and respond to these chapter books:

- *On My Honor* (Bauer, 1986), a story about a boy who breaks a promise to his father, with disastrous results.
- *Freckle Juice* (Blume, 1971), a humorous story about a boy who tries to rid himself of his freckles.
- *Shiloh* (Naylor, 1991), a heartwarming boy-and-dog story that has been made into a movie.

- *Bunnicula: A Rabbit-Tale of Mystery* (Howe & Howe, 1979), a fantasy about a bunny who just might be a vampire.
- *How to Eat Fried Worms* (Rockwell, 1973), a humorously revolting story about a boy who makes a bet that he can eat 15 worms in 15 days.
- *Bridge to Terabithia* (Paterson, 1977), a touching story of friendship between two lonely children.

All six of these books are good stories and popular with middle-grade students. Two have won the Newbery

Medal for excellence, and one is a Newbery Honor Book (runner-up for the Newbery
Medal). Mrs. Donnelly chose these books after reflecting on the interests and needs of the students in the
classroom, and based on requests and recommendations from her students. The reading levels of the books range from second to fifth grade.

Mrs. Donnelly has a set of six of each of these books, and she introduced them using a book talk. Students had a day to preview the books and sign up for one of the groups. After students get into groups, Mrs. Donnelly holds a class meeting to set the guidelines for this unit. Students will have 75 minutes each day for 5 days to read and respond to the books. Students in each group set their own schedules for reading, discussing the book, and writing in reading logs. They decide how they will read the book, plan for at least three grand conversations, write at least three entries in their reading logs, and develop a presentation to share their book with the class at the end of the unit. Mrs. Donnelly distributes a "Book Club Notes" sheet for students to use to keep track of their schedules and the assignments. A copy of this sheet is shown in the box on page 382. Students keep this sheet and their reading logs in their book club folders.

The students in each book club talk about their books and make plans. Four of the groups decide to write their first reading log entry before beginning to read, and the other two groups begin reading right away. As the students read, write, and talk about their books, Mrs. Donnelly moves from group to group and writes anecdotal notes to monitor students' progress.

Mrs. Donnelly joins the *Bridge to Terabithia* group as they finish reading the first chapter, and one student asks about the dedication. Mrs. Donnelly shares that she read that Katherine Paterson wrote this book after the child of a friend of hers died, and she guesses that the Lisa mentioned in the dedication is that child. Another child asks about the setting of the story, and from the information in the first chapter, the group deduces that the story is set in a rural area outside Washington, DC. Several students comment on how vividly Paterson describes Jesse and his family. After speculating on who might be moving into the old Perkins place, they continue reading.

Next, Mrs. Donnelly moves to the book club reading *Freckle Juice* and helps them set up their group schedule. The students in this group decide to read together. They will take turns reading aloud as the other group members follow along and help with unfamiliar words. Mrs. Donnelly stays with this group as they read the first three pages. Then she encourages them to continue reading and moves on to another group.

The next day, the book club reading *Bunnicula: A Rabbit-Tale of Mystery* asks Mrs. Donnelly to meet with them. They have a lot of questions and confusions about vampires and Dracula. Mrs. Donnelly is prepared for their requests, and she brings with her the "V" and "D" volumes of an encyclopedia and several other books about vampires. She spends 20 minutes with the group, helping them find information and clarify confusions.

Book Club Notes

Name _____ Date _____

Book _____

Schedule

1	2	3	4	5

Requirements

☐ Read the book

☐ Discuss the book 1 ____ 2 ____ 3 ____

☐ Write in a reading log 1 ____ 2 ____ 3 ____

☐ Make a project

Assessment Tools

She also joins with the *How to Eat Fried Worms* book club as they read chapter 3. The students ask Mrs. Donnelly what "monshure" is, and she explains that Alan is pretending to speak French. As they continue reading chapters 4 and 5, she points out similar instances. Once they finish reading, the group discusses the chapters they have read and talks about whether they would have made a similar bet. They compare themselves to Billy, the boy who eats the worms, and talk about how real the story seems and how they feel themselves tasting the worm as Billy eats it. Mrs. Donnelly seizes the moment for an impromptu lesson on reading strategies, and she explains that good readers often seem to connect with or become a character in a story and can see, hear, smell, and even taste the same things the character does.

A few days later, Mrs. Donnelly meets with the *Shiloh* book club as they are writing in their reading logs. Students in this group decided to write double-entry journals: They write interesting quotes from the book in one column and their reactions to the quotes in the other. Students are writing quotes and reactions from the last three chapters of the book. Todd chooses "I begin to see now I'm no better than Judd Travers—willing to look the other way to get something I want" (p. 124), and writes:

> *Marty IS better than Judd Travers. This book makes you realize that things are not just right and wrong and most of the time right and wrong and good and bad and fair and not fair get a little mixed up. Marty is keeping quiet about the doe for a real important reason. The deer is dead and that can't be helped but Marty can save Shiloh. He must save the dog. He's a much better person*

Check the Compendium of Instructional Procedures, which follows Chapter 14, for more information on highlighted terms.

than he thinks even though he did do some wrong. Part of the reason you know he is a good person is that he knows he did the wrong things. He has a conscience. Judd don't have a conscience, none at all.

Next, Mrs. Donnelly meets with the *On My Honor* book club as they discuss the end of the book. Kara comments, "I don't think Joel should feel so guilty about Tony dying. It wasn't his fault." Mrs. Donnelly asks, "Whose fault was it?" Several children say it was Tony's fault. Will explains, "He knew he couldn't swim and he went swimming anyway. That was just crazy." "What about Joel's dad?" Mrs. Donnelly asks, "Was it his fault, too?" Brooke says, "His dad seems like he thinks he's guilty and he tells Joel he's sorry." Jared offers another opinion, "It was just an accident. I don't think it was anyone's fault. No one killed Tony on purpose. He just died." The group continues to talk about the effect of Tony's death on his own family and on Joel and his family.

Mrs. Donnelly and the students in this multiage classroom have created a community of learners. They have learned to work together in small groups. They are responsible for assignments and are supportive of their classmates. They know the literacy routines and procedures to use during the book club unit. The classroom is arranged to facilitate their learning; they know where supplies are kept and how to use them. Mrs. Donnelly assumes a number of roles during the unit: She chooses books, organizes the unit, provides information and encouragement, teaches lessons, monitors students' progress, and assesses their work.

On the fifth day, students in each book club share their projects with the class. The purpose of these projects is to celebrate the reading experience and bring closure to it. An added benefit is that students "advertise" the books during these sharing sessions, and then other students want to read them. Each group takes approximately 5 to 10 minutes to share their projects. The *How to Eat Fried Worms* group goes first; they present a book commercial. Group members tell a little about the story and dare students to eat the worms—big earthworms or night crawlers—that they have brought to school. One student, Nathan, explains that it is perfectly safe to eat the worms and extols their nutritional benefits. Even so, no one volunteers. Next, the group reading *Freckle Juice* shares two projects: Two students display a graph they have made showing how many children in the class have freckles, and the other students present a commercial to sell a bottle of guaranteed "freckle juice."

The group reading *Bunnicula: A Rabbit-Tale of Mystery* explains that they've read a mystery about vegetables turning white, and they show some vegetables they have made out of light-colored clay as evidence. They point out two tiny marks on each vegetable. One student, Bill, pretends to be Harold, the family dog who wrote the book, and he explains that their pet rabbit—Bunnicula—who seemed to be harmless at first, may be responsible for sucking the vegetable juices out of the vegetables. Dolores displays a stuffed animal bunny dressed in a black cape to look like a vampire. The group recommends that classmates read this book if they want to find out what happens to Bunnicula.

The *Shiloh* group shares information from the local ASPCA, and Angelica reads an "I Am" poem about Marty that the group has written:

I am a boy who knows right from wrong
but I will do anything to save that dog.
I know how to treat a dog.
I say, "Please don't kick him like that."
I am afraid of Judd Travers.
But I will do anything to save Shiloh.

I dream of Shiloh being mine.
I have a secret hiding place for him.
I catch Judd Travers killing a doe out of season.
I will make mean Mr. Travers sell Shiloh to me.
I work hard for 20 hours to earn $40 to buy him.
I learn that nothing is as simple as it seems.
I am a boy who knows right from wrong
but I will do anything to save my dog.

The group reading *Bridge to Terabithia* presents a tabletop diorama they have made of the magical kingdom of Terabithia.

Last, Hector and Carlos from the group reading *On My Honor* role-play Joel and Tony, the two boys in the story. They reenact the scene where the boys decide to go swimming. They explain that Tony drowns, and then the boy playing Joel describes what it was like to search for Tony and then pretend that he didn't know what had happened to him. Then the other group members ask their classmates what they would have done after Tony died if they had been Joel.

After all the projects have been presented, many students trade books with classmates, and students spend the next 2 days independently reading any book they choose. Many students read one of the other books read during the book clubs, but some bring other books from home to read or choose a different book from the class library.

Mrs. Donnelly's students are motivated readers because they love books and enjoy reading and discussing them. Many of them choose to read as a leisure-time activity. Books of children's literature carry readers to far-off lands and times, stretch their imaginations, expand their knowledge of people and the world, and transform them by giving life new meaning. Charlotte Huck (1998) explains: "I believe in the transforming power of literature to take you out of yourself and return you to yourself—a changed self" (p. 4). Powerful experiences with literature, like those that Mrs. Donnelly's students experienced, heighten children's interest in reading and at the same time expand their reading abilities.

One of the best ways to nurture children's love of reading and ensure that they become lifelong readers is through literature circles—small, student-led book discussion groups that meet regularly in the classroom. In the vignette, Mrs. Donnelly called her literature circles "book clubs" (Raphael, Pardo, & Highfield, 2002), but some teachers call them "literature study groups" (Peterson & Eeds, 1990; Smith, 1998) or "literature discussion groups" (Evans, 2001).

In literature circles, children meet in small groups to read and discuss self-selected books. Harvey Daniels (1994) calls literature circles "a new kind of reading group" (p. 6). The reading materials are quality books of children's literature, including stories, poems, biographies, and informational books, but what matters most is that students are reading something that interests them and is manageable. In these groups, students choose the books they want to read and form temporary groups to read. Next, they set a reading and discussion schedule. Then they read independently or with buddies and come together to talk about their reading in discussions that are like grand conversations. Sometimes the teacher meets with the group, and at other times, the group meets independently. After finishing the book, students also prepare projects in order to share the book with classmates. A literature circle on one book may last from a day or two to a week or two, depending on the length of the book and the age of the students.

Literature circles embody three student-centered learning theories: sociolinguistics, reader response, and critical literacy. Sociolinguistics suggests that learning is a social process, and in literature circles, students read and discuss books in small groups. Classmates share ideas and support each other through social interaction as they deepen their comprehension and think about the important ideas in the book. Students incorporate the reader response theory because they read aesthetically and make connections between the book and their own lives, the world around them, and other literature they have read. Because students are reading high-quality, powerful literature during literature circles, they grapple with important cultural and social issues such as equality and discrimination. Students apply the critical literacy theory as they think about these social issues and develop projects that evolve from the books they have read to increase people's awareness of injustices and ameliorate these wrongs.

In this chapter, you will read about how to implement literature circles. Teachers often use literature circles to provide students with the opportunity to read authentic literature with a supportive group of classmates. Many times, teachers alternate literature focus units and literature circles so that students can have both more teacher-directed and more student-directed experiences. The feature on page 386 shows how literature circles fit into a balanced literacy program. As you continue reading this chapter, you will learn more about the ideas presented in the feature.

KEY FEATURES OF LITERATURE CIRCLES

Visit Chapter 12 on the Companion Website at *www.prenhall.com/ tompkins* to connect to web links related to literature circles.

The three key features of literature circles are choice, literature, and response. As teachers organize for literature circles, they make decisions about these features. They structure the program so that students can make choices about the literature they read, and they develop a plan for response so that students can think deeply about books they are reading and respond to them.

Choice

Students make many choices in literature circles. They choose the books they will read and the groups in which they participate. They share in setting the schedule for reading and discussing the book, and they choose the roles they assume in the discussions. They also choose how they will share the book with classmates. Teachers structure literature circles so that students have these opportunities, but even more important, they prepare students for making choices by creating a community of learners in their classrooms in which students assume responsibility for their learning and can work collaboratively with classmates. In traditional classrooms, children often work competitively with classmates, but in literature circles, students collaborate in order to set schedules, discuss their reading, and develop responses.

How Literature Circles Fit Into a Balanced Literacy Program

Component	Description
Reading	Students read independently or with partners and discuss their reading in small groups during literature circles.
Phonics and Other Skills	Students apply phonics and other skills as they read.
Strategies	Students apply strategies as they read books independently and assume roles to discuss books.
Vocabulary	Students learn new words as they read and respond to books, and they examine words during group discussions.
Comprehension	Students think inferentially and critically as they think, talk, and write about books they are reading.
Literature	Students read high-quality, thought-provoking literature and study genres and story structure during literature circles.
Content-Area Study	Sometimes students read stories and informational books related to content-area units.
Oral Language	Students assume roles and participate in discussions to extend their comprehension.
Writing	Students write in reading logs and use the writing process as they write stories, poems, and other projects.
Spelling	Spelling is not an important component in literature circles.

Literature

The books chosen for literature circles should be interesting to students and at their reading level. Books that are likely to lead to good discussions have interesting plots, richly developed characters, vivid language, and thought-provoking themes (Samway & Whang, 1996). The books must seem manageable to the students, especially during their first literature circles. Samway and Whang recommend choosing shorter books or picture books at first so that students don't become bogged down. It's also important that teachers have read and liked the books because otherwise they won't be able to do a convincing book talk. In addition, they won't be able to contribute to the book discussions.

Students typically read stories during literature circles, but they can also read informational books or informational books paired with stories (Stien & Beed, 2004). Students read informational books related to thematic units or biographies, or they may choose from the Magic Tree House series of easy-to-read chapter books that features pairs of fiction and nonfiction books, including *Hour of the Olympics* (Osborne, 1998) and *Olympics of Ancient Greece* (Osborne & Boyce, 2004), or the popular Magic School Bus picture-book series, including *The Magic School Bus on the Ocean Floor* (Cole, 1994).

Response

Students meet several times during a literature circle to discuss the book and extend their comprehension of it. Through these discussions, students summarize their reading, make personal, world, and literary connections, learn vocabulary, explore the author's use of story structure, and note literary language. Students learn that comprehension develops in layers. From an initial comprehension gained through reading, students deepen and expand their understanding through the discussions. They learn to return to the text to reread sentences and paragraphs in order to clarify a point or state an opinion. They also refine their ability to respond to books through these discussions.

How often students meet to discuss a book varies according to the book and the students. When students are reading a picture book, for example, they usually read the entire book before meeting to discuss it. But when they are reading chapter books, students usually meet after reading the first few chapters for an initial discussion and then several more times as they continue reading the book, as Mrs. Donnelly's students did in the vignette at the beginning of this chapter.

Karen Smith (1998) describes the discussions her students have after they finish reading a book as "intensive study." They often involve several group meetings. At the first session, students share personal responses. They talk about the characters and events of the story, share favorite parts, and ask questions to clarify confusions. At the end of the first session, students and the teacher decide what they want to study at the next session. They may choose to focus on an element of story structure—character development or foreshadowing, for example. Students prepare for the second discussion by rereading excerpts from the book related to the focus they have chosen. Then, during the second session, students talk about how the author used an element of

Literature Circles

These eighth graders are participating in a discussion during a literature circle featuring Rodman Philbrick's *Freak the Mighty* (1993), the memorable story of two unlikely friends. The students talk about events in the story, returning to the book to read sentences aloud. They also check the meaning of several words in a dictionary that one student keeps on his desk. They've read half of the book so far, and their conversation focuses on the friendship Max and Kevin have formed. They talk about their own friends and what it means to be a friend, and they make predictions about how the story will end.

story structure in the book, and they often make charts and diagrams, such as a plot profile or an open-mind portrait, to organize their thoughts.

The reason why students examine the structural elements of stories is to help them develop literary insights. Teachers assist by providing information, offering comments, asking insightful questions, and guiding students to make comments. Many teachers ask questions to probe students' thinking; a list of possible questions is presented in Figure 12–1. However, Smith (1998) cautions that simply asking a list of questions is rarely productive. Teachers should adapt questions and use them judiciously to help students think more deeply about the stories. Eeds and Peterson (1991) advise teachers to listen carefully to what students say as they talk about a book and to introduce literary terminology such as *conflict, foreshadowing*, and *theme* when appropriate.

Instead of asking, for example, "What are the conflicts in the story?" teachers ask themselves that question and then comment about one conflict in the story that they found interesting. Then they invite students to talk about other conflicts they noticed, and finally, students reflect on the importance of the various conflict situations. Or, teachers can take advantage of a comment that a student makes about a conflict situation and then guide the discussion toward conflict situations.

Students need many opportunities to respond to literature before they will be successful in literature circles. One of the best ways to prepare students for literature circle discussions is by reading aloud to them every day and involving them in grand conversations (Smith, 1998). Teachers create a community of learners through these read-aloud experiences, and they can demonstrate ways to respond to literature that are reflective and thoughtful. They also encourage students to respond to the books, and they reinforce students' comments when they share their thoughts and feelings,

Figure 12-1	Questions to Help Students Focus on Literary Elements
Element	**Questions**
Plot	What are the conflicts in the story? How does the author develop the conflicts? What events lead to the high point in the story? What devices did the author use to develop the plot?
Character	Which characters are fully developed and which are flat? How does the author tell us about the characters? By what they do? By how they look? By what they say? By what they think? How does the story show the development of the characters? If you were a character in the story, which one would you be? Why?
Setting	How does the setting influence the story? Is the setting important to the story? How is time marked in the story? Does the author use flashbacks or foreshadowing? How much time passes in the story?
Point of View	Is the story written from first person or third person? Are the characters' feelings and thoughts presented? How does the author describe the characters?
Theme	What symbols does the author use? What universal truths does the story present?

Adapted from Eeds & Peterson, 1991; Peterson & Eeds, 1990.

Part 3 How Do Teachers Organize Literacy Instruction?

examine the structure of texts, and talk about their use of literacy strategies as they listened to the teacher read aloud.

Gilles (1998) examined children's talk during literature circle discussions and identified four types.

1. *Talk about the book.* Children summarize their reading and talk about the book by applying what they have learned about the structure of stories and other texts as they:
   - retell events
   - identify main ideas
   - summarize the plot
   - discuss characters
   - examine the setting
   - explore themes and symbols

2. *Talk about the reading process.* Students think metacognitively and reflect on the process they used to read the book as they:
   - reflect on how they used strategies
   - explain their reading problems and how they solved them
   - identify sections that they reread and why they reread them
   - talk about their thinking as they were reading
   - identify parts they understood or misunderstood

3. *Talk about connections.* Students make connections between the book and their own lives, the world, and to other literature they have read as they:
   - explain connections to their lives
   - compare this book to another book
   - make connections to a film or television show they have viewed

4. *Talk about group process and social issues.* Children use talk to organize the literature circle and maintain the discussion. They also use talk to examine social issues and current events related to the book, such as homelessness and divorce, as they:
   - decide who will be group leader
   - determine the schedule, roles, and responsibilities
   - draw in nonparticipating students
   - bring the conversation back to the topic
   - extend the discussion to social issues and current events

Some teachers have students assume roles and complete assignments in preparation for discussion group meetings (Daniels, 1994; Daniels & Bizar, 1998). One student is the discussion director, and he or she assumes the leadership role and directs the discussion. To prepare, the discussion director chooses topics and formulates questions to guide the discussion. Other students prepare by selecting a passage to read aloud, identifying vocabulary words for study, making personal and literary connections, summarizing the reading or identifying big ideas for a nonfiction text, drawing a picture or making a graphic related to the book, and investigating a topic related to the book. These seven roles are detailed in Figure 12–2. Having students assume specific roles may seem artificial, but it teaches them about the types of responses they can make in literature circles.

Figure 12-2   Roles Students Play in Literature Circles

Role	Responsibilities
Discussion Director	The discussion director guides the group's discussion and keeps the group on task. To get the discussion started or to redirect the discussion, the discussion director may ask: • What did the reading make you think of? • What questions do you have about the reading? • What do you predict will happen next?
Passage Master	The passage master focuses on the literary merits of the book. This student chooses several memorable passages to share with the group and tells why he or she chose each one.
Word Wizard	The word wizard is responsible for vocabulary. This student identifies four to six important, unfamiliar words from the reading and looks them up in the dictionary. He or she selects the most appropriate meaning and other interesting information about the word to share with the group.
Connector	The connector makes connections between the book and the students' lives. These connections might include happenings at school or in the community, current events or historical events from around the world, or something from the connector's own life. Or the connector can make comparisons with other books by the same author or on the same topic.
Summarizer	The summarizer prepares a brief summary of the reading to convey the big ideas to share with the group. This student often begins the discussion by reading the summary aloud to the group.
Illustrator	The illustrator draws a picture or diagram related to the reading. The illustration might relate to a character, an exciting event, or a prediction. The student shares the illustration with the group, and the group talks about it before the illustrator explains it.
Investigator	The investigator locates some information about the book, the author, or a related topic to share with the group. This student may search the Internet, check an encyclopedia or library book, or interview a person with special expertise on the topic.

Adapted from Daniels, 1994; Daniels & Bizar, 1998.

Teachers often prepare assignment sheets for each of the roles their students assume during a literature circle and then pass out copies before students begin reading. Students complete one of the assignment sheets before each discussion. Figure 12–3 shows a "word wizard" assignment sheet that an eighth grader completed as he read *Holes* (Sachar, 1998), the story of a boy named Stanley Yelnats who is sent to a hellish correctional camp where he finds a real friend, a treasure, and a new sense of himself. As word wizard, this student chooses important words from the story to study. In the first column on the assignment sheet, the student writes the word and the number of the page on which it was found. Then, in the second column, the student checks the dictionary for the word's meaning, lists several meanings when possible, and places check marks next to the meanings that are appropriate for how the word is used in the book. Students also check the etymology of the word in the dictionary, and in the third column, they list the language the word came from and when it entered English.

During the discussion about the second section of *Holes*, the word *callused* became important. The student explained that *callused* means "toughened" and "hardened," and that in the story, Stanley and the other boys' hands became callused. He continued to say that the third meaning, "unsympathetic," didn't make sense. This comment provided an opportunity for the teacher to explain how *callused* could mean "unsympathetic," and students decided to make a chart to categorize characters in the story who had callused hands and those who were unsympathetic. The group concluded that the boys with callused hands were sympathetic to each other, but the adults at the correctional camp who didn't have callused hands were often unsympathetic and had callused hearts. Talking about the meaning of a single word—*callused*—led to a new and different way of looking at the characters in the story.

Literature circles are an effective instructional approach because of the three key features—choice, literature, and response. As students read and discuss books with classmates, they often become more engaged and motivated than in other more teacher-directed approaches. The feature on page 392 presents an overview of literature circles.

Figure 12-3 **An Eighth Grader's Literature Circle Role Sheet**

Word Wizard

Name _Ray_   Date _Dec. 7_   Book _Holes_

You are the Word Wizard in this literature circle. Your job is to look for important words in the book and learn about them. Complete this chart before your literature circle meets.

Word and Page Number	Meanings	Etymology
callused p. 80 "his callused hands"	✓ to toughen ✓ to make hard ? unsympathetic	Latin 1565
penetrating p. 82 "a penetrating stare"	? to enter ✓ sharp or piercing	Latin 1520
condemned p. 88 "a condemned man"	✓ found guilty	Latin 1300
writhed p. 91 "his body writhed with pain"	✓ to twist the body in pain	English 900

Literature Circles

Topic	Description
Purpose	To provide students with opportunities for authentic reading and literary analysis activities.
Components	Students form literature circles to read and discuss books that they choose themselves. They often assume roles for the book discussion and sometimes create projects to extend their learning after reading.
Theory Base	Literature circles reflect sociolinguistic, reader response, and critical literacy theories because students work in small, supportive groups to read and discuss books, and the books they read often involve cultural and social issues that require students to think critically.
Applications	Teachers often use literature circles in conjunction with a basal reading program or literature focus units so students have opportunities to do independent reading and literary analysis.
Strengths	• Books are available at a variety of reading levels. • Students are more strongly motivated because they choose the books they read. • Students have opportunities to work with their classmates. • Students participate in authentic literacy experiences. • Activities are student directed, and students work at their own pace. • Teachers may participate in discussions to help students clarify misunderstandings and think more critically about the book.
Limitations	• Teachers often feel a loss of control because students are reading different books. • Students must learn to be task oriented and use time wisely in order to be successful. • Sometimes students choose books that are too difficult or too easy for them.

IMPLEMENTING LITERATURE CIRCLES

Teachers organize and manage literature circles using a six-step series of activities.

1. ***Select the Books.*** Teachers prepare text sets with five to seven related titles and collect six or seven copies of each book. They give a brief book talk to introduce the new books, and then students sign up for the book they want to read. One way to do this is to set each book on the chalk tray and have students sign their names on the chalkboard above the book they want to read. Or, teachers can set the books on a table and place a sign-up sheet beside each one. Students need time to preview

These two boys are participating in a literature circle on Roald Dahl's fantasy story *Charlie and the Chocolate Factory* (1964). The boys often read together, but they vary how they read: Sometimes they take turns reading to each other, and at other times, they read silently. After they read several pages, they usually stop to talk about their reading—making predictions, asking questions, and summarizing big ideas. By reading together, they stay on-task, and they enjoy the reading experience more than they would if they read independently. They are also more successful, especially when they are reading challenging books like this one.

the books, and then they choose the book they want to read after considering the topic and the difficulty of the text. Once in a while, students don't get to read their first choice, but they can always read it another time, perhaps during another literature circle or during reading workshop.

2. **Form Literature Circles.** Students form literature circles to read each book; usually no more than six or seven students participate in a literature circle. The group begins by setting a schedule for reading and discussing the book within the time limits that the teacher has set. Sometimes students also choose discussion roles so that they can prepare for the discussion after reading.

3. **Read the Book.** Students read all or part of the book independently or with a partner, depending on the difficulty level of the book. After reading, students

Scaffolding Struggling Readers

Should my struggling readers participate in literature circles?

Struggling students benefit from a combination of instructional approaches, just like their classmates do, and literature circles present opportunities for students to read and discuss literature with their classmates that aren't possible in other instructional approaches. In literature circles, struggling readers collaborate with classmates, develop responsibility for completing tasks and being prepared, and learn ways to respond to literature. They read grade-appropriate literature that interests and intrigues them, usually with the assistance of classmates who buddy-read with them. They have opportunities to practice word-identification and comprehension strategies they are learning, study vocabulary words, and participate in thought-provoking discussions about issues that concern them. Literature circles aren't frivolous! It's through literature circles that students learn to love literature, and students who love literature are far more likely to become lifelong readers.

Learn more about grand conversations and other instructional procedures discussed in this chapter on the DVD that accompanies this text.

prepare for the discussion by doing the assignment for the role they assumed, writing in their reading logs, or completing other assignments.

4. ***Participate in a Discussion.*** Students meet to talk about the book; these grand conversations usually last about 30 minutes. The discussion director or another student who has been chosen as the leader begins the discussion, and then classmates continue the discussion as in any other grand conversation. The talk is meaningful because students share what interests them in the book, make text-to-self, text-to-world, and text-to-text connections, ask questions, and discuss social issues and other themes.

5. ***Develop Projects.*** Sometimes students develop a project to apply their reading: They may write a sequel, analyze the story's structure, learn about the author, or research a topic related to the book. At other times, they prepare a brief presentation about the book to share with the class.

6. ***Share With the Class.*** Students in each literature circle share the book they have read with their classmates through a book talk or another presentation.

As students participate in literature circles, they are involved in activities representing all five stages of the reading process. Figure 12–4 shows how students move through the reading process.

Using Literature Circles With Young Children

First and second graders can meet in small groups to read and discuss books, just as older, more experienced readers do (Martinez-Roldan & Lopez-Robertson, 1999/2000; Frank, Dixon, & Brandts, 2001; Marriott, 2002). These young children can choose books at their reading levels, listen to the teacher read a book aloud, or participate in a shared reading activity. Literature circles also can grow out of reading workshop, and children can come together to discuss different books. Children probably benefit from listening to a book read aloud two times or reading it several times before participating in the discussion.

Figure 12-4	How Students Apply the Reading Process During Literature Circles
Stage	**Activity**
Prereading	After the teacher gives a book talk, students choose books to read, form groups, and make schedules for reading and group meetings.
Reading	Students read the books they have selected independently or with a partner.
Responding	Students talk about the book during literature circle discussions. Students take responsibility to come to the discussion prepared to participate actively.
Exploring	Students study vocabulary, examine genre and elements of story structure, write summaries, or research a topic related to the book and share what they learn with their classmates during group meetings.
Applying	Sometimes students create projects after reading, and sometimes they give a brief presentation about the book to the class.

In preparation for the literature circle, children often draw and write reading log entries to share with the group. Or, they can write a letter to their group telling about the book (Frank et al., 2001). The literature circle often begins with one child sharing a reading log entry or letter with the small group.

Children meet with the teacher in a literature circle to talk about a book; these grand conversations usually last about 30 minutes. The teacher guides the discussion at first and models how to share ideas and to participate in a grand conversation. Just like any other grand conversation, the talk is meaningful because children share what interests them in the book, make text-to-self, text-to-world, and text-to-text connections, point out illustrations and other book features, ask questions, and discuss social issues and other themes. Young children don't usually assume roles in the discussion as older students do, but teachers often notice a few of the first and second graders beginning to take on leadership roles. During a literature circle, the other children in the classroom are usually reading books or writing in reading logs in preparation for their upcoming literature circle meeting with the teacher.

Monitoring and Assessing Students' Learning

Teachers have a variety of options for monitoring students' work and assessing their learning during literature circles: They can observe students as they participate in literature circles, monitor their work and progress using checklists and assignment sheets, assess students' written work, and examine their self-assessments. Specifically, teachers can participate in these four types of activities:

1. *Observing students*
   - Observe students collaborating with classmates.
   - Observe students reading independently.
   - Observe students participating in discussions.
   - Observe students' sharing of books and projects.

2. *Monitoring students' progress*
   - Monitor students' schedules and assignment sheets.
   - Monitor the sheets students complete for their roles in literature circles.

3. *Assessing students' work*
   - Assess students' reading log entries.
   - Assess students' projects.

4. *Examining students' reflections*
   - Read students' self-assessment letters.
   - Examine students' responses on a self-assessment checklist.
   - Conference with students about their assessment.

Students can write self-reflections in which they discuss their participation in their group, their reactions to the book they read and discussed, and their reading process. They also can complete assessment forms and checklists in which they assess their own work. Figure 12–5 shows a second-grade assessment checklist, which students complete at the end of a literature circle. They then meet with the teacher to discuss their learning.

Benefits of Using Literature Circles

Literature circles are one of the four ways to organize literacy instruction, and they are an important component of a balanced reading program. Students have opportunities

Figure 12–5 A Second-Grade Evaluation Form for Literature Circles

Literature Circles Report Card

Name _____ Book _____

1. How did you help your group?

2. What did you think of your book?

3. What did you say in the conversation?

4. What did you learn about your book?

5. What grade does the book get?

✴	✴✴	✴✴✴

6. What grade do you get?

✴	✴✴	✴✴✴

Assessment Tools

to read and discuss stories and other books with their classmates in a supportive community of learners. These are some of the benefits of using literature circles:

- Students view themselves as readers.
- Students have opportunities to read high-quality books that they might not have chosen on their own.
- Students read widely.
- Students are inspired to write.
- Students develop reading preferences.
- Students have many opportunities to develop critical and creative thinking.
- Students learn responsibility for completing assignments.
- Students learn to self-assess their learning and work habits. (Hill, Johnson, & Noe, 1995; Samway & Whang, 1996)

Other teacher-researchers echo these benefits and also conclude that literature circles are very effective in their classrooms (Day, Spiegel, McLellan, & Brown, 2002; Short & Pierce, 1998).

Complete a self-assessment to check your understanding of the concepts presented in this chapter on the Companion Website at *www. prenhall.com/tompkins*

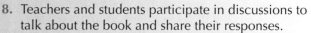

Review: How Effective Teachers Orchestrate Literature Circles

1. Teachers incorporate choice, literature, and response into literature circles.

2. Teachers prepare text sets with multiple copies of six or seven books.

3. Teachers give book talks to interest students in particular books.

4. Teachers have students choose the book they want to read, but provide guidance when needed.

5. Teachers allow students to set their own reading and discussion schedules.

6. Teachers have students read books independently or with a buddy, but they provide assistance when students are struggling.

7. Teachers often have students assume roles to learn about the types of responses.

8. Teachers and students participate in discussions to talk about the book and share their responses.

9. Teachers have students create projects after they finish reading and share the projects with the class.

10. Teachers monitor and assess students' learning as they participate in literature circles.

Professional References

Alderman, M. K. (1999). *Motivation for achievement: Possibilities for teaching and learning.* Mahwah, NJ: Erlbaum.

Daniels, H. (1994). *Literature circles: Voice and choice in the student-centered classroom.* York, ME: Stenhouse.

Daniels, H., & Bizar, M. (1998). *Methods that matter: Six structures for best practice classrooms.* York, ME: Stenhouse.

Day, J. P., Spiegel, D. L., McLellan, J., & Brown, V. B. (2002). *Moving forward with literature circles.* New York: Scholastic.

Dweck, C. S. (1986). Motivational processes affecting learning. *American Psychologist, 41,* 1040–1048.

Eeds, M., & Peterson, R. (1991). Teacher as curator: Learning to talk about literature. *The Reading Teacher, 45,* 118–126.

Evans, K. S. (2001). *Literature discussion groups in the intermediate grades: Dilemmas and possibilities.* Newark, DE: International Reading Association.

Frank, C. R., Dixon, C. N., & Brandts, L. R. (2001). Bears, trolls, and pagemasters: Learning about learners in book clubs. *The Reading Teacher, 54,* 448–462.

Gilles, C. (1998). Collaborative literacy strategies: "We don't need a circle to have a group." In K. G. Short & K. M. Pierce (Eds.), *Talking about books: Literature discussion groups in K–8 classrooms* (pp. 55–68). Portsmouth, NH: Heinemann.

Good, T., & Brophy, J. E. (2000). *Looking in classrooms* (2nd ed.). New York: Longman.

Hill, B. C., Johnson, N. J., & Noe, K. L. S. (Eds.). (1995). *Literature circles and response.* Norwood, MA: Christopher-Gordon.

Huck, C. S. (1998). The power of children's literature in the classroom. In K. G. Short & K. M. Pierce (Eds.), *Talking about books: Literature discussion groups in K–8 classrooms* (pp. 3–15). Portsmouth, NH: Heinemann.

Ivey, G., & Broaddus, K. (2001). "Just plain reading": A survey of what makes students want to read in middle school classrooms. *Reading Research Quarterly, 36,* 350–377.

Johnston, P., & Winograd, P. (1985). Passive failure in reading. *Journal of Reading Behavior, 17,* 279–301.

Kelly, P. R. (1990). Guiding young students' response to literature. *The Reading Teacher, 43,* 464–470.

Kohn, A. (1993). *Punished by rewards: The trouble with gold stars, incentive plans, A's, praise, and other bribes.* Boston: Houghton Mifflin.

Marriott, D. (2002). *Comprehension right from the start: How to organize and manage book clubs for young readers.* Portsmouth, NH: Heinemann.

Martinez-Roldan, C. M., & Lopez-Robertson, J. M. (1999/2000). Initiating literature circles in a first grade bilingual classroom. *The Reading Teacher, 53,* 270–281.

Oldfather, P. (1995). Commentary: What's needed to maintain and extend motivation for literacy in the middle grades. *Journal of Reading, 38,* 420–422.

Paris, S. G., Wasik, B. A., & Turner, J. C. (1991). The development of strategic readers. In R. Barr, M. L. Kamil, P. B. Mosenthal, & P. D. Pearson (Eds.), *Handbook of reading research* (vol. 2, pp. 609–640). New York: Longman.

Peterson, R., & Eeds, M. (1990). *Grand conversations: Literature groups in action.* New York: Scholastic.

Pressley, M., Dolezal, S. E., Raphael, L. M., Mohan, L., Roehrig, A. D., & Bogner, K. (2003). *Motivating primary-grade students.* New York: Guilford Press.

Raphael, T. E., Pardo, L. S., & Highfield, K. (2002). *Book club: A literature-based curriculum* (2nd ed.). Lawrence, MA: Small Planet Communications.

Robb, L. (1993). A cause for celebration: Reading and writing with at-risk students. *The New Advocate, 6,* 25–40.

Ruddell, R. B. (1995). Those influential literacy teachers: Meaning negotiators and motivation builders. *The Reading Teacher, 48,* 454–463.

Samway, K. D., & Whang, G. (1996). *Literature study circles in a multicultural classroom.* York, ME: Stenhouse.

Short, K. G. , & Pierce, K. M. (Eds.). (1998). *Talking about books: Literature discussion groups in K–8 classrooms.* Portsmouth, NH: Heinemann.

Smith, K. (1998). Entertaining a text: A reciprocal process. In K. G. Short & K. M. Pierce (Eds.), *Talking about books:*

Literature discussion groups in K–8 classrooms (pp. 17–31). Portsmouth, NH: Heinemann.

Stien, D., & Beed, P. L. (2004). Bridging the gap between fiction and nonfiction in the literature circle setting. *The Reading Teacher, 57,* 510–518.

Stipek, D. J. (1993). *Motivation to learn: From theory to practice* (2nd ed.). Boston: Allyn & Bacon.

Strickland, D. S., Ganske, K., & Monroe, J. K. (2002). *Supporting struggling readers and writers: Strategies for classroom intervention 3–6.* Portland, ME: Stenhouse.

Turner, J., & Paris, S. G. (1995). How literacy tasks influence children's motivation for literacy. *The Reading Teacher, 48,* 662–673.

Unrau, N. (2004). *Content area reading and writing: Fostering literacies in middle and high school cultures.* Upper Saddle River, NJ: Merrill/Prentice Hall.

Children's Book References

Bauer, M. D. (1986). *On my honor.* Boston: Houghton Mifflin.

Blume, J. (1971). *Freckle juice.* New York: Bradbury Press.

Cole, J. (1994). *The magic school bus on the ocean floor.* New York: Scholastic.

Dahl, R. (1964). *Charlie and the chocolate factory.* New York: Knopf.

Howe, D., & Howe, J. (1979). *Bunnicula: A rabbit-tale of mystery.* New York: Atheneum.

Naylor, P. R. (1991). *Shiloh.* New York: Atheneum.

Osborne, M. P. (1998). *Hour of the Olympics.* New York: Random House.

Osborne, M. P., & Boyce, N. P. (2004). *Olympics of Ancient Greece.* New York: Random House.

Paterson, K. (1977). *Bridge to Terabithia.* New York: Harper & Row.

Philbrick, R. (1993). *Freak the mighty.* New York: Blue Sky Press.

Rockwell, T. (1973). *How to eat fried worms.* New York: Franklin Watts.

Sachar, L. (1998). *Holes.* New York: Farrar, Straus & Giroux.

Implementing Reading and Writing Workshop

- What are the components of reading workshop?
- What are the components of writing workshop?
- How do students apply the reading and writing processes in this instructional approach?
- How do teachers manage a workshop classroom?
- Why do teachers use this instructional approach?

First Graders Participate in Writing Workshop

The 20 first graders in Mrs. Ockey's class participate in writing workshop from 10:20 to 11:30 each morning. Here is the schedule for writing workshop:

10:20–10:40 Shared reading/minilesson

10:40–11:15 Writing and conferencing with Mrs. Ockey

11:15–11:30 Author's chair

Mrs. Ockey devotes 70 minutes each morning to writing workshop because she wants her students to have time to talk about their experiences, extend their vocabulary, and manipulate basic English syntactic patterns through writing and talking. Many of these 5- and 6-year-olds are English learners whose parents or grandparents immigrated to the United States from southeast Asia and speak Hmong, Khmer, or Lao at home. They are learning to speak English as they learn to read and write in English.

The writing workshop begins with a 20-minute whole-class meeting. Mrs. Ockey either reads a big book using shared reading procedures or teaches a minilesson, often using something from the big book she has read previously as an example. Yesterday, Mrs. Ockey read *An Egg Is an Egg* (Weiss, 1990), an

informational book about egg-laying animals. After reading the big book twice, Mrs. Ockey and the children participated in an instructional conversation and talked about animals that lay eggs and those that don't.

Today, Mrs. Ockey rereads *An Egg Is an Egg,* and the children join in to read familiar words. Afterward, she reads the book again, asking the children to look for words on each page with *ou* and *ow* spellings. In a previous minilesson, Mrs. Ockey explained that usually these spellings are pronounced /ou/ as in *ouch*, but sometimes *ow* is pronounced /ō/ as in *snow*, and they began a chart of words with each spelling or pronunciation. The first graders locate several more words to add to their chart. After adding the new words from the big book, Shaqualle suggests *hour* and Leticia suggests *found*, words they noticed in books they were reading. The children practice reading the lists of words together, and Der reads the lists by himself. He smiles proudly as his classmates clap. Their chart is shown in the box below.

Mrs. Ockey quickly reviews the rules for writing because two children have recently joined the class, and she has noticed that some of the other children aren't on task during the writing and conferencing period. The class's rules for writing are posted on a chart that the children wrote using interactive writing earlier in the school year. Mrs. Ockey rereads each rule and then asks a child to explain the rule in his or her own words. Here are the rules:

1. Think about your story.
2. Draw pictures on a storyboard.
3. Write words by the pictures.
4. Tell your story to 1 editor.
5. Write your story.
6. Read your story to 2 editors.

The First Graders' Chart of *ou* and *ow* Words		
ou	ow	ow (long o)
loud	clown	low
sound	brown	blowing
cloud	down	tow
outside	town	slowly
flour	flower	sown
around	tower	snows
shout	now	
hour		
found		

7. Illustrate your story.

8. Publish your story.

Check the Compendium of Instructional Procedures, which follows Chapter 14, for more information on highlighted terms.

The second part of writing workshop is writing and conferencing. The children use a process approach to write personal narratives, stories about their families, pets, and events in their lives. To begin, the children plan their stories using storyboards, sheets of paper divided into four, six, or eight blocks. (These are different from story boards, which are described in the Compendium.) They sketch a drawing in each numbered block and then add a word or two to describe the picture. Next they use their storyboards to tell their stories to one of five first graders who are serving as editors that day; today's editors are Pauline, Lily, Mai, Destiny, and Khammala. You can tell the editors in Mrs. Ockey's classroom because they are wearing neon-colored plastic visors with the word "Editor" printed on them.

After this rehearsal, the children write their stories using one sheet of paper for each block on their planning sheets. Next, they read their writing to two editors, who often ask the child to add more detail or a word or phrase that has been omitted. Then the children draw and color a picture to complement and extend the words on each page. Sometimes the children add a cover and a title page and staple their stories together, and at other times, they turn in their drafts for the bilingual aide in the classroom to word process.

Children complete an editing sheet when they share their writing with two classmate editors. A copy of the editing sheet that they complete is shown in the box on the next page. The author writes his or her name and the title of the story at the top of the sheet, and then the editors check off each box as they read their classmate's story; they sign their names at the bottom of the page. Mrs. Ockey often calls herself their third editor, and the children know that they must complete this editing sheet with two classmates before they ask Mrs. Ockey to edit their writing.

Mrs. Ockey has divided the class into five conference groups; she meets with one group each day while the other children are working on their stories. The children bring their writing folders to the conference table and talk with Mrs. Ockey about their work. They are working at their own pace, so they are at different stages of the writing process.

Mrs. Ockey begins by asking the children to explain what they are writing about and where they are in the writing process. Then she examines each child's storyboard or writing and offers compliments, asks questions, and provides feedback about their work. She also makes notes about each child's progress.

Today, she is meeting with Lily, Der, Dalany, and Matthew. Lily begins by showing Mrs. Ockey her storyboard for a story about her cousin's birthday. She has developed eight blocks for her story, and she talks about each one, working to express her ideas in a sentence or two. Mrs. Ockey praises Lily for tackling such a long story and for including a beginning, middle, and end in her story. She encourages Lily to begin writing, and a week later, Lily completes her book and shares it with her classmates. Here is Lily's published story, "My Cousin's Birthday":

Page 1	This is my cousin's birthday.
Page 2	I bought her a present.
Page 3	I have clothes for her present.
Page 4	She makes a wish on her birthday cake.
Page 5	We eat cake.
Page 6	We play games.
Page 7	My cousin is happy.
Page 8	We went to sleep.

Name _____

Title of your story _____

Check Your Work!

Does the story make sense?	□	□
Punctuation marks	□	□
Capital letters	□	□
Spelling	□	□

My editors are:

_____   _____

Assessment Tools

Next, Mrs. Ockey turns to Der, who thinks he is working on a storyboard for a story about his grandmother's cat, but he can't find it. Mrs. Ockey checks her notes and recalls that Der couldn't find his storyboard for the same story last week, so she asks him to get a new storyboard and start again. They talk out the story together. Der wants to describe what his grandmother's cat looks like and then tell all the things she can do. He begins drawing a picture in the first block while Mrs. Ockey watches. After he draws the picture, Mrs. Ockey will help him add one or two key words in the block. Then she'll help him do a second block.

Once Der is working, Mrs. Ockey turns her attention to Matthew, who is finishing his ninth book, "The Soccer Game." He reads it to Mrs. Ockey:

Page 1   Me and my friends play soccer.
Page 2   I won a trophy.
Page 3   I won another point.
Page 4   I played at the soccer field.
Page 5   I won again.
Page 6   I went home.

Then they read it over again, and Mrs. Ockey helps him correct the spelling of *trophy* and *soccer* and correct several letters that were printed backward. He also shows her his editing sheet, which indicates that he had already edited his story with Pauline and Sammy. Matthew tells Mrs. Ockey that he wants to finish the book today so that he can share it at the author's chair. Mrs. Ockey sends him over to write his name on the sharing list posted beside the author's chair.

Dalany is next. She reminds Mrs. Ockey that she finished her book, "The Apple Tree," last week, and she is waiting for it to be word processed. Mrs. Ockey tells her that it is done and gives her the word-processed copy. They read it over together and Dalany returns to her desk to draw the illustrations. Here is Dalany's book, "The Apple Tree":

Page 1	*I see the apple tree.*
Page 2	*I picked the apple up.*
Page 3	*I ate the apple.*
Page 4	*I see another girl pick up the apple.*
Page 5	*The girl ate the apple.*
Page 6	*We are friends.*

Page 5 from Dalany's word-processed book with hand-drawn illustrations is shown in the box below.

After the children write their stories, an aide types them on the computer and prints them out along with a title page, a dedication page, and a "Readers' Comments" page. The child draws an illustration on each page. Then Mrs. Ockey laminates the title page and adds a back cover and the child staples the book together. The author shares the book at that day's author's chair, and then the book is placed in the classroom library. Children take turns reading each other's books and adding com-

A Page From a First Grader's Story About "The Apple Tree"

The girl ate the apple.

ments on the back page. Children take great pride in reading their classmates' comments in their books. Mrs. Ockey and the first graders have written these comments in Matthew's book about playing soccer:

I have a trophy. Der
I like Matthew play soccer. Pauline
You are a good soccer player! Mrs. Ockey
Nice story. Rosemary
You good soccer play. Jesse
Do you win and win? Lily
I like play soccer. Michael

Although not all of the comments are grammatically correct, Matthew can read them all, and he has walked around and thanked each person for his or her comment. It is important to him that lots of people read his book and write comments.

The third part of writing workshop is author's chair. Each day, three children sit in a special chair called the "author's chair" and share their published stories. After children read their stories, their classmates offer comments and ask clarifying questions. Then they clap for the author, and the published book is ceremoniously placed in a special section of the classroom library for everyone to read and reread.

Students are involved in authentic reading and writing projects during reading and writing workshop. They read and respond to self-selected books and write and publish books, as the first graders did in Mrs. Ockey's classroom. The workshop approach involves three key characteristics: time, choice, and response. First, in a workshop, students have large chunks of time and the opportunity to read and write. Instead of being add-ons for when students finish schoolwork, reading and writing become the core of the literacy curriculum.

Second, students have ownership of their learning through self-selection of books they read and their topics for writing. Instead of reading books selected by the teacher or reading the same book together as a group or class, students select the books they want to read, books that are suitable to their interests and reading levels. Usually students choose whatever book they want to read—a story, a book of poems, or an informational book—but sometimes teachers set parameters. During writing workshop, students plan their writing projects: They choose topics related to hobbies, content-area units, and other interests, and they also select the format for their writing. Often they choose to construct books.

The third characteristic is response. In reading workshop, students respond to books they are reading in reading logs that they share during conferences with the teacher. Similarly, in writing workshop, students share with classmates rough drafts of books and other compositions they are writing, and they share their completed and published compositions with genuine audiences.

Reading workshop and writing workshop are different types of workshops. Reading workshop fosters real reading of self-selected stories, poems, and informational books. Students read hundreds of books during reading workshop. At the first-grade level, students might read or reread three or four books each day, totaling close to a thousand books during the school year, and older students read fewer, longer books. Even so, Cora Lee Five, a fifth-grade teacher, reported that her students read between 25 and 144 books (Five, 1988).

Similarly, writing workshop fosters real writing (and the use of the writing process) for genuine purposes and for authentic audiences. Each student writes and publishes as many as 50 to 100 short books in the primary grades and 20 to 25 longer books in the middle and upper grades. As they write, students come to see themselves as authors and become interested in learning about the authors of the books they read.

Teachers often use both workshops, or if their schedule does not allow, they may alternate the two. Schedules for reading and writing workshop at the first-, third-, sixth-, and eighth-grade levels are presented in Figure 13–1.

Reading and writing workshop can be used as the primary instructional approach in a classroom, or it can be used along with other instructional approaches to provide additional authentic opportunities for students to read and write. This approach is student centered because students make many choices and work independently as they read and write. Providing authentic activities and independent work opportunities reflects the constructivist learning theory, which emphasizes that learners create their own knowledge through exploration and experimentation. Also, encouraging students to read aesthetically and respond to what they read reflects the reader response theory, which emphasizes students' active engagement with text. The feature on page 408 shows how reading and writing workshop fit into a balanced approach to literacy development.

READING WORKSHOP

Nancie Atwell introduced reading workshop in 1987 as an alternative to traditional reading instruction. In reading workshop, students read books that they choose themselves and respond to books through writing in reading logs and conferences with teachers and classmates (Atwell, 1998). This approach represented a change in what we believe about how children learn and how literature should be used in the classroom. Whereas traditional reading programs emphasized dependence on a teacher's guide to determine how and when particular strategies and skills should be taught, reading workshop is an individualized reading program. Atwell developed reading workshop with her middle school students, but it has been adapted and used successfully at every grade level, first through eighth (Hornsby, Parry, & Sukarna, 1992; Hornsby, Sukarna, & Parry, 1986; McWhirter, 1990). There are several versions of reading workshop, but they usually contain five components: reading, responding, sharing, teaching minilessons, and reading aloud to students.

Visit Chapter 13 on the Companion Website at *www.prenhall. com/tompkins* to connect to web links related to reading workshop.

Component 1: Reading

Students spend 30 to 60 minutes independently reading books and other written materials. Frank Smith (1984) claims that to learn to read, children need to read every day, and several times each day for varied purposes. Teachers need to provide plenty of time in class, and not simply assume that students will practice at home what they are learning at school. For example, McWhirter (1990) surveyed her eighth graders and found that 97% reported that they do not read on their own for pleasure. Moreover, research suggests that higher achievement is associated with more time allocated to academic activities (Brophy & Good, 1986).

Students choose the books they read during reading workshop; often they depend on recommendations from classmates. They also read books on particular topics— horses, science fiction, dinosaurs—or by favorite authors, such as Judy Blume, Chris

Figure 13-1 Schedules for Reading and Writing Workshop

First Grade

9:00–9:10	The teacher rereads several familiar big books with students. Then the teacher introduces a new big book and reads it with the students.
9:10–9:30	Students read matching small books independently and reread other familiar books.
9:30–9:40	Students choose one of the books they have read or reread during independent reading to draw and write a quickwrite.
9:40–9:50	Students share the favorite book and quickwrite.
9:50–10:05	The teacher teaches a reading/writing minilesson.
10:05–10:30	Students write independently on self-selected topics and conference with the teacher.
10:30–10:40	Students share their published books with classmates.
10:40–10:45	The class uses choral reading to enjoy poems and charts hanging in the classroom.

Third Grade

10:30–11:00	Students read self-selected books and respond to the books in reading logs.
11:00–11:15	Students share with classmates books they have finished reading and do informal book talks about them. Students often pass the "good" books to classmates who want to read them next.
11:15–11:30	The teacher teaches a reading/writing minilesson.
11:30–11:55	The teacher reads aloud picture books or chapter books, one or two chapters each day. After reading, students talk about the book in a grand conversation.
	—Continued after lunch—
12:45–1:15	Students write books independently.
1:15–1:30	Students share their published books with classmates.

Sixth Grade

8:20–8:45	The teacher reads aloud a chapter book to students, and students talk about their reactions in a grand conversation.
8:45–9:30	Students write independently using the writing process. They also conference with the teacher.
9:30–9:40	The teacher teaches a reading/writing minilesson.
9:40–10:25	Students read self-selected books independently.
10:25–10:40	Students share published writings and give book talks about books they have read with classmates.

Eighth Grade

During alternating months, students participate in reading workshop or writing workshop.

1:00–1:45	Students read or write independently.
1:45–2:05	The teacher presents a minilesson on a reading or writing procedure, concept, strategy, or skill.
2:05–2:15	Students share with their classmates books they have read or compositions they have published.

How Reading and Writing Workshop Fit Into a Balanced Literacy Program

Component	Description
Reading	Students gain necessary reading practice during reading workshop and are more likely to become lifelong readers.
Phonics and Other Skills	Students practice reading and writing skills through workshop activities.
Strategies	Students apply the strategies they are learning in reading and writing activities.
Vocabulary	The most important way that students learn vocabulary is through reading and reading, workshop provides an extended opportunity for students to read.
Comprehension	Students' focus is on comprehension as they read during reading workshop and write during writing workshop.
Literature	Students choose the books they read during reading workshop from classroom libraries. It is important that teachers have a wide selection of books and other reading materials available for students to choose from.
Content-Area Study	Students can read books related to thematic units during reading workshop and write reports and other compositions on content-area topics during writing workshop.
Oral Language	Students listen to books read aloud during reading workshop and give book talks to share the books they've read. During writing workshop, classmates discuss their compositions.
Writing	Writing is at the heart of a writing workshop. Students use the writing process to draft, refine, and polish their compositions.
Spelling	Students apply their knowledge of spelling as they participate in writing workshop.

Van Allsburg, and Dr. Seuss. Ohlhausen and Jepsen (1992) developed a strategy for choosing books that they called the "Goldilocks Strategy." These teachers created three categories of books—"Too Easy" books, "Too Hard" books, and "Just Right" books—using "The Three Bears" folktale as their model. The books in the "Too Easy" category were those students had read before or could read fluently; "Too Hard" books were unfamiliar and confusing; and books in the "Just Right" category were interesting and had just a few unfamiliar words. The books in each category vary according to the student's reading level. This approach works at any grade level. Figure 13–2 presents a chart about choosing books using the Goldilocks Strategy.

When students choose their own books, they take ownership of the reading. Students' reading fluency and enjoyment of reading are related to sustained encounters with interesting texts (Smith, 1984). Reading and responding to literature are the heart of reading workshop.

Teachers often read their own books and magazines or read a book of children's literature during reading workshop. Through their example, they are modeling and communicating the importance of reading. Teachers also conference with students about the books they are reading. As they conference, they talk briefly and quietly with students about their reading. Students may also read aloud favorite quotes or an interesting passage to the teacher.

Students read all sorts of books during reading workshop, including stories, informational books, biographies, and books of poetry. They also read magazines. Most of their reading materials are selected from the classroom library, but students also bring other books from home and borrow books from classmates, from the public library, and from the school library. Students read many award-winning books during reading workshop, but they also read series of popular books and technical books related to their hobbies and special interests. These books are not necessarily the same books that

Figure 13-2 **A Third-Grade Chart Applying the Goldilocks Strategy**

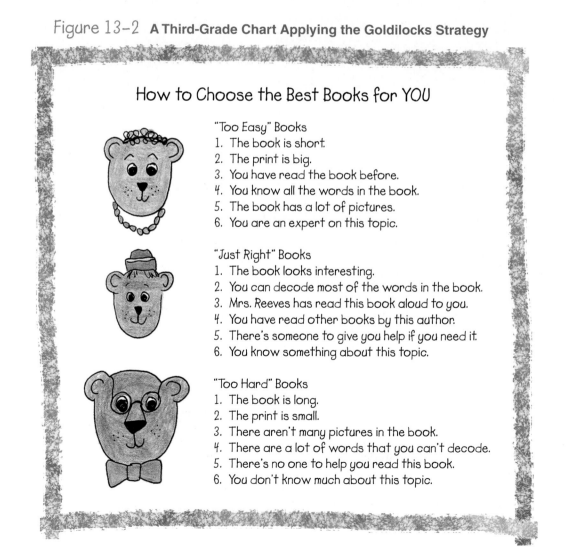

How to Choose the Best Books for YOU

"Too Easy" Books
1. The book is short.
2. The print is big.
3. You have read the book before.
4. You know all the words in the book.
5. The book has a lot of pictures.
6. You are an expert on this topic.

"Just Right" Books
1. The book looks interesting.
2. You can decode most of the words in the book.
3. Mrs. Reeves has read this book aloud to you.
4. You have read other books by this author.
5. There's someone to give you help if you need it.
6. You know something about this topic.

"Too Hard" Books
1. The book is long.
2. The print is small.
3. There aren't many pictures in the book.
4. There are a lot of words that you can't decode.
5. There's no one to help you read this book.
6. You don't know much about this topic.

Classroom Library

These third graders choose books to read during reading workshop from their classroom library. The students have dubbed the library their "book world." It is well organized and inviting, with space to sit and browse. The library is stocked with stories, informational books, and books of poetry that reflect the students' interests and their reading levels. Nonfiction books are arranged in one bookcase and fiction and poetry in another, and books related to thematic units are displayed on the top of the bookcases. This library works so well because students are responsible for keeping it neat and clean.

teachers use for literature focus units, but students often choose to reread books they have read earlier in the school year or the previous year in literature studies.

Teachers need to have literally hundreds of books in their class libraries, including books written at a range of reading levels, in order to have enough books so that every student can read during reading workshop. Primary teachers often worry about finding books that their students can handle independently. Alphabet books, predictable books, leveled books, and books the teacher has read aloud several times are often the most accessible for kindergartners and first graders. Primary-grade children often read and reread easy-to-read books such as those in the Scholastic Bookshelf series and the Wright Group's Story Box kits.

Teachers need to introduce students—especially reluctant readers—to the books in the classroom library so that they can more effectively choose books to read during reading workshop. The best way to preview books is using a very brief book talk to interest students in the book. In a book talk, teachers tell students a little about the book, show the cover, and perhaps read the first paragraph or two (Prill, 1994–1995); they also give book talks to introduce text sets of books. Students give book talks as they present books they have read to the class during the sharing part of reading workshop.

Component 2: Responding

Students usually keep reading logs in which they write their initial responses to the books they are reading. Sometimes students dialogue with the teacher about the book they are reading; a journal allows for ongoing written conversation between the teacher and individual students (Atwell, 1998; Staton, 1988). Responses often demonstrate students' reading strategies and offer insights into their thinking about literature. Seeing how students think about their reading helps teachers guide their learning.

Teachers play an important role in helping students expand and enrich their responses to literature (Hancock, 1993). They help students move beyond writing summaries and toward reflecting and making connections between literature and their own lives (Barone, 1990; Kelly, 1990). In addition, they collect students' journals periodically to monitor their responses. Wollman-Bonilla (1989) recommends writing back and forth with students, with the idea that students write more if the teacher responds. Also, teachers can model and support students' responses in their comments. However, because responding to students' journals is very time-consuming, teachers should keep their responses brief and not respond to every entry.

Teachers and researchers have examined students' responses and noticed patterns in them. Hancock (1992, 1993) identified these three categories of response patterns: personal meaning making, character and plot development, and literary evaluation. The categories and the various patterns that exemplify each category are summarized in Figure 13–3. In most reading log entries, students write responses

Figure 13-3 **Categories of Response in Students' Reading Log Entries**

Categories	Response Patterns	Descriptions
Personal Meaning Making	Monitoring Understanding	Students get to know the characters and explain how the story is making sense to them. These responses usually occur at the beginning of a book.
	Making Inferences	Students share their insights into the feelings and motives of a character. They often begin their comments with "I think."
	Making, Validating, or Invalidating Predictions	Students speculate about what will happen later in the story and also confirm or refute predictions they made previously.
	Expressing Wonder or Confusion	Students reflect on the way the story is developing. They ask "I wonder why" questions and write about confusions.
Character and Plot Development	Character Interaction	Students show that they are personally involved with a character, sometimes writing "If I were _____ , I would . . ." They express empathy and share related experiences from their own lives. Also, they may give advice to the character.
	Character Assessment	Students judge a character's actions and often use evaluative terms such as *nice* and *dumb*.
	Story Involvement	Students reveal their involvement in the story as they express satisfaction with how the story is developing. They may comment on their desire to continue reading or may use terms such as *disgusting, weird,* and *awesome* to react to sensory aspects of the story.
Literary Evaluation	Literary Criticism	Students offer "I liked/I didn't like" opinions and praise or condemn an author's style. Sometimes students compare the book with others they have read or compare the author with other authors with whom they are familiar.

Adapted from Hancock, 1992, 1993.

that address several patterns as they reflect on the story and explore their understanding. However, if they are writing in response to a specific prompt that addresses a single pattern, such as making a prediction, their entry might address only one pattern.

In the first category, personal meaning making, students indicate whether the book is making sense to them. They make inferences about characters, offer predictions, ask questions, or discuss confusions. Sixth graders' meaning-making responses excerpted from the reading logs about *Bunnicula: A Rabbit-Tale of Mystery* (Howe & Howe, 1979) include:

> *I think the Monroes will find out what Chester and Harold are doing.*

> *Can a bunny be a vampire? I don't think so. A bunny couldn't suck the blood out of a vegetable. They don't even have blood.*

> *I guess Bunnicula really is a vampire.*

> *I was right! I knew Harold and Chester would try to take care of Bunnicula. What I didn't know was that the Monroes would come home early.*

> *I wonder why the vegetables are turning white. I know it's not Bunnicula but I don't know why.*

In the second category, character and plot development, students show that they are personally involved with a character, often giving advice or judging a character's actions. They reveal their own involvement in the story as they express satisfaction with how the story is developing. Examples of responses include:

> *I know how Chester and Harold feel. It's like when I got a new baby sister and everyone paid attention to her. I got ignored a lot.*

> *If I were Bunnicula, I'd run away. He's just not safe in that house!*

> *Gross!!! The vegetables are all white and there are two little fang holes in each one.*

> *My dog is a lot like Harold. He gets on my bed with me and he loves snacks, but you should never feed a dog chocolate.*

> *I just can't stop reading. This book is so cool. And it's funny, too.*

In the third category, literary evaluation, students evaluate books they have read and reflect on their own literary taste. They offer opinions, sometimes saying "I liked . . . " or "I didn't like . . . " and compare the book to others they have read. Examples of responses include:

> *This is a great book! I know stuff like this couldn't happen but it would be awesome if it could. It's just fantasy but it's like I believe it.*

> *This book is like* Charlotte's Web *because the animals can talk and have a whole life that the people in the story don't know about. But the books are different because* Bunnicula *is much funner than* Charlotte's Web. *It made me laugh and* Charlotte's Web *made me cry.*

These categories can extend the possibilities of response by introducing teachers and students to a wide variety of response options. Hancock (1992, 1993) recommends that teachers begin by assessing the kinds of responses students are currently making; they can read students' journals, categorize entries, and make an assessment. Often students use only a few types of responses, not the wide range that is available. In that event, teachers can teach minilessons and model the types of responses that students aren't using, and they can ask questions in journals to prompt students to think in new ways about the story they are reading.

Some students write minimal responses in journals. It is important that students read books they find personally interesting and that they feel free to share their thoughts, feelings, and questions with a trusted audience—usually the teacher. Sometimes writing entries on a computer and using e-mail to share them with students in another class or with other interested readers increase students' interest in writing more elaborate responses.

During reading and responding time, there is little or no talking because students are engrossed in reading and writing independently. Rarely do students interrupt classmates, go to the rest room, or get drinks of water, except in case of emergency, nor do they use reading workshop time to do homework or other schoolwork.

Component 3: Sharing

For the last 15 minutes of reading workshop, the class gathers together to discuss books they have finished reading. Students talk about the book and why they liked it. Sometimes they read a brief excerpt aloud or formally pass the book to a classmate who wants to read it. Sharing is important because it helps students form a community to value and celebrate each other's accomplishments (Hansen, 1987).

Component 4: Teaching Minilessons

The teacher spends 5 to 15 minutes teaching minilessons on reading workshop procedures and reading strategies and skills. Topics for minilessons are usually drawn from students' observed needs, comments students make during conferences, and procedures that students need for reading workshop. Figure 13–4 lists possible minilesson topics.

Minilessons are sometimes taught to the whole class, and at other times, they are taught to small groups. At the beginning of the school year, teachers teach minilessons to the whole class on choosing books to read; later in the year, they teach minilessons on noticing literary language, visualizing, and other strategies. Teachers can teach minilessons on particular authors when they introduce their stories to the whole class. They also can teach minilessons on literary genres—contemporary realism, science fiction, historical fiction, folktales—when they set out collections of books representing each genre in the classroom library.

Component 5: Reading Aloud to Students

Teachers often read picture books and chapter books aloud to the class as part of reading workshop. They choose high-quality literature that students might not be able to read themselves, award-winning books that they feel every student should be exposed to, or books that relate to a social studies or science unit. After reading, students participate in a grand conversation to talk about the book and share the reading experience. This activity is important because students listen to a story read aloud and respond to it together as a community of learners, not as individuals.

 Learn more about grand conversations and other instructional procedures discussed in this chapter on the DVD that accompanies this text.

Figure 13-4 Minilesson Topics for Reading and Writing Workshop

Activity	Procedures	Concepts	Strategies/Skills
Reading Workshop	Choose a book Abandon a book Listen to book read aloud Read independently Decode unfamiliar words Respond in reading logs Use double-entry journals Give a book talk Participate in a conference	Aesthetic reading Efferent reading Comprehension Story genres Story elements Intertextuality Literary devices Author information	Identify unfamiliar words Visualize Predict and confirm Engage with text Identify with characters Elaborate on the plot Notice opposites Monitor understanding Connect to one's own life and the world Connect to previously read stories Value the story Evaluate the story
Writing Workshop	Choose a topic Cluster ideas Make a table of contents Participate in writing groups Proofread Use the dictionary Conference with the teacher Write an "All About the Author" page Make hardcover books Share published writing Use author's chair Use rubrics	The writing process Audience Purposes for writing Qualities of good writing Writing genres Proofreaders' marks Authors Illustration techniques Wordplay	Gather ideas Organize ideas Draft Revise Use metaphors and similes Use imagery Combine sentences Edit Identify and correct spelling errors Use capital letters correctly Use punctuation marks correctly Use dialogue Value the composition

Even though reading workshop is different from other instructional approaches, students work through the same five stages of the reading process. It's obvious that students read during reading workshop, but they also participate in prereading, responding, exploring, and applying activities. Figure 13–5 explains how students apply the reading process in reading workshop.

Is Sustained Silent Reading the Same as Reading Workshop?

Sustained Silent Reading (SSR) is an independent reading time set aside during the school day for students in one class or the entire school to silently read self-selected books. In some schools, everyone—students, teachers, principals, secretaries, and custodians—stops to read, usually for 15 to 30 minutes. SSR is a popular reading activity in schools that is known by a variety of names, including Drop Everything and Read (DEAR), Sustained Quiet Reading Time (SQUIRT), and Our Time to Enjoy Reading (OTTER).

Figure 13–5	How Students Apply the Reading Process in Reading Workshop
Stage	**Activity**
Prereading	In this student-centered instructional approach, students choose books to read, activate background knowledge, and preview the text as they look at the cover and think about the title.
Reading	Students read the books they have selected independently.
Responding	Students talk about the book when they conference with the teacher, and they often write responses in reading logs.
Exploring	Teachers teach students about genres, structural elements, authors and illustrators, and comprehension strategies during minilessons and when they read books aloud.
Applying	Students often give book talks to their classmates about books they have finished reading.

Teachers use SSR to increase the amount of reading students do every day and to develop their ability to read silently and without interruption (Hunt, 1967; Mc-Cracken & McCracken, 1978). A number of studies have shown that SSR is beneficial in developing students' reading ability (Krashen, 1993; Pilgreen, 2000). In addition, SSR promotes a positive attitude toward reading and encourages students to develop the habit of daily reading. It is based on these guidelines:

- Students choose the books they read.
- Students read silently.
- The teacher serves as a model by reading during SSR.
- Students choose one book or other reading material for the entire reading time.
- The teacher sets a timer for a predetermined, uninterrupted time period, usually between 15 and 30 minutes.
- All students in the class or school participate.
- Students do not write book reports or participate in other after-reading activities.
- The teacher does not keep records or evaluate students on their performance. (Pilgreen, 2000)

Even though SSR was specifically developed without follow-up activities, teachers often use a few carefully selected, brief follow-up activities to sustain students' interest in books. Sometimes students discuss their reading with a partner, or volunteers give book talks to tell the whole class about their books. As students listen to one another, they get ideas about books that they might like to read in the future. In some classrooms, students develop a ritual of passing on the books they have finished reading to interested classmates, much like students do during reading workshop.

Reading workshop and Sustained Silent Reading (SSR) are similar. The goal of both programs is to provide opportunities for students to read self-selected books independently, and the reading component of reading workshop is similar to SSR. Both programs work best in classrooms where the teacher and students have created a community of learners. It seems obvious that students need to feel relaxed and comfortable in order to read for pleasure, and a community of learners is a place where students do feel comfortable because they are respected and valued by classmates and the teacher.

There are important differences, however. Reading workshop has five components—reading, responding, sharing, teaching minilessons, and reading aloud to students—whereas SSR has only one—reading. Reading workshop is recognized as an instructional approach because it includes both independent reading and instruction through minilessons. In contrast, SSR is a supplemental program. Students read books and sometimes do book talks to share their favorite books with classmates, but there is not an instructional component to SSR. Both reading workshop and SSR have been found to be effective, but teachers need to determine their instructional goals before choosing to implement reading workshop or SSR in their classrooms.

WRITING WORKSHOP

Visit Chapter 13 on the Companion Website at *www.prenhall.com/tompkins* to connect to web links related to writing workshop.

Writing workshop is the best way to implement the writing process (Atwell, 1998; Calkins, 1994; Fletcher & Portalupi, 2001; Gillet & Beverly, 2001; Graves, 1994). Students write on topics that they choose themselves, and they assume ownership of their writing and learning. At the same time, the teacher's role changes from being a provider of knowledge to serving as a facilitator and guide. The classroom becomes a community of writers who write and share their writing. There is a spirit of pride and acceptance in the classroom.

In a writing workshop classroom, students have writing folders in which they keep all papers related to the writing project they are working on. They also keep writing notebooks in which they jot down images, impressions, dialogue, and experiences that they can build upon for writing projects (Calkins, 1991). Students have access to different kinds of paper, some lined and some unlined, as well as writing instruments such as pencils and red and blue pens. They also have access to the classroom library; many times, students' writing grows out of favorite books they have read. They may write a sequel to a book or retell a story from a different viewpoint. Primary-grade students often use patterns from books they have read to structure a book they are writing.

As they write, students sit at desks or tables arranged in small groups. The teacher circulates around the classroom, conferencing briefly with students, and the classroom atmosphere is free enough that students converse quietly with classmates and move around to assist others or share ideas. There is space for students to meet for writing groups, and often a sign-up sheet for writing groups is posted in the classroom. A table is available for the teacher to meet with individual students or small groups for conferences, writing groups, proofreading, and minilessons.

Writing workshop in a 60- to 90-minute period scheduled each day. During this time, students are involved in three components: writing, sharing, and minilessons. Sometimes a fourth activity, reading aloud to students, is added to writing workshop when it is not used in conjunction with reading workshop. The feature on the next page presents an overview of the workshop approach.

Component 1: Writing

Students spend 30 to 45 minutes or longer working independently on writing projects. Just as students in reading workshop choose books and read at their own pace, in writing workshop, students work at their own pace on writing projects they have chosen themselves. Most students move at their own pace through all five stages of the writing process—prewriting, drafting, revising, editing, and publishing—but young children often use an abbreviated process consisting of prewriting, drafting, and

Reading and Writing Workshop

Topic	Description
Purpose	To provide students with opportunities for authentic reading and writing activities.
Components	Reading workshop involves reading, responding, sharing, teaching minilessons, and reading aloud to students. Writing workshop consists of writing, sharing, and teaching minilessons.
Theory Base	The workshop approach reflects constructivism and reader response theories because students participate in authentic activities that encourage them to become lifelong readers and writers.
Applications	Teachers often use reading workshop in conjunction with a basal reading program or literature focus units so students have opportunities to do independent reading. They often add writing workshop to any of the other instructional approaches so students have more sustained opportunities to use the writing process to develop and refine compositions.
Strengths	• Students read books appropriate for their reading levels. • Students are more motivated because they choose the books they read. • Students work through the stages of the writing process. • Activities are student directed, and students work at their own pace. • Teachers have opportunities to work individually with students during conferences.
Limitations	• Teachers often feel a loss of control because students are reading different books and working at different stages of the writing process. • Teachers have responsibility to teach minilessons on strategies and skills to students, both in whole-class groups and to individual students. • Students must learn to be task oriented and to use time wisely in order to be successful.

publishing. Teachers often begin writing workshop by reviewing the five stages of the writing process, setting guidelines for writing workshop, and taking students through one writing activity together. A seventh-grade class's set of rules for writing workshop is presented in Figure 13–6.

Teachers conference with students as they write. Many teachers prefer moving around the classroom to meet with students rather than having the students come to a table to meet with them: Too often, a line forms as students wait, and they lose precious writing time. Some teachers move around the classroom in a regular pattern, meeting with one-fifth of the students each day. In this way, they can conference with every student during the week.

Figure 13-6 **A Seventh-Grade Class's Rules for Writing Workshop**

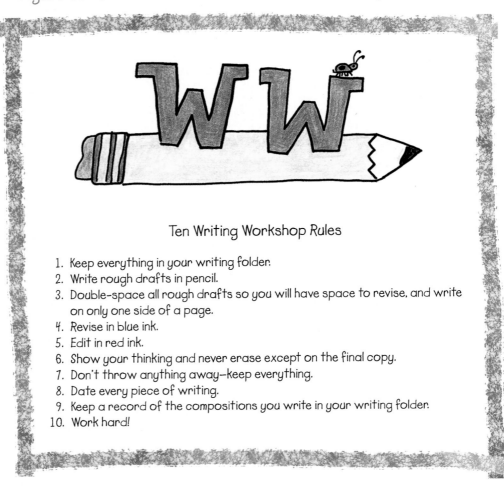

Ten Writing Workshop Rules

1. Keep everything in your writing folder.
2. Write rough drafts in pencil.
3. Double-space all rough drafts so you will have space to revise, and write on only one side of a page.
4. Revise in blue ink.
5. Edit in red ink.
6. Show your thinking and never erase except on the final copy.
7. Don't throw anything away—keep everything.
8. Date every piece of writing.
9. Keep a record of the compositions you write in your writing folder.
10. Work hard!

Other teachers spend the first 15 to 20 minutes of writing workshop stopping briefly to check on 10 or more students each day. Many use a zigzag pattern to get to all parts of the classroom each day. These teachers often kneel down beside each student, sit on the edge of the student's seat, or carry their own stool to each student's desk. During the 1- or 2-minute conference, teachers ask students what they are writing, listen to students read a paragraph or two, and then ask what they plan to do next. Then these teachers use the remaining time during writing workshop to conference more formally with students who are revising and editing their compositions; students often sign up for these conferences. The teachers identify strengths in students' writing, ask questions, and discover possibilities during these revising conferences. Some teachers like to read the pieces themselves, and others like to listen to students read their papers aloud. As they interact with students, teachers model the kinds of responses that students are learning to give to each other.

As students meet to share their writing during revising and editing, they continue to develop their sense of community. They share their rough drafts with classmates in writing groups composed of four or five students. In some classrooms, teachers join the writing groups whenever they can, but students normally run the groups themselves. They take turns reading their rough drafts to each other and listen as their classmates offer compliments and suggestions for revision. Students also participate in revising and editing centers that are set up in the classroom. They know how to work at each center and the importance of working with classmates to make their writing better.

After proofreading their drafts with a classmate and then meeting with the teacher for final editing, students make the final copy of their writings. They often want to print out their writings using the computer so that their final copies will appear professional. Many times, students compile their final copies to make books during writing workshop, but sometimes they attach their writing to artwork, make posters, write letters that will be mailed, or perform scripts as skits or puppet shows. Not every piece is necessarily published, however. Sometimes students decide not to continue with a piece of writing: They file that piece in their writing folders and start something new.

Component 2: Sharing

For the last 10 to 15 minutes of writing workshop, the class gathers together to share their new publications and make other related announcements. Younger students often

Writing Conferences

These students are meeting with their teacher for a writing conference. The teacher sits at a table, and students come and join her. Whenever there is an empty seat, a student can join the conference. What the teacher does during the conference depends on what the students need: Some students may need to talk about ideas in order to get started, and others may want the teacher to read and respond to their writing or do a final editing for them. The students sitting at the conference table often join in discussions and add their suggestions or assist with editing.

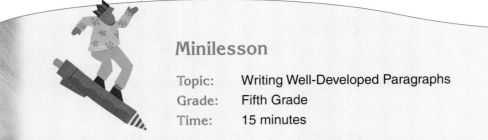

Minilesson

Topic: Writing Well-Developed Paragraphs

Grade: Fifth Grade

Time: 15 minutes

Ms. Hodas's fifth graders are writing reports about inventions during writing workshop. Together as a class, students developed clusters with information about the inventions they had studied, and then they worked independently to write rough drafts using the information from their clusters. More than half of the students have finished their rough drafts and are participating in revising groups. As Ms. Hodas conferences with students about their writing, she notices that many of them are not breaking their writing into paragraphs or writing well-developed paragraphs. She decides to bring the class together for a brief minilesson on paragraphing.

1. Introduce Topic

"Let's stop for a minute and talk about paragraphs," Ms. Hodas says. "What do you know about paragraphs?" Students talk about organizing ideas into paragraphs, keeping to one topic in a paragraph, using a topic sentence and a concluding sentence, and indenting paragraphs. Ms. Hodas is pleased that students remember what she has taught them about paragraphing and refers them to the chart on paragraphs posted in the classroom that they created earlier in the school year.

2. Share Examples

Ms. Hodas asks students to reread their rough drafts to themselves. Afterward, she asks them to check that they have organized their writing into paragraphs. The students who have not written in paragraphs add the paragraph indent symbol to indicate where new paragraphs should begin.

3. Provide Information

"Now let's look at your first paragraph," Ms. Hodas says. She asks each student to reread his or her first paragraph, checking for a topic sentence, detail sentences that stick to the topic, and a final sentence that sums up the paragraph. Students who find that their paragraphs are not well developed start revising or writing notes in the margin of their papers about how they want to revise the paragraph. They continue rereading their rough drafts, checking that all paragraphs are well crafted.

4. Guide Practice

Ms. Hodas asks for a volunteer to read a paragraph aloud for the class to examine. Jonas reads his first paragraph—a well-crafted paragraph—aloud to the class, and the students pick out the topic sentence, the detail sentences, and the concluding sentence. They agree that all sentences stick to the topic. Next, William reads another strong paragraph aloud, and students pick out all of the components. Then Ms. Hodas asks for other students to volunteer to read aloud paragraphs that they need to revise so that classmates can give some suggestions. Because Ms. Hodas has created a community of learners in the classroom, students are willing to share their paragraphs even when they are not their best work. Three students each read a paragraph aloud, and classmates identify the missing pieces and offer suggestions.

5. Assess Learning

The minilesson ends with Ms. Hodas inviting students who want more assistance to meet with her at the conferencing table. The other students return to working independently or with partners at their desks.

sit in a circle or gather together on a rug for sharing time. If an author's chair is available, each student sits in the special chair to read his or her composition. After each reading, classmates clap and offer compliments. They may also make other comments and suggestions, but the focus is on celebrating completed writing projects, not on revising the composition to make it better. Classmates help celebrate after the child shares by clapping; perhaps the best praise is having a classmate ask if he or she can read the newly published book.

Component 3: Teaching Minilessons

During this 5- to 15-minute period, teachers provide minilessons on writing workshop procedures, qualities of good writing, and writing strategies and skills, such as organizing ideas, proofreading, and using quotation marks to mark dialogue. In the middle and upper grades, teachers often make a transparency of an anonymous student's piece of writing (often a student in another class or from a previous year) and then display it using an overhead projector. Students read the writing, and the teacher uses it to teach the lesson, which may focus on giving suggestions for revision, combining sentences, proofreading, or writing a stronger lead sentence. Teachers also select excerpts from books students are reading for minilessons to show how published authors use writing skills and strategies. Refer to Figure 13–4 for a list of minilessons for writing workshop; these minilessons are similar to those taught in reading workshop. And for other ideas for minilessons, check *Craft Lessons: Teaching Writing K–8* (Fletcher & Portalupi, 1998), *Writing Rules! Teaching Kids to Write for Life, Grades 4–8* (Brusko, 1999), and *Reviser's Toolbox* (Lane, 1999).

Many minilessons occur during writing workshop when students ask questions or when the teacher notices that students misunderstand or misapply a procedure, concept, strategy, or skill. In the minilesson featured on the next page, Ms. Hodas reviews paragraphing skills with her fifth-grade class after she notices that students are not dividing their text into paragraphs or crafting well-developed paragraphs. Teachers also share information during minilessons about authors and how they write. For students to think of themselves as writers, they need to know what writers do. Each year, there are more autobiographies written by authors. James Howe, author of *Bunnicula: A Rabbit-Tale of Mystery* (Howe & Howe, 1979), has written an autobiography, *Playing With Words* (1994), in which he reflects on his desire since childhood to make people laugh and describes his writing routine and how he makes time to read and write every day. Other books in the Meet the Author series include *Firetalking*, by Patricia Polacco (1994), *Surprising Myself*, by Jean Fritz (1992), and *Making a Difference in the World*, by Lynne Cherry (2000).

Writing workshop is the best way for students to apply the writing process: Teachers teach students how to do the activities during each stage of the writing process, and then students practice what they have learned during writing workshop. They move through the five stages of the writing process as they plan, draft, revise, edit, and finally publish their writing. Figure 13–7 details how students apply the writing process in writing workshop.

MANAGING A WORKSHOP CLASSROOM

It takes time to establish a workshop approach in the classroom because students need to assume more responsibility for their own learning. They need to develop new ways of working and learning, and they have to form a community of readers and writers in the classroom (Gillet & Beverly, 2001). For reading workshop, students need to know how to select books and other reading workshop procedures. For writing workshop, students need to know how to develop and refine a piece of writing, how to make books and booklets for their compositions, and other writing workshop procedures. Sometimes students

Figure 13-7 How Students Apply the Writing Process in Writing Workshop

Stage	Activity
Prewriting	Students move through the stages of the writing process during the writing period. To begin, they create graphic organizers as they gather and organize ideas.
Drafting	Students write books and other compositions, usually on self-selected topics. They generally work independently.
Revising	Students participate in writing groups to share their rough drafts and to get feedback to help them revise their compositions.
Editing	Students work with classmates to proofread and correct mechanical errors in their compositions. They also meet with the teacher for a final editing.
Publishing	During sharing time, students usually sit in the author's chair to read their compositions to classmates.

complain that they don't know what to write about, but in time, they learn how to brainstorm possible topics and to keep a list of topics in their writing workshop notebooks.

Teachers establish the workshop environment in their classroom beginning on the first day of the school year by allowing students to choose the books they read and their topics for writing. Teachers provide time for students to read and write and teach them how to respond to books and to their classmates' writing. Through their interactions with students, the respect they show to students, and the way they model reading and writing, teachers establish the classroom as a community of learners.

Teachers develop a schedule for reading and writing workshop with time allocated for each component, as was shown in Figure 13–1. In their schedules, teachers allot as much time as possible for students to read and write. After developing the schedule, teachers post it in the classroom and talk with students about the activities and discuss their expectations. Teachers teach the workshop procedures and continue to model them as students become comfortable with the routines. As students share what they are reading and writing at the end of workshop sessions, their enthusiasm grows and the workshop approaches are successful.

Students keep two folders—one for reading workshop and one for writing workshop. In the reading workshop folder, students keep a list of books they have read, notes from minilessons, reading logs, and other materials. In the writing workshop folder, they keep all rough drafts and other compositions, a list of all compositions, topics for future pieces, and notes from minilessons.

Scaffolding Struggling Readers

How can I help my struggling writers who don't accomplish much during writing workshop?

Struggling students often resist writing; some don't know what to write, and others don't know how to write. One thing they have in common is that they don't expect to be successful, so it's important to teach struggling writers how to write and to structure writing activities so they can be successful. Teach students how to use the writing process and how to choose topics they're interested in writing about, share sample compositions when assigning writing so students know what's expected of them, and write collaborative compositions with them for practice. Teachers also use the Language Experience Approach when they want to focus on generating, organizing, and revising ideas, and interactive writing to review mechanical skills. In addition, students' first writing experiences should be brief to build their confidence.

Figure 13–8 "State of the Class" Chart

Names	Dates 3/13	3/14	3/15	3/16	3/17	3/20	3/21	3/22
Writing Workshop Chart								
Antonio	4	5	5	5	5	1	1	1 2
Bella	2	2	2 3	2	2	4	5	5
Charles	3	3 1	1	2	2 3	4	5	5
Dina	4 5	5	5	1	1	1	1	2 3
Dustin	3	3	4	4	4	5	5 1	1
Eddie	2 3	2	2 4	5	5	1	1 2	2 3
Elizabeth	2	3	3	4	4	4 5	5	1 2
Elsa	1 2	3 4	4 5	5	5	1	2	2

Code:
1 = Prewriting   2 = Drafting   3 = Revising   4 = Editing   5 = Publishing

Assessment Tools

Many teachers use a classroom chart to monitor students' work on a daily basis. At the beginning of reading workshop, students (or the teacher) record what book they are reading or if they are writing in a reading log, waiting to conference with the teacher, or browsing in the classroom library. For writing workshop, students identify the writing project they are involved in or the stage of the writing process they are in. A sample writing workshop chart is shown in Figure 13–8. Teachers can also use the chart to award weekly "effort" grades, to have students indicate their need to conference with the teacher, or to have students announce that they are ready to share the book they have read or publish their writing. Nancie Atwell (1998) calls this chart "the status of the class." Teachers can review students' progress and note which students need to meet with the teacher or receive additional attention. When students fill in the chart themselves, they develop responsibility for their actions and a stronger desire to accomplish tasks they set for themselves.

To monitor primary-grade students, teachers often use a pocket chart and have students place a card in their pocket to indicate whether they are choosing a new book, reading, or responding during reading workshop, or in which stage of the writing process they are working during writing workshop.

Teachers should take time during reading and writing workshop to observe students as they interact and work together in small groups. Researchers who have observed in reading and writing workshop classrooms report that some students, even as young as first graders, are excluded from group activities becasue of gender, ethnicity, ans socioeconomic status (Henkin, 1995; Lensmire, 1992); the socialization patterns in classrooms seem to reflect society's. Henkin recommends that teachers be alret to the possibility that boys might share books only with other boys or that some students won't find anyone willing to be their editing partner. If teachers see instances of discrimination in their classrooms, they should confront the situation directly and work to foster a classroom environment where student treat each other equitably.

Benefits of Reading and Writing Workshop

There are many reasons to recommend the workshop approach. In reading workshop, students select and read genuine literature that is interesting and written at their reading level. The literature has complex sentence patterns and presents challenging concepts and vocabulary. Through reading workshop, students become more fluent readers and learn to deepen their appreciation of books and reading. As students read, they are developing lifelong reading habits. They are introduced to different genres and choose favorite authors. Most important, they come to think of themselves as readers.

In writing workshop, students create their own compositions and come to see themselves as writers. They practice writing strategies and skills and learn to choose words carefully to articulate their ideas. Perhaps most important, they see firsthand the power of writing to entertain, inform, and persuade.

Samway, Whang, and their students (1991) reported that the two most important benefits of reading workshop are that students become a community of learners and that they view themselves as readers. As students read and respond to books, they understand themselves and their classmates better and gain confidence in themselves as readers. In addition, their ability to choose reading materials becomes more sophisticated during the school year. Students are much more enthusiastic about reading workshop than traditional reading approaches. The authors offer advice to teachers about the necessary components of reading workshop: Students want to read complete books, not excerpts; they want to choose the books they read; and they need plenty of time to read and talk about books.

Many teachers fear that their students' scores on standardized achievement tests will decline if they implement a workshop approach in their classrooms, even though many teachers have reported either an increase in test scores or no change at all (Five, 1988; Swift, 1993). Kathleen Swift (1993) reported the results of a yearlong study comparing two groups of her students; one group read basal reader stories, and the other participated in reading workshop. The reading workshop group showed significantly greater improvement, and Swift also reported that students participating in reading workshop showed more positive attitudes toward reading.

Complete a self-assessment to check your understanding of the concepts presented in this chapter on the Companion Website at *www.prenhall.com/tompkins*

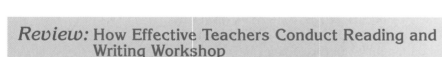

Review: How Effective Teachers Conduct Reading and Writing Workshop

1. Teachers allow students to choose the books they want to read.

2. Teachers teach students how to select books using the Goldilocks Strategy.

3. Teachers recognize reading workshop as an instructional approach and provide plenty of time for students to read and respond to books.

4. Teachers use conferences and responses students write in reading logs to monitor their reading progress.

5. Teachers build students' enthusiasm for reading and books through book talks and sharing.

6. Teachers teach minilessons and have students apply what they have learned through reading and writing.

7. Teachers allow students to choose their own topics and forms for writing.

8. Teachers teach students to use the writing process to develop and refine their compositions.

9. Teachers encourage students to publish their writing in books.

10. Teachers have students celebrate their completed writings and share them using an author's chair.

Professional References

Atwell, N. (1998). *In the middle: New understandings about reading and writing with adolescents* (2nd ed.). Upper Montclair, NJ: Boynton/Cook.

Barone, D. (1990). The written responses of young children: Beyond comprehension to story understanding. *The New Advocate, 3,* 49–56.

Brophy, J. E., & Good, T. L. (1986). Teacher behavior and student achievement. In M. C. Wittrock (Ed.), *Handbook of research on teaching* (3rd ed., pp. 328–375). New York: Macmillan.

Brusko, M. (1999). *Writing rules! Teaching kids to write for life, grades 4–8.* Portsmouth, NH: Heinemann.

Calkins, L. M. (1991). *Living between the lines.* Portsmouth, NH: Heinemann.

Calkins, L. M. (1994). *The art of teaching writing* (Rev. ed.). Portsmouth, NH: Heinemann.

Five, C. L. (1988). From workbook to workshop: Increasing children's involvement in the reading process. *The New Advocate, 1,* 103–113.

Fletcher, R., & Portalupi, J. (1998). *Craft lessons: Teaching writing K–8.* York, ME: Stenhouse.

Fletcher, R., & Portalupi, J. (2001). *Writing workshop: The essential guide.* Portsmouth, NH: Heinemann.

Gillet, J. W., & Beverly, L. (2001). *Directing the writing workshop: An elementary teacher's handbook.* New York: Guilford Press.

Graves, D. H. (1994). *A fresh look at writing.* Portsmouth, NH: Heinemann.

Hancock, M. R. (1992). Literature response journals: Insights beyond the printed page. *Language Arts, 69,* 36–42.

Hancock, M. R. (1993). Exploring and extending personal response through literature journals. *The Reading Teacher, 46,* 466–474.

Hansen, J. (1987). *When writers read.* Portsmouth, NH: Heinemann.

Henkin, R. (1995). Insiders and outsiders in first-grade writing workshops: Gender and equity issues. *Language Arts, 72,* 429–434.

Hornsby, D., Parry, J., & Sukarna, D. (1992). *Teach on: Teaching strategies for reading and writing workshops.* Portsmouth, NH: Heinemann.

Hornsby, D., Sukarna, D., & Parry, J. (1986). *Read on: A conference approach to reading.* Portsmouth, NH: Heinemann.

Hunt, L. (1967). Evaluation through teacher-pupil conferences. In T. C. Barrett (Ed.), *The evaluation of children's reading achievement* (pp. 111–126). Newark, DE: International Reading Association.

Johnson, B. (1999). *Never too early to write: Adventures in the K–1 writing workshop.* Gainesville, FL: Maupin House.

Kelly, P. R. (1990). Guiding young students' response to literature. *The Reading Teacher, 43,* 464–470.

Krashen, S. (1993). *The power of reading.* Englewood, CO: Libraries Unlimited.

Lane, B. (1999). *Reviser's toolbox.* Shoreham, VT: Discover Writing Press.

Lensmire, T. (1992). *When children write.* New York: Teachers College Press.

McCracken, R., & McCracken, M. (1978). Modeling is the key to sustained silent reading. *The Reading Teacher, 31,* 406–408.

McWhirter, A. M. (1990). Whole language in the middle school. *The Reading Teacher, 43,* 562–565.

Ohlhausen, M. M., & Jepsen, M. (1992). Lessons from Goldilocks: "Somebody's been choosing my books but I can make my own choices now!" *The New Advocate, 5,* 31–46.

Pilgreen, J. L. (2000). *The SSR handbook: How to organize and manage a sustained silent reading program.* Portsmouth, NH: Boynton/Cook/Heinemann.

Prill, P. (1994–1995). Helping children use the classroom library. *The Reading Teacher, 48,* 363–364.

Samway, K. D., Whang, G., Cade, C., Gamil, M., Lubandina, M. A., & Phommachanh, K. (1991). Reading the skeleton, the heart, and the brain of a book: Students' perspectives on literature study circles. *The Reading Teacher, 45,* 196–205.

Smith, F. (1984). *Reading without nonsense.* New York: Teachers College Press.

Staton, J. (1988). ERIC/RCS report: Dialogue journals. *Language Arts, 65,* 198–201.

Swift, K. (1993). Try reading workshop in your classroom. *The Reading Teacher, 46,* 366–371.

Wollman-Bonilla, J. E. (1989). Reading to participate in literature. *The Reading Teacher, 43,* 112–120.

Children's Book References

Cherry, L. (2000). *Making a difference in the world.* Katonah, NY: Richard C. Owen.

Fritz, J. (1992). *Surprising myself.* Katonah, NY: Richard C. Owen.

Howe, D., & Howe, J. (1979). *Bunnicula: A rabbit-tale of mystery.* New York: Atheneum.

Howe, J. (1994). *Playing with words.* Katonah, NY: Richard C. Owen.

Polacco, P. (1994). *Firetalking.* Katonah, NY: Richard C. Owen.

Weiss, N. (1990). *An egg is an egg.* New York: Putnam.

Reading and Writing in the Content Areas

- How do teachers make content-area textbooks more reader friendly or "considerate"?
- Why aren't content-area textbooks a complete program?
- Why should students use informational books, stories, and poems as well as textbooks to learn in content areas?
- How do teachers develop thematic units?

Mrs. Zumwalt's Third Graders Create Multigenre Projects

Mrs. Zumwalt's third graders are studying ocean animals, and her focus is adaptation: How do animals adapt to survive in the ocean? As her students learn about ocean life, they take special notice of how individual animals adapt. For example, Alyssa has learned that whelks have hard shells for protection, Aidan knows that some small fish travel together in schools, Cody reports that clams burrow into the sand to be safe, and Christopher has read that sea otters have thick fur to keep them warm in the cold ocean water. Students are adding what they are learning about adaptation to a chart hanging in the classroom.

More than a month ago, Mrs. Zumwalt began the thematic unit by passing out a collection of informational picture books from the text set on ocean animals for her students to peruse. After they examined the books and read excerpts for 30 minutes or so, she brought them together to begin a K-W-L chart. This huge chart covers half of the back wall of the classroom. There are three sheets of poster paper hanging vertically side by side. The sheet on the left is labeled "K—What We Know About Ocean Animals." The middle sheet is labeled "W—What We Wonder About Ocean Animals," and one on the right is labeled "L—What We Learned About Ocean Animals." Mrs. Zumwalt began by asking students what they already knew about ocean animals, and they offered many facts, including "sea stars can grow a lot of arms," "sharks have three rows of teeth," and "jellyfish and puffer fish are poisonous," which Mrs. Zumwalt recorded in the K column. They also asked questions, including "How can an animal live inside a jelly fish?" "Is it true that father seahorses give birth?" and "How do some fish light up?" which she wrote in the W column. Students continued to think of questions for several days, and Mrs. Zumwalt added them to the W column. Later, at the end of the unit, the students will finish the chart by adding facts they've learned to the L column.

Mrs. Zumwalt talked about the six ocean habitats—seashore, open ocean, deep ocean, seabed, coral reefs, and polar seas—and the animals living in each one. She began with the seashore, and the students took a field trip to the Monterey Bay Aquarium to learn about the animals that live at the seashore. She focused on several animals in each habitat, reading aloud books about animals and emphasizing how animals have adapted. As they studied each habitat, they made a class chart about it, and students recorded information in their learning logs. They hung the charts in the classroom, and after all six habitats were introduced, Mrs. Zumwalt set out a pack of cards with names of animals and pictures of them for students to sort according to habitat. The box on page 428 shows the habitat sort.

Students have learning logs that Mrs. Zumwalt compiled and stapled into booklets. Each learning log contains 20 sheets of lined paper for writing, 10 sheets of unlined paper for drawing and charting, and 15 information sheets about ocean animals. There's also a page for their personal word walls that is divided into nine boxes and labeled with letters of the alphabet; students record some of the words from the class word wall on their personal word walls. The class word wall is displayed on one wall of the classroom; it is shown in the box on page 429. Mrs. Zumwalt introduces new words during her presentations and as she reads aloud books from the text set on ocean animals; she adds them to the word wall as she talks about them.

Eight of her 20 third graders come from homes where Spanish is spoken, and these students struggle with oral and written English. Mrs. Zumwalt brings these students together most days for an extra lesson while their classmates work on other activities. She either previews the next lesson she will teach or the next book she will read or reviews the last lesson she taught or the last book she read. In this small-group setting, students talk about what they are learning, ask questions, examine artifacts and pictures, and practice vocabulary. They often create interactive writing charts to share what they've discussed with their classmates. Here is their chart about schools of fish:

There are two kinds of schools. Kids go to school to be smart and little fish travel in schools or groups. Fish are safer when they stick together in schools.

Once the students became familiar with a variety of ocean animals, each student picked a favorite animal to study. The third graders chose sting rays, dolphins, squids, sea anemones, sand dollars, great white sharks, seals, penguins, sea turtles, jellyfish,

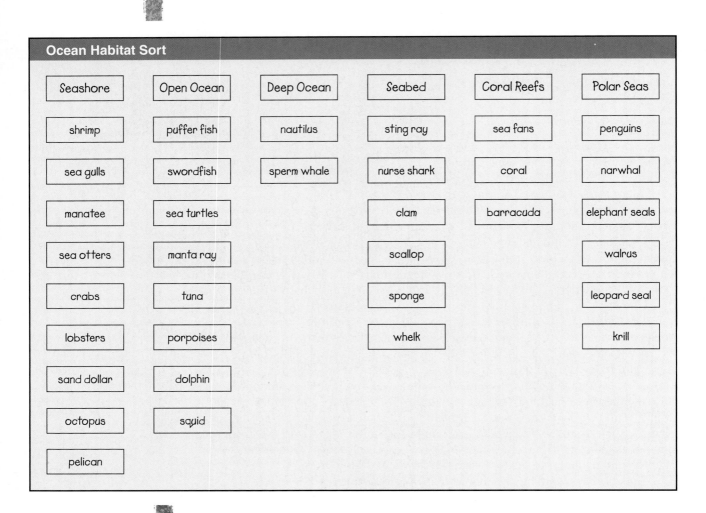

Ocean Habitat Sort

Seashore	Open Ocean	Deep Ocean	Seabed	Coral Reefs	Polar Seas
shrimp	puffer fish	nautilus	sting ray	sea fans	penguins
sea gulls	swordfish	sperm whale	nurse shark	coral	narwhal
manatee	sea turtles		clam	barracuda	elephant seals
sea otters	manta ray		scallop		walrus
crabs	tuna		sponge		leopard seal
lobsters	porpoises		whelk		krill
sand dollar	dolphin				
octopus	squid				
pelican					

octopuses, seahorses, pelicans, killer whales, barracudas, tunas, electric eels, lobsters, manatees, and squid. They researched their animals using Internet resources and books and encyclopedias in the text set; one of their best resources was the 11-volume encyclopedia *Aquatic Life of the World* (2001). Once they became experts, Mrs. Zumwalt introduced the idea of developing multigenre projects about the animals they had studied. In a multigenre project, students create three or more items representing different genres and package them in a box, on a display board, or in a notebook. For example, students might write reports, stories, poems; create artifacts; and design posters and charts. Earlier in the year, the students worked collaboratively to develop a class multigenre project on bees, so they were familiar with multigenre projects.

The students decided to develop four items in their multigenre projects: an informational book with chapters about their animal's physical traits, diet, habitat, and enemies along with three other items. Among the other items students might include are an adaptation poster, a life cycle chart, a poem, an alliterative sentence, a diagram of the animal, and a pack of true/false cards about the animal. They will package their projects in cereal boxes that they bring to school from home, and they will decorate the packages with pictures, interesting information, and a big idea statement about how that animal has adapted to ocean life.

The third graders used the writing process to prepare their informational books. These students have learned about how writers develop, draft, and refine their writing, and earlier in the year, they developed charts describing each stage of the writing process that now hang in the classroom. For prewriting, they used large, multicolored index cards to jot notes; the green one is for "Physical Traits," the yellow one is for "Diet," the blue one is for "Habitat," the purple one is for "Enemies," and the pink one is for other interesting information.

After students took notes using book resources from the text set and Internet resources, they shared the information they've gathered one-on-one with classmates, who asked questions about things that confused them and encouraged the students to add more information about incomplete topics. Next, students wrote rough drafts and shared them with the partners they worked with earlier. Then they met in writing groups with Mrs. Zumwalt and several classmates and revised their rough drafts using the feedback they got from their writing groups.

Now students are proofreading and correcting their revised drafts and creating their published books. Once they have corrected their mechanical errors and met with Mrs. Zumwalt for a final editing conference, they recopy their drafts in their best handwriting, add illustrations, and compile the pages into a hardbound book. They are also preparing the boxes and the other items for their multigenre projects.

Christian researched pelicans; his informational book is shown in the box on page 430. For his other three items, he drew a life-cycle chart showing a pelican egg, a newly hatched bird in the nest, a young adult bird flapping its wings, and an older adult diving into the ocean for food, he made a Venn diagram comparing white and brown pelicans, and he wrote an alliterative sentence about pelicans using only words that begin with *p*. His multigenre project box is decorated with pictures of pelicans and interesting information he collected, including "their wings are nine feet long" and "pelicans can live to be 25 years old." The adaptation statement on his multigenre box reads, "Pelicans have web feet and they can dive underwater to catch their food to eat. That's how they can survive at the seashore."

Check the Compendium of Instructional Procedures, which follows Chapter 14, for more information on highlighted terms.

Mrs. Zumwalt's Word Wall on Ocean Animals					
ABC		**DEF**		**GHI**	
crab	coral reef	dolphin		hermit crab	
colony	anal fin	dorsal fin		gill	
algae				invertebrate	
blubber					
crustacean					
Atlantic Ocean					
JKL		**MNO**		**PQR**	
larvae		ocean		Pacific Ocean	plankton
krill		Monterey Bay Aquarium		predator	pectoral fin
		mammal		prey	pelvic fin
		mollusk		penguin	porpoise
		mucus		reptile	
		manta ray		polyp	
STU		**VWX**		**YZ**	
tuna	spawning			whelk	
sea otter	suckers	vertebrate			
tide	tentacle				
school	seashore				
shark	seabed				
scavenger					

Christian's Informational Book About Pelicans

Chapter 1
Introduction
Pelicans are birds that live on the seashore. They have web feet for walking on sand and swimming. They can drive underwater to catch their food. That's how they live near the ocean.

Chapter 2
Physical Traits
Pelicans have some interesting physical traits. The pelican is easy to identify. They have big pouches and you can tell them by their big necks and plump bodies. The pelican has big legs and colors brown and white.

Chapter 3
Diet
Diet is what an animal eats. The pelican swallows a lot of fish. Pelicans gobble up meat. Pelicans attack sea stars and they chomp on seahorses.

Chapter 4
Habitat
A habitat is where an animal lives. The pelican lives in many countries. Pelicans are found where there's air and where it's warm. Some pelicans are now living in Monterey. Pelicans live by water, too.

Chapter 5
Enemies
Most animals are both prey and predator. That means animals are usually both the hunted and the hunter. The pelican eats seahorses and sea stars. Pelicans are hunted by sharks and people. Why do people hurt these birds? People dump waste into the water and it kills the fishes that the pelicans eat!

Chapter 6
Conclusion
I hope pelicans will always live in Monterey Bay but they could die if people dump pollution into the ocean and that would be very sad.

Today, Mrs. Zumwalt is meeting with students for a final editing before they create their published books. She meets with two students at a time; they work together to identify and correct any remaining spelling, capitalization, punctuation, and grammar errors, and use red pens to mark their corrections so they will be sure to notice them when they recopy their chapters.

Next, the students finish the K-W-L chart by adding comments about what they've learned about ocean animals. Cody offers that "octopuses can change shape and color to camouflage themselves," Hernan reports that "dolphins' tails go up and down and fishes' tails go side to side," and Carlos adds that "jellyfish are related to sea anemones because neither one has teeth."

Next Monday afternoon, the third graders will share their multigenre boxes with second graders, and that evening, they will share them with their parents at back-to-school night. In preparation for this sharing, the students have been taking turns sharing their projects in the classroom. Each day, three students sit in the author's chair to show their projects and read their informational books aloud to the class. Only five students still need to share, so they will be ready to share with other classes.

Students read and write all through the day as they learn science, social studies, and other content areas. Just as Mrs. Zumwalt's third graders learned about ocean animals through reading and writing, students at all grade levels—even kindergartners and first graders—read and write to learn about insects, the water cycle, pioneers, astronomy, and World War II. Teachers organize content-area study into thematic units, and together with students, they identify big ideas to investigate. Units are time-consuming because student-constructed learning takes time. Teachers can't try to cover every topic; if they do, their students will learn very little. Teachers make careful choices as they plan units, because only a relatively few topics can be presented in depth during a school year. During thematic units, students need opportunities to question, discuss, explore, and apply what they are learning (Harvey, 1998). It takes time for students to become deeply involved in learning so that they can apply what they are learning in their own lives.

Visit Chapter 14 on the Companion Website at *www.prenhall.com/ tompkins* to connect to web links related to content-area reading and writing.

Content-area textbooks are important resources that students use to learn about social studies, science, and other content areas, but they should never be considered a complete program. Students need to know how to read content-area textbooks because these books differ from other reading materials: They have unique conventions and structures that students can learn to use as aids in reading and remembering what they have read. They also need to be able to identify and remember the big ideas and connect them with their background knowledge. Because many students find textbooks more challenging to read than other books, teachers need to know how to support their students' reading so that they will be successful.

As you read this chapter, you'll learn about the role of content-area learning in a balanced approach to literacy instruction. As the balanced literacy feature on page 432 shows, students apply what they are learning about reading and writing as they learn social studies, science, and other content areas.

CONNECTING READING AND WRITING

Researchers agree that reading and writing should be connected because reading has a powerful impact on writing, and vice versa (Tierney & Shanahan, 1996): When students read about a topic before writing, their writing is enhanced because of what they learn about the topic, and when they write about the ideas in a book they are reading, their comprehension is deepened because they are exploring ideas and relationships. Making this connection is especially important when students are learning content-area information because of the added challenges that unfamiliar topics and technical vocabulary present.

There are other reasons for connecting reading and writing, too. Comprehension is the goal of both reading and writing: Students activate background knowledge, set purposes, and use many of the same strategies for both reading and writing. In addition, the reading and writing processes are virtually the same. Through both reading and writing, students learn a multistep process for developing and expanding meaning.

Writing as a Learning Tool

Students use writing as a learning tool as they read content-area textbooks and during thematic units: They take notes, categorize ideas, draw graphic organizers, and write summaries. The focus is on using writing to help students learn, not on spelling every word correctly or writing legibly. Nevertheless, students should use classroom resources, such as word walls, to spell most words correctly and write as neatly as possible so that they can reread their writing.

How Content-Area Learning Fits Into a Balanced Literacy Program

Component	Description
Reading	Reading content-area textbooks is a special kind of reading, and students need to know how to read efferently and use comprehension aids to read more effectively.
Phonics and Other Skills	Students apply phonics knowledge as they decode multisyllabic technical terms, and they identify big ideas to remember as they read and study.
Strategies	Students activate background knowledge, notice text structures, summarize, and use other strategies as they read informational books and content-area textbooks.
Vocabulary	Teachers develop word walls to spotlight important technical terms and involve students in a variety of vocabulary activities.
Comprehension	Teachers use a variety of activities to make informational books and inconsiderate content-area textbooks easier for students to read and understand.
Literature	Students read stories, informational books, and poems from text sets to support and extend what they are learning through content-area textbooks.
Content-Area Study	Content-area textbooks are designed for content-area study, but textbooks are not a complete program. Instead, textbooks should be used as part of thematic units.
Oral Language	Students work in small groups and talk as they complete graphic organizers, brainstorm ideas, make posters to share their learning, and create projects.
Writing	Students complete graphic organizers, write in learning logs, and do other compositions to demonstrate their learning.
Spelling	Students learn to spell content-related vocabulary as they make word walls, participate in vocabulary activities, and write reports and other compositions.

Learning Logs. Students use learning logs to record and react to what they are learning in social studies, science, or other content areas. Laura Robb (2003) explains that learning logs are "a place to think on paper" (p. 60). Students write in these journals to discover gaps in their knowledge and to explore relationships between what they are learning and their past experiences. Through these activities, students practice taking notes, writing descriptions and directions, and making graphic organizers. Figure 14–1 presents a page from a second grader's learning log about penguins. The chart shows that penguins have three enemies—leopard seals, skua gulls, and people.

Figure 14-1 **A Page From a Second Grader's Learning Log on Penguins**

Double-Entry Journals. Double-entry journals are just what the name suggests: Students divide their journal pages into two parts and write different types of information in each part (Barone, 1990). Students write important facts in one column and their reactions to the facts in the other column, or questions about the topic in the left column and answers in the right column. Figure 14–2 shows a sixth grader's double-entry journal written during a unit on drug prevention. In the left column, the student wrote information she was learning, and in the right column, she made personal connections to the information.

Simulated Journals. In some stories, such as *Catherine, Called Birdy* (Cushman, 1994), the author assumes the role of a character and writes a series of diary entries from the character's point of view. Here is an excerpt from one of Birdy's entries, which describes life in the Middle Ages:

12th Day of October

No more sewing and spinning and goose fat for me!
Today my life is changed. How it came about it this:
We arrived at the abbey soon after dinner, stopping just outside the entry gate at the guesthouse next to the mill. The jouncing cart did my stomach no kindness after jellied eel and potted lamb, so I was most relieved to alight. (Cushman, 1994, p. 25)

These books can be called simulated journals. They are rich with historical details and feature examples of both the vocabulary and sentence structure of the period. At the end of the book, authors often include information about how they researched the period and explanations about the liberties they took with the characters or events that are recorded.

Scholastic Books has created two series of historical journals; one series is for girls, and one is for boys. *A Journey to the New World: The Diary of Remember Patience Whipple* (Lasky, 1996), *A Picture of Freedom: The Diary of Clotee, a Slave Girl* (McKissack, 1997), and *Across the Wide and Lonesome Prairie: The Oregon Trail Diary of Hat-*

Figure 14-2 **A Page From a Sixth Grader's Double-Entry Journal**

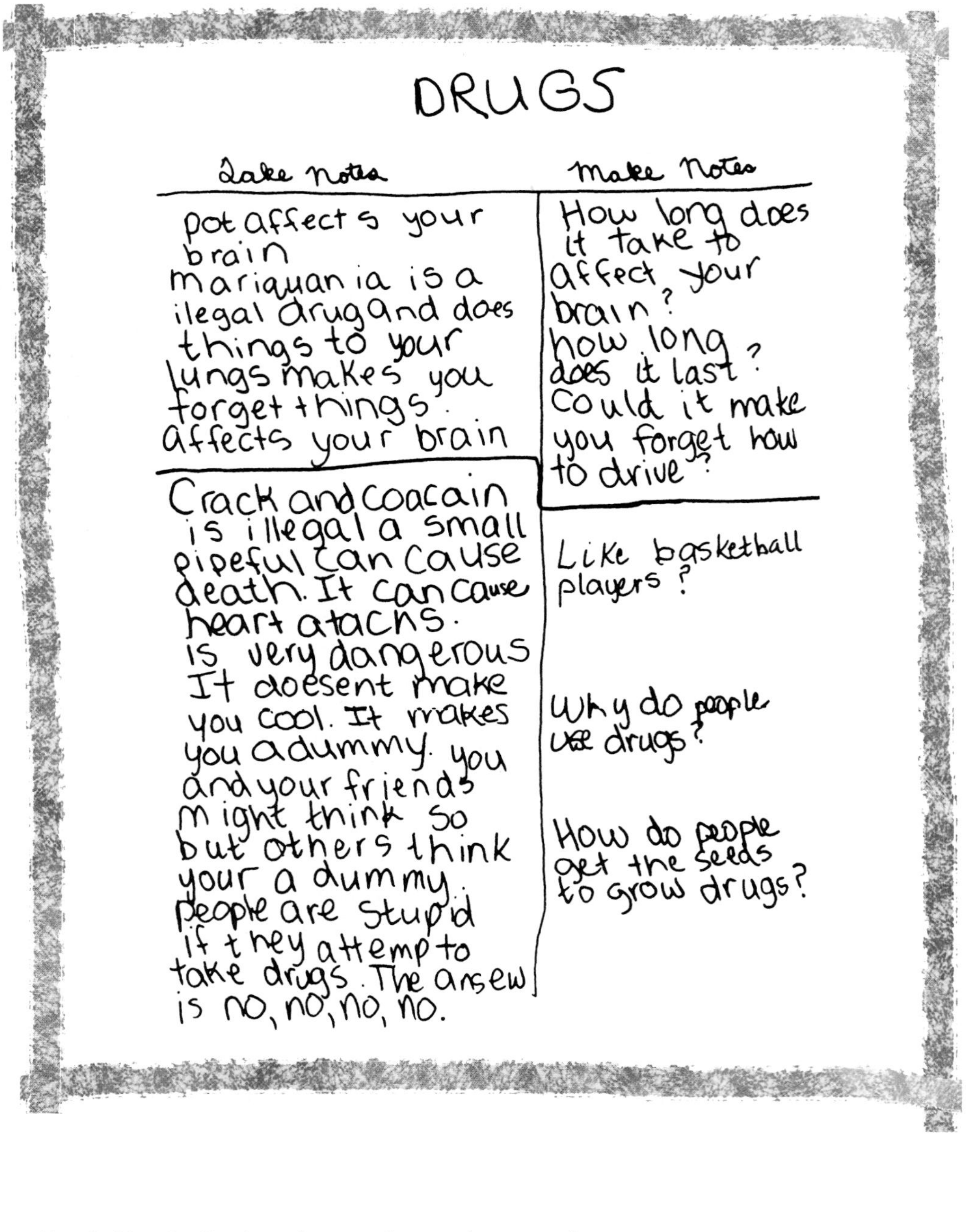

Part 3 How Do Teachers Organize Literacy Instruction?

tie Campbell (Gregory, 1997) are from the Dear America series; each book provides a glimpse into American history from a young girl's perspective. The My Name Is America series features books written from a boy's point of view. Three examples are *The Journal of Patrick Seamus Flaherty: United States Marine Corps* (White, 2002), *The Journal of Ben Uchida: Citizen 13559, Mirror Lake Internment Camp* (Denenberg, 1999), and *The Journal of William Thomas Emerson: A Revolutionary War Patriot* (Denenberg, 1998). These books are handsomely bound to look like old journals with heavy paper rough cut around the edges.

Students, too, can write simulated journals by assuming the role of another person and writing from that person's viewpoint. They assume the role of a historical figure when they read biographies or as part of social studies units. As they read stories, students assume the role of a character in the story. In this way, they gain insight into other people's lives and into historical events. When students write from the viewpoint of a famous person, they begin by making a "life line," a time line of the person's life. Then they pick key dates in the person's life and write entries about those dates. A look at a series of diary entries written by a fifth grader who has assumed the role of Benjamin Franklin shows how the student chose the important dates for each entry and wove in factual information:

December 10, 1719

Dear Diary,

My brother James is so mad at me. He just figured out that I'm the one who wrote the articles for his newspaper and signed them Mistress Silence Dogood. He says I can't do any more of them. I don't understand why. My articles are funny. Everyone reads them. I bet he won't sell as many newspapers anymore. Now I have to just do the printing.

February 15, 1735

Dear Diary,

I have printed my third "Poor Richard's Almanack." It is the most popular book in America and now I am famous. Everyone reads it. I pretend that somebody named Richard Saunders writes it, but it's really me. I also put my wise sayings in it. My favorite wise saying is "Early to bed, early to rise, makes a man healthy, wealthy, and wise."

June 22, 1763

Dear Diary,

I've been an inventor for many years now. There are a lot of things I have invented like the Franklin stove (named after me) and bifocal glasses, and the lightning rod, and a long arm to get books off of the high shelves. That's how I work. I see something that we don't have and if it is needed, I figure out how to do it. I guess I just have the knack for inventing.

May 25, 1776

Dear Diary,

Tom Jefferson and I are working on the Declaration of Independence. The patriots at the Continental Congress chose us to do it but it is dangerous business. The Red Coats will call us traitors and kill us if they can. I like young Tom from Virginia. He'll make a good king of America some day.

April 16, 1790

Dear Diary,

I am dying. I only have a day or two to live. But it's OK because I am 84 years old. Not very many people live as long as I have or do so many things in a life. I was a printer by trade but I have also been a scientist, an inventor, a writer, and a statesman. I have lived to see the Philadelphia that I love so very much become part of a new country. Good-bye to my family and everyone who loves me.

Students can use simulated journals in two ways: as a journal or as a refined and polished composition—a demonstration of learning project. When students use simulated journals as a tool for learning, they write the entries as they are reading a book in order to get to know the character better, or during a thematic unit as they are learning about the historical period. In these entries, students are exploring concepts and making connections between what they are learning and what they already know. These journal entries are less polished than when students write a simulated journal as a culminating project for a unit. For a project, students plan out their journals carefully, choose important dates, and use the writing process to draft, revise, edit, and publish their journals. They often add covers typical of the historical period. For example, a simulated journal written as part of a unit on ancient Greece might be written on a long sheet of butcher paper and rolled like a scroll, or a pioneer journal might be backed with paper cut from a brown grocery bag to resemble an animal hide.

Quickwriting. Quickwriting is a strategy in which students explore what they know about a topic, generate words and ideas, and make connections among the ideas. Students write on a topic for 5 to 10 minutes and let their thoughts flow from their minds to their pens without focusing on mechanics or revisions. Younger students can do quickwrites in which they draw pictures to explore ideas.

During a thematic unit on the solar system, for example, fourth graders each chose a word from the word wall to quickwrite about. This is one student's quickwrite on Mars:

Mars is known as the red planet. Mars is Earth's neighbor. Mars is a lot like Earth. On Mars one day lasts 24 hours. It is the fourth planet in the solar system. Mars may have life forms. Two Viking ships landed on Mars. Mars has a dusty and rocky surface. The Viking ships found no life forms. Mars' surface shows signs of water long ago. Mars has no water now. Mars has no rings.

Quickwrites provide a good way of checking on what students are learning and an opportunity to clarify misconceptions. After students write, they usually share their quickwrites in small groups, and then one student in each group shares with the class. Sharing also takes about 10 minutes, so the entire activity can be completed in 20 minutes or less.

Writing to Demonstrate Learning

Students also use writing to demonstrate their learning. This type of writing is more formal, and students use the writing process to revise and edit their writing before making a final copy.

Reports. Reports are the best-known type of writing to demonstrate learning; students write many types of reports, ranging from posters to class collaborations and individual reports. Too often, students are not exposed to report writing until they are faced with writing a term paper in high school, and then they are overwhelmed with learning how to take notes on note cards, how to organize and write the paper, and how to compile a bibliography. There is no reason to postpone report writing until students reach high school; early, successful experiences with informative writing teach students about content-area topics as well as how to write reports (Harvey, 1998; Tompkins, 2004).

Posters. Students combine visual and verbal elements when they make posters (Moline, 1995). They draw pictures and diagrams and write labels and commentary. For example, students might:

- draw detailed diagrams of the inner and outer planets in the solar system
- chart the life cycle of frogs or the steps in mummification
- identify the parts of a complex machine
- label the clothing a Revolutionary War soldier wore and the supplies he carried
- create time lines of a historical period
- identify important events of a person's life on a life line
- chart the explorers' voyages to America and around the world on a world map

Students use a process approach to create posters. They plan the information they want to include in the poster and consider how to devise attention-getting displays using headings, illustrations and diagrams, captions, boxes, and rules. Students prepare a rough draft of the sections of their posters and revise and edit the sections as they go through the writing process. Then they make a final copy of each section, glue the sections onto a sheet of posterboard, and share their posters with classmates as they would share finished pieces of writing. As part of a reading and writing workshop on informational books, a fifth grader read *The Magic School Bus Inside a Beehive* (Cole, 1996) and created a poster to share what he had learned. The poster is shown in Figure 14–3.

"All About . . . " Books. The first reports that young children write are "All About. . . " books, in which they provide information about familiar topics, such as "Signs of Fall" and "Sea Creatures" (Bonin, 1988; Sowers, 1985). Young children write an entire booklet on a single topic. Usually one piece of information and an illustration appear on each page. A page from a first grader's "All About Penguins" book is shown in Figure 14–4.

Alphabet Books. Students use the letters of the alphabet to organize the information they want to share in an alphabet book. These collaborative report books incorporate the sequence structure, because the pages are arranged in alphabetical order. Alphabet books such as *Ashanti to Zulu: African Traditions* (Musgrove, 1976), about African cultures, *Z Is for Zamboni: A Hockey Alphabet* (Napier, 2002), *The Queen's Progress: An Elizabethan Alphabet* (Mannis, 2003), and *Illuminations* (Hunt, 1989), about medieval life, can be used as models. Students begin by brainstorming information related to the topic being studied and identify a word or fact for each letter of the alphabet. Then they work individually, in pairs, or in small groups to compose pages for the book. The format for the pages is similar to the one used in alphabet books written by professional authors: Students write the letter in one corner of the page, draw an illustration, and write a sentence or paragraph to describe the word or fact. The text usually begins "_____ is for _____," and then a sentence or paragraph description follows. The "U" page from a fourth-grade class's alphabet book on the California missions is shown in Figure 14–5.

Figure 14-3 **A Fifth Grader's Poster About Bees**

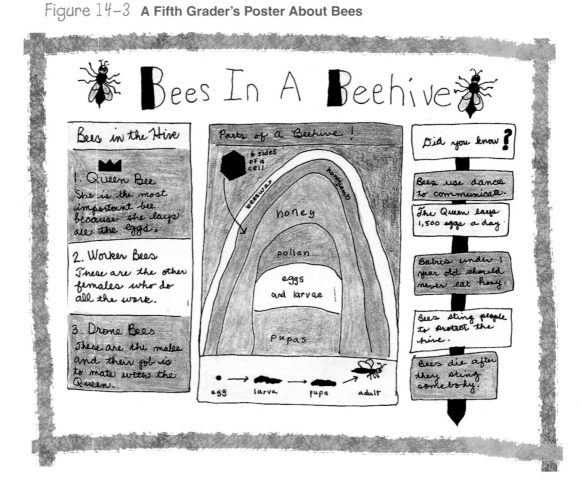

Class Collaborations. Students work together to write class collaborations. Sometimes students each write one page for the report, or they can work together in small groups to write chapters. Students create collaborative reports on almost any science or social studies topic.

Students might write collaborative biographies; each student or small group writes about one event or accomplishment in the subject's life, and then the pages are assembled in chronological order. Or, students work in small groups to write chapters for a collaborative report on the planets in the solar system, ancient Egypt, or the Oregon Trail.

Individual Reports. Students also write individual reports as projects during thematic units. Toby Fulwiler (1985) recommends that students do "authentic" research, in which they explore topics that interest them or hunt for answers to questions that puzzle them. When students become immersed in content-area study, questions arise that they want to explore. Increasingly students are turning to the Internet to research topics.

Poetry. Students often write poems as projects after reading books and as part of thematic units. They write formula poems by beginning each line or stanza with a word or line, they create free-form poems, and they follow the structure of model poems as they create their own poems.

"I Am" Poems. Students assume the role of a person and write a poem from that person's viewpoint. They begin and end the poem (or each stanza) with "I am _____" and begin all the other lines with "I." In this poem, an eighth grader writes from the viewpoint of John F. Kennedy after reading a biography about the 35th president:

I am John Fitzgerald Kennedy.
I commanded a PT boat in World War II.
I saved my crew after a Japanese ship hit us.
I became a politician because that's what my dad wanted me to do.
I was elected the 35th president of the United States.

Figure 14–4 **A Page From a First Grader's "All About Penguins" Book**

Penguins lay eggs and keep them worm with ther feets and ther stomechs.

Figure 14-5 The "U" Page From a Fourth-Grade Class's Alphabet Book

Some of the Indians thought life was UNBEARABLE at the missions. They thought this because they couldn't hunt or do the things they were used to. Once they were at the missions they couldn't leave. They were sometimes beaten if they did.

I said, "Ask not what your country can do for you—
ask what you can do for your country."
I believed in equal rights for blacks and whites.
I began the Peace Corps to help the world live free.
I cried the tears of assassination because
Lee Harvey Oswald shot me dead.
I left my young family in America's love.
I am John Fitzgerald Kennedy.

Poems for Two Voices. In this unique type of free verse, poems are written in two columns, side by side. The columns are read together by two readers or two groups of readers: One reader reads the left column, and the other reader reads the right column. When both readers have words—either the same words or different words—written on the same line, they read them simultaneously so that the poem sounds like a musical duet.

The two best-known books of poems for two readers are Paul Fleischman's *I Am Phoenix: Poems for Two Voices* (1985), which is about birds, and his Newbery Award–winning *Joyful Noise: Poems for Two Voices* (1988), which is about insects. Students, too, can write poems for two voices; Lorraine Wilson (1994) suggests that topics with contrasting viewpoints are the most effective.

A pair of eighth graders wrote this poem for two voices as a project during a unit on slavery; the students read about Harriet Tubman and her work with the Underground Railroad. The left column is written from the slave's perspective, and their right column from the condustor's.

FREEDOM!.	*FREEDOM!*
	I hide slaves in my house;
	It is my moral duty.
I dodge the law wherever I go;	
I follow the north star.	
	I feed them until they get
	to the next stop.
I hide in closets and cellars	
and sleep whenever I can.	
	It is a big risk.
I am in grave danger.	
BUT IT'S WORTH IT!	*BUT IT'S WORTH IT!*
Harriet Tubman is the Moses	
of our people.	
	I am a conductor,
	helping her and her passengers
	along the way.
Once we reach Canada,	
we're free.	
Will freedom be sweet?	
	Oh, yes it will.
FREE AT LAST	*FREE AT LAST!.*

Found Poems. Students create poems by culling words and phrases from a story they are reading or from an informational book or content-area textbook and arranging the words and phrases to create a free-form poem. Fourth graders created this found poem about a Saguaro cactus in the desert after reading *Cactus Hotel* (Guiberson, 1991):

A young cactus sprouts up.
After 10 years only four inches high,
after 25 years two feet tall,
after 50 years 10 feet all.
A welcoming signal across the desert.
A Gila woodpecker,
a white-winged dove,
an elf owl
decide to stay.
After 60 years an arm grows,
the cactus hotel is 18 feet tall.

After 150 years 7 long branches
and holes of every size
in the cactus hotel.

Multigenre Projects. Students explore a science or social studies topic through several genres in a multigenre project (Allen, 2001; Romano, 1995, 2000). They combine content-area study with writing in significant and meaningful ways. Tom Romano (2000) explains that the benefit of this approach is that each genre offers ways of learning and understanding that the others do not; students gain different understandings, for example, by writing a simulated journal entry, an alphabet book, and a cubing. Teachers or students identify a *repetend*, a common thread or unifying feature for the project, which helps students move beyond the level of remembering facts to a deeper, more analytical level of understanding. In the vignette at the beginning of the chapter, Mrs. Zumwalt's repetend was adaptation; in their multigenre projects, her students highlighted how the animal they studied adapted to life in the ocean.

Depending on the information they want to present and their repetend, students use a variety of genres for their projects. Figure 14–6 presents a list of 25 genres, including clusters, reports, poems, maps, letters, and data charts, that students can use in their multigenre projects. Students generally use three or more genres in a multigenre project and include both textual and visual genres. What matters most is that the genres amplify and extend the repetend.

Not only can students create multigenre projects, but some authors/illustrators use the technique in children's trade books. *The Magic School Bus on the Ocean Floor* (Cole, 1992) and other books in the Magic School Bus series are examples of multi-

Multigenre Projects

These third graders are completing work on their multigenre project on honeybees. They are finishing poems that will go into one pocket on the project board. Classmates have written a flipbook with facts on honeybees, a collection of riddles, and a report about their trip to interview a beekeeper. Their teacher has added a list of content standards, vocabulary cards, and photos of their activities. After they finish the project, they will share their multigenre project with other classes. Students will go to the classroom to introduce the project and then leave it there on display for a few days.

Figure 14-6 Genres for Multigenre Projects

Genre	Description
Acrostics	Students spell a key word vertically and then write a phrase or sentence beginning with each letter to create a poem or other composition.
Biographical Sketch	Students write a biographical sketch of a person related to the topic being studied.
Cartoons	Students draw a cartoon or copy a published cartoon from a book or Internet article.
Charts	Students organize and display textual and visual information on a chart.
Clusters	Students draw clusters or other diagrams to display information concisely.
Cubes	Students examine a topic from six perspectives.
Data Charts	Students create a data chart to list and compare information.
Found Poems	Students collect words and phrases from a book or article and arrange them to make a poem.
"I Am" Poems	Students create an "I am" poem about a person or a topic.
Letters	Students write simulated letters or make copies of real letters related to the topic.
Life Lines	Students draw life lines and mark important dates related to a person's life.
Maps	Students make copies of actual maps or draw maps related to the topic.
Newspaper Articles	Students make copies of actual newspaper articles or write simulated articles related to the topic.
Open-Mind Portraits	Students draw open-mind portraits of people related to the topic.
Photos	Students download photos from the Internet or make copies of photos in books.
Postcards	Students create postcards with a picture on one side and a message on the other.
Questions-Answers	Students write a series of questions and answers related to the topic.
Quotes	Students collect quotes about the topic from materials they are reading.
Riddles	Students write riddles with information related to the topic.
Simulated Journals	Students write simulated-journal entries from the viewpoint of a person related to the topic.
Songs	Students write lyrics about the topic that are sung to familiar tunes.
Stories	Students write stories related to the topic.
Time Lines	Students draw time lines to sequence events related to the topic.
Venn Diagrams	Students draw Venn diagrams to compare the topic with something else.
Word Wall	Students make an alphabetized word wall or word cards of key words related to the topic.

genre books. Each book features a story about Ms. Frizzle and her students on a fantastic science adventure, and on the side panels of pages, a variety of explanations, charts, diagrams, and essays are presented. Together the story and informational side panels present a more complete, multigenre presentation or project. Other multigenre books for older students are *To Be a Slave* (Lester, 1968), *Nothing But the Truth* (Avi,

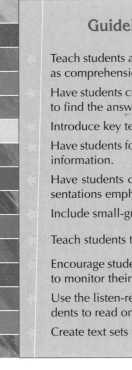

1991), *Tears of a Tiger* (Draper, 1994), and *Ernest L. Thayer's Casey at the Bat: A Ballad of the Republic Sung in the Year 1888* (Bing, 2000).

CONTENT-AREA TEXTBOOKS

Textbooks have traditionally been the centerpiece of social studies, science, and other content-area classes, but these textbooks have shortcomings that limit their effectiveness. Too often, content-area textbooks are unappealing to students, too difficult for students to read and understand, and cover too many topics superficially. It is up to teachers to plan instruction to make content-area textbooks more comprehensible and to supplement students' learning with other reading and writing activities during thematic units. A list of guidelines for using content-area textbooks is presented in the box above.

Unique Conventions of Content-Area Textbooks

Content-area textbooks look different than other types of books and have unique conventions, including:

Headings and subheadings to direct readers' attention to the big ideas

Photographs and drawings to illustrate the big ideas

Charts and maps to provide detailed information visually

Margin notes to provide supplemental information or to direct readers to additional information on a topic

Highlighted words to identify key vocabulary

Figure 14-7 Ways to Make Content-Area Textbooks More Comprehensible

Stage	Purposes	Activities
Prereading	Activate background knowledge Build background knowledge Develop interest and motivation Introduce key concepts and vocabulary Preview the text Set purposes	K-W-L charts Field trips Films and videos Quickwriting Trade books Anticipation guides Exclusion brainstorming Concept maps Word wall Prereading plan Graphic organizers Possible sentences Text walk
Reading	Ensure fluent reading Identify big ideas Organize ideas and details	Listen before reading Read with a buddy Small-group read and share Reciprocal teaching Highlighting Graphic organizers Say something
Responding	Clarify understanding Reflect on big ideas Summarize Make connections	Instructional conversations Think-pair-square-share Learning logs Double-entry journals Write summaries
Exploring	Study vocabulary words Review big ideas Connect big ideas and details	Word walls Word maps and posters Word sorts Read-arounds Data charts Semantic feature analysis Graphic organizers Skim and scan Question-answer-relationships (QAR)
Applying	Draw conclusions Expand knowledge Personalize learning Share knowledge	Read other books Conduct research Write stories, reports, and poems Cubings Create PowerPoint presentations Present oral reports

An index to assist readers in locating specific information

A glossary to assist readers in pronouncing and defining vocabulary words

Study questions at the end of the chapter to check readers' comprehension

These conventions make the textbook easier to read. It is important that students learn to use them to make reading content-area textbooks more effective and improve their comprehension (Harvey & Goudvis, 2000). Teachers teach minilessons about these conventions and how to use them to read more effectively.

Making Content-Area Textbooks More Comprehensible

Teachers use a variety of activities during each stage of the reading process to make content-area textbooks more "reader friendly" and to improve students' comprehension of what they have read. Figure 14–7 lists ways teachers can make content-area textbooks more comprehensible at each stage of the reading process. Teachers choose one or more activities at each stage to support their students' reading, but they never try to do all of the activities listed in the figure during a single reading assignment.

Stage 1: Prereading. Teachers play an important role during the prereading stage; they often feel that what they do during this stage determines the success of students' reading experience. There are six purposes:

- Activate students' background knowledge.
- Build new background knowledge about the topic.
- Develop students' interest and motivation for reading.
- Introduce key concepts and vocabulary related to the reading assignment.
- Preview the text.
- Set purposes for reading.

Teachers use a variety of activities to prepare students to read a textbook chapter, and the activities often serve more than one purpose. K-W-L charts (Ogle, 1986, 1989) are a good example. In this activity, students and the teacher make a chart of the things they already know about a topic and the things they want to learn as they read about the topic. As students participate in this activity, their background knowledge is activated and developed, and as they share their knowledge and develop questions about what they want to learn, they become more motivated and set their own purposes for reading.

Other ways to activate and build students' background knowledge about the topic include showing films and videos, taking students on field trips, having students write quickwrites, and reading aloud stories and informational books. Teachers use the gamelike formats of anticipation guides (Head & Readence, 1986) and exclusion brainstorming (Johns, Van Leirsburg, & Davis, 1994) to develop students' interest and motivation. In anticipation guides, teachers introduce a set of statements on the topic of the chapter, students agree or disagree with each statement and then read the assignment to see if they are right. In exclusion brainstorming,

Scaffolding Struggling Readers

How can I help my struggling students read content-area textbooks more effectively?

Struggling readers generally approach all reading assignments the same way—they open to the first page and read it straight through. That's a mistake, however, because content-area textbooks are different from novels, and students need to take advantage of a textbook's special features to make reading easier. You can teach students to activate prior knowledge by previewing a textbook chapter: They read the introduction, the headings, conclusion, and end-of-chapter questions and examine illustrations. They locate highlighted vocabulary words, use context clues to figure out their meaning, and check unfamiliar words in the glossary. Next, as they read, have students focus on the big ideas and stop after reading each section to summarize. Finally, after reading the entire chapter, have students make sure they can answer the end-of-chapter questions.

students examine a list of words and decide which ones are related to the reading assignment. As students complete these activities, they become more interested in the topic and want to read the textbook chapter to check their answers.

Teachers introduce key concepts and vocabulary through all prereading activities, but they emphasize key concepts when they create a prereading plan in which they introduce a key concept discussed in the chapter and then have students brainstorm words and ideas related to the concept (Langer, 1981). They also begin a word wall and introduce graphic organizers that students complete during reading and discuss afterward. Another activity is possible sentences (Moore & Moore, 1992; Stahl & Kapinus, 1991), in which students compose sentences that might be in the textbook chapter using two or more vocabulary words from the chapter. Later, as they read the chapter, students check to see if their sentences are included or are accurate enough so that they could be used in the chapter.

To preview the chapter before reading, teachers take students on a "text walk" through the chapter. They examine the chapter, noting main headings, looking at illustrations, and reading diagrams and charts. Sometimes students turn the main headings into questions and prepare to read to find the answers to the questions.

Students need to have a purpose when they read content-area textbooks so that they can be purposefully involved in finding an answer. Teachers set purposes through a variety of prereading activities, including K-W-L charts, anticipation guides, exclusion brainstorming, and graphic organizers. Teachers can also have students read the questions at the end of the chapter, assume responsibility for finding the answer to a specific question, and then read to find the answer. After reading, students share their answers with the class.

Learn more about K-W-L charts and other instructional procedures discussed in this chapter on the DVD that accompanies this text.

Stage 2: Reading. Students read the assigned textbook chapter in this stage, and teachers make sure that students can read it and are prepared to identify the big ideas. There are three purposes:

Ensure that students can read the assignment fluently.

Assist students in identifying the big ideas.

Help students organize ideas and details.

Students won't be successful if they can't read the textbook assignment. Sometimes activating and building background knowledge and introducing key vocabulary are all teachers need to do to ensure that students can read the assignment fluently, but sometimes students need more support than that. When students can't read the chapter, teachers have several options. For example, they can read the chapter aloud to the class before students read it independently. In this way, students will be familiar with the big ideas and vocabulary when they begin reading. Or, students can read with a buddy or partner and stop at the end of each paragraph to "say something" to help them identify the big ideas and remember what they just read. Teachers also can divide the reading assignment into sections and assign groups of students to read each section and report back to the class. In this way, the reading assignment is shorter, and students can read aloud to classmates or read along with them. Students learn the material from the entire chapter as they listen to classmates share their sections. After this sharing experience, students may then be able to go back and read the chapter.

Teachers help students identify and organize the big ideas and details as they highlight parts of the text using marking pens or small sticky notes or by completing graphic organizers as they read. Students can also turn the headings into questions and then take notes to answer the questions after they read each section.

Stage 3: Responding. Teachers help students develop and refine their comprehension in this stage as they think, talk, and write about the information they have read. There are four purposes:

Clarify students' misunderstandings.

Encourage students to reflect on the big ideas from the reading assignment.

Help students summarize the big ideas.

Make connections to students' lives and the world.

Students react to the chapter, ask questions to clarify confusions, and make connections to their own lives as they participate in instructional conversations, which are similar to grand conversations (Goldenberg, 1992/1993). In these discussions, the big ideas are discussed and students make comments, ask questions, and connect the information they are learning to background knowledge and to their own lives. Teachers are the discussion leaders, and they ask questions to stimulate thinking, provide information, expand students' language using vocabulary from the chapter, and coax students to participate in the conversation.

Students also talk about their reading in small groups and with partners. One popular strategy is think-pair-square-share, in which students begin by thinking about a topic individually for several minutes. Next, they pair up with classmates to share their thoughts and hear other points of view. Then each pair of students gets together with another pair, forming a square, a group of four students, to share their thinking. Finally, students come back together as a class to discuss the topic.

Writing is another way for students to deepen their understanding. They reflect on their reading by writing in learning logs about important ideas and interesting details. Or, students can use double-entry journals to record quotes or important information from the chapter and then write to reflect on this information.

Students also write summaries in which they concisely synthesize the big ideas and describe the relationships among them. They also make generalizations or draw conclusions. Summary writing requires students to use complex cognitive strategies as they analyze what they read to determine which parts are important and which are unnecessary and to figure out the relationships among the ideas. Students use what they have learned about the structure of narrative, expository, and poetic texts when they summarize because the structure points to the big ideas and the relationships among them. Researchers indicate that students summarize events in their lives every day, but because the thinking is unconscious, they often have trouble when asked to summarize an oral presentation or a reading assignment in school (Brozo & Simpson, 2003; Marzano, Norford, Paynter, Pickering, & Gaddy, 2001). The minilesson feature on the next page shows how Mr. Surabian teaches his fourth graders to write summaries.

Stage 4: Exploring. Teachers ask students to dig into the text during the exploring stage to focus on vocabulary, examine the text, and analyze the big ideas. There are three purposes:

Have students study vocabulary words.

Review the big ideas in the chapter.

Help students to connect the big ideas and details.

As they study the important vocabulary words in the chapter, students post words on word walls, make word maps and posters to study the meaning of words, or do word sorts according to the big ideas. To focus on the big ideas and details, students

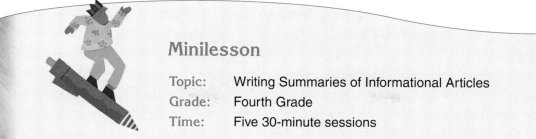

Minilesson

Topic: Writing Summaries of Informational Articles
Grade: Fourth Grade
Time: Five 30-minute sessions

Mr. Surabian plans to teach his students how to write a summary; only a few of his students seem familiar with the term *summary writing,* and none of the fourth graders know how to write one. Writing a summary is one of the state's fourth-grade standards, and the prompt for the state's fourth-grade writing assessment often requires summary writing. The teacher recognizes that his students need both instruction in how to write a summary and many opportunities to practice summary writing if they are to be successful on the state's achievement tests.

1. Introduce the Topic

Mr. Surabian explains that a summary is a brief statement of the main points of an article. He presents a poster with these characteristics of a summary:

- A summary tells the big ideas.
- A summary is organized to show connections between the big ideas.
- A summary has a generalization or a conclusion.
- A summary is written in a student's own words.
- A summary is brief.

2. Share Examples

Mr. Surabian shares a one-page article about Wilbur and Orville Wright and the summary he has written about it. The students check that the summary meets all of the characteristics on the poster. Then he shares a second article about mummification, and the students pick out the big ideas and highlight them. Next, Mr. Surabian draws a diagram to show the relationships among the ideas, and they develop a generalization or conclusion statement. Then he shares his summary, and the fourth graders check that he included the big ideas and that the summary meets all of the characteristics on the poster.

3. Provide Information

The next day, Mr. Surabian reviews the characteristics of a summary and shares an article about motorcycles. Together the students read it, identify and highlight the big ideas, draw a diagram to illustrate the relationships among the ideas, and create a generalization or conclusion statement. After this preparation, they write a summary of the article. They check that their summary meets the characteristics listed on the classroom poster. On the third day, Mr. Surabian and his students repeat the process with another article about rain forests.

4. Guide Practice

On the fourth day, Mr. Surabian shares an article about the Mississippi River. The students read and discuss it, identifying the big ideas, relationships among the ideas, and possible conclusions. Then the teacher divides the students into small groups, and each group writes a summary. Afterward, they share their summaries and check them against the poster. The class repeats this activity the next day; this time, they read about porpoises. Mr. Surabian shortens the time spent discussing the article and identifying the big ideas and conclusions so that students must assume more responsibility for developing and writing the summary.

5. Assess Learning

Mr. Surabian assesses students' learning by monitoring them as they work in small groups. He identifies several students who need practice, and he plans more additional minilessons with them.

Figure 14-8 **A Fourth Grader's Data Chart on California**

REGION	VEGETATION	ANIMALS	PLACES	HISTORY	ECONOMY
North	Redwood tres	Grizzly Bears Salmon	Eureka Napa Valley	Sutter's Fort GOLD!	Logging Wine
North Coast	Redwood trees Giant Sequoia tres	seals Sea Otters Monarch Butterflies	San Francisco	Chinatown Cable Cars Earthquake	Computers Ghirardelli chocolate Levis
South Coast	Palm tres Orange tres	Gray whales Condors	Los Angeles Hollywood	El Camino Real missions O.J. Simpson Earthquake	Disneyland TV + movies airplanes
Central Valley	Poppies	Quail	Fresno Sacramento	capital Pony Express Railroad	grapes Peaches Cotton Almond
Sierra Nevada	Giant Sequoia Lupine	Mule Deer Golden eagles Black Baers	Yosemite	John Muir	Skiing

make data charts and list information according to the big ideas. Figure 14–8 shows a data chart that fourth graders made as they studied the regions of their state. Students often hold onto these charts and use them to write reports or for other projects. They can also complete a semantic feature analysis to chart important information.

Students share their completed graphic organizers to review the big ideas in the chapter, or they can work in small groups to make posters to highlight the big ideas and details from sections of the chapter. Then each group presents the information to the class and displays the poster on the wall.

Students learn to use two special types of reading—skimming and scanning—in content-area textbook activities. In skimming, students read quickly and superficially to get the general idea; in scanning, they reread quickly to locate specific information. Students skim as they preview or to locate a word for the word wall. In contrast, students use scanning to locate details for data charts and to find specific sentences for a read-around.

Stage 5: Applying. Teachers support students as they extend their learning and apply what they have learned in a variety of projects and other activities. There are four purposes:

Expand students' knowledge about the topic.

Encourage students to draw conclusions.

Have students personalize their learning.

Expect students to share their knowledge.

Students read other books, consult the Internet, interview people, and conduct research to extend their knowledge about the topic. As they write and develop presentations and use the information they have learned, they often draw conclusions. Cubing (Neeld, 1986) is a good way to encourage students to think about a topic and consider it from different viewpoints. To make a cube, students describe a topic, compare it to something else, associate the topic with something else, analyze the topic, apply the topic, and argue for or against it.

Students often write reports, create PowerPoint presentations, or present oral reports to share what they have learned, but many other projects are possible. Students can write poems, present dramatic presentations, or create paper or cloth quilts with information recorded on each square.

Learning How to Study

Students are often asked to remember content-area material that they've read for an instructional conversation or other discussion, to take a test, or for an oral or written project. The traditional way to study is to try to memorize a list of facts, but researchers have found that other strategies—those that require students to think critically and to elaborate ideas—are the most effective (Brozo & Simpson, 2003). As they study, students need to:

- restate the big ideas in their own words
- make connections among the big ideas
- add details to each of the big ideas
- ask questions about the importance of the ideas
- monitor whether they understand the ideas

Students use these five strategies as they study class notes, complete graphic organizers to highlight the big ideas, and orally rehearse by explaining the big ideas to themselves.

Taking Notes. When students take notes, they identify what is most important and then restate it in their own words. They select and organize the big ideas, identify organizational patterns, paraphrase and summarize information, and use abbreviations and symbols to take notes more

Scaffolding Struggling Readers

How can I get my struggling students to study?

It rarely works simply to tell struggling students to study because they often don't know how to do it. You need to teach students how to study effectively. Studying involves three parts. First, students activate background knowledge as they prepare to read a content-area textbook chapter. Second, as they read each section, students take notes or complete study guides. Teachers ensure that students understand the big ideas and key vocabulary words as they participate in instructional conversations, and they check students' notes and study guides for accuracy and completeness. Finally, students review their notes: They reread their notes, draw diagrams to show the organization among the ideas, and orally rehearse answers to questions the teacher has supplied or to questions they have generated.

quickly. Copying information verbatim is less effective than restating information because students are less actively involved in understanding what they are reading.

Students take notes in different ways: They can make outlines or bulleted lists, draw flow charts, clusters, and other graphic organizers, or make double-entry journals with notes in one column and their interpretations in the other column. Or, if students can mark on the text they are reading, they underline or highlight the big ideas and write notes in the margin.

Too often, teachers encourage students to take notes without teaching them how to do it. It is important that teachers share copies of notes they've taken so students see different styles of note taking, and that they demonstrate note taking—identifying the big ideas, organizing them, and restating information in their own words—as students read an article or excerpt from a content-area textbook. Once students understand how to identify the big ideas and to state them in their own words, they need opportunities to practice note taking. First, they work in small groups to take notes collaboratively, and then they work with a partner.

Teachers often use study guides to direct students toward the big ideas when they read content-area textbooks. Teachers create the study guides using diagrams, charts, lists, and sentences, and students complete them as they read using information and vocabulary from the chapter. Afterward, they review their completed study guides with partners, small groups, or the whole class and check that their work is correct.

It's also important that teachers teach students how to review notes to study for quizzes and tests. Too often, students think they're done with notes once they've written them because they don't understand that the notes are a study tool.

Question-Answer-Relationships (QAR). Students use Taffy Raphael's question-answer-relationships (QAR) technique (Raphael & McKinney, 1983; Raphael & Wonnacott, 1985) to understand how to answer questions written at the end of content-area textbook chapters. The technique teaches students to be consciously aware of whether they are likely to find the answer to a question "right there" on the page, between the lines, or beyond the information provided in the text. By being aware of the requirements posed by a question, students are in a better position to be able to answer it correctly and to use the activity as a study strategy.

The SQ3R Study Strategy. Students in the seventh and eighth grades also need to learn how to use the SQ3R study strategy, a five-step technique in which students survey, question, read, recite, and review as they study a content-area reading assignment. This study strategy, which incorporates before-, during-, and after-reading components, was devised in the 1930s and has been researched and thoroughly documented as a very effective technique (Anderson & Armbruster, 1984; Caverly & Orlando, 1991; Topping & McManus, 2002).

Teachers introduce the SQ3R study strategy and provide opportunities for students to practice each step. At first, students can work together as a class as they use the strategy with a text the teacher is reading to them. Then they can work with partners and in small groups before using the strategy individually. Teachers need to emphasize that if students simply begin reading the first page of the assignment without doing the first two steps, they won't be able to remember as much of what they read. When students are in a hurry and skip some of the steps, the strategy will not be as successful.

Why Aren't Content-Area Textbooks Enough?

Sometimes content-area textbooks are used as the entire instructional program in social studies or science, but that's not a good idea. Textbooks typically only survey top-

Text Sets

These eighth graders are reading a novel as part of a text set about medieval life. As they read, they enjoy the story and learn information at the same time. Other books in the text set include informational books and their social studies textbook. After finishing the novel, the students will preview the unit in their textbook, read other books in the text set, and then return to the textbook to read it thoroughly. The text set helps students expand their knowledge base about medieval life, prepares them to read the textbook, and extends their learning.

ics; other instructional materials are needed to provide depth and understanding. Students need to read, write, and discuss topics. It is most effective to use the reading process and then extend students' learning with projects. Developing thematic units with content-area textbooks as one resource is a much better idea than using content-area textbooks as the only reading material.

THEMATIC UNITS

Thematic units are interdisciplinary units that integrate reading and writing with social studies, science, and other curricular areas. Students are often involved in planning the thematic units and identifying some of the questions they want to explore and the activities that interest them. Students are involved in authentic and meaningful learning activities, not reading chapters in content-area textbooks in order to answer the questions at the end of the chapter. Textbooks are often used as a resource, but only one of many available resources. Students explore topics that interest them and research answers to questions they have posed and are genuinely interested in answering. Students share their learning at the end of the unit, as Mrs. Zumwalt's students did in the vignette at the beginning of the chapter, and are assessed on what they have learned as well as the processes they used in learning and working in the classroom.

How to Develop a Thematic Unit

To begin planning a thematic unit, teachers choose the general topic and then identify three or four key concepts that they want to develop through the unit. The goal

Visit
Chapter 14 on the Companion Website at *www.prenhall.com/ tompkins* to check into your state's standards for content-area literacy.

of a unit is not to teach a collection of facts but to help students grapple with several big understandings (Tunnell & Ammon, 1993). Next, teachers identify the resources they have available for the unit and develop their teaching plan. An overview of nine important considerations in developing a thematic unit is presented in Figure 14–9 and discussed in the following sections.

1. *Collect a text set of stories, informational books, magazine and Internet articles, and poems.* Teachers collect books, magazine and Internet articles, and reference books for the text set related to the unit. The text set is placed in the special area in the classroom library for materials related to the unit. Teachers plan to read some books aloud to students, and others will be read independently or in small groups. These materials can also be used for minilessons—to teach students, for example, about expository text structures or how to take notes. Other books can be used as models or patterns for writing projects. Teachers also write poems on charts to share with students or arrange a bulletin board display of the poems.

2. *Coordinate content-area textbook readings.* Teachers review the content-area textbook chapter related to the unit and decide how to use it most effectively in the unit. They might decide to use the textbook to introduce the unit, have students read it along with other activities, or use it at the end of the unit to review the big ideas. They also think about how they can make the textbook more comprehensible and decide on activities for each stage of the reading process.

3. *Locate Internet and other multimedia materials.* Teachers locate videos, CD-ROMs, Internet websites, computer programs, maps, models, and other materials to be used in connection with the unit. Some materials are used to develop students' background knowledge about the unit, and others are used in teaching the key concepts. Teachers use some multimedia materials for lessons and set up other materials in centers. Also, students create multimedia materials during the unit to display in the classroom.

4. *Identify potential words for the word wall.* Teachers preview books in the text set and identify potential words for the word wall. This list is useful in planning vocabulary activities, but teachers do not simply use their word lists for the class room word wall: Students and the teacher develop the classroom word wall together as they read and discuss the key concepts and other information related to the unit.

5. *Plan how students will use learning logs.* Teachers plan for students to keep learning logs in which they can take notes, write questions, make observations, clarify their thinking, and write reactions to what they read during thematic units (Tompkins, 2004).

Figure 14-9 The Steps in Developing a Thematic Unit

1. **Collect a Text Set of Reading Materials**
   - Include books, magazine and Internet articles, and reference books in the text set.
   - Place the text set in a special area in the classroom library.
   - Identify some books to read aloud to students.
   - Identify other books for literature circles, minilessons, or other special projects.

2. **Coordinate Content-Area Textbook Readings**
   - Review textbook chapter(s) related to the unit.
   - Decide how and when to use the textbook.
   - Identify ways to make the textbook more comprehensible.
   - Prepare anticipation guides, graphic organizers, and other materials to support textbook use.

3. **Locate Internet and Other Multimedia Materials**
   - Collect multimedia materials related to the unit.
   - Review the multimedia materials.
   - Decide which materials to use to develop students' background knowledge.
   - Decide which materials to use to teach key concepts.
   - Decide which materials to use in centers and for students' projects.

4. **Identify Potential Words for the Word Wall**
   - Preview the content-area textbook and books in the text set to identify potential words for the word wall.
   - Plan vocabulary activities using these words.

5. **Plan How Students Will Use Learning Logs**
   - Decide how to use learning logs.
   - Make a sample learning log.

6. **Identify Literacy Skills and Strategies to Teach**
   - Choose skills and strategies to introduce or review.
   - Plan minilessons to teach these literacy skills and strategies using content-area materials.

7. **Design Centers to Support Content-Area and Literacy Learning**
   - Plan centers to practice literacy skills and strategies.
   - Design other centers to examine content-area concepts and vocabulary.

8. **Brainstorm Possible Projects**
   - Identify a list of possible culminating projects.
   - Collect needed materials and supplies.

9. **Plans for the Unit Assessment**
   - Decide how to assess students' learning.
   - Create checklists, rubrics, and other assessment forms.

---

6. ***Identify literacy skills and strategies to teach during the unit.*** Teachers plan minilessons to teach literacy skills and strategies, such as using an index, skimming and scanning a text, researching on the Internet, writing an alphabet book, and conducting an interview. Students have opportunities to apply what they are learning in minilessons in reading and writing activities.

7. ***Design centers to support content-area and literacy learning.*** Teachers plan centers where students work independently or in small groups to practice strategies and skills that were first presented to the whole class and to explore topics and materials related to the unit. Possible centers include a computer research center, a reading center with text set books and other reading materials, a listening center, a writing center, a word work center, a map- and chart-making center, a learning log center, and a project center.

8. ***Brainstorm possible projects students can create to apply their learning.*** Teachers think about projects students can choose to develop to apply and personalize their learning during the unit. This planning makes it possible for teachers to collect needed supplies and to have suggestions ready for students who need assistance in choosing a project. Students work on the project independently or in small groups and then share it with the class at the end of the theme. Projects involve reading, writing, talk, art, music, or drama. Following are some suggestions:

- Read a biography related to the unit.
- Create a poster to illustrate a big idea.
- Do a cubing to examine the topic from different viewpoints.
- Make a quilt about the unit.
- Create and present a PowerPoint project.
- Write a story related to the unit.
- Perform a readers theatre production, puppet show, or other dramatization related to the unit.
- Write a poem, song, or rap related to the unit.
- Write a report about one of the big ideas.
- Create a commercial or advertisement related to the unit.
- Create a tabletop display or diorama about the unit.

9. ***Plan for the assessment of the unit.*** Teachers consider how they will assess students' learning as they make plans for activities and assignments. In this way, they can explain to students at the beginning of the unit how they will be assessed and check to see that their assessment will emphasize students' learning of the big ideas.

Teachers consider the resources they have available, brainstorm possible activities, and then develop clusters to guide their planning. The goal in developing plans for a thematic unit is to consider a wide variety of resources that integrate listening, talking, reading, and writing with the content of the theme (Pappas, Kiefer, & Levstik, 1990).

A First-Grade Unit on Trees

During this 4-week unit, students learn about trees and their importance to people and animals. Students observe trees in their community and learn to identify the parts of a tree and types of trees. Teachers read aloud books from the text set and list important words on the word wall. A collection of leaves, photos of trees, pictures of animals that live in trees, and products that come from trees is displayed in the classroom, and students learn about categorizing as they sort types of leaves, shapes of trees, foods that grow on trees and those that don't, and animals that live in trees and those that don't. Students learn how to use writing as a tool for learning as they make entries in learning logs. Teachers use the Language Experience Approach and interactive writing to make charts to explore the big ideas and projects to demonstrate students' learning. As a culminating activity, students plant a tree at their school or participate in a community tree-planting campaign. Figure 14–10 shows the planning cluster for this unit.

A Fourth-Grade Unit on Desert Ecosystems

During this 3-week unit, students investigate the plants, animals, and people that live in the desert and how they support each other. They keep learning logs in which they take notes and write reactions to books they are reading. Students divide into book clubs during the first week to read books about the desert. During the second week of the unit, students participate in an author study of Byrd Baylor, a woman who lives in the desert and writes about desert life, and they read many of her books. During the third week, students participate in a reading workshop to read other desert books and reread favorite books. To apply their learning, students participate in projects, including writing desert riddles, making a chart of a desert ecosystem, and drawing a desert mural. Together as a class, students can write a desert alphabet book or a class collaboration about deserts. A planning cluster for a unit on desert life is presented in Figure 14–11.

A Sixth-Grade Unit on Ancient Egypt

Students learn about this great ancient civilization during a monthlong unit. Key concepts include the influence of the Nile River on Egyptian life, the contributions of this civilization to contemporary America, a comparison of ancient to modern Egypt, and the techniques Egyptologists use to locate tombs of the ancient rulers and to decipher Egyptian hieroglyphics. Students will read books in literature circles and choose other books from the text set to read during reading workshop. Students and the teacher will add vocabulary to the word wall, and students will use the words in a variety of activities.

Teachers will teach minilessons on writing simulated journals, map-reading skills, Egyptian gods, mummification, and writing poems for two voices. Students will also work in writing workshop as they write reports, biographies, or collections of poetry related to the thematic unit. As a culminating activity, students will create individual projects and share them on Egypt day, when they assume the roles of ancient Egyptians, dress as ancient people did, and eat foods of the period. Figure 14–12 presents a planning cluster for a sixth-grade unit on ancient Egypt.

Complete a self-assessment to check your understanding of the concepts presented in this chapter on the Companion Website at *www.prenhall.com/ tompkins*

Figure 14-10 A Planning Cluster for a First-Grade Unit on Trees

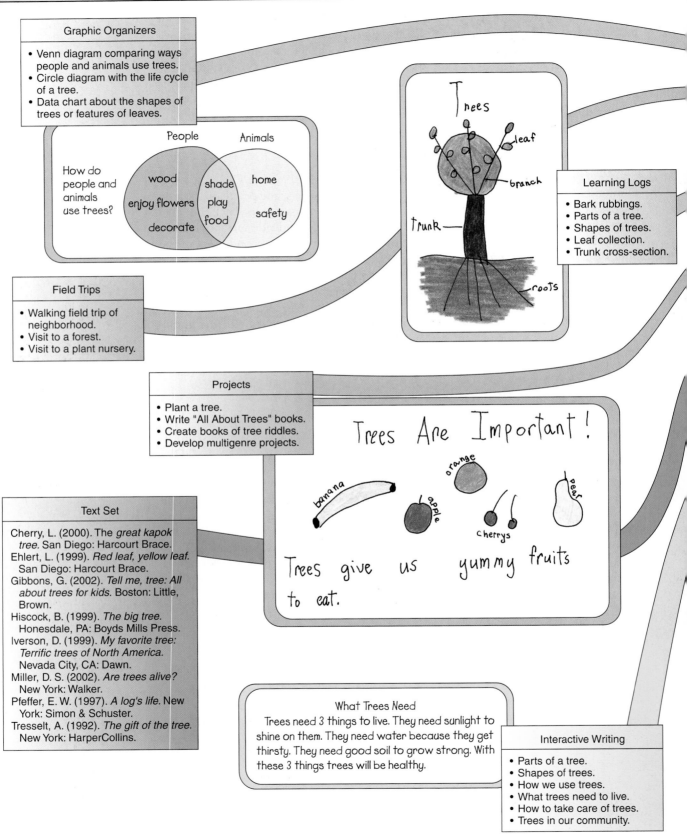

Graphic Organizers
- Venn diagram comparing ways people and animals use trees.
- Circle diagram with the life cycle of a tree.
- Data chart about the shapes of trees or features of leaves.

How do people and animals use trees?

People / Animals
- wood
- enjoy flowers
- decorate
- shade
- play
- food
- home
- safety

Trees
- leaf
- branch
- trunk
- roots

Learning Logs
- Bark rubbings.
- Parts of a tree.
- Shapes of trees.
- Leaf collection.
- Trunk cross-section.

Field Trips
- Walking field trip of neighborhood.
- Visit to a forest.
- Visit to a plant nursery.

Projects
- Plant a tree.
- Write "All About Trees" books.
- Create books of tree riddles.
- Develop multigenre projects.

Trees Are Important!
banana   orange   apple   cherrys   pear
Trees give us yummy fruits to eat.

Text Set
Cherry, L. (2000). The *great kapok tree*. San Diego: Harcourt Brace.
Ehlert, L. (1999). *Red leaf, yellow leaf*. San Diego: Harcourt Brace.
Gibbons, G. (2002). *Tell me, tree: All about trees for kids*. Boston: Little, Brown.
Hiscock, B. (1999). *The big tree*. Honesdale, PA: Boyds Mills Press.
Iverson, D. (1999). *My favorite tree: Terrific trees of North America*. Nevada City, CA: Dawn.
Miller, D. S. (2002). *Are trees alive?* New York: Walker.
Pfeffer, E. W. (1997). *A log's life*. New York: Simon & Schuster.
Tresselt, A. (1992). *The gift of the tree*. New York: HarperCollins.

What Trees Need
Trees need 3 things to live. They need sunlight to shine on them. They need water because they get thirsty. They need good soil to grow strong. With these 3 things trees will be healthy.

Interactive Writing
- Parts of a tree.
- Shapes of trees.
- How we use trees.
- What trees need to live.
- How to take care of trees.
- Trees in our community.

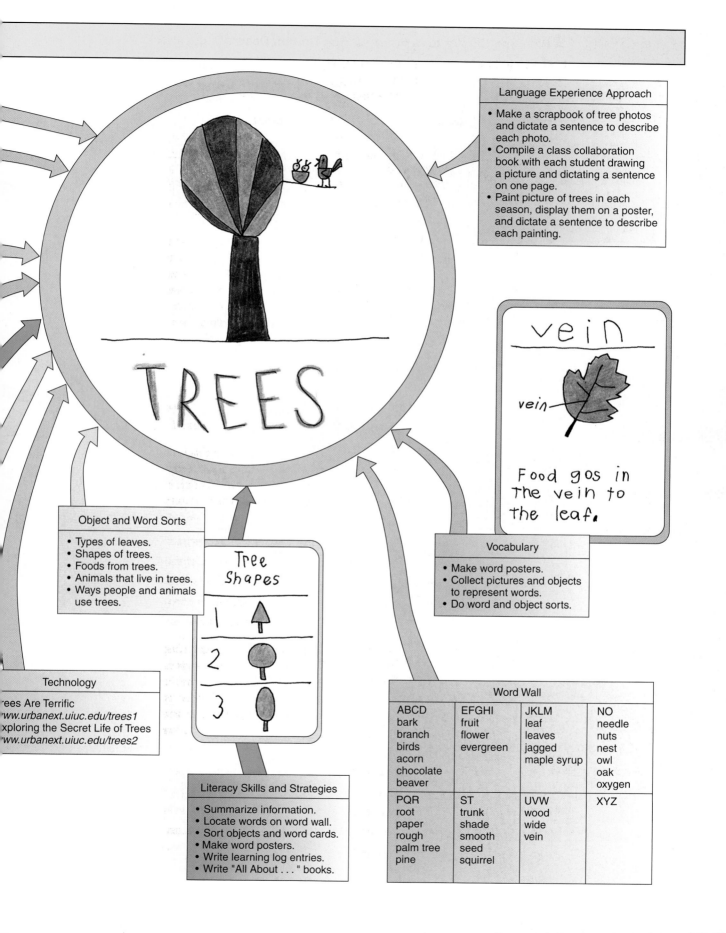

Language Experience Approach

- Make a scrapbook of tree photos and dictate a sentence to describe each photo.
- Compile a class collaboration book with each student drawing a picture and dictating a sentence on one page.
- Paint picture of trees in each season, display them on a poster, and dictate a sentence to describe each painting.

vein

vein

Food gos in the vein to the leaf.

Object and Word Sorts

- Types of leaves.
- Shapes of trees.
- Foods from trees.
- Animals that live in trees.
- Ways people and animals use trees.

Tree Shapes

1
2
3

Vocabulary

- Make word posters.
- Collect pictures and objects to represent words.
- Do word and object sorts.

Technology

rees Are Terrific
rww.urbanext.uiuc.edu/trees1
xploring the Secret Life of Trees
rww.urbanext.uiuc.edu/trees2

Literacy Skills and Strategies

- Summarize information.
- Locate words on word wall.
- Sort objects and word cards.
- Make word posters.
- Write learning log entries.
- Write "All About . . . " books.

Word Wall			
ABCD	EFGHI	JKLM	NO
bark	fruit	leaf	needle
branch	flower	leaves	nuts
birds	evergreen	jagged	nest
acorn		maple syrup	owl
chocolate			oak
beaver			oxygen
PQR	ST	UVW	XYZ
root	trunk	wood	
paper	shade	wide	
rough	smooth	vein	
palm tree	seed		
pine	squirrel		

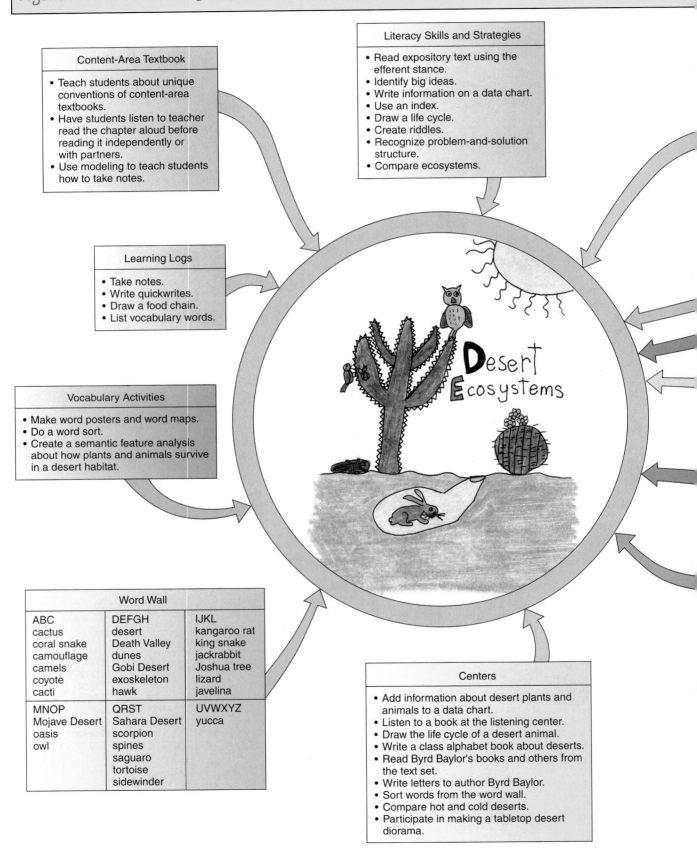

Content-Area Textbook

- Teach students about unique conventions of content-area textbooks.
- Have students listen to teacher read the chapter aloud before reading it independently or with partners.
- Use modeling to teach students how to take notes.

Literacy Skills and Strategies

- Read expository text using the efferent stance.
- Identify big ideas.
- Write information on a data chart.
- Use an index.
- Draw a life cycle.
- Create riddles.
- Recognize problem-and-solution structure.
- Compare ecosystems.

Learning Logs

- Take notes.
- Write quickwrites.
- Draw a food chain.
- List vocabulary words.

Vocabulary Activities

- Make word posters and word maps.
- Do a word sort.
- Create a semantic feature analysis about how plants and animals survive in a desert habitat.

Word Wall

ABC	DEFGH	IJKL
cactus	desert	kangaroo rat
coral snake	Death Valley	king snake
camouflage	dunes	jackrabbit
camels	Gobi Desert	Joshua tree
coyote	exoskeleton	lizard
cacti	hawk	javelina
MNOP	QRST	UVWXYZ
Mojave Desert	Sahara Desert	yucca
oasis	scorpion	
owl	spines	
	saguaro	
	tortoise	
	sidewinder	

Centers

- Add information about desert plants and animals to a data chart.
- Listen to a book at the listening center.
- Draw the life cycle of a desert animal.
- Write a class alphabet book about deserts.
- Read Byrd Baylor's books and others from the text set.
- Write letters to author Byrd Baylor.
- Sort words from the word wall.
- Compare hot and cold deserts.
- Participate in making a tabletop desert diorama.

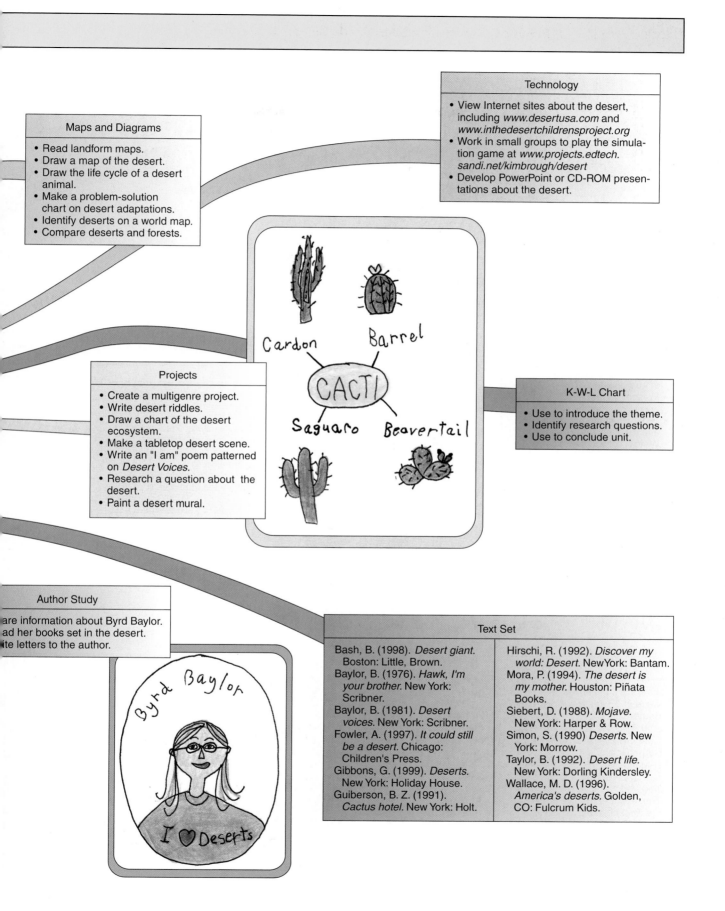

Maps and Diagrams

- Read landform maps.
- Draw a map of the desert.
- Draw the life cycle of a desert animal.
- Make a problem-solution chart on desert adaptations.
- Identify deserts on a world map.
- Compare deserts and forests.

Technology

- View Internet sites about the desert, including *www.desertusa.com* and *www.inthedesertchildrensproject.org*
- Work in small groups to play the simulation game at *www.projects.edtech.sandi.net/kimbrough/desert*
- Develop PowerPoint or CD-ROM presentations about the desert.

Projects

- Create a multigenre project.
- Write desert riddles.
- Draw a chart of the desert ecosystem.
- Make a tabletop desert scene.
- Write an "I am" poem patterned on *Desert Voices*.
- Research a question about the desert.
- Paint a desert mural.

Cardon   Barrel

CACTI

Saguaro   Beavertail

K-W-L Chart

- Use to introduce the theme.
- Identify research questions.
- Use to conclude unit.

Author Study

are information about Byrd Baylor.
ad her books set in the desert.
ite letters to the author.

Byrd Baylor

I ♥ Deserts

Text Set

Bash, B. (1998). *Desert giant.* Boston: Little, Brown.
Baylor, B. (1976). *Hawk, I'm your brother.* New York: Scribner.
Baylor, B. (1981). *Desert voices.* New York: Scribner.
Fowler, A. (1997). *It could still be a desert.* Chicago: Children's Press.
Gibbons, G. (1999). *Deserts.* New York: Holiday House.
Guiberson, B. Z. (1991). *Cactus hotel.* New York: Holt.

Hirschi, R. (1992). *Discover my world: Desert.* New York: Bantam.
Mora, P. (1994). *The desert is my mother.* Houston: Piñata Books.
Siebert, D. (1988). *Mojave.* New York: Harper & Row.
Simon, S. (1990) *Deserts.* New York: Morrow.
Taylor, B. (1992). *Desert life.* New York: Dorling Kindersley.
Wallace, M. D. (1996). *America's deserts.* Golden, CO: Fulcrum Kids.

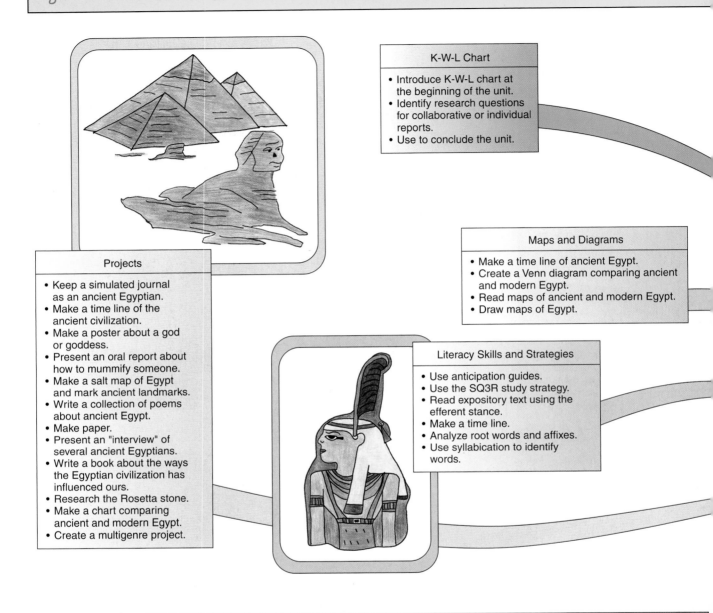

K-W-L Chart
- Introduce K-W-L chart at the beginning of the unit.
- Identify research questions for collaborative or individual reports.
- Use to conclude the unit.

Projects
- Keep a simulated journal as an ancient Egyptian.
- Make a time line of the ancient civilization.
- Make a poster about a god or goddess.
- Present an oral report about how to mummify someone.
- Make a salt map of Egypt and mark ancient landmarks.
- Write a collection of poems about ancient Egypt.
- Make paper.
- Present an "interview" of several ancient Egyptians.
- Write a book about the ways the Egyptian civilization has influenced ours.
- Research the Rosetta stone.
- Make a chart comparing ancient and modern Egypt.
- Create a multigenre project.

Maps and Diagrams
- Make a time line of ancient Egypt.
- Create a Venn diagram comparing ancient and modern Egypt.
- Read maps of ancient and modern Egypt.
- Draw maps of Egypt.

Literacy Skills and Strategies
- Use anticipation guides.
- Use the SQ3R study strategy.
- Read expository text using the efferent stance.
- Make a time line.
- Analyze root words and affixes.
- Use syllabication to identify words.

Text Set

Aliki. (1979). *Mummies made in Egypt.* New York: HarperCollins.

Carter, D. S. (1987). *His majesty, Queen Hatshepsut.* New York: HarperCollins.

Der Manueliàn, P. (1991). *Hieroglyphs from A to Z.* New York: Scholastic.

Giblin, J. C. (1990). *The riddle of the Rosetta stone.* New York: HarperCollins.

Gregory, K. (1999). *Cleopatra VII, daughter of the Nile.* New York: Scholastic.

Harris, G. (1992). *Gods and pharaohs from Egyptian mythology.* New York: Peter Bedrick.

Hart, G. (2004). *Ancient Egypt.* New York: DK Publishing.

Honan, L. (1999). *Spend the day in ancient Egypt.* New York: Wiley.

Katan, N. J., & Mintz, B. (1981). *Hieroglyphs: The writing of ancient Egypt.* New York: McElderry.

Lattimore, D. N. (1992). *The winged cat: A tale of ancient Egypt.* New York: HarperCollins.

Macaulay, D. (1975). *Pyramid.* Boston: Houghton Mifflin.

McMullen, K. (1992). *Under the mummy's spell.* New York: Farrar, Straus & Giroux.

Perl, L. (1987). *Mummies, tombs, and treasure: Secrets of ancient Egypt.* New York: Clarion.

Stanley, D., & Vennema, P. (1994). *Cleopatra.* New York: Morrow.

Stolz, M. (1988). *Zekmet the stone carver: A tale of ancient Egypt.* San Diego: Harcourt Brace.

Ventura, P., & Ceserani, G. P. (1985). *In search of Tutankh-amun.* Morristown, NJ: Silver Burdett.

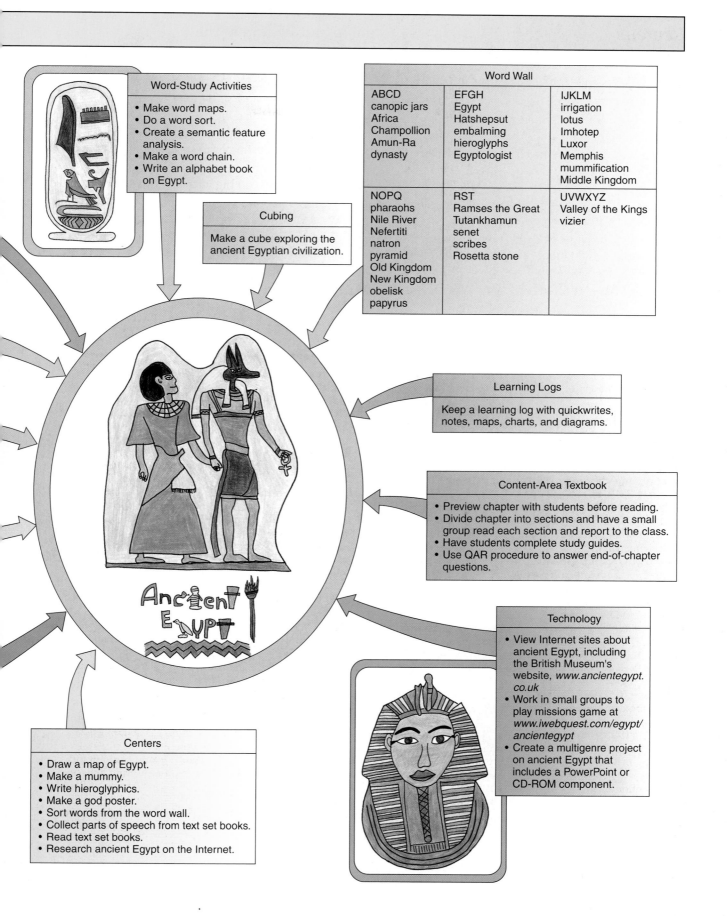

Word-Study Activities

- Make word maps.
- Do a word sort.
- Create a semantic feature analysis.
- Make a word chain.
- Write an alphabet book on Egypt.

Cubing

Make a cube exploring the ancient Egyptian civilization.

Word Wall

ABCD	EFGH	IJKLM
canopic jars	Egypt	irrigation
Africa	Hatshepsut	lotus
Champollion	embalming	Imhotep
Amun-Ra	hieroglyphs	Luxor
dynasty	Egyptologist	Memphis
		mummification
		Middle Kingdom
NOPQ	**RST**	**UVWXYZ**
pharaohs	Ramses the Great	Valley of the Kings
Nile River	Tutankhamun	vizier
Nefertiti	senet	
natron	scribes	
pyramid	Rosetta stone	
Old Kingdom		
New Kingdom		
obelisk		
papyrus		

Learning Logs

Keep a learning log with quickwrites, notes, maps, charts, and diagrams.

Content-Area Textbook

- Preview chapter with students before reading.
- Divide chapter into sections and have a small group read each section and report to the class.
- Have students complete study guides.
- Use QAR procedure to answer end-of-chapter questions.

Technology

- View Internet sites about ancient Egypt, including the British Museum's website, *www.ancientegypt. co.uk*
- Work in small groups to play missions game at *www.iwebquest.com/egypt/ ancientegypt*
- Create a multigenre project on ancient Egypt that includes a PowerPoint or CD-ROM component.

Centers

- Draw a map of Egypt.
- Make a mummy.
- Write hieroglyphics.
- Make a god poster.
- Sort words from the word wall.
- Collect parts of speech from text set books.
- Read text set books.
- Research ancient Egypt on the Internet.

Review: How Effective Teachers Use Reading and Writing in the Content Areas

1. Teachers teach students about the unique conventions of content-area textbooks.

2. Teachers use content-area textbooks as one resource in thematic units.

3. Teachers recognize the characteristics of considerate texts.

4. Teachers use a variety of activities during each stage of the reading process to make content-area textbooks more comprehensible.

5. Teachers provide students with opportunities to talk and write about what they are reading in content-area textbooks.

6. Teachers teach students how to take notes and study effectively.

7. Teachers develop text sets of books, magazines, and Internet resources to supplement content-area textbooks.

8. Teachers focus on big ideas in content-area units.

9. Teachers list important words on word walls and use a variety of activities to teach vocabulary.

10. Teachers have students create projects to apply and share their learning.

Professional References

Allen, C. A. (2001). *The multigenre research paper: Voice, passion, and discovery in grades 4–6.* Portsmouth, NH: Heinemann.

Anderson, T. H., & Armbruster, B. B. (1984). Studying. In P. D. Pearson, R. Barr, M. L. Kamil, & P. Mosenthal (Eds.), *Handbook of reading research* (pp. 657–679). New York: Longman.

Barone, G. (1990). The written responses of young children: Beyond comprehension to story understanding. *The New Advocate, 3,* 49–56.

Bonin, S. (1988). Beyond storyland: Young writers can tell it other ways. In T. Newkirk & N. Atwell (Eds.), *Understanding writing* (2nd ed., pp. 47–51). Portsmouth, NH: Heinemann.

Brozo, W. G., & Simpson, M. L. (2003). *Readers, teachers, learners: Expanding literacy across the content areas* (4th ed.). Upper Saddle River, NJ: Merrill/Prentice Hall.

Caverly, D. C., & Orlando, V. P. (1991). Textbook study strategies. In D. C. Caverly & V. P. Orlando (Eds.), *Teaching reading and study strategies at the college level* (pp. 86–165). Newark, DE: International Reading Association.

Fulwiler, T. (1985). Research writing. In M. Schwartz (Ed.), *Writing for many roles* (pp. 207–230). Upper Montclair, NJ: Boynton/Cook.

Goldenberg, C. (1992/1993). Instructional conversations: Promoting comprehension through discussion. *The Reading Teacher, 46,* 316–326.

Harvey, S. (1998). *Nonfiction matters: Reading, writing, and research in grades 3–8.* York, ME: Stenhouse.

Harvey, S., & Goudvis, A. (2000). *Strategies that work: Teaching comprehension to enhance understanding.* York, ME: Stenhouse.

Head, M. H., & Readence, J. E. (1986). Anticipation guides: Meaning through prediction. In E. K. Dishner, T. W. Bean, J. E. Readence, & D. W. Moore (Eds.), *Reading in the content areas* (2nd ed., pp. 229–234). Dubuque, IA: Kendall/Hunt.

Johns, J. L., Van Leirsburg, P., & Davis, S. J. (1994). *Improving reading: A handbook of strategies.* Dubuque, IA: Kendall/Hunt.

Langer, J. A. (1981). From theory to practice: A prereading plan. *Journal of Reading, 25,* 152–157.

Marzano, R. J., Norford, J. S., Paynter, D. E., Pickering, D. J., & Gaddy, B. B. (2001). *A handbook for classroom instruction that works.* Alexandria, VA: Association for Supervision and Curriculum Development.

Moline, S. (1995). *I see what you mean: Children at work with visual information.* York, ME: Stenhouse.

Moore, D. W., & Moore, S. A. (1992). Possible sentences: An update. In E. K. Dishner, T. W. Bean, J. E. Readence, & D. W. Moore (Eds.), *Reading in the content areas* (3rd ed., pp. 303–310). Dubuque, IA: Kendall/Hunt.

Neeld, E. C. (1986). *Writing* (2nd ed.). Glenview, IL: Scott Foresman.

Ogle, D. M. (1986). K-W-L: A teaching model that develops active reading of expository text. *The Reading Teacher, 39,* 564–570.

Ogle, D. M. (1989). The know, want to know, learn strategy. In K. D. Muth (Ed.), *Children's comprehension of text: Research into practice* (pp. 205–223). Newark, DE: International Reading Association.

Pappas, C. C., Kiefer, B. Z., & Levstik, L. S. (1990). *An integrated language perspective in the elementary school: Theory into action.* New York: Longman.

Raphael, T., & McKinney, J. (1983). Examination of fifth- and eighth-grade children's question-answering behavior: An instructional study in metacognition. *Journal of Reading Behavior, 15,* 67–86.

Raphael, T., & Wonnacott, C. (1985). Heightening fourth grade students' sensitivity to sources of information for answering comprehension questions. *Reading Research Quarterly, 20,* 282–296.

Raphael, T. E. (1986). Teaching question-answer-relationships, revisited. *The Reading Teacher, 39,* 516–523.

Robb, L. (2003). *Teaching reading in social studies, science, and math.* New York: Scholastic.

Romano, T. (1995). *Writing with passion: Life stories, multiple genres.* Portsmouth, NH: Heinemann/Boynton/Cook.

Romano, T. (2000). *Blending genre, alternating style: Writing multiple genre papers.* Portsmouth, NH: Heinemann/Boynton/Cook.

Sowers, S. (1985). The story and the "all about" book. In J. Hansen, T. Newkirk, & D. Graves (Eds.), *Breaking ground: Teachers relate reading and writing in the elementary school* (pp. 73–82). Portsmouth, NH: Heinemann.

Stahl, S. A., & Kapinus, B. (1991). Possible sentences: Predicting word meanings to teach content area vocabulary. *The Reading Teacher, 45,* 36–43.

Tierney, R. J., & Shanahan, T. (1996). Research on the reading-writing relationship: Interactions, transactions, and outcomes. In R. Barr, M. L. Kamil, P. Mosenthal, & P. D. Pearson (Eds.), *Handbook of reading research* (vol. 2, pp. 246–280). Mahwah, NJ: Lawrence Erlbaum.

Tompkins, G. E. (2004). *Teaching writing: Balancing process and product* (4th ed.). Upper Saddle River, NJ: Merrill/Prentice Hall.

Topping, D., & McManus, R. (2002). *Real reading, real writing: Content-area strategies.* Portsmouth, NH: Heinemann.

Tunnell, M. O., & Ammon, R. (Eds.). (1993). *The story of ourselves: Teaching history through children's literature.* Portsmouth, NH: Heinemann.

Wilson, L. (1994). *Write me a poem: Reading, writing, and performing poetry.* Portsmouth, NH: Heinemann.

Children's Book References

Aquatic life of the world. (2001). New York: Marshall Cavendish.

Avi. (1991). *Nothing but the truth.* New York: Orchard.

Bing, C. (2000). *Ernest L. Thayer's Casey at the bat: A ballad of the republic sung in the year 1888.* Brooklyn, NY: Handprint Books.

Cole, J. (1992). *The magic school bus on the ocean floor.* New York: Scholastic.

Cole, J. (1996). *The magic school bus inside a beehive.* New York: Scholastic.

Cushman, K. (1994). *Catherine, called Birdy.* New York: HarperCollins.

Denenberg, B. (1998). *The journal of William Thomas Emerson: A Revolutionary War patriot.* New York: Scholastic.

Denenberg, B. (1999). *The journal of Ben Uchida: Citizen 13559, Mirror Lake Internment Camp.* New York: Scholastic.

Draper, S. M. (1994). *Tears of a tiger.* New York: Atheneum.

Fleischman, P. (1985). *I am phoenix: Poems for two voices.* New York: HarperCollins.

Fleischman, P. (1988). *Joyful noise: Poems for two voices.* New York: HarperCollins.

Gregory, K. (1997). *Across the wide and lonesome prairie: The Oregon Trail diary of Hattie Campbell.* New York: Scholastic.

Guiberson, B. Z. (1991). *Cactus hotel.* New York: Henry Holt.

Hunt, J. (1989). *Illuminations.* New York: Bradbury Press.

Lasky, K. (1996). *A journey to the new world: The diary of Remember Patience Whipple.* New York: Scholastic.

Lester, J. (1968). *To be a slave.* New York: Dial Books.

Lowry, L. (1989). *Number the stars.* Boston: Houghton Mifflin.

Macaulay, D. (1977). *Castle.* Boston: Houghton Mifflin.

Macaulay, D. (1983). *Castle* (video). Washington, DC: Unicorn Projects Inc.

Mannis, C. D. (2003). *The queen's progress: An Elizabethan alphabet.* New York: Viking.

McKissack, P. C. (1997). *A picture of freedom: The diary of Clotee, a slave girl.* New York: Scholastic.

Musgrove, M. (1976). *Ashanti to Zulu: African traditions.* New York: Dial Books.

Napier, M. (2002). *Z is for Zamboni: A hockey alphabet.* Chelsea, MI: Sleeping Bear Press.

Steele, P. (1998). *Knights.* New York: Kingfisher.

White, E. E. (2002). *The journal of Patrick Seamus Flaherty: United States Marine Corps.* New York: Scholastic.

Compendium of Instructional Procedures

The instructional procedures in this Compendium, which effective teachers use in teaching reading and writing, are presented with step-by-step directions. You have read about grand conversations, minilessons, guided reading, interactive writing, and other procedures in this text; they were highlighted to cue you to consult the Compendium for more detailed information. These nine instructional procedures are also featured on the DVD that accompanies this text:

- **Grand Conversations**
- **Guided Reading**
- **Instructional Conversations**
- **Interactive Writing**
- **K-W-L Charts**
- **Making Words**
- **Shared Reading**
- **Word Sorts**
- **Word Walls**

You will see how experienced teachers use instructional procedures in real classroom settings. Sometimes the steps merge or repeat as they customize the procedures to meet the students' needs and the content being presented.

The Compendium and the DVD are handy resources to use as you develop lesson plans and teach in kindergarten through eighth-grade classrooms.

Notice in these photos which instructional procedures Mrs. Donnelly is using with her third graders during reading and writing workshop.

Anticipation guides (Head & Readence, 1986) are lists of statements about a topic that students discuss at the beginning of a thematic unit or before reading a content-area textbook. They are used to stimulate students' interest in the topic and activate their prior knowledge during the prereading stage of the reading process. Teachers prepare a list of statements about the topic; some of the statements are true, and others are incorrect or based on misconceptions. Students discuss each statement and agree or disagree with it, and then they discuss the statements again at the end of the unit or after reading. A fifth-grade anticipation guide about Canada is shown in Figure 1.

Teachers follow these steps to develop an anticipation guide:

1. *Consider students' background knowledge.* At the beginning of a thematic unit or before reading a chapter in a content-area textbook, teachers consider their students' knowledge about the topic and any misconceptions they might have, and they identify ideas for the anticipation guide.

2. *Develop a list of four to eight statements.* Teachers write statements for the anticipation guide based on their consideration of students' background knowledge and likely misconceptions. These statements should be general enough to pique students' interest and stimulate discussion. The list can be written on a chart, or individual copies can be made for each student.

3. *Discuss the statements on the anticipation guide.* Teachers introduce the anticipation guide and have students talk about the statements in small groups or together as a class and decide whether they agree or disagree with each one.

4. *Have students mark their opinions.* Students mark whether they agree or disagree with each statement in the "before reading" column of the class chart or on individual copies of the chart.

5. *Involve students in activities to learn about the topic.* Students participate in instructional activities or read the chapter in the content-area textbook, and they try to

Figure 1 **Anticipation Guide on Canada**				
Before Reading		Statements	After Reading	
Agree	Disagree		Agree	Disagree
		Canada is the second largest country in the world.		
		The official language of Canada is English.		
		Canada is very much like the United States.		
		Canada's economy is based on its wealth of natural resources.		
		Canada has always fought on the American side during wars.		
		Today, most Canadians live within 200 miles of the American border.		

make connections between the statements on the anticipation guide and what they are learning.

6. *Have students mark their opinions again.* Students reread the statements on the anticipation guide and mark their opinions in the "after reading" column on the class chart or on their individual copies.

7. *Discuss the statements again.* The students talk about the statements, and decide whether each statement is true or false. They give reasons for their decisions, and compare their "before reading" and "after reading" opinions.

Students can also try their hand at writing anticipation guides. When students are reading informational books in literature circles, for example, they can create an anticipation guide after reading and then share the guide with classmates when they present the book during a sharing time.

BOOK TALKS

Book talks are brief teasers that teachers present to interest students in particular books. During this prereading activity, teachers introduce students to books in the classroom library, books for literature circles, or a text set of books for a thematic unit or an author study featuring books written by a particular author.

Book talks involve these steps:

1. *Select a book to share.* Teachers select a book to share, and they read it if they are unfamiliar with it or review it if they have read it previously.

2. *Plan a brief presentation about the book.* Teachers decide what they will say about the book and how they will present this information. If they plan to read a brief excerpt, they mark it with a bookmark and then rehearse it so that they will read expressively.

3. *Give the presentation.* During the 1- to 3-minute presentation, teachers tell the title and author of the book, show the book, and give a brief summary. Sometimes they read a short excerpt and show an illustration. They also explain why they liked it and why students might be interested in it.

4. *Display the book.* Teachers show the book during the book talk and then display it on a chalk tray or shelf to encourage students' interest.

Students also give book talks to share books they have read during reading workshop; they follow the same steps as they prepare and present their book talks.

CHORAL READING

Teachers use choral reading to develop students' reading fluency. Poems are usually the texts chosen for choral reading, but other texts that lend themselves to group reading can also be used. Students practice rereading a familiar poem or other text in this exploring-stage activity. As they read aloud, they practice chunking words together, varying their reading speed, and reading more expressively. Students take turns reading lines or sentences of the text as they read together as a class or in small groups. Choral reading can follow one of these arrangements:

To read how a second-grade teacher uses choral reading, turn to page 154.

- *Echo reading.* The leader reads each line, and the group repeats it.
- *Leader and chorus reading.* The leader reads the main part of the poem, and the group reads the refrain or chorus in unison.

- *Small-group reading.* The class divides into two or more groups, and each group reads one part of the poem.
- *Cumulative reading.* One student or one group reads the first line or stanza, and another student or group joins in as each line or stanza is read so that a cumulative effect is created.

Here are the steps in choral reading:

1. *Select a poem for choral reading.* Teachers select a poem or other text to use for choral reading and copy it onto a chart large enough for the class to read, prepare an overhead transparency to be shown on a large screen, or make multiple copies for students to read.

2. *Arrange the text for choral reading.* Teachers work with students to decide how to arrange the text for reading. They add marks to each line of text so that they can follow the arrangement.

3. *Do the choral reading.* Students read the poem or other text together several times, and teachers emphasize that they should pronounce words clearly and read with expression. Teachers may want to tape-record students' reading so that they can hear themselves.

4. *Experiment with other arrangements.* Students change the arrangement of the text and then read it again. Sometimes students experiment with three or four arrangements before they are satisfied with the effect they create through the choral reading.

Choral reading makes students active participants in the poetry experience, and it helps them learn to appreciate the sounds, feelings, and magic of poetry. Choral reading is especially effective for English learners because it is an enjoyable, low-anxiety activity that helps children learn English intonation patterns and improve their reading fluency.

CLASS COLLABOR- ATIONS

Turn to page 6 to read about fourth graders who collaborated to write an introduction for their collection of stories, page 101 for a page from a kindergarten class collaboration book, and page 440 for an excerpt from a class alphabet book.

Class collaborations are books that students work together to make. Students each contribute one page or work with a classmate to write a page or a section of the book. They use the writing process as they draft, revise, and edit their pages. The benefit of collaborative books is that students share the work of creating a book so that the books are made much more quickly and easily than individual books (Tompkins, 2004). Because students write only one page or section, it takes less time for teachers to conference with students and help them to revise and edit their writing. Teachers often make class collaborations with students as a first bookmaking project and to introduce the stages of the writing process. Students at all grade levels can write collaborative books to retell a favorite story, illustrate a poem with one line or a stanza on each page, or write an informational book or biography.

Teachers follow these steps in making a collaborative book:

1. *Choose a topic.* Teachers choose a topic related to a literature focus unit or thematic unit. Then students choose specific topics or pages to prepare.

2. *Introduce the page or section design for the book.* Teachers explain the design or share a sample book. They show students how to write their pages or sections for the class book. For a class alphabet book, for example, teachers explain the arrangement— where to place the letter, the featured word, the illustration, and the text. Teachers often model the procedure and have the class write one page of the book together before students begin working on their pages.

3. *Have students make rough drafts of their pages.* They share the pages in writing groups. After getting feedback from classmates, students revise their pictures and text. Then they correct mechanical errors and make the final copy of their pages.

4. *Compile the pages to complete the book.* Students add a title page and covers. Older students might also prepare a table of contents, an introduction, and a conclusion, and add a bibliography at the end. To make the book sturdier, teachers often laminate the covers (or all pages in the book) and have the book bound.

5. *Make copies of the book for students.* Teachers can make copies of the book for each student. The specially bound copy is often placed in the class or school library.

Students create class collaborations as part of literature focus units and thematic units, retelling familiar stories and creating innovations or new versions of a story. They can make a class book to illustrate a poem or song by writing one line or stanza on each page and then drawing an illustration. *The Lady With the Alligator Purse* (Westcott, 1988) and *America the Beautiful* (Bates, 1993) are examples of song and poem retellings that have been published as picture books; students can examine these books before they write their own. Students also write informational books, reports, and biographies collaboratively to share knowledge they have learned in a thematic unit.

CUBING

Students use cubing to explore a topic from six viewpoints in this applying-stage activity (Neeld, 1986). This activity is called *cubing* because cubes have six sides, and students consider a topic from six viewpoints:

- *Describe the topic.* Students represent the topic in words, including its colors, shapes, and sizes, to create a mental image.
- *Compare the topic to something else.* Students consider how it is similar to or different from this other thing.
- *Associate the topic with something else.* Students explain why the topic makes them think of this other thing.
- *Analyze the topic.* Students tell how it is made or what it is composed of.
- *Apply the topic.* Students explain how it can be used or what can be done with it.
- *Argue for or against the topic.* Students take a stand and list reasons to support their argument.

Cubing involves these steps:

1. *Construct a cube.* Students construct a cube from cardboard, or they can use a square cardboard box, such as a department store gift box. Next, they cut six squares of paper to fit the sides of the cube; later, they will write and draw their responses on these square pieces of paper and attach them to the cube.

2. *Divide students into groups.* Students form six small groups, and each group chooses one of the viewpoints for the cubing activity.

3. *Have each group examine one viewpoint.* Students consider the topic from their viewpoint and brainstorm ideas to use in the paragraph they will write.

4. *Draft and refine a paragraph.* Students use the ideas they have brainstormed to draft a paragraph about the topic. They revise and edit their paragraph and make the final copy on a square piece of paper that has been cut to fit the cube.

5. *Complete the cube.* Students attach their completed responses to each side of the cube and then share their work with classmates.

Cubing is a useful procedure for helping students to think more deeply about the big ideas presented in content-area units. Middle- and upper-grade students can cube topics such as Antarctica, the U.S. Constitution, endangered animals, the Underground Railroad, and ancient Greece.

DATA CHARTS

Data charts are grids that students make and use to collect and organize information about a topic (McKenzie, 1979). They are often used as an exploring-stage activity. After reading an informational article about how animals protect themselves, for example, students make a data chart and write big ideas, such as "camouflage," across the top of the chart and names of animals in the left column. Then students complete the chart by explaining how each animal protects itself. Sometimes students have learned enough information to complete the chart, and sometimes filling in the chart interests them in searching for more information about a topic. Students create data charts to make notes after reading. At other times, data charts are used as a prewriting activity in which students gather and organize information before beginning to write.

To see examples of data charts, turn to pages 358 and 450.

These steps are involved in using data charts:

1. *Design the data chart.* The teacher or students choose a topic and decide how to set up the data chart, such as listing the big ideas related to the topic across the top of the chart and examples or resources in the left column.

2. *Draw the chart.* Teachers or students create a skeleton chart on butcher paper for a class project or on a sheet of unlined paper for an individual project. Then they write the big ideas across the top of the chart and the examples or resources down the left column.

3. *Complete the chart.* Students complete the chart by adding words, pictures, sentences, or paragraphs in each cell.

4. *Use the chart.* Students use the information recorded on the data chart for an activity.

Teachers use data charts in many different ways. In literature focus units, for example students record on data charts information about versions of folktales and fairy tales, such as "Cinderella" stories, or about a collection of books by an author, such as Eric Carle, Eve Bunting, or Chris Van Allsburg. In content-area units, data charts are used to record information about the big ideas students are learning about the solar system, Native American tribes, or ancient civilizations.

DIRECTED READING-THINKING ACTIVITY (DRTA)

Teachers actively involve students in reading stories or listening to stories read aloud when they use the Directed Reading-Thinking Activity (DRTA) because students make predictions and then read or listen to confirm their predictions (Stauffer, 1975). DRTA is a useful approach for teaching students how to use the predicting strategy. DRTA is used with both picture-book and chapter-book stories but not with informational books and content-area textbooks because students do not predict what non-fiction books will be about; instead, they read to locate the big ideas.

DRTA involves these steps:

1. *Introduce the story.* Teachers discuss the topic or show objects and pictures related to the story to activate or build students' background knowledge. They show the cover of the book and ask students to make a prediction about the story using one or more of these questions:

- What do you think a story with a title like this might be about?
- What do you think might happen in this story?
- Does this picture give you any ideas about what might happen in this story?

If necessary, the teacher reads the first paragraph or two to provide more information for students to use in making their predictions. After a brief discussion in which all students commit themselves to one or another of the alternatives presented, the teacher asks these questions:

- Which of these ideas do you think would be the likely one?
- Why do you think that idea is a good one?

2. *Read the beginning of the story.* Teachers have students read the beginning of the story or listen to it read aloud. Then students confirm or reject their predictions by responding to questions such as:

- What do you think now?
- What do you think will happen next?
- What do you think would happen if . . . ?
- Why do you think that idea is a good one?

3. *Continue reading and predicting.* Students continue reading or the teacher continues reading aloud, stopping again at several key points to make new predictions, read, and then confirm or reject the predictions.

4. *Have students reflect on their predictions.* Students reflect on the predictions they made as they read or listened to the story read aloud, and they talk about how making predictions helped them to comprehend the story. Teachers ask these questions to help students think about their predictions:

- What predictions did you make?
- What in the story made you think of that prediction?
- What in the story supports that idea?

The Directed Reading-Thinking Activity is useful only when students are reading or listening to an unfamiliar story so that they can be actively involved in the prediction-confirmation cycle.

DOUBLE-ENTRY JOURNALS

Students write double-entry journals so that they can think more deeply about stories they are reading and information they are learning during thematic units (Barone, 1990; Berthoff, 1981). They divide the journal pages into two columns. In the left column, students write quotes from the story or informational book they are reading, and in the right column, they reflect on each quote. They may relate a quote to their own lives, react to it, write a question, or make some other comment. Excerpts from a fifth grader's double-entry journal about *The Lion, the Witch and the Wardrobe* (Lewis, 1994) are shown in Figure 2.

To see examples of double-entry journals, turn to pages 222 and 434.

Here are the steps for using double-entry journals:

1. *Design journal pages.* Students divide the pages in their reading logs or learning logs into two columns, labeling the left column "In the Text" or "Quotes" and the right column "My Responses," "Comments," or "Reflections."

2. *Write quotes in journals.* Students copy one or more important or interesting quotes in the left column of the logs.

3. *Reflect on the quotes.* Students reread the quotes and make notes in the right column about their reasons for selecting each one. Sometimes it is easier if students share the quotes with a reading buddy or in a grand conversation before they write comments or reflections in the right column.

Double-entry journals can be used in several other ways, too. For example, instead of recording quotes from the story, students can write "Reading Notes" in the left column and then add "Reactions" in the right column. In the left column, students can write about the events they read about in the chapter, and in the right column, make personal connections to the events. Younger students can use the double-entry format for a prediction journal (Macon, Bewell, & Vogt, 1991): They label the left column "Predictions" and the right column "What Happened." In the

---

Figure 2 Excerpts From a Fifth Grader's Double-Entry Journal About *The Lion, the Witch and the Wardrobe*

Quotes	Reflections
Chapter 1 I will tell you this is the sort of house where no one is going to mind what we do.	I remember the time that I went to Beaumont, Texas to stay with my aunt. My aunt's house was very large. She had a piano and she let us play it. She told us that we could do whatever we wanted to.
Chapter 5 "How do you know?" he asked, "that your sister's story is not true?"	It reminds me of when I was little and I had an imaginary place. I would go there in my mind. I made up all kinds of make-believe stories about myself in this imaginary place. One time I told my big brother about my imaginary place. He laughed at me and told me I was silly. But it didn't bother me because nobody can stop me from thinking what I want.
Chapter 15 Still they could see the shape of the great lion lying dead in his bonds.	When Aslan died I thought about when my Uncle Carl died.
They're nibbling at the cords.	This reminds me of the story where the lion lets the mouse go and the mouse helps the lion.

474

left column, they write or draw a picture of what they predict will happen in the story or chapter before reading it. Then after reading, they draw or write what actually happened in the right column.

Exclusion brainstorming is a prereading-stage activity that teachers use to activate students' prior knowledge and expand their understanding about a social studies or science topic before reading (Blachowicz, 1986). Teachers present a list of words, and students identify words on the list that they think relate to the topic as well as those that do not belong. As they talk about the words and try to decide which ones are related to the topic, students refine their knowledge of the topic, are introduced to some key vocabulary words, and set a purpose for reading. Then, after reading, students review the list of words and decide whether they chose the correct words.

Teachers follow these steps to lead an exclusion brainstorming activity:

1. *Create a list of words.* Teachers choose words related to a book students will read or a thematic unit they will study and include a few words that do not fit with the topic. Then they write the list on chart paper and make individual copies for students.

2. *Mark the list.* Students read the list of words and work in small groups or together as a class to decide which ones are related to the topic. Then they circle the words they think are not related.

3. *Learn about the topic.* Students read the book or study the unit, noting when the words in the exclusion brainstorming activity are mentioned.

4. *Check the list.* After reading or studying the unit, students check their exclusion brainstorming list and make corrections based on their new knowledge. They cross out unrelated words, whether or not they circled them earlier.

Figure 3   **An Exclusion Brainstorming About** *The Ballad of Lucy Whipple*

Exclusion brainstorming can also be used with literature when teachers want to focus on a historical setting or another social studies or science concept before reading the story. A fourth-grade teacher created the exclusion brainstorming list shown in Figure 3 before reading *The Ballad of Lucy Whipple* (Cushman, 1996), the story of a young girl who travels with her family to California during the gold rush. The teacher used this activity to introduce some of the vocabulary in the story and to help students develop an understanding of life during the California gold rush. Students circled seven words before reading, and after reading, they crossed out three words, all different from the ones they had circled earlier.

GIST PROCEDURE

The GIST procedure (Cunningham, 1982) is a procedure for summarizing expository text. GIST stands for <u>G</u>enerating <u>I</u>nteractions between <u>S</u>chemata and <u>T</u>ext. Although the procedure can be tedious, it does improve students' ability to comprehend the big ideas in a paragraph. In this reading-stage activity, students create summaries of up to 15 words for increasingly larger amounts of text, beginning with a few sentences and working up to a paragraph. Teachers introduce the procedure with the whole class, but after students learn how to craft the summaries, they can work in small groups and then individually.

Teachers follow these steps to use the GIST procedure:

1. *Choose a paragraph for the activity.* Teachers choose a paragraph-long text, often taken from a content-area textbook or informational book with three to five sentences that can be summarized in a sentence.

2. *Prepare summary sheets.* Teachers create a summary sheet with space for students to write summary sentences of approximately 15 words each.

3. *Read the first sentence.* The teacher reads the first sentence, and students reread it. Then the sentence is covered and students retell it in their own words.

4. *Craft a summary sentence.* Students summarize the first sentence with a 15-word sentence, and teachers write this "rough draft" sentence on the chalkboard or on an overhead. Students refine it until they are satisfied, and then they reread the original sentence to be sure that their summary statement reflects the original sentence. Then students copy the "final" summary sentence on the first row of their summary sheets.

5. *Read the second sentence and revise their summary sentence.* Students reread the first sentence and read the second sentence, and then they revise their first summary sentence to reflect both the first and second sentences. Once students are satisfied with it, they copy it on the second row of their summary sheets.

6. *Continue reading and summarizing each sentence in the paragraph.* Students repeat the fifth step for each sentence in the paragraph; the summary sentence that they write for the final sentence should summarize the entire paragraph.

Once students learn how to craft summary sentences, they can move on to longer texts with three or more paragraphs and focus on crafting multiparagraph summaries, in which they read one entire paragraph and then craft a summary sentence that they refine after reading the second paragraph and each succeeding paragraph. Working with paragraphs prepares students for summarizing on their own as they read longer texts.

A grand conversation is a discussion about literature in which students deepen their comprehension, make connections, and reflect on their reading experience during the responding stage of the reading process (Eeds & Wells, 1989; Peterson & Eeds, 1990). In these discussions, which often last about 30 minutes, students sit in a circle so that they can see each other. The teacher serves as a facilitator, but the talk is primarily among the students. Traditionally, literature discussions have been "gentle inquisitions"; here the talk changes to dialoguing among students.

Here are the steps in conducting a grand conversation:

1. *Read the book.* Students prepare for the grand conversation by reading a chapter of the book or the entire book, depending on its length, or by listening to the teacher read it aloud.

2. *Prepare for the grand conversation.* Students draw pictures, quickwrite, or write in a reading log to think about the story. This step is optional and is often used when students don't talk much.

3. *Have small-group conversations.* Teachers have students share their ideas about the story in small groups before beginning the whole-class conversation. This, too, is an optional step and is often used when students don't talk much.

4. *Begin the conversation.* Students come together as a class for the conversation, and they sit in a circle. Teachers begin by asking: "Who would like to begin?" or "What did you think?" One student shares an idea about an event, a character, a favorite quote, the author's craft, or an illustration. Students take turns talking about the idea introduced by the first speaker; they continue until that idea has been exhausted. Students may share their drawings or read from their quickwrites or reading log entries.

5. *Continue the conversation.* A student introduces a new idea and the students talk about it, sharing ideas, asking for clarifications, and reading excerpts from the story to make a point. Students limit their comments to the idea being discussed, and after students finish discussing one idea, a new one is introduced. So that everyone gets to participate, many teachers ask students to make no more than two or three comments until everyone has spoken once. The talk is primarily among the students, but teachers ask questions and make comments to share their ideas and direct the conversation when necessary.

6. *Ask questions.* Teachers ask questions to focus students' attention on an aspect of the story that was missed. For example, teachers may focus on a big idea, an element of story structure, or the author's craft, or they may ask students to compare this book with a similar book, the film version of the story, or other books by the same author.

7. *Conclude the conversation.* Teachers bring the conversation to a close by summarizing, drawing conclusions, or making predictions about the next chapter after all students have shared and the big ideas have been explored.

8. *Reflect on the conversation.* Teachers may have students write (or write again) in reading logs. This step is optional, but students often have many ideas for reading log entries after participating in the discussion. Also, students may record their predictions before continuing to read chapter books.

Grand conversations are discussions about stories; discussions about informational books and content-area textbooks are called instructional conversations, and their focus is slightly different.

GRAND CONVER-SATIONS

 Turn to page 44 to read how a seventh-grade teacher conducts a grand conversation and to page 354 to read about how second graders talk about "The Three Little Pigs." Also view the DVD that accompanies this text to see a grand conversation in a sixth-grade classroom.

GRAPHIC ORGANIZERS

To see examples of graphic organizers, turn to pages 253, 265, 274–275 and 433.

Graphic organizers are schematic diagrams of big ideas in a chapter or part of a chapter that highlight the relationships among the ideas (Readence, Moore, & Rickelman, 2000; Tierney & Readence, 2000). These diagrams take different forms, ranging from clusters to flow charts to hierarchical maps, depending on the organization of the text. This spatial representation is what makes graphic organizers more effective than traditional outlines. Students use graphic organizers as a framework or structure for previewing, reading, and studying a chapter in a content-area textbook, informational book, or other text. This procedure spans the reading process because teachers introduce the graphic organizer as a prereading activity and students follow the diagram as they read the text. Students complete the diagram either while they are reading or immediately after reading. Later, students can use the graphic organizer as a study tool. Researchers have found that graphic organizers enhance students' comprehension because they provide an instructional framework of the text and give students the tools for structuring and relating the big ideas (Beck, Omanson, & McKeown, 1982).

Here are the steps in using graphic organizers:

1. *Identify big ideas.* Teachers read a chapter or a section of a chapter in a content-area textbook or other informational book to identify the big ideas and notice how the ideas are related.

2. *Create a graphic organizer.* Teachers create a diagram that emphasizes the big ideas and reflects the relationships among them. Graphic organizers should take the form that best represents the text's structure, and coordinate ideas should be shown as equally important. Teachers create a complete diagram with labels added and a second incomplete diagram with empty boxes and lines for students to fill in.

3. *Present the graphic organizer to students.* Teachers draw the diagram on the chalkboard or display it on an overhead projector so that all students can see it, and they also distribute individual copies to students. Teachers talk students through the diagram, explaining relationships and encouraging discussion to introduce big ideas. Or, teachers have students preview text to locate the big ideas and then fill them in on the graphic organizer.

4. *Read the text.* Students read the text individually or in small groups and compare what they are reading to the graphic organizer.

5. *Complete the graphic organizer.* Students complete the diagram either while reading or immediately after reading. Students write big ideas and key vocabulary words in the boxes and on the lines to complete the graphic organizer. They are expected to spell words accurately because they are using words taken directly from the text.

6. *Review the completed graphic organizer.* Students and the teacher complete the graphic organizer displayed on the chalkboard or overhead projector using the information students have recorded on their own diagrams. Teachers review the big ideas and key vocabulary words and clarify any misconceptions.

7. *Use the graphic organizer as a resource.* Students keep the completed graphic organizer in a thematic unit folder or learning log and use it as a resource for other activities and as a study guide when preparing for a test.

Once students are familiar with graphic organizers and understand how they highlight the big ideas and reflect the organization of the text, they can construct their own diagrams after reading. Graphic organizers serve another purpose as well: Students can create them as a prewriting activity to generate and organize their ideas before beginning to write.

Teachers use guided reading to read a book with a small group of students who read at approximately the same reading level (Clay, 1991). They select a book that students can read at their instructional level, that is, with approximately 90–94% accuracy. Teachers use the reading process and support students' reading and their use of reading strategies during guided reading (Depree & Iversen, 1996; Fountas & Pinnell, 1996). Students do the actual reading themselves, and they usually read silently at their own pace through the entire book. Emergent readers often mumble the words softly as they read, which helps the teacher keep track of students' reading and the strategies they are using. Guided reading is not round-robin reading, in which students take turns reading pages aloud to the group.

Here are the steps in a guided reading lesson:

1. *Choose an appropriate book for the small group of students.* The students should be able to read the book with 90–94% accuracy. Teachers collect copies of the book for each student in the group.

2. *Introduce the book to the group.* Teachers show the cover, reading the title and the author's name, and activating students' prior knowledge on a topic related to the book. They often use key vocabulary as they talk about the book, but they don't use vocabulary flash cards to drill students on new words before reading. Students also "picture walk" through the book, looking at the illustrations and talking about them.

3. *Have students read the book independently.* Teachers provide support to students with decoding and reading strategies as needed. Students either read silently or "mumble" read softly. Teachers observe students as they read and assess their use of word-identification and comprehension strategies. They help individual students decode unfamiliar words, deal with unfamiliar sentence structures, and comprehend ideas presented in the text whenever assistance is required.

4. *Provide opportunities for students to respond to the book.* Students talk about the book, ask questions, and relate it to others they have read, as in a grand conversation.

5. *Involve students in one or two exploring activities.* Examples: teach a phonics concept, word-identification skill, or reading strategy; review vocabulary words; examine an element of story structure.

6. *Provide opportunities for independent reading.* Teachers place the book in a book basket or in the classroom library so that students can reread it independently during reading workshop.

During guided reading, students read books they have not read before. Emergent readers usually read small picture books at one sitting, but older students who are reading longer chapter books take several days to several weeks to read them.

Instructional conversations are like grand conversations except that they are about nonfiction topics, not about literature. These conversations provide opportunities for students to talk about the big ideas in content-area units and enhance both students' conceptual knowledge and the technical vocabulary they are learning (Goldenberg, 1992/1993). Like grand conversations, these responding-stage discussions are interesting and engaging, and students are active participants, building on classmates' ideas with their own comments. Teachers are participants in the conversation, making comments much like the students do, but they also clarify misconceptions, ask questions,

Turn to page 81 to read how a primary teacher teaches a guided reading lesson. Also see the DVD that accompanies this text for another guided reading lesson.

INSTRUCTIONAL CONVERSATIONS

To see fourth graders have an instructional conversation, view the DVD that accompanies this text.

and provide instruction. Goldenberg has identified these content and linguistic elements of an instructional conversation:

- The conversation focuses on a content-area topic.
- Students activate or build knowledge about the topic during the instructional conversation.
- Teachers provide information and directly teach concepts when necessary.
- Teachers promote students' use of more complex vocabulary and language to express the ideas being discussed.
- Teachers encourage students to support the ideas they present with information presented in content-area textbooks, text sets, and other unit-related resources in the classroom.
- Students and teachers ask higher-level questions, often questions with more than one answer, during the instructional conversation.
- Students participate actively in the instructional conversation and make comments that build upon and expand classmates' comments.
- The classroom is a community of learners where both students' and teachers' comments are respected and encouraged.

Instructional conversations involve these steps:

1. _Choose a focus._ Teachers choose a focus for the instructional conversation related to the goals of a content-area unit or big ideas presented in an informational book or in a content-area textbook.

2. _Present information._ Teachers present information in preparation for the discussion, or students read an informational book or selection from a content-area textbook to learn about the topic.

3. _Prepare for the instructional conversation._ Sometimes teachers have students complete a graphic organizer together as a class or in small groups, or they may have students write learning log entries before beginning the conversation. This step is optional; it is used when students need additional opportunities to think about the information they are learning.

4. _Have small-group conversations._ Students share their ideas in small groups before beginning the whole-class instructional conversation. Sometimes teachers give students in each group a question or topic to talk about so that they are prepared to begin the whole-class conversation. This step is optional, too, and is often used with English learners and struggling students.

5. _Begin the conversation._ Students come together as a class and sit in a circle. Teachers begin the conversation with a question related to the focus they have identified. Students take turns responding; they share information they have learned, ask questions, and make connections. Teachers assist students as they make comments, helping them extend their ideas and use appropriate vocabulary. Sometimes teachers write students' comments on chart paper in a list or a graphic organizer.

6. _Continue the conversation._ Teachers continue the conversation by asking additional questions, and students take turns responding to the questions and exploring the big ideas.

7. _Conclude the conversation._ Teachers conclude the conversation by summarizing the big ideas or assisting students in drawing conclusions. Teachers often review the charts they have developed and explain how students will apply what they have learned in upcoming lessons.

8. *Reflect on the conversation.* Students write and draw in learning logs and record the big ideas discussed during the instructional conversation. Students may refer to the chart that the teacher made during the conversation.

Instructional conversations are useful in helping students grapple with important ideas they are learning in social studies, science, and other content areas. When students are talking about literature, they should use grand conversations.

INTERACTIVE WRITING

Watch a first-grade teacher conducting an interactive writing lesson on the DVD that accompanies this text, and turn to page 103 to see two samples of young children's interactive writing.

Students and the teacher "share the pen" as they write messages on chart paper in interactive writing (Button, Johnson, & Furgerson, 1996). This instructional strategy shows novice writers how writing works and how to construct words using their knowledge of sound-symbol correspondences and spelling patterns (Fountas & Pinnell, 1996). Teachers follow the writing process as students compose the message, and they guide students to write the message word by word on chart paper. Students take turns writing known letters and familiar words, adding punctuation marks, and marking spaces between words.

Teachers follow these steps to lead an interactive writing activity:

1. *Collect materials.* Teachers collect chart paper, colored marking pens, white correction tape, an alphabet chart, magnetic letters, and a pointer. For individual students' writing, they also collect small white boards, dry-erase pens, and erasers.

2. *Set a purpose for the activity.* Teachers present a stimulus activity or set a purpose for the interactive writing activity. Often they read aloud a trade book as a stimulus, but students also write daily news, compose a letter, or brainstorm information they are learning in a social studies or science unit.

3. *Pass out writing supplies.* Teachers pass out the small white boards, dry-erase pens, and erasers for students to use to write the text individually as it is written on chart paper. Teachers periodically ask students to hold up their white boards so they can see what the students are writing.

4. *Choose a sentence to write.* Teachers negotiate the sentence to write with students. Students repeat the sentence several times and segment it into words. They also count the number of words in the sentence. The teacher also helps the students remember the message as it is written.

5. *Write the first sentence.* Students and the teacher write the sentence word by word. They slowly pronounce the word, "pulling" it from their mouths and "stretching" it out. Then students take turns writing the letters in the word on chart paper. The teacher chooses students to write each sound or the entire word, depending on students' spelling knowledge. Students use one color of pen for the letters they write, and teachers use another color to write the parts of words that students can't spell so that they can keep track of how much writing students are able to do. A poster with upper- and lowercase letters is available nearby for students to refer to when they are unsure how to form a letter, and white correction tape is available to cover spelling errors and poorly formed letters. After each word is written, one student serves as the "spacer" and uses his or her hand to mark the space between words. Students reread the sentence from the beginning each time a new word is completed; when appropriate, teachers call children's attention to capital letters, punctuation marks, and other conventions of print.

6. Repeat for additional sentences. Teachers repeat this procedure to write additional sentences to complete the message.

7. Display the message. After the message is written, teachers display it in the classroom and have students reread it independently or using shared reading. Students often reread interactive charts when they "read the room." They may also add artwork to "finish" the chart.

When students begin interactive writing in kindergarten, they write letters to represent the beginning sounds in words and write familiar words such as *the, a,* and *is.* The first letters that students write are often the letters in their own names. As students learn more about sound-symbol correspondences and spelling patterns, they do more of the writing. Once they are writing words fluently, they can continue to do interactive writing as they work in small groups. Each student in the group uses a particular color pen and takes turns writing letters, letter clusters, and words. They also learn to use white correction tape to correct poorly formed letters and misspelled words.

K-W-L Charts

Turn to page 250 or 426 to read how teachers create K-W-L charts with their classes, and view the DVD for another example of K-W-L charts.

Teachers use K-W-L charts during content-area units (Ogle, 1986, 1989). The letters *K, W,* and *L* stand for What We K̲now, What We W̲onder, and What We L̲earned. Teachers introduce a K-W-L chart at the beginning of a content-area unit to activate students' background knowledge and identify questions that often stimulate students' interest in the topic. At the end of the unit, students complete the last section of the chart, listing what they have learned. This instructional procedure helps students to combine new information with prior knowledge and develop their vocabularies. A third-grade class's K-W-L chart is shown in Figure 4.

Here are the steps in creating a K-W-L chart:

1. Post a K-W-L chart. Teachers post a large sheet of butcher paper on a classroom wall, dividing it into three columns and labeling the columns K (What We Know), W (What We Wonder), and L (What We Learned).

2. Complete the K column. At the beginning of the unit, teachers ask students to brainstorm what they know about the topic. Teachers write this information in phrases or complete sentences in the K (What We Know) column. When students offer incorrect information, teachers suggest rephrasing it into a question so they can learn more about it and then add it to the W column. Students also suggest questions they would like to explore, and these, too, are added to the W column.

3. Complete the W column. Teachers write the questions that students suggest in the W (What We Wonder) column, and they continue to add questions to the W column throughout the unit.

4. Complete the L column. At the end of the unit, students reflect on what they have learned and brainstorm a list of newly learned information to complete the L column of the chart. Students do not try to answer each question listed in the W column, although the questions may trigger some newly learned information. Teachers write the newly learned information in the L column.

Figure 4	**Third-Grade K-W-L Chart on the Water Cycle**	
K What We Know	W What We Wonder	L What We Learned
Water is very important. Animals and plants need water to drink. People need water, too. Water comes from the water pipes and the faucet in the kitchen. Water comes from oceans and rivers and ponds. We get water from the rain. Water sinks into the ground when it rains.	Where does water come from? Is snow like rain? How does rain get in the clouds? Why are clouds white? What is the water cycle? Why does it rain? What would happen if it never rained?	Water goes up into the air and makes clouds. The water cycle happens over and over. Water vapor goes up into the clouds. Another word for rain is precipitation. Water goes up, makes a cloud, comes down, and it starts all over. Evaporation is when water changes from a liquid to a gas. Condensation is the opposite of evaporation. Condensation is when water vapor changes into a liquid—water. You can't see water vapor because it is invisible.

Older students can make K-W-L charts in small groups or create individual charts to document their learning. Class charts, however, are more effective for younger children and for older students who have not made K-W-L charts before. Individual K-W-L charts can be made like flip books: Students fold 8 1/2 × 13-inch sheets of paper in half lengthwise and make two cuts to create K, W, and L flip pages, as shown in Figure 5. They write the letters on the flip pages and lift each page to write information in each column.

One variation is K-W-L-Plus (Carr & Ogle, 1987): Teachers add a fourth section to the K-W-L chart called Categories of Information We Expect to Use, in which students categorize their knowledge and questions. This section is usually placed across the bottom of the K, W, and L columns, but it can also be placed on a separate chart. Categorizing the information is important because it emphasizes the big ideas. If the topic is the rain forest, for example, the categories might include animals, plants, people, products from the rain forest, and threats to survival. Later, when students complete the L section of the K-W-L chart, they categorize what they have learned and can use the categories in creating a cluster or other graphic organizer with the information.

Figure 5   A Fourth Grader's Flip Chart on Spiders

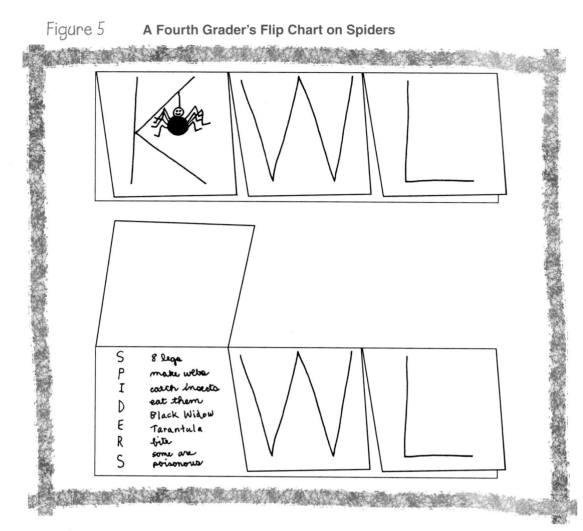

LANGUAGE EXPERIENCE APPROACH

To read how a second-grade teacher uses the Language Experience Approach, turn to page 154.

Children dictate words and sentences about an experience in the Language Experience Approach (LEA), and teachers write the dictation for them (Ashton-Warner, 1965; Lee & Allen, 1963; Stauffer, 1970). In this shared writing activity, reading and writing are integrated because students are actively involved in reading what they have written. The text they develop together becomes the reading material. Because the language comes from the children themselves and because the content is based on their experiences, children usually are able to read the text easily.

A kindergartner's LEA writing is shown in Figure 6. The child drew this picture of the Gingerbread Baby and dictated the sentence after listening to the teacher read Jan Brett's *Gingerbread Baby* (1999), a new version of "The Gingerbread Man" story.

LEA involves these steps:

1. *Provide an experience.* Teachers provide an experience to serve as the stimulus for the writing. For group writing, it can be reading a book aloud, taking a field trip, or an experience that all children are familiar with, such as having a pet or playing in the snow. For individual writing, the stimulus can be any experience that is important for the particular child.

2. *Talk about the experience.* The teacher and children talk about the experience to generate words, and they review the experience so that the children's dictation will

Figure 6   A Kindergartner's LEA Writing Sample About *Gingerbread Baby*

The Gingerbread Baby runs and runs into the gingerbread house.

be more interesting and complete. Teachers often begin with an open-ended question, such as "What are you going to write about?" As children talk about their experiences, they clarify and organize ideas, use more specific vocabulary, and extend their understanding.

3. *Record the child's dictation.* Teachers write texts for individual children on sheets of paper or in small booklets and group texts on chart paper. Teachers print neatly and spell words correctly, but they preserve students' language as much as possible: Although it is a great temptation to change the child's language to the teacher's own, in either word choice or grammar, editing should be kept to a minimum so that children do not get the impression that their language is inferior or inadequate. For individual texts, teachers take the child's dictation and write until the child finishes or hesitates. If the child hesitates, the teacher rereads what has been written and encourages the child to continue. For group texts, children take turns dictating sentences, and the teacher rereads each sentence after writing it.

4. *Read the text aloud, pointing to each word.* Teachers read the text aloud to remind children of the content of the text and demonstrate how to read it aloud with appropriate intonation. Then children join in the reading. After reading group texts together, individual children can take turns rereading. Group texts can also be duplicated so each child has a copy to read independently.

5. *Extend the experience.* Teachers encourage children to extend the experience through one or more of these activities:

- Add illustrations to their writing.
- Read their texts to classmates from the author's chair.
- Take their texts home to share with family members.
- Add this text to a collection of their writings.
- Pick out words from their texts that they would like to learn to read.

The Language Experience Approach is an effective way to help children emerge into reading. Even students who have not been successful with other types of reading activities can read what they have dictated.

LEARNING LOGS

Turn to page 152 to see a second grader's learning log entry.

Students write in learning logs during content-area units. Learning logs, like other types of journals, are booklets of paper in which students record information they are learning, write questions and reflections about their learning, and make graphic organizers. Students often make entries as a responding-stage activity, but they may also use their learning logs at other stages in the reading process.

Here are the steps in using learning logs:

1. *Prepare learning logs.* Students make learning logs at the beginning of a unit. They typically staple together sheets of lined writing paper and plain paper for drawing diagrams and add construction paper covers.

2. *Write entries.* Students make entries in their learning logs as part of content-area unit activities. They take notes, draw diagrams, and do quickwrites.

3. *Monitor students' entries.* Teachers read students' entries, and in their responses, they answer students' questions and clarify confusions.

Students' writing is impromptu in learning logs, and the emphasis is on using writing as a learning tool rather than creating polished products. Even so, students should work carefully and spell words found on the word wall correctly.

MAKING WORDS

View the DVD that accompanies this text to see a third-grade teacher conducting a making words lesson.

Making words is an exploring-stage activity in which students arrange letter cards to spell words. As they spell words, they practice phonics and spelling concepts (Cunningham & Cunningham, 1992; Gunning, 1995). Teachers choose words that exemplify particular phonics or spelling patterns for students to practice from books students are reading or from a content-area unit. Then they prepare a set of letter cards that students use to spell words. The teacher leads students to create progressively longer words with the letters until they use every letter to spell the "big" word. Figure 7 shows the results of a making words activity that a sixth-grade class completed while studying ancient Egypt.

Here are the steps in a making words activity:

1. *Make letter cards.* Teachers make a set of small letter cards (1-inch-square cards) for students to use in word-making activities. For high-frequency letters (vowels, *s*, *t*, and *r*) they make three or four times as many letter cards as there are students in the class. They make fewer cards for less frequently used letters. Teachers package cards with each letter separately in small boxes, plastic trays, or plastic bags. They may also make a set of large letter cards (3- to 6-inch-square cards) to display in a pocket chart or on the chalkboard during the activity.

486

Figure 7   A Sixth-Grade Making Words Activity Using the Word *Hieroglyphics*

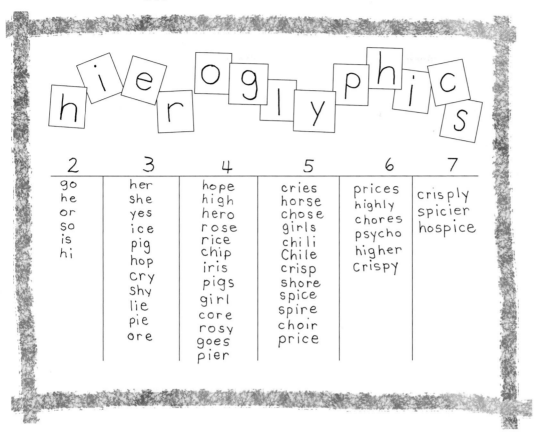

2	3	4	5	6	7
go	her	hope	cries	prices	crisply
he	she	high	horse	highly	spicier
or	yes	hero	chose	chores	hospice
so	ice	rose	girls	psycho	
is	pig	rice	chili	higher	
hi	hop	chip	Chile	crispy	
	cry	iris	crisp		
	shy	pigs	shore		
	lie	girl	spice		
	pie	core	spire		
	ore	rosy	choir		
		goes	price		
		pier			

2. *Choose a word for the activity.* Teachers choose a "big" word for the word-making activity, but they do not tell students what it is. The word is often taken from a word wall in the classroom and relates to a book students are reading or to a content-area unit. The word should be long enough and have enough vowels that students can easily make at least 10 words with the letters.

3. *Distribute letter cards.* A student distributes the needed letter cards to small groups of students, and students arrange them on one side of their desks. It is crucial that students have letter cards to manipulate; it is not sufficient to write the letters on the chalkboard, because manipulating the cards makes the activity more meaningful.

4. *Name the letter cards.* Teachers name the letter cards, clarifying confusing letters such as *n/u* and *m/w*. Teachers also ask students to identify the vowels and to separate the letters into consonant and vowel groups.

5. *Make small words using the cards.* Students manipulate the letter cards to spell two-letter words, and then they list the words they spell on a sheet of paper divided into columns according to the number of letters in the word. After spelling all possible two-letter words, students spell three- and four-letter words, and they record them on their charts. Teachers circulate around the classroom, providing assistance as needed.

6. *Make longer and longer words with the cards.* Students continue to spell longer words and record them on their charts. They use strategies for creating longer words by adding inflectional endings and prefixes and suffixes. They also use dictionaries to check for additional words.

7. *Figure out the "big" word using all the letters.* Students use all the letter cards to spell the "big" word. They often make it a contest to be first to figure out the "big" word, and once they have found it, they keep it secret. Students often have a good idea of the word from other words they have created, but if they have difficulty figuring it out, teachers can provide semantic and morphological clues.

8. *List the words.* After students have made as many words as they can, teachers conclude the making words activity by creating a class chart of all the words on the chalkboard or on chart paper. Students take turns naming two-letter words, three-letter words, and so on, and the teacher writes them on the chart. Teachers use the large letter cards to help students correctly spell a tricky word or to review a spelling skill that confuses the students. Finally, the students who first figured out the "big" word come to the chalkboard to spell the word with the teacher's large letter cards.

9. *Put the activity in a center.* Teachers put a set of letter cards in a spelling center so that students can practice the word-making activity.

Students also can use letter cards to practice spelling rimes. For example, to practice the -*ake* rime, students use the *b, c, f, h, l, m, r, s, t,* and *w* letter cards and the -*ake* rime card to make these words: *bake, shake, cake, make, flake, rake, lake, take,* and *wake.* Teachers often add several other letter cards, such as *d, p,* and *v,* to make the activity more challenging.

MINILESSONS

Turn to pages 120, 133, 140, 163, 172, 198, 242, 271, 421, and 449 to read sample minilessons.

Teachers teach minilessons on literacy procedures, concepts, strategies, and skills (Atwell, 1998). These lessons are brief, often lasting only 20 to 30 minutes, but they may continue over several days. Minilessons are usually taught during the exploring stage of the reading process or during the editing stage of the writing process, but they can be used at other times as well.

Here are the steps in conducting a minilesson:

1. *Introduce the topic.* Teachers begin the minilesson by introducing the procedure, concept, strategy, or skill. They name the topic and provide essential information about it.

2. *Share examples.* Teachers share examples of the topic taken from books students are reading or from students' own writing projects.

3. *Provide information.* Teachers provide additional information about the procedure, concept, strategy, or skill and make connections to students' reading or writing.

4. *Involve students in a guided practice activity.* Teachers involve students in guided practice activities so that they can apply what they are learning in a structured format. Teachers are also available to provide assistance.

5. *Assess students' learning.* Teachers check that students understand the procedure, concept, strategy, or skill well enough to apply it independently. They often monitor students during guided practice or review students' work, but sometimes teachers administer a quiz or other more formal assessment.

Teachers present minilessons to the whole class or to small groups to introduce or review a topic. The best time to teach a minilesson is when students will have immediate opportunities to apply what they are learning. Afterward, students use what they have learned in meaningful ways and in authentic literacy activities.

To help students think more deeply about a character and reflect on story events from the character's viewpoint, students draw open-mind portraits of characters as exploring- or applying-stage activities. These portraits have two parts: The face of the character is drawn on the first page, and the mind of the character is explored on several pages placed behind the first page. An excerpt from a fourth grader's open-mind portrait of Sarah, the mail-order bride in *Sarah, Plain and Tall* (MacLachlan, 1983), is shown in Figure 8.

Open-mind portraits involve these steps:

1. *Make a portrait of a character.* Students draw and color a large portrait of the head and neck of a character in a book they are reading.

2. *Assemble the open-mind project.* Students cut out the character's portrait and trace around the character's head on several more sheets of paper. Students include several "mind" pages to show what the character is thinking at important points in the story. Next, they cut out the "mind" pages and place them in order: The portrait goes on top, and the "mind" pages go behind it. Then they attach the portrait and

Figure 8   **An Open-Mind Portrait of Sarah From *Sarah, Plain and Tall***

489

"mind" pages with a brad or staple to a sheet of heavy construction paper or cardboard; it is important to place the fastener at the top of the portrait so that there will be space to write and draw on the "mind" pages.

3. Design the "mind" pages. Students lift the portrait and draw and write about the character, from the character's viewpoint, on the "mind" pages. They focus on what the character is thinking and doing at various points in the story.

4. Share completed open-mind portraits. Students share their portraits with classmates and talk about the words and pictures they chose to include in the "mind" pages.

Teachers also can use open-mind portraits when students are reading biographies or doing an autobiographical project: Instead of exploring the mind of a story character, they think about the person they are reading about in the biography or about themselves at different points in their lives.

PREREADING PLAN

Teachers use prereading plans before students read informational books and content-area textbooks (Tierney, Readence, & Dishner, 1995). This prereading-stage strategy helps them determine students' prior knowledge so that they can provide necessary background information to prepare students to understand what they will be reading.

Here are the steps in a prereading plan:

1. Discuss a big idea. Teachers introduce a big idea, using a word, phrase, or picture to initiate a discussion. Then students brainstorm words about the topic and record their ideas on a chart. Teachers help students make connections among the brainstormed ideas and present additional key vocabulary and clarify any misconceptions, if necessary.

2. Quickwrite about the big idea. Students write a quickwrite or draw pictures about the big ideas using words from the brainstormed list.

3. Share the quickwrites. Students share their quickwrites with classmates, and teachers ask questions to help students clarify and elaborate their quickwrites.

This activity is especially important for students who have little technical vocabulary or background knowledge about a topic and for English learners.

QUESTION-ANSWER RELATIONSHIPS (QARs)

Students learn how to find the answers to comprehension questions when they use the question-answer-relationship (QAR) technique (Raphael & McKinney, 1983; Raphael & Wonnacott, 1985). QAR differentiates among four types of questions and the kinds of thinking required to answer them; some questions require only literal thinking whereas others demand higher inferential or evaluative levels of thinking. There are four types of questions:

- **Right There Questions.** Readers find the answer "right there" in the text, usually in the same sentence as words from the question. These are literal-level questions.
- **Think and Search Questions.** The answer is in the text, but readers must search for it in different parts of the text and put the ideas together. These are inferential-level questions.

- *Author and Me Questions.* Readers use a combination of the author's ideas and their own ideas to answer the question. These questions require inferential and evaluative thinking.
- *On My Own Questions.* Readers use their own ideas to answer the question; sometimes it is not even necessary to read the text to answer the question. These are evaluative-level questions.

The first two types of questions are known as "in the book" questions because the answers can be found in the book, and the last two types are "in the head" questions because they require information and ideas not presented in the book (Raphael, 1986). By being aware of the requirements posed by a question, students are in a better position to be able to answer it.

Here are the steps in the QAR procedure:

1. *Read the questions before reading the text.* Students read the questions as a preview before reading the text to give them an idea of what to think about as they are reading.

2. *Predict how to answer the questions.* Students consider which of the four types of questions each question represents and the level of thinking required to answer it.

3. *Read the text.* Students read the text while thinking about the questions they will answer afterward.

4. *Answer the questions.* Students reread the questions, determine where to find the answers, locate the answers, and then write the answers.

5. *Share answers.* Students read their answers aloud and explain how they answered the questions. Students should again refer to the type of questions and whether the answer was "in the book" or "in the head."

After practicing the QAR procedure, students should use it whenever they are reading narrative or expository texts and have comprehension questions to answer afterward.

QUICKWRITING

Students use quickwriting to generate and explore relationships among ideas, ramble on paper, make connections, reflect on learning, and do other types of impromptu writing. It is a way for students to use writing as a tool for thinking because the focus is on content, with little emphasis on mechanics. Young children often do quickwrites in which they draw pictures and add labels. Some students do a mixture of writing and drawing. Figure 9 presents a fifth grader's quickwrites written while reading *The Breadwinner* (Ellis, 2000), the story of a girl who pretended to be a boy to earn money to buy food for her family when the Taliban ruled Afghanistan. For each quickwrite, the teacher provided several words, such as *Taliban, breadwinner, Parvana,* and *burqa,* and the students selected one word as the topic of each quickwrite. She also asked students to include information from the story and to make connections to their own lives.

Quickwriting involves these steps:

1. *Choose a topic.* Teachers identify a topic for the quickwrite, and students write it at the top of the paper.

2. *Write or draw about the topic.* Students write sentences or paragraphs and/or draw a picture related to the topic. They focus on interesting ideas, make connections between the topic and their own lives, and reflect on their reading or learning.

Figure 9 **A Fifth Grader's Quickwrites About** *The Breadwinner*

Parvana

I feel sorry for Parvana and no, I would not want to be her. I would hate to carry water all the time and have to stay inside with my Mom. I think I would like to go to work with my Dad but I would be very sad if a bomb blew his leg off and that happened to Parvana's Dad. If I lived over there in Afghanistan my life would be very bad. I would be very scared. I would be afraid my family would die and I would be all alone. There would be no one to take care of me. I think this book is about war and the theme is that war is bad. I'm not sure but that's what I think now.

A Breadwinner

A breadwinner is the person in your family who goes to work every day to make money to take care of your family. I have two breadwinners in my family. My Mom is a teacher and my Dad is a plumber. They both make money. They pay for our house and buy food and clothes and lots of other stuff. I would not want to be the breadwinner because I'm a kid and I would be scared. I don't think I could make enough money to pay for everything. I feel sorry for Parvana because she has to be the breadwinner because the soldiers came and took her Dad to prison.

Burqas

The Taliban made the women wear these ugly clothes called burqas if they went outside. There was just a little opening for their eyes and nothing else at all. I don't know why the Taliban did it. I guess they just hate women. I would try to stay close to my Mom so I wouldn't get lost because in the book it said that it was hard for kids to find their Moms because they all looked alike in the burqas. Women could never go outside without their burqas and if they did terrible things happened to them. That is very mean and I am glad it could not happen in the U.S.A.

3. *Share quickwrites.* After students write, they usually share their quickwrites in small groups or during grand conversations, and then one student in each group shares with the class.

Students do quickwrites during almost every stage of the reading process:

- Prereading: to activate background knowledge before reading
- Reading: to record predictions
- Reading: to summarize

- Responding: as an entry for reading logs
- Exploring: to define or explain a word on the word wall
- Exploring: to think about a big idea in a content-area chapter
- Exploring: to describe a favorite character or analyze the theme of a story
- Exploring: to compare book and film versions of a story
- Applying: to discuss a project being created

Students also do quickwrites during the writing process.

QUILTS

Students make squares out of construction paper and arrange them to make a quilt to celebrate a book they have read or to present information they have learned in a content-area unit. Quilts about stories are designed to highlight the theme, reinforce symbolism, and recall favorite sentences from the book students have read; quilts about content-area units are designed to highlight the big ideas students have learned and key vocabulary.

Making a quilt involves these steps:

1. *Design the quilt square.* Teachers and students choose a design for the quilt square that is appropriate for the story or the topic of the content-area unit. Students either choose a quilt design that quilt makers use or create their own design, and they choose colors for their quilt that emphasize important ideas or concepts.

2. *Make the squares.* Students each make a square and add an important piece of information from the unit or a favorite sentence from the story around the outside of the quilt square or in a designated section of the square.

3. *Assemble the quilt.* Teachers tape the squares together and back the quilt with butcher paper, or they staple the squares side by side on a large bulletin board.

Quilts also can be made of cloth. Teachers cut out squares of light-colored cloth, and students use fabric markers to draw pictures and write words. Then teachers or other adults sew the squares together and add a border to complete the quilt.

To read how seventh graders created a quilt about *The Giver*, turn to page 45; turn to page 188 to see how fifth and sixth graders made a vocabulary quilt.

READ-AROUNDS

Read-arounds are celebrations of stories and other books, usually performed as an applying-stage activity at the end of literature focus units or literature circles. Students choose favorite passages from a book to read aloud. Read-arounds are sometimes called "Quaker readings" because of their "unprogrammed" format.

Teachers follow these steps to conduct a read-around:

1. *Choose a favorite passage.* Students skim a book they have read to locate one or more favorite passages (a sentence or paragraph) and mark them with bookmarks.

2. *Practice reading the passage.* Students rehearse reading the passages so that they can read them fluently.

3. *Read the passages.* Teachers begin the read-around by asking a student to read a favorite passage aloud to the class. Then there is a pause and another student begins to read. Teachers don't call on students; any student may begin reading when no one else is reading. The passages can be read in any order, and more than one student can read the same passage. Teachers, too, read their favorite passages. The read-around continues until everyone who wants to read has done so.

Students like participating in read-arounds because the featured book is like a good friend. They enjoy listening to classmates read favorite passages and noticing literary language. They seem to move back and forth through the story, remembering events and reliving the story.

READERS THEATRE

Readers theatre is a dramatic production of a script by a group of readers (Martinez, Roser, & Strecker, 1998/1999). Each student assumes a role and reads the character's lines in the script. Readers interpret a story without using much action; they carry the whole communication of the plot, characterization, mood, and theme through their voices, gestures, and facial expressions. The emphasis is not on production quality; rather, it is on the interpretive quality of the readers' voices and expressions.

Here are the steps in a readers theatre presentation:

1. Select a script. Students and the teacher select a script from a trade book or a textbook and read and discuss it as they would any story. Or, students can create their own scripts.

2. Choose parts. Students volunteer to read each part and mark their lines on the script. They also decide how to use their voice, gestures, and facial expressions to interpret the character they are reading.

3. Rehearse the production. Students read the script several times, striving for accurate pronunciation, voice projection, and appropriate inflections. Less rehearsal is needed for an informal, in-class presentation than for a more formal production; nevertheless, interpretations should always be developed as fully as possible.

4. Stage the production. Readers theatre can be presented on a stage or in a corner of the classroom. Students stand or sit in a row and read their lines in the script. They stay in position through the production or enter and leave according to the characters' appearances "onstage." If readers are sitting, they may stand to read their lines; if they are standing, they may step forward to read. Costumes and props are unnecessary; however, adding a few small props enhances interest and enjoyment as long as they do not interfere with the interpretive quality of the reading.

Readers theatre avoids many of the restrictions inherent in theatrical productions: Students don't memorize their parts or spend long, tedious hours rehearsing; and elaborate props, costumes, and backdrops are not needed.

READING LOGS

Turn to page 105 to see young children's reading log entries and to page 43 for seventh graders' reading log entries.

Students write in reading logs about books they are reading or listening to the teacher read aloud. The primary purpose of reading logs is for students to relate the book to their own lives, to the world around them, or to other literature, but they also summarize their reading, list interesting or unfamiliar words, jot down quotable quotes, and take notes about characters, plot, or other story elements. Students also add lists of words from the word wall, diagrams about story elements, and information about authors and genres (Tompkins, 2004). Students typically make single entries for picture-book stories, and for chapter books, they write after reading every chapter or two.

Reading logs involve these steps:

1. Prepare the reading logs. Students make reading logs by stapling paper into booklets. They write the title of the book on the cover and add an appropriate illustration.

2. *Write entries.* Students write about the story or chapter they have read or listened to the teacher read aloud. Sometimes students choose their own topics for these entries, but at other times, teachers identify the topic in order to help students think more deeply about the story they are reading. The writing is informal, but teachers expect students to write legibly and to spell familiar words, including names of characters, correctly.

3. *Read and respond to the entries.* Teachers read students' entries and write comments back to them. Some teachers read and respond to all entries, and other teachers, because of time limitations, read and respond selectively.

Teachers have students write in reading logs during literature focus units, literature circles, and reading workshop. This responding-stage activity is an important tool for helping students think more deeply about the stories they are reading and for teachers to monitor students' comprehension.

RECIPROCAL TEACHING

Reciprocal teaching is a scaffolded discussion procedure incorporating four comprehension strategies—predicting, questioning, clarifying, and summarizing (Palinscar & Brown, 1984). This procedure improves students' comprehension by teaching them to integrate their use of multiple strategies. Reciprocal teaching is a reading-stage activity: Students apply the four strategies as they read and then reflect in a discussion on what they have accomplished. When they are learning to use the procedure, students also pause while reading with whole-class and small groups of classmates to think aloud and to demonstrate their strategy use.

Fiction and nonfiction texts, including big books, picture-book stories, novels, basal readers, content-area textbooks, magazine articles, and informational books, can be used for reciprocal teaching. At first, students practice the procedure as they read short sections of text, a paragraph or a page in length. As they gain experience, they read increasingly longer sections, up to a chapter, an entire article, or a picture book.

Reciprocal teaching involves these steps:

1. *Teach the comprehension strategies.* Teachers teach students to predict, question, clarify, and summarize as they read stories and informational books. They model how to use each strategy, and they think aloud to show students their thinking. They often develop charts about each strategy and post them in the classroom to prompt students to use the strategies.

2. *Introduce reciprocal teaching.* Teachers explain that reciprocal teaching is a way to get more involved in the reading experience and to understand the big ideas better. They use shared reading to model how to use the four strategies as they read aloud a short text, stopping often to share their thinking. While thinking aloud, teachers make predictions, ask questions, clarify confusing words and ideas, and summarize what they have read. Afterward, they discuss what they have read and how each strategy enhanced their comprehension of the text.

3. *Practice in teacher-led small groups.* Students practice reciprocal teaching in guided reading groups or other small groups. Teachers scaffold students as they read short sections of text and use the four comprehension strategies. Students often begin by making predictions and then reading silently. They pause partway through the text to modify the predictions they made earlier, ask questions and clarify the meanings of unfamiliar words and other confusions. Then they continue reading;

depending on the length and complexity of the text, they may pause again. After they finish reading, they summarize, ask additional questions, and clarify any confusions. The order in which students use strategies varies depending on the students and the text they are reading. Students can use small self-stick notes to record their thinking and then refer to these notes when they discuss how they used each strategy.

4. *Practice in student-led small groups.* Students form literature circles or other small groups to use the procedure to read novels, chapters in content-area textbooks, or other texts. Students can continue to use self-stick notes to track their strategy use, or they can make strategy charts by dividing a sheet of paper or a page in their reading logs into four sections where they record their predictions in one section, and their questions, clarifications, and summaries in the other sections. After reading, students discuss their strategy use and share the notes they made or the charts they created.

5. *Continue to use reciprocal teaching with longer texts.* After students become proficient at reading and comprehending short sections of text, teachers have them use reciprocal teaching to read increasingly longer sections of text.

This approach was developed for struggling seventh and eighth graders, but it can be used effectively with younger students (Oczkus, 2003). The biggest difference is that teachers provide more scaffolding as students learn to integrate the four comprehension strategies.

REPEATED READINGS

Repeated readings is an instructional procedure to help students increase their reading fluency and accuracy through rereading (Samuels, 1979). This procedure is useful for struggling students and for English learners who don't read fluently. When teachers monitor students' reading on a regular basis, students become more careful readers. Making a graph to document growth is an important component of the procedure, because the graph provides concrete evidence of students' growth.

Here are the steps in the individualized procedure:

1. *Conduct a pretest.* The student chooses a book at his or her independent reading level and reads a passage from it aloud while the teacher records the reading time and any errors.

2. *Practice reading the passage.* The student rereads the passage orally or silently several times.

3. *Conduct a posttest.* The student rereads the passage while the teacher again records the reading time and notes any errors.

4. *Compare pre- and posttest results.* The student compares his or her reading times and accuracy of the first and last readings. Then he or she prepares a graph to document growth between the first and last readings.

Repeated readings is not the same as rereading. The repeated readings procedure is an individualized fluency-building activity; on the other hand, rereading is a multi-purpose activity—teachers often encourage students to reread parts of a featured book for specific purposes during literature focus units and to reread favorite books during reading workshop to develop reading stamina, comprehension, and a love of reading.

In this reading-stage activity, teachers observe individual students as they read aloud and make notes to assess their reading fluency (Clay, 1985). Through a running record, teachers calculate the percentage of words the student reads correctly and then analyze the miscues or errors. Teachers make a check mark on a sheet of paper as the student reads each word correctly; they use other marks to indicate words that the student doesn't know or mispronounces.

Here are the steps in conducting a running record:

To read how a first-grade teacher takes running records, turn to page 292.

1. *Choose a book.* Teachers have the student choose an excerpt 100 to 200 words in length from a book he or she is reading. For beginning readers, the text can be shorter.

2. *Take the running record.* As the student reads the excerpt aloud, the teacher makes a record of the words read correctly as well as those read incorrectly. The teacher makes check marks on a blank sheet of paper for each word read correctly. Errors are marked in these ways:

- If the student reads a word incorrectly, the teacher writes the incorrect word and the correct word under it:

    take
    ——
    taken

- If the student self-corrects an error, the teacher writes SC (for "self-correction") following the incorrect word:

    for SC
    ——
    from

- If the student attempts to pronounce a word, the teacher records each attempt and adds the correct text underneath:

    be-bēf–before
    ——————
    before

- If the student skips a word, the teacher marks the error with a dash:

    —
    ——
    the

- If the student says words that are not in the text, the teacher writes an insertion symbol (caret) and records the inserted words:

    not
    ——
    ^

- If the student can't identify a word and the teacher supplies the word for the student, the teacher writes T:

    T
    ——
    which

- If the student repeats a word or phrase, the repetition is not scored as an error, but the teacher notes the repetition by drawing a line under the word or phrase (marked in the running record with check marks) that was repeated:

    ✓ ✓ ✓
    ————

3. *Calculate the percentage of miscues.* Teachers calculate the percentage of miscues or oral reading errors. When the student makes 5% or fewer errors, the book is considered to be at the independent level for that child. When there are 6–10% errors,

the book is at the instructional level, and when there are more than 10% errors, the book is too difficult—the frustration level.

4. *Analyze the miscues.* Teachers look for patterns in the miscues in order to determine how the student is growing as a reader and what skills and strategies the student should be taught.

Many teachers conduct running records with all their students at the beginning of the school year and at the end of grading periods. In addition, teachers do running records more often during guided reading groups and with students who are not making expected progress in reading in order to track their growth as readers and to make instructional decisions.

SEMANTIC FEATURE ANALYSIS

Teachers use semantic feature analysis to help students examine the characteristics of vocabulary words or content-area concepts (Pittelman, Heimlich, Berglund, & French, 1991). They create a grid for the analysis with words or concepts listed on one axis and the characteristics or components listed on the other axis. Students reading a novel, for example, can do a semantic feature analysis with vocabulary words listed on one axis and the characters' names on the other; they decide which words relate to which characters and use pluses and minuses to mark the relationships on the grid. Or, in a social studies unit, students can do a semantic feature analysis to review what they are learning about

Figure 10 Fifth Graders' Semantic Feature Analysis on Immigration

	Arrived in the 1600s	Arrived in the 1700s	Arrived in the 1800s	Arrived in the 1900s	Came to to Ellis Island	Came for religious freedom	Came for safety	Came for opportunity	Were refugees	Experienced prejudice
English	+	+	−	−	−	+	−	+	−	−
Africans	+	+	+	−	−	−	−	−	−	+
Irish	−	−	+	−	−	−	+	+	+	+
Other Europeans	−	+	+	+	+	−	+	+	+	+
Jews	−	−	+	+	+	+	+	−	+	+
Chinese	−	−	+	−	−	−	−	−	−	+
Latinos	−	−	−	+	−	−	−	+	−	+
Southeast Asians	−	−	−	+	−	−	+	+	+	+

Code: + = yes
− = no
? = don't know

America as a culturally pluralistic society, listing the groups of people who immigrated to the United States on one axis and historical features on the other axis. Then students complete the analysis by marking each cell on the grid. A fifth-grade class's semantic feature analysis on immigration is shown in Figure 10. After completing this grid, the students examined the grid for patterns and identified three big ideas:

- Different peoples immigrated to America at different times.
- The Africans who came as slaves were the only people who were brought to America against their will.
- The English were the only immigrants who didn't suffer prejudice.

Here are the steps in doing a semantic feature analysis:

1. *Create a grid.* Teachers create a grid with vocabulary or concepts listed on the vertical axis and characteristics or categories on the horizontal axis.

2. *Complete the grid.* Students complete the grid, cell by cell, by considering the relationship between each item on the vertical axis and the items on the horizontal axis. Then they mark the cell with a plus to indicate a relationship, a minus to indicate no relationship, and a question mark when they are unsure.

3. *Reflect on the grid.* Students and the teacher examine the grid for patterns and then make insights or draw conclusions based on the patterns.

Teachers often do semantic feature analysis with the whole class, but students can work in small groups or individually to complete the grid. The reflection should be done as a whole-class activity, however, so that students can share their insights.

Teachers use shared reading to read books and other texts with students who could not read those materials independently (Holdaway, 1979). Students and the teacher read the text aloud and in unison. When doing shared reading with young children, teachers use enlarged texts, including big books, poems written on charts, Language Experience stories, and interactive writing charts, so that both small groups and whole-class groups can see the text and read along with the teacher. Teachers focus on concepts about print, including left-to-right direction of print, words, letters, and punctuation marks. They model what fluent readers do as they involve students in enjoyable reading activities (Depree & Iversen, 1996; Fountas & Pinnell, 1996).

Here are the steps in a shared reading lesson:

1. *Introduce the text.* Teachers talk about the book or other text by activating or building background knowledge on topics related to the book and by reading the title and the author's name aloud.

2. *Read the text aloud.* Teachers read the story aloud to students, using a pointer (a dowel rod with a pencil eraser on the end) to track the text as they read. They invite students to join in the reading if the story is repetitive.

3. *Have a grand conversation.* Teachers invite students to talk about the story, ask questions, and share their responses.

4. *Reread the story.* Students take turns using the pointer to track the reading and turning pages. Teachers invite students to join in reading familiar and predictable words. Also, they take opportunities to teach and use graphophonic cues and reading strategies while reading.

SHARED READING

Turn to page 78 to read about a shared reading lesson in a primary classroom, and view the DVD that accompanies this text to see a shared reading lesson.

5. *Repeat the process.* Teachers reread the story with students several more times over a period of several days, again having students turn pages and take turns using the pointer to track the text while reading. They encourage students who can read the text to read along with them.

6. *Have students read independently.* After students become familiar with the text, teachers distribute individual copies of the book or other text for students to read independently and use for a variety of activities.

Shared reading is a step between reading to children and independent reading by students (Parkes, 2000). For older students, teachers use shared reading techniques to read books that students could not read themselves. Students each have a copy of the text—a chapter book, content-area textbook, or other book—and the teacher and students read together. The teacher or another fluent reader reads aloud while other students follow along in the text, reading to themselves.

SQ3R STUDY STRATEGY

The best-known study strategy is the SQ3R study strategy (Anderson & Armbruster, 1984). Students use five steps—survey, question, read, recite, and review—to read and remember information from content-area reading assignments. This strategy has been shown to be very effective when students apply it correctly.

SQ3R involves these steps:

1. *Survey.* Students preview the reading assignment, noting headings and skimming (rapidly reading) the introduction and summary. They note the big ideas that are presented. This step helps students activate prior knowledge and organize what they will read.

2. *Question.* Students turn each heading into a question before reading the section. Reading to find the answer to the question gives students a purpose for reading.

3. *Read.* Students read the section to find the answer to the question they have formulated. They read each section separately.

4. *Recite.* Immediately after reading each section, students recite from memory the answer to the question they formulated and other important information they have read. They can answer the questions orally or in writing.

5. *Review.* After finishing the entire reading assignment, students take a few minutes to review what they have read. They ask themselves the questions they developed from each heading and try to recall the answers they learned by reading. If students took notes or wrote answers to the questions in the fourth step, they should try to review without referring to the written notes.

STORY BOARDS

Story boards are cards to which the illustrations and text (or only the illustrations) from a picture book have been attached. Teachers make story boards by cutting apart two copies of a picture book. Students use story boards to sequence the events of a story, to examine a picture book's illustrations, and for other exploring-stage activities.

Here are the steps in making story boards:

1. *Collect two copies of a book.* Teachers purchase two paperback copies of the book. In a few picture books, however, all illustrations are on either the right-hand or left-hand pages, so only one copy of these books is needed for illustration-only story boards. In Chris Van Allsburg's *The Mysteries of Harris Burdick* (1984), for example, all illustrations are on the right-hand pages.

2. ***Cut the books apart.*** Teachers remove the covers and separate the pages. Next, they trim the cut edges.

3. ***Attach the pages to pieces of cardboard.*** Teachers glue each page or double-page spread to a piece of cardboard, making sure to include each page in the story.

4. ***Laminate the cards.*** Teachers laminate the cards so that they can withstand use by students.

5. ***Use the cards in sequencing activities.*** Teachers pass out the cards in random order to students. Students examine their pages, think about the sequence of events in the story, and arrange themselves in a line around the classroom to sequence the story events.

For chapter books, students can create their own story boards, one for each chapter. Students can divide into small groups, and each group works on a different chapter. Students make a poster with a picture illustrating the chapter and a paragraph-length summary of the chapter. A group of eighth graders created the story board presented in Figure 11; it summarizes chapter 2 of *Dragonwings* (Yep, 1975),

Figure 11   **An Eighth-Grade Story Board From *Dragonwings***

Chapter 2
"The Company"

Moon Shadow meets his Uncle Bright Star. He had worked in the California Gold Rush and building the railroad. Then Windrider, Moon Shadow's dad, shows Moon Shadow around, to make him feel safe at home. They go past the Barbary Coast where the white demons live to his new home in Chinatown, the town of the Tang People. It looks like his old home in China. Moon Shadow's dad gave him a kite to fly. It was like a blue and green butterfly. Moon Shadow loved his new kite. Moon Shadow hasn't flown his kite yet, but I bet that he can't wait! They all go into a big house called the Company of the Peach Order Vow and then Uncle Bright Star's son named Black Dog comes. He is in a gang and he takes drugs. He tells everyone that the demons hate them and want to kill them. Then they heard the sound of a window shattering. So they went downstairs and they saw that a window was broken and the white demons were yelling and shouting at them. Moon Shadow is scared but Windrider protects him.

the story of Moon Shadow, a young boy who comes to San Francisco from China in 1903 to join the father he has never met.

Sustained Silent Reading (SSR)

Sustained Silent Reading (SSR) is an independent reading time set aside during the school day for students in one class or the entire school to silently read self-selected books. In some schools, everyone—students, teachers, principals, secretaries, and custodians—stops to read, usually for a 15- to 30-minute period. SSR is a popular reading activity in schools that is known by a variety of names, including "drop everything and read" (DEAR), "sustained quiet reading time" (SQUIRT), and "our time to enjoy reading" (OTTER).

Teachers use SSR to increase the amount of reading students do every day and to develop their ability to read silently and without interruption (Hunt, 1967; McCracken & McCracken, 1978). Through numerous studies, SSR has been found to be beneficial in developing students' reading ability (Krashen, 1993; Pilgreen, 2000). In addition, it promotes a positive attitude toward reading and encourages students to develop the habit of daily reading. Because students choose the books they will read, they have the opportunity to develop their own tastes and preferences as readers. SSR is based on these guidelines:

- Students choose the books they read.
- Students read silently.
- The teacher serves as a model by reading during SSR.
- Students choose one book or other reading material for the entire reading time.
- The teacher sets a timer for a predetermined, uninterrupted time period, usually from 15 to 30 minutes.
- All students in the class or school participate.
- Students do not write book reports or participate in other after-reading activities.
- The teacher does not keep records or evaluate students on their performance. (Pilgreen, 2000)

For a successful SSR program, students need to have access to lots of books in a classroom library or the school library and know how to use the Goldilocks Strategy (see p. 408) to choose books at their reading level. If students don't have books that interest them written at their reading level, they won't be able to read independently for extended periods of time.

SSR involves these steps:

1. *Set aside a time for SSR.* Teachers allow time every day for uninterrupted, independent reading; it may last for only 10 minutes in a first-grade classroom or 20 to 30 minutes or more in the upper grades. Teachers often begin with a 10-minute SSR period and then extend the period as students build endurance and ask for more time.

2. *Ensure that students have books to read.* For capable readers, SSR is a time for independent reading. Students keep a book at their desks to read during SSR, and they use a bookmark to mark their place in the book. Beginning readers may read new books or choose three or four leveled readers that they have already read to reread during SSR. For children who cannot read on their own, partner reading may be substituted for independent reading.

3. Set a timer for a predetermined time. Teachers keep a kitchen timer in the classroom, and after everyone gets out a book to read, they set the timer for the SSR reading period. To ensure that students are not disturbed during SSR, some teachers place a "do not disturb" sign on the door.

4. Read along with students. Teachers read a book, magazine, or newspaper for pleasure while students read. This way, teachers model what capable readers do and that reading is a pleasurable activity.

Even though SSR was specifically developed without follow-up activities, many teachers use a few carefully selected and brief follow-up activities to sustain students' interest in reading books (Pilgreen, 2000). Students often discuss their reading with a partner, or volunteers give book talks to tell the whole class about their books. As students listen to one another, they get ideas about books they might like to read in the future. Sometimes students develop a ritual of passing on the books they have finished reading to interested classmates.

Students examine words and their meanings, sound-symbol correspondences, or spelling patterns using word sorts (Morris, 1982; Schlagal & Schlagal, 1992). Students sort a group of words (or objects or pictures) according to one of these characteristics:

- Conceptual relationships, such as words related to one of several characters in a story or words related to the inner or outer planets in the solar system
- Rhyming words, such as words that rhyme with *ball*, *hit*, or *flake*
- Consonant sounds, such as names of objects (actual objects or pictures) beginning with *r* or *l*
- Sound-symbol relationships, such as words in which the final *y* sounds like long *i* (*cry*) and words in which the final *y* sounds like long *e* (*baby*)
- Spelling patterns and rules, such as long-*e* words with various spelling patterns (*sea, greet, be, Pete*)
- Number of syllables, such as *pig, happy, afternoon*, and *television*
- Syllable division rules, using words such as *mag-net, can-dle, ti-ger, stor-y*, and *po-et*
- English, Latin, and Greek etymologies of words, using words such as *teeth* (English), *nation* (Latin), and *thermometer* (Greek)

WORD SORTS

 Check the third-grade word sort on ocean habitats on page 428, and view the DVD that accompanies this text to see a group of sixth graders do a word-sorting activity.

Sometimes teachers determine the categories for the sort, and at other times, students choose the categories; when teachers determine the categories, it is a closed word sort, and when students choose them, it is an open word sort (Bear, Invernizzi, Templeton, & Johnston, 2004).

Here are the steps in this exploring-stage activity:

1. Compile a list of words. Teachers compile a list of 10 to 20 words that exemplify a particular pattern and write the words on small cards. With younger children, small objects or picture cards can be used.

2. Determine the categories for the sort. Teachers determine the categories for the sort and tell students, or students read the words, group them, and determine the categories themselves. They can work individually or together in small groups or as a class.

3. Sort the cards. Students sort the words into two or more categories and write the groups of words on a chart or glue the cards onto a piece of chart paper.

4. Share the completed sorts. Students share their word sort with classmates, emphasizing the categories they created.

The words chosen for word sorts should come from phonics and spelling lessons, high-frequency word walls, books students are reading, or content-area units. Figure 12 shows two word sorts using words from *Holes* (Sachar, 1998); the first word sort is a conceptual sort, and the second is a grammar sort.

WORD WALLS

For examples of high-frequency word walls turn to pages 141, 159, and 160. Check page 429 for a content-area word wall and pages 210 and 356 for literature word walls. To see a fourth-grade teacher use a content-area word wall, view the DVD that accompanies this text.

Word walls are collections of words posted in the classroom that students use for word-study activities and refer to when they are reading and writing. Words for the word wall can be written on large sheets of butcher paper or on word cards that are then attached to the butcher paper. The words are arranged in alphabetized boxes so that students can locate them more easily.

There are three types of word walls. One type is a high-frequency word wall, where primary teachers post some or all of the 100 highest-frequency words (Cunningham, 2000). A second type is a content-area word wall, on which teachers and students write important words related to the unit they are studying. A third type of word wall is a literature word wall, where teachers and students write interesting, confusing, and important words from the story they are reading. The three types of word walls should be posted separately in the classroom because if the words are mixed, students will have difficulty categorizing them.

Here are the steps in using a literature word wall:

1. Prepare the word wall. Teachers hang a long sheet of butcher paper on a blank wall in the classroom and divide it into alphabetical categories, and then they prepare a stack of cards, if they are using word cards. They write the title of the book at the top of the word wall.

2. Introduce the word wall. Teachers introduce the word wall and add several words, such as the characters' names.

3. Add words to the word wall. After reading a picture book or after reading each chapter of a chapter book, students suggest additional "important" words for the word wall. Students may be familiar with some of these words, and others may be new to them. Students or the teacher writes the words in alphabetical categories on the butcher paper or on word cards, making sure to write large enough so that most students can see them.

4. Use the word wall for exploring-stage activities. Students refer the word wall words for a variety of vocabulary activities, such as creating word sorts and completing graphic organizers.

Word walls are useful because they make vocabulary words more visible in the classroom—and when words are visible, students learn to read and write them more readily.

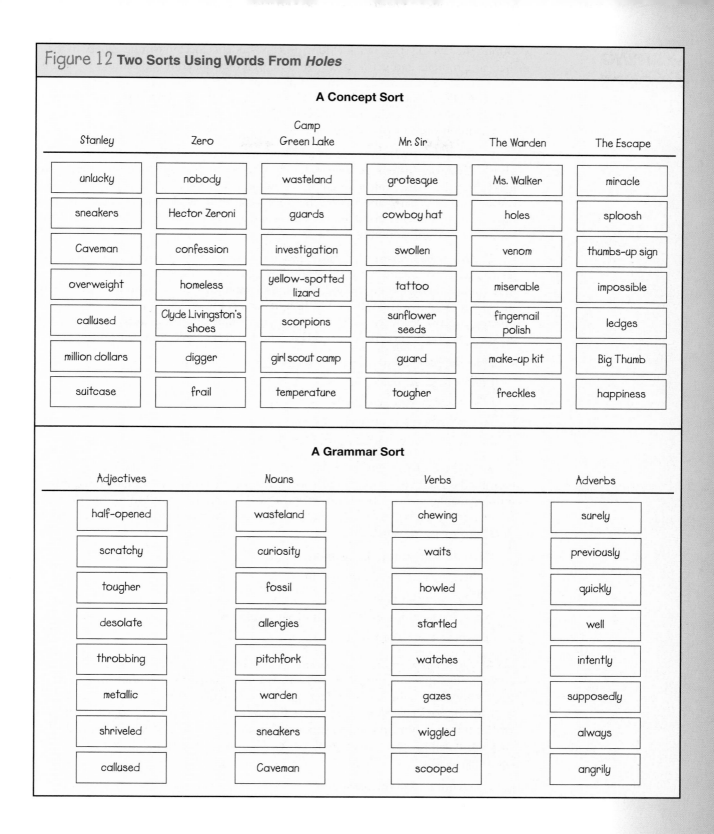

Figure 12 Two Sorts Using Words From *Holes*

A Concept Sort

Stanley	Zero	Camp Green Lake	Mr. Sir	The Warden	The Escape
unlucky	nobody	wasteland	grotesque	Ms. Walker	miracle
sneakers	Hector Zeroni	guards	cowboy hat	holes	sploosh
Caveman	confession	investigation	swollen	venom	thumbs-up sign
overweight	homeless	yellow-spotted lizard	tattoo	miserable	impossible
callused	Clyde Livingston's shoes	scorpions	sunflower seeds	fingernail polish	ledges
million dollars	digger	girl scout camp	guard	make-up kit	Big Thumb
suitcase	frail	temperature	tougher	freckles	happiness

A Grammar Sort

Adjectives	Nouns	Verbs	Adverbs
half-opened	wasteland	chewing	surely
scratchy	curiosity	waits	previously
tougher	fossil	howled	quickly
desolate	allergies	startled	well
throbbing	pitchfork	watches	intently
metallic	warden	gazes	supposedly
shriveled	sneakers	wiggled	always
callused	Caveman	scooped	angrily

WRITING GROUPS

During the revising stage of the writing process, students meet in writing groups to share their rough drafts and get feedback on how well they are communicating (Tompkins, 2004). Revising is probably the most difficult part of the writing process: Students can have trouble evaluating their writing objectively, so it is especially important that they learn how to work together in writing groups and provide useful feedback to classmates.

Writing groups involve these steps:

1. ***Read drafts aloud.*** Students take turns reading their rough drafts aloud to the group. Everyone listens politely, thinking about compliments and suggestions to make after the writer finishes reading. Only the writer looks at the composition, because when classmates and the teacher look at it, they quickly notice and comment on mechanical errors, even though the emphasis should be on content. Listening keeps the focus on content.

2. ***Offer compliments.*** After listening to the rough draft read aloud, classmates offer compliments, telling the writer what they liked about the composition. These positive comments should be specific, focusing on strengths, rather than the often-heard "I liked it" or "It was good"; even though such comments are positive, they do not provide effective feedback. Comments can focus on organization, introductions, word choice, voice, sequence, dialogue, theme, and so on. Possible comments include:

> I like the part where . . .
>
> I'd like to know more about . . .
>
> I like the way you described . . .
>
> Your writing made me feel . . .
>
> I like the order you used in your writing because . . .

3. ***Ask clarifying questions.*** Writers ask for assistance with trouble spots they identified earlier when rereading their writing, or they may ask questions that reflect more general concerns about how well they are communicating. Admitting the need for help from one's classmates is a major step in learning to revise. Here are possible questions to ask classmates:

> What do you want to know more about?
>
> Is there a part I should throw out?
>
> What details can I add?
>
> What do you think the best part of my writing is?
>
> Are there some words I need to change?

4. ***Offer other revision suggestions.*** Members of the writing group ask questions about things that were unclear to them and make suggestions about how to revise the composition. Almost any writer resists constructive criticism, but it is especially difficult for novice writers to appreciate suggestions. It is important to teach students what kinds of comments and suggestions are acceptable so that they will word what they say in helpful rather than hurtful ways. Comments and suggestions that students can offer include:

> I got confused in the part about . . .
>
> Do you need a closing?
>
> Could you add more about about . . . ?
>
> I wonder if your paragraphs are in the right order because . . .
>
> Could you combine some sentences?

5. *Repeat the process.* The writing group members repeat the process so that all students have an opportunity to share their rough drafts.

6. *Make plans for revision.* Students each make a commitment to revise their writing based on the comments and suggestions they received. The decision on what to revise always rests with the writers themselves, but with the understanding that their rough drafts are not perfect comes the realization that some revision will be necessary. When students verbalize their planned revisions, they are more likely to complete the revision stage.

Students make revisions after the group disbands. Sometimes they decide to conference with the teacher or meet again with classmates for more advice about how to revise their rough drafts.

Professional References

Anderson, T. H., & Armbruster, B. B. (1984). Studying. In P. D. Pearson, R. Barr, M. L. Kamil, & P. Mosenthal (Eds.), *Handbook of reading research* (pp. 657–679). New York: Longman.

Ashton-Warner, S. (1965). *Teacher.* New York: Simon & Schuster.

Atwell, N. (1998). *In the middle: New understandings about writing, reading, and learning* (2nd ed.). Portsmouth, NH: Heinemann.

Barone, D. (1990). The written responses of young children: Beyond comprehension to story understanding. *The New Advocate, 3,* 49–56.

Bear, D. R., Invernizzi, M., Templeton, S., & Johnston, F. (2004). *Words their way: Word study for phonics, vocabulary, and spelling instruction.* Upper Saddle River, NJ: Merrill/Prentice Hall.

Beck, I. L., Omanson, R. C., & McKeown, M. G. (1982). An instructional redesign of reading lessons: Effects on comprehension. *Reading Research Quarterly, 17,* 462–481.

Berthoff, A. E. (1981). *The making of meaning.* Montclair, NJ: Boynton/Cook.

Blachowicz, C. L. Z. (1986). Making connections: Alternatives to the vocabulary notebook. *Journal of Reading, 29,* 643–649.

Button, K., Johnson, M. J., & Furgerson, P. (1996). Interactive writing in a primary classroom. *The Reading Teacher, 49,* 446–454.

Carr, E. M., & Ogle, D. (1987). K-W-L-Plus: A strategy for comprehension and summarization. *Journal of Reading, 28,* 626–631.

Clay, M. M. (1985). *The early detection of reading difficulties* (3rd ed.). Portsmouth, NH: Heinemann.

Clay, M. M. (1991). *Becoming literate: The construction of inner control.* Portsmouth, NH: Heinemann.

Cunningham, J. W. (1982). Generating interactions between schemata and text. In J. A. Niles & L. A. Harris (Eds.), *New inquiring in reading research and instruction: Thirty-first yearbook of the National Reading Conference* (pp. 42–47). Washington, DC: National Reading Conference.

Cunningham, P. M. (2000). *Phonics they use: Words for reading and writing* (3rd ed.). New York: HarperCollins.

Cunningham, P. M., & Cunningham, J. W. (1992). Making words: Enhancing the invented spelling-decoding connection. *The Reading Teacher, 46,* 106–115.

Depree, H., & Iversen, S. (1996). *Early literacy in the classroom: A new standard for young readers.* Bothell, WA: Wright Group.

Eeds, M., & Wells, D. (1989). Grand conversations: An exploration of meaning construction in literature study groups. *Research in the Teaching of English, 23,* 4–29.

Fountas, I. C., & Pinnell, G. S. (1996). *Guided reading: Good first teaching for all children.* Portsmouth, NH: Heinemann.

Goldenberg, C. (1992/1993). Instructional conversations: Promoting comprehension through discussion. *The Reading Teacher, 46,* 316–326.

Gunning, T. G. (1995). Word building: A strategic approach to the teaching of phonics. *The Reading Teacher, 48,* 484–488.

Head, M. H., & Readence, J. E. (1986). Anticipation guides: Meaning through prediction. In E. K. Dishner, T. W. Bean, J. E. Readence, & D. W. Moore (Eds.), *Reading in the content areas* (2nd ed. pp. 229–234). Dubuque, IA: Kendall/Hunt.

Holdaway, D. (1979). *Foundations of literacy.* Auckland, NZ: Ashton Scholastic.

Hunt, L. (1967). Evaluation through teacher-pupil conferences. In T. C. Barrett (Ed.), *The evaluation of children's reading achievement* (pp. 111–126). Newark, DE: International Reading Association.

Krashen, S. (1993). *The power of reading.* Englewood, CO: Libraries Unlimited.

Lee, D. M. , & Allen, R. V. (1963). *Learning to read through experience* (2nd ed.). New York: Meredith.

Macon, J. M., Bewell, D., & Vogt, M. E. (1991). *Responses to literature, grades K–8.* Newark, DE: International Reading Association.

Martinez, M., Roser, N. L., & Strecker, S. (1998/1999). "I never thought I could be a star": A readers theatre ticket to fluency. *The Reading Teacher, 52,* 326–334.

McCracken, R., & McCracken, M. (1978). Modeling is the key to sustained silent reading. *The Reading Teacher, 31,* 406–408.

McKenzie, G. R. (1979). Data charts: A crutch for helping pupils organize reports. *Language Arts, 56,* 784–788.

Morris, D. (1982). "Word sort": A categorization strategy for improving word recognition. *Reading Psychology, 3,* 247–259.

Neeld, E. C. (1986). *Writing* (2nd ed.). Glenview, IL: Scott Foresman.

Oczkus, L. D. (2003). *Reciprocal teaching at work: Strategies for improving reading comprehension.* Newark, DE: International Reading Association.

Ogle, D. M. (1986). K-W-L: A teaching model that develops active reading of expository text. *The Reading Teacher, 39,* 564–570.

Ogle, D. M. (1989). The know, want to know, learn strategy. In K. D. Muth (Ed.), *Children's comprehension of text: Research into practice* (pp. 205–223). Newark, DE: International Reading Association.

Palinscar, A. M., & Brown, A. L. (1984). Reciprocal teaching of comprehension-fostering and comprehension-monitoring activities. *Cognition and Instruction, 1,* 117–175.

Parkes, B. (2000). *Read it again! Revisiting shared reading.* York, ME: Stenhouse.

Peterson, R., & Eeds, M. (1990). *Grand conversations: Literature groups in action.* New York: Scholastic.

Pilgreen, J. L. (2000). *The SSR handbook: How to organize and manage a sustained silent reading program.* Portsmouth, NH: Boynton/Cook/Heinemann.

Pittelman, S. D., Heimlich, J. E., Berglund, R. L., & French, M. P. (1991). *Semantic feature analysis: Classroom applications.* Newark, DE: International Reading Association.

Raphael, T., & McKinney, J. (1983). Examination of fifth- and eighth-grade children's question-answering behavior: An instructional study in metacognition. *Journal of Reading Behavior, 15,* 67–86.

Raphael, T., & Wonnacott, C. (1985). Heightening fourth grade students' sensitivity to sources of information for answering comprehension questions. *Reading Research Quarterly, 20,* 282–296.

Raphael, T. E. (1986). Teaching question-answer-relationships, revisited. *The Reading Teacher, 39,* 516–523.

Readence, J. E., Moore, D. W., & Rickelman, R. J. (2000). *Prereading activities for content area reading and writing.* Newark, DE: International Reading Association.

Samuels, S. J. (1979). The method of repeated readings. *The Reading Teacher, 32,* 403–408.

Schlagal, R. C., & Schlagal, J. H. (1992). The integral character of spelling: Teaching strategies for multiple purposes. *Language Arts, 69,* 418–424.

Stauffer, R. G. (1970). *The language experience approach to the teaching of reading.* New York: Harper & Row.

Stauffer, R. G. (1975). *Directing the reading-thinking process.* New York: Harper & Row.

Tierney, R. J., & Readence, J. E. (2000). *Reading strategies and practices: A compendium* (5th ed.). Boston: Allyn & Bacon.

Tierney, R. J., Readence, J. E., & Dishner, E. K. (1995). *Reading strategies and practices: A compendium* (4th ed.). Boston: Allyn & Bacon.

Tompkins, G. E. (2004). *Teaching writing: Balancing process and product* (4th ed.). Upper Saddle River, NJ: Merrill/Prentice Hall.

Children's Book References

Bates, K. L. (1993). *America the beautiful.* New York: Atheneum.

Brett, J. (1999). *Gingerbread baby.* New York: Putnam.

Cushman, K. (1996). *The ballad of Lucy Whipple.* New York: Clarion Books.

Ellis, D. (2000). *The breadwinner.* Toronto, Ontario: Groundwood Books.

Lewis, C. S. (1994). *The lion, the witch and the wardrobe.* New York: HarperCollins.

MacLachlan, P. (1983). *Sarah, plain and tall.* New York: Harper & Row.

Sachar, L. (1998). *Holes.* New York: Farrar, Straus & Giroux.

Van Allsburg, C. (1984). *The mysteries of Harris Burdick.* Boston: Houghton Mifflin.

Westcott, N. B. (1988). *The lady with the alligator purse.* Boston: Little, Brown.

Yep, L. (1975). *Dragonwings.* New York: HarperCollins.

Glossary

Aesthetic reading Reading for pleasure.

Affix A syllable added to the beginning (prefix) or end (suffix) of a word to change the word's meaning (e.g., *il-* in *illiterate* and *-al* in *national*).

Alphabetic principle The assumption underlying alphabetical language systems that each sound has a corresponding graphic representation (or letter).

Antonyms Words with opposite meanings (e.g., *good–bad*).

Applying The fifth stage of the reading process, in which readers go beyond the text to use what they have learned in another literacy experience, often by making a project or reading another book.

Background knowledge A student's knowledge or previous experiences about a topic.

Basal readers Reading textbooks that are leveled according to grade.

Basal reading program A collection of student textbooks, workbooks, teacher's manuals, and other materials and resources for reading instruction used in kindergarten through sixth grade.

Big books Enlarged versions of picture books that teachers read with children, usually in the primary grades.

Blend To combine the sounds represented by letters to pronounce a word.

Bound morpheme A morpheme that is not a word and cannot stand alone (e.g., *-s, tri-*).

Closed syllable A syllable ending in a consonant sound (e.g., *make, duck*).

Cluster A spiderlike diagram used to collect and organize ideas after reading or before writing; also called a map or a web.

Comprehension The process of constructing meaning using both the author's text and the reader's background knowledge for a specific purpose.

Concepts about print Basic understandings about the way print works, including the direction of print, spacing, punctuation, letters, and words.

Consonant A speech sound characterized by friction or stoppage of the airflow as it passes through the vocal tract; usually any letter except *a, e, i, o,* and *u*.

Consonant digraph Two adjacent consonants that represent a sound not represented by either consonant alone (e.g., *th–this, ch–chin, sh–wash, ph–telephone*).

Content-area reading Reading in social studies, science, and other areas of the curriculum.

Context clue Information from the words or sentences surrounding a word that helps to clarify the word's meaning.

Cueing systems The phonological, semantic, syntactic, and pragmatic information that students rely on as they read.

Decoding Using word-identification strategies to pronounce and attach meaning to an unfamiliar word.

Diphthong A sound produced when the tongue glides from one sound to another; it is represented by two vowels (e.g., *oy–boy, ou–house, ow–how*).

Drafting The second stage of the writing process, in which writers pour out ideas in a rough draft.

Echo reading The teacher or other reader reads a sentence and a group of students reread or "echo" what was read.

Editing The fourth stage of the writing process, in which writers proofread to identify and correct spelling, capitalization, punctuation, and grammatical errors.

Efferent reading Reading for information.

Elkonin boxes A strategy for segmenting sounds in a word that involves drawing a box to represent each sound in a word.

Emergent literacy Children's early reading and writing development before conventional reading and writing.

Environmental print Signs, labels, and other print found in the community.

Etymology The origin and history of words; the etymological information is enclosed in brackets in dictionary entries.

Explicit instruction Systematic instruction of concepts, strategies, and skills that builds from simple to complex.

Exploring The fourth stage of the reading process, in which readers reread the text, study vocabulary words, and learn strategies and skills.

Expository text Nonfiction.

Fluency Reading smoothly, quickly, and with expression.

Free morpheme A morpheme that can stand alone as a word (e.g., *book, cycle*).

Frustration level The level of reading material that is too difficult for a student to read successfully.

Genre A category of literature such as folklore, science fiction, biography, or historical fiction.

Goldilocks principle A strategy for choosing "just right" books.

Grand conversation A small-group or whole-class discussion about literature.

Grapheme A written representation of a sound using one or more letters.

Graphic organizers Diagrams that provide organized visual representations of information from texts.

Graphophonemic Referring to sound-symbol relationships.

Guided reading Students work in small groups to read as independently as possible a text selected and introduced by the teacher.

High-frequency word A common English word, usually a word among the 100 or 300 most common words.

Homographic homophones Words that sound alike and are spelled alike but have different meanings (e.g., baseball *bat* and the animal *bat*).

Homographs Words that are spelled alike but are pronounced differently (e.g., a *present* and to *present*).

Homonyms Words that sound alike but are spelled differently (e.g., *sea–see, there–their–they're*); also called homophones.

Hyperbole A stylistic device involving obvious exaggerations.

Imagery The use of words and figurative language to create an impression.

Independent reading level The level of reading material that a student can read independently with high comprehension and an accuracy level of 95–100%.

Inferential comprehension Using background knowledge and determining relationships between objects and events in a text to draw conclusions not explicitly stated in the text.

Inflectional endings Suffixes that express plurality or possession when added to a noun (e.g., *girls, girl's*), tense when added to a verb (e.g., *walked, walking*), or comparison when added to an adjective (e.g., *happier, happiest*).

Informal Reading Inventory (IRI) An individually administered reading test composed of word lists and graded passages that are used to determine students' independent, instructional, and frustration levels and listening capacity levels.

Instructional reading level The level of reading material that a student can read with teacher support and instruction with 90–94% accuracy.

Interactive writing A writing activity in which students and the teacher write a text together, with the students taking turns to do most of the writing themselves.

Invented spelling Students' attempts to spell words that reflect their developing knowledge about the spelling system.

K-W-L An activity to activate background knowledge and set purposes for reading an informational text and to bring closure after reading. The letters stand for What I (We) Know, What I (We) Wonder, and What I (We) Learned.

Language Experience Approach (LEA) A student's oral composition is written by the teacher and used as a text for reading instruction; it is usually used with beginning readers.

Leveling books A method of estimating the difficulty level of a text.

Lexile scores A method of estimating the difficulty level of a text.

Listening capacity level The highest level of graded passage that can be comprehended well when read aloud to the student.

Literacy The ability to read and write.

Literal comprehension The understanding of what is explicitly stated in a text.

Literature circle An instructional approach in which students meet in small groups to read and respond to a book.

Literature focus unit An approach to reading instruction in which the whole class reads and responds to a piece of literature.

Long vowels The vowel sounds that are also names of the alphabet letters: /ā/ as in *make*, /ē/ as in *feet*, /ī/ as in *ice*, /ō/ as in *coat*, and /ū/ as in *mule*.

Lowercase letters The letters that are smaller and usually different from uppercase letters.

Metacognition Students' thinking about their own thought and learning processes.

Metaphor A comparison expressed directly, without using *like* or *as*.

Minilesson Explicit instruction about literacy procedures, concepts, strategies, and skills that are taught to individual students, small groups, or the whole class, depending on students' needs.

Miscue analysis A strategy for categorizing and analyzing a student's oral reading errors.

Mood   The tone of a story or poem.

Morpheme   The smallest meaningful part of a word; sometimes it is a word (e.g., *cup, hope*), and sometimes it is not a whole word (e.g., *-ly, bi-*).

Narrative   A story.

Onset   The part of a syllable (or one-syllable word) that comes before the vowel (e.g., *str* in *string*).

Open syllable   A syllable ending in a vowel sound (e.g., *sea*).

Orthography   The spelling system.

Personification   Figurative language in which objects and animals are represented as having human qualities.

Phoneme   A sound; it is represented in print with slashes (e.g., /s/ and /th/).

Phoneme-grapheme correspondence   The relationship between a sound and the letter that represents it.

Phonemic awareness   The ability to manipulate the sounds in words orally.

Phonics   Predictable relationships between phonemes and graphemes.

Phonics instruction   Teaching the relationships between letters and sounds and how to use them to read and spell words.

Phonological awareness   The ability to identify and manipulate phonemes, onsets and rimes, and syllables; it includes phonemic awareness.

Phonology   The sound system of language.

Polysyllabic   Containing more than one syllable.

Pragmatics   The social use system of language.

Prediction   A strategy in which students predict what will happen in a story and then read to verify their guesses.

Prefix   A syllable added to the beginning of a word to change the word's meaning (e.g., *re-* in *reread*).

Prereading   The first stage of the reading process, in which readers activate background knowledge, set purposes, and make plans for reading.

Prewriting   The first stage of the writing process, in which writers gather and organize ideas for writing.

Proofreading   Reading a composition to identify and correct spelling and other mechanical errors.

Publishing   The fifth stage of the writing process, in which writers make the final copy of their writing and share it with an audience.

Quickwrite   An activity in which students explore a topic through writing.

Readability formula   A method of estimating the difficulty level of a text.

Reading   The second stage of the reading process, in which readers read the text for the first time using independent reading, shared reading, or guided reading, or by listening to it read aloud.

Reading workshop   An approach in which students read self-selected texts independently.

Responding   The third stage of the reading process, in which readers respond to the text, often through grand conversations and by writing in reading logs.

Revising   The third stage of the writing process, in which writers clarify meaning in the writing.

Rhyming   Words with the same rime sound (e.g., *white, bright*).

Rime   The part of a syllable (or one-syllable word) that begins with the vowel (e.g., *ing* in *string*).

Scaffolding   The support a teacher provides to students as they read and write.

Segment   To pronounce a word slowly, saying each sound distinctly.

Semantics   The meaning system of language.

Shared reading   The teacher reads a book aloud with a group of children as they follow along in the text, often using a big book.

Short vowels   The vowel sounds represented by /ă/ as in *cat*, /ĕ/ as in *bed*, /ĭ/ as in *big*, /ŏ/ as in *hop*, and /ŭ/ as in *cut*.

Simile   A comparison expressed using *like* or *as*.

Skill   An automatic processing behavior that students use in reading and writing, such as sounding out words, recognizing antonyms, and capitalizing proper nouns.

Strategy   A problem-solving behavior that students use in reading and writing, such as predicting, monitoring, visualizing, and summarizing.

Suffix   A syllable added to the end of a word to change the word's meaning (e.g., *-y* in *hairy*, *-ful* in *careful*).

Sustained Silent Reading (SSR)   Independent reading practice in which everyone in the class or in the school stops what they are doing and spends time (20–30 minutes) reading a self-selected book.

Syllable   An uninterrupted segment of speech that includes a vowel sound (e.g., *get, a-bout, but-ter-fly, con-sti-tu-tion*).

Symbol   The author's use of an object to represent something else.

Synonyms   Words that mean nearly the same thing (e.g., *road–street*).

Syntax   The structural system of language or grammar.

Trade book   A published book that is not a textbook; the type of books in bookstores and libraries.

Uppercase letters   The letters that are larger and are used as first letters in a name or at the beginning of a sentence; also called "capital letters."

Vowel A voiced speech sound made without friction or stoppage of the airflow as it passes through the vocal tract; the letters *a, e, i, o, u,* and sometimes *w* and *y.*

Vowel digraph Two or more adjacent vowels in a syllable that represent a single sound (e.g., *bread, eight, pain, saw*).

Word families Groups of words that rhyme (e.g., *ball, call, fall, hall, mall, tall,* and *wall*).

Word identification Strategies that students use to decode words, such as phonic analysis, analogies, syllabic analysis, and morphemic analysis.

Word sort A word-study activity in which students group words into categories.

Word wall An alphabetized chart posted in the classroom listing words students are learning.

Writing process The process in which students use prewriting, drafting, revising, editing, and publishing to develop and refine a composition.

Writing workshop An approach in which students use the writing process to write books and other compositions on self-selected topics.

Zone of proximal development The distance between a child's actual developmental level and his or her potential developmental level that can be reached with scaffolding by the teacher or classmates.

Author and Title Index

Hirschi, R., 461
His Majesty, Queen Hatshepsut, 462
Hiscock, B., 458
Hitchcock, M. E., 156
Hoang Anh: A Vietnamese-American Boy, 277
Hoban, T., 273
Hobbit, The, 310
Hoberman, M. A., 119, 278
Hodges, R. E., 11
Hoffman, J. V., 24, 337–338
Hoffman, M., 363
Hog-Eye, 264, 365
Holdaway, D., 53, 84, 96, 499
Holes, 179, 262, 264, 308, 390–391, 504, 505
Holling, H. C., 150
Holloway, J. H., 37
Homeless Bird, 15, 179, 366
Honan, L., 462
Honoring Children's Rights to Excellent Reading Instruction, 11
Hooks, W. H., 258, 356, 357
Hop on Pop, 99, 119, 120
Hopkins, L. B., 278
Hopkinson, D., 220
Horn, E., 126, 141
Horns, Antlers, Fangs, and Tusks, 276
Hornsby, D., 51, 406
Horrible Harry books, 178
Horvatic, A., 277
Hour of the Olympics, 386
House for a Hermit Crab, A, 99, 150–154, 156
House on Mango Street, The, 363
How Come? Planet Earth, 277
How Do Apples Grow?, 276
How Sweet It Is (and Was): The History of Candy, 275
How to Eat Fried Worms, 380–384
How to Talk to Your Dog, 277
How We Crossed the West: The Adventures of Lewis and Clark, 277
How We Learned the Earth Is Round, 277
Howe, D., 10, 212, 257, 264, 272, 307, 308, 310, 318, 373, 380, 412
Howe, J., 10, 178, 212, 257, 264, 272, 307, 308, 310, 318, 373, 380, 412, 420
Hoyt-Goldsmith, D., 277
Huck, C., 384
Hundred Penny Box, The, 307, 308, 363
Hungry, Hungry Sharks, 334, 336
Hungry Thing, The, 119
Hunt, J., 273

Hunt, L., 415, 502
Hutchins, P., 100, 119, 121, 256, 308, 365, 372
Hutton, W., 258
Hyman, T. S., 256

I Am Phoenix: Poems for Two Voices, 282, 441
I Am the Dog, I Am the Cat, 70
"I Can't," Said the Ant, 119
I Know an Old Lady Who Swallowed a Fly, 119
I Spy, 113
I Want to Be, 70
I Went Walking, 308
If the Dinosaurs Came Back, 106, 365
If You Give a Mouse a Cookie, 99, 105, 106, 365
If You Give an Author a Pencil, 377
If You Made a Million, 273
If You Traveled on the Underground Railroad, 229
...If You Traveled West in a Covered Wagon, 276
If You Were There When They Signed the Constitution, 245
Iktomi and the Boulder, 258, 261
Illuminations, 273
I'm in Charge of Celebrations, 70
In a Pickle and Other Funny Idioms, 186, 206
In Search of Tutankhamun, 277, 462
In the Desert, 100
Inside-Outside Book of Washington, D.C., The, 277
Inside the Titanic, 187
Invernizzi, M., 87, 135, 136, 142, 212, 316, 503
Ira Sleeps Over, 226, 264
Irwin, J. W., 223
Is Your Mama a Llama?, 99
It Could Still Be a Desert, 461
It's Christmas, 278
It's Raining Pigs and Noodles, 278
Iversen, S., 52, 345, 479, 499
Iverson, D., 458
Ivey, G., 25, 130, 237

Jabberwocky, 278
Jack and the Beanstalk, 257
Jack's Garden, 99
Jacobs, V. A., 173
Jaffe, N., 258
Jake Baked the Cake, 99
Jamberry, 119
James and the Giant Peach, 10

Janeczko, P. B., 186, 278
Jazz Fly, The, 119
Jepsen, M., 408
Jeremy Thatcher, Dragon Hatcher, 261
Jigsaw Jones Mysteries, 178
Jiménez, F., 216–217, 220, 363
Jin Woo, 363
Jipson, J., 361
Joey Pigza Loses Control, 218, 221, 231, 241, 243, 260, 264
Johnny Appleseed, 258
Johns, J. L., 446
Johnson, D., 226
Johnson, D. D., 173
Johnson, M. J., 28, 102, 481
Johnson, N. J., 396
Johnson, R. L., 298, 326
Johnson, T., 100
Johnson, T. D., 146, 265
Johnston, F., 135, 136, 142, 212, 316, 503
Johnston, P., 238
Jolliffe, D. A., 238, 239, 240
Jones, C., 257
Jones, H., 278, 363
Jones, L. A., 243
Jones, M. T., 178
Josefina Story Quilt, The, 242, 310
Jouanah: A Hmong Cinderella, 258
Journal of Ben Uchida, The: Citizen 13559, Mirror Lake Internment Camp, 363, 435
Journal of Patrick Seamus Flaherty, The: United States Marine Corps, 435
Journal of William Thomas Emerson, The: A Revolutionary War Patriot, 435
Journey of English, The, 186
Journey of Oliver K. Woodman, The, 70
Journey to the New World, A: The Diary of Remember Patience Whipple, 434
Journey to Topaz, 362, 363, 366
Joyful Noise: Poems for Two Voices, 278, 282, 441
Juel, C., 89, 124, 164, 345
Julie of the Wolves, 262, 267, 366
Jumanji, 4, 5, 6, 56, 267, 285
Junebug, 363
Junie B. Jones and Her Big Fat Mouth, 113
Junie B. Jones and the Stupid Smelly Bus, 177, 308
Junie B. Jones books, 113, 178
Just a Dream, 5, 9

Kalan, K., 99
Kalman, B., 186

Kame'enui, E., 194, 298
Kapinus, B., 447
Kaplan, R., 150, 153
Karnowski, L., 257
Karr, K., 10
Kasza, K., 259
Katan, N. J., 462
Kawakami-Arakaki, A., 92
Kear, D. J., 317
Keene, E. O., 240
Kellogg, S., 258, 261, 357, 365
Kelly, P. R., 411
Kennedy, D. M., 278
Kennedy, X. J., 278, 279
Kentley, E., 187
Kidder, E. B., 146
Kids in Ms. Colman's Class
    books, The, 178
Kiefer, B. Z., 456
Kimmell, E. A., 99
King, M., 66
King-Smith, D., 272
King Who Rained, The, 186, 202
Kintsch, W., 255
Kitchener, R. F., 12
Klesius, J. P., 124
Kline, S., 178
Knights, 273
Knights of the Kitchen Table, 259
Knock at a Star: A Child's Introduction
    to Poetry, 278
Knots on a Counting Rope, 363
Koch, K., 284, 286
Kohn, A., 236
Koskinen, P. S., 175
Krashen, S., 415, 502
Kraus, B., 99
Kraus, R., 308
Kremer, K. E., 223
Kruse, A. E., 301, 303
Kuhs, T. M., 298, 326
Kuskin, K., 119, 278

La Mariposa, 216–217, 220
Laase, L., 320, 323, 324
LaBerge, D., 94, 156, 174
Lady with the Alligator Purse, The, 99,
    119, 278, 471
Laird, D., 357
L'Allier, S., 37
Lamb, H., 66
Lane, B., 420
Langer, J. A., 61, 64, 447
Langford, K. G., 146
Lansky, B., 278
Lapp, D., 162, 255

Larrick, N., 276–277
Lasker, J., 277
Lasky, K., 434
Lattimore, D. N., 462
Lauber, P., 277
Lawson, L. L., 130
Lear, E., 278, 279
Lee, D. M., 484
Lee, J. J., 195
Leedy, L., 70
Legend of the Bluebonnet, The,
    258, 363
Lehr, F., 116
Lehr, S. S., 269
L'Engle, M., 267
Leslie, L., 311
Lest We Forget: The Passage from Africa
    to Slavery and Emancipation, 277
Lester, H., 266, 365, 373
Lester, J., 443
Levine, E., 229, 276
Levine, G. C., 258
Levstik, L. S., 456
Levy, E., 245
Lewis, C. S., 259, 261, 264, 308,
    310, 475
Lewis, J., 186
Lewison, M., 15–16
Lewkowicz, N. K., 119
Lin, G., 363
Lincoln: A Photobiography, 272
Lindbergh, R., 99
Lindfors, J. W., 19
Lion, the Witch and the Wardrobe, The,
    259, 261, 264, 308, 310, 366,
    475, 476
Lion and the Rat, The, 257
Lionni, L., 259
Listen to the Desert/Oye al Desierto, 100
Listening Walk, The, 119
Little House in the Big Woods, 10
Little Pigeon Toad, A, 186, 202
Little Red Hen (Galdone), 99
"Little Red Hen, The," 52
Little Red Hen, The (Zemach), 269
Little Women, 310
Livingston, M. C., 278
The Llama Who Had No Pajama: 100
    Favorite Poems, 278
Lobel, A., 279
Locker, T., 70
Locomotion, 363
Logan, J. W., 195
Log's Life, A, 458
Lomax, R. G., 124
Longfellow, H. W., 277, 279

Looking for Your Name: A Collection of
    Contemporary Poems, 278
Lopez-Robertson, J. M., 394
Loser, 179, 260
Lotus Seed, The, 220
Louie, A. L., 220, 258
Louis, D. R., 265
Lowell, S., 356, 357
Lowry, L., 42–46, 208, 257, 260, 261,
    264, 267, 268, 269, 282, 308, 310,
    365, 366, 373, 376, 441
Luke, A., 15
Lukens, R. J., 260, 262, 267, 268,
    269, 270
Lundberg, I., 303

Macaulay, D., 275, 310, 366, 462
Macedo, D., 15
Mack, S., 99
MacLachlan, P., 14, 175–176, 261,
    264, 272, 282, 307, 365, 373, 489
Macon, J. M., 474
Mad as a Wet Hen! And Other Funny
    Idioms, 186
Maestro, B., 276
Maestro, G., 202
Magic School Bus and the Electric Field
    Trip, The, 193–194
Magic School Bus books, 178,
    273–274, 386, 443
Magic School Bus Inside a Beehive, The,
    274, 437
Magic School Bus Lost in the Solar
    System, The, 297
Magic School Bus on the Ocean Floor,
    The, 310, 386, 442–443
Magic Tree House books, 113, 178,
    226, 386
Make Way for Ducklings, 78–79, 267
Making a Difference in the World, 420
Mammano, J., 186
Man and Mustang, 276
Mannis, J., 437
Markle, S., 277
Marriott, D., 394
Marshall, E. & J., 178
Marshall, J., 178, 354–355, 357,
    359, 365
Martin, A., 178, 363, 365
Martin, B., 363, 365
Martin, B., Jr., 56, 99, 106, 119, 208,
    245, 267, 365
Martin, N., 60
Martin, R., 258
Martinez, M., 177, 494
Martinez-Roldan, C. M., 394

Subject Index

assessment tools for, 309–311
background knowledge and, 225–226
in balanced literacy programs, 26, 224, 256
capable *vs.* less capable students, 238–240
content-area textbooks and, 445, 446–447
fluency and, 227
inferences and, 232–234
informational books and, 270–276
motivation and attention, 234–238
overview of factors, 225
poetry and, 276–286
purpose of, 227
reader factors, 216–248
routines for, 243
stories and, 255–270
teaching, 240–246
text factors, 225, 250–290
vignettes, 216–222, 250–254
young children and, 85
Comprehension center, 335
Comprehension factors, 225
Comprehension instruction, 240–246
comprehension through reading, 243–245
comprehension through writing, 245–246
connections between reading and writing, 246
explicit, 241–243
guidelines for strategy instruction, 243
instructional procedures, 244
teaching routines, 243
teaching strategies, 216–222, 241–243
Comprehension routines, 243
Comprehension strategies, 228–232
books for teaching, 220
as comprehension factor, 225
connecting strategy, 228–229
connections between reading and writing, 246
evaluating strategy, 232
explicit instruction, 241–243
guidelines for teaching, 243
identifying big ideas strategy, 231
minilessons on, 241, 242
monitoring strategy, 232
overview, 229
predicting strategy, 228
questioning strategy, 230–231
summarizing strategy, 231

teaching, 216–222, 241–243
visualizing, 230
Computer center, 113, 335, 350
Computer literacy, 11
Computers
drafting and, 63
in vignette, 80
Concept knowledge, and struggling readers, 208
Concepts
alphabet concepts, 88–89
key concepts, 447
phonics concepts, 125–130
print concepts, 86, 300–301, 302
word concepts, 87–88
Concepts About Print Test (CAP Test), 300–301, 302
Conditional knowledge, 241
Conferences
book discussion conferences, 319
editing conferences, 67, 319
minilesson conferences, 319
for monitoring student progress, 319
on-the-spot, 319
for portfolios, 319, 321, 324
for prereading or prewriting, 319
for reading and writing workshop, 402–404
revising conferences, 319
writing conferences, 419
Conflict in plot, 262–264
Connecting strategy, 218, 228–229, 244
Connections
instruction and assessment, 31–34
reading and writing, 71–73, 246, 431–444
text-to-self, 228–229
text-to-text, 228–229
text-to-world, 228–229
Connections chart, 219
Connector role, 390
Consonant blends, 126, 133
Consonant digraphs, 126
Consonants, 126
Constructivism, 12, 13
Constructivist learning theory, 406
Containers, letter, 90
Contemporary stories, 260, 261
Content
of leveled books, 307
vocabulary and, 225, 246
Content-area instruction, 426–465
in balanced literacy programs, 26, 432
connecting reading and writing, 431–444
multigenre projects, 426–430

thematic units, 453–463
vignette, 426–430
writing as learning tool, 431–436
writing to demonstrate learning, 436–444
young children and, 85
Content-area textbooks, 431, 444–453
comprehension and, 445, 446–447
applying, 445, 451
exploring, 445, 448, 450
prereading, 445, 446–447
reading, 445, 447
responding, 445, 448
guidelines for using, 444
learning how to study, 451–452
question-answer-relationships (QARs), 452
SQ3R study strategy, 452
taking notes, 451–452
need to supplement, 452–453
purpose and, 447
struggling readers and, 446
unique conventions of, 444–446
Content-area word walls, 504
Context clues, 193–194
Continuum of literacy instruction, 27
Contractions, 151, 152–153
Contrast, as context clue, 193
Conventional spelling, 102
Conversations. *See* Grand conversations; Instructional conversations
Copying from chalkboard, 180–181
Core books, 360
Correcting errors, 66–67
Correction tape, 102
Counting books, 273
Critical literacy, 13, 15–16, 359, 385
Critical pedagogy, 15
Critical Reading Inventory, 311
Cross-checking strategy, 93
Cubing, 471–472
in applying stage, 451
for multigenre projects, 443
purpose setting and, 49
Cueing systems, 16–20, 132
English learners and, 18
miscue analysis and, 304–305
phonological, 16–18
pragmatic, 20
relationships among, 17
semantic, 19–20
syntactic, 18–19
Cultural consciousness, 362
Cultural literacy, 11
Cumulative reading, 470
Cumulative stories, 99, 257

nonfiction genres and, 273–274
in vignette, 9
Fantastic stories, 261
Fiction. *See also* Stories
historical, 365, 366
novels, 256–257
realistic, 259–260
science fiction, 259, 261, 366
Figurative meanings of words, 205–208
First-person viewpoint, 268–269
Five-senses poems, 286
Flip charts, 483, 484
Fluency, 154–156, 173–181. *See also*
Reading fluency; Writing fluency
assessing, 181, 295
assessment tools for, 302–305
in balanced literacy programs, 155
capable *vs.* less capable students
and, 239
comprehension and, 225, 227, 246
explicit instruction and, 173
high-frequency words and, 305
sentence fluency, 69, 70
Fluent literacy, 91
Fluent reading and writing stage,
89–90, 94–96
instructional practices for, 97
Flynt-Cooter Reading Inventory for the
Classroom, 311
Focus Wall, 111, 112
Folk literature, 257
Folklore, 257–258, 261
Folktales, 257, 261, 365
Form, for prewriting, 60–61
Found poems, 283, 441–442, 443
Fourth-grade slump, 173
Frames, letter, 90
Franklin, Benjamin, 435–436
Free morphemes, 168
Free verse, 281–283
French loan words, 203
Frustration reading level, 304
Fry Readability Graph, 306, 307
Fry's New Instant Word Lists, 305
Full word knowledge, 191

Games center, 83
Gender bias, 361
Genres, 225, 246
literature focus units on, 376
multigenre projects, 426–430,
442–444
narrative genres, 257–260
nonfiction genres, 273–274
writing genres, 61, 62
GIST procedure, 231, 476

Goldilocks Strategy, 408, 409, 502
Grades, 324–326
unit assignment sheets, 325–326
Gradual release, 241
Grammar, 15, 18
as context clue, 193
Grammar center, 335
Grand conversations, 245, 477
English learners, 369
in literature circles, 395
in responding stage, 55–56
in vignettes, 9, 78, 82, 84,
219–220, 221
Graphemes, 16, 115, 116
Graphic organizer center, 65
Graphic organizers, 61, 231,
274–275, 478
Graphophonemic relationships, 115
Greek affixes, 170, 171
Greek root words, 168, 169, 205
Guided reading, 28–29, 479
applying stage and, 348, 349
basal reading programs and,
345–348
beginning reading and, 94
comparison of reading types, 54
in continuum of literacy
instruction, 27
exploring stage and, 347–348, 349
groups for, 113
prereading and, 346, 349
reading process and, 346–348
reading stage and, 52–53,
346–347, 349
responding stage and, 347, 349
steps in, 349
struggling readers and, 241
Guided writing, 27, 28–29

Haiku, 279–281
Handwriting, manuscript, 103–104
Hermit crabs, 150–154, 180
High fantasy, 259, 261
High-frequency word walls, 139, 141,
151–152, 158–161, 175, 504
High-frequency words, 139, 141
assessment with, 295, 305
choral reading and, 154
English learners and, 161
fluency and, 305
lists of, 141, 157, 160
minilesson on, 162, 163
struggling readers and, 158
in vignette, 150–154
word recognition, 156–158
High-level word knowledge, 196

Highlighting center, 65
Historical fiction, 365, 366
Historical journals, 434–435
Historical stories, 260, 261
History of English language, 203–205
Homographs, 188
Homonyms, 65, 188, 202–203, 204
Homophone posters, 203, 204
Homophones, 188, 202–203, 204
Homophones center, 65
Houghton Mifflin Reading, 111
Housekeeping center, 88
Hyperbole, 270, 272

"I Am. . ." poems, 439–440, 443
"I Wish. . ." poems, 284
Ideas
assessing fluency and, 181
gathering and organizing, 61
identifying big ideas, 229, 231, 244,
245, 447
as quality of good writing, 69, 70
Identifying big ideas, 229, 231, 244,
245, 447
Idiom posters, 206, 207
Idioms, 205–208
"If I Were. . ." poems, 286
Illustrations
as context clue, 193
in leveled books, 307
Illustrators
literature circles and, 390
literature focus units and, 376–378
Imagery, 270, 272
Immigration, 198
Important sentences, 57
Incentives, 236
Incidental word learning, 192–193
Independent reading, 29–30
basal reading programs and, 342
comparison of reading types, 54
in continuum of literacy
instruction, 27
in reading stage, 51
vocabulary growth and, 192
Independent reading level, 304
Independent writing, 10, 27, 29–30
Individual reports, 438
Inference charts, 233, 234, 235
Inferences
comprehension and, 225,
232–234, 246
in vignette, 8, 9
Inflectional suffices, 168, 170
Informal reading inventories (IRIs),
310–311

basal reading program and, 110–115
concepts, 125–130
   blending into words, 127
   consonants, 126
   phonics generalizations, 128–130
   rimes and rhymes, 127–128
   vowels, 126–127
as controversial topic, 132, 134
dictation and, 297
guidelines for teaching, 132
interactive writing and, 132
minilesson on, 130, 132
sequence of instruction, 131
teaching, 130–132
   direct instruction, 130, 132
   teachable moments, 132
young children and, 85
Phonics center, 113, 350
Phonics generalizations, 128–130
Phonological cueing system, 16–18
Phonology, 124
Photos, for multigenre projects, 443
Phrasing, 181
Picture books, 178, 277–278. *See also*
   Big books
   literature focus units on, 372–373
   wordless, 256
Planning
   for basal reading programs, 342
   for literature focus units, 369–370
   for prereading, 50, 490
   for reading, 50
Play centers, 88
Plot, 260–266, 388
Plot development, 263–265, 411
Plot diagrams, 263, 265
Plot profiles, 265–266
Pocket charts center, 83, 350
Poems for two voices, 282–283,
   440–441
Poetry, 61, 276–286
   acrostic poems, 285, 443
   color poems, 46, 284–285
   comprehension and, 276–286
   five-senses poems, 285
   found poems, 283, 441–442, 443
   free verse, 281–283
   haiku and related forms, 279–281
   "I Am. . ." poems, 439–440, 443
   "I Wish. . ." poems, 284
   "If I Were. . ." poems, 286
   in literature focus units, 365, 366
   narrative poems, 279
   poems for two voices, 282–283,
      440–441
   poetic forms, 278–286

preposition poems, 286
rhymed verse, 279
types of poetry books, 276–278
writing to demonstrate learning,
   438–442
Poetry center, 350
Poetry collections, 278
Poetry unit, 280
Poetry writing, 62, 438–442
Point of view, 264, 268–269, 388
Pop literature, 176
Portfolios, 319–324
   benefits of, 320
   collecting work in, 320–323
   review conferences, 324
   showcasing, 324
   student self-assessment, 323–324
Possible sentences, 447
Postcards, for multigenre projects, 443
Posters
   homophone posters, 203, 204
   idiom posters, 206, 207
   letter posters, 90
   monitoring poster, 216, 217
   word posters, 211
   writing to demonstrate learning,
      437, 438
Pragmatic cueing system, 17, 20
Preassessing, 32
Predictability, of basal readers, 338
Predictable books, 98–100
Predicting strategy, 216–221, 228,
   229, 244
Prediction journals, 474
Prefixes, 19, 168, 170, 200
Preposition poems, 286
Prereading center, 335
Prereading stage, 48–50
   activating background knowledge,
      48–49
   comprehension and, 445, 446–447
   conferences for, 319
   content-area textbooks and, 446–447
   guided reading and, 346, 349
   K-W-L charts and, 446
   learning logs and, 50
   literature circles and, 394
   planning for reading, 50, 490
   prewriting and, 72
   reading process and, 98
   setting purposes, 49–50
Previewing, 50
Prewriting, 7, 58–61
   audience, 60
   choosing a topic, 59
   conferences for, 319

form for, 60–61
gathering and organizing ideas, 61
prereading and, 72
purpose for, 60
Print, environmental, 87, 90
Print concepts, 86, 300–301, 302
Printing press, 203
Problem and solution, 274, 275,
   276, 277
Procedural knowledge, 241
Projects, 230
   applying stage and, 57, 58–59
   drama projects, 59
   literature circles and, 394
   multigenre, 426–430, 442–444
   for thematic units, 456
Proofreading, 66, 142–143
Proofreading center, 350
Prosody, 174, 175–176, 181
Publishing, 7, 60, 67–69, 429–430
   applying stage and, 72
   making books, 67–68
   sharing writing, 68–69
Punctuation, 65
Punctuation center, 65
Puppets center, 350
Purpose
   capable *vs.* less capable readers, 239
   as comprehension factor, 225,
      227, 246
   for reading content-area textbooks, 447
   of writing, 60
Purpose setting, in prereading, 49–50

Qualitative Inventory of Spelling
   Development, 316
Qualitative Reading Inventory, 3, 311
Question-and-answer books, 276
Question-answer-relationships (QARs),
   231, 452, 490–491
Questioning strategy, 229, 230–231,
   242, 244
Questions-answers, for multigenre
   projects, 443
Quickwriting, 50, 180, 436, 491–493
Quilts, 45, 56, 189, 493
Quotes, for multigenre projects, 443

Racial bias, 361
Rain forest, 332–336
Read-arounds, 45, 177, 493–494
Readability formulas, 306–307
Reader factors, of comprehension,
   216–248
Reader response theory, 13, 14–15, 55,
   359, 385, 406

Reader Self-Perception Scale, 317
Readers, capable and less capable, 238–249
Readers theatre, 28, 177, 494
Readiness activities, 84
Reading, 50–54. *See also* Basal reading programs; Guided reading; Independent reading; Literacy; Prereading stage; Shared reading
aesthetic, 14–15, 49, 272
assisted, 177
in balanced literacy programs, 26, 47
balanced reading movement, 337
beginning reading, 89, 93–94, 97
buddy reading, 51, 54, 393
choral, 469–470
in classroom center, 350
comparison of five types of, 54
competence in, 237
comprehension development with, 243–245
connecting reading and writing, 71–73
constructing meaning with, 11, 46–47
cumulative, 470
developmental stages of, 91
drafting and, 72
echo reading, 176, 469
efferent, 14–15, 49, 270–271
fluent reading and writing stage, 89–90, 94–96, 97
instructional practices for stages of, 97
interactive, 27, 28, 94
involvement in, 234–238
as key feature in reading process, 48
letter knowledge and, 89
modeled, 26–27, 92
phonemic awareness and, 124
as predictor of vocabulary growth, 192
principles of reading programs, 11–16
round-robin, 53–54, 179
unison reading, 176
young children and, 85
Reading aloud, 82, 192–193
literature focus units and, 52, 53–54
reading workshop and, 413–414
to struggling readers, 373
Reading center, 335
Reading development, 89–96
fourth-grade slump, 173
Matthew effect and, 192
stages of, 91
Reading fluency, 175–179. *See also* Fluency
assessing, 181
developing reading stamina, 177, 179

enhancing word recognition, 175
improving reading speed, 175
reading practice, 176–177
round-robin reading, 179
teaching prosody, 175–176
Reading instruction, in continuum of literacy instruction, 27
Reading Is Fundamental (RIF), 37–38
Reading logs, 494–495
English learners and, 55
responding stage and, 55, 411–413
shared reading and, 100
writing centers and, 105
Reading practice, 176–177
Reading process, 46–57
applying stage, 57
in balanced literacy programs, 47
exploring stage, 56–57
examining the author's craft, 56
focusing on words and sentences, 57
rereading the selection, 56
teaching minilessons, 57
key features of, 48
literature circles and, 394
prereading stage, 48–50
activating background knowledge, 48–49
planning for reading, 50
setting purposes, 49–50
reading stage, 50–54
buddy reading, 51
guided reading, 52–53
independent reading, 51
reading aloud to students, 53–54
shared reading, 53
reading workshop and, 415
responding stage, 55–56
participating in discussions, 55–56
writing in reading logs, 55
shared reading and, 53, 98
vignette, 42–46
Reading projects, 59
Reading rate, 94
Reading Recovery, 307, 345
Reading speed, 173–174, 175, 181
Reading stage, 50–54
buddy reading, 51
guided reading and, 52–53, 346–347, 349
independent reading, 51
literature circles and, 394
reading aloud to students, 53–54
shared reading, 53
Reading stamina, 177, 179
Reading the room center, 83

Reading workshop, 30–31, 33, 177, 237, 406–416
applications, 417
in balanced literacy approach, 408
components of, 417
independent reading in, 51
managing a workshop classroom, 422–424
minilessons for, 413, 414
overview of, 417
purpose of, 417
purpose setting in, 49
reading aloud to students, 413–414
reading component, 406–410
reading process and, 415
responding component, 410–413
schedules for, 407
sharing in, 413
strengths and limitations, 417
Sustained Silent Reading *vs.*, 414–416
theory base, 417
vignette, 81–82
vocabulary growth and, 192
Realistic fiction, 259–260, 261, 365
Reciprocal teaching, 243, 495–496
Rehearsal activities, 61
Repeated readings, 175, 496
Repetend, 442
Repetition
in leveled books, 307
in vocabulary instruction, 196
Repetitive sentences, 99
Reports, 436–437
individual, 438
Rereading, 56
rough drafts, 63–64
Rereading center, 65
Research center, 83
Research projects, 59
Responding
comprehension and, 445, 448
content-area textbooks and, 448
reading workshop component, 410–413
Responding stage, 48, 55–56, 229
grand conversations in, 55–56
guided reading and, 347, 349
instructional conversations in, 55–56, 448
literature circles and, 394
participating in discussions, 55–56
reading logs and, 55, 411–413
revising *vs.*, 72
shared reading and, 98
writing in reading logs, 55